Oxford Starter F

Also available from Oxford University Press

Oxford Take off in French
Language learning course with almost 5 hours of audio
Book + 4 × 75 minute cassettes: 0–19–860274–X
Book + 4 × 75 minute CDs: 0–19–860298–7
Book only: 0–19–860299–5

Oxford Take off in French Dictionary
0–19–860331–2
(available in the UK only)

The Oxford Colour French Dictionary
Colour headwords throughout
0–19–860191–3
0–19–860190–5 (US edition)

Pocket Oxford–Hachette French Dictionary
An ideal dictionary for higher examinations
0–19–860279–0

Oxford French Verbpack
0–19–860338–X

Oxford French Wordpack
0–19–860335–5

Oxford French Grammar
0–19–860341–X

The Oxford Starter French Dictionary

Revised edition

Edited by

Marie-Hélène Corréard
and Mary O'Neill

OXFORD
UNIVERSITY PRESS

OXFORD
UNIVERSITY PRESS

Great Clarendon Street, Oxford OX2 6DP

Oxford University Press is a department of the University of Oxford.
It furthers the University's objective of excellence in research, scholarship,
and education by publishing worldwide in

Oxford New York

Athens Auckland Bangkok Bogotá Buenos Aires Calcutta
Cape Town Chennai Dar es Salaam Delhi Florence Hong Kong Istanbul
Karachi Kuala Lumpur Madrid Melbourne Mexico City Mumbai
Nairobi Paris São Paulo Singapore Taipei Tokyo Toronto Warsaw

with associated companies in Berlin Ibadan

Published in the United States
by Oxford University Press Inc., New York

British Library Cataloguing in Publication Data
Data available

Library of Congress Cataloging in Publication Data
Data available

ISBN 0-19-860328-2
ISBN 0-19-968013-2 (educational edition)

10 9 8 7 6 5 4 3 2 1

Typeset in Swift and Arial by Latimer Trend & Company Ltd.
Printed in Italy

Contents

Introduction   vi

The structure of French–English entries   viii

The structure of English–French entries   ix

How to use the dictionary   xi

Glossary of grammatical terms   xiii

Guide to French pronunciation   xix

French–English dictionary   1

Dictionary know-how   171

English–French dictionary   185

French verbs   381

Numbers in French   417

Index of lexical and grammar notes   419

A guide to French grammar   421

Contributors

Chief Editor
Marie-Hélène Corréard

Associate Editor
Mary O'Neill

Editors
Gearóid Cronin
Françoise de Peretti
Natalie Pomier

Lexical usage notes
Henri Béjoint
Richard Wakely

Data-capture
Alison Curr
Diane Diffley

Administration
Isabelle Lemoine

Proofreading
Alison Curr
Isabelle Lemoine

North American English
Tim Horner
Carol Petersen

Introduction
Glossary of grammatical terms
Graham Bishop
Mary O'Neill

Dictionary know-how
A guide to French grammar
Martyn Bird

Design
Information Design Unit
Jane Stevenson

Introduction

A fresh approach

Created to meet the specific needs of English speakers who are starting to learn French, the *Oxford Starter French Dictionary* takes a completely fresh approach to helping you make sense of the new language. We have changed the design of the entries to make them different from entries in traditional dictionaries. What exactly is it that makes the entries so different?

- they have a new, clearer layout

- they are designed to provide the information you need in a helpful, readable way with the minimum of clutter

- since you will be using the English–French and the French–English sides of the dictionary for different tasks, each side works differently and it shows in the way the information is presented.

Because of these major changes, you will find that the *Oxford Starter French Dictionary* is a far more efficient language-learning tool for you as a beginner. Finding the right information quickly and easily will make French more satisfying to learn.

A clearer layout

Each page of the dictionary presents the information you will need in entries which are well-spaced, easy to read, and which have a consistent layout both in English and French. The main features of the new design are:

- bullet points and numbers to indicate the various uses of each word

- different typefaces as well as the symbol = to indicate the switch from one language to the other

- use of the symbol ! to indicate important grammar points

- use of the symbol ✱ to indicate informal or colloquial words

- use of the symbol ☞ to indicate words which should be used with care.

More helpful and easy to use

The entries have been designed so that you can find the information you need quickly. Many of the conventions in traditional dictionaries which you may find confusing or offputting have been avoided, so:

- PARTS OF SPEECH and grammatical terms are written out in full for you. A separate section explains all the terms used if you should need to find out more about them

- explanations of specific grammar points and notes on how a word is actually used are provided in short paragraphs at appropriate places in the dictionary text

- groups of words which behave in a similar way, or which present similar difficulties, are treated in a consistent manner which you will quickly

Words in capital letters are found in the glossary

come to recognize. In many entries, you are guided to other parts of the dictionary, to VERB tables, for instance, where you will find all the forms of the main French verbs. You will also find handy language notes which deal with such concepts as colours, countries, and dates.

* the language used in the examples and in the signposts to the right translation has been carefully chosen to ensure that it is clear and up to date.

This dictionary, with its precise and lively examples, contains all the words you will need as a beginner and includes plenty of examples of British as well as American English in both the English–French and French–English texts.

Using the two sides of the dictionary to do different things

Each side of the dictionary has been separately designed to take account of the different ways in which you will use it.

The English–French side is longer. Since you are moving from your own language into French, you will need more detailed guidance. We have provided regular reminders about essential grammar rules. The signposts which pinpoint the precise context in which a word is used are there to help you choose the right translation. These 'sense indicators' are also supported with a wide selection of useful examples.

The French–English side makes the most of what you already know about your own language. The presentation of translations from French is therefore more streamlined. There is detailed treatment of the more irregular and unpredictable features of French which you may come across in newspapers and magazines, for example. A particularly useful feature is that the variations in spelling of IRREGULAR VERBS, ADJECTIVES and PLURAL NOUNS are all listed as separate entries in the WORD LIST. These words then send you to the main dictionary form where you will find the translation you are looking for.

Special features

To help you make the most of your Starter Dictionary, we have provided in this introductory section the following features:

A Guide to Pronunciation
Definitions of Grammatical Terms
A Key to the Design of the Entries
A Guide to Using the Dictionary
A Word Games section

Words in capital letters are found in the glossary

The structure of French–English entries

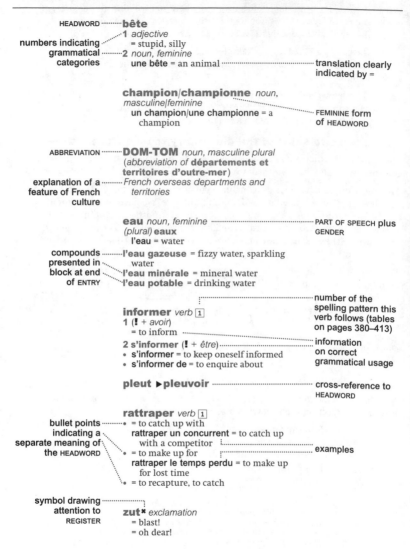

HEADWORD ⸱⸱⸱⸱ **bête**
1 *adjective*
numbers indicating ⸱⸱⸱⸱ = stupid, silly
grammatical ⸱⸱⸱⸱ 2 *noun, feminine*
categories   une bête = an animal ⸱⸱⸱⸱ translation clearly
indicated by =

champion/championne *noun,*
masculine/feminine
un champion/une championne = a ⸱⸱⸱⸱ FEMININE form
champion   of HEADWORD

ABBREVIATION ⸱⸱⸱⸱ **DOM-TOM** *noun, masculine plural*
(*abbreviation of* **départements et**
territoires d'outre-mer)
explanation of a ⸱⸱⸱⸱ *French overseas departments and*
feature of French *territories*
culture

eau *noun, feminine* ⸱⸱⸱⸱ PART OF SPEECH plus
(*plural*) **eaux** GENDER
l'eau = water
compounds ⸱⸱⸱⸱ l'eau gazeuse = fizzy water, sparkling
presented in ⸱⸱⸱⸱ water
block at end ⸱⸱⸱⸱ l'eau minérale = mineral water
of ENTRY l'eau potable = drinking water

    number of the
spelling pattern this
informer *verb* 1 verb follows (tables
1 (! + *avoir*) on pages 380–413)
= to inform ⸱⸱⸱⸱
2 s'informer (! + *être*) ⸱⸱⸱⸱ information
• s'informer = to keep oneself informed on correct
• s'informer de = to enquire about grammatical usage

pleut ▶ **pleuvoir** ⸱⸱⸱⸱ cross-reference to
HEADWORD

rattraper *verb* 1
bullet points ⸱⸱⸱⸱ • = to catch up with
indicating a ⸱⸱⸱⸱ rattraper un concurrent = to catch up
separate meaning of ⸱⸱⸱⸱ with a competitor
the HEADWORD • = to make up for ⸱⸱⸱⸱ examples
rattraper le temps perdu = to make up
for lost time
• = to recapture, to catch

symbol drawing ⸱⸱⸱⸱
attention to **zut ✕** *exclamation*
REGISTER = blast!
= oh dear!

Words in capital letters are found in the glossary

The structure of English–French entries

HEADWORD ⋯⋯ **circus** *noun*
a circus = un cirque

⋯⋯ GENDER of French NOUNS made clear

delicious *adjective*
= délicieux/délicieuse ⋯⋯ FEMININE form of ADJECTIVES made clear

PART OF SPEECH ⋯⋯ made clear

fed up *adjective*
to be fed up = en avoir marre✱ ⋯⋯ symbol drawing attention to REGISTER

fire
numbers indicating ⋯⋯ **1** *noun*
grammatical categories
fire = le feu ⋯⋯ indicators which spell out the different meanings of the HEADWORD
a fire (*for heat*) = un feu
(*causing damage*) = un incendie
to catch fire = prendre feu
to be on fire = être en feu
2 *verb*
bullet points ⋯⋯ • (*to shoot*) = tirer
indicating a ⋯⋯ • (*to dismiss*) = renvoyer
separate meaning
of the HEADWORD

fireman *noun* ▶ **315** ⋯⋯ page number where more information is given
a fireman = un pompier
separate entries for ⋯⋯ **fire station** *noun*
COMPOUND NOUNS
a fire station = une caserne de pompiers

⋯⋯ translation clearly indicated by =

kick *verb*
to kick someone = donner un coup de pied à quelqu'un
he kicked the ball = il a donné un coup de pied dans le ballon
PHRASAL VERBS ⋯⋯ **kick off** = donner le coup d'envoi
presented in ⋯⋯ **kick out**
separate
blocks
to kick someone out = mettre quelqu'un à la porte

need *verb*
• (*to have to*) ⋯⋯ basic structure to use as a model
you don't need to ask permission = tu n'es pas obligé de demander la permission
they'll need to come early = il va falloir qu'ils viennent de bonne heure

information on ⋯⋯ **!** *Note that the subjunctive is used after*
correct grammatical *falloir que.*
usage

• (*to want*) = avoir besoin de
they need [money|help|friends...] = ils ont
example of a model ⋯⋯ besoin [d'argent|d'aide|d'amis...]
structure which can we need to see the doctor = nous avons
be imitated besoin de voir le médecin
everything you need = tout ce qu'il vous faut

Words in capital letters are found in the glossary

How to use the dictionary

Where to look for a word

Bilingual dictionaries are divided into two sections. The first section gives you a list of French words followed by their English equivalents as well as information about the contexts in which they are used.

The second section gives you a list of English words followed by the French words which match their exact meaning according to the contexts in which they are used.

* *Decide first which section you need to look at.*

Your Starter Dictionary is particularly good at listing as HEADWORDS the various forms that VERBS, NOUNS, and ADJECTIVES may take in French when they are being used to indicate TENSE, GENDER, or NUMBER. From these more unpredictable forms, you will be referred to the main entry of the BASE FORM for the meaning and any further information.

What information does the dictionary provide you with?

Your dictionary gives you information which falls into three broad categories:

1. information about meaning
2. information about the grammatical characteristics of the words
3. information about the circumstances in which a word may be safely used – either from the point of view of CONTEXT (e.g. medical, sport, school contexts) or REGISTER (e.g. formal, polite, informal registers)

How to recognize the information given in the dictionary

Study carefully the diagrams given on pages x–xi **The Structure of French–English and English–French entries**. There you will see how the three categories of information mentioned above are displayed to help you. If you need help finding out what PART OF SPEECH you are dealing with, have a look at the **Definitions of Grammatical Terms** on page xv.

Finding meanings and translating

When you are looking up words for meaning in order to translate them either from your own language or from French, dictionaries can only give you lists of choices. You must look carefully at the information provided to help you choose the right translation in English or in French for the CONTEXT you are in.

If you look up the French word for '**right**', you need to be clear whether you mean '**right**' as opposed to '**left**' or whether you mean '**right** 'as opposed to '**wrong**'.

Scan the whole entry to find the word in French which matches the meaning you need. The context indicators or 'signposts' will help you to pinpoint this meaning. This will be easier to select when you are looking up French words to translate into English since you will know what each of the choices given in English means and how it is used.

If the entry is a long one, first identify the PART OF SPEECH of the word you want to translate. When you have found the right section of the entry, check the range of meanings covered in that section to find the appropriate one. For example:

* '**ring**' could be a verb, in which case the correct French translation may be '**sonner**' which is also a verb;

Words in capital letters are found in the glossary

- **'ring'** could be a noun, in which case the correct French equivalent might be **'une bague'** (*a piece of jewellery*) or **'la piste'** (*in a circus*) or **'un cercle'** (*a circle*).

Your Starter Dictionary will give you the context clearly so that you can decide on the appropriate word.

Using the entries to find information about a word other than the meaning

- Sometimes you will want to use your dictionary simply to check the spelling of the FEMININE or PLURAL form of a NOUN or ADJECTIVE.
- You may wish to check to see if the word has ACCENTS.
- You may wish to check the GENDER of a noun.
- You may wish to find out how a verb is spelled in a particular TENSE.
- The entry will often tell you which pattern of CONJUGATION the VERB follows by referring you to the tables at the back of the book (see pages 381–397).

How to use the verb tables

Where you see a French verb followed by a number in a box, look at the back of the dictionary where you will find tables of verbs. The number given against the verb indicates the spelling pattern that the verb follows.

For example: **'arriver'** and **'informer'** are both followed by the number 1. In the verb tables this spelling pattern is represented by the verb **'chanter'**.

Verbs can be split into two parts: the *stem* and the *ending*.

     e.g. **arriv** + **er**; **inform** + **er**

The endings of **'chant** + **er'** should be used with the stems of **arriv** + **er** and **inform** + **er** to form the tenses you need.

Where the verb is REGULAR the stem does not change, only the endings.

Where the verb is IRREGULAR the stem may alter as well. Just follow the pattern indicated.

     e.g. 19 **rappeler**   [**rappel** + **er**]   note the change from **'l'** to double **'ll'**
          52 **comprendre** [**comprend** + **re**]   note how the **'d'** is not always there
          56 **joindre**   [**joind** + **re**]   note how the **'d'** is not always there and the change to **'gn'** from **'nd'** in certain TENSES

Getting to know your dictionary

In the central section of this dictionary (pages 171–184) you will find a short section of games and exercises which will help you get to know your dictionary better and to use it more effectively. Your dictionary is a very important study aid which can greatly help you to find out how the French language works and how to expand your vocabulary.

Words in capital letters are found in the glossary

Glossary of grammatical terms

The list of words and definitions below contains most of the words which you will come across when learning a language and its grammar. Some are used in this dictionary; others you will see in grammars and textbooks.

Abbreviation	a shortened form of a word or phrase, e.g. (English) exam ▶ examination; (French) imper ▶ imperméable
Accent	**1.** (in writing) a mark associated with a letter, usually showing how the letter is pronounced, e.g. grave accent (è); acute accent (é); circumflex (â) **2.** (in speech) a person's way of speaking
Adjective	a word describing a noun, e.g. a *green* shirt = une chemise *verte*; a *small* girl = une *petite* fille
Adverb	a word that describes or modifies the meaning of a verb, an adjective or another adverb, e.g. he speaks *quickly* = il parle *vite*; fairly big = *assez* grand; very slowly = *très* lentement
Agree, Agreement	when a word agrees with another, its spelling changes to match the number of that other word, e.g. one child = un enfant; two children = deux enfant**s**; it must also match it for gender, e.g. the **big** dog = **le grand** chien; the **big** house = **la grande** maison
Article	the definite article 'the'; the indefinite article 'a' or 'an'; the partitive articles 'some', 'any' are all used before a noun (see grammar box on page 352 and also the glossary entry DETERMINER)
Auxiliary, Auxiliary verb	either of the verbs être or avoir which are used to form the perfect, pluperfect, or future perfect tenses, e.g. j'*ai* mangé = I have eaten; je *suis* revenu = I came back; ils *avaient* vu Bob = they had seen Bob
Base form	see DICTIONARY FORM
Clause	a self-contained section of a sentence which contains a subject and a verb
Cognates	words which resemble each other in more than one language and which historically have the same origin, e.g. republic, république. They do not always retain the same meaning. See FAUX AMI
Colloquial	refers to a word or an expression used in relaxed, everyday situations. Colloquial language is usually spoken, or used in personal letters or informal writing
Comparative	the form of the adjective or adverb which allows a comparison to be made, e.g. big*ger* = *plus* grand; *more* intelligent = *plus* intelligent; clever*er* = *plus* malin
Compound noun	A noun formed from two or more separate words: an airport = un aéroport

Conditional	the form of the verb that expresses what might happen IF something else occurred first, e.g. *if* it tasted good, I **would eat** it = *si* c'était bon, je le **mangerais**
Conjunction	a word used to join clauses together, e.g. *and, but, because*
Consonant	a letter representing a sound such as b, c, d, p, t, s, z, etc. Consonants cannot form a complete sound unit or syllable without a vowel. See VOWEL
Construction	the way the words in a phrase or sentence work together grammatically
Context	the environment or surroundings within which a word occurs and which affect its meaning. Compare *the* **tank** *fired first* with *he filled the petrol* **tank**. Information about the context of a word helps to pinpoint its exact sense. Knowing the sense and then using the dictionary signposts will guide you to the right translation
Definite Article	See ARTICLE
Determiner	a word which is used before a noun to make clear what is being referred to. It describes the function of definite and indefinite articles as well as words like *this, my,* and *certain,* e.g. *this* money = *cet argent; my* room = *ma chambre; certain* people = *certaines* personnes. In French, the determiner will match the gender and the number of the noun it is referring to
Dictionary form	the form of a word given in the dictionary WORD LIST. For verbs, it is the spelling of the infinitive in English and French; for French nouns, the spelling of the masculine singular form (or the feminine singular form if there is no masculine form); for French adjectives, the spelling of the masculine singular form
Direct object	the noun or pronoun directly affected by the verb, e.g. she bought *the book* = elle a acheté *le livre;* he carried *it* = il l'a porté; help *me* = aidez-*moi*
Ending	that part of a noun or an adjective which can be changed to show gender or number and of a verb to show number or tense. The ending doesn't change the basic meaning of the word
Entry	the information given in a dictionary about the word you have looked up; also the word itself. See HEADWORD
Exclamation	a sound, word or remark expressing a strong feeling such as anger, fear, or joy, e.g. ouch! = aïe!
Faux ami	one of a pair of words from two different languages which look alike but which do not have the same meaning, e.g. *sensible* (English) = *having good sense* and *sensible* (French) = *sensitive*
Feminine	one of the two genders for nouns in French, which is most clearly indicated by the article used with the noun, e.g. *the* girl = *la* fille; *a* table = *une* table. Pronouns and adjectives also carry gender information e.g., *she* eats = *elle* mange; a black dress = une robe noir*e* (because the noun *robe* is feminine)

Gender	marks words in French as being either masculine or feminine (whether they refer to persons *or things*) whereas English does not make the distinction. The gender of a French noun is important because it will affect the form of adjectives which describe it, e.g. a white cow = **une** vache blanc**he**; a white horse = **un** cheval blanc. Gender will also affect the form of pronouns which replace a French noun, e.g. the boy laughed ▶ he laughed = **il** a ri; the beach (feminine) is clean ▶ it is clean = **elle** est propre
Headword	the word which is used in the dictionary word list to begin each separate entry.
Imperative	a verb form for expressing commands, e.g. *close* the door = *ferme* la porte; *be quiet!* = *taisez-vous!*; *let's go!* = *allons-y!*
Imperfect tense	the tense of the verb which refers to a continuous action or state in the past, e.g. I *was singing* = je *chantais;* or to something that used to happen regularly, e.g. he *used to eat* meat = il *mangeait* la viande; I *took* the bus every day = je *prenais* le bus tous les jours
Impersonal verb	a verb whose action is not performed by a person or a thing, e.g. *it is raining* = *il* pleut; *it's going to snow* = *il* va neiger
Indefinite article	See ARTICLE
Indefinite pronoun	a pronoun that does not identify a specific person or object, e.g. *you* never know = *on* ne sait jamais; *one* wonders why = *on* se demande pourquoi; *it's* raining = *il* pleut
Indicative	a verb form which is used when indicating or stating a fact, e.g. I don't understand = je ne comprends pas; it was true = c'était vrai. See SUBJUNCTIVE
Indirect object	the noun or pronoun indirectly affected by the verb and often following a preposition, e.g. I wrote *to him* = je *lui* ai écrit. The direct object also has an effect on the indirect object, e.g. she gave the book *to the boy* = elle a donné le livre *au garçon*; he tells *us* stories = il *nous* raconte des histoires
Infinitive	the basic part or 'name' of a verb before it is altered to indicate tense or number, e.g. to sing = chanter; to drive = conduire. See DICTIONARY FORM
Interrogative	a form of wording used to ask questions
Intonation	the quality in a human voice which indicates an emotion (surprise, shock) or which shows that a speaker is asking a question, stating a fact or giving an order
Inverted commas	punctuation marks used to indicate direct speech, e.g. "come here," she said. They are also referred to as quotation marks.
Irregular verb	a verb whose spelling is not predictable or does not follow a regular pattern when it changes to express tense. See REGULAR VERB

Masculine	one of the two genders for nouns in French, which is most clearly indicated by the article used with the noun, e.g. *the* boy = *le* garçon; *a* dog = *un* chien. Pronouns and adjectives also carry gender information e.g., *he* eats = *il* mange; a black hat = un chapeau *noir* (because the noun *chapeau* is masculine)
Noun	a word which names a person, an animal, an object, a feeling or an event, e.g. a student = un étudiant; a dog = un chien; a house = une maison; envy = l'envie; the storm = l'orage
Number	a form of the word indicating whether it is singular, e.g. a boy = un garçon, or plural, e.g. two boy*s* = deux garçon*s*
Object	the person, thing or idea affected by or referred to by a verb, e.g. he walked *the dog* = il a promené *le chien*; we crossed *the road* = nous avons traversé *la rue*. See also DIRECT OBJECT, INDIRECT OBJECT
Part of speech	the grammatical term which describes the function of a word and categorizes it as *noun, verb, adjective, adverb*, etc. All the entries in this dictionary carry information about the part of speech of the word you look up.
Past participle	the part of the verb used to form compound tenses in combination with an auxiliary verb, e.g. I have *sung* = j'ai *chanté*; we had *stayed* = nous étions *restés;* she's *gone* to bed = elle s'est *couchée*
Past simple	the tense of the verb which refers to past events which have been completed. In French, it is a verb form which is mostly used in written language
Perfect tense	the tense of the verb which refers to past events which have been completed, e.g. we *have finished* the work = nous *avons terminé* le travail. She *left* yesterday = elle *est partie* hier. It is also called the *passé composé* in French and is used in spoken language as well as in print
Person	the 'person' of a verb shows you **who** or **what** is carrying out the action referred to by the verb. There are six persons in the singular: *I, you, he, she, it, one* and three in the plural: *we, you, they*
Phonetics	the system of sounds of a language. The word can also refer to the symbols used to represent these sounds. The most common system of symbols is the International Phonetic Alphabet
Phrasal verb	a form of the English verb which combines with a preposition or an adverb to produce a particular meaning, e.g. to *turn up* = *arriver*; to *carry on* working = *continuer* à travailler
Phrase	1. a self-contained section of a sentence which does not contain a full verb 2. an expression which has a particular meaning which can make it more difficult to translate word for word, e.g. to lay the table = mettre la table; to hang around = traîner
Pluperfect tense	the tense of the verb referring to (1) past events which precede (2) other events taking place in a more recent past, e.g. he (1) *had sold* the car when (2) he *told me* about it = il (1) *avait vendu* la voiture quand (2) il *m'en a parlé*

Plural	the form of nouns and pronouns which refers to more than one of something, e.g. *boys, we, they.* French ADJECTIVES also have plural forms, e.g. red shoes = des chaussures rouge**s** to agree with the noun they are describing
Preposition	a word which stands in front of a noun or pronoun, connecting it to the rest of a sentence, e.g. *between* the chairs = *entre* les chaises; *with* us = *avec* nous; *to* Paris = *à* Paris; *from* Bob = *de* Bob
Present tense	the tense of the verb referring to something that is happening now, e.g. I *am watching* television = je *regarde* la télévision; she *understands* = elle *comprend*
Pronoun	a word which takes the place of a noun, e.g. is it *your dog*? ▶ is it *yours*?; I sold *the car* ▶ I sold *it*
Reflexive verb	a verb whose object is the same as its subject, e.g. *he* washed *himself* = il s'est lavé; I hurt *myself* = je me suis blessé
Register	the style of language used in speech and writing which is suited (and which you can adapt) to the circumstances. These may range from very formal situations to very relaxed or informal contexts
Regular verb	a verb which follows a set pattern in its different forms and tenses and can be classified in a fixed group of verbs. In French, there are many verbs ending in, for example, -er (*aim**er**, chant**er**, tourn**er***) which behave regularly. See IRREGULAR VERB
Sentence	a set of words usually containing a subject and a verb, which can stand alone and make sense, e.g. she's gone = elle est partie; who is it? = qui est-ce?; (you) leave me alone! = laisse-moi tranquille!
Singular	the form of nouns and pronouns which refers to just one of something, e.g. *boy, I, it.* See PLURAL
Stem	the part of the verb to which endings which indicate tense, number and gender are added, e.g. the regular verb *chanter* is made up of the stem *chant-* and the ending *-er.* When a verb is regular, the stem doesn't change. When it is irregular, the stem as well as the endings change
Subject	the noun or pronoun which causes the action of a verb and can usually be identified by asking **who..?** or **what..?**, e.g. *he* wants to leave = il veut partir; *the computer's* broken down = l'ordinateur est en panne
Subjunctive	a verb form that is used to express a desire, doubt or unlikelihood, e.g. I'm not sure he'll come = je ne suis pas sûr qu'il vienne. It often indicates how the speaker feels about something rather than the fact itself, e.g. I'm happy *that you are back* = je suis content que tu sois rentré
Superlative	the form of the adjective which makes it 'the most', e.g. the big*gest* = le plus grand; the small*est* = le plus petit; the most intelligent = le plus intelligent
Syllable	part of a word which can form a spoken unit built around the VOWEL it contains, e.g. the word **in-tel-li-gent** has four syllables
Synonym	a word which has the same (or almost the same) meaning as another, e.g. *enormous* and *gigantic*, *sure* and *certain*

Tense	the form of the verb which indicates a particular time frame – past: I *had* = j'*avais*; present: I *have* = j'*ai*; future: I *will have* = j'*aurai*
Verb	a word which indicates what is being done or which describes a situation, e.g. he *left* the house = il *a quitté* la maison; you *seem* happy = tu *as* l'air heureux; I *am* tired = je *suis* fatigué
Vowel	a sound which forms the basis of the syllable and which can be spoken by itself, e.g. *a, i, e, o, u*. See CONSONANT, SYLLABLE
Word list	the list of headwords or vocabulary items which is found in a dictionary

A guide to French pronunciation

While phonetics have not been given for entries in the present dictionary, a simplified, user-friendly table summarizing the main features of French pronunciation and spelling follows.

This table is designed
(a) to help English speakers to bridge the gap between the sound systems of English and French
(b) to connect French sounds to the most frequent written representations of those sounds, illustrating the link by means of examples from basic French vocabulary.

Learners will find in it a useful point of departure for a more advanced study of French phonetics at a later stage. It is not, however, meant to take the place of either a human model—a teacher, for example—or a recording of the same sounds produced by a native speaker.

The table is subdivided into three main categories of phonetic sounds: *vowels, semi-vowels,* and *consonants.* The French sounds are presented in order of increasing complexity when compared with the English sound system. In many cases, the sounds are broadly similar, if not actually the same. In others, however, it is only possible in the present format to give an approximation in English terms of the French sound. This is indicated by the symbol ≈. This is particularly true of the French vowels which are nasalized (represented by ɛ̃, ɑ̃, ɔ̃, and œ̃ in the International Phonetic Alphabet) and those which require a marked degree of lip-rounding (represented by ø, œ, y, and ɥ).

A major distinguishing feature of written French is the mute h, as in **homme, hôtel.** It functions in the same way as a vowel and spelling or pronunciation adjust accordingly **l'homme, cet homme, les hommes** [lezɔm]. We have systematically included the mute h in the column dealing with French spelling forms while notes throughout the dictionary text regularly draw users' attention to this important feature.

M. O'N.

Vowels

phonetic symbol	sounds like English	written in French as	examples
a	cat, flat	a, à, ha-	acheter, basse, patte, **à**, voilà, hameau (*note also* femme)
ɑ	arm, car	â, as	âgé, gâteau, pâte, bas, las
e	hay, tray but *shorter*	-er, -es, -ez, -é, -ée, é-, hé-	aller, des, nez, âgé, année, étage, hélas
ɛ	pet, threat	è-, ê-, e-, ai, -ais, ait, -ei-, aî-, -ë-, -et	règle, très, être, bête, elle, cet, aide, faible, français, lait, était, pleine, connaître, Noël, secret
i	treat, fleet	i, -ie, -is, î-, hi, y, -ï	il, immeuble, libre, pile, vie, pris, île, hibou, elle y va, type, maïs
o	horse, course	au, eau, aux, eaux, o, os, ô, hô-	aussi, gauche, tuyau, beau, château, chevaux, eaux, chose, orage, loto, gros, côte, hôtel (*note also* trop)
ɔ	hot, what	o-, ho-, hô-	objet, dommage, randonnée, botte, horaire, hôpital

French pronunciation

Vowels

phonetic symbol	sounds like English	written in French as	examples
u	hoot, flute	ou, où, -oû-, -oo-, hou-, -oux	ouvrir, trou, mourir, amour, où, goûter, football, houx, roux (*note also* août)
ə	ago, gather (*British English*)	e (*silent at the end of words and may even be left out*)	mère, elle, j'aime, même, premier, grenouille, menu, le, ne, de, petit, fera, chemin, médecin
ø	purr, her but shorter	eu, eux	Europe, peu, neveu, bleu, chanteuse, heureux, cheveux, yeux
œ	≈ fun, son	eu, œu-, heu-, œ	peur, déjeuner, meuble, humeur, fauteuil, œuf, sœur, heure, œil
y	ee but with rounded lips	u, û, hu	une, utile, rue, vendu, mûr, sûr, humeur, hurler (*note also* eu)
ɛ̃	an/am + nasal twang	in, im, ain, -ein, -yn, ym, -en, -aim, hein	intéressant, matin, imbécile, train, copain, plein, peindre, syndicat, sympa, italien, rien, faim, hein
ɑ̃	awn/alm + nasal twang	an, -ant, en, em-, -ent, am-	an, chanter, chant, entrer, ennui, empêcher, tempête, souvent, rampe (*note also* temps, paon, banc, sang *and* champ)
ɔ̃	on + nasal twang	on, om, hon-	onze, bon, montrer, jambon, ombre, sombre, tromper, honte
œ̃	fun, son + nasal twang	un, -um	un, brun, lundi, parfum

Semi-Vowels

phonetic symbol	sounds like English	written in French as	examples
j	yes, player	-i-, y, -il, -ill-	bien, ciel, tiède, il y a, yaourt, payer, soleil, travail, feuille, fille, billet
w	≈ was	oi, -oî-, ou, -oê-, w-	oiseau, voir, besoin, quoi, oui, jouet, boîte, poêle, K-way
ɥ	≈ we, tweet but with rounded lips	-ui-, hui, -uî-, huî-	nuit, lui, aujourd'hui, huit, huître

Consonants

phonetic symbol	sounds like English	written in French as	examples
b	as English	b, -bb-	bain, robe, abbaye
d	as English	d, -dd-	devoir, aide, addition
f	as English	f, -ff-, ph	fête, neuf, affaires, photo, téléphone
k	as English	c, qu-, -q, -cc-, k, -ck-, -ch-	café, sac, quartier, marquer, coq, occupé, kilomètre, kayak, ticket, orchestre
l	as English	l, -ll-	lettre, pile, mal, ville, salle
m	as English	m, -mm-	mère, madame, femme, sommeil
n	as English	n, -nn-	non, animal, panne, donner
p	as English	p, -pp-, -bs-	pomme, chapeau, hop, appuyer, observer
s	as English	s, -ss-, c, ç-, sc-	son, festival, assiette, poisson, chasse, cette, tracer, cil, garçon, ça, reçu, scène, piscine (*note also* six, dix)
t	as English	t, -tt-, th	tour, auto, patte, thé, bibliothèque
v	as English	v, w	venir, lever, grave, wagon, W-C
z	as English	-s-, z, -x-	maison, loisirs, brise, zoo, bizarre, dix-huit, sixième
g	as English	g, gu-, -gg-	goût, bagarre, gai, guitare, blague, aggressif
ʒ	leisure, seizure	j, g-, ge-	j'ai, jeune, déjeuner, plage, geler, gifler, gîte, nageons
ʃ	ra*sh*, *sh*oe	ch, sh	château, achats, riche, poche, short
ɲ	*n*ew, o*n*ion	gn	ignorer, vignoble, soigner, champignon (*note also* oignon)
ŋ	si*ng*, wro*ng*	-ng	camping, parking
R	≈ a very soft lo*ch* sound produced at the *back* of the throat	r, -rr-, rh-	rouge, partir, arrêter, marre, rhume

French–English

a ▶ avoir ⑧

à *preposition*
(**!** à + le *becomes* au; à + les *becomes* aux)
> **!** *You will find translations for phrases with* à *such as* à côté de, à l'étranger, penser à, *etc. under the entries* côté, étranger, penser, *etc.*

• (*showing destination*) = to
  se rendre [à Nice | à l'école | aux courses …]
  = to go [to Nice | to school | to the races …]
• (*showing location*) = in
  = at
  = on
  habiter [à la campagne | au Portugal | aux États-Unis …] = to live [in the country | in Portugal | in the United States …]
• (*in a description*) = with
  la maison aux volets verts = the house with the green shutters
• (*showing ownership*)
  le livre est [à moi | à eux | à Isabelle …] = the book is [mine | theirs | Isabelle's …]
• (*indicating a time, a speed, a price*) = at
  à minuit = at midnight
  un timbre à trois francs = a three-franc stamp
• (*meaning during a period of time*) = in
  au printemps = in (the) spring
• (*indicating a distance*)
  à cinq kilomètres = five kilometres away
• (*showing how something is done*)
  écrire au crayon = to write in pencil
  à pied = on foot

abandonner *verb* ①
• = to abandon
• = to give up

abeille *noun, feminine*
  une abeille = a bee

abîmer *verb* ①
1 (**!** + *avoir*)
  = to damage, to spoil
2 s'abîmer (**!** + *être*)
  s'abîmer = to get damaged

abonné/abonnée *noun, masculine/feminine*
  un abonné/une abonnée = a subscriber

abonnement *noun, masculine*
  un abonnement = a subscription

abonner: **s'abonner à** *verb* ① (**!** + *être*)
  s'abonner à = to subscribe to

abord: **d'abord** *adverb*
  d'abord = first, at first
  tout d'abord = first of all

abri *noun, masculine*
  un abri = (a) shelter

abricot *noun, masculine*
  un abricot = an apricot

abriter *verb* ①
1 (**!** + *avoir*)
  = to shelter
2 s'abriter (**!** + *être*)
  s'abriter = to shelter, to take shelter

absent/absente *adjective*
  = absent, missing

absolument *adverb*
  = absolutely

accélérer *verb* ⑭
  = to accelerate

accepter *verb* ①
• = to accept
• = to agree to

accès *noun, masculine* (**!** *never changes*)
  l'accès = access
  'accès interdit' = 'no entrance', 'do not enter'

accident *noun, masculine*
  un accident = an accident

accompagner *verb* ①
• = to accompany, to go with
• = to take

accomplir *verb* ③
  = to carry out, to accomplish

accord *noun, masculine*
• **un accord** = an agreement
• **d'accord!** = OK!, all right!
  je suis d'accord avec toi = I agree with you

accorder *verb* ①
  = to give, to grant

accotement *noun, masculine*
  un accotement = a verge, a shoulder
  accotement non stabilisé = soft verge, soft shoulder

accroc *noun, masculine*
  un accroc (*in material*) = a tear, a rip

accrocher *verb* ①
1 (**!** + *avoir*)
  = to hang
2 s'accrocher (**!** + *être*)
  s'accrocher = to hang on, to cling
  accroche-toi à la branche = hang on to the branch

accueil *noun, masculine*
  un accueil = a welcome, a reception
  ils nous ont fait bon accueil = they made us welcome, they made us feel at home
  la famille d'accueil = the host family

accueillir verb 27
* (*if it's a host*) = to welcome
* (*if it's a stadium, a hotel*) = to accommodate

achat noun, masculine
  un achat = a purchase
  faire des achats = to do some shopping

acheter verb 18
  = to buy

acheteur/acheteuse noun,
masculine/feminine
  un acheteur/une acheteuse = a buyer, a
  purchaser

acteur/actrice noun,
masculine/feminine
  un acteur/une actrice = an actor/an actress

actif/active adjective
  = active

activité noun, feminine
  une activité = an activity

actrice ▶ acteur

actualité
1 noun, feminine
  l'actualité = current affairs, current events
2 **actualités** noun, feminine plural
  les actualités = the news

actuel/actuelle adjective
  = present, current

actuellement adverb
  = currently, at the moment

addition noun, feminine
* (*in a restaurant, a café*)
  l'addition = the bill, the check
* (*in arithmetic*)
  une addition = an addition

additionner verb 1
  = to add

adhérent/adhérente noun,
masculine/feminine
  un adhérent/une adhérente = a member

adhésion noun, feminine
  l'adhésion = membership

adieu noun, masculine
  (*plural*) **adieux**
  = goodbye, farewell
  faire ses adieux = to say goodbye

adjectif noun, masculine
  un adjectif = an adjective

admettre verb 60
* = to admit
* = to allow
* **être admis à un examen** = to pass an
  exam, to pass a test
* **admettons qu'il vienne** = (let's) suppose he
  comes

admis/admise ▶ admettre 60

admission noun, feminine
  l'admission = admission

adolescent/adolescente noun,
masculine/feminine
  un adolescent/une adolescente = a
  teenager, an adolescent

adorer verb 1
  = to love, to adore

adresse noun, feminine
  une adresse = an address
  changer d'adresse = to move

adresser verb 1
1 (**!** + *avoir*)
* = to send
* = to address
2 **s'adresser** (**!** + *être*)
* **s'adresser à un employé** = to talk to an
  employee
* **s'adresser à la banque** = to contact the
  bank

adroit/adroite adjective
* = skil(l)ful
* = clever, smart

adversaire noun, masculine/feminine
  un adversaire/une adversaire = an
  opponent

aérer verb 14
  = to air

aérien/aérienne adjective
  = air

aérobic noun, masculine
  l'aérobic = aerobics

aérogare noun, feminine
  une aérogare = an air terminal

aéroglisseur noun, masculine
  un aéroglisseur = a hovercraft

aéroport noun, masculine
  un aéroport = an airport

affaire
1 noun, feminine
  une affaire = a bargain
2 **affaires** noun, feminine plural
* **les affaires** = business
* **mes affaires** = my things, my belongings

affairer: s'affairer verb 1 (**!** + *être*)
  s'affairer = to bustle about, to hurry
  around

affectueusement adverb
  = affectionately
  (*ending a letter*) = love

affectueux/affectueuse adjective
  = affectionate

affiche noun, feminine
  une affiche = a poster
  = a notice

afficher verb ⓵
- = to put up, to hang up
- = to display
  afficher complet = to be fully booked

affoler verb ⓵
1 (**!** + avoir)
= to throw into a panic
2 s'affoler (**!** + être)
  s'affoler = to get into a panic

affreux/affreuse adjective
= awful

afin
1 afin de preposition
  afin de = in order to
2 afin que conjunction
  afin que = so that

africain/africaine adjective
= African

Afrique noun, feminine
  l'Afrique = Africa

agacer verb ⓬
= to annoy, to irritate

âge noun, masculine
  l'âge = age
  quel âge as-tu? = how old are you?

âgé/âgée adjective
- = old, elderly
- **être âgé de 18 ans** = to be 18 years old

agence noun, feminine
  une agence = an agency
  une agence immobilière = an estate
  agent's, a real estate agency
  une agence de voyages = a travel
  agency

agenda noun, masculine
  un agenda = a diary, a date book

agent noun, masculine
  un agent = an agent
  un agent de la circulation = a traffic
  policeman
  un agent de police = a policeman, a
  police officer

agglomération noun, feminine
  une agglomération = a town
  = a village

agile adjective
= agile

agir verb ⓷
1 (**!** + avoir)
= to act
2 s'agir de (**!** + être)
  s'agir de = to be about
  de quoi s'agit-il? = what's it about?

agitation noun, feminine
- **l'agitation** = (the) bustle
- **l'agitation** = (the) excitement

agité/agitée adjective
  (describing the sea) = rough, choppy

agiter verb ⓵
1 (**!** + avoir)
- **agiter un mouchoir** = to wave a
  handkerchief
- **agiter un flacon** = to shake a bottle
2 s'agiter (**!** + être)
- **s'agiter** = to fidget
- **s'agiter** = to become restless

agneau noun, masculine
(plural) **agneaux**
- (the animal)
  un agneau = a lamb
- (the meat)
  l'agneau = lamb

agréable adjective
= pleasant

agressif/agressive adjective
= aggressive

agression noun, feminine
- **une agression** = an attack
- **une agression** = a mugging

agricole adjective
= agricultural

agriculteur/agricultrice noun,
masculine/feminine
  un agriculteur/une agricultrice = a farmer

ai ▶ avoir ⓼

aide
1 noun, feminine
  l'aide = help
  = assistance
2 noun, masculine/feminine
  un aide/une aide = an assistant

aider verb ⓵
1 (**!** + avoir)
= to help
2 s'aider de (**!** + être)
  s'aider de = to use

aïe exclamation
= ouch!

aigle noun, masculine
  un aigle = an eagle

aigre adjective
- (tasting unpleasant) = sour
- (sounding unpleasant) = sharp

aiguille noun, feminine
- **une aiguille** = a needle
  une aiguille à tricoter = a knitting needle
- **les aiguilles d'une montre** = the hands on
  a watch

ail noun, masculine
  l'ail = garlic

aile noun, feminine
  une aile = a wing

aille ▶ aller 1 ⓽

ailleurs
1 *adverb*
  ailleurs = elsewhere, somewhere else
2 d'ailleurs = besides

aimable *adjective*
  = kind, friendly

aimer *verb* [1]
* = to love
  aimer ses enfants = to love one's children
* = to like, to be fond of
  j'aime mieux le vin = I prefer wine

aîné/aînée *adjective*
  = eldest, oldest
  = elder, older

ainsi
1 *adverb*
* = in this way
  et ainsi de suite = and so on
* = so
  ainsi tu t'en vas? = so you're leaving?
2 ainsi que = and, as well as

air *noun, masculine*
* **l'air** = (the) air
  en plein air = in the open (air), outdoors
  allons prendre l'air = let's go and get some
    fresh air
* **de l'air** = a wind, a breeze
* (*appearance*)
  un air = a look
  avoir l'air heureux = to look happy
  il n'a pas l'air de comprendre = he doesn't
    seem to understand
* (*for a song*)
  un air = a tune

aire *noun, feminine*
  une aire = an area
  une aire de jeux = a playground
  une aire de loisirs = a recreation area

aise: **à l'aise** *adverb*
  à l'aise = at ease

ajouter *verb* [1]
1 (**!** + *avoir*)
  = to add
2 s'ajouter à (**!** + *être*)
  s'ajouter à = to be added to

alarme *noun, feminine*
  donner l'alarme = to raise the alarm

album *noun, masculine*
  un album = an album
  un album à colorier = a colo(u)ring book

alcool *noun, masculine*
  l'alcool = alcohol
  sans alcool = nonalcoholic, alcohol-free

alcoolisé/alcoolisée *adjective*
  = alcoholic

alcootest *noun, masculine*
  un alcootest = a Breathalyzer   test

algèbre *noun, feminine*
  l'algèbre = algebra

Alger *noun*
  = Algiers

Algérie *noun, feminine*
  l'Algérie = Algeria

algérien/algérienne *adjective*
  = Algerian

aliment *noun, masculine*
  un aliment = a food

alimentation *noun, feminine*
* (*the foods usually eaten*)
  une alimentation saine = a healthy diet
* (*food retailing*)
  un magasin d'alimentation = a grocery
    store

allais ▶ **aller 1** [9]

allée
1 *noun, feminine*
  une allée = a path
  (*wider*) = an avenue
  (*leading to a garage*) = a drive, a driveway
2 allées *noun, feminine plural*
  leurs allées et venues = their comings
    and goings

Allemagne *noun, feminine*
  l'Allemagne = Germany

allemand/allemande
1 *adjective*
  = German
2 allemand *noun, masculine*
  l'allemand = German

aller
1 *verb* [9] (**!** + *être*)
* = to go
  où vas-tu? = where are you going?
  il faut que j'aille les voir = I must go and
    see them
  allons-y! = let's go!
* (*when talking about the near future*) = to be
  going to
  = to be about to
  attention, tu vas tomber! = careful, you're
    going to fall!
  j'allais partir quand il est arrivé = I was
    about to leave when he arrived
* (*when talking about health, business*)
  comment vas-tu?, comment allez-vous?
    = how are you?
  je vais bien = I'm fine
  qu'est-ce qui ne va pas? = what's the
    matter?

  ! *For more examples, see* **ça.**

* (*to be flattering or convenient*) = to suit, to
  be good for
  le rouge te va bien = red suits you, red is
    right for you
* (*to be of the right size*) = to fit
  son costume ne lui va plus = his suit
    doesn't fit him any more
* (*when urging or encouraging*)
  allons, taisez-vous! = come on, be quiet!
  allez-y, tirez! = go on, pull!

2 s'en aller verb (**!** + être)
* (if it's a person)
 s'en aller = to leave, to be off, to go (away)
 va-t'en!, allez-vous-en! = go away!
* (if it's a stain)
 s'en aller = to come out
3 noun, masculine
 un aller simple = a single (ticket), a one-way ticket
 un aller retour = a return ticket, a round trip ticket

allô exclamation
 allô! = hello!

allonger verb 13
1 (**!** + avoir)
* = to lengthen
* = to stretch out
2 s'allonger (**!** + être)
* **s'allonger** = to lie down
* **s'allonger** = to get longer

allumer verb 1
* = to light
* = to turn on

allumette noun, feminine
 une allumette = a match

allure noun, feminine
* **l'allure** = the speed
 = the pace
 à toute allure = at top speed
* **une allure** = an appearance
 = a look

alors
1 adverb
* = so
 et alors? = so what?
* = then
 alors je prendrai le bleu = I'll take the blue one then, OK I'll take the blue one
* **ça alors!** = my goodness!, oh dear!
2 alors que = while
 = even though

alouette noun, feminine
 une alouette = a lark

alpinisme noun, masculine
 l'alpinisme = climbing, mountaineering

alpiniste noun, masculine/feminine
 un alpiniste/une alpiniste = a mountain-climber

altitude noun, feminine
 l'altitude = the altitude
 = the height

amande noun, feminine
 une amande = an almond

amateur noun, masculine
* (a keen person)
 un amateur = an enthusiast
* (not a professional)
 un amateur = an amateur

ambassade noun, feminine
 une ambassade = an embassy

ambiance noun, feminine
 l'ambiance = the atmosphere
 il y a de l'ambiance = it's pretty lively

ambition noun, feminine
 l'ambition = ambition

âme noun, feminine
 une âme = a soul

amélioration noun, feminine
 une amélioration = an improvement

améliorer verb 1
 = to improve

aménagé/aménagée adjective
* = fully-equipped
* = converted

aménager verb 13
* = to equip
 = to fit out
* = to convert
 aménager une grange = to convert a barn

amende noun, feminine
 une amende = a fine

amener verb 16
 = to bring
 amenez vos amis = bring your friends

amer/amère adjective
 = bitter

américain/américaine
1 adjective
 = American
2 américain noun, masculine
 l'américain = American English

Amérique noun, feminine
 l'Amérique = America
 l'Amérique du Nord = North America

ami/amie noun, masculine/feminine
 un ami/une amie = a (male) friend/a (female) friend
 un petit ami/une petite amie = a boyfriend/a girlfriend

amical/amicale adjective
(plural) **amicaux/amicales**
 = friendly

amicalement adverb
* = in a friendly way
* (ending a letter) = best wishes

amitié noun, feminine
* **l'amitié** = friendship
* (ending a letter)
 amitiés = kindest regards, fondly

amour noun, masculine
 l'amour = love

amoureux/amoureuse adjective
 = in love

ampoule noun, feminine
* (for lighting)
  une ampoule = a light bulb
* (on the skin)
  une ampoule = a blister

amusant/amusante adjective
= entertaining
= funny

amuser verb ⒈
1 (! + avoir)
= to amuse
2 s'amuser (! + être)
s'amuser = to enjoy oneself
= to have fun

an noun, masculine
un an = one year
avoir seize ans = to be sixteen years old

ananas noun, masculine (! never changes)
un ananas = a pineapple

ancêtre noun, masculine/feminine
un ancêtre/une ancêtre = an ancestor

anchois noun, masculine (! never changes)
un anchois = an anchovy

ancien/ancienne adjective
* (if placed before the noun) = former
  l'ancienne mairie = the former town hall
* (if placed after the noun) = old
  = antique

âne noun, masculine
un âne = a donkey

ange noun, masculine
un ange = an angel

angine noun, feminine
une angine = a throat infection, tonsillitis

anglais/anglaise
1 adjective
= English
2 anglais noun, masculine
l'anglais = English

Anglais/Anglaise noun, masculine/feminine
un Anglais/une Anglaise = an Englishman/an Englishwoman
les Anglais = the English

angle noun, masculine
* **un angle** = an angle
* **un angle** = a corner
  le magasin qui fait l'angle = the shop on the corner

Angleterre noun, feminine
l'Angleterre = England

animal noun, masculine
(plural) **animaux**
un animal = an animal
un animal de compagnie = a pet

animé/animée adjective
= lively

anneau noun, masculine
(plural) **anneaux**
un anneau = a ring

année noun, feminine
une année = a year
Bonne année! = Happy New Year!
les années 60 = the sixties

anniversaire noun, masculine
un anniversaire (of one's birth) = a birthday
(of an event) = an anniversary
Joyeux anniversaire! = Happy birthday!

annonce noun, feminine
* **une annonce** = an advertisement
  les petites annonces = classified advertisements
* **une annonce** = an announcement

annoncer verb ⒓
1 (! + avoir)
= to announce
2 s'annoncer (! + être)
ça s'annonce bien = it looks promising

annuaire noun, masculine
un annuaire (téléphonique) = a telephone directory, a phone book
l'annuaire électronique = the electronic telephone directory on Minitel

annuler verb ⒈
= to cancel

antigel noun, masculine
l'antigel = antifreeze

antillais/antillaise adjective
= West Indian

Antilles noun, feminine plural
les Antilles = the West Indies

antipathique adjective
= unpleasant

antivol noun, masculine
un antivol = an antitheft device

anxieux/anxieuse adjective
= anxious

août noun, masculine
août = August

apercevoir verb ⒌
1 (! + avoir)
= to catch sight of
= to see
2 s'apercevoir (! + être)
s'apercevoir que = to realize that
= to notice that

aperçu/aperçue
1 ▶ **apercevoir** ⒌
2 aperçu noun, masculine
un aperçu = a general idea

aplatir verb ⒊
= to flatten

appareil noun, masculine
* un appareil = a device, a gadget
 = an appliance
* un appareil = a telephone
 Victor à l'appareil = (this is) Victor speaking
* un appareil = an aeroplane, an airplane
* un appareil (photo) = a camera

apparence noun, feminine
 l'apparence = appearance

appartement noun, masculine
 un appartement = a flat, an apartment

appartenir verb 36
 appartenir à = to belong to
 à qui appartiennent les clés? = whose keys are they?

appel noun, masculine
* (in order to attract attention)
 un appel = a call
* (at school)
 l'appel = registration
 faire l'appel = to take the register, to call the roll

appeler verb 19
 1 (! + avoir)
* = to call
* = to phone
 2 s'appeler (! + être)
 s'appeler = to be called
 comment t'appelles-tu? = what's your name?

appendicite noun, feminine
 l'appendicite = appendicitis

appétissant/appétissante adjective
 = appetizing

appétit noun, masculine
 l'appétit = appetite
 bon appétit! = enjoy your meal!

applaudir verb 3
 = to applaud, to clap

applaudissements noun, masculine plural
 des applaudissements = applause

appliquer verb 1
 1 (! + avoir)
* (on the skin, on a surface) = to apply
* (to enforce) = to implement
 2 s'appliquer (! + être)
* (to do one's best)
 s'appliquer = to apply oneself
* (to be relevant)
 s'appliquer = to apply

apporter verb 1
 = to bring

apprécier verb 2
 = to like, to appreciate

apprendre verb 52
* (to get knowledge) = to learn
 ils ont appris à lire = they've learned to read
* (to give lessons) = to teach
 elle m'apprenait à conduire = she was teaching me to drive
 ça t'apprendra! = that'll teach you!
* (to receive information) = to hear
 j'ai appris qu'elle était partie = I heard that she'd left
* (to give information) = to tell

apprentissage noun, masculine
* l'apprentissage = training
* l'apprentissage du russe = learning Russian

appris/apprise ▶ **apprendre** 52

approcher verb 1
 1 (! + avoir)
* = to get nearer, to get closer
* = to bring nearer, to bring closer
 2 approcher de (! + avoir)
 approcher de = to be getting close to
 3 s'approcher de (! + être)
 s'approcher de = to go closer to
 = to come closer to

approuver verb 1
 = to approve of

approximativement adverb
 = approximately

appuyer verb 22
 1 (! + avoir)
* = to press, to push
* = to rest
* = to lean
 2 s'appuyer (! + être)
 s'appuyer = to lean

après
 1 preposition
 = after
 2 adverb
 = afterward(s), after
 = later
 3 d'après
 d'après moi = in my opinion
 d'après [lui | eux | le journal ...] = according to [him | them | the newspaper ...]

après-demain adverb
 = the day after tomorrow

après-midi noun, masculine or feminine (! never changes)
 un or une après-midi = an afternoon

après-vente adjective (! never changes)
 le service après-vente = after-sales service

aquarium noun, masculine
 un aquarium = an aquarium, a fish tank

arabe
 1 adjective
 = Arab
 = Arabic

2 *noun, masculine*
l'**arabe** = Arabic

Arabe *noun, masculine|feminine*
un **Arabe**/une **Arabe** = an Arab

araignée *noun, feminine*
une **araignée** = a spider

arbitre *noun, masculine*
un **arbitre** = a referee

arbre *noun, masculine*
un **arbre** = a tree
un **arbre de Noël** = a Christmas tree

arc *noun, masculine*
un **arc** (*a weapon*) = a bow

arc-en-ciel *noun, masculine*
(*plural*) **arcs-en-ciel**
un **arc-en-ciel** = a rainbow

arche *noun, feminine*
une **arche** = an arch

ardoise *noun, feminine*
l'**ardoise** = slate

arête *noun, feminine*
• (*in a fish*)
une **arête** = a fishbone
• (*of a mountain*)
l'**arête** = the ridge

argent *noun, masculine*
• (*metal*)
l'**argent** = silver
• (*currency*)
l'**argent** = money
l'**argent liquide** = cash
l'**argent de poche** = pocket money,
spending money

argot *noun, masculine*
l'**argot** = slang

arme *noun, feminine*
une **arme** = a weapon
une **arme à feu** = a firearm

armée *noun, feminine*
une **armée** = an army

armoire *noun, feminine*
une **armoire** = a wardrobe, a closet
une **armoire à pharmacie** = a medicine
cupboard, a medicine cabinet

arracher *verb* ⒈
• = to pull out
• = to tear out
• = to snatch

arranger *verb* ⒔
1 (**!** + *avoir*)
• = to arrange
• = to fix, to repair
• = to tidy, to clean up
• = to suit
ça m'**arrange** d'y aller avec eux = it suits
me to go with them

2 s'**arranger** (**!** + *être*)
• s'**arranger** = to improve
le temps s'est **arrangé** = the weather has
improved
• s'**arranger** = to sort itself out, to work out
• s'**arranger** = to come to an agreement

arrestation *noun, feminine*
une **arrestation** = an arrest

arrêt *noun, masculine*
un **arrêt** = a stop
un **arrêt d'autobus** = a bus stop

arrêter *verb* ⒈
1 (**!** + *avoir*)
• = to stop
arrête de crier = stop shouting
arrête! = stop it!
• = to arrest
2 s'**arrêter** (**!** + *être*)
s'**arrêter** = to stop

arrhes *noun, feminine plural*
des **arrhes** = a deposit

arrière
1 *adjective*
= back
= rear
2 *noun, masculine*
• (*the rear part*)
l'**arrière** = the back
• (*in sport*)
un **arrière** = a fullback
= a defender
3 en **arrière** *adverb*
• = backward(s)
se pencher en **arrière** = to lean back
• = behind
rester en **arrière** = to stay behind

arrivée *noun, feminine*
• (*of a plane, a passenger*)
une **arrivée** = an arrival
aller chercher un ami à l'**arrivée du train**
= to meet a friend off the train, to meet
a friend from the train
• (*of a race*)
l'**arrivée** = the finish

arriver *verb* ⒈ (**!** + *être*)
• = to arrive
• = to come
j'**arrive**! = I'm coming!
ils sont **arrivés** en courant = they came up
running, they ran up
• = to reach
arriver à faire = to manage to do, to
succeed in doing
je n'y **arrive** pas = I can't manage it, I can't
do it
• = to happen
c'est **arrivé** à mon frère = it happened to
my brother
que t'est-il **arrivé**? = what happened to
you?
il m'**arrive** d'oublier = I sometimes forget

arrondir verb ③
  arrondir un chiffre = to round off a figure

arrondissement noun, masculine
  un arrondissement = an arrondissement, a
  district

arroser verb ①
  = to water
  = to spray

arrosoir noun, masculine
  un arrosoir = a watering can

art noun, masculine
  l'art = art
les arts ménagers = home economics

artichaut noun, masculine
  un artichaut = an artichoke

article noun, masculine
• (in grammar)
  un article = an article
• (in a shop)
  un article = an item
  des articles de sport = sports equipment
  des articles de toilette = toiletries

artificiel/artificielle adjective
  = artificial
  = man-made

artisan noun, masculine
  un artisan = a craftsman

artisanal/artisanale adjective
(plural) **artisanaux/artisanales**
  une méthode artisanale = a traditional
    method
  de fabrication artisanale = hand-crafted,
    hand-made
  = home-made

artisanat noun, masculine
  l'artisanat = the craft industry
  magasin d'artisanat = arts and crafts shop

artiste noun, masculine/feminine
  un artiste/une artiste = an artist
  (in films, plays) = an actor/an actress
  un artiste peintre = a painter

as¹ ▶ **avoir** ⑧

as² noun, masculine (**!** never changes)
  un as = an ace

ascenseur noun, masculine
  un ascenseur = a lift, an elevator

ascension noun, feminine
  une ascension = an ascent

Ascension noun, feminine
  l'Ascension = Ascension

asiatique adjective
  = from the Far East, Asian

Asie noun, feminine
  l'Asie = Asia

asperge noun, feminine
  des asperges = asparagus

asphyxier: s'asphyxier verb ②
(**!** + être)
  s'asphyxier = to suffocate

aspirateur noun, masculine
  un aspirateur = a vacuum cleaner

assassin noun, masculine
  un assassin = a murderer

assassinat noun, masculine
  un assassinat = a murder

assassiner verb ①
  = to murder

asseoir: s'asseoir verb ㉞ (**!** + être)
  s'asseoir = to sit (down)
  (in bed) = to sit up

assez adverb
  = enough
  = quite, pretty

assiette noun, feminine
  une assiette = a plate
une assiette anglaise = assorted cold
  meats, cold cuts

assis/assise
1 ▶ **asseoir** ㉞
2 adjective
  = seated

assister verb ①
• assister à = to attend, to be at
• assister à = to witness

association noun, feminine
  une association sportive = a sports
    association, a (sports) club

assorti/assortie adjective
• = matching
• = assorted

assurance noun, feminine
• (a feeling)
  l'assurance = (self-)confidence
• (against accidents)
  une assurance = insurance
l'assurance maladie = health insurance
l'assurance au tiers = third-party
  insurance
l'assurance tous risques
  = comprehensive insurance

assuré/assurée
1 adjective
• = confident
• = certain
2 noun, masculine/feminine
  l'assuré/l'assurée = the insured party

assurer verb ①
1 (**!** + avoir)
• (to tell confidently) = to assure
  il m'a assuré que c'était vrai = he assured
    me that it was true
• (against accidents) = to insure
2 s'assurer (**!** + être)
• s'assurer = to take out insurance
• s'assurer que = to make sure that

astrologue noun, masculine|feminine
  un astrologue/une astrologue = an
    astrologer

astronaute noun, masculine|feminine
  un astronaute/une astronaute = an
    astronaut

astuce noun, feminine
• une astuce = a trick
• l'astuce = cleverness
  = shrewdness

astucieux/astucieuse adjective
  = clever, smart
  = shrewd

atelier noun, masculine
  un atelier (for a craftsman) = a workshop
  (for a painter) = a studio

athlétisme noun, masculine
  l'athlétisme = athletics

Atlantique noun, masculine
  l'(océan) Atlantique = the Atlantic (Ocean)

atout noun, masculine
• (at cards)
  un atout = a trump
  atout trèfle! = clubs are trumps!
• (in life)
  un atout = an asset, an advantage

attacher verb 1
1 (! + avoir)
  = to tie
  = to fasten
2 s'attacher à (! + être)
  s'attacher à = to become attached to

attaquer verb 1
1 (! + avoir)
  = to attack
2 s'attaquer à (! + être)
  s'attaquer à = to attack

atteindre verb 55
• = to reach
• = to hit
• être atteint d'une maladie = to suffer from
    a disease

atteint/atteinte ▶ atteindre 55

attendre verb 6
1 (! + avoir)
• = to wait
  = to wait (for)
• = to expect
  j'attends une visite = I'm expecting a visit
2 s'attendre à (! + être)
  s'attendre à = to expect
  il fallait s'y attendre = it was to be expected

attendu/attendue ▶ attendre 6

attentat noun, masculine
  un attentat (on a person) = an
    assassination attempt
  (on a group, a building) = an attack

attente noun, feminine
  l'attente = wait(ing)

attention noun, feminine
  l'attention = attention
  faire attention (to take care) = to be careful
  (to concentrate) = to pay attention
  attention! = careful!, watch out!
  attention à la marche! = mind the step!,
    watch the step!

attentivement adverb
  = attentively

atterrir verb 3
  = to land

atterrissage noun, masculine
  un atterrissage = a landing

attirer verb 1
1 (! + avoir)
  = to attract
2 s'attirer (! + être)
  s'attirer des ennuis = to get into trouble

attraction noun, feminine
• l'attraction = attraction
• des attractions = entertainment
  un parc d'attractions = an amusement
    park

attraper verb 1
  = to catch

au ▶ à

auberge noun, feminine
  une auberge = an inn
  une auberge de jeunesse = a youth
    hostel

aucun/aucune
1 adjective
  = no, not any
  en aucun cas = under no circumstances
  aucune idée! = I've no idea!
2 pronoun
  = none, not any
  aucun d'entre nous = none of us
  aucune des deux = neither of them

audace noun, feminine
  l'audace (bravery) = boldness
  (guts) = audacity, nerve

audacieux/audacieuse adjective
  = bold

au-delà de preposition
  = beyond
  = over

au-dessous de preposition
  = below
  = under

au-dessus de preposition
  = above
  = over

auditeur/auditrice noun,
masculine|feminine
  un auditeur/une auditrice = a listener

augmenter verb 1
= to increase

aujourd'hui adverb
• = today
• = nowadays

aurai ▶ avoir 8

aussi
1 adverb
• = also, as well
= too
eux aussi ont faim = they are hungry too
• = so
je ne savais pas que c'était aussi cher = I didn't know it was so expensive
il n'avait jamais vu un aussi gros chien = he'd never seen such a large dog
• = as
aussi [riche | vieux | petit ...] que = as [rich | old | small ...] as
2 conjunction
= so, consequently
aussi sommes-nous partis = (and) so we left

aussitôt
1 adverb
= immediately, right away
2 aussitôt que = as soon as

Australie noun, feminine
l'Australie = Australia

australien/australienne adjective
= Australian

autant adverb
1 autant que = as much as
il gagne autant que toi = he earns as much as you
2 autant de = as much
= as many
autant de [valeur | patience | temps ...] que = as much [value | patience | time ...] as
autant de [fautes | lettres | soucis ...] que = as many [mistakes | letters | worries ...] as

auteur noun, masculine
l'auteur (of a book) = the author
(of a song) = the composer

auto noun, feminine
une auto = a car

autobus noun, masculine (**!** never changes)
un autobus = a bus

autocar noun, masculine
un autocar = a coach, a bus

autocollant/autocollante
1 adjective
= self-adhesive
2 autocollant noun, masculine
un autocollant = a sticker

auto-école noun, feminine
(plural) **auto-écoles**
une auto-école = a driving school

automne noun, masculine
l'automne = autumn, fall

automobile noun, feminine
une automobile = a (motor)car, an automobile

automobiliste noun, masculine|feminine
un automobiliste/une automobiliste = a motorist

autoritaire adjective
= authoritarian

autoroute noun, feminine
une autoroute = a motorway, a highway

auto-stop noun, masculine
l'auto-stop = hitchhiking
faire de l'auto-stop = to hitchhike

autour de preposition
= around

autre
1 determiner
= other
l'autre jour = the other day
rien d'autre = nothing else
2 d'autre part = besides
= on the other hand

autrefois adverb
= in the past
= before

autrement adverb
• = in a different way, differently
autrement dit = in other words
• (if not) = otherwise
autrement il ne viendra pas = otherwise he won't come

Autriche noun, feminine
l'Autriche = Austria

autrichien/autrichienne adjective
= Austrian

autruche noun, feminine
une autruche = an ostrich

aux ▶ à

avais ▶ avoir 8

avaler verb 1
= to swallow

avance
1 noun, feminine
• (of an army)
l'avance = the advance
• (on a competitor)
une avance = a lead
• (money)
une avance = an advance
2 à l'avance = in advance
3 d'avance
• **payer d'avance** = to pay in advance
• **avoir cinq minutes d'avance** = to be five minutes early

avoir　*verb* 8

present	imperfect	future	past participle
j'ai	j'avais	j'aurai	eu / eue
tu as	tu avais	tu auras	
il / elle a	ill / elle avait	il / elle aura	
nous avons	nous avions	nous aurons	
vous avez	vous aviez	vous aurez	
ils / elles ont	ils / elles avaient	ils / elles auront	

● **1 avoir** functions as an ordinary verb:

= to have (got)

　ils **ont** un chien　　　= *they have a dog*

● = to get

　réussir à **avoir** des billets = *to manage to get tickets*

2 avoir is used as an auxiliary verb to conjugate most other verbs, except all reflexive verbs and those verbs labelled (**!** + *être*):

　elle **a** bu son lait　　= *she drank her milk*
　ils **auraient** aimé te voir = *they would have liked to see you*

3 avoir is used in the phrase **il y a**:

　il y **a**　　　　　　= *there is* or *there are*
　il y **aura**　　　　　= *there will be*

4 avoir is used in expressions like **avoir faim, avoir soif, avoir l'air, avoir besoin de** etc. You will find translations at **faim, soif, air, besoin** etc.

---

4 en avance
　arriver en avance = to arrive early
　être en avance sur les autres = to be
　　ahead of the others

avancer *verb* 12
1 (**!** + *avoir*)
● = to move forward
　avancer d'un mètre = to move forward one
　　metre
● = to make progress
　avancer lentement = to make slow
　　progress
● = to be fast
　ta montre avance de cinq minutes = your
　　watch is five minutes fast
● = to bring forward
　avancer une réunion = to bring a meeting
　　forward, to push a meeting up
● = to lend
　avancer de l'argent à un ami = to lend
　　money to a friend
2 s'avancer (**!** + *être*)
　s'avancer = to move forward
　il s'est avancé vers la table = he moved
　　toward(s) the table

avant
1 *noun, masculine*
● (*the front part*)
　l'avant = the front

● (*in sport*)
　un avant = a forward
2 *adjective* (**!** *never changes*)
　= front
　les roues avant = the front wheels
3 *preposition*
　= before
　juste avant de partir = just before leaving
4 *adverb*
　= before
　= first
　que faisait-il avant? = what was he doing
　　before?
　la semaine d'avant = the week before
　la dame était avant = the lady was first
5 en avant = forward(s)
● **se pencher en avant** = to lean forward(s)
● **partir en avànt** = to go (on) ahead

avantage *noun, masculine*
　un avantage = an advantage

avant-hier *adverb*
　= the day before yesterday

avare *adjective*
　= mean, miserly

avec *preposition*
　= with

avenir *noun, masculine*
　l'avenir = the future
　à l'avenir = in (the) future

✲ in informal situations

aventure *noun, feminine*
  une aventure = an adventure
  partir à l'aventure = to set off in search of
    adventure

aventurier/aventurière *noun,*
masculine/feminine
  un aventurier/une aventurière = an
    adventurer

averse *noun, feminine*
  une averse = a shower, a downpour

avertir *verb* ③
* = to warn
* = to inform

aveugle *adjective*
  = blind

avez ▶ **avoir** ⑧

avion *noun, masculine*
  un avion = an aeroplane, an airplane
  un avion = a jet (plane)

aviron *noun, masculine*
* **l'aviron** = rowing
* **un aviron** = an oar

avis *noun, masculine* (**!** *never changes*)
* (*a belief*)
  un avis = an opinion
  changer d'avis = to change one's mind
* (*an announcement*)
  un avis = a notice, a sign

avocat¹ *noun, masculine*
  un avocat = an avocado

avocat²/avocate *noun,*
masculine/feminine
  un avocat/une avocate = a lawyer
  = a barrister, an attorney

avoir *verb* ⑧
▶ See the boxed note.

avons ▶ **avoir** ⑧

avouer *verb* ①
  = to confess

avril *noun, masculine*
  avril = April

ayant ▶ **avoir** ⑧

baby-foot *noun, masculine* (**!** *never*
changes)
  le baby-foot = table football

bac, **baccalauréat** *noun, masculine*
  le baccalauréat = the baccalaureate (*a*
    school-leaving diploma taken at 17–18)

badaud *noun, masculine*
  un badaud = an onlooker

bagage *noun, masculine*
  un bagage = a piece of luggage

bagarre *noun, feminine*
  une bagarre = a fight

bagarrer; se bagarrer *verb* ① (**!** + *être*)
  se bagarrer = to fight

bague *noun, feminine*
  une bague = a ring

baguette *noun, feminine*
* (*bread*)
  une baguette = a baguette, a French stick,
    French bread
* (*a thin piece of wood*)
  une baguette = a stick
  une baguette magique = a magic wand

baie *noun, feminine*
* (*on the coast*)
  une baie = a bay
* (*fruit*)
  une baie = a berry

baignade *noun, feminine*
  la baignade = swimming

baigner; se baigner *verb* ① (**!** + *être*)
  se baigner = to go for a swim

baignoire *noun, feminine*
  une baignoire = a bathtub

bâiller *verb* ①
  = to yawn

bain *noun, masculine*
* (*at home*)
  un bain = a bath
  prendre un bain = to have a bath, to take a
    bath
* (*at the swimming pool*)
  le grand bain = the (main) pool
  le petit bain = the shallow pool, the
    learners' pool

baiser *noun, masculine*
  un baiser = a kiss

baisser *verb* ①
1 (**!** + *avoir*)
* = to lower
  baisser le store = to lower the blinds
* = to drop
  la température a baissé = the temperature
    has dropped
2 se baisser (**!** + *être*)
  se baisser = to bend down, to reach down

bal *noun, masculine*
  un bal = a dance, a ball

balade *noun, feminine*
  une balade (*on foot*) = a walk, a stroll
  (*by car*) = a drive
  (*on a bicycle*) = a ride

balader:**se balader** verb [1] (**!** + *être*)
  se balader (*on foot*) = to go for a walk
  (*by car*) = to go for a drive
  (*on a bicycle*) = to go for a ride

baladeur *noun, masculine*
  un baladeur = a walkman

balai *noun, masculine*
  un balai = a broom

balance *noun, feminine*
  une balance = scales

Balance *noun, feminine*
  la Balance = Libra

balançoire *noun, feminine*
  une balançoire = a swing
  = a see-saw

balayer *verb* [21]
  = to sweep

balcon *noun, masculine*
  un balcon = a balcony

baleine *noun, feminine*
  une baleine = a whale

balle *noun, feminine*
• (*for playing*)
  une balle = a (small) ball
• (*for a gun*)
  une balle = a bullet

ballerine *noun, feminine*
• (*a person*)
  une ballerine = a ballerina
• (*footwear*)
  une ballerine (*for dancing*) = a ballet
  pump, a ballet slipper
  (*for walking*) = a flat pump, a slipper

ballon *noun, masculine*
  un ballon = a (large) ball

bambou *noun, masculine*
  le bambou = bamboo

banal/**banale** *adjective*
  = commonplace, ordinary

banane *noun, feminine*
• **une banane** = a banana
• **une banane** = a bum bag, a fanny pack

banc *noun, masculine*
  un banc = a bench

bancaire *adjective*
  = bank, banking

bande *noun, feminine*
• (*of people*)
  une bande = a group, a bunch
• (*with sound*)
  une bande = a tape
• (*something long and narrow*)
  une bande = a strip
une bande dessinée = a comic strip

bandeau *noun, masculine*
(*plural*) **bandeaux**
  un bandeau (*holding the hair*) = a
  hairband, a headband
  (*over the eyes*) = a blindfold

banlieue *noun, feminine*
  la banlieue = the suburbs

banque *noun, feminine*
  une banque = a bank

banquette *noun, feminine*
  une banquette = a seat

banquier *noun, masculine*
  un banquier = a banker

baptême *noun, masculine*
  un baptême = a christening

bar *noun, masculine*
  un bar = a bar

barbant/**barbante*** *adjective*
  = boring

barbare *noun, masculine*/*feminine*
  un barbare/**une barbare** = a barbarian

barbe *noun, feminine*
• **une barbe** = a beard
• **quelle barbe*****! = what a bore!
la barbe à papa = candyfloss, cotton
candy

barber:**se barber*** [1] (**!** + *être*)
  se barber = to be bored

barboter *verb* [1]
  = to paddle

barbu *noun, masculine*
  un barbu = a bearded man

barque *noun, feminine*
  une barque = a (small) boat

barrage *noun, masculine*
• (*on a river*)
  un barrage = a dam
• (*on a road*)
  un barrage de police = a police roadblock

barre *noun, feminine*
• (*of metal, chocolate*)
  une barre = a bar
• (*a line*)
  une barre = a stroke, a mark
• (*on a ship*)
  la barre = the tiller, the helm

barreau *noun, masculine*
(*plural*) **barreaux**
  un barreau (*on a cage*) = a bar

barrer *verb* [1]
• = to cross out
• = to block

barrière *noun, feminine*
• (*enclosing an area*)
  une barrière = a fence

✶ in informal situations

* (an obstacle)
  une barrière = a barrier

bar-tabac noun, masculine
(plural) **bars-tabac**
  un bar-tabac = a café (also selling stamps and cigarettes)

bas/basse
1 adjective
  = low
2 bas adverb
* = low
  voir plus bas = see below
* = quietly
  parler tout bas = to speak in a whisper
3 bas noun, masculine (! never changes)
* (the lower part)
  le bas = the bottom
  en bas = downstairs
  à bas les patrons! = down with bosses!
* (a garment)
  un bas = a stocking

basculer verb [1]
* (to fall over) = to topple over
* (to tilt) = to tip up

basilic noun, masculine
  le basilic = basil

basket
1 noun, masculine
  le basket = basketball
2 noun, feminine
  des baskets = trainers, sneakers

basse ▶ bas 1

bassin noun, masculine
  un bassin = a pool

bataille noun, feminine
  une bataille = a battle
  la bataille navale = battleships

bateau noun, masculine
(plural) **bateaux**
  un bateau = a boat
  faire du bateau = to go boating
  = to go sailing

bateau-mouche noun, masculine
(plural) **bateaux-mouches**
  un bateau-mouche a large river boat for sightseeing

bâtiment noun, masculine
  un bâtiment = a building

bâtir verb [3]
  = to build

bâton noun, masculine
  un bâton = a stick

batterie noun, feminine
* (in a car)
  la batterie = the battery
* (in a band)
  la batterie = the percussion, the drums

battre verb [61]
1 (! + avoir)
  = to beat
  battre un record = to break a record
* **le cœur battant** = with a beating heart
* **battre des mains** = to clap
2 se battre (! + être)
  se battre = to fight

battu/battue ▶ battre [61]

baudruche noun, feminine
  un ballon en baudruche = a balloon

bavard/bavarde adjective
  = talkative

bavarder verb [1]
  = to chat

bazar noun, masculine
  un bazar (a shop) = a general store

BD noun, feminine
  une BD = a comic strip

beau/belle adjective
(plural) **beaux/belles**

  ! bel is used instead of beau before masculine nouns beginning with a vowel or a mute h. The plural of bel is **beaux**.

  = beautiful, handsome
  = fine
  il fait beau = the weather is fine

beaucoup adverb
  = a lot
  = much
  c'est beaucoup trop = it's far too much
  beaucoup de [patience | temps | livres …] = a lot of [patience | time | books …]
  il ne me reste plus beaucoup d'argent = I haven't got much money left

beau-frère noun, masculine
(plural) **beaux-frères**
  un beau-frère = a brother-in-law

beau-père noun, masculine
(plural) **beaux-pères**
  un beau-père = a father-in-law
  = a stepfather

beauté noun, feminine
  la beauté = beauty

beaux-arts noun, masculine plural
  les beaux-arts = fine arts

bébé noun, masculine
  un bébé = a baby

bec noun, masculine
  un bec = a beak

bêche noun, feminine
  une bêche = a spade, a shovel

beignet noun, masculine
  un beignet = a fritter
  = a doughnut, a donut

bel ▶ **beau**

belge *adjective*
= Belgian

Belgique *noun, feminine*
la Belgique = Belgium

Bélier *noun, masculine*
le Bélier = Aries

belle ▶ **beau**

belle-fille *noun, feminine*
(*plural*) **belles-filles**
une belle-fille = a daughter-in-law

belle-mère *noun, feminine*
(*plural*) **belles-mères**
une belle-mère = a mother-in-law
= a stepmother

belle-sœur *noun, feminine*
(*plural*) **belles-sœurs**
une belle-sœur = a sister-in-law

bénéfice *noun, masculine*
faire un bénéfice = to make a profit

béquille *noun, feminine*
une béquille = a crutch

berceau *noun, masculine*
(*plural*) **berceaux**
un berceau = a cradle

bercer *verb* 12
= to rock

berge *noun, feminine*
la berge (de la rivière) = the (river)bank

berger/bergère *noun,*
masculine/feminine
un berger/une bergère = a shepherd/a
shepherdess
un berger allemand = a German
shepherd dog, an Alsatian

bermuda *noun, masculine*
un bermuda = bermuda shorts

besoin *noun, masculine*
un besoin = a need
avoir besoin d'argent = to need money

bête
1 *adjective*
= stupid, silly
2 *noun, feminine*
une bête = an animal

bêtise *noun, feminine*
• **la bêtise** = stupidity
• **faire une bêtise** = to do something silly
dire des bêtises = to talk nonsense

béton *noun, masculine*
le béton = concrete

betterave *noun, feminine*
une betterave = a beetroot, a beet

✶ in informal situations

beurre *noun, masculine*
le beurre = butter

bibelot *noun, masculine*
un bibelot = an ornament

biberon *noun, masculine*
un biberon = a (baby's) bottle, a (nursing)
bottle

bibliothèque *noun, feminine*
une bibliothèque (*a room or a building*) = a
library
(*a piece of furniture*) = a bookcase

bic *noun, masculine*
un bic = a biro , a ballpoint pen

bicyclette *noun, feminine*
• (*the equipment*)
une bicyclette = a bicycle
• (*the sport*)
faire de la bicyclette = to cycle, to go
cycling

bidon
1 *adjective*✶ (**!** *never changes*)
= bogus, phoney
2 *noun, masculine*
un bidon = a can
= a drum

bidonville *noun, masculine*
un bidonville = a shanty town

bien
1 *adjective* (**!** *never changes*)
• = good
2 *adverb*
• = well
ils vont bien = they're well
ça s'est bien passé = it went well
c'est bien fait pour lui! = it serves him
right!
• = very
c'est bien triste = it's very sad
je l'espère bien = I very much hope so, I
hope so
• = exactly
• = definitely
c'est bien ce que je pensais = that's
(exactly) what I thought
la voiture rouge est bien à eux = the red
car is definitely theirs
je te l'avais bien dit! = I told you so!
3 *noun, masculine*
le bien = good
c'est pour ton bien = it's for your own good
4 **bien sûr** = of course
5 **bien entendu** = naturally

bientôt *adverb*
= soon

bienvenu/bienvenue *adjective*
= welcome

bière *noun, feminine*
la bière = beer
la bière (à la) pression = draught beer,
draft beer

la bière blonde = lager, light beer
la bière brune = stout

bifteck noun, masculine
le bifteck = steak

bifurquer verb [1]
• (if it's a road) = to fork
• (if it's a driver) = to turn off

bijou noun, masculine
(plural) **bijoux**
un bijou = a piece of jewellery, a piece of
jewelry

bijouterie noun, feminine
une bijouterie = a jeweller's, a jewellery
shop, a jewelry store

bijoutier/bijoutière noun,
masculine/feminine
un bijoutier/une bijoutière = a jeweller, a
jeweler

bilingue adjective
= bilingual

billard noun, masculine
le billard = billiards
le billard américain = pool
le billard anglais = snooker

bille noun, feminine
une bille = a marble

billet noun, masculine
• (on a train, at the theatre)
un billet = a ticket
• (money)
un billet (de banque) = a (bank)note, a bill

biscotte noun, feminine
une biscotte ≈ a rusk

bise✻ noun, feminine
une bise✻ = a kiss

bisou✻ noun, masculine
un bisou✻ = a kiss

bissextile adjective
une année bissextile = a leap year

bistro(t)✻ noun, masculine
un bistro(t)✻ = a bistro, a café

bizarre adjective
= strange, peculiar

blague✻ noun, feminine
• une blague✻ = a funny story
• (a piece of mischief)
une blague✻ = a trick
faire une blague✻ à un ami = to play a trick
on a friend

blanc/blanche
1 adjective
• = white
• = blank
2 **blanc** noun, masculine
un blanc (a space) = a blank
un blanc d'œuf = an egg white

du blanc de poulet = a piece of chicken
breast

blanchisserie noun, feminine
une blanchisserie = a laundry, a dry
cleaner's

blé noun, masculine
le blé = wheat, corn

blessé/blessée
1 adjective
= injured
= wounded
2 noun, masculine/feminine
un blessé/une blessée = an injured
person
= a casualty

blesser verb [1]
1 (**!** + avoir)
= to hurt
= to wound
2 **se blesser** (**!** + être)
se blesser = to hurt oneself
elle s'est blessée à la jambe = she hurt
her leg

blessure noun, feminine
une blessure = an injury
= a wound

bleu/bleue
1 adjective
= blue
bleu marine = navy blue
2 **bleu** noun, masculine
un bleu = a bruise

bloc
1 noun, masculine
(for writing)
un bloc = a notepad
2 **à bloc** = completely
vissé à bloc = tightly screwed
gonflé à bloc = fully inflated

blond/blonde adjective
(describing hair) = blonde, blond
(describing tobacco) = light, Virginia

bloquer verb [1]
1 (**!** + avoir)
• = to block
• = to jam
• **bloquer les salaires** = to freeze wages
2 **se bloquer** (**!** + être)
se bloquer = to jam

blouse noun, feminine
• (worn for protection)
une blouse = an overall
• (a kind of shirt)
une blouse = a blouse

blouson noun, masculine
un blouson = a blouson, a jacket

bobo✻ noun, masculine
ce n'est qu'un bobo✻ = it's only a scratch

B

bocal *noun, masculine*
(*plural*) **bocaux**
  un bocal = a jar

bœuf *noun, masculine*
• (*the animal*)
  un bœuf = an ox
• (*the meat*)
  le bœuf = beef

boire *verb* 51
  = to drink

bois
1 ▶ **boire** 51
2 *noun, masculine* (**!** *never changes*)
• (*timber*)
  le bois = wood
• (*a place*)
  un bois = a wood

boisson *noun, feminine*
  une boisson = a drink

boîte *noun, feminine*
  une boîte = a box
une boîte de conserve = a tin, a can
une boîte aux lettres = a postbox, a
  mailbox
  = a letter box, a mailbox
une boîte de nuit = a nightclub
une boîte de vitesses = a gearbox

boiter *verb* 1
  = to limp

boiteux/boiteuse *adjective*
  = lame

bol *noun, masculine*
  un bol = a bowl

bombe *noun, feminine*
• (*a weapon*)
  une bombe = a bomb
• (*an aerosol*)
  une bombe = a spray

bon/bonne[1]
1 *adjective*
• = good
• = right
  la bonne réponse = the right answer
• = valid
  le billet est encore bon = the ticket is still
  valid
• **bon anniversaire!** = happy birthday!
  bonne journée! = have a nice day
2 **bon** *adverb*
  il fait bon dehors = it's nice outside
  sentir bon = to smell nice
3 **bon** *noun, masculine*
  un bon = a coupon
  = a voucher
4 **bon** *exclamation*
  bon! = right!
  ah bon? = really?

bon marché = cheap
le bon sens = common sense

bonbon *noun, masculine*
  un bonbon = a sweet, a candy

bonbonne *noun, feminine*
  une bonbonne (*for wine*) = a demijohn
  (*for gas*) = a cylinder

bond *noun, masculine*
  un bond = a leap

bondé/bondée *adjective*
  = packed

bondir *verb* 3
  = to leap

bonhomme✶ *noun, masculine*
(*plural*) **bonshommes**
  un bonhomme✶ = a chap, a guy, a fellow
un bonhomme de neige = a snowman

bonjour *noun, masculine*
  bonjour! = hello!, good morning!, good
  afternoon!

bonne[2] *noun, feminine*
  une bonne = a maid

bonnet *noun, masculine*
  un bonnet = a cap, a hat

bonsoir *noun, masculine*
  bonsoir = good evening!, good night!

bonté *noun, feminine*
  la bonté = kindness

bord
1 *noun, masculine*
  le bord (*of a bed, a cliff*) = the edge
  (*of a road*) = the side
  (*of a river*) = the bank
  des vacances au bord de la mer = seaside
  holidays, a seaside vacation
2 **à bord** = on board, aboard

bordeaux
1 *adjective* (**!** *never changes*)
  = burgundy
2 *noun, masculine* (**!** *never changes*)
  le Bordeaux = Bordeaux wine

bordure *noun, feminine*
  la bordure (*the limit*) = the edge
  (*ornamental*) = the border

bosse *noun, feminine*
  une bosse (*on the head*) = a lump
  (*on the back*) = a hump
  (*on a car*) = a dent

botte *noun, feminine*
• (*footwear*)
  une botte = a boot
• (*a bundle*)
  une botte = a bunch

bouc *noun, masculine*
• (*an animal*)
  un bouc = a billy goat

✶ in informal situations

* (*a beard*)
  un bouc = a goatee

bouche *noun, feminine*
  la bouche = the mouth
une bouche de métro = a tube entrance,
  a subway entrance

bouchée *noun, feminine*
  une bouchée = a mouthful

boucher[1] *verb* [1]
* = to plug
  = to fill up
* = to block
  = to clog up
* = to cork

boucher[2]/**bouchère** *noun,*
masculine/feminine
  le boucher/la bouchère = the butcher

boucherie *noun, feminine*
  une boucherie = a butcher's (shop)

bouchon *noun, masculine*
* (*on a bottle*)
  un bouchon = a cork
  = a top
* (*on the road*)
  un bouchon = a traffic jam

boucle *noun, feminine*
* (*on a belt*)
  une boucle = a buckle
* (*of hair*)
  une boucle = a curl
* (*a curved shape*)
  une boucle = a loop
une boucle d'oreille = an earring

bouclé/bouclée *adjective*
  = curly

boucler *verb* [1]
* = to buckle
* = to fasten

boudin *noun, masculine*
  le boudin = black pudding, blood pudding

boue *noun, feminine*
  la boue = mud

bouffer✕ *verb* [1]
  = to eat

bouger *verb* [13]
  = to move

bougie *noun, feminine*
* (*for lighting*)
  une bougie = a candle
* (*in an engine*)
  une bougie = a sparking plug, a spark
  plug

bouillir *verb* [31]
  = to boil

bouilloire *noun, feminine*
  une bouilloire = a kettle

bouillotte *noun, feminine*
  une bouillotte = a hot-water bottle

boulanger/boulangère *noun,*
masculine/feminine
  un boulanger/une boulangère = a baker

boulangerie *noun, feminine*
  une boulangerie = a baker's (shop)

boule *noun, feminine*
* (*a shape*)
  une boule = a ball
  une boule de neige = a snowball
* (*in games*)
  une boule = a bowl
  = a boule

boulevard *noun, masculine*
  un boulevard = an avenue

boulot✕ *noun, masculine*
* **le boulot**✕ = work
* **un boulot**✕ = a job

boum✕ *noun, feminine*
  une boum✕ = a party

bouquet *noun, masculine*
  un bouquet = a bunch

bouquin✕ *noun, masculine*
  un bouquin✕ = a book

bourgeon *noun, masculine*
  un bourgeon = a bud

bousculer *verb* [1]
* = to bump into
  = to jostle
* = to rush
  ne me bouscule pas = don't rush me

boussole *noun, feminine*
  une boussole = a compass

bout *noun, masculine*
* **un bout** = a piece
* **le bout** = the end
  = the tip

bouteille *noun, feminine*
  une bouteille = a bottle
  une bouteille de gaz = a gas cylinder

boutique *noun, feminine*
  une boutique = a shop

bouton *noun, masculine*
* (*on a coat, for a doorbell*)
  un bouton = a button
* (*on the skin*)
  un bouton = a spot, a pimple
* (*on an appliance*)
  un bouton = a switch
* (*on a plant*)
  un bouton = a bud

boxe *noun, feminine*
  la boxe = boxing

bracelet *noun, masculine*
  un bracelet = a bracelet
  = a bangle

B

un bracelet de montre = a watchstrap, a watchband

branche noun, feminine
* (on a tree)
  une branche = a branch
* (an area of work, study)
  une branche = a field

branché/branchée✶ adjective
= trendy, cool

brancher verb 1
= to plug in
= to connect

braquer verb 1
* **braquer un revolver sur quelqu'un** = to aim a gun at someone
* **braquer le volant à gauche** = to turn the wheel hard (to the) left

bras noun, masculine (! never changes)
un bras = an arm
en bras de chemise = in one's shirtsleeves

brasserie noun, feminine
* (for meals)
  une brasserie = a brasserie, a café
* (a factory)
  une brasserie = a brewery

bravo exclamation
= bravo!, well done!

brebis noun, feminine (! never changes)
une brebis = a ewe

bref/brève
1 adjective
= brief, short
2 **(en) bref** adverb
= in short

Bretagne noun, feminine
la Bretagne = Brittany

breton/bretonne
1 adjective
= Breton
2 **breton** noun, masculine
le breton = Breton

brève ▶ bref 1

brevet noun, masculine
un brevet (a qualification) = a certificate
un brevet des collèges = a certificate of general education
un brevet de pilote = a pilot's licence

bricolage noun, masculine
le bricolage = DIY, do-it-yourself

brillant/brillante adjective
* = shiny
* = brilliant

briller verb 1
= to shine

brin noun, masculine
un brin (of parsley, mimosa) = a sprig
(of grass) = a blade

brioche noun, feminine
une brioche = a brioche, a (sweet) bun

briquet noun, masculine
un briquet = a cigarette lighter

britannique adjective
= British

brocante noun, feminine
une brocante = a flea market

brocanteur/brocanteuse noun, masculine/feminine
un brocanteur/une brocanteuse = a bric-à-brac dealer

broche noun, feminine
* (an ornament)
  une broche = a brooch, a pin
* (for cooking)
  une broche = a spit

brochette noun, feminine
une brochette = a kebab, a brochette

brochure noun, feminine
une brochure = a brochure

broder verb 1
= to embroider

bronzage noun, masculine
un bronzage = a (sun)tan

bronzé/bronzée adjective
= tanned, brown

bronzer verb 1
= to get a tan, to go brown

brosse noun, feminine
une brosse = a brush
avoir les cheveux (taillés) en brosse = to have a crew cut
une brosse à dents = a toothbrush

brosser verb 1
= to brush

brouillard noun, masculine
le brouillard = fog

brouillé/brouillée adjective
= jumbled, mixed up

brouillon noun, masculine
un brouillon = a rough draft

broussailles noun, feminine plural
les broussailles = the undergrowth

brugnon noun, masculine
un brugnon = a nectarine

bruit noun, masculine
le bruit = noise

brûlant/brûlante adjective
= burning hot

✶ in informal situations

brûlé noun, masculine
  ça sent le brûlé = there's a smell of
    burning

brûler verb [1]
1 (**!** + avoir)
* = to burn
* brûler un feu (rouge) = to jump the lights,
  to run the lights
2 se brûler (**!** | être)
  se brûler = to burn oneself

brume noun, feminine
  la brume = mist

brumeux/brumeuse adjective
  = misty

brun/brune adjective
* = brown, dark
* = dark-haired

brunir verb [3]
  = to tan

brusque adjective
* = abrupt
* = sudden

Bruxelles noun
  = Brussels

bruyant/bruyante adjective
  = noisy

bu/bue ▶ **boire** [51]

bûche noun, feminine
  une bûche = a log

buffet noun, masculine
* (a piece of furniture)
  un buffet = a sideboard
* (a meal, a place)
  un buffet = a buffet

buisson noun, masculine
  un buisson = a bush
  = a shrub

buissonnière adjective, feminine
  faire l'école buissonnière = to play truant,
    to play hooky

bulle noun, feminine
* (of soap)
  une bulle = a bubble
  faire des bulles = to blow bubbles
* (in a cartoon)
  une bulle = a speech bubble

bulletin noun, masculine
  un bulletin = a report
  = a form
  = a certificate
un bulletin météorologique = a weather
  report
un bulletin scolaire = a school report, a
  report card

bureau noun, masculine
(plural) **bureaux**
* (a piece of furniture)
  un bureau = a desk
* (a room)
  un bureau = an office
le bureau de poste = the post office
le bureau des renseignements = the
  information office, the information desk

bus noun, masculine (**!** never changes)
  un bus = a bus

but noun, masculine
* (what one has in mind)
  un but = a goal
  = an aim, a purpose
  = an intention
  dans le but de = with the intention of
* (in football)
  un but = a goal

buvable adjective
  = drinkable
  (on a medicine label) = to be taken orally

buveur/buveuse noun,
masculine/feminine
  un buveur/une buveuse = a drinker

Cc

c' ▶ **ce**

ça pronoun
* = this
  = that
  donne-moi ça = give me that
  ça, c'est bizarre = that's strange
* = it
  ça ne fait rien = it doesn't matter
  c'est ça! = that's right!, that's it!
  c'est pour ça que ... = that's why ...
  et avec ça? = anything else?
* où ça? = where?
* comment ça va? = how are you?
  ça va mal = things are bad
  ça y est, j'ai fini = that's it, I've finished

cabane noun, feminine
  une cabane = a hut, a shack

cabillaud noun, masculine
  le cabillaud = cod

cabine noun, feminine
  une cabine (for sleeping) = a cabin
  (for changing) = a cubicle, a changing
    room
une cabine d'essayage = a fitting room
une cabine téléphonique = a telephone
  box, a telephone booth

cabinet noun, masculine
* (a place of work)
  un cabinet = an office
  (for a doctor) = a surgery, an office
* (a W.C.)
  le cabinet, les cabinets = the toilet, the bathroom
un cabinet de toilette = washing facilities

câble noun, masculine
  un câble = a cable

cacahuète noun, feminine
  une cacahuète = a peanut

cacao noun, masculine
  le cacao = cocoa

cache-cache noun, masculine (**!** never changes)
  jouer à cache-cache = to play hide and seek

cacher verb [1]
  = to hide

cachet noun, masculine
* (a medicine)
  un cachet = a tablet, a pill
* (on a form)
  un cachet = a stamp

cachette noun, feminine
  une cachette = a hiding place
  en cachette = secretly

c-à-d conjunction
(abbreviation of **c'est-à-dire**)
  c-à-d = i.e.

cadeau noun, masculine
(plural) **cadeaux**
  un cadeau = a present, a gift

cadet/cadette adjective
  = younger, youngest

cadre noun, masculine
* (for a picture)
  un cadre = a frame
* (an employee)
  un cadre = an executive
* (the space around a person or a thing)
  le cadre = the surroundings

cafard noun, masculine
* **un cafard** = a cockroach
* **avoir le cafard** = to feel down, to feel blue

café noun, masculine
* (a product)
  le café = coffee
* (a place)
  un café = a café, a diner
un café crème = an espresso with milk
un café au lait = a coffee with milk

cafetière noun, feminine
  une cafetière = a coffee maker

✗ in informal situations

cage noun, feminine
  une cage = a cage

cahier noun, masculine
  un cahier = an exercise book
un cahier de brouillon = a rough book, a notebook
un cahier de textes = a homework notebook

caillou noun, masculine
(plural) **cailloux**
  un caillou = a stone

Caire noun, masculine
  le Caire = Cairo

caisse noun, feminine
* (for goods)
  une caisse = a crate
* (for money)
  une caisse = a till, a cash register
* (where you pay in a shop)
  la caisse = the cash desk
  = the checkout

calcul noun, masculine
* (the study of numbers)
  le calcul = arithmetic
* (an operation)
  un calcul = a calculation

calculatrice noun, feminine
  une calculatrice = a (pocket) calculator

calculer verb [1]
  = to calculate, to work out

calé/calée✗ adjective
  = clever

caleçon noun, masculine
  un caleçon (for men) = boxer shorts
  (for women) = leggings
un caleçon long = long johns

calendrier noun, masculine
  un calendrier = a calendar

caler verb [1]
* (in order to fix in a position) = to wedge
* (when driving) = to stall

calmant noun, masculine
  un calmant = a sedative

calmar noun, masculine
  un calmar = a squid

calme
1 adjective
  = calm, quiet
2 noun, masculine
  le calme = peace (and quiet)

calmer verb [1]
1 (**!** + avoir)
  = to calm (down)
2 se calmer (**!** + être)
  se calmer = to calm down

camarade noun, masculine/feminine
  un camarade/une camarade = a friend

cambriolage *noun, masculine*
  un cambriolage = a burglary

cambrioler *verb* 1
  = to burgle

caméra *noun, feminine*
  une caméra = a (cine-)camera, a movie camera

caméscope *noun, masculine*
  un caméscope = a camcorder

camion *noun, masculine*
  un camion = a lorry, a truck

camionnette *noun, feminine*
  une camionnette = a van

campagne *noun, feminine*
* *(the area around towns)*
  la campagne = the country
  = the countryside
* *(for an election, in war)*
  une campagne = a campaign

camper *verb* 1
  = to camp

campeur/campeuse *noun, masculine/feminine*
  un campeur/une campeuse = a camper

camping *noun, masculine*
* *(the activity)*
  le camping = camping
* *(the place)*
  un camping = a campsite, a campground

camping-car *noun, masculine*
(plural) **camping-cars**
  un camping-car = a camper-van, an RV

Canada *noun, masculine*
  le Canada = Canada

canadien/canadienne *adjective*
  = Canadian

canal *noun, masculine*
(plural) **canaux**
* *(a waterway)*
  un canal = a canal
* *(in telecommunications)*
  un canal = a channel

canapé *noun, masculine*
  un canapé = a settee, a sofa

canard *noun, masculine*
  un canard = a duck

Cancer *noun, masculine*
  le Cancer = Cancer

candidat/candidate *noun, masculine/feminine*
  un candidat/une candidate *(in an examination, an election)* = a candidate
  (for a job) = an applicant

caniche *noun, masculine*
  un caniche = a poodle

canif *noun, masculine*
  un canif = a penknife, a pocketknife

canne *noun, feminine*
  une canne = a (walking) stick, a cane
  une canne à pêche = a fishing rod

canoë *noun, masculine*
* *(the equipment)*
  un canoë = a (Canadian) canoe
* *(the sport)*
  le canoë = canoeing

canot *noun, masculine*
  un canot = a (small) boat, a dinghy
  un canot de sauvetage = a lifeboat

cantine *noun, feminine*
  une cantine = a canteen

caoutchouc *noun, masculine*
  le caoutchouc = rubber

CAP *noun, masculine* ▶ **certificat**

capitaine *noun, masculine*
  un capitaine = a captain

capitale *noun, feminine*
* *(a town)*
  une capitale = a capital (city)
* *(a letter)*
  une capitale = a capital

capot *noun, masculine*
  le capot = the bonnet, the hood

Capricorne *noun, masculine*
  le Capricorne = Capricorn

capuchon *noun, masculine*
* *(for the head)*
  un capuchon = a hood
* *(for a pen)*
  un capuchon = a cap

car
1 *noun, masculine*
  un car = a coach, a bus
2 *conjunction*
  car = because, for

caractère *noun, masculine*
* *(a personality)*
  un caractère = a character, a nature
* *(in writing)*
  un caractère = a letter

Caraïbes *noun, feminine plural*
  les Caraïbes = the Caribbean islands

carambolage *noun, masculine*
  un carambolage = a pile-up

caramel *noun, masculine*
* *(on ice cream, custard)*
  le caramel = caramel
* *(a sweet)*
  un caramel = a toffee

caravane *noun, feminine*
  une caravane = a caravan, a trailer

carburateur noun, masculine
  le carburateur = the carburettor

caresser verb 1
  = to stroke

carnet noun, masculine
* (in which to write)
  un carnet = a notebook
* (a set of tickets, stamps)
  un carnet = a book
un carnet d'adresses = an address book
un carnet de chèques = a cheque book,
  a checkbook

carotte noun, feminine
  une carotte = a carrot

carré/carrée adjective
  = square

carreau noun, masculine
(plural) **carreaux**
* (on a window)
  un carreau = a window pane
* (on the wall, the floor)
  un carreau = a tile
  du tissu à carreaux = check(ed) material,
    chequered material
* (at cards)
  carreau = diamonds

carrefour noun, masculine
  le carrefour = the crossroads

carrière noun, feminine
* (a profession)
  une carrière = a career
* (a place)
  une carrière = a quarry

carrosserie noun, feminine
  la carrosserie = bodywork

cartable noun, masculine
  un cartable = a satchel, a schoolbag
    = a briefcase

carte noun, feminine
* (in games)
  une carte = a card
* (of a country)
  une carte = a map
* (in a restaurant)
  la carte = the menu
une carte bleue = a credit card
une carte grise = a logbook
une carte d'identité = an ID card
une carte orange = a season ticket (in the
  Paris area)
une carte postale = a postcard
une carte à puce = a smart card
une carte de visite = a visiting card
    = a business card
une carte de vœux = a greeting(s) card

carton noun, masculine
* (the substance)
  le carton = cardboard
* (a container)
  un carton = a cardboard box

cas noun, masculine (! never changes)
  un cas = a case

case noun, feminine
  une case = a box

casier noun, masculine
  un casier (for messages) = a pigeonhole
  (for keeping things organized) = a locker

casque noun, masculine
* (for protection)
  un casque = a helmet
    = a hard hat
* (for listening to music)
  un casque = headphones

casquette noun, feminine
  une casquette = a cap

casse-croûte noun, masculine (! never
changes)
  un casse-croûte = a snack

casser verb 1
1 (! + avoir)
  = to break
2 se casser (! + être)
  se casser = to break
  je me suis cassé le poignet = I broke my
    wrist

casserole noun, feminine
  une casserole = a saucepan, a pan

cassis noun, masculine (! never changes)
  le cassis = blackcurrants

catastrophe noun, feminine
  une catastrophe = a disaster

catch noun, masculine
  le catch = wrestling

catéchisme noun, masculine
  le catéchisme = catechism

catégorie noun, feminine
  une catégorie = a category

cauchemar noun, masculine
  un cauchemar = a nightmare

cause noun, feminine
  la cause = the cause
  à cause de = because of

causer verb 1
* = to cause
  causer un accident = to cause an accident
* ✷ = to chat, to talk

caution noun, feminine
  une caution = a deposit

cave noun, feminine
  une cave = a cellar

✷ in informal situations

ce¹/cette *adjective*
(*plural*) **ces**

> **!** **cet** *is used instead of* **ce** *before a masculine noun beginning with a vowel or a mute h. The plural of* **cet** *is* **ces**.

= this, that
  ce livre(-ci) = this book
  cet oiseau(-là) = that bird
  ces enfants = these children, those children

ce² *pronoun* (**c'** *before e*)
* (*when the verb* **être** *is in the singular*)
  c'est un cadeau = it's a present
  ce serait dommage = it would be a shame
  qui est-ce? = who is it?
  qu'est-ce que c'est? = what is it?
  c'est moi qui l'ai cassé = I was the one who broke it
* (*when the verb* **être** *is in the plural*)
  ce sont des insectes = they're insects
  ce sont des détails sans importance = these are unimportant details
* **voilà ce que j'ai dit** = that's what I said
  prenez ce dont vous avez besoin = take what you need
  c'est ce qui les inquiète = that's what worries them
  ce qui m'ennuie le plus, c'est qu'il faudra se lever tôt = what bothers me most is that we'll have to get up early
  il est venu, ce qui est étonnant = he came, which is surprising

> **!** *Look up the verb* **être** *for translations of* **est-ce que**.

ceci *pronoun*
= this

céder *verb* 14
* = to give up
* = to give in
  céder le passage = to give way, to yield
* = to collapse

cédille *noun, feminine*
  une cédille = a cedilla

CEE *noun, feminine* ▶ **communauté**

ceinture *noun, feminine*
  une ceinture = a belt
  une ceinture de sécurité = a seatbelt

cela *pronoun*
= it, that

célèbre *adjective*
= famous

célébrer *verb* 14
= to celebrate

céleri *noun, masculine*
  le céleri = celery

célibataire
1 *adjective*
= single

2 *noun, masculine/feminine*
  un célibataire/une célibataire = a single man/woman

celle ▶ **celui**

celle-ci ▶ **celui-ci**

celle-là ▶ **celui-là**

celles-ci ▶ **celui-ci**

celles-là ▶ **celui-là**

celui/celle *pronoun*
(*plural*) **ceux/celles**
  celui/celle = the one
  ceux/celles = the ones
  = those
  celle de ma sœur = my sister's

celui-ci/celle-ci *pronoun*
(*plural*) **ceux-ci/celles-ci**
  celui-ci/celle-ci = this one
  ceux-ci/celles-ci = these

celui-là/celle-là *pronoun*
(*plural*) **ceux-là/celles-là**
  celui-là/celle-là = that one
  ceux-là/celles-là = those

cendre *noun, feminine*
  la cendre = ash

cendrier *noun, masculine*
  un cendrier = an ashtray

Cendrillon *noun, feminine*
  Cendrillon = Cinderella

censé/censée *adjective*
  être censé = to be meant to

cent *number*
= hundred
  pour cent = per cent

centaine *noun, feminine*
  une centaine = about a hundred

centième *number*
= hundredth

centime *noun, masculine*
  un centime = a centime

centimètre *noun, masculine*
* (*a unit of length*)
  un centimètre = a centimetre, a centimeter
* (*a measuring device*)
  un centimètre = a tape measure

central/centrale¹
(*plural*) **centraux/centrales**
1 *adjective*
= central
2 central *noun, masculine*
  le central (téléphonique) = the (telephone) exchange

centrale² *noun, feminine*
  une centrale = a power station

centre *noun, masculine*
le centre = the centre, the center
un centre aéré = a children's outdoor activity centre
un centre commercial = a shopping centre, a shopping mall

centre-ville *noun, masculine*
(*plural*) **centres-villes**
le centre-ville = the town centre, the town center

cependant *conjunction*
= however

cercle *noun, masculine*
un cercle = a circle

cercueil *noun, masculine*
un cercueil = a coffin

céréale *noun, feminine*
une céréale = a cereal, a grain

cérémonie *noun, feminine*
une cérémonie = a ceremony

cerf *noun, masculine*
un cerf = a stag

cerf-volant *noun, masculine*
(*plural*) **cerfs-volants**
un cerf-volant = a kite

cerise *noun, feminine*
une cerise = a cherry

cerisier *noun, masculine*
un cerisier = a cherry tree

certain/certaine
1 *adjective*
= certain, sure
2 *determiner*
= some
3 certains/certaines *pronoun, plural*
= some
certains d'entre vous = some of you

certainement *adverb*
= most probably
= certainly

certificat *noun, masculine*
un certificat = a certificate
un certificat d'aptitude professionnelle, un CAP = a vocational training qualification
un certificat médical = a doctor's certificate
un certificat de naissance = a birth certificate

cerveau *noun, masculine*
(*plural*) **cerveaux**
le cerveau = the brain

cervelle *noun, feminine*
la cervelle = the brain

✖ in informal situations

ces ▶ **ce**[1]

CES *noun, masculine* ▶ **collège**

cesser *verb* [1]
= to stop

c'est-à-dire *adverb*
= that is (to say)

cet ▶ **ce**[1]

CET *noun, masculine* ▶ **collège**

cette ▶ **ce**[1]

ceux ▶ **celui**

chacun/chacune *pronoun*
• = each (one)
chacun d'entre vous = each one of you
• = everybody

chahut *noun, masculine*
du chahut = a racket

chaîne *noun, feminine*
• (*linked metal rings*)
une chaîne = a chain
• (*on television*)
une chaîne = a channel
• (*in a factory*)
la chaîne = the assembly line
une chaîne hi-fi = a hi-fi system
une chaîne laser = a CD system
une chaîne de montagnes = a mountain range

chair *noun, feminine*
la chair = flesh
la chair de poule = goose pimples, goose bumps

chaise *noun, feminine*
une chaise = a chair
une chaise longue = a deckchair

chaleur *noun, feminine*
la chaleur = heat, warmth

chambre *noun, feminine*
une chambre = a room, a bedroom
une chambre pour une personne = a single room
une chambre pour deux personnes = a double room
une chambre d'hôte = a room in a B & B
'chambres d'hôte' = 'bed and breakfast'

chameau *noun, masculine*
(*plural*) **chameaux**
un chameau = a camel

champ
1 *noun, masculine*
un champ = a field
2 à tout bout de champ✖ = all the time

champignon *noun, masculine*
un champignon = a mushroom

champion/championne *noun, masculine/feminine*
un champion/une championne = a champion

championnat *noun, masculine*
  un championnat = a championship

chance *noun, feminine*
* (*good fortune*)
  la chance = luck
* (*possibility*)
  avoir des chances de gagner = to stand a
    chance of winning

change *noun, masculine*
  le taux de change = the exchange rate

changement *noun, masculine*
  un changement = a change

changer *verb* 13
  = to change
  changer d'avis = to change one's mind
  changer d'adresse = to move

chanson *noun, feminine*
  une chanson = a song

chant *noun, masculine*
  un chant = a song

chanter *verb* 1
  = to sing

chanteur/chanteuse *noun,
masculine/feminine*
  un chanteur/une chanteuse = a singer

chantier *noun, masculine*
  un chantier = a building site

chantilly *noun, feminine* (! *never
changes*)
  la chantilly = whipped cream

chapeau *noun, masculine*
(*plural*) **chapeaux**
* un chapeau = a hat
* (*when praising*)✗
  chapeau✗! = well done!, good job!
  un chapeau melon = a bowler hat,
    a derby hat

chapitre *noun, masculine*
  un chapitre = a chapter

chaque *determiner*
  = each, every

char *noun, masculine*
* (*in a carnival*)
  un char = a float
* (*a military vehicle*)
  un char = a tank

charcuterie *noun, feminine*
* (*a shop*)
  une charcuterie = a pork butcher's
* (*a type of food*)
  la charcuterie = cooked pork meats

charcutier/charcutière *noun,
masculine/feminine*
  un charcutier/une charcutière = a pork
    butcher

charger *verb* 13
1 (! + *avoir*)

* = to load
  charger un camion de légumes = to load a
    truck with vegetables
* = to ask
  charger quelqu'un [de poster une lettre |
    d'arroser les plantes | de transmettre un
    message …] = to ask someone [to post a
    letter | to water the plants | to pass on a
    message …]
* ils sont chargés de surveiller les enfants
    = they're responsible for looking after the
    children
2 se charger (! + *être*)
  se charger d'une tâche = to take
    responsibility for a job, to see to a job
  je me charge de le leur dire = I'll tell them

chariot *noun, masculine*
  un chariot = a trolley, a cart

charité *noun, feminine*
  la charité = charity

charmant/charmante *adjective*
  = charming

chasse *noun, feminine*
  la chasse = hunting
  la chasse d'eau = the (toilet) flush

chasse-neige *noun, masculine* (! *never
changes*)
  un chasse-neige = a snowplough,
    a snowplow

chasser *verb* 1
* = to hunt
* = to shoot
* = to drive away

chasseur *noun, masculine*
  un chasseur = a hunter

chat *noun, masculine*
  un chat = a cat

châtaigne *noun, feminine*
  une châtaigne = a (sweet) chestnut

châtain *adjective*
  = brown

château *noun, masculine*
(*plural*) **châteaux**
  un château = a castle
  un château fort = a fortified castle

chaton *noun, masculine*
  un chaton = a kitten

chatte *noun, feminine*
  une chatte = a (female) cat

chaud/chaude
1 *adjective*
  = hot, warm
2 chaud *adverb*
  il fait chaud ici = it's hot in here
3 chaud *noun, masculine*
  avoir chaud = to be hot

chaudière *noun, feminine*
  une chaudière = a boiler

chauffage noun, masculine
le chauffage = the heating

chauffard✶ noun, masculine
un chauffard✶ = a reckless driver

chauffer verb 1
* = to heat
* = to overheat
  le moteur chauffe = the engine is
  overheating
* = to give out heat, to give off heat
  le poêle chauffe bien = the stove gives out
  a lot of heat
  le soleil chauffe aujourd'hui = the sun is
  hot today

chauffeur noun, masculine
un chauffeur = a driver

chaumière noun, feminine
une chaumière = a thatched cottage

chaussée noun, feminine
la chaussée = the road, the highway
'chaussée déformée' = 'uneven road
surface'

chausser verb 1
chausser du 39 = to take a size 39 (in
shoes), to take a size 6

chaussette noun, feminine
une chaussette = a sock

chausson noun, masculine
* (footwear)
  un chausson = a slipper
* (a cake)
  un chausson = a turnover

chaussure noun, feminine
une chaussure = a shoe
des chaussures de ski = ski boots

chauve adjective
= bald

chauve-souris noun, feminine
(plural) **chauves-souris**
une chauve-souris = a bat

chef
1 noun, masculine
* (the person in charge)
  le chef = the leader
* (in a restaurant)
  un chef (cuisinier) = a chef
2 en chef
l'ingénieur en chef = the chief engineer
un chef d'entreprise = a company
manager
un chef d'État = a head of state
un chef de gare = a station master
un chef d'orchestre = a conductor

chef-d'œuvre noun, masculine
(plural) **chefs-d'œuvre**
un chef-d'œuvre = a masterpiece

chemin noun, masculine
* un chemin = a country lane, a path
* le chemin = the way
le chemin de fer = the railway, the
railroad

cheminée noun, feminine
une cheminée = a chimney
= a fireplace
= a mantelpiece, a mantel

chemise noun, feminine
une chemise = a shirt

chemisier noun, masculine
un chemisier = a blouse

chêne noun, masculine
un chêne = an oak (tree)

chenille noun, feminine
une chenille = a caterpillar

chèque noun, masculine
un chèque = a cheque, a check
un chèque sans provision = a bad
cheque, a dud check

chèque-voyage noun, masculine
(plural) **chèques-voyage**
un chèque-voyage = a traveller's cheque, a
traveler's check

chéquier noun, masculine
un chéquier = a cheque book, a checkbook

cher/chère adjective
* = dear
* = expensive

chercher verb 1
* = to look for
* aller chercher de l'eau = to go and get
some water

chère ▶ cher

chéri/chérie noun, masculine/feminine
(mon) chéri/(ma) chérie = (my) darling

cheval noun, masculine
(plural) **chevaux**
* (an animal)
  un cheval = a horse
  monter à cheval = to ride (a horse)
* (the sport)
  le cheval = horseriding, horseback riding
* (meat)
  le cheval = horsemeat

chevalier noun, masculine
un chevalier = a knight

chevet noun, masculine
une lampe de chevet = a bedside lamp

cheveu noun, masculine
(plural) **cheveux**
les cheveux = hair

cheville noun, feminine
une cheville = an ankle

✶ in informal situations

chèvre noun, feminine
une chèvre = a goat

chez preposition
* = at
je serai chez moi = I'll be at home
il est chez eux ce matin? = is he at their place this morning?
* = to
aller chez le dentiste = to go to the dentist's

chic adjective
* (elegant) = chic, smart
* (kind, obliging)✶ = nice

chien noun, masculine
* un chien = a dog
un chien d'aveugle = a guide dog
* il fait un temps de chien✶ = the weather is awful

chienne noun, feminine
une chienne = a female dog, a bitch

chiffon noun, masculine
un chiffon = a rag, a cloth
un chiffon (à poussière) = a duster, a dust cloth

chiffre noun, masculine
un chiffre = a figure

chignon noun, masculine
un chignon = a bun, a chignon

chimie noun, feminine
la chimie = chemistry

chimique adjective
= chemical

chinois/chinoise
1 adjective
= Chinese
2 **chinois** noun, masculine
le chinois = Chinese

chiot noun, masculine
un chiot = a puppy

chips noun, feminine (! never changes)
une chips = a crisp, a (potato) chip

chirurgien noun, masculine
un chirurgien = a surgeon

choc noun, masculine
un choc = a shock

chocolat noun, masculine
le chocolat = chocolate

choisir verb ③
= to choose

choix noun, masculine (! never changes)
un choix = a choice
des produits de choix = choice products
de premier choix = top quality

chômage noun, masculine
le chômage = unemployment
être au chômage = to be unemployed

chômeur/chômeuse noun, masculine/feminine
un chômeur/une chômeuse = an unemployed man/woman

choquer verb ①
= to shock

chorale noun, feminine
une chorale = a choir

chose noun, feminine
une chose = a thing
quelque chose = something = anything
pas grand chose = not much

chou noun, masculine
(plural) **choux**
* (a vegetable)
un chou = a cabbage
* (a cake)
un chou = a choux bun, a pastry shell
* (a person)
mon chou = my darling
un chou de Bruxelles = a Brussels sprout
un chou à la crème = a cream puff

choucroute noun, feminine
la choucroute = sauerkraut

chouette
1 adjective✶
= nice, great
2 noun, feminine
une chouette = an owl

chou-fleur noun, masculine
(plural) **choux-fleurs**
un chou-fleur = a cauliflower

chronométrer verb ⑭
= to time

chrysanthème noun, masculine
un chrysanthème = a chrysanthemum

chuchoter verb ①
= to whisper

chut exclamation
chut! = shh!, hush!

chute noun, feminine
une chute = a fall

cicatrice noun, feminine
une cicatrice = a scar

ci-contre adverb
= opposite

ci-dessous adverb
= below

ci-dessus adverb
= above

cidre noun, masculine
le cidre = cider, hard cider

ciel noun, masculine
* le ciel = the sky
* le ciel = heaven

cieux noun, masculine plural
les cieux = heaven

cigale noun, feminine
une cigale = a cicada

ci-joint/ci-jointe adjective
= enclosed

cil noun, masculine
un cil = an eyelash

cime noun, feminine
la cime = the top

cimetière noun, masculine
un cimetière = a graveyard, a cemetery

ciné✗ noun, masculine
le ciné✗ = the pictures, the movies

cinéma noun, masculine
* un cinéma = a cinema, a movie theater
* le cinéma = the cinema, the movies

cinglé/cinglée✗ adjective
= mad, crazy

cinq number
= five

cinquantaine noun, feminine
une cinquantaine = about fifty

cinquante number
= fifty

cinquième
1 number
= fifth
2 noun, feminine
la cinquième = the class for secondary school students aged 12 to 13

cirage noun, masculine
le cirage = shoe polish

circuit noun, masculine
* (visiting several places)
un circuit = a tour
* (in a race)
un circuit = a circuit

circulation noun, feminine
la circulation = the traffic

circuler verb 1
* = to move
* = to run
ce train ne circule pas le dimanche = this train doesn't run on Sundays
* = to circulate

cirque noun, masculine
le cirque = the circus

ciseaux noun, masculine plural
des ciseaux = scissors

citadelle noun, feminine
une citadelle = a fortress

cité noun, feminine
* une cité = a city, a town
* une cité = a housing estate, a housing development
une cité universitaire = student halls of residence, dormitories

citoyen/citoyenne noun, masculine/feminine
un citoyen/une citoyenne = a citizen

citron noun, masculine
un citron = a lemon
un citron pressé = a freshly squeezed lemonade

citronnade noun, feminine
la citronnade = lemon squash, (still) lemonade

clair/claire
1 adjective
* = clear
* = light
2 clair noun, masculine
le clair de lune = moonlight

claqué/claquée✗ adjective
= exhausted

claquer verb 1
* = to slam
claquer la porte = to slam the door
* = to bang
une porte claquait = a door was banging
* faire claquer ses doigts = to snap one's fingers
il claque des dents = his teeth are chattering

claquettes noun, feminine plural
les claquettes = tap dancing

clarinette noun, feminine
une clarinette = a clarinet

classe noun, feminine
* (a room)
une (salle de) classe = a classroom
aller en classe = to go to school
* (a category)
une classe = a class
un billet de première classe = a first-class ticket
une classe de mer = a seaside trip (with a school)
une classe de neige = a skiing trip (with a school)
une classe verte = a field trip (with a school)

classeur noun, masculine
un classeur = a folder

clavier noun, masculine
un clavier = a keyboard

clé noun, feminine
* (for a lock)
une clé = a key
fermer à clé = to lock

✗ in informal situations

• (*a tool*)
une clé = a spanner, a wrench
• **le mot(-)clé** = the key word

clef ▶ clé

client/cliente *noun, masculine/feminine*
un client/une cliente = a customer, a client

clignotant *noun, masculine*
un clignotant = an indicator, a turn signal

climat *noun, masculine*
le climat = the climate

climatisation *noun, feminine*
la climatisation = air-conditioning

clinique *noun, feminine*
une clinique = a (private) clinic

clochard/clocharde *noun,*
masculine/feminine
un clochard/une clocharde = a tramp, a
bum

cloche *noun, feminine*
• **une cloche** = a bell
• **une cloche✶** = an idiot

cloche-pied: **à cloche-pied** *adverb*
sauter à cloche-pied = to hop

clocher *noun, masculine*
un clocher = a steeple
= a church tower, a bell tower

clochette *noun, feminine*
une clochette = a small bell

cloison *noun, feminine*
une cloison = a partition

cloque *noun, feminine*
une cloque = a blister

clos/close *adjective*
• = enclosed
• = closed

clôture *noun, feminine*
une clôture = a fence

clou
1 *noun, masculine*
un clou = a nail
2 clous *noun, masculine plural*
les clous = the pedestrian crossing, the
crosswalk

clouer *verb* 1
= to nail (down)

clouté *adjective, masculine*
un passage clouté = a pedestrian crossing,
a crosswalk

clown *noun, masculine*
un clown = a clown
faire le clown = to clown around

club *noun, masculine*
un club = a club

cobaye *noun, masculine*
un cobaye = a guinea pig

coca *noun, masculine*
un coca = a Coke , a Coca-Cola

cocher *verb* 1
= to tick, to check (off)

cochon *noun, masculine*
un cochon = a pig
un cochon d'Inde = a guinea pig

coco *noun, masculine*
une noix de coco = a coconut

cocotier *noun, masculine*
un cocotier = a coconut tree

code
1 *noun, masculine*
un code = a code
2 codes *noun, masculine plural*
les codes = dipped headlights, dimmed
headlights
se mettre en codes = to dip one's
headlights, to dim one's headlights
un code confidentiel (d'identification)
= a personal identification number
un code postal = a postcode, a zip code
le code de la route = the highway code,
the rules of the road

cœur
1 *noun, masculine*
• **le cœur** = the heart
avoir mal au cœur = to feel sick, to feel
nauseous
avoir bon cœur = to be kind-hearted
• (*at cards*)
cœur = hearts
2 par cœur = by heart

coffre *noun, masculine*
• **un coffre** (*for storage*) = a chest, a trunk
(*for valuables*) = a safe
• (*in a car*)
le coffre = the boot, the trunk

coffre-fort *noun, masculine*
(*plural*) **coffres-forts**
un coffre-fort = a safe

cognac *noun, masculine*
le cognac = brandy

coiffer: **se coiffer** *verb* 1 (**!** + *être*)
se coiffer = to do one's hair

coiffeur/coiffeuse *noun,*
masculine/feminine
un coiffeur/une coiffeuse = a hairdresser, a
hairstylist

coin *noun, masculine*
• (*an angle*)
un coin = a corner
au coin de la rue = on the corner of the
street
au coin du feu = by the fire
• (*a place*)
un coin = a spot
un petit coin tranquille = a nice quiet spot

• (the surrounding area)
  le coin = the neighbo(u)rhood
  le café du coin = the local café
  dans le coin = in the area

coincer verb 12
= to jam, to wedge

col noun, masculine
• (on a garment)
  un col = a collar
  un col roulé = a polo neck, a turtleneck
• (in the mountain)
  un col = a pass

colère noun, feminine
  la colère = anger

coléreux/coléreuse adjective
= quick-tempered, short-tempered

colique noun, feminine
  la colique = diarrh(o)ea

colis noun, masculine (! never changes)
  un colis = a parcel, a package

collant/collante
1 adjective
= sticky
2 **collant** noun, masculine
  un collant = (a pair of) tights, pantyhose

colle noun, feminine
  la colle = glue

collectionner verb 1
= to collect

collège noun, masculine
  **un collège (d'enseignement secondaire),
  un CES** = a secondary school, ≈ a junior
  high school (for students aged 11 to 14)
  **un collège d'enseignement technique, un
  CET** = a technical secondary school (for
  students aged 11 to 14)

collègue noun, masculine/feminine
  un collègue/une collègue = a colleague

coller verb 1
• = to stick, to glue
• (in an examination)✶
  se faire coller✶ à un examen = to fail an
  examination

collier noun, masculine
  un collier (on a person) = a necklace
  (on an animal) = a collar

colline noun, feminine
  une colline = a hill

colonie noun, feminine
  une colonie = a colony
  une colonie de vacances = a holiday
  camp, a summer camp (for children)

colonne noun, feminine
  une colonne = a column

colorier verb 2
= to colo(u)r

coloris noun, masculine (! never changes)
  un coloris = a colo(u)r

combien
1 adverb
  combien (de) = how much, how many
2 noun (! never changes)
  le combien sommes-nous? = what's the
  date today?
  du combien chaussez-vous? = what size
  shoe do you take?

combinaison noun, feminine
  une combinaison (a fashion garment) = a
  jumpsuit
  (protective clothing) = overalls, coveralls
  une combinaison de plongée = a
  wetsuit
  une combinaison de ski = a ski-suit

combiné noun, masculine
  le combiné = the handset, the receiver

comédie noun, feminine
• (a play)
  une comédie = a comedy
• (pretence)
  de la comédie = an act

comédien/comédienne noun,
masculine/feminine
  un comédien/une comédienne = an
  actor/an actress

comestible adjective
= edible

comique adjective
• = comic
• = funny

commandant noun, masculine
  le commandant = the major
  le commandant de bord = the captain

commande noun, feminine
• (for goods)
  une commande = an order
• (a device)
  une commande = a control
  être aux commandes = to be at the
  controls

commander verb 1
• (in a restaurant) = to order
• (in a group) = to be in command

comme
1 adverb
  comme c'est beau! = it's so beautiful!
2 conjunction
• = like
  il conduit comme un fou = he drives like a
  maniac
• = as
  comme toujours = as always
  gros comme mon poing = as big as my fist

✶ in informal situations

- = as, since
  comme il pleuvait, je ne suis pas sorti = as it was raining I didn't go out
- = as a
  travailler comme serveuse = to work as a waitress
  comme ci comme ça* = so so
3 **comme il faut** = properly, correctly

commencer verb $\boxed{12}$
= to start, to begin

comment adverb
- = how
  comment allez-vous? = how are you?
- = what
  comment s'appelle-t-il? = what's his name?
  comment trouves-tu leur jardin? = what do you think of their garden?
  c'est comment? = what's it like?
- (when asking someone to repeat)
  comment? = sorry?, pardon?, excuse me?

commentaire noun, masculine
- (on a text, on a match)
  un commentaire = a commentary
- (a remark)
  un commentaire = a comment

commerçant/commerçante noun, masculine/feminine
  un commerçant/une commerçante = a shopkeeper

commerce noun, masculine
- (a place)
  un commerce = a shop, a store
- (an activity)
  le commerce = trade

commettre verb $\boxed{60}$
  commettre un meurtre = to commit a murder
  commettre une erreur = to make a mistake

commis/commise ▶ **commettre** $\boxed{60}$

commissariat noun, masculine
  le commissariat (de police) = the police station

commode
1 adjective
  = convenient, handy
2 noun, feminine
  une commode = a chest of drawers, a dresser

commun/commune adjective
  = common

communauté noun, feminine
  une communauté = a community
la Communauté Européenne, la CE = the European Community, the EC

communication noun, feminine
  une communication (téléphonique) = a (phone) call

communiquer verb $\boxed{1}$
  = to communicate

compagne noun, feminine
  une compagne = a (female) companion

compagnie noun, feminine
- (a firm, a group of actors)
  une compagnie = a company
- (the presence of other people)
  la compagnie = company
une compagnie aérienne = an airline

compagnon noun, masculine
  un compagnon = a (male) companion

comparaison noun, feminine
  une comparaison = a comparison

comparer verb $\boxed{1}$
  = to compare

compartiment noun, masculine
  un compartiment = a compartment

compétition noun, feminine
- **la compétition** = competition, rivalry
- **une compétition (sportive)** = a sporting event

complet/complète adjective
- = complete
- = full

compliment noun, masculine
  un compliment = a compliment
  tous mes compliments! = congratulations!

compliqué/compliquée adjective
  = complicated

comporter verb $\boxed{1}$
1 (**!** + avoir)
  = to consist of
2 **se comporter** (**!** + être)
  se comporter = to behave

composer verb $\boxed{1}$
1 (**!** + avoir)
- = to dial
  composer un numéro = to dial a number
- = to put together
  composer un menu = to put a menu together
- = to make up
  les joueurs qui composent l'équipe = the players who make up the team
  composé de = made up of
- = to compose
  qui a composé la musique du film? = who composed the score for the film?
2 **se composer de** (**!** + être)
  se composer de = to be made up of

compositeur/compositrice noun, masculine/feminine
  un compositeur/une compositrice = a composer

composter verb $\boxed{1}$
  = to punch

compote noun, feminine
  la compote de pommes = stewed apple
comprendre verb 52
1 (! + avoir)
* = to understand
* = to include
2 se comprendre (! + être)
* se comprendre = to understand each other
* se comprendre = to be understandable
comprimé noun, masculine
  un comprimé = a tablet, a pill
compris/comprise
1 ▶ comprendre 52
2 adjective
  = included
3 y compris = including
compte noun, masculine
* (in a bank, a post office)
  un compte = an account
* se rendre compte = to realize
* tenir compte de = to take into account
* travailler à son compte = to be self-employed
compter verb 1
* = to count
* = to intend
* compter sur = to count on
comptoir noun, masculine
  le comptoir (in a shop) = the counter
  (in a café) = the bar, the counter
con✹ noun, masculine
  un con✹ = a stupid jerk
concerner verb 1
* = to concern
* = to affect
concessionnaire noun, masculine/feminine
  un concessionnaire/une concessionnaire = a distributor, an agent
concierge noun, masculine/feminine
  un concierge/une concierge = a caretaker, a superintendent
concombre noun, masculine
  un concombre = a cucumber
concours noun, masculine (! never changes)
* (a game, an event)
  un concours = a competition, a contest
* (an examination)
  un concours = a competitive examination
concurrence noun, feminine
  la concurrence = competition
concurrent/concurrente noun, masculine/feminine
  un concurrent/une concurrente = a competitor

condamner verb 1
* (to declare someone guilty) = to convict
* (to punish) = to sentence
  être condamné à une amende = to be fined
condition noun, feminine
  une condition = a condition
  à condition de, à condition que = provided (that), on condition that
condoléances noun, feminine plural
  des condoléances = condolences
conducteur/conductrice noun, masculine/feminine
  un conducteur/une conductrice = a driver
conduire verb 62
1 (! + avoir)
* = to drive
* = to lead
  le sentier conduit au village = the path leads to the village
2 se conduire (! + être)
  se conduire = to behave
conduite noun, feminine
  ta conduite = your behavio(u)r
  = your conduct
confection noun, feminine
  la confection = ready-to-wear clothes
confiance noun, feminine
* (in someone's honesty)
  la confiance = trust
  faire confiance = to trust
* (in someone's ability)
  la confiance = confidence
  la confiance en soi = (self-)confidence
confier verb 2
1 (! + avoir)
  = to entrust
2 se confier (! + être)
  se confier à quelqu'un = to confide in someone
confiserie noun, feminine
  une confiserie = a sweet shop, a candy store
confisquer verb 1
  = to confiscate
confiture noun, feminine
  la confiture = jam, jelly
  la confiture d'orange = marmalade
confort noun, masculine
  le confort = comfort
confortable adjective
  = comfortable
congé noun, masculine
  un congé = a holiday, a vacation
  être en congé = to be on holiday, to be on vacation
  un congé de maladie = sick leave

---

congélateur *noun, masculine*
un congélateur = a freezer

conjuguer *verb* 1
= to conjugate

connaissance *noun, feminine*
* **la connaissance** = knowledge
* **une connaissance** = an acquaintance
  j'ai fait la connaissance de leur fils = I met their son
* **perdre connaissance** = to lose consciousness
  sans connaissance = unconscious

connaître *verb* 63
1 (**!** + *avoir*)
= to know
2 se connaître (**!** + *être*)
* **se connaître** = to know each other
* **se connaître** = to know oneself
3 s'y connaître en (**!** + *être*)
  s'y connaître en = to know about
  tu t'y connais en voitures? = do you know about cars?

connu/connue
1 ▶ **connaître** 63
2 *adjective*
= well-known

consciencieux/consciencieuse
adjective
= conscientious

conseil *noun, masculine*
* (*an opinion*)
  un conseil = a piece of advice
  des conseils = advice
* (*a group of people*)
  un conseil = a council
un conseil de classe = a staff meeting
  (*for those teaching a given class*)
le conseil municipal = the town council

conseiller¹ *verb* 1
* = to advise
* = to recommend

conseiller²/conseillère *noun,*
masculine/feminine
* (*an expert*)
  un conseiller/une conseillère = an adviser, a consultant
* (*an elected member*)
  un conseiller/une conseillère = a councillor
un conseiller d'éducation = a supervisor
un conseiller municipal = a town councillor
un conseiller d'orientation = a careers adviser

conservatoire *noun, masculine*
un conservatoire = an academy, a conservatory

conserve *noun, feminine*
les conserves (*in tins*) = canned food

(*in jars*) = preserves
une boîte de conserve = a can (of food)

conserver *verb* 1
* = to keep
* = to preserve

consigne *noun, feminine*
* **la consigne** = the left luggage office
* **la consigne** = orders, instructions
la consigne automatique = the left luggage lockers, the baggage lockers

consoler *verb* 1
= to comfort
= to console

consommateur/consommatrice
noun, masculine/feminine
un consommateur/une consommatrice (*of goods, services*) = a consumer
(*in a café*) = a customer

consommation *noun, feminine*
* (*in a café*)
  une consommation = a drink
* (*of gas, food*)
  la consommation = consumption

consommer *verb* 1
= to consume

constater *verb* 1
= to notice

construire *verb* 62
= to build

construit ▶ **construire** 62

consulat *noun, masculine*
un consulat = a consulate

consulter *verb* 1
= to consult

contacter *verb* 1
= to contact, to get in touch with

contagieux/contagieuse *adjective*
= contagious

conte *noun, masculine*
un conte = a story, a tale
un conte de fées = a fairy tale

contenir *verb* 36
* = to contain
* = to hold

content/contente *adjective*
= happy, pleased, glad
il est content de te voir = he's happy to see you

contenu/contenue
1 ▶ **contenir** 36
2 contenu *noun, masculine*
le contenu = the contents

continuellement *adverb*
= continuously

continuer *verb* 1
= to continue

contourner verb 1
= to go (a)round
= to bypass

contraire adjective
= opposite

contrarier verb 2
= to upset

contravention noun, feminine
une contravention = a fine

contre
1 preposition
= against
2 noun, masculine
le pour et le contre = the pros and cons
3 par contre = on the other hand

contrebande noun, feminine
la contrebande = smuggling
des produits de contrebande = smuggled
goods

contrebasse noun, feminine
une contrebasse = a double bass, an
upright bass

contribuer verb 1
contribuer à = to contribute to

contrôle noun, masculine
* (a way of checking)
un contrôle = a check
= an inspection
(in class) = a test
un contrôle de qualité = a quality check
un contrôle des billets = a ticket
inspection
* (over a vehicle)
le contrôle = control
le contrôle (continu) des
connaissances = (continuous)
assessment

contrôler verb 1
= to check
= to inspect

contrôleur/contrôleuse noun,
masculine/feminine
un contrôleur/une contrôleuse = an
inspector

convaincre verb 57
= to convince
= to persuade

convaincu/convaincue ▶
convaincre 57

convenable adjective
* = suitable
* = proper

convenir verb 36
convenir à = to suit
= to be suitable for

✗ in informal situations

convenu/convenue ▶ convenir 36

convoi noun, masculine
un convoi = a convoy

convoquer verb 1
= to summon
= to send for

copain noun, masculine
mon copain = my friend
= my boyfriend

copie noun, feminine
* (of a letter, a painting)
une copie = a copy
* (a piece of schoolwork)
une copie = a paper

copier verb 2
= to copy

copine noun, feminine
ma copine = my friend
= my girlfriend

coq noun, masculine
un coq = a cock, a rooster

coquillage noun, masculine
* un coquillage = a shell
* les coquillages = shellfish

coquille noun, feminine
une coquille = a shell
une coquille Saint-Jacques = a scallop

cor noun, masculine
un cor = a horn

corbeau noun, masculine
(plural) **corbeaux**
un corbeau = a crow

corbeille noun, feminine
une corbeille = a basket
une corbeille à papier = a wastepaper
basket

corde noun, feminine
* une corde = a rope
* (on a violin, a bow, a racket)
une corde = a string
une corde à sauter = a skipping rope, a
jumprope

corne noun, feminine
une corne = a horn

cornet noun, masculine
* (for ice cream)
un cornet = a cornet
* (for fries, sweets)
un cornet = a bag

Cornouailles noun, feminine
la Cornouailles = Cornwall

corps noun, masculine (**!** never changes)
le corps = the body

correct/correcte adjective
* = correct

• = proper
• = polite

correspondance *noun, feminine*
• (*when travelling*)
  une correspondance = a connection
• (*when writing letters*)
  la correspondance = correspondence

correspondant/correspondante
noun, masculine/feminine
  un correspondant/une correspondante = a
  penfriend, a penpal

correspondre *verb* 6
• = to write
• **correspondre à** = to correspond to, to
  match

corrigé *noun, masculine*
  le corrigé = the correct version

corriger *verb* 13
• = to correct
• = to mark, to grade

Corse *noun, feminine*
  la Corse = Corsica

cortège *noun, masculine*
  un cortège = a procession

corvée *noun, feminine*
  une corvée = a chore

costaud* *adjective*
  = strong, sturdy

costume *noun, masculine*
• (*a man's outfit*)
  un costume = a suit
• (*worn by actors*)
  un costume = a costume

côte
1 *noun, feminine*
• (*by the sea*)
  la côte = the coast
• (*an incline*)
  une côte = a hill
  = a slope
• (*in the body*)
  une côte = a rib
2 côte à côte = side by side

côté
1 *noun, masculine*
  un côté = a side
2 à côté = nearby
  j'habite à côté = I live nearby
  la maison d'à côté = the house next door
3 à côté de = next to

Côte-d'Ivoire *noun, feminine*
  la Côte-d'Ivoire = the Ivory Coast

côtelette *noun, feminine*
  une côtelette = a chop, a cutlet

cotisation *noun, feminine*
  une cotisation = a subscription

coton *noun, masculine*
• (*a natural fibre*)
  le coton = cotton
• (*fluffy wadding*)
  le coton (hydrophile) = cotton wool,
  (absorbent) cotton

cou *noun, masculine*
  le cou = the neck

couche *noun, feminine*
• (*a thickness*)
  une couche = a layer
• (*on a baby*)
  une couche = a nappy, a diaper

coucher
1 *verb* 1 (**!** + *avoir*)
• = to put to bed
• = to sleep
2 se coucher *verb* 1 (**!** + *être*)
• **se coucher** = to go to bed
  ils sont couchés = they're in bed
• **se coucher** = to lie (down)
• **se coucher** = to set, to go down
  le soleil se couche vers 8 heures = the sun
  sets at about 8 o'clock
3 *noun, masculine*
  le coucher du soleil = sunset

couchette *noun, feminine*
  une couchette = a couchette, a berth

coucou *exclamation*
  coucou! = peekaboo!

coude *noun, masculine*
  un coude = an elbow

coudre *verb* 66
  = to sew

couette *noun, feminine*
• (*on a bed*)
  une couette = a duvet, a comforter
• (*a hairstyle*)
  des couettes = bunches, pigtails

couler *verb* 1
  = to flow

couleur *noun, feminine*
  une couleur = a colo(u)r

couloir *noun, masculine*
  un couloir = a corridor, a hallway
  = a passage

coup *noun, masculine*
  ! *For translations of phrases such as* **coup**
  de foudre, coup de fil, coup de soleil *etc*
  look up the entries at **foudre, fil, soleil** *etc.*

• (*a hard hit*)
  un coup = a blow
  donner un coup de [pied | poing | couteau ...]
  à quelqu'un = [to kick | to punch | to stab ...]
  someone
  à coups de marteau = with a hammer

* (*a loud noise*)
  un coup = a knock
  frapper trois coups à la porte = to knock three times on the door
* (*the firing of a gun*)
  un coup de [feu | fusil | revolver …] = a shot
  tué d'un coup de fusil = shot dead
* (*an attempt, an occasion*)
  du premier coup = first time
  à chaque coup = every time
  ce coup-ci = this time
  sur le coup = at the time
  = instantly
  tout d'un coup, tout à coup = suddenly, all of a sudden

coupable
1 *adjective*
= guilty
2 *noun, masculine/feminine*
un coupable/une coupable = a culprit

coupe *noun, feminine*
* (*a trophy*)
  une coupe = a cup
* (*at the hairdresser's*)
  une coupe = a haircut
* (*a container*)
  une coupe = a bowl

couper *verb* ⑴
1 (**!** + *avoir*)
= to cut off
2 se couper (**!** + *être*)
  se couper = to cut oneself
  se couper le doigt = to cut one's finger

cour *noun, feminine*
* (*an enclosed area*)
  une cour = a yard
  = a courtyard
  = a farmyard
* (*a play area at school*)
  une cour (de récréation) = a playground, a schoolyard
* (*for royalty, trials*)
  la cour = the court

courageux/courageuse *adjective*
= courageous, brave

couramment *adverb*
* = fluently
* = widely

courant
1 ▶ courir ㉖
2 *noun, masculine*
un courant = a current
3 au courant
  être au courant de ce qui se passe = to know what's going on
  je vous tiendrai au courant = I'll keep you informed
un courant d'air = a draught, a draft

coureur/coureuse *noun, masculine/feminine*
un coureur/une coureuse = a runner
un coureur cycliste = a racing cyclist

courir *verb* ㉖
* = to run
* = to race
* = to rush

couronne *noun, feminine*
* (*on a king's head*)
  une couronne = a crown
* (*on a grave*)
  une couronne = a wreath

courrier *noun, masculine*
  le courrier = the post, the mail
  = letters
  par retour du courrier = by return (post), by return mail
le courrier du cœur = the problem page, the advice column

cours *noun, masculine* (**!** *never changes*)
* (*a teaching session*)
  un cours = a lesson, a class
  faire cours = to teach
* (*a series of lessons*)
  un cours = a course
* (*on the foreign exchange*)
  le cours du dollar = the (exchange) rate for the dollar
* **au cours de la journée** = during the course of the day
  en cours de route = along the way
un cours d'eau = a waterway
un cours du soir = an evening class

course
1 *noun, feminine*
* (*a competition*)
  une course = a race
* (*some business to attend to*)
  une course = an errand
2 courses *noun, feminine plural*
  des courses = shopping

coursier/coursière *noun, masculine/feminine*
  un coursier/une coursière = a messenger, a dispatch rider

court/courte *adjective*
= short
de courte durée = short-lived

couru/courue ▶ courir ㉖

cousin/cousine *noun, masculine/feminine*
  un cousin/une cousine = a cousin

coussin *noun, masculine*
  un coussin = a cushion

cousu/cousue ▶ coudre ㉖㉖

coût *noun, masculine*
  le coût = the cost

couteau *noun, masculine*
(*plural*) **couteaux**
  un couteau = a knife

---

coûter verb [1]
= to cost

coûteux/coûteuse adjective
= costly

coutume noun, feminine
une coutume = a custom

couture noun, feminine
• (an activity)
la couture = sewing
• (in a garment)
une couture = a seam

couvercle noun, masculine
un couvercle = a lid

couvert¹ noun, masculine
un couvert = a place setting
mettre le couvert = to set the table

couvert²/couverte ▶ couvrir [32]

couverture noun, feminine
• (on a bed)
une couverture = a blanket
• (on a book)
une couverture = a cover

couvrir verb [32]
= to cover

crabe noun, masculine
un crabe = a crab

cracher verb [1]
• = to spit
• = to spit out

craie noun, feminine
la craie = chalk

craindre verb [54]
• = to fear, to be afraid
ne craignez rien = don't be afraid
• = to be sensitive to

craint/crainte¹ ▶ craindre [54]

crainte¹ noun, feminine
la crainte = fear

cramoisi/cramoisie adjective
= crimson

crampe noun, feminine
une crampe = a cramp

crâne noun, masculine
le crâne = the skull

crapaud noun, masculine
un crapaud = a toad

craquer verb [1]
• = to break
• = to creak
• (emotionally)✻ = to crack up

cravate noun, feminine
une cravate = a tie

crayon noun, masculine
un crayon = a pencil

un crayon à bille = a ballpoint pen
un crayon de couleur = a colo(u)red pencil
un crayon feutre = a felt-tip pen

crèche noun, feminine
• (for babies)
une crèche = a day-nursery, a nursery
• (a Christmas scene)
une crèche = a crib, a crèche

crédit noun, masculine
le crédit = credit
acheter à crédit = to buy on credit
'la maison ne fait pas de crédit' = 'no credit'

créer verb [11]
• = to create
• = to set up, to found

crème
1 noun, feminine
la crème = cream
2 noun, masculine
un crème = an espresso with milk

crémerie noun, feminine
une crémerie = a cheese shop, a cheese store

crêpe noun, feminine
une crêpe = a pancake

crêperie noun, feminine
une crêperie = a pancake restaurant

cresson noun, masculine
le cresson = watercress

crête noun, feminine
• (of a hill, a wave)
la crête = the crest
• (of a roof)
la crête = the ridge
• (on a bird)
la crête = the comb

creuser verb [1]
• = to dig
• l'exercice, ça creuse✻! = exercise gives you an appetite!

creux/creuse adjective
= hollow

crevaison noun, feminine
une crevaison = a puncture

crevant/crevante✻ adjective
• = exhausting
• = hilarious

crevé/crevée✻ adjective
• = exhausted
• = flat, punctured

crever verb [16]
• = to have a puncture
• = to burst
= to puncture
• = to die
un chat crevé = a dead cat

- (*to exhaust*)✖ = to wear out
  la course m'a crevé✖ = the race wore me out

crevette *noun, feminine*
  une crevette grise = a shrimp
  une crevette rose = a prawn

cri *noun, masculine*
- (*by a person*)
  un cri = a cry, a shout
  = a scream
  pousser un cri = to scream
- (*by an animal*)
  un cri = a cry
  = a call

crier *verb* [2]
  = to shout
  = to scream

crime *noun, masculine*
  un crime (*a criminal action*) = a crime
  (*an unlawful killing*) = a murder

criminel/criminelle
1 *adjective*
  = criminal
2 *noun, masculine/feminine*
  un criminel/une criminelle = a criminal
  = a murderer

crise *noun, feminine*
- (*a difficult situation*)
  une crise = a crisis
- (*an outburst*)
  une crise = a fit
- (*a sudden illness*)
  une crise = an attack
  une crise cardiaque = a heart attack

critiquer *verb* [1]
  = to criticize

crochet *noun, masculine*
- (*a piece of bent metal*)
  un crochet = a hook
- (*on a journey*)
  un crochet = a detour

croire *verb* [53]
1 (**!** + *avoir*)
- = to believe
  je te crois = I believe you
- = to think
  je ne crois pas = I don't think so
2 **se croire** (**!** + *être*)
  il se croit malin = he thinks he's smart

croisement *noun, masculine*
  un croisement = a junction, an intersection

croiser *verb* [1]
1 (**!** + *avoir*)

- = to cross
  les jambes croisées = legs crossed
  les bras croisés = arms folded
- = to pass
  croiser une voiture = to pass a car (coming the other way)
2 **se croiser** (**!** + *être*)
- **se croiser** = to cross
- **se croiser** = to pass each other

croisière *noun, feminine*
  une croisière = a cruise

croissance *noun, feminine*
  la croissance = growth

croissant *noun, masculine*
- (*a pastry*)
  un croissant = a croissant
- (*a shape*)
  un croissant = a crescent

croix *noun, feminine* (**!** *never changes*)
  une croix = a cross

croque-monsieur *noun, masculine*
(**!** *never changes*)
  un croque-monsieur = a grilled ham and cheese sandwich

crotte *noun, feminine*
  de la crotte de chien = dog mess, dog poop

croûte *noun, feminine*
- (*on bread*)
  la croûte = the crust
- (*on cheese*)
  la croûte = the rind
- (*on the skin*)
  une croûte = a scab

croûton *noun, masculine*
  un croûton = a crouton

CRS *noun, masculine* (**!** *never changes*)
  un CRS a member of the French riot police

cru/crue
1 ▶ **croire** [53]
2 *adjective*
  = raw

crudités *noun, feminine plural*
  des crudités = raw vegetables

cruel/cruelle *adjective*
  = cruel

cueillir *verb* [27]
  = to pick

cuiller, cuillère *noun, feminine*
  une cuiller, une cuillère = a spoon
**une cuillère à café, une petite
cuillère** = a teaspoon
une cuillère à soupe = a soup spoon

✖ in informal situations   ☛ may be considered offensive

cuillerée noun, feminine
  une cuillerée = a spoonful

cuir noun, masculine
  le cuir = leather

cuire verb 62
  = to cook
  = to bake

cuisine noun, feminine
• (a room)
  une cuisine = a kitchen
• (the preparation of food)
  la cuisine = cooking

cuisinier/cuisinière¹ noun,
masculine/feminine
  un cuisinier/une cuisinière = a cook

cuisinière² noun, feminine
  une cuisinière = a cooker, a stove, a range

cuisse noun, feminine
  une cuisse = a thigh
  des cuisses de grenouille = frog's legs

cuit/cuite ▶ cuire 62

cul⚬ noun, masculine
  le cul⚬ = the arse, the ass

culot✱ noun, masculine
  le culot✱ = cheek, nerve

culotte noun, feminine
  une culotte = pants, panties, knickers

cultiver verb 1
• = to cultivate
• = to grow

cure noun, feminine
  une cure = a course of treatment (in a
    spa)

curé noun, masculine
  un curé = a (parish) priest

curieux/curieuse
1 adjective
• = inquisitive
• = odd, strange
2 **curieux** noun, masculine plural
  les curieux = onlookers

curiosité noun, feminine
  la curiosité = curiosity

cuvette noun, feminine
  une cuvette = a bowl

CV noun, masculine
• (personal details)
  un CV = a CV, a résumé
• (a unit of power)
  un CV = one HP

cyclable adjective
  une piste cyclable = a cycle lane

cycliste noun, masculine/feminine
  un cycliste/une cycliste = a cyclist

cygne noun, masculine
  un cygne = a swan

cyprès noun, masculine (**!** never changes)
  un cyprès = a cypress

Dd   **D**

---

d' ▶ de

dactylo noun, masculine/feminine
  un dactylo/une dactylo = a typist

daim noun, masculine
• (an animal)
  un daim = a deer
• (a type of leather)
  le daim = suede

dame
1 noun, feminine
  une dame = a lady
2 **dames** noun, feminine plural
  les dames = draughts, checkers

Danemark noun, masculine
  le Danemark = Denmark

danger noun, masculine
  le danger = danger
  'danger de noyade' = 'unsafe for
    swimming'

dangereux/dangereuse adjective
  = dangerous

danois/danoise
1 adjective
  = Danish
2 **danois** noun, masculine
  le danois = Danish

dans preposition
• = in
  vivre dans une ville = to live in a town
  être dans les affaires = to be in business
  aller dans la bonne direction = to go in the
    right direction
  dans une semaine = in a week's time
• = into
  entrer dans une maison = to go into a
    house
  sortir dans le jardin = to go out into the
    garden
• = on
  être dans un train = to be on a train
  monter dans un avion = to get on a plane
  dans l'ensemble = on the whole
• = through
  fouiller dans un sac = to rummage
    through a bag
• = out of
  prendre un verre dans un placard = to take
    a glass out of a cupboard

danse noun, feminine
• la danse = dancing
• une danse = a dance
la danse classique = ballet dancing

danser verb 1
= to dance

danseur/danseuse noun,
masculine/feminine
un danseur/une danseuse = a dancer

date noun, feminine
la date = the date
'date limite de consommation' = 'use-by date'

dater verb 1
= to date
dater de = to date from

datte noun, feminine
une datte = a date

daube noun, feminine
la daube beef stew cooked in wine

dauphin noun, masculine
un dauphin = a dolphin

davantage adverb
• = more
• = longer

de (**d'** before vowel or mute h; de + le becomes du; de + les becomes des)

! You will find translations for phrases with de such as d'abord, pomme de terre, chemin de fer etc under the words abord, pomme, chemin, etc.

1 preposition
• = of
un verre d'eau = a glass of water
la voiture de mon père = my father's car
• = from
le paquet vient de Paris = the package comes from Paris
du matin au soir = from morning till night
• = by
un tableau de Picasso = a painting by Picasso
il était suivi de son chien = he was followed by his dog
• = about
elle parle des voisins = she's talking about the neighbo(u)rs
de quoi s'agit-il? = what's it about?
• = than
plus de trois heures après mon arrivée = more than three hours after I'd arrived
moins de dix pour cent = less than ten per cent
2 determiner
= some
= any
voulez-vous de la bière? = would you like some beer?
il n'a pas de monnaie = he hasn't got any change
as-tu des courses à faire? = have you got any shopping to do?

dé noun, masculine
• (in games)
un dé = a dice
• (in sewing)
un dé = a thimble

déballer verb 1
• = to unpack
• = to display

débarquer verb 1
• = to disembark, to get off
• = to unload

débarras noun, masculine (! never changes)
• (a room)
un débarras = a junk room
• bon débarras! = good riddance!

débarrasser verb 1
1 (! + avoir)
• = to clear (out)
débarrasser (la table) = to clear the table
débarrasser une pièce = to clear out a room
• = to rid
je vous débarrasse de votre manteau? = shall I take your coat?
2 se débarrasser de (! + être)
se débarrasser de = to get rid of

débattre: se débattre verb 61 (! + être)
se débattre = to struggle

déborder verb 1
= to overflow

débouché noun, masculine
un débouché = an opening

déboucher verb 1
• = to open
déboucher une bouteille = to open a bottle
• = to unblock, to unclog
déboucher un évier = to unblock a sink
• = to lead to
le sentier débouche sur une route = the path leads to a road
• = to come out
la voiture a débouché d'une petite rue = the car came out of a side street

debout adverb
• = standing
se mettre debout = to stand up
rester debout = to stand
• = upright
mets la caisse debout = stand the crate in an upright position
• = up
être debout à six heures du matin = to be up at six in the morning
debout! = get up!

déboutonner verb 1
= to unbutton

débraillé/débraillée adjective
= dishevelled

débrancher verb 1
= to unplug

débrayer verb 21
= to put the clutch in

débris noun, masculine (**!** never changes)
• (of glass, china)
  un débris = a fragment
• (of car, plane)
  un débris = a piece of wreckage

débrouiller verb 1
1 (**!** + avoir)
• = to unscramble
• = to disentangle
2 **se débrouiller** (**!** + être)
• **se débrouiller** = to manage
  se débrouiller pour avoir des billets = to
    manage to get tickets
• **se débrouiller** = to get by
  se débrouiller en anglais = to get by in
    English

début noun, masculine
  le début = the beginning
  au début = at the beginning
  début avril = at the beginning of April, in
    early April

débutant/débutante noun,
masculine/feminine
  un débutant/une débutante = a beginner

décacheter verb 20
= to unseal

décaféiné/décaféinée adjective
= decaffeinated

décalage noun, masculine
  le décalage horaire = the time difference
  = jet lag

décapsuleur noun, masculine
  un décapsuleur = a bottle-opener

décéder verb 14
= to die
  être décédé = to be dead

décembre noun, masculine
  décembre = December

déception noun, feminine
  une déception = a disappointment

décès noun, masculine (**!** never changes)
  un décès = a death

décevant/décevante adjective
= disappointing

décevoir verb 5
= to disappoint

déchaîner: se déchaîner verb 1
(**!** + être)
  se déchaîner = to go wild

décharger verb 13
= to unload

déchets noun, masculine plural
  les déchets = waste

déchiffrer verb 1
= to decipher
= to decode

déchirer verb 1
1 (**!** + avoir)
= to tear (up)
2 **se déchirer** (**!** + être)
  se déchirer = to tear

décidément adverb
= really

décider verb 1
1 (**!** + avoir)
• = to decide
  elle a décidé de les inviter = she's decided
    to invite them
  c'est décidé = it's settled
• = to persuade
  j'ai décidé mes amis à venir = I persuaded
    my friends to come
2 **se décider** (**!** + être)
  se décider = to make up one's mind

déclarer verb 1
1 (**!** + avoir)
• = to declare
  rien à déclarer = nothing to declare
• = to report
  déclarer un vol = to report a theft
2 **se déclarer** (**!** + être)
  se déclarer = to break out
  un incendie s'est déclaré = a fire broke
    out

déclencher verb 1
= to set off
= to trigger

décollage noun, masculine
  le décollage = take-off

décoller verb 1
1 (**!** + avoir)
• = to peel off
  décoller une étiquette = to peel off a label
• = to take off
  l'avion va décoller = the plane is about to
    take off
2 **se décoller** (**!** + être)
  se décoller = to come off

décolleté/décolletée adjective
= low-cut

décolorer verb 1
• = to bleach
• = to cause to fade

décombres noun, masculine plural
  les décombres = the rubble

décongeler verb 17
= to defrost

décontracté/décontractée
adjective
• = relaxed, laid-back
• = casual

D

décorer verb [1]
= to decorate

découper verb [1]
= to cut out
= to cut up
= to carve

décourager verb [13]
= to discourage

découvert/découverte¹
▶ **découvrir** [32]

découverte² noun, feminine
une découverte = a discovery

découvrir verb [32]
• = to discover
• = to uncover

décrire verb [42]
= to describe

décrocher verb [1]
• (to remove from its hook) = to take down
  décrocher le téléphone = to pick up the
  receiver
  = to take the phone off the hook
• (in a competition, an exam)✖ = to pass
  = to get
  décrocher✖ son permis = to pass one's
  driving test

déçu/déçue ▶ **décevoir** [5]

dedans adverb
= inside

défaire verb [10]
1 (! + avoir)
• = to undo
  défaire sa valise = to unpack one's
  suitcase
2 se défaire (! + être)
  se défaire = to come undone

défaut noun, masculine
un défaut = a fault

défavorisé/défavorisée adjective
• = underprivileged
• = disadvantaged

défectueux/défectueuse adjective
= faulty

défendre verb [6]
1 (! + avoir)
• = to forbid
  je vous défends de sortir = I forbid you to
  go out
  c'est défendu = it's forbidden, it's not
  allowed
• = to defend
2 se défendre (! + être)
  se défendre = to defend oneself

défendu/défendue ▶ **défendre** [6]

défense noun, feminine
• (an order)
  'défense de fumer' = 'no smoking'
• (against an attack, an accusation)
  la défense = the defence, the defense
  prendre la défense d'un ami = to stand up
  for a friend
  sans défense = helpless, defenceless,
  defenseless
• (of an elephant, a walrus)
  une défense = a tusk

défilé noun, masculine
• (a military display)
  un défilé = a parade
• (people filing past)
  un défilé = a procession
  = a march
• (a constant flow of people)
  un défilé de visiteurs = a stream of visitors

défiler verb [1]
= to march past

défoncer verb [12]
  défoncer une porte = to break down a
  door

déformé/déformée adjective
= distorted
= misshapen
  'chaussée déformée' = 'uneven road
  surface'

dégager verb [13]
1 (! + avoir)
• = to clear
  ciel dégagé = clear sky
• = to free
• = to give off
  dégager de la chaleur = to give off heat
2 se dégager (! + être)
• se dégager = to clear
  le temps s'est dégagé = the weather has
  cleared
• se dégager (de) = to free oneself (from)

dégâts noun, masculine plural
  les dégâts = the damage

dégonfler verb [1]
1 (! + avoir)
• = to deflate, to let down
2 se dégonfler (! + être)
• se dégonfler = to deflate, to go down
• (when faced with a challenge)✖
  se dégonfler✖ = to lose one's nerve, to
  chicken out

dégoûtant/dégoûtante adjective
• = filthy
• = disgusting

degré noun, masculine
• (a unit of measurement)
  un degré = one degree

✖ in informal situations

• (*a level*)
l'enseignement du second degré
= secondary education, high school
education (*for students aged 11 to 18*)

dégringoler* verb [1]
= to take a tumble
= to tumble down

déguiser verb [1]
1 (**!** + *avoir*)
= to disguise
2 se déguiser (**!** + *être*)
• **se déguiser** = to disguise oneself
• **se déguiser** = to dress up

dégustation noun, feminine
une dégustation de vin = a wine tasting

déguster verb [1]
• = to taste, to sample
• = to enjoy

dehors adverb
= outside

déjà adverb
= already

déjeuner
1 noun, masculine
• (*in the middle of the day*)
le déjeuner = lunch
• (*in the morning*)
le (petit) déjeuner = breakfast
2 verb
• = to have lunch
• = to have breakfast

delà: au delà de preposition
au delà de = beyond

délabré/délabrée adjective
= dilapidated

délai noun, masculine
• (*time allowed*)
dans un délai de 24 heures = within 24
hours
sans délai = immediately
mardi, dernier délai = Tuesday at the latest
• (*additional time*)
un délai = an extension

délasser verb [1]
= to refresh
= to relax

délicieux/délicieuse adjective
= delicious

délit noun, masculine
un délit = an offence, an offense

délivrer verb [1]
• = to free
délivrer un prisonnier = to free a prisoner
• = to issue
délivrer un passeport = to issue a passport

deltaplane noun, masculine
• (*the equipment*)
un deltaplane = a hang-glider

• (*the sport*)
le deltaplane = hang-gliding

demain adverb
= tomorrow
à demain = see you tomorrow

demande noun, feminine
• **une demande** = an application
= a request
faire une demande de prêt = to apply for a
loan
'demandes d'emploi' = 'jobs wanted'
• (*in business*)
l'offre et la demande = supply and
demand

demander verb [1]
1 (**!** + *avoir*)
• = to ask (for)
elle a demandé de l'argent à ses parents
= she's asked her parents for money
• = to require
ça demande trop d'efforts = it requires too
much effort
2 se demander (**!** + *être*)
se demander = to wonder

démarrer verb [1]
• (*if it's a vehicle*) = to pull away
• (*if it's a driver*) = to drive off

démarreur noun, masculine
le démarreur = the starter

déménagement noun, masculine
• (*going to live elsewhere*)
un déménagement = a move
• (*transporting furniture*)
un déménagement = a removal

déménager verb [13]
= to move (house)

demeurer verb [1]
• = to live
• = to remain

demi/demie[1]
1 adjective
• **demi-** (**!** *comes before the noun, never
changes*)
= half
= semi
une demi-heure = half an hour
un demi-tarif = a half-price ticket
une demi-finale = a semi-final
• **et demi/et demie** (**!** *comes after the noun,
never plural*)
= and a half
deux et demi = two and a half
à cinq heures et demie = at half past five,
at five-thirty
2 demi noun, masculine
• (*a drink*)
un demi = a glass of beer
• (*in rugby*)
un demi de mêlée = a scrum half
3 à demi = half
à demi éveillé = half awake

demie² *noun, feminine*
la demie = half past
il est déjà la demie = it's already half past

demi-frère *noun, masculine*
(*plural*) **demi-frères**
un demi-frère = a stepbrother, a half-brother

demi-pension *noun, feminine*
la demi-pension = half board,
accommodation with one meal only

demi-sœur *noun, feminine*
(*plural*) **demi-sœurs**
une demi-sœur = a stepsister, a half-sister

démissionner *verb* 1
= to resign

demi-tour *noun, masculine*
(*plural*) **demi-tours**
un demi-tour = a half-turn
faire demi-tour = to turn back

démodé/démodée *adjective*
= old-fashioned

demoiselle *noun, feminine*
une demoiselle = a young lady
une demoiselle d'honneur = a
bridesmaid

démolir *verb* 3
= to demolish

démonter *verb* 1
• = to take apart, to dismantle
• = to remove, to take off

démontrer *verb* 1
= to demonstrate

denrée *noun, feminine*
une denrée = a product

dent *noun, feminine*
une dent = a tooth
avoir mal aux dents = to have (a)
toothache

dentelle *noun, feminine*
la dentelle = lace

dentifrice *noun, masculine*
le dentifrice = toothpaste

dentiste *noun, masculine|feminine*
un dentiste/une dentiste = a dentist

dépannage *noun, masculine*
'service de dépannage' = 'breakdown
service', 'emergency service'

dépanner *verb* 1
• = to fix, to repair
• (*if someone's in difficulty*)✶ = to help out

dépanneur/dépanneuse¹ *noun,
masculine|feminine*
un dépanneur/une dépanneuse = an
engineer

dépanneuse² *noun, feminine*
une dépanneuse = a breakdown truck, a
tow truck

dépareillé/dépareillée *adjective*
= odd

départ *noun, masculine*
• (*the act of leaving*)
le départ = the departure
• (*the beginning*)
le départ = the start
au départ = at first

département *noun, masculine*
un département = a department (*an
administrative district*)

dépasser *verb* 1
• = to overtake, to pass
• = to exceed
elle le dépasse de 5 centimètres = she's 5
centimetres taller than him
• = to be ahead of, to outstrip
• = to stick out
• = to pass, to go past
nous avons dépassé l'école = we've gone
past the school

dépêcher: se dépêcher *verb* 1
(✶ + *être*)
se dépêcher = to hurry up
dépêchez-vous! = hurry up!

dépendre *verb* 6
dépendre de = to depend on
ça dépendra du temps = it'll depend on
the weather
ça dépend! = it depends!

dépense *noun, feminine*
la dépense du ménage = the household
expenditure
faire une dépense = to spend some money

dépenser *verb* 1
= to spend (money)

déplacer *verb* 12
1 (✶ + *avoir*)
= to move
2 se déplacer (✶ + *être*)
• se déplacer = to move
• se déplacer = to travel

dépliant *noun, masculine*
un dépliant = a leaflet

déplier *verb* 2
= to unfold

déposer *verb* 1
1 (✶ + *avoir*)
• déposer des ordures = to dump rubbish,
to dump garbage
• déposer une gerbe = to lay a wreath
• déposer de l'argent sur un compte = to
deposit money in an account
• déposer une valise à la consigne
automatique = to leave a suitcase in a left-
luggage locker

✶ in informal situations

- **déposer un passager** = to drop a passenger off
- **déposer une plainte** = to lodge a complaint, to make a complaint
- **une marque déposée** = a registered trademark

2 se déposer(! + *être*)
  se déposer = to settle
  = to collect

dépositaire*noun, masculine/feminine*
  un dépositaire/une dépositaire = an agent, a representative
  un dépositaire de journaux = a newsagent, a newsdealer

dépôt*noun, masculine*
- (*for goods*)
  un dépôt = a warehouse
- (*in a shop*)
  faire dépôt de gaz = to sell bottled gas
- (*in a bottle*)
  un dépôt = a deposit, a residue

déprime✕ *noun, feminine*
  la déprime✕ = depression

déprimer*verb* ⊞
- (*to cause sadness*) = to depress
- (*to feel sadness*)✕ = to be depressed

déprogrammer*verb* ⊞
  = to cancel

depuis
1*preposition*
- = since
  depuis lundi = since Monday
  depuis quand est-il à Paris? = how long has he been in Paris?
- = for
  depuis un an = for a year
  je le connais depuis longtemps = I've known him for a long time
  il pleuvait depuis trois jours = it had been raining for three days
  depuis combien de temps le sais-tu? = how long have you known?
2*adverb*
  = since
  je n'ai pas de nouvelles depuis = since then I haven't heard any news
3 depuis que = since, ever since

député*noun, masculine*
  un député = a Member of the National Assembly
  un député européen = a member of the European Parliament, a Euro-MP

dérailler*verb* ⊞
  = to be derailed

déranger*verb* ⊡
1(! + *avoir*)
- = to bother, to disturb
  excusez-moi de vous déranger = I'm sorry to bother you
  ça vous dérange si je mets la radio? = do you mind if I turn the radio on?
- = to disturb, to upset, to mess up

2 se déranger(! + *être*)
- **se déranger** = to get up
  = to move
- **se déranger** = to put oneself out

déraper*verb* ⊞
  = to skid

dériveur*noun, masculine*
  un dériveur = a dinghy

dernier/dernière
1*adjective*
  = last
  = latest
  au dernier étage = on the top floor
2*noun, masculine/feminine*
- **le dernier/la dernière** = the last one
  c'est le dernier qui me reste = it's my last one
  arriver le dernier = to arrive last
  être le dernier de la classe = to be bottom of the class, to be last in the class
- **ce dernier/cette dernière** = the latter
3 en dernier = lastly
  = last

dernièrement*adverb*
  = recently, lately

derrière
1*preposition*
  = behind
2*adverb*
  = behind
  = at the back, in the back
3*noun, masculine*
- (*the rear*)
  le derrière = the back
  la porte de derrière = the back door
- (*part of the body*)✕
  le derrière✕ = the behind, the backside

des▶ de

dès
1*preposition*
  = from
  dès ce soir = from tonight
  dès mon arrivée = as soon as I arrive(d)
2 dès que = as soon as

désagréable*adjective*
  = unpleasant

désastre*noun, masculine*
  un désastre = a disaster

descendre*verb* ⊡
1(! + *être*)
- = to go down, to come down
  il est descendu au village = he's gone down to the village
  tu es descendu à pied? = did you walk down?
  nous sommes descendus en courant = we ran down
- = to go downstairs, to come downstairs
- = to get off
  je descendrai à la prochaine gare = I'll get off at the next station

- (*other uses*)
  descendre dans un hôtel = to stop (off) at a hotel
2 (**!** + *avoir*)
- = to go down
  descendre la rue = to go down the street
  il a descendu l'escalier en courant = he ran down the stairs
- = to take down, to bring down
  je dois descendre mes bagages = I must take my luggage down
  peux-tu me descendre mes lunettes? = can you bring my glasses down to me?

descente *noun, feminine*
- (*a steep surface*)
  une descente = a slope
- (*in a plane*)
  la descente = the descent
- (*in a skiing competition*)
  la descente = the downhill event

désert/déserte
1 *adjective*
  = deserted
2 désert *noun, masculine*
  le désert = the desert

désespéré/désespérée *adjective*
  (*describing a person*) = in despair
  (*describing a situation*) = hopeless

désespoir *noun, masculine*
  le désespoir = despair
  être au désespoir = to be in despair

déshabiller *verb* ⊡
1 (**!** + *avoir*)
  = to undress
2 se déshabiller (**!** + *être*)
  se déshabiller = to get undressed

désigner *verb* ⊡
- = to point out
- = to choose, to designate

désirer *verb* ⊡
  = to want
  que désirez-vous? = what would you like?

désobéir *verb* ⊡
- = to be disobedient
- = to disobey
  désobéir à son père = to disobey one's father

désobéissant/désobéissante
adjective
  = disobedient

désolé/désolée *adjective*
  je suis désolé = I'm sorry

désordre *noun, masculine*
- (*in a room*)
  le désordre = untidiness, messiness
  quel désordre! = what a mess!
  être en désordre = to be untidy
  mettre du désordre dans une pièce = to make a room untidy, to make a room messy

- (*unrest*)
  le désordre = disorder

désormais *adverb*
  = from now on
  = from then on

dessert *noun, masculine*
  un dessert = a dessert

dessin *noun, masculine*
- (*a picture*)
  un dessin = a drawing
- (*a subject*)
  le dessin = art, drawing
  = design
un dessin animé = a cartoon (film)

dessinateur/dessinatrice *noun,*
masculine/feminine
  un dessinateur/une dessinatrice = a draughtsman, a draftsman
  = an illustrator
  = a designer

dessiner *verb* ⊡
  = to draw

dessous
1 *adverb*
  = underneath
2 *noun, masculine* (**!** *never changes*)
  le dessous = the underside
  = the bottom
  le drap de dessous = the bottom sheet
  les voisins du dessous = the people who live (on the floor) below
3 en dessous = underneath
  la taille en dessous = the next size down, the smaller size
4 en dessous de = below
  en dessous de la moyenne = below average

dessus
1 *adverb*
  = on top
  écris ton nom dessus = write your name on it
2 *noun, masculine* (**!** *never changes*)
  le dessus = the top
  le drap de dessus = the top sheet
  les voisins du dessus = the people who live (on the floor) above

destinataire *noun, masculine/feminine*
  le destinataire/la destinataire = the addressee

destination
1 *noun, feminine*
  une destination = a destination
2 à destination de = bound for
  vol 802 à destination de Nice = flight 802 to Nice

détacher *verb* ⊡
1 (**!** + *avoir*)
- = to undo
  = to untie
  = to unfasten
- = to tear off, to detach

2 se détacher (**!** + *être*)
• **se détacher** = to come undone
• **se détacher** = to come off

détail *noun, masculine*
• (*a minor point*)
  un détail = a detail
  des détails supplémentaires = extra
    information
• (*selling direct to the public*)
  le détail = retail

détendre *verb* 6
1 (**!** + *avoir*)
• = to relax
• = to be relaxing
2 se détendre (**!** + *être*)
  se détendre = to relax

détenu/détenue *noun,*
masculine/feminine
  un détenu/une détenue = a prisoner

détester *verb* 1
  = to detest, to hate

détraquer *verb* 1
  = to damage

détresse *noun, feminine*
  la détresse = distress

détroit *noun, masculine*
  un détroit = a strait

détruire *verb* 62
  = to destroy

dette *noun, feminine*
  une dette = a debt

deuil *noun, masculine*
• **un deuil** = a bereavement
• **le deuil** = mourning

deux *number*
  = two
  ils iront tous les deux = both of them will
    go

deuxième *number*
  = second

deux-roues *noun, masculine* (**!** *never*
changes)
  un deux-roues = a two-wheeler

devant
1 *preposition*
• = in front of
  le livre est devant toi = the book is in front
    of you
• = ahead of
  Paul était loin devant nous = Paul was (a
    long) way ahead of us
• = outside
  attends-moi devant la bibliothèque = wait
    for me outside the library
• = past
  passer devant un magasin = to walk past
    a shop

2 *adverb*
  = in front
  = at the front
3 *noun, masculine*
  le devant = the front
  la fenêtre de devant = the front window

devenir *verb* 36 (**!** + *être*)
  = to become

déviation *noun, feminine*
  une déviation = a diversion, a detour

deviner *verb* 1
  = to guess

devinette *noun, feminine*
  une devinette = a riddle

devis *noun, masculine* (**!** *never changes*)
  un devis = an estimate

devise *noun, feminine*
• (*money*)
  une devise = a currency
• (*a short saying*)
  une devise = a motto

devoir
1 *noun, masculine*
• (*work set by a teacher*)
  un devoir = a piece of homework, an
    assignment
  faire ses devoirs = to do one's homework
• (*responsibility*)
  le devoir = duty
  faire son devoir = to do one's duty
2 *verb* 44
• = to owe
  devoir de l'argent à un ami = to owe a
    friend money
  je leur dois des excuses = I owe them an
    apology
• (*to be obliged to*) = to have to
  je dois aller travailler = I have to go to
    work, I must go to work
  tu aurais dû téléphoner = you should have
    phoned
  vous devriez les remercier = you ought to
    thank them
• (*meaning that something is likely*) = must
  il doit être arrivé = he must have arrived
  elle devait avoir 11 ans = she must have
    been 11
  ils ont dû oublier = they must have
    forgotten
• (*meaning that something is certain or
  expected*)
  cela devait arriver = it was bound to
    happen
  le train doit partir vers neuf heures = the
    train is due to leave at about nine
    o'clock

devrai ▶ devoir 2 44

diabétique *adjective*
  = diabetic

diabolo menthe *noun, masculine*
(*plural*) **diabolos menthe**
   un diabolo menthe = a mint cordial and
   lemonade, a mint cordial and soda

diamètre *noun, masculine*
   le diamètre = the diameter

diapositive *noun, feminine*
   une diapositive = a slide

diarrhée *noun, feminine*
   la diarrhée = diarrh(o)ea

dictée *noun, feminine*
   une dictée = a dictation

dicter *verb* $\boxed{1}$
   = to dictate

dictionnaire *noun, masculine*
   un dictionnaire = a dictionary

diète *noun, feminine*
   être à la diète = to be on a restricted diet

diététicien/diététicienne *noun,*
masculine/feminine
   un diététicien/une diététicienne = a
   dietician

dieu *noun, masculine*
(*plural*) **dieux**
   un dieu = a god
   mon Dieu! = my God!

différence *noun, feminine*
   une différence = a difference
   à la différence des animaux = unlike
   animals

difficile *adjective*
 • = difficult
 • = fussy

difficulté *noun, feminine*
   une difficulté = a difficulty

difforme *adjective*
   = deformed

diffuser *verb* $\boxed{1}$
   (*on radio*) = to broadcast

dimanche *noun, masculine*
   dimanche = Sunday

dinde *noun, feminine*
   une dinde = a turkey

dîner
1 *noun, masculine*
   le dîner = dinner
   à l'heure du dîner = at dinner time
2 *verb* $\boxed{1}$
   = to have dinner

dingue✶ *adjective*
   = crazy

✶ in informal situations

diplôme *noun, masculine*
   un diplôme = a diploma
   = a qualification

dire *verb* $\boxed{40}$
1 (**!** + *avoir*)
 • = to say
   on dit que l'usine va fermer = they say the
   factory is going to close down
 • = to tell
   dire des mensonges = to tell lies
   dites-leur de venir = tell them to come
 • = to think
   qu'est-ce que tu en dis? = what do you
   think?
   on ne dirait pas qu'elle a 20 ans = you
   wouldn't think she was 20, she doesn't
   look 20
   on dirait qu'il va pleuvoir = it looks like
   rain
 • vouloir dire = to mean
   qu'est-ce que ça veut dire? = what does it
   mean?
 • ça ne me dit rien = it doesn't appeal to me,
   I don't feel like it
   = it doesn't mean anything to me, it
   doesn't ring a bell
2 se dire (**!** + *être*)
 • se dire = to tell oneself
 • se dire = to claim to be
   il se dit médecin = he claims to be a doctor
 • ça ne se dit pas = you can't say that

direct/directe
1 *adjective*
   = direct
2 direct *noun, masculine*
 • (*a train*)
   un direct = an express (train)
 • (*on radio, TV*)
   le direct = live broadcasting
   en direct de Rome = live from Rome

directement *adverb*
 • = straight
 • = directly

directeur/directrice *noun,*
masculine/feminine
 • (*in a school*)
   le directeur/la directrice = the headteacher,
   the principal
 • (*in an organization, a business*)
   un directeur/une directrice = a director
   = a manager

direction *noun, feminine*
 • (*when moving*)
   une direction = a direction
   dans quelle direction? = which way?
   en direction de Calais = toward(s) Calais
 • (*in an organization*)
   la direction = (the) management
 • (*on a car*)
   la direction = the steering

directrice ▶ directeur

diriger verb 13
1 (! + avoir)
- **diriger une affaire** = to manage a business, to run a business
- **diriger une opération** = to direct an operation
- **diriger un orchestre** = to conduct an orchestra
2 se diriger (! + être)
- **se diriger vers Paris** = to make for Paris, to head toward(s) Paris
- **se diriger dans le noir** = to find one's way in the dark

disco noun, masculine
le disco = disco music

discothèque noun, feminine
- (a library)
  une discothèque = a record library
- (a nightclub)
  une discothèque = a disco(theque)

discours noun, masculine (! never changes)
un discours = a speech

discuter verb 1
- = to chat, to talk
- = to argue
- **discuter de** = to discuss

disparaître verb 63
- = to disappear
- = to die

disparition noun, feminine
la disparition = the disappearance

disparu/disparue ▶ disparaître 63

disponible adjective
= available

disposer verb 1
1 (! + avoir)
- = to arrange, to position
- **disposer de** = to have (at one's disposal)
2 se disposer (! + être)
- **se disposer à partir** = to prepare to leave, to be about to leave

dispute noun, feminine
une dispute = an argument, a quarrel

disputer: **se disputer** verb 1 (! + être)
se disputer = to argue, to quarrel

disque noun, masculine
- (in music)
  un disque = a record, an LP
  un disque compact = a compact disc
- (in sport)
  le disque = the discus

disquette noun, feminine
une disquette = a diskette, a floppy disk

dissimuler verb 1
= to conceal, to hide

distance noun, feminine
la distance = distance
à une distance de 25 kilomètres = 25 kilometres away
la ville est à quelle distance? = how far is the town?
commande à distance = remote control

distingué/distinguée adjective
= distinguished

distraction noun, feminine
- (leisure activity)
  une distraction = entertainment
- (lack of concentration)
  la distraction = absent-mindedness

distraire verb 58
1 (! + avoir)
- = to entertain, to amuse
- = to distract
2 se distraire (! + être)
se distraire = to amuse oneself

distrait/distraite
1 ▶ distraire 58
2 adjective
= absent-minded

distribuer verb 1
= to give out, to distribute
distribuer le courrier = to deliver the mail
distribuer les cartes = to deal

distributeur noun, masculine
un distributeur automatique de billets = a cash dispenser

divan noun, masculine
un divan = a sofa

divers/diverse adjective
- = various
- = miscellaneous

diviser verb 1
= to divide

divorcé/divorcée noun, masculine/feminine
un divorcé/une divorcée = a divorcee

divorcer verb 12
= to get divorced

dix number
= ten

dix-huit number
= eighteen

dix-huitième number
= eighteenth

dixième number
= tenth

dix-neuf number
= nineteen

dix-neuvième number
= nineteenth

dix-sept *number*
= seventeen

dix-septième *number*
= seventeenth

dizaine *noun, feminine*
une dizaine = about ten
= ten

docteur *noun, masculine*
un docteur = a doctor

documentaire *noun, masculine*
un documentaire = a documentary

documentation *noun, feminine*
de la documentation = brochures,
literature

dodo✱ *noun, masculine*
au dodo✱! = beddy-byes!, bed time!

doigt *noun, masculine*
• (*on the hand*)
un doigt = a finger
montrer du doigt = to point at
un doigt de pied = a toe
• (*small amount*)
un doigt de vin = a drop of wine

dois ▶ **devoir** 2 44

doive ▶ **devoir** 2 44

domestique
1 *adjective*
= domestic
2 *noun, masculine/feminine*
un domestique/une domestique = a
servant

domicile
1 *noun, masculine*
un domicile = a (place of) residence
2 **à domicile**
travailler à domicile = to work from home
livrer à domicile = to deliver, to do home
deliveries

domicilié/domiciliée *adjective*
être domicilié à Londres = to live in
London

dominer *verb* 1
1 (**!** + *avoir*)
• = to dominate
• = to tower over
le monument dominait le village = the
monument towered over the village
• = to control
dominer sa peur = to overcome one's fear
• = to be predominant
2 **se dominer** (**!** + *être*)
se dominer = to control oneself

domino *noun, masculine*
un domino = a domino

---

dommage *noun, masculine*
• (*in expressions of regret*)
(quel) dommage! = what a pity!, what a
shame!
• (*harm*)
un dommage = damage
des dommages et intérêts = damages

DOM-TOM *noun, masculine plural*
(*abbreviation of* **départements et
territoires d'outre-mer**)
French overseas departments and territories

don *noun, masculine*
• (*talent*)
un don = a gift
• (*something given*)
un don = a donation

donc *conjunction*
= so, therefore
il est malade, donc il restera au lit = he's
unwell, so he'll stay in bed
taisez-vous donc! = be quiet, will you?
sers-toi donc! = do help yourself!

donjon *noun, masculine*
un donjon = a keep

donner *verb* 1
• = to give
donner un jouet à un enfant = to give a
child a toy
donner des coups à un animal = to hit an
animal
• donner une veste à nettoyer = to take a
jacket to be dry-cleaned
• donner sur = to overlook
la chambre donne sur la baie = the
bedroom overlooks the bay

dont *pronoun*
• = whose
voici le chauffeur dont la voiture a pris feu
= this is the driver whose car caught
fire
• = of which
= of whom
c'est le dessin dont il est si fier = it's the
drawing of which he's so proud
ils ont cinq fils, dont deux sont étudiants
= they've got five sons, two of whom are
students
j'ai lu le livre dont tu m'avais parlé = I read
the book that you'd told me about
il a pris les outils dont il avait besoin = he's
taken the tools that he needed
le pays dont elle vient = the country she
comes from
la façon dont il parle = the way he talks
c'est tout ce dont je me souviens = that's
all I can remember

doré/dorée *adjective*
= gilt
= golden
= gold

dormir *verb* 30
= to sleep

dortoir *noun, masculine*
　un dortoir = a dormitory

dos *noun, masculine* (**!** *never changes*)
　le dos = the back
　avoir mal au dos = to have (a) backache
　je l'ai vu de dos = I saw him from behind

dose *noun, feminine*
　une dose = a dose

dossier *noun, masculine*
* (*part of a seat*)
　le dossier = the back(rest)
* (*documents*)
　un dossier = a file

douane *noun, feminine*
　la douane = the customs

douanier/douanière *noun,*
masculine/feminine
　un douanier/une douanière = a customs
　　officer

double
1 *adjective*
　= double
2 *noun, masculine*
* (*a quantity*)
　payer le double = to pay twice as much
　le double de la taille normale = twice the
　　normal size
* (*a duplicate*)
　un double = a copy
　le double des clés = a spare set of keys

doubler *verb* 1
* (*to increase twofold*) = to double
* (*in a car*) = to overtake, to pass
* (*for a film*) = to dub
* (*in dressmaking*) = to line

douce ▶ **doux**

doucement *adverb*
* = gently
* = softly
* = slowly

douche *noun, feminine*
　une douche = a shower

doucher. **se doucher** *verb* 1 (**!** + *être*)
　se doucher = to take a shower

doué/douée *adjective*
　= gifted, talented

douleur *noun, feminine*
* une douleur = a pain
* la douleur = grief

douloureux/douloureuse *adjective*
　= painful

doute
1 *noun, masculine*
　le doute = doubt
　ça ne fait aucun doute = there's no doubt
　　about it
2 sans doute = probably

Douvres *noun*
　= Dover

doux/douce
1 *adjective*
* = soft
　une voix douce = a soft voice
* = mild
　un temps doux = mild weather
* = gentle
　une pente douce = a gentle slope
2 doux *adverb*
　doux = mild
　il fait doux aujourd'hui = it's mild today

douzaine *noun, feminine*
　une douzaine = a dozen
　= about twelve

douze *number*
　= twelve

douzième *number*
　= twelfth

dragée *noun, feminine*
　une dragée = a sugared almond

draguer* *verb* 1
　= to chat up, to come on to

drap *noun, masculine*
　un drap = a sheet

drapeau *noun, masculine*
(*plural* **drapeaux**)
　un drapeau = a flag

dresser *verb* 1
1 (**!** + *avoir*)
* = to train
　dresser un animal = to train an animal
* = to put up
　dresser une tente = to put up a tent
* = to raise
　dresser la tête = to raise one's head
　dresser l'oreille = to prick up one's ears
2 se dresser (**!** + *être*)
　se dresser = to stand (up)

drogue *noun, feminine*
　la drogue = drugs

drogué/droguée *noun,*
masculine/feminine
　un drogué/une droguée = a drug addict

droguer. **se droguer** *verb* 1 (**!** + *être*)
　se droguer = to take drugs

droguerie *noun, feminine*
　une droguerie = a hardware shop, a
　　hardware store

droguiste *noun, masculine/feminine*
　un droguiste/une droguiste = a hardware
　　dealer, an ironmonger

D

droit/droite[1]
1 *adjective*
- = straight
- = upright
- = right
  du côté droit = on the right-hand side

2 droit *adverb*
= straight
continuez tout droit = carry straight on

3 droit *noun, masculine*
- (*something one is entitled to*)
  un droit = a right
  avoir le droit d'aller où l'on veut = to have the right to go wherever one wants
  = to be allowed to go wherever one wants
- (*money that has to be paid*)
  un droit = a fee
  = a tax
- (*a course of study*)
  le droit = law
  les droits de douane = customs duties

droite[2] *noun, feminine*
la droite = the right

droitier/droitière *noun, masculine/feminine*
un droitier/une droitière = a right-handed person

drôle *adjective*
= funny

du ▶ de

dû/due ▶ devoir 2 44

duc *noun, masculine*
un duc = a duke

dur/dure
1 *adjective*
= hard, tough
= harsh
2 dur *adverb*
travailler dur = to work hard

durée *noun, feminine*
- (*of a reign, of a course*)
  la durée = the length
  = the duration
  un séjour de courte durée = a short stay
- (*of a cassette*)
  la durée = the playing time
- (*of a battery*)
  la durée = the life
  pile longue durée = long-life battery

durer *verb* 1
= to last

duvet *noun, masculine*
- (*for sleeping in*)
  un duvet = a sleeping bag
- (*feathers*)
  le duvet = down

dynamique *adjective*
= dynamic

Ee

eau *noun, feminine*
(*plural*) **eaux**
l'eau = water
l'eau gazeuse = fizzy water, sparkling water
l'eau minérale = mineral water
l'eau potable = drinking water

eau-de-vie *noun, feminine*
(*plural*) **eaux-de-vie**
l'eau-de-vie = brandy

éboueur *noun, masculine*
un éboueur = a dustman, a garbage collector

éboulement *noun, masculine*
un éboulement (de rochers) = a rockfall

écarlate *adjective*
= scarlet

écarter *verb* 1
1 (**!** + *avoir*)
- (*to open*) = to spread
  = to part
- (*to remove*) = to push aside
  = to move away
2 s'écarter (**!** + *être*)
s'écarter = to move out of the way
= to move away

échafaudage *noun, masculine*
un échafaudage = scaffolding

échalote *noun, feminine*
une échalote = a shallot

échange
1 *noun, masculine*
un échange = an exchange
faire un échange = to swap
2 en échange (de) = in exchange (for), in return (for)

échanger *verb* 13
= to exchange

échangeur *noun, masculine*
un échangeur = an interchange, a clover junction

échapper: s'échapper *verb* 1
(**!** + *être*)
s'échapper = to escape

écharpe *noun, feminine*
une écharpe = a scarf

échasse *noun, feminine*
une échasse = a stilt

échauffer: s'échauffer *verb* 1
(**!** + *être*)
s'échauffer = to warm up

échec
1 noun, masculine
un échec = a failure
2 échecs noun, masculine plural
les échecs = chess

échelle noun, feminine
* (a piece of equipment)
une échelle = a ladder
faire la courte échelle à Roger = to give Roger a leg-up
* (on a map)
l'échelle = the scale

échiquier noun, masculine
un échiquier = a chessboard

échouer verb [1]
1 (! + avoir)
= to fail
échouer à un examen = to fail an examination
2 s'échouer (! + être)
s'échouer = to run aground

éclair noun, masculine
* (in the sky)
un éclair = a flash of lightning
* (a cake)
un éclair = an eclair

éclairage noun, masculine
l'éclairage = the lighting

éclaircie noun, feminine
une éclaircie = a sunny spell

éclairer verb [1]
1 (! + avoir)
* = to light
* = to give light
2 s'éclairer (! + être)
s'éclairer (if it's a face, a screen) = to light up

éclater verb [1]
(if it's a tyre, a pipe) = to burst
(if it's a bomb) = to explode
(if it's a storm) = to break
(if it's war) = to break out
éclater de rire = to burst out laughing

école noun, feminine
une école = a school
une école libre = an independent school
une école maternelle = a nursery school (for children aged 2 to 6)
une école primaire = a primary school (for children aged 6 to 11)
une école secondaire = a secondary school (for students aged 11 to 18)
une école publique = a state school (in the US) = a public school

écolier/écolière noun, masculine/feminine
un écolier/une écolière = a schoolboy/a schoolgirl

écologie noun, feminine
l'écologie = ecology

écologiste noun, masculine/feminine
* (a scientist)
un écologiste/une écologiste = an ecologist
* (a person who is against pollution)
un écologiste/une écologiste = an environmentalist

économe adjective
= thrifty

économie noun, feminine
une économie = a saving
faire des économies = to save up, to save money

écorce noun, feminine
l'écorce (on a tree) = the bark
(on an orange) = the peel

écossais/écossaise adjective
* = Scottish
* une veste écossaise = a tartan jacket, a plaid jacket

Écosse noun, feminine
l'Écosse = Scotland

écouter verb [1]
= to listen to
écouter un disque = to listen to a record

écran noun, masculine
* (on a television set)
un écran = a screen
* (protection from the sun)
une crème écran total = a sun block

écraser verb [1]
1 (! + avoir)
* = to crush
* = to run over
se faire écraser = to get run over
2 s'écraser (! + être)
s'écraser = to crash

écrevisse noun, feminine
une écrevisse = a crayfish, a crawfish

écrire verb [42]
1 (! + avoir)
= to write
2 s'écrire (! + être)
* s'écrire = to write (to each other)
* s'écrire = to be spelled

écriture noun, feminine
* (the activity)
l'écriture = writing
* (the way one writes)
ton écriture = your handwriting

écrivain noun, masculine
un écrivain = a writer

écrou noun, masculine
un écrou = a nut

écrouler: s'écrouler verb [1] (! + être)
s'écrouler = to collapse

écurie noun, feminine
une écurie = a stable

écusson noun, masculine
  un écusson (on a garment) = a (cloth)
    badge

éducation noun, feminine
• (teaching)
  l'éducation = education
• (politeness)
  l'éducation = manners
  l'éducation physique = PE, physical
  education

effacer verb 12
  = to erase
  = to delete
  effacer le tableau = to wipe the board, to
    erase the board

effet
1 noun, masculine
• (result)
  un effet = an effect
  n'avoir aucun effet = to have no effect
  faire de l'effet = to be effective
• (impact)
  un effet = an impression
  faire bon effet = to make a good
    impression
  ça m'a fait un drôle d'effet = it made me
    feel strange
2 en effet = indeed

efficace adjective
• = effective
• = efficient

effondrer: s'effondrer verb 1 (**!** + être)
  s'effondrer = to collapse

effort noun, masculine
  un effort = an effort

effrayant/effrayante adjective
  = frightening

effrayer verb 21
  = to frighten, to scare

effronté/effrontée adjective
  = cheeky

égal/égale adjective
(plural) **égaux/égales**
  = equal
  ça m'est égal = I don't mind either way
  = I don't care

égaler verb 1
  = to be equal to

égalité noun, feminine
  l'égalité = equality

égarer verb 1
1 (**!** + avoir)
  = to lose
2 s'égarer (**!** + être)
  s'égarer = to get lost

✱ in informal situations

église noun, feminine
  une église = a church

égoïste adjective
  = selfish

eh bien exclamation
  eh bien! = well!

électricien/électricienne noun,
masculine/feminine
  un électricien/une électricienne = an
    electrician

électroménager
1 adjective, masculine
  un appareil électroménager = an electrical
    household appliance
2 noun, masculine
  l'électroménager = electrical household
    appliances

électrophone noun, masculine
  un électrophone = a record player

élégant/élégante adjective
  = elegant

éléphant noun, masculine
  un éléphant = an elephant

élève noun, masculine/feminine
  un élève/une élève = a pupil, a student

élevé/élevée adjective
• = high
• **bien élevé** = well brought-up, well-
  mannered
  mal élevé = ill-mannered

élever verb 16
1 (**!** + avoir)
• (if it's children) = to bring up, to raise
• (if it's animals) = to breed
• (if it's a wall, a statue) = to erect, to raise
2 s'élever (**!** + être)
• **s'élever** = to rise
• **s'élever à 500 francs** = to add up to 500
  francs

éliminer verb 1
• = to eliminate
  = to knock out, to eliminate
  être éliminé en quart de finale = to be
    knocked out in the quarter final
• = to rule out

elle pronoun, feminine
(plural) **elles**
• = she
  = it
  elles n'ont rien dit = they said nothing
  elle est cassée = it's broken
• = her
  à cause d'elle = because of her
  la valise bleue est à elle = the blue
    suitcase is hers
  c'est à elle de jouer = it's her turn to play
  les livres sont pour elles = the books are
    for them

elle-même *pronoun, feminine*
(*plural*) **elles-mêmes**
= herself
= itself
elles-mêmes = themselves

elles ▶ elle

éloigné/éloignée *adjective*
= distant
éloigné de = far from

éloigner: s'éloigner *verb* 1 (**!** + *être*)
s'éloigner = to move away

Élysée *noun, masculine*
(**le palais de**) **l'Élysée** = the Élysée palace
(*the official residence of the French President*)

emballage *noun, masculine*
l'emballage = the packaging
= the wrapping

embarquer *verb* 1
1 (**!** + *avoir*)
• = to load
• = to board
2 s'embarquer (**!** + *être*)
s'embarquer = to board

embêtant/embêtante *adjective*
= annoying

embêter *verb* 1
1 (**!** + *avoir*)
• = to annoy
= to pester
• **ça m'embête d'y aller** = I don't really want to go
2 s'embêter (**!** + *être*)
s'embêter = to be bored

emblée: d'emblée *adverb*
d'emblée = right away, straightaway

embouteillage *noun, masculine*
un embouteillage = a traffic jam

embrasser *verb* 1
1 (**!** + *avoir*)
= to kiss
2 s'embrasser (**!** + *être*)
s'embrasser = to kiss (each other)

embrayage *noun, masculine*
l'embrayage = the clutch

émeute *noun, feminine*
une émeute = a riot

émigrer *verb* 1
= to emigrate

émission *noun, feminine*
une émission = a broadcast, a
program(me)

emménager *verb* 13
= to move in

emmener *verb* 16
= to take
= to take away

empêcher *verb* 1
1 (**!** + *avoir*)
• = to prevent
empêcher un enfant de sortir = to prevent
a child from going out, to stop a child
from going out
• (**il**) **n'empêche que** = all the same,
nevertheless
2 s'empêcher (**!** + *être*)
je n'ai pas pu m'empêcher de rire
= I couldn't help laughing

empiffrer: s'empiffrer* *verb* 1
(**!** + *être*)
s'empiffrer = to stuff oneself

emplacement *noun, masculine*
un emplacement (*for a building*) = a site
(*for a tent*) = a pitch
(*for a vehicle*) = a parking space

emploi *noun, masculine*
• (*a post*)
un emploi = a job
• (*the job market*)
l'emploi = employment
• (*of a word, a product*)
l'emploi = the use
un emploi du temps = a timetable

employé/employée *noun,
masculine/feminine*
un employé/une employée = an employee
un employé de banque = a bank clerk
un employé de bureau = an office
worker

employer *verb* 23
• = to employ
• = to use

empoisonné/empoisonnée
adjective
= poisoned

emporter *verb* 1
1 (**!** + *avoir*)
• = to take
emporte un parapluie = take an umbrella
• = to take away
'**plats à emporter**' = 'take away food',
'food to go'
• = to sweep away
le pont a été emporté = the bridge has
been swept away
• **l'emporter** = to win
l'emporter sur = to get the better of, to
beat
2 s'emporter (**!** + *être*)
s'emporter = to lose one's temper

empreinte *noun, feminine*
une empreinte (*left by a foot*) = a footprint
les empreintes digitales = fingerprints

emprunter *verb* 1
= to borrow
emprunter de l'argent à la banque = to
borrow money from the bank

en

| ! You will find translations for phrases with en such as en train de, s'en aller etc at the entries train, aller, etc.

1 *preposition*
* = in
  vivre en France = to live in France
  en mai = in May
  faire le trajet en deux heures = to do the journey in two hours
* = to
  = into
  aller en Espagne = to go to Spain
  aller en ville = to go into town
  monter en voiture = to get into the car
* = by
  voyager en [train | bateau | voiture …] = to travel by [train | boat | car …]
* = made of
  c'est en bois = it's (made of) wood
  une chaîne en or = a gold chain
* (showing that two things are done at the same time) = while
  chanter en travaillant = to sing while working
  j'ai lu le journal en attendant = I read the paper while I was waiting
* (showing the manner in which something is done)
  sortir en courant = to run out
  se réveiller en pleurant = to wake up crying
  j'ai fini le travail en me levant tous les jours à six heures = I finished the work by getting up at six every day
* (showing the circumstances in which something occurs)
  il est tombé en traversant la rue = he fell as he was crossing the street
  tu t'es trompé en mesurant la pièce = you made a mistake when you measured the room

2 *pronoun*
* = of it
  = of them
  il en boit beaucoup = he drinks a lot of it
  il y en a quatre = there are four (of them)
  combien en voulez-vous? (if it's cheese) = how much (of it) would you like?
  (if it's cakes) = how many (of them) would you like?
  je m'en souviens = I remember
* = some/any
  encore un peu de thé? il en reste = a little more tea? there's some left
  des roses? il n'y en a plus = roses? there aren't any left
* (representing a place)
  j'en arrive à l'instant = I've just got back from there

enchanter *verb* [1]
= to delight
enchanté (de faire votre connaissance) = pleased to meet you

enchères *noun, feminine plural*
une vente aux enchères = an auction

encombré/encombrée *adjective*
(describing a street) = congested
(describing a room, a cupboard) = cluttered

encombrement *noun, masculine*
l'encombrement (on the road) = traffic congestion

encore *adverb*
* = still
  tu es encore jeune = you're still young
* = again
  il a encore écrit = he's written again
* = more
  = another
  tu veux encore un peu de thé? = would you like some more tea?
  essaie encore une fois = try again
  encore un gâteau? = another cake?
* pas encore = not yet
  elle n'est pas encore arrivée = she hasn't arrived yet
* encore plus = even more
  c'est encore plus cher = it's even more expensive
  il fait encore plus chaud ici = it's even hotter here

encourager *verb* [13]
= to encourage

encre *noun, feminine*
l'encre = ink

endormi/endormie *adjective*
= asleep

endormir *verb* [30]
1 (! + *avoir*)
= to put to sleep
la télévision m'endort = television puts me to sleep
2 s'endormir (! + *être*)
s'endormir = to fall asleep
= to get to sleep

endroit *noun, masculine*
* (a spot)
  un endroit = a place
  au bon endroit = in the right place
  par endroits = in places
  à quel endroit? = where?
* (a side)
  l'endroit = the right side
  à l'endroit = the right way round, the right way around

énergie *noun, feminine*
l'énergie = energy

énergique *adjective*
= energetic

énervé/énervée *adjective*
= irritable
= on edge

énerver verb 1
1 (! + avoir)
= to irritate
ça m'énerve = it irritates me, it gets on my nerves
2 s'énerver (! + être)
s'énerver = to get irritable, to get annoyed

enfance noun, feminine
l'enfance = childhood

enfant noun, masculine/feminine
un enfant/une enfant = a child

enfer noun, masculine
l'enfer = Hell
un bruit d'enfer = a hell of a noise

enfermer verb 1
1 (! + avoir)
= to lock up
2 s'enfermer (! + être)
s'enfermer = to lock oneself in

enfin adverb
• = finally
• = at last
• **mais enfin, cesse de crier!** = for heaven's sake, stop shouting!

enflammer: **s'enflammer** verb 1
(! + être)
s'enflammer = to go up in flames
= to catch fire

enfler verb 1
= to swell (up)

enfoncer verb 12
1 (! + avoir)
• = to push in
enfoncer un clou = to drive a nail in
enfoncer une épingle = to stick a pin in
enfoncer ses mains dans ses poches = to dig one's hands into one's pockets
• **enfoncer une porte** = to break down a door
2 s'enfoncer (! + être)
• **s'enfoncer** = to sink
s'enfoncer dans la boue = to sink in the mud
s'enfoncer dans un fauteuil = to sink back into an armchair
• **s'enfoncer une épine dans le doigt** = to get a thorn in one's finger

enfreindre verb 55
enfreindre le règlement = to break the rules

enfuir: **s'enfuir** verb 29 (! + être)
s'enfuir = to run away
= to escape

engin noun, masculine
• **un engin** = a device
• **un engin** = a vehicle

engorger verb 13
= to block
= to clog up

enlever verb 16
1 (! + avoir)
• = to remove
• = to kidnap
2 s'enlever (! + être)
s'enlever = to come off

enneigé/enneigée adjective
= covered in snow

ennui noun, masculine
• **un ennui** = a problem
• **l'ennui** = boredom

ennuyer verb 22
1 (! + avoir)
• = to bore
• = to bother
= to annoy
ça t'ennuie qu'il vienne? = do you mind if he comes?
2 s'ennuyer (! + être)
s'ennuyer = to be bored

ennuyeux/ennuyeuse adjective
• = boring
= tedious
• = annoying

énorme adjective
= huge, enormous

énormément adverb
= tremendously, immensely

enquête noun, feminine
• (into a crime)
une enquête = an inquiry, an investigation
• (on opinions, lifestyles)
une enquête = a survey

enquêteur/enquêtrice noun, masculine/feminine
un enquêteur/une enquêtrice = an investigator

enregistrement noun, masculine
• (for sound)
un enregistrement = a recording
• (for air passengers)
l'enregistrement = checking-in

enregistrer verb 1
• (if it's sound, statistics) = to record
• (if it's luggage) = to register
(at an airport) = to check in

enrhumer: **s'enrhumer** verb 1
(! + être)
s'enrhumer = to catch a cold
être enrhumé = to have a cold

enseignant/enseignante noun, masculine/feminine
un enseignant/une enseignante = a teacher

enseigne noun, feminine
une enseigne = a sign

enseignement noun, masculine
* (as a career)
  l'enseignement = teaching
* (a system)
  l'enseignement = education
l'enseignement par correspondance
= correspondence courses

ensemble
1 adverb
= together
2 noun, masculine
* (clothes)
  un ensemble = an outfit
  = a lady's suit
* (the entirety)
  l'ensemble = the whole
  = all
  une vue d'ensemble = an overall view
* (a collection)
  un ensemble = a set
  = a group
  un grand ensemble = a high-density
  housing complex, a high-rise housing
  complex
3 dans l'ensemble = on the whole

ensoleillé/ensoleillée adjective
= sunny

ensuite adverb
= then
= later
= next

entendre verb [6]
1 (! + avoir)
= to hear
j'ai entendu dire qu'il était de retour = I've
heard that he's back
as-tu entendu parler de ce film? = have
you heard about this film?
2 s'entendre (! + être)
s'entendre = to get on, to get along
elles s'entendent bien = they get on well,
they get along well

entendu/entendue
1 ▶ entendre [6]
2 adjective
= agreed
entendu! = OK then!
3 bien entendu = of course

enterrement noun, masculine
un enterrement = a funeral

enterrer verb [1]
= to bury

enthousiasmer verb [1]
1 (! + avoir)
= to fill with enthusiasm
2 s'enthousiasmer (! + être)
s'enthousiasmer = to get enthusiastic

enthousiaste adjective
= enthusiastic

entier/entière adjective
= whole, entire

entourer verb [1]
* = to surround
  des collines entourent la ville = the town
  is surrounded by hills
  un jardin entouré d'une haie = a garden
  surrounded by a hedge
* = to circle
  entourer une date en rouge = to circle a
  date in red
* **entourer son doigt d'un mouchoir** = to put
  a handkerchief round one's finger

entracte noun, masculine
un entracte = an interval, an intermission

entraînement noun, masculine
l'entraînement (for an athlete) = training
(for a musician) = practice

entraîner verb [1]
1 (! + avoir)
* = to lead to
  entraîner des problèmes = to lead to
  problems, to cause problems
* = to drag along
  entraîner un ami à la plage = to drag a
  friend along to the beach
* = to coach, to train
  entraîner une équipe = to coach a team
2 s'entraîner (! + être)
s'entraîner = to train
= to practise, to practice

entraîneur noun, masculine
un entraîneur = a coach

entre preposition
= between
l'un d'entre eux = one of them

entrée noun, feminine
* (way in)
  l'entrée = the entrance
  = the (entrance) hall
* (access)
  l'entrée = entry
  = admission
  'entrée interdite' = 'no entry', 'do not
  enter'
  'entrée gratuite' = 'free admission'
* (on a menu)
  une entrée = a starter, an appetizer

entreprise noun, feminine
une entreprise = a firm
= a company

entrer verb [1] (! + être)
= to enter, to go in
= to enter, to come in
entrez! = come in!
entrer dans la cuisine = to go into the
kitchen
= to come into the kitchen

entretien noun, masculine
* **un entretien** (a conversation) = a
  discussion
  (for a job) = an interview

- l'entretien (*of a house, a garden*) = the upkeep, the maintenance
(*of clothes, furniture*) = the care

enveloppe *noun, feminine*
une enveloppe = an envelope

envelopper *verb* 1
= to wrap

envers
1 *preposition*
= toward, towards, to
2 *noun, masculine* (**!** *never changes*)
l'envers = the back
= the wrong side
= the reverse
3 à l'envers = the wrong way

envie *noun, feminine*
une envie = a desire
avoir envie de pleurer = to want to cry, to feel like crying

environ *adverb*
= about

environs *noun, masculine plural*
les environs = the surrounding area

envoler: s'envoler *verb* 1 (**!** + *être*)
s'envoler (*if it's a bird*) = to fly away
(*if it's a plane*) = to take off

envoyer *verb* 24
- = to send
- = to throw

épais/épaisse *adjective*
= thick

épaule *noun, feminine*
une épaule = a shoulder

épeler *verb* 19
= to spell

épice *noun, feminine*
une épice = a spice

épicerie *noun, feminine*
une épicerie = a grocer's, a grocery store

épicier/épicière *noun, masculine/feminine*
un épicier/une épicière = a grocer

épinards *noun, masculine plural*
des épinards = spinach

épine *noun, feminine*
une épine = a thorn

épingle *noun, feminine*
une épingle = a pin
une épingle à nourrice, une épingle de sûreté = a safety pin

épisode *noun, masculine*
un épisode = an episode
un roman à épisodes = a serialized novel

éplucher *verb* 1
= to peel

épluchure *noun, feminine*
des épluchures = peelings

éponge *noun, feminine*
- (*a type of material*)
l'éponge = (terry-)towelling, terrycloth
- (*a sea creature*)
une éponge = a sponge

époque *noun, feminine*
une époque = a period, an era
à notre époque = nowadays, in our times
à l'époque = at the time

épouse *noun, feminine*
une épouse = a wife

épouser *verb* 1
= to marry

épouvantable *adjective*
= dreadful

épouvante *noun, feminine*
l'épouvante = terror
= horror
un film d'épouvante = a horror film, a horror movie

époux (**!** *never changes*)
1 *noun, masculine singular*
un époux = a husband
2 *noun, masculine plural*
les époux = the (married) couple
les jeunes époux = the newly weds

épreuve *noun, feminine*
une épreuve (*at school*) = an examination
(*in sport*) = an event

éprouver *verb* 1
= to feel

EPS *noun, feminine* (**!** *never changes*)
l'EPS = PE

épuisé/épuisée *adjective*
= exhausted

équateur *noun, masculine*
l'équateur = the equator

équilibre *noun, masculine*
l'équilibre = balance
perdre l'équilibre = to lose one's balance
en équilibre = balanced

équilibrer *verb* 1
= to balance

équipage *noun, masculine*
un équipage = a crew

équipe *noun, feminine*
- (*of players, workers*)
une équipe = a team
- (*in a factory*)
l'équipe de nuit = the night shift

équipement *noun, masculine*
l'équipement = the equipment

équitation *noun, feminine*
l'équitation = (horse-)riding

E

erreur *noun, feminine*
une erreur = a mistake

es ▶ être 7

escalade *noun, feminine*
l'escalade = rock climbing

escalader *verb* 1
= to climb

escalier *noun, masculine*
• un escalier = a staircase
= (a flight of) stairs
• les escaliers = the stairs
un escalier roulant = an escalator

escargot *noun, masculine*
un escargot = a snail

esclave *noun, masculine|feminine*
un esclave/une esclave = a slave

escrime *noun, feminine*
l'escrime = fencing

escroc *noun, masculine*
un escroc = a crook

espace *noun, masculine*
• l'espace = space
• un espace = a space, a gap
un espace vert = an open space, a green
area, a park

Espagne *noun, feminine*
l'Espagne = Spain

espagnol/espagnole
1 *adjective*
= Spanish
2 espagnol *noun, masculine*
l'espagnol = Spanish

espèce *noun, feminine*
• *(a sort)*
une espèce de roue = a kind of wheel
• *(a group of animals or plants)*
une espèce = a species

espérer *verb* 14
= to hope (for)

espionnage *noun, masculine*
l'espionnage = espionage, spying

esquimau/esquimaude
(plural) **esquimaux/esquimaudes**
1 *adjective*
= Eskimo
2 esquimau *noun, masculine*
un esquimau = a choc-ice, an ice cream
bar

essayer *verb* 21
• = to try
essayer d'ouvrir la porte = to try to open
the door
• = to try on
essayer un chapeau = to try on a hat

essence *noun, feminine*
l'essence = petrol, gas(oline)

l'essence sans plomb = unleaded petrol,
unleaded gas

essorage *noun, masculine*
l'essorage = spinning

essuie-glace *noun, masculine*
(plural) **essuie-glaces**
un essuie-glace = a windscreen wiper, a
windshield wiper

essuyer *verb* 22
1 (! + *avoir*)
• = to dry
• = to wipe (up)
2 s'essuyer (! + *être*)
s'essuyer = to wipe oneself
= to dry oneself
s'essuyer les mains = to wipe one's hands

est¹ ▶ être 7

est²
1 *noun, masculine*
l'est = the east
2 *adjective* (! *never changes*)
= east
= eastern

est-ce que ▶ être 7

estivant/estivante *noun,*
masculine|feminine
un estivant/une estivante = a summer
visitor

estomac *noun, masculine*
l'estomac = the stomach

et *conjunction*
= and
et avec ceci? = anything else?

étage *noun, masculine*
un étage = a floor, a story
habiter au premier étage (*in Britain*) = to
live on the first floor
(*in the US*) = to live on the second floor
à l'étage = upstairs

étagère *noun, feminine*
une étagère (*a flat piece of wood, glass*)
= a shelf
(*a piece of furniture*) = a bookshelf

étais ▶ être 7

étaler *verb* 1
= to spread (out)

étang *noun, masculine*
un étang = a pond

étant ▶ être 7

étape *noun, feminine*
• *(a place)*
une étape = a stop
faire étape à Nice = to stop in Nice
• *(part of a journey)*
une étape = a stage
(*in a race*) = a leg

état *noun, masculine*
 un état = a state

États-Unis *noun, masculine plural*
 les États-Unis = the United States

été
1 ▶ être 7
2 *noun, masculine*
 l'été = summer

éteindre *verb* 55
1 (**!** + *avoir*)
• = to put out
• = to switch off, to turn off
2 s'éteindre (**!** + *être*)
• s'éteindre = to go out
• s'éteindre = to go off

éteint/éteinte ▶ éteindre 55

étendre *verb* 6
1 (**!** + *avoir*)
• (*to put down flat*)
 étendre une nappe = to spread out a tablecloth
• (*to put out to dry*)
 étendre le linge = to hang out the washing, to hang out the laundry
2 s'étendre (**!** + *être*)
• (*if it's a person*)
 s'étendre = to lie down
• (*if it's land*)
 s'étendre = to stretch
• (*if it's a conflict*)
 s'étendre = to spread

étendu/étendue¹
1 ▶ étendre 6
2 *adjective*
 = extensive

étendue² *noun, feminine*
• (*of land, water*)
 une étendue = an expanse
 = a stretch
• (*of a disaster*)
 l'étendue = the scale, the size

éternuer *verb* 1
 = to sneeze

êtes ▶ être 7

étiquette *noun, feminine*
 une étiquette = a label
 = a tag

étirer, s'étirer *verb* 1 (**!** + *être*)
 s'étirer = to stretch

étoile *noun, feminine*
 une étoile = a star

étonnant/étonnante *adjective*
 = surprising
 = amazing

étonner *verb* 1
1 (**!** + *avoir*)
 = to surprise
2 s'étonner (**!** + *être*)
 s'étonner = to be surprised

étouffant/étouffante *adjective*
 = stifling

étouffer *verb* 1
1 (**!** + *avoir*)
• = to smother
• = to suffocate
 on étouffe ici! = it's stifling in here!
2 s'étouffer (**!** + *être*)
 s'étouffer = to choke

étourdi/étourdie *adjective*
 = scatterbrained

étrange *adjective*
 = strange

étranger/étrangère
1 *adjective*
 = foreign
2 *noun, masculine/feminine*
 un étranger/une étrangère (*from another country*) = a foreigner
 (*an unknown person*) = a stranger
3 à l'étranger = abroad

être *verb* 7 (**!** + *avoir*)
▶ 64 | *See the boxed note.*

étroit/étroite *adjective*
 = narrow

étude
1 *noun, feminine*
• (*an activity*)
 l'étude = study
• (*a room in a school*)
 l'étude = the study room, the study hall
• (*on the school timetable*)
 'étude' = 'private study'. 'study hall'
2 études *noun, feminine plural*
 les études = studies, higher education
 faire des études = to study, to be a student

étudiant/étudiante *noun, masculine/feminine*
 un étudiant/une étudiante = a student

étudier *verb* 2
• = to study
• = to examine

étui *noun, masculine*
 un étui = a case
 un étui à lunettes = a glasses case

eu/eue ▶ avoir 8

eurochèque *noun, masculine*
 un eurochèque = a Eurocheque

Europe *noun, feminine*
 l'Europe = Europe

européen/européenne *adjective*
 = European

eux *pronoun*
• = them
 à cause d'eux = because of them

E

être verb 7

present	imperfect	future	past participle
je suis	j'étais	je serai	été
tu es	tu étais	tu seras	
il / elle est	il / elle était	il / elle sera	
nous sommes	nous étions	nous serons	
vous êtes	vous étiez	vous serez	
ils / elles sont	ils / elles étaient	ils / elles seront	

1 être functions as an ordinary verb:

● (*showing a quality or state*) = to be

je **suis** fatigué	= *I'm tired*
le ciel **est** bleu	= *the sky is blue*
elle **est** fatiguée	= *she is tired*
sois sage!	= *be good!*
ils **ont été** malades	= *they've been ill*

● (*showing ownership*)

la maison **est** à Pierre	= *the house belongs to Pierre, the house is Pierre's*
à qui **sont** ces gants?	= *who do these gloves belong to, whose gloves are they?*
ils **sont** à moi	= *they belong to me, they're mine*

2 être is used as an auxiliary verb to conjugate some verbs, notably reflexive verbs and a few others, all of which are labelled (**!** + *être*):

je **suis** né en Italie	= *I was born in Italy*
elle n'**est** pas encore rentrée	= *she hasn't come home yet*
ils **sont** partis	= *they've left*
tu t'**es** lavé les mains?	= *did you wash your hands?*

3 être is used to form questions in the phrase **est-ce que**:

est-ce que tu aimes le jazz?	= *do you like jazz?*
est-ce qu'il fait froid?	= *is it cold?*
est-ce que tu viendras?	= *will you come?*
est-ce qu'ils ont fini?	= *have they finished?*
est-ce que tu as de l'argent?	= *have you got any money?*

- (*indicating possession, turn*)
  le chien est à eux = the dog is theirs
  c'est à eux de jouer = it's their turn to play
- (*when used for emphasis*) = they
  je suis resté, mais eux sont partis = I stayed but they left

eux-mêmes *pronoun*
  = themselves

évaluer *verb* 1
- = to assess
- = to estimate
- = to value

évanouir: s'évanouir *verb* 3 (**!** + *être*)
  s'évanouir = to faint

évasion *noun, feminine*
  une évasion = an escape

événement *noun, masculine*
  un événement = an event

éventail *noun, masculine*
  un éventail = a fan

éventuellement *adverb*
- = possibly
- = if necessary

évidemment *adverb*
  = obviously
  = of course

évident/évidente *adjective*
  = obvious

évier *noun, masculine*
  un évier = a (kitchen) sink

éviter *verb* 1
  = to avoid

exact/exacte *adjective*
- = correct
- = exact

✘ in informal situations

exactement *adverb*
= exactly

exagérer *verb* 14
= to exaggerate

examen *noun, masculine*
• *(for pupils, students)*
un **examen** = an examination, an exam, a test
passer un **examen** = to take an exam
réussir à un **examen** = to pass an exam
• *(by a doctor)*
un **examen** = an examination

examiner *verb* 1
= to examine

excursion *noun, feminine*
une **excursion** = an excursion, a trip
faire une **excursion** = to go on an excursion

excuse *noun, feminine*
• *(a reason)*
une **excuse** = an excuse
• *(when saying that one is sorry)*
des **excuses** = an apology
présenter des **excuses** = to apologize

excuser *verb* 1
1 (**!** + *avoir*)
= to excuse
excusez-moi *(when apologizing)* = I'm sorry
(when interrupting) = excuse me
2 s'excuser (**!** + *être*)
s'**excuser** = to apologize

exemple *noun, masculine*
un **exemple** = an example
par **exemple** = for example, for instance

exercer: s'exercer *verb* 12 (**!** + *être*)
s'**exercer** = to practise, to practice
s'**exercer à sauter à la corde** = to practise skipping

exercice *noun, masculine*
un **exercice** = an exercise

exiger *verb* 13
= to demand
= to require

expédier *verb* 2
= to send

expéditeur/expéditrice *noun, masculine/feminine*
un **expéditeur/une expéditrice** = a sender

expérience *noun, feminine*
• *(skill, knowledge)*
l'**expérience** = experience
• *(a test)*
une **expérience** = an experiment

expliquer *verb* 1
= to explain

explorateur/exploratrice *noun, masculine/feminine*
un **explorateur/une exploratrice** = an explorer

exploser *verb* 1
= to explode

exposer *verb* 1
• *(in a shop window)* = to display
• *(in a gallery)* = to exhibit
• *(to the sun, to a danger)* = to expose

exposition *noun, feminine*
une **exposition** = an exhibition

exprès *adverb*
= on purpose

express *noun, masculine* (**!** *never changes*)
un **express** = an express, a fast train

exprimer *verb* 1
= to express

extérieur/extérieure
1 *adjective*
= outside
2 extérieur *noun, masculine*
l'**extérieur** = the outside
à l'**extérieur de la boîte** = outside the box

externe
1 *adjective*
= external
2 *noun, masculine/feminine*
un **externe/une externe** = a day pupil, a day student

extra *adjective*
= first-class, great

extrait *noun, masculine*
un **extrait** = an extract

F

Ff

fabrication *noun, feminine*
la **fabrication** = manufacture

fabriquer *verb* 1
• = to make, to manufacture
• **qu'est-ce que tu fabriques*?** = what are you up to?

façade *noun, feminine*
la **façade** = the front

face
1 *noun, feminine*
la **face** *(on a box)* = the side
(of a coin) = the heads side
pile ou face = heads or tails

2 de face = from the front
3 en face (de) = opposite

fâcher: se fâcher verb 1
se fâcher = to get angry

facile adjective
= easy

facilement adverb
= easily

façon noun, feminine
une façon = a way
la façon dont il parle = the way he talks
de toute façon = anyway

façonner verb 1
= to shape, to mould

facteur/factrice noun,
masculine/feminine
un facteur/une factrice = a postman/a
postwoman, a mail carrier

facture noun, feminine
une facture = a bill, an invoice

faible adjective
= weak

faillir verb 28
j'ai failli y aller = I (very) nearly went, I
almost went

faim noun, feminine
la faim = hunger
avoir faim = to be hungry

fainéant/fainéante adjective
= lazy

faire verb 10
! You will find translations for phrases with
faire such as faire attention, faire le clown,
faire pousser etc under the words
attention, clown, pousser etc.

1 (! + avoir)
* = to make
  faire [un gâteau | un effort | une faute ...] = to
  make [a cake | an effort | a mistake ...]
* = to do
  faire [la vaisselle | ses devoirs | un travail ...]
  = to do [the dishes | one's homework | a job ...]
  que fait-il? (for a living) = what does he do?
  (at this very moment) = what's he doing?
* = to go
  faire [de l'escalade | du vélo | des courses ...]
  = to go [climbing | cycling | shopping ...]
* (when talking about the weather)
  il fait [chaud | gris | du vent ...] = it's [hot |
  overcast | windy ...]
  il faisait 30° à l'ombre = it was 30° in the
  shade
  il fera beau demain = the weather will be
  fine tomorrow

* (when talking about a particular length of
  time)
  ça fait deux heures que j'attends = I've
  been waiting for two hours
  ça fait longtemps qu'il est parti = he left a
  long time ago
* (when talking about measurements)
  faire 1,75 m = to be 1.75 m tall
  faire du 42 = to take a size 42
* (to cause something to happen)
  il m'a fait [tomber | manquer le train |
  travailler ...] = he made me [fall | miss the
  train | work ...]
* (to get something done)
  faire nettoyer une veste = to have a jacket
  cleaned
* (some other uses)
  ça ne fait rien = it doesn't matter
  qu'est-ce que ça peut bien te faire?
  = what's it to you?
  fais comme tu veux = do as you like
  faites comme chez vous = make yourself
  at home
2 se faire (! + être)
* (to do something for oneself)
  se faire = to make
  elle s'est fait du café = she made herself
  some coffee
  se faire des amis = to make friends
  se faire comprendre = to make oneself
  understood
* (to get someone to do something for you)
  se faire couper les cheveux = to have one's
  hair cut
  elle s'est fait faire une robe = she's had a
  dress made
* (when something is done to you)
  se faire [attraper | menacer | écraser ...] = to be
  [caught | threatened | run over ...]
* (other uses)
  ça ne se fait pas = it isn't the done thing,
  it isn't the thing to do
3 s'en faire (! + être)
s'en faire = to worry
ne t'en fais pas = don't worry

faire-part noun, masculine (! never
changes)
un faire-part = an announcement card

fais ▶ faire 10

faisable adjective
= feasible
c'est faisable = it can be done

faisais ▶ faire 10

faisan noun, masculine
un faisan = a pheasant

faisons ▶ faire 10

fait/faite
1 ▶ faire 10
2 adjective
* = done
  un travail bien fait = a job well done
  c'est bien fait pour lui! = it serves him
  right!

• **tout fait** = ready-made
  des rideaux tout faits = ready-made
  curtains, store-bought drapes
• **c'est fait pour nettoyer les vitres** = it's
  meant for cleaning windows
3 fait *noun, masculine*
  un fait = a fact
4 au fait = by the way
5 en fait = in fact
un fait divers = a (short) news item

faites ▶ faire ⑩

falaise *noun, feminine*
  une falaise = a cliff

falloir *verb* ㊿
  il faut une clé pour ouvrir la porte = you
  need a key to open the door
  il me fallait de l'argent = I needed some
  money
  allons, il faut partir = come on, we've got to
  go
  il ne faut jamais arriver en retard = one
  must never be late
  achète ce qu'il faut pour le jardin = buy
  whatever is necessary for the garden
  il le fallait = it was necessary
  il faudra que tu ailles au garage = you will
  have to go to the garage
  il va falloir que vous le fassiez = you will
  have to do it

fallu ▶ falloir ㊿

familial/familiale *adjective*
(*plural*) **familiaux/familiales**
  = family

familier/familière *adjective*
  = familiar

famille *noun, feminine*
  une famille = a family
  en famille = with the family
  = as a family

fana✻ *noun, masculine|feminine*
  un fana✻/une fana✻ = a fanatic

fantastique *adjective*
  = fantastic

fantôme *noun, masculine*
  un fantôme = a ghost

farce *noun, feminine*
• (*a trick*)
  une farce = a practical joke
• (*in cooking*)
  la farce = the stuffing

farci/farcie *adjective*
  = stuffed

fard *noun, masculine*
  le fard = make-up

farfelu/farfelue✻ *adjective*
• = scatterbrained
• = eccentric

farine *noun, feminine*
  la farine = flour

fasse ▶ faire ⑩

fatigant/fatigante *adjective*
  = tiring

fatigue *noun, feminine*
  la fatigue = tiredness

fatigué/fatiguée
  = tired

fauché/fauchée✻ *adjective*
  = broke

F

faudra ▶ falloir ㊿

faune *noun, feminine*
  la faune = wildlife

fausse ▶ faux

faut ▶ falloir ㊿

faute *noun, feminine*
• (*an error*)
  une faute = a mistake
• (*responsibility*)
  c'est (de) ta faute = it's your fault

fauteuil *noun, masculine*
  un fauteuil = an armchair
un fauteuil roulant = a wheelchair

faux/fausse
1 *adjective*
• (*not right*) = wrong
• (*not genuine*) = false
  = fake
2 faux *adverb*
  chanter faux = to sing out of tune

favori/favorite *adjective*
  = favo(u)rite

féculent *noun, masculine*
  un féculent = a starchy food

fêlé/fêlée *adjective*
  = cracked

félicitations *noun, feminine plural*
  des félicitations = congratulations

femme *noun, feminine*
  une femme = a woman
  = a wife
une femme d'affaires = a businesswoman
une femme de ménage = a cleaning lady

fenêtre *noun, feminine*
  une fenêtre = a window

fente *noun, feminine*
  une fente (*for a coin*) = a slot
  (*in a wall*) = a crack
  (*in a mask*) = a slit

fer *noun, masculine*
  le fer = iron
  un fer à repasser = an iron

ferai ▶ **faire** [50]

férié/fériée *adjective*
un jour férié = a public holiday, a holiday

ferme *noun, feminine*
une ferme = a farm

fermer *verb* [1]
= to close, to shut

fermeture *noun, feminine*
• (*of a shop*)
la fermeture = closing (down)
'fermeture annuelle' = 'annual closing'
• (*a device*)
une fermeture = a fastener
une fermeture éclair = a zip(per)

fermier/fermière *noun, masculine/feminine*
un fermier/une fermière = a farmer

féroce *adjective*
= fierce

ferroviaire *adjective*
= rail, railroad

fesse *noun, feminine*
une fesse = a buttock

fête *noun, feminine*
• (*a special day in a country*)
une fête = a public holiday, a holiday
• (*a special day for a person*)
ma fête = my (saint's) name-day
bonne fête! = happy saint's day!
• (*an organized event*)
une fête = a festival
• (*at home*) = a celebration
= a party
faire une fête = to have a party
une fête foraine = a funfair, a carnival
la fête des Mères = Mother's day
(*celebrated in France on the last Sunday in May*)
la fête du travail = May Day

fêter *verb* [1]
= to celebrate

feu *noun, masculine*
(*plural*) **feux**
• (*flames*)
un feu = a fire
mettre le feu à une maison = to set fire to a house
au feu! = fire!
en feu = on fire
• (*the flame from a match or a lighter*)
du feu = a light
demander du feu = to ask for a light
• (*on a car, in the street*)
un feu = a light
les feux = the traffic lights
un feu d'artifice = a fireworks display
les feux de détresse = hazard lights
les feux de signalisation, les feux tricolores = the traffic lights

feuille *noun, feminine*
• (*on a tree*)
une feuille = a leaf
• (*paper*)
une feuille = a sheet

feuilleter *verb* [20]
= to flick through

feuilleton *noun, masculine*
un feuilleton = a serial
= a soap opera

feutre *noun, masculine*
un feutre = a felt-tip pen

fève *noun, feminine*
• **une fève** = a broad bean, a fava bean
• **une fève** = a lucky charm (*hidden in the galette des rois*)

février *noun, masculine*
février = February

fiançailles *noun, feminine plural*
des fiançailles = an engagement

fiancer: **se fiancer** *verb* [12] (**!** + *être*)
se fiancer = to get engaged

ficelle *noun, feminine*
• (*around a parcel*)
de la ficelle = string
• (*bread*)
une ficelle = a thin baguette

fiche *noun, feminine*
une fiche = a form
= card

ficher✖ *verb* [1]
1 (**!** + *avoir*)
• = to do
il n'a rien fiché✖ *or* **fichu✖ de la journée** = he's done nothing all day
• **ficher✖ à la poubelle** = to bin, to throw out
• **fiche-moi la paix✖!** = leave me alone!
2 se ficher✖ (**!** + *être*)
• **se ficher de quelqu'un✖**
(*to mock*) = to make fun of someone
(*to lack consideration*) = to mess someone around
• **je m'en fiche✖** = I couldn't care less
je me fiche✖ de ce qu'on dit = I couldn't care less what people say

fichu/fichue✖
1 ▶ **ficher** [1]
2 *adjective*
• = rotten, nasty
avoir un fichu✖ caractère = to have a nasty temper
• = done for
ma voiture est fichue✖ = my car's had it
s'il pleut c'est fichu✖ = if it rains that's the end of that
• **être fichu✖ de faire** = to be capable of doing

✖ in informal situations

fidèle *adjective*
= faithful

fier/fière *adjective*
= proud

fièvre *noun, feminine*
une fièvre = a fever
avoir de la fièvre = to have a temperature

fiévreux/fiévreuse *adjective*
= feverish

figue *noun, feminine*
une figue = a fig

figure *noun, feminine*
• la figure = the face
• une figure = a figure
= a diagram

figurer *verb* [1]
1 (! + *avoir*)
= to appear, to feature
figurer sur une liste = to appear on a list
2 se figurer (! + *être*)
se figurer = to think, to imagine

fil *noun, masculine*
• (*for sewing*)
le fil = thread
• (*connecting a telephone*)
un fil = a wire
un coup de fil = a phone call
passe-moi un coup de fil = give me a call
le fil de fer = wire

file *noun, feminine*
• (*a row of people or cars*)
une file = a line
(*at a cinema, a bus stop, a store*)
une file d'attente = a queue, a line
• (*part of a road*)
une file = a lane

filer* *verb* [1]
• (*if it's time*) = to fly by
• (*to leave*)✗ = to go off
• (*to escape*)✗ = to get away

filet *noun, masculine*
un filet = a net
un filet à provisions = a string bag

fille *noun, feminine*
une fille = a girl
= a daughter

fillette *noun, feminine*
une fillette = a little girl

filleul/filleule *noun, masculine/feminine*
un filleul/une filleule = a godson/a
goddaughter

film *noun, masculine*
un film = a film, a movie
un film d'animation = a cartoon (film)
un film policier = a detective film

fils *noun, masculine* (! *never changes*)
un fils = a son

fin¹ *noun, feminine*
la fin = the end
en fin de matinée = late in the morning
en fin de compte = in the end, finally

fin²/fine *adjective*
= thin
= slender
= fine

finalement *adverb*
= finally, in the end

finir *verb* [3]
• = to finish
j'ai fini d'écrire = I've finished writing
• = to end
il a fini par avoir un accident = he ended
up having an accident
l'histoire finit bien = the story has a happy
ending

fioul *noun, masculine*
le fioul = fuel oil

firme *noun, feminine*
une firme = a firm

fixe *adjective*
un prix fixe = a fixed price
une résidence fixe = a permanent address
manger à heure fixe = to eat at a set time

flamme *noun, feminine*
une flamme = a flame

flan *noun, masculine*
un flan ≈ custard
= a custard tart, a custard flan

flâner *verb* [1]
= to stroll

flaque *noun, feminine*
une flaque = a puddle

flèche *noun, feminine*
une flèche = an arrow

fléchette *noun, feminine*
une fléchette = a dart

fleur *noun, feminine*
une fleur = a flower

fleuriste *noun, masculine/feminine*
un fleuriste/une fleuriste = a florist

fleuve *noun, masculine*
un fleuve = a (large) river

flic* *noun, masculine*
un flic✗ = a cop, a policeman

flipper *noun, masculine*
le flipper (*the machine*) = the pinball
machine
(*the device in the machine*) = the flipper
(*the game*) = pinball

flocon *noun, masculine*
un flocon de neige = a snowflake

flotter *verb* [1]
= to float

F

flotteur noun, masculine
un flotteur = a float

fluo adjective (**!** never changes)
= fluorescent

fluorescent/fluorescente adjective
= fluorescent

flûte noun, feminine
• (an instrument)
une flûte = a flute
une flûte à bec = a recorder
• (bread)
une flûte = a French stick, French bread

foie noun, masculine
le foie = (the) liver

foire noun, feminine
une foire = a fair
= a trade fair

fois
1 noun, feminine (**!** never changes)
encore une fois = one more time
une fois = once
deux fois = twice
trois fois = three times
une fois qu'il aura fini = once he's finished
une fois pour toutes = once and for all
2 à la fois = at the same time
= at once
3 des fois* = sometimes

folklorique adjective
= folk

folle ▶ fou

foncé/foncée adjective
= dark

foncer verb [12]
foncer sur quelqu'un = to charge at
someone

fonctionnaire noun, masculine/feminine
un fonctionnaire/une fonctionnaire = a
civil servant

fonctionner verb [1]
= to work

fond
1 noun, masculine
• (the deepest part)
le fond = the bottom
au fond du verre = at the bottom of the
glass
• (the furthest part)
le fond (of a cupboard, a shop) = the back
(of a room, a yard) = the far end
(on a picture) = the background
2 à fond
respirer à fond = to breathe deeply
appuyer à fond = to press hard

3 au fond, dans le fond
au fond, ce n'est pas bête = it's a rather
good idea
dans le fond, il a raison = he's right, really
un fond de teint = a foundation, a make-
up base

fonder verb [1]
= to found

fondre verb [6]
= to melt
faire fondre = to melt

fondu/fondue adjective
= melted

font ▶ faire [10]

fontaine noun, feminine
une fontaine = a fountain

foot* noun, masculine
le foot* = football, soccer

football noun, masculine
le football = football, soccer

footing noun, masculine
le footing = jogging

force
1 noun, feminine
• (energy)
la force = strength
avoir de la force = to be strong
• (violence)
la force = force
de force = by force
2 à force de
réussir à force de travailler = to succeed by
dint of hard work
j'ai mal au bras à force d'écrire = I've done
so much writing that my arm hurts

forcer verb [12]
1 (**!** + avoir)
= to force
forcer un enfant à manger = to force a
child to eat
2 se forcer (**!** + être)
se forcer = to force oneself

forêt noun, feminine
une forêt = a forest

forfaitaire adjective
= inclusive

forgeron noun, masculine
un forgeron = a blacksmith

formation noun, feminine
• (the learning of skills)
la formation = training
• (the process of creating or developing)
la formation = the formation

*** in informal situations　　　*̒ may be considered offensive**

forme *noun, feminine*
• (*an outline*)
  une forme = a shape
  = a form
  en forme de T = T-shaped
• (*a person's energy*)
  avoir la forme = to be in good form
  être en (pleine) forme = to be in (very)
    good form

former *verb* $\boxed{1}$
• = to form
• = to train

formidable *adjective*
• = tremendous
• = great

formulaire *noun, masculine*
  un formulaire = a form

fort/forte
1 *adjective*
• (*not weak*) = strong
• (*not slim*) = stout
  = broad
• (*not soft*) = loud
• (*not slight*)
  de fortes pluies = heavy rain
  une forte chaleur = intense heat
  une forte pente = a steep slope
• (*gifted*)
  fort en = good at
  être fort en chimie = to be good at
    chemistry
2 fort *adverb*
• = hard
  taper fort = to hit hard
• = loudly
  parler fort = to speak loudly

fortement *adverb*
  = strongly
  = deeply

fortune *noun, feminine*
  une fortune = a fortune
  faire fortune = to make one's fortune

fossé *noun, masculine*
  un fossé = a ditch

fou/folle
1 *adjective*
  = mad, crazy
  être fou✗/folle✗ de quelqu'un = to be mad
    about someone
2 *noun, masculine/feminine*
  un fou/une folle = a madman/a
    madwoman

foudre *noun, feminine*
• **la foudre** = lightning
• **le coup de foudre** = love at first sight

fouiller *verb* $\boxed{1}$
• = to search
• **fouiller dans un tiroir** = to rummage
  around in a drawer

foulard *noun, masculine*
  un foulard = a scarf

foule *noun, feminine*
  la foule = the crowd

fouler: se fouler *verb* $\boxed{1}$ (**!** + *être*)
  se fouler la cheville = to sprain one's ankle

four *noun, masculine*
  un four = an oven
  faire cuire au four = to roast
  = to bake
  un four à micro-ondes = a microwave
  (oven)

fourche *noun, feminine*
  une fourche = a garden fork
  = a pitchfork

fourchette *noun, feminine*
  une fourchette = a fork

fourgonnette *noun, feminine*
  une fourgonnette = a (small) van

fourmi *noun, feminine*
  une fourmi = an ant

fournir *verb* $\boxed{3}$
  = to provide, to supply

fourrer✗ *verb* $\boxed{1}$
1 (**!** + *avoir*)
  = to shove, to put
  fourrer✗ des lettres dans un sac = to shove
    letters into a bag
2 se fourrer✗ (**!** + *être*)
  se fourrer = to put oneself

fourrure *noun, feminine*
  la fourrure = fur

foutre: se foutre de✗ *verb* $\boxed{6}$ (**!** + *être*)
  se foutre de✗ = not to give a damn about
  je m'en fous✗ = I couldn't care less, I don't
    give a damn

foyer *noun, masculine*
• (*for a large group*)
  un foyer = a hostel
• (*where a family lives*)
  un foyer = a home
• (*in a fireplace*)
  le foyer = the hearth

fracture *noun, feminine*
  une fracture = a fracture

fragile *adjective*
  = fragile
  = delicate

fraîche ▶ frais 1

frais/fraîche
1 *adjective*
• = cool
  = chilled
  des boissons fraîches = cool drinks, cold
    drinks
  '**servir frais**' = 'serve chilled'

F

• = fresh
des légumes frais = fresh vegetables
des nouvelles fraîches = fresh news
2 frais adverb
• = cool
= chilly
il fait frais ce matin = it's cool this morning
= it's chilly this morning
3 frais noun, masculine (**!** never changes)
'**garder au frais**' = 'keep in a cool place'
prendre le frais = to take a breath of fresh air
4 frais noun, masculine plural
des frais = expenses

fraise noun, feminine
une fraise = a strawberry

framboise noun, feminine
une framboise = a raspberry

franc/franche
1 adjective
= frank
2 franc noun, masculine
un franc = one franc

français/française
1 adjective
= French
2 français noun, masculine
le français = French

Français/Française noun,
masculine/feminine
un Français/une Française = a Frenchman/a Frenchwoman
les Français = the French

France noun, feminine
la France = France

franchement adverb
= frankly

franchir verb ③
• = to cross
franchir une frontière = to cross a border
• = to get over
franchir une clôture = to get over a fence
• = to cover
franchir dix kilomètres = to cover ten kilometres

francophone adjective
= French-speaking

frange noun, feminine
une frange = a fringe, bangs

frapper verb ①
• = to hit
• = to knock

fraternité noun, feminine
la fraternité = fraternity

frein noun, masculine
un frein = a brake
le frein à main = the handbrake
donner un coup de frein = to brake

freiner verb ①
= to brake

fréquenter verb ①
• = to mix with, to associate with
fréquenter des voyous = to mix with hooligans
• = to go to
= to visit
= to attend

frère noun, masculine
un frère = a brother

frigidaire noun, masculine
un frigidaire = a refrigerator

frigo✱ noun, masculine
un frigo✱ = a fridge

frimeur/frimeuse✱ noun,
masculine/feminine
un frimeur✱/une frimeuse✱ = a show-off

fringues✱ noun, feminine plural
des fringues✱ = clothes

frire verb ㉟
= to fry

frisé/frisée adjective
= curly

frisson noun, masculine
un frisson = a shiver
= a shudder

frit/frite adjective
= fried

frites noun, feminine plural
les frites = chips, French fries

froid/froide
1 adjective
= cold
2 froid adverb
il fait froid = it's cold
3 froid noun, masculine
le froid = the cold
avoir froid = to feel cold, to be cold
prendre froid = to catch (a) cold

fromage noun, masculine
le fromage = cheese
le fromage blanc ≈ fromage frais

front noun, masculine
le front = the forehead

frontière noun, feminine
une frontière = a border, a frontier

frotter verb ①
= to rub

fruit noun, masculine
un fruit = a piece of fruit
des fruits = fruit
des fruits de mer = seafood

fuir verb ㉙
• (if it's a person) = to flee
• (if it's a tap, a hose) = to leak

✱ in informal situations

fuite *noun, feminine*
- (*of a person*)
la fuite = the flight
= the escape
- (*in a pipe, a hose*)
une fuite = a leak

fumée *noun, feminine*
la fumée = smoke

fumer *verb* 1
= to smoke

fumeur/fumeuse *noun, masculine/feminine*
un fumeur/une fumeuse = a smoker

funiculaire *noun, masculine*
un funiculaire = a funicular (railway)

fur: au fur et à mesure *adverb*
au fur et à mesure = as one goes along
au fur et à mesure que = as
au fur et à mesure qu'on fait des progrès = as one improves

furieux/furieuse *adjective*
= furious, angry

fuseau *noun, masculine*
(*plural*) **fuseaux**
un fuseau = ski pants
un fuseau horaire = a time zone

fusée *noun, feminine*
une fusée = a rocket

fusil *noun, masculine*
un fusil = a (shot)gun
= a rifle
un coup de fusil = a shot

gâcher *verb* 1
= to waste
= to spoil

gaffe* *noun, feminine*
- une gaffe = a blunder
- faire gaffe* = to watch out

gagnant/gagnante
1 *adjective*
= winning
2 *noun, masculine/feminine*
un gagnant/une gagnante = a winner

gagner *verb* 1
- = to win
- = to earn
Il gagne bien sa vie = he makes a good living

= to save
gagner du temps = to save time
gagner de la place = to make more room

gai/gaie *adjective*
= happy
= cheerful

gain *noun, masculine*
c'est un gain de temps = it saves time

gala *noun, masculine*
un gala = a gala, a gala event

galerie *noun, feminine*
- (*a passage*)
une galerie = a gallery
- (*on a car*)
la galerie = the roof rack
- une galerie d'art = an art gallery
une galerie marchande = a shopping centre, a shopping mall

galet *noun, masculine*
un galet = a pebble

galette *noun, feminine*
une galette = a biscuit, a cookie
= a pancake
la galette des rois = the Twelfth Night cake (*eaten on the Epiphany*)

Galles *noun, plural*
le pays de Galles = Wales

gallois/galloise
1 *adjective*
= Welsh
2 gallois *noun, masculine*
le gallois = Welsh

galop *noun, masculine*
un galop = a gallop
au galop = at a gallop

galoper *verb* 1
= to gallop

gamin/gamine* *noun, masculine/feminine*
un gamin*/une gamine* = a kid, a child

gamme *noun, feminine*
- (*of products*)
une gamme = a range
- (*in music*)
une gamme = a scale

gant *noun, masculine*
un gant = a glove
un gant de toilette = a face flannel, a wash cloth

garage *noun, masculine*
un garage = a garage
un garage à vélos = a bicycle shed

garagiste *noun, masculine/feminine*
un garagiste/une garagiste = a garage owner
= a car mechanic

G

garantie *noun, feminine*
 une garantie = a guarantee
 = a warranty
 un bon de garantie = a guarantee

garçon *noun, masculine*
• un garçon = a boy
 = a young man
• un garçon (de café) = a waiter
 un garçon d'honneur = a best man
 un garçon manqué = a tomboy

garde
1 *noun, feminine*
• la garde (*of a child*) = the care
 (*of a building*) = guarding
• être de garde (*if it's a doctor*) = to be on call
 (*if it's a pharmacist*) = to be on duty
2 *noun, masculine*
 un garde = a guard
 un garde du corps = a bodyguard

garde-chasse *noun, masculine*
(*plural*) **gardes-chasses**
 un garde-chasse = a game warden
 = a gamekeeper

garde-fou *noun, masculine*
(*plural*) **garde-fous**
 un garde-fou = a parapet
 = a safeguard

garder *verb* 1
• = to keep (on)
• = to look after
• = to guard

gardien/gardienne *noun,*
masculine/feminine
 un gardien/une gardienne (*in a prison*) = a
 warder, a guard
 (*in a museum*) = an attendant, a museum
 security guard
 (*on work premises*) = a security guard
 (*in an apartment block*) = a caretaker, a
 janitor
 un gardien de but = a goalkeeper
 une gardienne d'enfant = a childminder,
 a day-care lady

gare
1 *noun, feminine*
 une gare = a railway station
2 *exclamation*
 gare à toi! = watch it!
 une gare maritime = a harbo(u)r station
 une gare routière = a coach station, a bus
 station

garer *verb* 1
1 (**!** + *avoir*)
 = to park
2 se garer (**!** + *être*)
 se garer = to park
 = to pull over

garni/garnie *adjective*
 = served with vegetables

gars✱ *noun, masculine* (**!** *never changes*)
• un (petit) gars✱ = a (young) lad, a (young)
 guy
• un gars✱ = a chap, a guy

gas-oil *noun, masculine*
 le gas-oil = diesel oil, fuel oil

gaspiller *verb* 1
 = to waste

gâteau *noun, masculine*
(*plural*) **gâteaux**
 un gâteau = a cake
 le gâteau de riz = rice pudding
 un gâteau sec = a biscuit, a cookie

gâter *verb* 1
1 (**!** + *avoir*)
• = to spoil
 un enfant gâté = a spoiled child
2 se gâter (**!** + *être*)
• (*if it's fruit*)
 se gâter = to go bad
• (*if it's the weather*)
 se gâter = to take a turn for the worse

gauche
1 *adjective*
• = left
• = awkward
 = clumsy
2 *noun, feminine*
 la gauche = the left
 tournez à gauche = turn left
 conduire à gauche = to drive on the left-
 hand side

gaucher/gauchère *adjective*
 = left-handed

gaufre *noun, feminine*
 une gaufre = a waffle

Gaulois/Gauloise *noun,*
masculine/feminine
 un Gaulois/une Gauloise = a Gaul

gaz *noun, masculine* (**!** *never changes*)
 le gaz = gas
 se chauffer au gaz = to have gas heating
 le gaz carbonique = carbon dioxide
 le gaz de ville = mains gas

gazeux/gazeuse *adjective*
 = fizzy, sparkling
 une boisson gazeuse = a fizzy drink

gazon *noun, masculine*
 le gazon = grass, lawn

géant/géante
1 *adjective*
 = huge
2 *noun, masculine/feminine*
 un géant/une géante = a giant/a giantess

gel *noun, masculine*
• (*in winter*)
 le gel = frost

✱ in informal situations

• (for hair)
  un gel coiffant = a styling gel

gelé/gelée¹ adjective
= frozen

gelée² noun, feminine
• (on the ground)
  la gelée = frost
• (in cooking)
  la gelée de groseilles = redcurrant jelly

geler verb 17
1 (**!** + avoir)
= to freeze
  il gèle = it's freezing
2 se geler* (**!** + être)
  se geler* = to be freezing

gélule noun, feminine
  une gélule = a capsule

Gémeaux noun, masculine plural
  les Gémeaux = Gemini

gémir verb 3
= to moan
= to whimper

gênant/gênante adjective
= embarrassing

gendarme noun, masculine
  un gendarme = a gendarme, a French
  policeman

gendarmerie noun, feminine
• **la gendarmerie (nationale)** = the
  gendarmerie
• **une gendarmerie** ≈ a police station

gendre noun, masculine
  un gendre = a son-in-law

généalogique adjective
  un arbre généalogique = a family tree

gêner verb 1
1 (**!** + avoir)
• = to disturb
• = to bother
  ça te gêne si j'allume? = do you mind if
  I switch the light on?
• = to be in the way
• = to embarrass
2 se gêner (**!** + être)
• **se gêner** = to get in each other's way
• **ne te gêne pas pour moi** = don't mind me

général/générale
(plural) **généraux/générales**
1 adjective
• = general
  de l'avis général = in most people's
  opinion
  dans l'intérêt général = in the public
  interest
• **en général** = generally
  = usually
2 général noun, masculine
  un général = a general

généralement adverb
= generally
= normally

généraliste adjective
• = non-specialized
• **un médecin généraliste** = a general
  practitioner, a GP, a family doctor

généreux/généreuse adjective
= generous

génétique adjective
= genetic

Genève noun
= Geneva

génial/géniale* adjective
(plural) **géniaux/géniales**
= brilliant

génie noun, masculine
  le génie = genius
  une idée de génie = a brainwave

genou noun, masculine
(plural) **genoux**
  un genou = a knee
  être sur les genoux de sa mère = to be on
  one's mother's lap
  à genoux = on one's knees
  se mettre à genoux = to kneel down

genre noun, masculine
• (a type)
  un genre = a kind
  ce genre de travail = this kind of work
  un peu dans le genre de ta robe = a little
  bit like your dress
• (a look)
  avoir un drôle de genre = to look a bit
  shady
  pour se donner un genre = to make
  oneself look different
• (in grammar)
  le genre = gender
• (in literature, cinema)
  un genre = a genre

gens noun, masculine plural
  les gens = people

gentil/gentille adjective
= kind, nice

gentillesse noun, feminine
  la gentillesse = kindness

gentiment adverb
= nicely, kindly

géographie noun, feminine
  la géographie = geography

gérant/gérante noun,
masculine/feminine
• (in a shop)
  un gérant/une gérante = a manager
• (for a property)
  un gérant/une gérante = a managing
  agent

G

gerboise noun, feminine
une gerboise = a gerbil

germain/germaine adjective
un cousin germain = a first cousin

geste noun, masculine
un geste = a movement
= a gesture

gibier noun, masculine
le gibier = game

gifle noun, feminine
une gifle = a slap in the face

gigantesque adjective
= huge, gigantic

gigot noun, masculine
un gigot d'agneau = a leg of lamb

gilet noun, masculine
• un gilet = a cardigan
• un gilet = a waistcoat, a vest
un gilet de sauvetage = a lifejacket

girafe noun, feminine
une girafe = a giraffe

gîte noun, masculine
un gîte rural = a self-catering cottage

givrant adjective, masculine
du brouillard givrant = freezing fog

givre noun, masculine
le givre = frost

glace noun, feminine
• (frozen water)
la glace = ice
• (a confection)
la glace = ice cream
une glace à la vanille = a vanilla ice cream
• (a looking glass)
une glace = a mirror

glacé/glacée adjective
• = ice-cold
= frozen
• = glossy

glaçon noun, masculine
un glaçon = an ice cube

glisser verb [1]
1 (! + avoir)
• = to slip
= to slide
• = to be slippery
2 se glisser (! + être)
se glisser dans = to slip into
= to sneak into
= to creep into

globe noun, masculine
le globe (terrestre) = the globe, the Earth

gloire noun, feminine
la gloire = glory, fame

goal noun, masculine
un goal = a goalkeeper

gogo: à gogo✱ adverb
à gogo✱ = galore

golfe noun, masculine
un golfe = a gulf

gomme noun, feminine
• une gomme = a rubber, an eraser
• la gomme = gum

gonflé/gonflée adjective
• = inflated
• = swollen
• être gonflé✱ = to have a nerve
= to have guts

gonfler verb [1]
• = to inflate
• = to swell (up)

gorge noun, feminine
la gorge = the throat
avoir mal à la gorge = to have a sore throat
avoir la gorge serrée = to have a lump in
one's throat

gorgée noun, feminine
une gorgée = a sip
= a gulp

gorille noun, masculine
• un gorille = a gorilla
• un gorille✱ = a bodyguard

gosse✱ noun, masculine/feminine
un gosse✱/une gosse✱ = a kid, a child

goudron noun, masculine
le goudron = tar

goudronner verb [1]
= to tarmac, to blacktop

gourde noun, feminine
une gourde = a gourd
= a flask

gourmand/gourmande adjective
être gourmand = to be fond of good food
(to like sweet things) = to have a sweet
tooth

goût noun, masculine
le goût = taste

goûter
1 verb [1]
= to taste
2 noun, masculine
• le goûter = an afternoon snack
• un goûter = a children's party

goutte noun, feminine
une goutte = a drop
goutte à goutte = drop by drop

grâce
1 noun, feminine
la grâce = grace
2 grâce à = thanks to

✱ in informal situations

gradins *noun, masculine plural*
les gradins = the terraces, the bleachers

graine *noun, feminine*
une graine = a seed

graisse *noun, feminine*
la graisse (*in food*) = fat
(*for machinery*) = grease

graisser *verb* $\boxed{1}$
= to grease
= to lubricate

grammaire *noun, feminine*
la grammaire = grammar

gramme *noun, masculine*
un gramme = a gram

grand/grande
1 *adjective*
• = tall
= big, large
= long
Théo est grand = Théo is tall
un grand jardin = a large garden
un grand voyage = a long journey
il n'y avait pas grand monde = there
weren't many people
faire de grands gestes = to wave one's
arms around
• = great
un grand homme = a great man
un train à grande vitesse = a high-speed
train
2 grand *adverb*
= wide
grand ouvert = wide open
voir grand = to think big
le grand bassin = the main pool
un grand magasin = a department store
le grand public = the general public
une grande personne = a grown-up
une grande surface = a supermarket
les grandes lignes = main train routes
les grandes vacances = the summer
holidays, the summer vacation

grand-chose *pronoun*
pas grand-chose = not much, not a lot
ça ne sert pas à grand-chose = it's not
much use

Grande-Bretagne *noun, feminine*
la Grande-Bretagne = Great Britain

grandir *verb* $\boxed{3}$
= to grow

grand-mère *noun, feminine*
(*plural*) **grands-mères**
une grand-mère = a grandmother

grand-père *noun, masculine*
(*plural*) **grands-pères**
un grand-père = a grandfather

grands-parents *noun, masculine plural*
des grands-parents = grandparents

grange *noun, feminine*
une grange = a barn

granulé *noun, masculine*
un granulé = a granule

graphique
1 *adjective*
= graphic
2 *noun, masculine*
un graphique = a graph

grappe *noun, feminine*
une grappe = a bunch
= a cluster

gras/grasse
1 *adjective*
• = greasy
= fatty
• = fat
• (*if it's a letter*) = bold
2 gras *noun, masculine* (**!** *never changes*)
le gras (*on meat*) = fat

gratin *noun, masculine*
un gratin = a gratin (*a dish topped with
browned cheese and breadcrumbs*)
un gratin de pommes de terre = potatoes
au gratin

gratis
1 *adjective* (**!** *never changes*)
= free
2 *adverb*
= free, for free

gratter *verb* $\boxed{1}$
1 (**!** + *avoir*)
• = to scratch
= to scrape (off)
• ça me gratte partout = I'm itching all over
2 se gratter (**!** + *être*)
se gratter = to scratch

gratuit/gratuite *adjective*
= free

gratuitement *adverb*
= free, for free
travailler gratuitement = to work for
nothing

grave *adjective*
• = serious
• = grave, solemn
• une voix grave = a deep voice

gravement *adverb*
• = seriously
• = gravely, solemnly

gravier *noun, masculine*
du gravier = gravel

gravillon *noun, masculine*
un gravillon = a bit of grit, some grit

grec/grecque
1 *adjective*
= Greek
2 grec *noun, masculine*
le grec = Greek

G

Grèce noun, feminine
la Grèce = Greece

grecque ▶ grec 1

grêle noun, feminine
la grêle = hail
il tombe de la grêle = it's hailing

grêlon noun, masculine
un grêlon = a hailstone

grelotter verb 1
= to shiver

grenier noun, masculine
un grenier = an attic, a loft

grenouille noun, feminine
une grenouille = a frog

grève noun, feminine
• (at work)
une grève = a strike
faire grève = to go on strike
• (by the sea)
la grève = the shore
une grève de la faim = a hunger strike

griffe noun, feminine
une griffe = a claw

griffer verb 1
= to scratch

grignoter verb 1
= to nibble

grillade noun, feminine
une grillade = grilled meat

grillage noun, masculine
le grillage = wire netting

grille noun, feminine
• (in a garden)
une grille = a gate
• (for a crossword)
une grille = a grid

grille-pain noun, masculine (! never changes)
un grille-pain = a toaster

griller verb 1
• (in cooking)
(faire) griller = to grill
= to toast
• griller* un feu = to go through a red light

grimace noun, feminine
une grimace = a (funny) face
faire des grimaces = to make faces
faire la grimace devant un plat = to turn one's nose up at a dish

grimper verb 1
= to climb

grippe noun, feminine
la grippe = flu

✱ in informal situations

gris/grise adjective
• = grey, gray
• = dull, dreary
un temps gris = dull weather

grive noun, feminine
une grive = a thrush

grognon adjective
= grumpy, grouchy

gros/grosse
1 adjective
• = big
• = heavy
un gros fumeur = a heavy smoker
2 gros adverb
• écrire gros = to write in big letters
• perdre gros = to lose a lot
3 gros noun, masculine (! never changes)
• le gros du travail = the bulk of the work
• le prix de gros = the wholesale price
4 en gros
• en gros = roughly
• en gros = wholesale
• en gros = in big letters
le gros lot = the first prize
un gros mot = a swearword
les gros titres = the headlines

groseille noun, feminine
une groseille = a redcurrant
une groseille à maquereau = a gooseberry

grosse ▶ gros 1

grossier/grossière adjective
• = rude
• = coarse

grotte noun, feminine
une grotte = a cave
= a grotto

groupe noun, masculine
un groupe = a group
un groupe scolaire = a school

guépard noun, masculine
un guépard = a cheetah

guêpe noun, feminine
une guêpe = a wasp

guère adverb
= hardly
il n'avait guère le choix = he didn't really have a choice

guérir verb 3
= to cure
= to heal
= to recover

guerre noun, feminine
une guerre = a war

guetter verb 1
= to watch
= to watch out for

gueule noun, feminine
une gueule = a mouth
avoir une grande gueule✶ = to have a big mouth

gui noun, masculine
le gui = mistletoe

guichet noun, masculine
un guichet (in a bank, a post office) = a counter
= a window
(in a museum, a station) = a ticket office
(in a theatre, a cinema) = a box office
un guichet automatique = an automatic cash dispenser

guide noun, masculine
un guide = a guide

guidon noun, masculine
le guidon = the handlebars

guignol noun, masculine
un guignol = a puppet show

guillemets noun, masculine plural
des guillemets = inverted commas
= quotation marks

guitare noun, feminine
une guitare = a guitar

gym✶ noun, feminine
• (at school)
la gym✶ = physical education
• (as a sport)
la gym✶ = gymnastics

gymnase noun, masculine
un gymnase = a gymnasium

gymnastique noun, feminine
la gymnastique (the sport) = gymnastics
(to keep fit) = exercise

habile adjective
= clever
= skil(l)ful

habiller verb [1]
1 (! + avoir)
= to dress
2 s'habiller (! + être)
s'habiller = to get dressed
= to dress up

habitant/habitante noun, masculine/feminine
un habitant/une habitante = an inhabitant

habiter verb [1]
= to live (in)
habiter la campagne = to live in the country
habiter à Paris = to live in Paris

habitude
1 noun, feminine
une habitude = a habit
avoir l'habitude de se lever tôt = to be in the habit of getting up early
= to be used to getting up early
avoir l'habitude des enfants = to be used to children
2 d'habitude = usually
comme d'habitude = as usual

habituel/habituelle adjective
= usual

haché/hachée adjective
= minced
= chopped

hachis noun, masculine (! never changes)
le hachis = mince, ground meat
le hachis Parmentier = shepherd's pie

haie noun, feminine
une haie = a hedge

haleine noun, feminine
l'haleine = the breath
hors d'haleine = out of breath

halte noun, feminine
une halte (a pause) = a stop
(a place) = a stopping place
faire halte = to stop

haltérophilie noun, feminine
l'haltérophilie = weightlifting

hameau noun, masculine
(plural) **hameaux**
un hameau = a hamlet

hameçon noun, masculine
un hameçon = a fish-hook

hanche noun, feminine
une hanche = a hip

handicapé/handicapée
1 adjective
= handicapped
2 noun, masculine/feminine
un handicapé/une handicapée = a handicapped person

hanté/hantée adjective
= haunted

hareng noun, masculine
un hareng = a herring

haricot noun, masculine
un haricot = a bean
les haricots verts = French beans

hasard noun, masculine
le hasard = chance
un hasard = a coincidence

H

hâte *noun, feminine*
- **la hâte** = haste
  à la hâte = hastily
- **j'ai hâte de partir** = I can't wait to leave

hausse *noun, feminine*
une hausse = a rise, an increase

hausser *verb* 1
= to raise
hausser les épaules = to shrug one's shoulders

haut/haute
1 *adjective*
- = high
  = tall
- **à haute voix** = aloud
  = loudly

2 haut *adverb*
- = high
  haut les mains! = hands up!
- = loud(ly)
  tout haut = aloud

3 haut *noun, masculine*
- **le haut** = the top
  les pièces du haut = the upstairs rooms
- **faire 15 mètres de haut** = to be 15 metres high

4 en haut = at the top
= upstairs

hauteur *noun, masculine*
la hauteur = the height

Haye *noun, feminine*
la Haye = the Hague

hebdomadaire *adjective*
= weekly

hébergement *noun, masculine*
l'hébergement = accommodation, lodging

héberger *verb* 13
= to put up

hein✱ *exclamation*
- **hein✱?** = what?
- **tu n'iras pas, hein✱?** = you won't go, will you?

hélas *exclamation*
hélas! = unfortunately!

hélice *noun, feminine*
une hélice = a propeller

hélicoptère *noun, masculine*
un hélicoptère = a helicopter

herbe *noun, feminine*
- **de l'herbe** = grass
- **une herbe** = a(n) herb
- **une mauvaise herbe** = a weed

hérisson *noun, masculine*
un hérisson = a hedgehog

héritage *noun, masculine*
un héritage = an inheritance

hériter *verb* 1
= to inherit

héritier/héritière *noun, masculine/feminine*
un héritier/une héritière = an heir/an heiress

héros *noun, masculine* (**!** *never changes*)
un héros = a hero

hésiter *verb* 1
= to hesitate

heure *noun, feminine*
- **l'heure** = the time
  quelle heure est-il? = what time is it?
  il est huit heures = it's eight o'clock
  il est huit heures dix = it's ten past eight
  il est huit heures moins dix = it's ten to eight
  l'heure du déjeuner = lunchtime
  être à l'heure = to be on time
  de bonne heure = early
  mettre sa montre à l'heure = to set one's watch
- **une heure** = an hour
  toutes les trois heures = every three hours
  faire du 100 à l'heure✱ = to do 100 km per hour

les heures d'affluence = peak times
les heures de pointe = the rush hour
les heures supplémentaires = overtime

heureuse ▶ **heureux**

heureusement *adverb*
= fortunately
= luckily

heureux/heureuse *adjective*
= happy

heurter *verb* 1
= to bump into
= to hit, to crash into

hibou *noun, masculine*
(*plural*) **hiboux**
un hibou = an owl

hier *adverb*
= yesterday
hier soir = yesterday evening

hippodrome *noun, masculine*
un hippodrome = a racecourse

hippopotame *noun, masculine*
un hippopotame = a hippopotamus

hirondelle *noun, feminine*
une hirondelle = a swallow

histoire *noun, feminine*
- **l'histoire** = history
- **une histoire** = a story
- **faire des histoires✱** = to make trouble

✱ in informal situations

historique *adjective*
- = historic
- = historical

hit-parade *noun, masculine*
(*plural*) **hit-parades**
le hit-parade = the charts

hiver *noun, masculine*
l'hiver = winter

HLM *noun, masculine or feminine*
un(e) HLM ≈ a council flat, a low-rent
apartment
= a block of council flats, a low-rent
apartment building

hocher *verb* [1]
hocher la tête (*in agreement*) = to nod
(*to say no*) = to shake one's head

hollandais/hollandaise
1 *adjective*
= Dutch
2 hollandais *noun, masculine*
le hollandais = Dutch

Hollande *noun, feminine*
la Hollande = Holland

homard *noun, masculine*
un homard = a lobster

homme *noun, masculine*
un homme = a man
un homme d'affaires = a businessman

Hongrie *noun, feminine*
la Hongrie = Hungary

hongrois/hongroise
1 *adjective*
= Hungarian
2 hongrois *noun, masculine*
le hongrois = Hungarian

honnête *adjective*
= honest

honoraire
1 *adjective*
= honorary
2 honoraires *noun, masculine plural*
les honoraires = the fee(s)

honte *noun, feminine*
la honte = shame
avoir honte = to be ashamed

hôpital *noun, masculine*
(*plural*) **hôpitaux**
un hôpital = a hospital

hoquet *noun, masculine*
le hoquet = hiccoughs, hiccups

horaire *noun, masculine*
un horaire = a timetable
**les horaires à la carte, les horaires
libres** = flexitime, flextime

horizon *noun, masculine*
l'horizon = the horizon
à l'horizon = on the horizon

horizontal/horizontale *adjective*
(*plural*) **horizontaux/horizontales**
= horizontal, flat

horizontalement *adverb*
- = horizontally
- (*in a crossword*) = across

horloge *noun, feminine*
une horloge = a clock

horloger/horlogère *noun,
masculine/feminine*
un horloger/une horlogère = a
watchmaker

horreur *noun, feminine*
- l'horreur = horror
quelle horreur! = how horrible!
= it's hideous!
- l'horreur = loathing
avoir horreur de laver la voiture = to loathe
washing the car

horrible *adjective*
= awful, horrible

hors *preposition*
hors (de) = outside, out of
hors d'haleine = out of breath
hors jeu = offside
hors de prix = ridiculously expensive
hors (de) saison = out of season
'hors service' = 'out of order'
hors taxes, HT (*describing a shop*) = duty-
free
(*describing a price*) = excluding tax
hors d'usage = worn out

hors-d'œuvre *noun, masculine* (! *never
changes*)
un hors-d'œuvre = a starter

hospitalité *noun, feminine*
l'hospitalité = hospitality

hôte
1 *noun, masculine*
un hôte = a host
2 *noun, masculine/feminine*
un hôte/une hôte = a guest

hôtel *noun, masculine*
un hôtel = a hotel
l'hôtel de ville = the town hall

hôtelier/hôtelière *noun,
masculine/feminine*
un hôtelier/une hôtelière = a hotel-keeper,
a hotel manager

hôtesse *noun, feminine*
- (*a person who has guests*)
une hôtesse = a hostess
- (*a person who deals with customers*)
une hôtesse (*in a firm*) = a receptionist
(*on a train, a boat*) = a stewardess
une hôtesse d'accueil = a receptionist
une hôtesse de l'air = a flight attendant,
an air hostess

H

houx *noun, masculine* (**!** *never changes*)
le houx = holly

HT ▶ hors

hublot *noun, masculine*
un hublot = a porthole

huile *noun, feminine*
l'huile = oil

huissier *noun, masculine*
un huissier (de justice) = a bailiff

huit *number*
= eight
huit jours = a week
= eight days
lundi en huit = a week on Monday

huitaine *noun, feminine*
une huitaine = about a week
= about eight

huitante *number*
= eighty

huitième *number*
= eighth

huître *noun, feminine*
une huître = an oyster

humain/humaine *adjective*
• = human
• = humane

humeur *noun, feminine*
une humeur = a mood
être de bonne humeur = to be in a good mood
être de mauvaise humeur = to be in a bad mood

humide *adjective*
= damp
= humid

hurlement *noun, masculine*
un hurlement = a howl

hurler *verb* 1
= to howl

hydroglisseur *noun, masculine*
un hydroglisseur = a hydrofoil

hydrophile *adjective*
= absorbent

hygiénique *adjective*
le papier hygiénique = toilet paper

hyper* *adverb*
= extremely

hypermarché *noun, masculine*
un hypermarché = a hypermarket, a large supermarket

I i

ici *adverb*
= here
venez par ici = come this way

idéal/idéale *adjective*
(*plural*) **idéaux/idéales**
= ideal

idée *noun, feminine*
une idée = an idea

identifier *verb* 2
= to identify

identité *noun, feminine*
l'identité = identity

idiot/idiote
1 *adjective*
= stupid
2 *noun, masculine/feminine*
un idiot/une idiote = an idiot

ignorer *verb* 1
• = not to know
j'ignore où il habite = I don't know where he lives
• = to ignore

il *pronoun, masculine*
1 (*referring to a person, an animal or a thing*)
= he
= it
ils = they
2 (*impersonal use*)
• = it
il fait froid = it's cold
il est facile d'obtenir des billets = it's easy to get tickets
• il y a = there is
= there are
il y a une fuite = there is a leak
• (*when talking about time*)
il y a une heure que j'attends = I've been waiting for an hour
il y a un an qu'il est parti = he left a year ago

île *noun, feminine*
une île = an island
les îles Anglo-Normandes = the Channel Islands

illégal/illégale *adjective*
(*plural*) **illégaux/illégales**
= illegal

illettré/illettrée *adjective*
= illiterate

illimité/illimitée *adjective*
= unlimited

illisible adjective
• = illegible
• = unreadable

illuminé/illuminée adjective
= lit up
= illuminated

illustre adjective
= illustrious

illustré noun, masculine
un illustré = an illustrated magazine
= a comic, a comic book

illustrer verb 1
= to illustrate

ils pronoun, masculine plural
= they

image noun, feminine
une image = a picture
= an image

imaginaire adjective
= imaginary

imaginer verb 1
= to imagine

imbattable adjective
= unbeatable

imbécile noun, masculine/feminine
un imbécile/une imbécile = an idiot
faire l'imbécile = to be silly

imiter verb 1
= to imitate

immatriculation noun, feminine
l'immatriculation = registration
= the registration number

immédiatement adverb
= immediately

immense adjective
= huge
= great

immeuble noun, masculine
un immeuble = a building
= a block of flats, an apartment block

immigré/immigrée adjective
= immigrant

immobile adjective
= still

immobilier noun, masculine
l'immobilier = property, real estate

impair/impaire adjective
les nombres impairs = odd numbers

imparfait/imparfaite
1 adjective
= imperfect
2 **imparfait** noun, masculine
l'imparfait = the imperfect (tense)

impasse noun, feminine
une impasse = a cul-de-sac, a dead end

impatienter: s'impatienter 1
(! + être)
s'impatienter = to get impatient

imper✱ noun, masculine
un imper✱ = a mac, a raincoat

imperméable
1 noun, masculine
un imperméable = a raincoat
2 adjective
= waterproof

impoli/impolie adjective
= impolite, rude

important/importante adjective
= important
= considerable
= sizeable

importer verb 1
• = to import
• = to be important
il importe de [faire | dire | savoir ...] = it's
important to [do | say | know ...]
n'importe
n'importe lequel = any
n'importe où = anywhere
n'importe quel = any
n'importe qui = anybody
n'importe quoi = anything

impôt noun, masculine
un impôt = a tax

impressionnant/impressionnante
adjective
= impressive

impressionner verb 1
= to impress

imprévu/imprévue adjective
= unexpected

imprimé/imprimée
1 adjective
= printed
2 **imprimé** noun, masculine
• (paper)
un imprimé = a leaflet
• (on material)
un imprimé = a print

imprimer verb 1
= to print

imprimeur noun, masculine
un imprimeur = a printer

improviser verb 1
= to improvise

improviste: à l'improviste adverb
à l'improviste = unexpectedly

imprudence noun, feminine
• l'imprudence = recklessness
• faire une imprudence = to do something
reckless

imprudent/imprudente adjective
= reckless

inabordable *adjective*
• (*describing a price*) = prohibitive, unaffordable
• (*describing a person*) = unapproachable

inadmissible *adjective*
= unacceptable

inattendu/inattendue *adjective*
= unexpected

incapable *adjective*
= incompetent
être incapable de conduire = to be incapable of driving
= to be unable to drive

incendie *noun, masculine*
un incendie = a fire

incident *noun, masculine*
un incident = an incident

inclus/incluse *adjective*
• = including
• = enclosed

inconnu/inconnue
1 *adjective*
= unknown
2 *noun, masculine/feminine*
un inconnu/une inconnue = a stranger
= an unknown man/woman

inconvénient *noun, masculine*
un inconvénient = a drawback, a disadvantage
si vous n'y voyez pas d'inconvénient = if you have no objection

incroyable *adjective*
= unbelievable

incroyablement *adverb*
= incredibly

inculpé/inculpée *noun, masculine/feminine*
l'inculpé/l'inculpée = the accused

inculper *verb* [1]
= to charge
on l'a inculpé de meurtre = he's been charged with murder

Inde *noun, feminine*
l'Inde = India

indemne *adjective*
= unharmed

indépendant/indépendante *adjective*
= independent

index *noun, masculine* (**!** *never changes*)
l'index = the index finger, the forefinger

indicateur *noun, masculine*
• (*a book giving information*)
un indicateur (*for trains*) = a timetable
(*for streets*) = a directory
• (*an instrument*)
un indicateur = a gauge

indicatif *noun, masculine*
• (*when making a phone call*)
l'indicatif = the dialling code, the area code
• (*of a radio or TV programme*)
l'indicatif = the signature tune, the theme music
• (*in grammar*)
l'indicatif = the indicative

indice *noun, masculine*
un indice = a sign, an indication
(*in a police inquiry*) = a clue

indien/indienne *adjective*
= Indian

indigestion *noun, feminine*
une indigestion = a stomach upset

indigner: s'indigner *verb* [1] (**!** + *être*)
s'indigner = to be indignant

indiquer *verb* [1]
• (*with one's hand*) = to indicate, to point to
• (*to give information*) = to tell
pouvez-vous m'indiquer la banque la plus proche? = could you tell me where the nearest bank is?
je leur ai indiqué le moyen d'entrer sans payer = I told them how to get in for free
il m'a indiqué un bon restaurant = he recommended a good restaurant
indiquez votre nom et votre adresse = give your name and address
• (*to display information*) = to show
le village n'est pas indiqué sur la carte = the village isn't shown on the map
• (*to be a sign or a clue*) = to suggest
rien n'indique qu'il changera d'avis = there's nothing to suggest that he'll change his mind

individu *noun, masculine*
un individu = an individual
= a person

individuel/individuelle *adjective*
= individual

industrie *noun, feminine*
l'industrie = industry

industriel/industrielle *adjective*
= industrial

inédit/inédite *adjective*
• = (previously) unpublished
• = new

infect/infecte *adjective*
= horrible, revolting

infecter: s'infecter *verb* [1] (**!** + *être*)
s'infecter = to become infected, to go septic

inférieur/inférieure *adjective*
• = lower
• = inferior

infirme
1 *adjective*
= disabled
2 *noun, masculine/feminine*
un infirme/une infirme = a disabled person

infirmerie *noun, feminine*
l'infirmerie = the sick bay

infirmier/infirmière *noun,*
masculine/feminine
un infirmier/une infirmière = a nurse

inflammable *adjective*
= flammable

infliger *verb* 13
= to inflict

informaticien/informaticienne
noun, masculine/feminine
un informaticien/une informaticienne = a
computer scientist

informations *noun, feminine plural*
les informations = the news

informatique *noun, feminine*
l'informatique = computer science,
computing

informer *verb* 1
1 (**!** + *avoir*)
= to inform
2 s'informer (**!** + *être*)
• s'informer = to keep oneself informed
• s'informer de = to enquire about

ingénieur *noun, masculine*
un ingénieur = an engineer

ingrat/ingrate *adjective*
• (*not thankful*) = ungrateful
• (*not pretty*) = unattractive

inhabité/inhabitée *adjective*
= uninhabited

inhabituel/inhabituelle *adjective*
= unusual

inhumer *verb* 1
= to bury

initiale *noun, feminine*
une initiale = an initial

injure *noun, feminine*
une injure = an insult

injuste *adjective*
= unfair

inquiet/inquiète *adjective*
= worried, anxious

inquiéter *verb* 14
1 (**!** + *avoir*)
= to worry
2 s'inquiéter (**!** + *être*)
s'inquiéter = to worry

inquiétude *noun, feminine*
l'inquiétude = worry

inscrire *verb* 42
1 (**!** + *avoir*)
• = to enrol(l), to register
• = to write down
2 s'inscrire (**!** + *être*)
s'inscrire = to register
= to enrol

inscrit/inscrite ▶ inscrire 42

insecte *noun, masculine*
un insecte = an insect

insolation *noun, feminine*
une insolation = sunstroke

insolent/insolente *adjective*
= insolent, cheeky

insomniaque *adjective*
= insomniac, unable to sleep

inspecter *verb* 1
= to inspect

inspecteur/inspectrice *noun,*
masculine/feminine
un inspecteur/une inspectrice = an
inspector
un inspecteur de police = a detective
constable, a police detective

inspirer *verb* 1
1 (**!** + *avoir*)
• = to inspire
• = to breathe in
2 s'inspirer de (**!** + *être*)
s'inspirer de = to be inspired by, to draw
one's inspiration from

installation
1 *noun, feminine*
• (*the fact of fitting*)
l'installation = installing, putting in
• (*going to new premises*)
une installation = a move
2 installations *noun, feminine plural*
des installations = facilities
des installations sanitaires = toilets

installer *verb* 1
1 (**!** + *avoir*)
• (*to fit*) = to install, to put in
(*if it's gas, water, electricity*) = to connect
faire installer le téléphone = to have the
telephone connected
• (*to position*)
installer une tente sous un arbre = to put
up a tent under a tree
installer un invité dans un fauteuil = to sit
a guest in an armchair
2 s'installer (**!** + *être*)
s'installer dans une ville = to settle in a
town
s'installer près du feu = to sit by the fire

instant *noun, masculine*
un instant = a moment
à chaque instant = constantly

instinctivement *adverb*
= instinctively

instituteur/institutrice *noun, masculine/feminine*
un instituteur/une institutrice = a (primary school) teacher

instruction *noun, feminine*
• des instructions = instructions
• l'instruction = education
l'instruction civique = social studies
l'instruction religieuse = religious education

instrument *noun, masculine*
un instrument = an instrument
un instrument de musique = a musical instrument

insuffisant/insuffisante *adjective*
= insufficient

insulter *verb* 1
= to insult

insupportable *adjective*
= unbearable

intelligent/intelligente *adjective*
= intelligent, clever

intention *noun, feminine*
une intention = an intention
avoir l'intention de voyager = to intend to travel

interdire *verb* 40
= to forbid
elle nous a interdit de sortir = she forbade us to go out

interdit/interdite *adjective*
= forbidden, not allowed
'baignade interdite' = 'no swimming'

intéressant/intéressante *adjective*
= interesting

intéresser *verb* 1
1 (**!** + *avoir*)
= to interest
ça ne m'intéresse pas = I'm not interested
2 s'intéresser (**!** + *être*)
s'intéresser à = to be interested in

intérêt *noun, masculine*
un intérêt = an interest

intérieur/intérieure
1 *adjective*
= inside
= inner
2 extérieur *noun, masculine*
l'intérieur = the inside
à l'intérieur de la boîte = inside the box

internat *noun, masculine*
un internat = a boarding school

interne
1 *adjective*
= internal

2 *noun, masculine/feminine*
un interne/une interne (*a pupil*) = a boarder, a boarding student

interprète *noun, masculine/feminine*
un interprète/une interprète = an interpreter

interro* *noun, feminine*
(*abbreviation of* **interrogation**)
une interro* = a test

interrogation *noun, feminine*
• (*in class*)
une interrogation = a test
une interrogation écrite = a written test
• (*in grammar*)
une interrogation = a question

interroger *verb* 13
• = to question
• = to test

interviewer *verb* 1
= to interview

intituler *verb* 1
1 (**!** + *avoir*)
= to call, to entitle
2 s'intituler (**!** + *être*)
s'intituler = to be called

intoxication *noun, feminine*
une intoxication alimentaire = food poisoning

introduire *verb* 62
1 (**!** + *avoir*)
= to insert
2 s'introduire dans (**!** + *être*)
s'introduire dans (*to go in*) = to enter

intrus/intruse *noun, masculine/feminine*
• (*a person*)
un intrus/une intruse = an intruder
• (*in a game*)
'cherchez l'intrus' = 'spot the odd one out', 'pick the one that doesn't fit'

inutile *adjective*
= useless
= pointless

inutilisable *adjective*
= unusable

inventer *verb* 1
• = to invent
• = to think up

inverse *noun, masculine*
l'inverse = the opposite

invité/invitée *noun, masculine/feminine*
un invité/une invitée = a guest

inviter *verb* 1
= to invite

irai ▶ aller 1 9

irlandais/irlandaise
1 *adjective*
= Irish

***** in informal situations

2 irlandais *noun, masculine*
l'irlandais = Irish

Irlande *noun, feminine*
l'Irlande = Ireland
la République d'Irlande = the Republic of Ireland
l'Irlande du Nord = Northern Ireland

irriter *verb* 1
= to irritate

islamique *adjective*
= Islamic

isolé/isolée *adjective*
= isolated
= lonely

issue *noun, feminine*
une issue = an exit, a way out
une issue de secours = an emergency exit
'voie sans issue' = 'no through road'

Italie *noun, feminine*
l'Italie = Italy

italien/italienne
1 *adjective*
= Italian
2 italien *noun, masculine*
l'italien = Italian

italique *noun, masculine*
en italique(s) = in italics

itinéraire *noun, masculine*
un itinéraire = a route, an itinerary
'itinéraire bis' = 'alternative route'

ivoire *noun, masculine*
l'ivoire = ivory

ivre *adjective*
= drunk

ivresse *noun, feminine*
l'ivresse = drunkenness, intoxication

ivrogne *noun, masculine/feminine*
un ivrogne/une ivrogne = a drunkard

j' ▶ **je**

jadis *adverb*
= in the past, a long time ago

jaloux/jalouse *adjective*
= jealous

jamaïcain/jamaïcaine *adjective*
= Jamaican

Jamaïque *noun, feminine*
la Jamaïque = Jamaica

jamais *adverb*
• (*at no time*) = never
= ever
il n'écrit jamais = he never writes
plus jamais = never again
rien n'est jamais certain = nothing is ever certain
• (*at any other time*) = ever
il fait plus froid que jamais = it's colder than ever

jambe *noun, feminine*
une jambe = a leg

jambon *noun, masculine*
le jambon = ham

janvier *noun, masculine*
janvier = January

Japon *noun, masculine*
le Japon = Japan

japonais/japonaise
1 *adjective*
= Japanese
2 japonais *noun, masculine*
le japonais = Japanese

jardin *noun, masculine*
un jardin = a garden, a yard
faire son jardin = to work in one's garden
un jardin potager = a vegetable garden
un jardin public = a park
un jardin zoologique = a zoo

jardinage *noun, masculine*
le jardinage = gardening

jardinier/jardinière *noun, masculine/feminine*
un jardinier/une jardinière = a gardener

jaune *adjective*
= yellow

javelot *noun, masculine*
un javelot = a javelin

J.-C. (*abbreviation of* **Jésus-Christ**)
avant J.-C. = BC
après J.-C. = AD

je (**j'** *before vowel or mute h*) *pronoun*
= I

jean *noun, masculine*
un jean = (a pair of) jeans

jetable *adjective*
= disposable

jeter *verb* 20
= to throw (away)

jeton *noun, masculine*
un jeton = a counter

jeu *noun, masculine*
(*plural*) **jeux**
• (*the activity*)
un jeu = a game
faire un jeu = to play a game

- (*the equipment*)
  un jeu = a set
  un jeu d'échecs = a chess set
un jeu de mots = a pun
le jeu de l'oie ≈ snakes and ladders, chutes and ladders
un jeu de société = a board game = a party game
un jeu télévisé = a game show
les jeux Olympiques = the Olympic Games

jeudi *noun, masculine*
jeudi = Thursday

jeun: **à jeun** *adverb*
être à jeun = to have had nothing to eat

jeune
1 *adjective*
= young
2 *noun, masculine*
un jeune = a youth, a lad
les jeunes = young people
une jeune fille = a girl
un jeune homme = a young man

jeunesse *noun, feminine*
- (*the young years*)
  la jeunesse = youth
- (*young boys and girls*)
  la jeunesse = young people

jf (*abbreviation of* **jeune fille**)
= young woman

jh (*abbreviation of* **jeune homme**)
= young man

Joconde *noun, feminine*
la Joconde = the Mona Lisa

joie *noun, feminine*
la joie = joy

joindre *verb* 56
1 (**!** + *avoir*)
- (*to add*) = to attach
  = to enclose
- (*to link, to fasten*) = to join
  = to put together
- (*to make contact*) = to get hold of
  = to get in touch with
2 se joindre à (**!** + *être*)
se joindre à = to join

joli/jolie *adjective*
= pretty, attractive
= nice

jongler *verb* 1
= to juggle

jongleur/jongleuse *noun, masculine/feminine*
un jongleur/une jongleuse = a juggler

jonquille *noun, feminine*
une jonquille = a daffodil

joue *noun, feminine*
une joue = a cheek

jouer *verb* 1
- = to play
  jouer à [cache-cache | la marelle | colin-maillard …] = to play [hide-and-seek | hopscotch | blind man's buff …]
  jouer aux cartes = to play cards
  à quoi jouez-vous? = what are you playing?
  jouer de [la guitare | la flûte | la harpe …] = to play [the guitar | the flute | the harp …]
  jouer du piano = to play the piano
  de quoi joue-t-il? = what does he play?
- = to gamble
- **qu'est-ce qu'on joue au théâtre?** = what's on at the theatre?, what's showing at the theater?

jouet *noun, masculine*
un jouet = a toy

joueur/joueuse *noun, masculine/feminine*
un joueur/une joueuse (*in a game, in sport*) = a player
(*at the casino*) = a gambler
être mauvais joueur = to be a bad loser

jour *noun, masculine*
- (*24 hours*)
  un jour = a day
  tous les jours = every day
  par jour = per day
  un jour de congé = a day off
  il y a quinze jours = a fortnight ago, two weeks ago
  de nos jours = nowadays
- (*the light*)
  le jour = daylight
  il fait jour = it's daylight
  en plein jour = in broad daylight
  voyager de jour = to travel by day, to travel in the daytime
le jour de l'An = New Year's (Day)
un jour férié = a bank holiday, a legal holiday
le jour J = D-day
un jour ouvrable = a working day

journal *noun, masculine*
(*plural*) **journaux**
- (*a publication*)
  un journal = a newspaper
- (*a private record*)
  un journal (intime) = a diary
le journal télévisé = the TV news

journaliste *noun, masculine/feminine*
un journaliste/une journaliste = a journalist

journée *noun, feminine*
une journée = a day
dans la journée = during the day

joyeux/joyeuse *adjective*
= happy

juger *verb* [13]
= to judge

juif/juive
1 *adjective*
= Jewish
2 *noun, masculine/feminine*
un juif/une juive = a Jew

juillet *noun, masculine*
juillet = July
le 14 juillet = Bastille Day

juin *noun, masculine*
juin = June

juive ▶ **juif**

jumeau/jumelle
(*plural*) **jumeaux/jumelles**
1 *adjective*
= twin
2 *noun, masculine/feminine*
un jumeau/une jumelle = a (male) twin/a (female) twin
des jumeaux/des jumelles = twins

jumelage *noun, masculine*
un jumelage = a (town) twinning

jumelé/jumelée *adjective*
= twinned
Oxford est jumelé avec Grenoble = the city of Oxford is twinned with Grenoble

jumelles *noun, feminine plural*
des jumelles = binoculars

jupe *noun, feminine*
une jupe = a skirt

jurer *verb* [1]
= to swear

jus *noun, masculine* (**!** *never changes*)
• (*from fruit*)
du jus = juice
un jus de fruit = a fruit juice
• (*from a roast*)
le jus = the gravy

jusque (**jusqu'** *before vowel*)
1 *preposition*
• = as far as
aller jusqu'à Rome = to go as far as Rome
• = up to
= down to
de l'eau jusqu'à la taille = water up to the waist
se pencher jusqu'à terre = to bend down to the ground
• = until, till
jusqu'à lundi = until Monday
jusqu'à l'an 2000 = until the year 2000
jusqu'ici, jusqu'à présent = till now, up to now
2 jusqu'à ce que = until

juste
1 *adjective*
• = right, correct
une réponse juste = a correct answer
• = fair
ce n'est pas juste = it's not fair, it's unfair
• = tight
2 *adverb*
• **chanter juste** = to sing in tune
• **il est huit heures juste** = it's exactly eight o'clock
• **tout juste** = only just
il arrive juste = he's (only) just arrived
juste à temps = just in time
3 au juste = exactly

justement *adverb*
= exactly

kaki
1 *adjective* (**!** *never changes*)
= khaki
2 *noun, masculine*
un kaki = a persimmon

kangourou *noun, masculine*
un kangourou = a kangaroo

karting *noun, masculine*
le karting = go-karting

kayak *noun, masculine*
• (*the equipment*)
un kayak = a kayak
• (*the sport*)
le kayak = canoeing

kermesse *noun, feminine*
une kermesse = a fête, a festival

kilo, kilogramme *noun, masculine*
un kilo, un kilogramme = a kilo, a kilogram

kilomètre *noun, masculine*
un kilomètre = a kilometre, a kilometer

kiosque *noun, masculine*
un kiosque = a kiosk
un kiosque à journaux = a newspaper kiosk, a newsstand
un kiosque à musique = a bandstand

klaxon *noun, masculine*
un klaxon = a (car) horn

klaxonner *verb* [1]
= to sound one's horn, to honk the horn

KO *adjective* (**!** *never changes*)
(*abbreviation of* **knocked out**)
• = KO'ed
mettre son adversaire KO = to KO one's
opponent
• **je suis KO✶** = I'm exhausted

K-way *noun, masculine*
un K-way = a windcheater, a windbreaker

L l

l'▶ le

la▶ le

là *adverb*
• (*indicating a place*) = there
j'habitais là = I used to live there
passez par là = go that way
c'est là qu'il est né = that's where he was
born
là où elle travaille = where she works
• (*indicating a time*) = then
d'ici là j'aurai fini = by then, I'll have
finished
ce jour-là = that day
en ce temps-là = in those days

là-bas *adverb*
= over there

laboratoire *noun, masculine*
un laboratoire = a laboratory

lac *noun, masculine*
un lac = a lake

lacet *noun, masculine*
• (*for shoes*)
un lacet = a lace
• (*in a road*)
un lacet = a hairpin bend, a hairpin turn
une route en lacets = a twisting road

lâcher *verb* 1
• (*to stop holding*) = to drop
= to let go of
• (*to collapse*) = to give way
• (*to stop working*) = to fail

là-dedans *adverb*
= in there

là-dessous *adverb*
= under there, under it

là-dessus *adverb*
• (*on a surface*) = there, on it
• (*on a subject*) = about it

✶ in informal situations

là-haut *adverb*
= up there
= upstairs

laid/laide *adjective*
= ugly

laine *noun, feminine*
la laine = wool
de laine, en laine = wool(l)en, wool

laisse *noun, feminine*
une laisse = a leash

laisser *verb* 1
1 (**!** + *avoir*)
• = to leave
laisser sa voiture à l'ombre = to leave one's
car in the shade
laissez-moi tranquille! = leave me alone!
• = to let
laisser couler l'eau = to let the water run
laisser tomber un verre = to drop a glass
2 se laisser (**!** + *être*)
• **se laisser influencer** = to allow oneself to
be influenced
• **se laisser tomber sur le sable** = to flop
down on the sand

lait *noun, masculine*
le lait = milk
le lait en poudre = powdered milk
le lait solaire = suntan lotion

laitier/laitière
1 *adjective*
les produits laitiers = dairy products
une vache laitière = a dairy cow
2 *noun, masculine/feminine*
un laitier/une laitière = a milkman/a
milkwoman

laitue *noun, feminine*
une laitue = a (head of) lettuce

lame *noun, feminine*
une lame = a blade
une lame de rasoir = a razor blade

lamentable *adjective*
= pitiful
= awful

lampadaire *noun, masculine*
un lampadaire (*in a house*) = a standard
lamp, a floor lamp
(*in the street*) = a streetlamp, a streetlight

lampe *noun, feminine*
une lampe = a lamp
une lampe de chevet = a bedside lamp
une lampe électrique = a torch, a
flashlight
une lampe de poche = a pocket torch, a
flashlight

lancer *verb* 12
1 (**!** + *avoir*)
• = to throw
• = to launch
2 se lancer (**!** + *être*)

- (to jump)
  se lancer = to throw oneself
- (to dare)
  se lancer = to take the plunge
- (to start)
  se lancer dans les affaires = to go into business

langage noun, masculine
un langage = a language

langouste noun, feminine
une langouste = a rock lobster

langue noun, feminine
- **la langue** = the tongue
- **une langue** = a language
la langue maternelle = the mother tongue
les langues vivantes = modern languages

languir verb ③
1 (**!** + avoir)
languir de revoir un ami = to be longing to see a friend
2 se languir de (**!** + être)
se languir de = to be pining for

lapin noun, masculine
- **un lapin** = a rabbit
- **poser un lapin✱ à quelqu'un** = to stand someone up

laquelle ▶ lequel

large
1 adjective
= wide
2 noun, masculine
- **faire trois mètres de large** = to be three metres wide
- **le large** = the open sea
  au large de la Bretagne = off the coast of Brittany

largement adverb
avoir largement le temps = to have plenty of time
c'est largement suffisant = it's more than enough

largeur noun, feminine
la largeur = the width

larme noun, feminine
une larme = a tear

las/lasse adjective
= tired, weary

lassant/lassante adjective
= tedious
= tiresome

lasser: se lasser de verb ① (**!** + être)
se lasser de = to grow tired of

latin noun, masculine
le latin = Latin

laurier noun, masculine
- **le laurier** = laurel
  = bay
- **une feuille de laurier** = a bay leaf

lavable adjective
= washable

lavabo noun, masculine
un lavabo = a washbasin, a wash-hand basin

lavage noun, masculine
le lavage = washing

lavande noun, feminine
la lavande = lavender

lave-linge noun, masculine (**!** never changes)
un lave-linge = a washing machine

laver verb ①
1 (**!** + avoir)
= to wash
2 se laver (**!** + être)
se laver = to wash oneself
se laver les mains = to wash one's hands

laverie noun, feminine
une laverie (automatique) = a launderette, a laundromat

lave-vaisselle noun, masculine (**!** never changes)
un lave-vaisselle = a dishwasher

le/la (**l'** before vowel or mute h)
(plural) **les**
1 determiner
- = the
  la fenêtre de la cuisine = the kitchen window
  les Martin = the Martins
- (not translated in some cases)
  apprendre le russe = to learn Russian
  aimer le café = to like coffee
  les enfants aiment les animaux = children like animals
- = a
  20 francs le kilo = 20 francs a kilo
  cent kilomètres à l'heure = one hundred kilometres an hour
- (used with nouns relating to a part of the body)
  avoir les yeux bleus = to have blue eyes
  se casser la jambe = to break one's leg
  il m'a serré la main = he shook my hand
- (used with a day of the week)
  travailler le lundi = to work on Mondays
  tous les mardis = every Tuesday
2 pronoun
- (referring to a person, an animal or a thing)
  = him/her
  = it
  (plural) = them
  il l'a invitée = he invited her
  où les as-tu achetés? = where did you buy them?

- (*other cases*)
  comme vous le savez = as you know
  je te l'avais dit = I told you
  il ne peut pas te le dire = he can't tell you
  espérons-le! = let's hope so!

lécher *verb* ①
= to lick

leçon *noun, feminine*
une leçon = a lesson

lecteur/lectrice
1 *noun, masculine/feminine*
un lecteur/une lectrice = a reader
2 lecteur *noun, masculine*
un lecteur de cassettes = a cassette player
un lecteur laser = a CD player

lecture *noun, feminine*
la lecture = reading

légendaire *adjective*
= legendary

légende *noun, feminine*
- (*a story*)
  une légende = a legend
- (*on a picture, a cartoon*)
  la légende = the caption
- (*on a map*)
  la légende = the key

léger/légère *adjective*
- (*not heavy*) = light
- (*not serious*) = slight
- (*not strong*)
  un café léger = a weak coffee
  une cigarette légère = a mild cigarette
  un vent léger = a light wind

légèrement *adverb*
= slightly

légume *noun, masculine*
un légume = a vegetable

lendemain *noun, masculine*
le lendemain = the next day, the following day
le lendemain matin = the next morning
le lendemain de mon arrivée = the day after I arrived

lent/lente *adjective*
= slow

lentement *adverb*
= slowly

lentille *noun, feminine*
- (*food*)
  des lentilles = lentils
- (*optical device*)
  une lentille = a lens
  les lentilles de contact = contact lenses

lequel/laquelle *pronoun*
(*plural*) **lesquels/lesquelles**
- = which one

lequel d'entre eux a payé? = which one of them paid?
lesquelles veux-tu? = which ones do you want?
- = which
  la situation dans laquelle je me trouve = the situation in which I find myself

les ▶ le

lesquels/lesquelles ▶ lequel

lessive *noun, feminine*
la lessive = the washing, the laundry

lettre *noun, feminine*
une lettre = a letter
en toutes lettres = in full

leur
1 *determiner*
= their
leur jardin = their garden
leurs sacs = their bags
2 *pronoun* (**!** *never changes*)
= them
il leur a prêté sa voiture = he lent them his car
je la leur ai envoyée = I sent it to them
3 *pronoun*
le leur/la leur/les leurs = theirs

levée *noun, feminine*
une levée (*from a post-box*) = a collection

lever
1 *verb* ⑯ (**!** + *avoir*)
= to raise
levez les bras = raise your arms
lever le doigt (*in class*) ≈ to put up one's hand
2 se lever *verb* ⑯ (**!** + *être*)
- (*if it's a person*)
  se lever = to get up
  = to stand up
- (*if it's the sun, the wind*)
  se lever = to rise
3 *noun, masculine*
au lever = when one gets up
= on getting up
le lever du soleil = sunrise

lèvre *noun, feminine*
une lèvre = a lip

levure *noun, feminine*
la levure = yeast
la levure chimique = baking powder

lexique *noun, masculine*
un lexique = a vocabulary list

libérer *verb* ⑭
= to release, to free

liberté *noun, feminine*
la liberté = freedom

libraire *noun, masculine/feminine*
un libraire/une libraire = a bookseller

librairie *noun, feminine*
  une librairie = a bookshop, a bookstore

libre *adjective*
• = free
  ils sont libres d'y aller = they're free to go
  'entrée libre' = 'admission free'
• = clear
  la route est libre = the road is clear
• = vacant
  une place libre = a vacant seat
• la ligne n'est pas libre = the line is
  engaged, the line is busy

librement *adverb*
  = freely

libre-service *noun, masculine*
(*plural*) **libres-services**
  un libre-service = a self-service

licence *noun, feminine*
  une licence (*a diploma*) = a degree

licencier *verb* 2
  = to dismiss, to lay off
  = to make redundant, to let go

lien *noun, masculine*
  un lien = a tie
  = a bond
  = a link

lieu *noun, masculine*
(*plural*) **lieux**
1 un lieu = a place
  un lieu de rencontre = a meeting place
  votre lieu de naissance = your place of
    birth
2 avoir lieu = to take place
3 au lieu de = instead of

lièvre *noun, masculine*
  un lièvre = a hare

ligne *noun, feminine*
  une ligne = a line

lilas *noun, masculine* (! *never changes*)
  le lilas = lilac

limande *noun, feminine*
  une limande (*a fish*) = a dab

limonade *noun, feminine*
  la limonade = lemonade

linge *noun, masculine*
• (*sheets, towels*)
  le linge (de maison) = (household) linen
  le linge sale = dirty linen
• (*when being laundered*)
  le linge = the washing, the laundry
  avoir du linge à laver = to have some
    washing to do

lion *noun, masculine*
  un lion = a lion

Lion *noun, masculine*
  le Lion = Leo

liquide *noun, masculine*
• un liquide = a liquid
• payer en liquide = to pay cash

lire[1] *verb* 41
  = to read

lire[2] *noun, feminine*
  la lire = the lira

lisse *adjective*
  = smooth

liste *noun, feminine*
  une liste = a list
  une liste d'attente = a waiting list
  être sur liste rouge = to be ex-directory, to
    have an unlisted number

lit *noun, masculine*
  un lit = a bed
  un lit de camp = a camp bed
  un grand lit = a double bed
  des lits superposés = bunk beds

litre *noun, masculine*
  un litre = a litre, a liter

littérature *noun, feminine*
  la littérature = literature

littoral *noun, masculine*
(*plural*) **littoraux**
  le littoral = the coast

livraison *noun, feminine*
  une livraison = a delivery

livre
1 *noun, masculine*
  un livre = a book
2 *noun, feminine*
  une livre = a pound

livrer *verb* 1
  = to deliver

livret *noun, masculine*
  un livret = a booklet
  un livret de famille = a family record
    book (*of births, marriages and deaths*)
  un livret scolaire = a school report book

local/locale
(*plural*) **locaux/locales**
1 *adjective*
  = local
2 local *noun, masculine*
  un local = a place

locataire *noun, masculine|feminine*
  un locataire/une locataire = a tenant

location *noun, feminine*
  la location (*of accommodation*) = renting
  (*of equipment*) = hiring
  (*of seats*) = booking, reservation
  'location de voitures' = 'car hire', 'car
    rental'

loge *noun, feminine*
• (*for a caretaker*)
  une loge = a lodge

L

- (*for an actor*)
  une loge = a dressing room

logé/logée *adjective*
= housed
être logé et nourri = to have room and board

logement *noun, masculine*
- **un logement** = accommodation
  = a flat, an apartment
- **le logement** = housing

loger *verb* 13
1 (! + *avoir*)
- (*to provide accommodation*) = to house
  (*for a short time*) = to put up
- (*to have accommodation*) = to live
  (*for a short time*) = to stay

2 se loger (! + *être*)
trouver à se loger = to find somewhere to live

logique *adjective*
= logical

loi *noun, feminine*
une loi = a law

loin *adverb*
- = a long way, far (away)
  c'est trop loin = it's too far
  c'est encore loin? = is it much further?
- **de loin** = from a distance
- **au loin** = in the distance

lointain/lointaine *adjective*
= distant

loisir *noun, masculine plural*
- (*spare time*)
  le loisir = leisure
- (*activity*)
  un loisir = a leisure activity, a pastime

Londres *noun*
= London

long/longue
1 *adjective*
= long
2 long *noun, masculine*
faire deux mètres de long = to be two metres long
marcher de long en large = to pace up and down
3 le long de = along

longer *verb* 13
= to follow

longtemps *adverb*
= (for) a long time
il y a longtemps qu'il est parti = he left a long time ago
ça fait longtemps que tu attends? = have you been waiting long?

✖ in informal situations

longue ▶ **long**

longuement *adverb*
= for a long time

longueur *noun, feminine*
la longueur = the length
à longueur de journée = all day long

lorsque (**lorsqu'** *before vowel or mute h*) *conjunction*
= (at the time) when

loterie *noun, feminine*
une loterie = a lottery

lotissement *noun, masculine*
un lotissement = a housing estate, a housing development

loto *noun, masculine*
le loto = lotto
= bingo

louche
1 *adjective*
= shady
2 *noun, feminine*
une louche = a ladle

louer *verb* 1
- (*as the owner*) = to rent out
  'à louer' = 'to let', 'for rent'
- (*as the tenant*) = to rent
  (*as the hirer*) = to hire, to rent

loufoque✖ *adjective*
= crazy

loup *noun, masculine*
un loup = a wolf

loupe *noun, feminine*
une loupe = a magnifying glass

lourd/lourde *adjective*
- (*weighty*) = heavy
- (*describing the weather*) = muggy, sultry
  il fait lourd = it's muggy

loyer *noun, masculine*
le loyer = the rent

lu/lue ▶ **lire**[1] 41

lucarne *noun, feminine*
une lucarne = a skylight

lueur *noun, feminine*
une lueur = a (faint) light
= a glow
= a gleam, a flash

luge *noun, feminine*
- (*the equipment*)
  une luge = a toboggan, a sled
- (*the sport*)
  la luge = tobogganing

lui
1 *pronoun, masculine*
• = him
  à cause de lui = because of him
  la voiture est à lui = the car belongs to him, the car is his
  c'est à lui de jouer = it's his turn to play
• = he
  elle est restée, mais lui est parti = she stayed, but he left
2 *pronoun, feminine*
  = her
  je lui ai prêté ma robe = I lent her my dress

lui-même *pronoun, masculine*
  = himself
  = itself

luire *verb* 62
  = to shine, to glow

luisant/luisante *adjective*
  = shining, glowing

lumière *noun, feminine*
  la lumière = light

lunch *noun, masculine*
  un lunch = a buffet lunch

lundi *noun, masculine*
  lundi = Monday

lune *noun, feminine*
  la lune = the moon

lunette
1 *noun, feminine*
  une lunette = a telescope
2 **lunettes** *noun, feminine plural*
  des lunettes = glasses, spectacles
  des lunettes de soleil = sunglasses

lustrer *verb* 1
  = to polish

lutin *noun, masculine*
  un lutin = an imp

lutte *noun, feminine*
• (*a fight*)
  une lutte = a struggle
• (*the sport*)
  la lutte = wrestling

lutter *verb* 1
  = to fight
  = to struggle

luxe *noun, masculine*
  le luxe = luxury

Luxembourg *noun, masculine*
  le Luxembourg = Luxembourg

lycée *noun, masculine*
  un lycée = a secondary school, ≈ a senior high school (*for students aged 15 to 18*)

lycéen/lycéenne *noun, masculine/feminine*
  un lycéen/une lycéenne = a secondary school student, a high school student (*aged 15 to 18*)

Mm

m *noun, masculine* (**!** *never changes*)
(*abbreviation of* **mètre**)
  m = m

m' ▶ **me**

M. (*abbreviation of* **Monsieur**)
  M. = Mr

ma ▶ **mon**

macaron *noun, masculine*
  un macaron = a macaroon

macédoine *noun, feminine*
• une macédoine de légumes = mixed diced vegetables
• une macédoine de fruits = a fruit salad

machin *noun, masculine*
  un machin✷ = a thing, a what's it

machine *noun, feminine*
  une machine = a machine
une machine à coudre = a sewing machine
une machine à écrire = a typewriter
une machine à laver = a washing machine
une machine à sous = a one-armed bandit

maçon *noun, masculine*
  un maçon = a bricklayer
  = a mason
  = a builder

madame *noun, feminine*
(*plural*) **mesdames**
  Madame Martin = Mrs Martin
  bonjour madame = good morning
  mesdames et messieurs = ladies and gentlemen

mademoiselle *noun, feminine*
(*plural*) **mesdemoiselles**
  Mademoiselle Martin = Miss Martin
  bonjour mademoiselle = good morning
  mesdames, mesdemoiselles et messieurs = ladies and gentlemen

magasin *noun, masculine*
  un magasin = a shop, a store
un grand magasin = a department store

magazine *noun, masculine*
  un magazine = a magazine

magique *adjective*
  = magic

magnétophone *noun, masculine*
  un magnétophone = a tape recorder

magnétoscope *noun, masculine*
  un magnétoscope = a video recorder

M

magnifique *adjective*
= magnificent
= wonderful

mai *noun, masculine*
mai = May
le 1er Mai = May Day

maigre *adjective*
• = thin
• = lean

maigrir *verb* 3
= to lose weight

maillot *noun, masculine*
un maillot (*for a dancer*) = a leotard
(*in football*) = a shirt, a jersey
(*for cyclists*) = a jersey
un maillot de corps = a vest, an
undershirt
un maillot de bain = a swimsuit

main *noun, feminine*
une main = a hand
fait (à la) main = handmade
se donner la main = to hold hands
se serrer la main = to shake hands
je vais te donner un coup de main = I'll
give you a hand
haut les mains! = hands up!

maintenant *adverb*
= now
= nowadays

maire *noun, masculine*
le maire = the mayor

mairie *noun, feminine*
la mairie = the town hall

mais *conjunction*
= but

maïs *noun, masculine* (! *never changes*)
le maïs = maize, corn
= sweetcorn

maison
1 *adjective* (! *never changes*)
= homemade
2 *noun, feminine*
la maison = the house
= home
rester à la maison = to stay at home
une maison de campagne = a house in
the country
une maison de la culture = a
community arts centre
**une maison des jeunes (et de la
culture)** = a youth club
une maison de retraite = a retirement
home

maître/maîtresse *noun, masculine/
feminine*

• (*in a school*)
le maître/la maîtresse = the teacher
• (*of a pet*)
le maître/la maîtresse = the master/the
mistress

majeur/majeure *adjective*
• = major, main
en majeure partie = for the most part
• être majeur = to be over 18 years of age

mal
1 *adjective* (! *never changes*)
= bad
c'est mal de mentir = it's bad to lie
les photos ne sont pas mal✱ = the photos
aren't bad
2 *adverb*
mal = badly
= not well
ils ont mal dormi = they slept badly
elle va mal = she isn't well at all
être mal élevé = to be bad mannered
3 **faire mal** = to hurt
ça me fait mal = it hurts
tu me fais mal = you're hurting me
je me suis fait mal = I hurt myself
4 **avoir mal**
avoir mal à la tête = to have a headache
avoir mal aux dents = to have (a)
toothache
avoir mal à la gorge = to have a sore throat
avoir mal au cœur = to feel sick
il a mal au genou = his knee hurts
avoir le mal de mer = to be seasick

malade
1 *adjective*
= ill, sick
tomber malade = to fall ill
2 *noun, masculine/feminine*
un malade/une malade = a patient
= a sick person

maladie *noun, feminine*
une maladie = an illness, a disease

maladroit/maladroite *adjective*
= clumsy

malaise *noun, masculine*
• (*faintness*)
un malaise = a dizzy turn
avoir un malaise = to feel faint
• (*nervousness*)
un malaise = unease

malfaiteur *noun, masculine*
un malfaiteur = a criminal

malgré *preposition*
= despite, in spite of

malheur *noun, masculine*
un malheur = a misfortune

malheureusement *adverb*
= unfortunately

✱ in informal situations

malheureux/malheureuse *adjective*
= unhappy
= unfortunate

malhonnête *adjective*
= dishonest

malin/maligne *adjective*
= clever
= crafty

malsain/malsaine *adjective*
= unhealthy

maltraiter *verb* 1
= to ill-treat

maman *noun, feminine*
une maman = a mum, a mom

mamie✗ *noun, feminine*
ma mamie✗ = my gran, my granny

manche
1 *noun, feminine*
une manche = a sleeve
sans manches = sleeveless
2 *noun, masculine*
un manche = a handle
un manche à balai = a broomstick
= a joystick

Manche *noun, feminine*
la Manche = the (English) Channel

mandat *noun, masculine*
un mandat = a money order

manège *noun, masculine*
un manège = a fairground ride

manger *verb* 13
= to eat
inviter des amis à manger = to invite
friends for a meal
manger au restaurant = to eat out

mangue *noun, feminine*
une mangue = a mango

manière *noun, feminine*
• (*a method*)
la manière = the way
c'est leur manière de remercier = it's their
way of saying thank you
• (*conduct*)
des manières = manners

manif✗ *noun, feminine*
une manif✗ = a demo

manifestation *noun, feminine*
une manifestation = a demonstration
une manifestation sportive = a
sporting event

mannequin *noun, masculine*
un mannequin (*in a shop window*) = a
dummy, a mannequin
(*a person*) = a (fashion) model

manquer *verb* 1
• (*to fail to catch, hit, reach, see, hear*) = to
miss
manquer le train = to miss the train
• mes amis me manquent = I miss my
friends
ça t'a manqué? = did you miss it?
• (*impersonal use*) = to be missing
il manque un bouton = there's a button
missing
je ne peux pas l'acheter, il me manque dix
francs = I can't buy it, I'm ten francs
short
il te manque cinq francs pour payer la note
= you need five francs more to pay the
bill
• manquer de = to be short of
= to lack
• manquer à sa promesse = to break one's
promise

mansarde *noun, feminine*
une mansarde = an attic room

manteau *noun, masculine*
(*plural*) **manteaux**
un manteau = a coat

maquereau *noun, masculine*
(*plural*) **maquereaux**
un maquereau = a mackerel

maquette *noun, feminine*
une maquette = a scale model

maquillage *noun, masculine*
le maquillage = make-up

maquiller: se maquiller *verb* 1
(**!** + *être*)
se maquiller = to put on make-up
= to wear make-up

marbre *noun, masculine*
le marbre = marble

marchand/marchande *noun,*
masculine/feminine
un marchand/une marchande = a
shopkeeper
= a stallholder

marchandise *noun, feminine*
de la marchandise = goods

marche *noun, feminine*
• (*stair*)
une marche = a step
les marches = the stairs
• (*the sport*)
la marche = walking
• (*when talking about a machine, a*
mechanism)
être en marche = to be running
mettre le moteur en marche = to start the
engine up
• (*when talking about a vehicle*)
un train en marche = a moving train
faire marche arrière = to reverse
la marche à suivre = the procedure

M

marché *noun, masculine*
• (*a place*)
  un marché = a market
  faire son marché = to go shopping
• (*in business*)
  un marché = a deal
• **être bon marché** = to be cheap
le Marché Commun = the Common Market
un marché aux puces = a flea market

marcher *verb* ⊡
• = to walk
• = to work
  comment marche la tondeuse? = how does the mower work?
• (*if it's an event, a fest*)✶ = to go well
  les affaires marchent✶ bien = business is going well
  l'examen a marché✶? = how did the exam go?

mardi *noun, masculine*
  mardi = Tuesday
Mardi gras = Shrove Tuesday

mare *noun, feminine*
  une mare = a pond

marée *noun, feminine*
  la marée = the tide
  la marée monte = the tide is coming in
  la marée descend = the tide is going out
une marée noire = an oil slick

marelle *noun, feminine*
  la marelle = hopscotch

marge *noun, feminine*
  la marge = the margin

mari *noun, masculine*
  un mari = a husband

mariage *noun, masculine*
  un mariage = a wedding
            = a marriage

marié/mariée
1 *adjective*
  = married
2 *noun, masculine/feminine*
  le marié/la mariée = the bridegroom/the bride

marier *verb* ⊡
1 (**!** + *avoir*)
  = to marry
  ils ont marié leur fille = they married their daughter
2 se marier (**!** + *être*)
  se marier = to get married, to marry
  elle s'est mariée avec son cousin = she got married to her cousin, she married her cousin

marin/marine¹
1 *adjective*

• **le sel marin** = sea salt
• **un pull marin** = a seaman's jersey
2 marin *noun, masculine*
  un marin = a sailor

marine² *noun, feminine*
  la marine = the navy

marionnette *noun, feminine*
  une marionnette = a puppet

Maroc *noun, masculine*
  le Maroc = Morocco

marocain/marocaine *adjective*
  = Moroccan

maroquinerie *noun, feminine*
  une maroquinerie = a leather shop, a leather store

marque *noun, feminine*
• (*in commerce*)
  une marque = a brand, a make
  de marque française = French
• (*a trace*)
  une marque = a mark

marquer *verb* ⊡
• = to note (down), to write
• = to score
• = to mark, to make an impression

marraine *noun, feminine*
  une marraine = a godmother

marrant/marrante✶ *adjective*
  = funny

marre✶ *adverb*
  en avoir marre✶ = to be fed up

marrer: se marrer✶ *verb* ⊡ (**!** + *être*)
• **se marrer✶** = to laugh
• **se marrer✶** = to have a good laugh

marron
1 *adjective* (**!** *never changes*)
  = brown
2 *noun, masculine*
  un marron = a chestnut
  un marron (d'Inde) = a horse chestnut
des marrons chauds = roast chestnuts

mars *noun, masculine*
  mars = March

Marseillaise *noun, feminine*
  la Marseillaise = the Marseillaise (*the French national anthem*)

marteau *noun, masculine*
(*plural*) **marteaux**
  un marteau = a hammer
un marteau piqueur = a pneumatic drill, a jackhammer

mas *noun, masculine* (**!** *never changes*)
  un mas = a farmhouse (*in Provence*)

masque *noun, masculine*
  un masque = a mask

✶ in informal situations

mât *noun, masculine*
  un mât = a mast

match *noun, masculine*
  un match de football = a football match, a football game

matelas *noun, masculine* (**!** *never changes*)
  un matelas = a mattress
  un matelas pneumatique = an air bed, an air mattress

matériel *noun, masculine*
  le matériel = the equipment

mathématiques *noun, feminine plural*
  les mathématiques = mathematics

maths* *noun, feminine plural*
  les maths* = math(s)

matière *noun, feminine*
• (*something studied*)
  une matière = a subject
• (*a substance*)
  une matière = a material
  les matières grasses = fats
  les matières premières = raw materials

matin *noun, masculine*
  un matin = a morning
  demain matin = tomorrow morning
  de bon matin = early in the morning

matinal/matinale *adjective*
(*plural*) **matinaux/matinales**
  = early
  être matinal = to be an early riser

matinée *noun, feminine*
  la matinée = the morning
  faire la grasse matinée = to have a lie-in, to sleep in

mauvais/mauvaise
1 *adjective*
• = bad
  le mauvais temps = bad weather
  être mauvais en algèbre = to be bad at algebra
• = wrong
  la mauvaise adresse = the wrong address
2 mauvais *adverb*
• il fait mauvais = the weather is bad
• ça sent mauvais = it smells
  une mauvaise herbe = a weed

maximum *noun, masculine*
  un maximum = a maximum
  100 francs au maximum = 100 francs at (the) most

mayonnaise *noun, feminine*
  la mayonnaise = mayonnaise

me (**m'** *before vowel or mute h*) *pronoun*
• = me
  il m'a vu = he saw me
  elle ne me parle pas = she won't speak to me

• = myself
  je me suis coupé = I cut myself

mec* *noun, masculine*
  un mec* = a bloke, a guy

mécanicien/mécanicienne
  un mécanicien/une mécanicienne (*in a garage*) = a mechanic
  (*on a train*) = an engine driver, a locomotive engineer

mécanique
1 *adjective*
  = mechanical
  (*describing a toy*) = clockwork
2 *noun, feminine*
  la mécanique = mechanics

méchant/méchante *adjective*
  = nasty, mean

méchoui *noun, masculine*
  un méchoui = a North African style barbecue

mécontent/mécontente *adjective*
  = dissatisfied, displeased

médaille *noun, feminine*
  une médaille = a medal

médecin *noun, masculine*
  un médecin = a doctor

médical/médicale *adjective*
(*plural*) **médicaux/médicales**
  = medical

médicament *noun, masculine*
  un médicament = a medicine, a drug

médiéval/médiévale *adjective*
(*plural*) **médiévaux/médiévales**
  = medieval

Méditerranée *noun, feminine*
  la (mer) Méditerranée = the Mediterranean (Sea)

méfiant/méfiante *adjective*
  = suspicious, mistrustful

méfier: se méfier *verb* **2** (**!** | *être*)
• se méfier = to distrust
  je me méfie de ce garçon = I don't trust that boy
• se méfier = to be careful
  méfie-toi! = be careful

meilleur/meilleure
1 *adjective*
• = better
  le film est meilleur que le roman = the film is better than the novel
• = best
  le meilleur vin de la région = the best wine in the area
2 *noun, masculine/feminine*
  le meilleur/la meilleure = the best one

M

3 meilleur *adverb*
= better
il fait meilleur qu'hier = the weather is better than yesterday

mélanger *verb* 13
- (*to combine*) = to mix
- (*to muddle up*) = to mix up

melon *noun, masculine*
un melon = a melon

membre *noun, masculine*
- (*a person*)
un membre = a member
- (*an arm, a leg*)
un membre = a limb

même
1 *adjective*
= same
les mêmes bottes que les miennes = the same boots as mine
2 *pronoun*
le même/la même = the same one
3 *adverb*
- (*used for emphasis*) = even
il n'a même pas répondu = he didn't even reply
j'irai, même s'il pleut = I'll go, even if it rains
- (*exactly*) = very
aujourd'hui même = this very day
ici même = in this very place, right here

mémé✱ *noun, feminine*
ma mémé✱ = my gran, my granny

mémoire *noun, feminine*
la mémoire = memory

mémoriser *verb* 1
= to memorize

menacer *verb* 12
= to threaten

ménage *noun, masculine*
- (*cleaning*)
le ménage = the housework
- (*the people*)
un ménage = a couple
= a household

ménager/ménagère¹ *adjective*
= domestic
= household

ménagère² *noun, feminine*
une ménagère = a housewife

mendiant/mendiante *noun, masculine/feminine*
un mendiant/une mendiante = a beggar

mener *verb* 16
- = to lead
- = to take

mensonge *noun, masculine*
un mensonge = a lie

mensuel/mensuelle *adjective*
= monthly

menteur/menteuse *noun, masculine/feminine*
un menteur/une menteuse = a liar

menthe *noun, feminine*
la menthe = mint
une menthe à l'eau = a mint cordial

mentionner *verb* 1
= to mention

mentir *verb* 30
= to lie

menton *noun, masculine*
le menton = the chin

menu/menue
1 *adjective*
= small
2 menu *adverb*
hacher menu = to chop finely
3 menu *noun, masculine*
le menu = the menu
le menu à prix fixe = the set menu

mer *noun, feminine*
la mer = the sea

merci *noun, masculine* (also *exclamation*)
merci! = thank you!

mercredi *noun, masculine*
mercredi = Wednesday

merde✶ *exclamation*
= shit!

mère *noun, feminine*
une mère = a mother

méridional/méridionale *adjective*
(*plural*) **méridionaux/méridionales**
= southern

mériter *verb* 1
= to deserve

merveille *noun, feminine*
une merveille = a marvel, a wonder
faire des merveilles = to work wonders

merveilleux/merveilleuse *adjective*
= marvellous, wonderful

mes ▶ mon

mesdames ▶ madame

mesdemoiselles ▶ mademoiselle

messe *noun, feminine*
une messe = a mass

messieurs ▶ monsieur

mesure *noun, feminine*
- (*when determining size*)
une mesure = a measurement
sur mesure = made to measure

✱ in informal situations   ✶ may be considered offensive

- (a decision, a step)
  une mesure = a measure

mesurer verb 1
= to measure
combien mesures-tu? = how tall are you?
Paul mesure 1,80 m = Paul is six foot tall

météo noun, feminine
la météo = the weather forecast
la météo marine = the shipping forecast
la météo annonce de la pluie = the forecast is for rain

méthode noun, feminine
- (a way of doing things)
  une méthode = a method
- (a book)
  une méthode = a handbook
  = a textbook

métier noun, masculine
un métier = a job
= a trade

mètre noun, masculine
- (a unit of measurement)
  un mètre = a metre, a meter
- (an instrument)
  un mètre = a tape measure

métro noun, masculine
le métro = the underground, the subway

mets ▶ mettre 60

mettre verb 60
1 (! + avoir)
- = to put
  j'ai mis la lettre sur la table = I put the letter on the table
- = to put on
  il a mis son chapeau = he put on his hat
- (other uses)
  mettre le couvert = to set the table
  elle met une heure pour aller au bureau = it takes her one hour to get to the office
2 se mettre (! + être)
- (to place oneself)
  se mettre debout = to stand up
  il s'est mis à table = he sat down at the table
- (to apply, to wear)
  se mettre = to put on
  se mettre du rouge à lèvres = to put lipstick on
- (to begin)
  se mettre à [chanter | pleurer | écrire ...] = to start [singing | crying | writing ...]
  se mettre en colère = to lose one's temper, to get angry
  se mettre en route = to set off

meuble noun, masculine
un meuble = a piece of furniture
des meubles = furniture

meubler verb 1
= to furnish

meurtre noun, masculine
un meurtre = a murder

micro noun, masculine
un micro = a microphone

microbe noun, masculine
un microbe = a germ, a microbe

midi noun, masculine
- = twelve o'clock, midday, noon
  il est midi et demi = it's half past twelve, it's twelve thirty
- = lunchtime

Midi noun, masculine
le Midi = the South of France

miel noun, masculine
le miel = honey

mien/mienne pronoun
le mien/la mienne = mine
les miens/les miennes = mine

miette noun, feminine
une miette = a crumb

mieux adverb, adjective (! never changes)
= better

mignon/mignonne adjective
= sweet, cute

mijoter verb 1
- = to simmer
- = to prepare

milieu
(plural) **milieux**
1 noun, masculine
- (the centre)
  le milieu = the middle
- (the world around)
  le milieu (nature) = the environment
  (family) = the background
2 **au milieu de** = in the middle of
= among

militaire
1 adjective
= military
2 noun, masculine
un militaire = a soldier

mille
1 number (! never changes)
= a thousand, one thousand
2 noun, masculine
un mille (marin) = a (nautical) mile

milliard noun, masculine
un milliard = a billion

millier noun, masculine
un millier = a thousand
= about a thousand

million noun, masculine
un million = a million, one million

M

minable* *adjective*
= pathetic
= shabby

mince
1 *adjective*
= slim, thin, slender
2 *exclamation**
mince*! (*expressing annoyance*) = damn!
(*expressing amazement*) = wow!

minéral/minérale *adjective*
(*plural*) **minéraux/minérales**
= mineral

mineur/mineure
1 *adjective*
• (*under 18*) = underage
• (*not important*) = minor
2 *noun, masculine|feminine*
un mineur/une mineure = a minor
3 mineur *noun, masculine*
un mineur = a miner

Minitel   *noun, masculine*
le Minitel = Minitel (*a terminal linking
phone users to interactive databases*)

minuit *noun, masculine*
minuit = twelve o'clock, midnight

minuscule *adjective*
= tiny, minute

minute *noun, feminine*
une minute = a minute, one minute

miroir *noun, masculine*
un miroir = a mirror

mis/mise ▶ mettre 60

misérable *adjective*
= poor
= wretched

misère *noun, feminine*
la misère = poverty

mistral *noun, masculine*
le mistral = the mistral (*a cold north wind*)

mite *noun, feminine*
une mite = a (clothes) moth

mixte *adjective*
= mixed
(*describing a school*) = coeducational

Mlle (*abbreviation of* **Mademoiselle**)
Mlle = Miss, Ms

Mme (*abbreviation of* **Madame**)
Mme = Mrs, Ms

mobilier *noun, masculine*
le mobilier = the furniture

mobylette   *noun, feminine*
une mobylette = a moped

moche* *adjective*
• = ugly
• = awful

mode
1 *noun, feminine*
une mode = a fashion
être à la mode (*if it's clothes*) = to be
fashionable
(*if it's a singer, an actor*) = to be popular
2 *noun, masculine*
un mode de vie = a lifestyle

modèle *noun, masculine*
un modèle = a model
= a pattern

modéré/modérée *adjective*
= moderate

moi *pronoun*
= me
moi non plus = nor me, me neither
donne-la-moi = give it to me
ce sac est à moi = this bag belongs to me,
this bag is mine
c'est à moi de jouer = it's my turn to play
viens chez moi = come to my house
moi, je reste ici = I'm staying here

moi-même *pronoun*
= myself

moineau *noun, masculine*
(*plural*) **moineaux**
un moineau = a sparrow

moins
1 *preposition*
• = minus
= less
il fait moins cinq (degrés) = it's minus five
(degrees)
550 francs, moins la caution = 550 francs,
minus the deposit
• (*when talking about time*) = to
il est une heure moins le quart = it's a
quarter to one
2 *adverb*
• = less
moins intéressant = less interesting
moins cher que d'habitude = cheaper than
usual
de moins en moins = less and less
deux fois moins cher = twice as cheap
• **moins de** = less
= fewer
= less than
= under
un peu moins de sucre = a little less sugar
il a moins d'amis maintenant = he has
fewer friends now
moins de la moitié = less than half
• **moins... moins...** = the less... the less...
moins... plus... = the less... the more...
**moins je travaille, moins j'ai envie de
travailler** = the less I work, the less I feel
like working

___

* in informal situations

- **le moins/la moins** = the least
  = the less
  le coin le moins ensoleillé du jardin = the least sunny spot in the garden
  le moins cher des deux = the cheaper of the two
- **3 au moins** = at least
- **4 du moins** = at least
- **4 à moins que, à moins de** = unless

mois *noun, masculine* (**!** *never changes*)
  un mois = a month
  au mois de mai = in May

moisson *noun, feminine*
  la moisson = the harvest

moitié *noun, feminine*
  une moitié = a half
  à moitié prix = half-price

molle▶ mou

moment *noun, masculine*
  un moment = a moment, one moment
  en ce moment = at the moment
  par moments = at times
  juste au moment où il allait partir = just as he was about to leave

mon/ma *determiner*
(*plural*) **mes**
  = my

monde *noun, masculine*
- **le monde** = the world
  faire le tour du monde en bateau = to sail around the world
  le monde des affaires = the business world
- **il y a du monde, il y a beaucoup de monde** = there are a lot of people
  tout le monde = everybody

moniteur/monitrice
1 *noun, masculine/feminine*
  un moniteur/une monitrice (*for skiers, drivers*) = an instructor
  (*in a holiday camp*) = a group leader, a counselor
2 moniteur *noun, masculine*
  un moniteur (*a screen*) = a monitor

monnaie *noun, feminine*
- **la monnaie** = change
- **une monnaie** = a currency

monsieur *noun, masculine*
(*plural*) **messieurs**
  un monsieur = a gentleman
  bonjour messieurs = good morning (gentlemen)
  Monsieur Martin = Mr Martin

monstre
1 *adjective*
  monstre* = huge
2 *noun, masculine*
  un monstre = a monster

montagne *noun, feminine*
  une montagne = a mountain

montagneux/montagneuse
adjective
  = mountainous

montant/montante
1 *adjective*
- **un col montant** = a high collar
- **la marée montante** = the rising tide
2 montant *noun, masculine*
  le montant (*on a bill*) = the total

monter *verb* ☐1
1 (**!** + *être*)
- = to go up
  elle est montée au village = she's gone up to the village
  tu es monté à pied? = did you walk up?
  nous sommes montés en courant = we ran up
- = to go upstairs
  montez, le bureau est à l'étage au-dessus = go upstairs, the office is on the next floor
- = to come up
  = to come upstairs
  je suis dans le grenier, monte = I'm in the attic, come up
- = to get in(to)
  = to get on
  elle est montée dans la voiture = she got into the car
  monter dans un avion = to get on a plane
- = to climb
  ne monte pas sur la table = don't climb onto the table
- = to rise, to go up
  les prix montent = prices are rising, prices are going up
- (*other uses*)
  monter à bicyclette = to ride a bicycle
  monter à cheval = to ride
2 (**!** + *avoir*)
- = to go up
  il a monté la colline en vélo = he cycled up the hill
- = to take up(stairs)
  je vais monter les bagages = I'm going to take the luggage up(stairs)
- = to bring up
  peux-tu me monter mes lunettes? = can you bring my glasses up to me?
- = to put up
  monter une tente = to put up a tent

montgolfière *noun, feminine*
  une montgolfière = a hot air balloon

montre *noun, feminine*
  une montre = a watch

montrer *verb* ☐1
  = to show

monument *noun, masculine*
  un monument = a monument
  un monument historique = a historical building
  un monument aux morts* = a war memorial

moquer: **se moquer de** *verb* 1
(**!** + *être*)
- (*to mock*)
  se moquer de = to make fun of
- (*to dismiss*)
  se moquer de = not to care about
  je m'en moque = I don't care

moquette *noun, feminine*
  une moquette = a fitted carpet, wall-to-wall carpeting

moral *noun, masculine*
  le moral = morale
  avoir le moral, avoir bon moral = to be in good spirits
  avoir le moral à zéro✱ = to feel very down

morceau *noun, masculine*
(*plural*) **morceaux**
  un morceau = a piece
  un morceau de sucre = a lump of sugar

mordre *verb* 6
  = to bite

morpion *noun, masculine*
  le morpion = noughts and crosses

mort¹ *noun, feminine*
  la mort = death

mort²/morte
1 ► **mourir** 25
2 *adjective*
  = dead
  être mort de peur = to be scared stiff
3 *noun, masculine|feminine*
  un mort/une morte = a dead man/a dead woman

mosquée *noun, feminine*
  une mosquée = a mosque

mot *noun, masculine*
- **un mot** = a word
- (*a message*)
  un mot = a note
  des mots croisés = a crossword puzzle

motard *noun, masculine*
  un motard = a motorcyclist, a biker
  = a police motorcyclist

mot-clé *noun, masculine*
(*plural*) **mots-clés**
  un mot-clé = a key word

moteur *noun, masculine*
  un moteur = an engine
  = a motor

moto *noun, feminine*
  une moto = a motorbike, a motorcycle

mou/molle *adjective*
- (*describing things*) = soft
  = limp

- (*describing a person*) = spineless
  = lethargic

mouche *noun, feminine*
  une mouche = a fly

mouchoir *noun, masculine*
  un mouchoir = a handkerchief

mouette *noun, feminine*
  une mouette = a seagull

mouiller *verb* 1
1 (**!** + *avoir*)
  = to wet
2 **se mouiller** (**!** + *être*)
  se mouiller = to get wet

moule
1 *noun, feminine*
  une moule = a mussel
2 *noun, masculine*
  un moule = a mould
  = a (baking) tin, a pan

mourir *verb* 25 (**!** + *être*)
  = to die
  il est mort en avril = he died in April
  je meurs [de faim | de soif | de froid …]! = I'm [starving | parched | freezing …]!
  il meurt d'envie de te le dire = he's dying to tell you

mousse *noun, feminine*
- (*a plant*)
  la mousse = moss
- (*bubbles*)
  la mousse = foam
  = lather
  = froth
- (*in cooking*)
  une mousse au chocolat = a chocolate mousse
- (*a material*)
  la mousse = foam rubber

moustache *noun, feminine*
- (*on a man*)
  une moustache = a moustache
- (*on an animal*)
  des moustaches = whiskers

moustique *noun, masculine*
  un moustique = a mosquito

moutarde *noun, feminine*
  la moutarde = mustard

mouton *noun, masculine*
  un mouton = a sheep

moyen/moyenne¹
1 *adjective*
  = average
  = medium
2 **moyen** *noun, masculine*
  un moyen = a means
  = a way
  un moyen de transport = a means of transport
  c'est le seul moyen = it's the only way

✱ in informal situations

3 moyens *noun, masculine plural*
  des moyens (*money*) = means
  je n'ai pas les moyens de voyager = I can't
    afford to travel
le Moyen Âge = the Middle Ages

moyenne² *noun, feminine*
• (*in statistics*)
  la moyenne = the average
  en moyenne = on average
• (*in an exam*)
  la moyenne = half marks, 50%

moyennement *adverb*
  = moderately
  = fairly

Moyen-Orient *noun, masculine*
  le Moyen-Orient = the Middle East

muet/muette *adjective*
• = dumb
• = silent

muguet *noun, masculine*
  le muguet = lily of the valley

multiplier *verb* 2
  = to multiply

municipal/municipale *adjective*
(*plural*) **municipaux/municipales**
  = municipal

municipalité *noun, feminine*
  la municipalité = the (local) council

munir: se munir de *verb* 3 (**!** + *être*)
  se munir de = to equip oneself with

mur *noun, masculine*
  un mur = a wall
le mur du son = the sound barrier

mûr/mûre¹ *adjective*
• (*describing fruit*) = ripe
• (*describing people*) = mature

muraille *noun, feminine*
  une muraille = a great wall

mûre² *noun, feminine*
  une mûre = a blackberry

murmurer *verb* 1
• = to murmur
• = to whisper

musclé/musclée *adjective*
  = muscular

musculation *noun, feminine*
  la musculation = body-building

musée *noun, masculine*
  un musée = a museum, a gallery

musicien/musicienne *noun,*
masculine/feminine
  un musicien/une musicienne = a musician

musique *noun, feminine*
  la musique = music

mutinerie *noun, feminine*
  une mutinerie = a mutiny

mystère *noun, masculine*
  un mystère = a mystery

mystérieux/mystérieuse *adjective*
  = mysterious

Nn

n' ▶ **ne**

nage *noun, feminine*
  la nage = swimming
  traverser le fleuve à la nage = to swim
    across the river

nager *verb* 13
  = to swim

nain/naine
1 *adjective*
  = dwarf
  = miniature
2 *noun, masculine/feminine*
  un nain/une naine = a dwarf

naissance *noun, feminine*
  la naissance = birth
  à ma naissance = when I was born

naître *verb* 64 (**!** + *être*)
  = to be born
  il est né le 10 janvier = he was born on 10
    January

nappe *noun, feminine*
  une nappe = a tablecloth
  une nappe de brouillard = a blanket of fog

narine *noun, feminine*
  une narine = a nostril

natal/natale *adjective*
(*plural*) **natals/natales**
  = native

natation *noun, feminine*
  la natation = swimming

national/nationale¹ *adjective*
(*plural*) **nationaux/nationales**
  = national

nationale² *noun, feminine*
  une nationale = a trunk road, a highway

nature
1 *adjective* (**!** *never changes*)
  = plain
  un yaourt nature = a plain yogurt
  un thé nature = a black tea

N

2 *noun, feminine*
 la nature = nature
 la protection de la nature = the protection
  of the environment
une nature morte = a still life

naturel/naturelle
1 *adjective*
  = natural
2 naturel *noun, masculine*
 • être d'un naturel timide = to be shy by
  nature
 • il manque de naturel = he's not very
  natural
 • du thon au naturel = tuna in brine

naufrage *noun, masculine*
 un naufrage = a shipwreck
 faire naufrage (*if it's a ship*) = to be
  wrecked
 (*if it's a crew*) = to be shipwrecked

nausée *noun, feminine*
 la nausée = nausea
 avoir la nausée = to feel sick, to feel
  nauseous

nautique *adjective*
 les sports nautiques = water sports

navet *noun, masculine*
 un navet = a turnip

navette *noun, feminine*
 une navette = a shuttle
  = a shuttle service
 faire la navette = to travel back and forth
  = to commute

navire *noun, masculine*
 un navire = a ship

navré/navrée *adjective*
 je suis vraiment navré = I'm terribly sorry
 avoir l'air navré = to look upset

ne (**n'** *before vowel or mute h*) *adverb*

 ! *In cases where* ne *is used with* aucun,
 guère, jamais, pas, personne, plus, rien
 *etc, one should consult the
 corresponding entry.* ne + verb + que *is
 treated in the entry below.*

 je ne sais pas = I don't know
 je n'ai que 10 francs = I've only got 10
  francs
 tu n'avais qu'à le dire = you only had to
  say so

né/née ▶ naître 64

néanmoins *adverb*
  = nevertheless

nécessaire
1 *adjective*
  = necessary

2 *noun, masculine*
 • faire le nécessaire pour les billets = to see
  about the tickets
 • le strict nécessaire = the bare essentials

néerlandais/néerlandaise
1 *adjective*
  = Dutch
2 néerlandais *noun, masculine*
 le néerlandais = Dutch

néfaste *adjective*
  = harmful

négatif/négative *adjective*
  = negative

négliger *verb* 13
  = to neglect

neige *noun, feminine*
 la neige = snow
 des blancs d'œufs battus en neige
  = stiffly beaten eggwhites

neiger *verb* 13
  = to snow
 il neige = it's snowing

nénuphar *noun, masculine*
 un nénuphar = a waterlily

nerf *noun, masculine*
 un nerf = a nerve
 il me tape sur les nerfs✱ = he gets on my
  nerves

nerveux/nerveuse *adjective*
  = nervous, tense

n'est-ce pas *adverb*
 c'est grand, n'est-ce pas? = it's big, isn't it?
 tu viendras, n'est-ce pas? = you will
  come, won't you?

net/nette
1 *adjective*
 • (*describing prices or weights*) = net
 • (*free from stains or clutter*) = clean
 • (*easy to see or understand*) = clear
2 net *adverb*
 s'arrêter net = to stop dead
 refuser net = to refuse flatly

nettoyer *verb* 23
  = to clean

neuf¹ *number*
  = nine

neuf²/neuve *adjective*
  = new
 une voiture toute neuve = a brand new car

neuvième *number*
  = ninth

neveu *noun, masculine*
 (*plural*) **neveux**
 un neveu = a nephew

nez *noun, masculine* (! *never changes*)
 le nez = the nose

✱ in informal situations

ni *conjunction*
 ni anglais ni espagnol = neither English nor Spanish
 elle ne veut pas le voir ni lui parler = she doesn't wish to see him or talk to him
 ni l'un ni l'autre = neither of them

niche *noun, feminine*
• (*for a dog*)
 une niche = a kennel, a doghouse
• (*in a wall*)
 une niche = a recess

nid *noun, masculine*
 un nid = a nest

nièce *noun, feminine*
 une nièce = a niece

nier *verb* 2
 = to deny

n'importe ▶ **importer** 1

niveau *noun, masculine*
(*plural*) **niveaux**
 un niveau = a level
 = a standard
 le niveau de vie = the standard of living

noce *noun, feminine*
 une noce = a wedding
 des noces d'argent = a silver wedding anniversary

nocturne *adjective*
 = nocturnal
 = night

Noël *noun, masculine*
 Noël = Christmas

nœud *noun, masculine*
 un nœud = a knot
 un nœud papillon = a bow tie

noir/noire *adjective*
• = black
• = dark

noisette *noun, feminine*
 une noisette = a hazelnut

noix *noun, feminine* (**!** *never changes*)
 une noix = a walnut, an English walnut

nom
1 *noun, masculine*
• **un nom** = a name
• **un nom** = a noun
2 au nom de = in the name of
 = on behalf of
 un nom de famille = a surname, a last name
 un nom de jeune fille = a maiden name

nombre *noun, masculine*
 un nombre = a number
 un certain nombre de personnes = some people

nombreux/nombreuse *adjective*
 = large
 = many
 une foule nombreuse = a large crowd
 de nombreuses personnes = many people
 ils sont peu nombreux = there are few of them

nommer *verb* 1
1 (**!** + *avoir*)
• = to name
 = to call
 nommer un enfant Olivier = to name a child Olivier
 une plage nommée 'La Salie' = a beach called 'La Salie'
• = to appoint
 être nommé à Paris = to be posted to Paris
2 se nommer (**!** + *être*)
 se nommer = to be called

non
1 *adverb*
• = no
 ah, ça non! = definitely not
 je pense que non = I don't think so
• = non
 non alcoolisé = nonalcoholic
2 non plus
 je ne suis pas d'accord non plus = I don't agree either
 il n'a pas aimé le film, moi non plus = he didn't like the film, neither did I

nonante *number*
 = ninety

nord
1 *noun, masculine*
 le nord = the north
2 *adjective* (**!** *never changes*)
 = north
 = northern

normal/normale *adjective*
(*plural*) **normaux/normales**
 = normal
 il est normal qu'il soit triste = it's natural that he should be sad

normalement *adverb*
 = normally

normand/normande *adjective*
 = Norman
 = from Normandy
 la côte normande = the Normandy coast

Normandie *noun, feminine*
 la Normandie = Normandy

Norvège *noun, feminine*
 la Norvège = Norway

norvégien/norvégienne
1 *adjective*
 = Norwegian
2 norvégien *noun, masculine*
 le norvégien = Norwegian

N

nos ▶ notre

note noun, feminine
- (in a hotel)
  la note = the bill, the check
- (in music)
  une note = a note
- (at school)
  une note = a mark, a grade
- (words taken down)
  des notes = notes

noter verb [1]
- = to write down
- = to notice
- = to mark, to grade

notre determiner
(plural) **nos**
= our

nôtre pronoun
le nôtre/la nôtre/les nôtres = ours

nouille noun, feminine
les nouilles = noodles, pasta

nourrir verb [3]
1 (! + avoir)
= to feed
= to nourish
2 se nourrir (! + être)
se nourrir = to feed
= to eat

nourriture noun, feminine
la nourriture = food

nous pronoun
- = we
  = us
  nous avons froid = we're cold
  donne-nous le livre = give us the book
  la voiture est à nous = the car is ours
  c'est à nous de jouer = it's our turn to play
  il nous l'a prêté = he lent it to us
- = ourselves
  nous nous soignons = we look after
    ourselves
  nous nous levons tôt = we get up early
- = each other
  nous nous aimons = we love each other

nouveau/nouvelle¹
(plural) **nouveaux/nouvelles**
1 adjective

> ! nouvel is used instead of nouveau
> before masculine nouns that begin with a
> vowel or a mute h. The plural of nouvel is
> nouveaux.

= new
le Nouvel An = the New Year
c'est tout nouveau = it's brand new
2 noun, masculine|feminine
le nouveau/la nouvelle (a pupil) = the new
  boy/the new girl

3 de nouveau = (once) again

nouveau-né noun, masculine
(plural) **nouveau-nés**
un nouveau-né = a newborn baby

nouvel ▶ nouveau 1

nouvelle² noun, feminine
une nouvelle = a piece of news
la nouvelle = the news
les nouvelles = the news
tu connais la nouvelle? = have you heard
  the news?

Nouvelle-Zélande noun, feminine
la Nouvelle-Zélande = New Zealand

novembre noun, masculine
novembre = November

noyau noun, masculine
(plural) **noyaux**
un noyau = a stone, a pit

noyé/noyée noun, masculine|feminine
un noyé/une noyée = a drowned person

noyer
1 noun, masculine
un noyer = a walnut tree
2 verb [23] (! + avoir)
= to drown
3 se noyer (! + être)
se noyer = to drown

nu/nue adjective
= naked, bare

nuage noun, masculine
un nuage = a cloud

nuageux/nuageuse adjective
= cloudy

nuance noun, feminine
- (a colour)
  une nuance = a shade
- (between two things)
  une nuance = a slight difference

nuée noun, feminine
une nuée = a swarm

nuire verb [62]
nuire à = to harm
= to be harmful to

nuisible adjective
= harmful

nuit noun, feminine
une nuit = a night
cette nuit = last night
= tonight
il fait nuit = it's dark
une nuit blanche = a sleepless night

nul/nulle
1 adjective
- (describing a person)✘ = hopeless
  (describing a piece of work)✘ = worthless
  (describing a film, a book)✘ = trashy

___
✘ in informal situations

- (*in sports*)
  un match nul = a draw, a tie
  faire match nul = to draw, to tie
2 *determiner*
  nul [homme | pays | besoin ...] = no [man | country | need ...]
  nul autre que vous = no-one else but you
3 *pronoun*
  = no-one
4 nulle part = nowhere

numéro *noun, masculine*
- (*for a house, a telephone, a ticket*)
  un numéro = a number
  un numéro de téléphone = a telephone number
- (*a magazine*)
  un numéro = a copy, an issue

nuque *noun, feminine*
  la nuque = the nape (of the neck)

obéir *verb* 3
  = to obey
  obéir à son maître = to obey one's master

obéissant/obéissante *adjective*
  = obedient

objet *noun, masculine*
  un objet = an object
  des objets de valeur = valuables
objets trouvés = lost property, lost and found

obligatoire *adjective*
  = compulsory

obliger *verb* 13
  obliger un enfant à manger = to make a child eat, to force a child to eat
  je suis obligé de partir = I have to go

obscur/obscure *adjective*
- = dark
- = obscure

obscurité *noun, feminine*
  l'obscurité = darkness

obsèques *noun, feminine plural*
  les obsèques = the funeral

observateur/observatrice *noun, masculine/feminine*
  un observateur/une observatrice = an observer

observer *verb* 1
- = to watch
- = to notice
- = to observe

obtenir *verb* 36
  = to get, to obtain

occasion *noun, feminine*
- (*a chance*)
  une occasion = an opportunity
- **une voiture d'occasion** = a second-hand car
- (*a circumstance*)
  une occasion = an occasion

occident *noun, masculine*
  l'occident = the west

occidental/occidentale *adjective*
(*plural*) **occidentaux/occidentales**
  = western

occupé/occupée *adjective*
- (*having a lot to do*) = busy
- (*not vacant*) = engaged

occuper *verb* 1
1 (! + *avoir*)
- = to occupy
- = to keep busy
  ça m'occupe = it keeps me busy
2 s'occuper (! + *être*)
- **s'occuper** = to keep oneself busy, to occupy oneself
- **s'occuper de** = to take care of, to look after

océan *noun, masculine*
  un océan = an ocean

octante *number*
  = eighty

octobre *noun, masculine*
  octobre = October

odeur *noun, feminine*
  une odeur = a smell

odieux/odieuse *adjective*
  = horrible, hateful

œil *noun, masculine*
(*plural*) **yeux**
  un œil = an eye

œillet *noun, masculine*
  un œillet = a carnation

œuf *noun, masculine*
  un œuf = an egg
  un œuf à la coque = a boiled egg
  un œuf dur = a hard-boiled egg
  un œuf sur le plat = a fried egg

œuvre *noun, feminine*
  une œuvre = a work

offense *noun, feminine*
  une offense = an insult

offenser *verb* 1
  = to offend

office *noun, masculine*
- (*in church*)
  un office = a service

O

- (*an organization*)
  un office = an office
  l'office du tourisme = the tourist office

offre *noun, feminine*
une offre = an offer
'offres d'emploi' = 'situations vacant'

offrir *verb* 4
1 (! + *avoir*)
- = to offer
- = to give
2 s'offrir (! + *être*)
s'offrir une croisière = to treat oneself to a cruise

oie *noun, feminine*
une oie = a goose

oignon *noun, masculine*
un oignon = an onion

oiseau *noun, masculine*
(*plural*) **oiseaux**
un oiseau = a bird

olivier *noun, masculine*
un olivier = an olive tree

ombre *noun, feminine*
- (*darkness*)
  l'ombre = shade
- (*a shape*)
  une ombre = a shadow

ombrelle *noun, feminine*
une ombrelle = a sunshade, a parasol

omnibus *noun, masculine* (! *never changes*)
un (train) omnibus = a slow train, a local train

omoplate *noun, feminine*
l'omoplate = the shoulder blade

on *pronoun*
- = someone
  on t'appelle = someone's calling you
- = we
  on a eu un accident = we had an accident
- = one
  = you
  = they
  on est obligé de payer à l'avance = one has to pay in advance
  = you have to pay in advance
  on vend des fleurs au supermarché = they sell flowers at the supermarket
- = people
  je me moque de ce qu'on dit = I don't care what people say
- (*other possible translations*)
  on m'a demandé ma carte = I was asked for my card
  on a réparé la route = the road has been repaired

oncle *noun, masculine*
un oncle = an uncle

ondulé/ondulée *adjective*
= wavy

ongle *noun, masculine*
un ongle = a nail

ont ▶ avoir 8

onze *number*
= eleven

onzième *number*
= eleventh

opération *noun, feminine*
- (*in mathematics*)
  une opération = a calculation
- (*on a patient*)
  une opération = an operation

opérer *verb* 14
= to operate
se faire opérer = to have an operation

opinion *noun, feminine*
une opinion = an opinion

opposé/opposée *adjective*
= opposite

optimiste *adjective*
= optimistic

or *noun, masculine*
l'or = gold
une montre en or = a gold watch

orage *noun, masculine*
un orage = a storm

orageux/orageuse *adjective*
= stormy

orchestre *noun, masculine*
un orchestre = an orchestra
= a band

ordinaire *adjective*
= ordinary

ordinateur *noun, masculine*
un ordinateur = a computer

ordonnance *noun, feminine*
une ordonnance = a prescription

ordre *noun, masculine*
- (*a command*)
  un ordre = an order
- (*a way of arranging things*)
  dans l'ordre = in order
- (*neatness*)
  l'ordre = tidiness
  mettre de l'ordre = to tidy up, to clean up

ordures *noun, feminine plural*
les ordures = rubbish, garbage, trash

oreille *noun, feminine*
une oreille = an ear

oreiller *noun, masculine*
un oreiller = a pillow

organisateur/organisatrice *noun,*
masculine/feminine
  un organisateur/une organisatrice = an
  organizer

organiser *verb* $\boxed{1}$
  1 (**!** + *avoir*)
  = to organize
  2 s'organiser (**!** + *être*)
  s'organiser = to get organized

organisme *noun, masculine*
  un organisme = an organization, a body

orge *noun, feminine*
  l'orge = barley

orgueil *noun, masculine*
  l'orgueil = pride

orgueilleux/orgueilleuse *adjective*
  = proud

orient *noun, masculine*
  l'orient = the east

oriental/orientale *adjective*
(*plural*) **orientaux/orientales**
  = eastern

originaire *adjective*
  être originaire d'un pays = to come from a
  country, to be a native of a country

original/originale *adjective*
(*plural*) **originaux/originales**
  • = original
  • = eccentric, unusual

origine *noun, feminine*
  l'origine = the origin

orner *verb* $\boxed{1}$
  = to decorate

orphelin/orpheline *noun,*
masculine/feminine
  un orphelin/une orpheline = an orphan

orteil *noun, masculine*
  un orteil = a toe

orthographe *noun, feminine*
  l'orthographe = spelling

ortie *noun, feminine*
  une ortie = a (stinging) nettle

os *noun, masculine* (**!** *never changes*)
  un os = a bone

oser *verb* $\boxed{1}$
  = to dare

osier *noun, masculine*
  l'osier = wicker

otage *noun, masculine*
  un otage = a hostage

ôter *verb* $\boxed{1}$
  = to take off, to remove

ou *conjunction*
  • = or
  ou bien = or else
  • ou (bien)... ou (bien)... = either... or...

où
  1 *adverb*
  = where
  d'où vient le bus? = where does the bus
  come from?
  2 *pronoun*
  • = where
  restez où vous êtes = stay where you are
  • = when
  juste au moment où il partait = just as he
  was leaving

oublier *verb* $\boxed{2}$
  = to forget

ouest
  1 *noun, masculine*
  l'ouest = the west
  2 *adjective* (**!** *never changes*)
  = west, western

ouf *exclamation*
  ouf! = phew!

oui *adverb*
  = yes
  je crois que oui = I think so

ouragan *noun, masculine*
  un ouragan = a hurricane

ourlet *noun, masculine*
  un ourlet = a hem

ours *noun, masculine* (**!** *never changes*)
  un ours = a bear
  un ours en peluche = a teddy bear

oursin *noun, masculine*
  un oursin = a sea urchin

outil *noun, masculine*
  un outil = a tool

outre-mer *adverb*
  = overseas

ouvert/ouverte
  1 ▶ **ouvrir** $\boxed{32}$
  2 *adjective*
  = open

ouverture *noun, feminine*
  une ouverture = an opening

ouvrable *adjective*
  un jour ouvrable = a working day

ouvrage *noun, masculine*
  un ouvrage = a (piece of) work, a project
  = a book, a work

ouvre-boîtes *noun, masculine* (**!** *never*
changes)
  un ouvre-boîtes = a can-opener

ouvreur/ouvreuse *noun,*
masculine/feminine
  un ouvreur/une ouvreuse = an usher/an
  usherette

O

ouvrier/ouvrière
1 *noun, masculine|feminine*
  un ouvrier/une ouvrière = a worker
2 *adjective*
  = working-class

ouvrir *verb* 32
1 (**!** + *avoir*)
  = to open
2 **s'ouvrir** (**!** + *être*)
  s'ouvrir = to open

Pp

pagaille✗
1 *noun, feminine*
  une pagaille✗ = a mess
  mettre la pagaille✗ = to cause chaos
2 **en pagaille✗**
  il y a du vin en pagaille✗ = there's loads of
  wine, there's lots of wine

page *noun, feminine*
  une page = a page

paille *noun, feminine*
  la paille = straw

pain *noun, masculine*
• **le pain** = bread
• **un pain** = a loaf
  le pain grillé = toast
  un petit pain = a bread roll

pair/paire¹
1 *adjective*
  les nombres pairs = even numbers
2 **au pair**
  une jeune fille au pair = an au pair

paire² *noun, feminine*
  une paire = a pair

paisible *adjective*
  = peaceful

paix *noun, feminine* (**!** *never changes*)
  la paix = peace
  = peace and quiet

palais *noun, masculine* (**!** *never changes*)
• **un palais** = a palace
• **le palais** = the palate

pâle *adjective*
  = pale

palier *noun, masculine*
  le palier = the landing

palmier *noun, masculine*
  un palmier = a palm tree

pamplemousse *noun, masculine*
  un pamplemousse = a grapefruit

panaché *noun, masculine*
  un (demi-)panaché = a shandy, a beer with
  lemonade

pancarte *noun, feminine*
  une pancarte = a notice, a sign
  = a placard

panier *noun, masculine*
  un panier = a basket

paniquer✗ *verb* 1
  = to panic

panne *noun, feminine*
  une panne = a breakdown
  tomber en panne = to break down
  tomber en panne d'essence = to run out
  of petrol, to run out of gas
une panne de courant = a power failure

panneau *noun, masculine*
(*plural*) **panneaux**
• **un panneau** = a panel
• **un panneau** = a sign
un panneau d'affichage = a noticeboard
un panneau de signalisation routière
  = a road sign

pansement *noun, masculine*
  un pansement = a dressing, a bandage
un pansement adhésif = a plaster, a
  Band-Aid

pantalon *noun, masculine*
  un pantalon = (a pair of) trousers, (a pair
  of) pants

pantoufle *noun, feminine*
  une pantoufle = a slipper

paon *noun, masculine*
  un paon = a peacock

papa *noun, masculine*
  un papa = a dad

pape *noun, masculine*
  le pape = the pope

papeterie *noun, feminine*
  une papeterie = a stationer's

papier *noun, masculine*
  le papier = paper
  le papier alu(minium) = aluminium foil,
  aluminum foil
le papier d'emballage = wrapping paper
le papier hygiénique = toilet paper
le papier peint = wallpaper
les papiers (d'identité) = (identity)
  papers

papillon *noun, masculine*
  un papillon = a butterfly

pâquerette *noun, feminine*
  une pâquerette = a daisy

Pâques *noun, masculine*
  Pâques = Easter

✗ in informal situations

paquet noun, masculine
• **un paquet** = a packet
• **un paquet** = a parcel, a package

par
1 preposition
• = by
  il a été piqué par une abeille = he was stung by a bee
  payer par carte de crédit = to pay by credit card
• = through
  le chemin passe par la forêt = the path goes through the forest
  par ici = this way, through here
• = per
  = a
  par personne = per person
  trois par [jour | mois | an ...] = three a [day | month | year ...]
• = in
  mettez-vous deux par deux = stand in twos
  sortir par mauvais temps = to go out in bad weather
• = on
  par une froide journée d'hiver = on a cold winter's day
• = out of
  regarder par la fenêtre = to look out (of) the window
  par bêtise = out of stupidity
2 par contre = on the other hand

parachute noun, masculine
• (the equipment)
  un parachute = a parachute
• (the sport)
  le parachute = parachuting

parages noun, masculine plural
  dans les parages = in the area

paraître verb 63
1 (! + avoir)
• (to create an impression) = to seem, to look
• (to be seen) = to appear
  paraître en public = to appear in public
2 (! + être)
  (if it's a book, a record) = to come out
3 il paraît que = apparently
  il paraît que non = apparently not

parapente noun, masculine
• (the equipment)
  un parapente = a paraglider
• (the sport)
  le parapente = paragliding

parapluie noun, masculine
  un parapluie = an umbrella

parasol noun, masculine
  un parasol = a sunshade, a beach umbrella

parc noun, masculine
  un parc = a park
un parc d'attractions = an amusement park

parce que (**parce qu'** before vowel or mute h) conjunction
  = because

par-ci adverb
  par-ci par-là = here and there

parcmètre noun, masculine
  un parcmètre = a parking meter

parcourir verb 26
• = to cover
  parcourir une distance = to cover a distance
• = to go all over
  parcourir toute la ville = to go all over the town
• = to glance through
  parcourir un article = to glance through an article

parcours noun, masculine (! never changes)
  un parcours = a journey
  = a route

parcouru/parcourue ▶ **parcourir** 26

pardessus noun, masculine (! never changes)
  un pardessus = an overcoat

pardon noun, masculine
• **le pardon** = forgiveness
  demander pardon = to apologize
  = to ask for forgiveness
• **pardon!** = sorry!
  pardon monsieur, je cherche la mairie = excuse me, I'm looking for the town hall

pardonner verb 1
  = to forgive

pare-brise noun, masculine (! never changes)
  un pare-brise = a windscreen, a windshield

pareil/pareille
1 adjective
• = the same
  = similar
  = identical
• = such
  je n'ai jamais vu un luxe pareil = I've never seen such luxury
2 pareil* adverb
  = the same
  faisons pareil* = let's do the same

parent/parente
1 noun, masculine/feminine
  un parent/une parente = a relative, a relation
2 parents noun, masculine plural
  les parents = parents

parenthèse noun, feminine
  entre parenthèses = between brackets

P

paresse noun, feminine
la paresse = laziness

paresseux/paresseuse adjective
= lazy

parfait/parfaite adjective
= perfect

parfois adverb
= sometimes

parfum noun, masculine
un parfum = a perfume
= a flavo(u)r

parfumé/parfumée adjective
= scented
= flavo(u)red

parier verb [2]
= to bet

parisien/parisienne adjective
= Parisian

parking noun, masculine
un parking = a car park, a parking lot

parler verb [1]
= to talk
= to speak

parmi preposition
= among

paroisse noun, feminine
une paroisse = a parish

parole noun, feminine
une parole = a word
prendre la parole = to speak
à vous la parole! = your turn to speak!

parrain noun, masculine
un parrain = a godfather

part
1 noun, feminine
• (when dividing)
une part (of food) = a portion
(of a legacy) = a share
• (meaning direction, place)
de toutes parts = from all sides, from
everywhere
nulle part = nowhere
quelque part = somewhere
d'une part... d'autre part = on the one
hand... on the other hand
faire part d'une naissance = to announce
a birth
2 de la part de = from
= on behalf of
elle m'a fait part de sa décision = she
informed me of her decision
3 à part = apart (from)

partager verb [13]
= to share

***** in informal situations

partenaire noun, masculine/feminine
un partenaire/une partenaire = a partner

parterre noun, masculine
• (in a garden)
un parterre = a bed
• (in a theatre)
le parterre = the stalls, the orchestra

participer verb [1]
• participer (à) = to take part (in)
• participer à = to share in

particulier/particulière adjective
= particular
= special

partie
1 noun, feminine
• (not the whole)
une partie = (a) part
• (at cards, in sport)
une partie = a game
2 en partie = partly, in part
3 faire partie de = to be part of
ça fait partie de mon travail = it's part of
my job
faire partie d'un club = to be a member of
a club

partir
1 verb [30] (! + être)
• = to leave
partir en courant = to run off
• = to go
partir à Paris = to go to Paris
• = to start
le sentier part du bois = the path starts in
the wood
2 à partir de = from
à partir de maintenant = from now on

partout adverb
= everywhere

paru ▶ paraître [63]

parvenir verb [36] (! + être)
• parvenir à = to achieve
parvenir à son but = to achieve one's goal
parvenir à faire = to manage to do
• parvenir à = to reach
parvenir à New York = to reach New York

parvenu/parvenue ▶ parvenir [36]

pas
1 adverb
= not
pas du tout = not at all
le film n'est pas mal***** = the film isn't bad
2 noun, masculine (! never changes)
• (a movement)
un pas = a step
c'est à deux pas d'ici = it's very near here
• (speed)
le pas = the pace
d'un pas lent = slowly

passage noun, masculine
• (a section of a text, a film)
un passage = a passage

- (*a means of access*)
  un passage = a way
  céder le passage = to give way, to yield
  'passage interdit' = 'no entry'
- **être de passage** = to be passing through
un passage à niveau = a level crossing, a
  grade crossing
un passage pour piétons = a pedestrian
  crossing, a crosswalk
un passage souterrain = a subway, a
  pedestrian underpass

passager/passagère *noun,*
masculine/feminine
  un passager/une passagère = a passenger
un passager clandestin = a stowaway

passant/passante *noun,*
masculine/feminine
  un passant/une passante = a passer-by

passé/passée
1 ▶ passer ①
2 *adjective*
- **l'an passé** = last year
- **il est cinq heures passées** = it's past five
  o'clock
3 passé *noun, masculine*
  le passé = the past

passer *verb* ①
1 (**!** + *avoir*)
- = to spend
  passer son temps à lire = to spend one's
    time reading
- = to take, to sit
  passer un examen = to take an
    examination

  ! *Note that* **réussir à un examen** *means to
  pass an exam.*

- = to show
  = to play
  passer un film = to show a film
  passer un disque = to play a record
- = to pass
  = to give
  peux-tu passer le sel? = can you pass the
    salt?
  il m'a passé son rhume = he gave me his
    cold
  je vous la passe (*on the telephone*) = I'll
    put her on
- (*to miss*)
  passer son tour = to pass
2 (**!** + *être*)
- (*to walk, to drive, to fly past*) = to go past, to
  go by
  un bus vient de passer = a bus has just
    gone past
  passer devant l'église = to go past the
    church, to pass the church
- (*to go a certain way*)
  passer par = to go through, to go by
  passer par la porte de derrière = to go
    through the back door

- (*to make one's way*) = to get past
  je ne peux pas passer = I can't get past
  laisser passer les enfants = to let the
    children past
- (*to call, to arrive*) = to come
  le facteur passe vers dix heures = the
    postman comes at about ten o'clock
- (*to pay a visit*) = to drop in
  passer voir un ami = to drop in on a friend
- (*to move to a different level*)
  passer dans la classe supérieure = to
    move up to the next class
- = to pass
  le temps passe trop vite = time passes too
    quickly
3 se passer (**!** + *être*)
- **se passer** = to happen
  qu'est-ce qui se passe? = what's
    happening?, what's going on?
- **se passer** = to go
  ça s'est bien passé = it went well
- **se passer de** = to do without

passerelle *noun, feminine*
  une passerelle = a footbridge
  = a gangway

passe-temps *noun, masculine* (**!** *never
changes*)
  un passe-temps = a hobby

passion *noun, feminine*
  une passion = a passion

passionnant/passionnante
adjective
  = fascinating
  – exciting

passionné/passionnée
1 ▶ passionner ①
2 *adjective*
  = passionate
3 *noun, masculine/feminine*
  un passionné/une passionnée de football
    = a football enthusiast, a football fan

passionner *verb* ①
1 (**!** + *avoir*)
  = to fascinate
2 se passionner pour (**!** + *être*)
  se passionner pour = to have a passion for

passoire *noun, feminine*
  une passoire = a colander
  = a strainer

pastèque *noun, feminine*
  une pastèque = a watermelon

pasteur *noun, masculine*
  un pasteur = a parson, a minister

pastille *noun, feminine*
  une pastille = a lozenge, a cough drop

patate* *noun, feminine*
  une patate* = a spud, a potato

patauger *verb* ⑬
  = to splash about

P

pâte
1 *noun, feminine*
• **la pâte** = pastry
  = dough
  = batter
• **une pâte** = a paste
2 pâtes *noun, feminine plural*
  des pâtes (alimentaires) = pasta

pâté *noun, masculine*
• **le pâté** = pâté
  un pâté (en croûte) = a pie
• **un pâté de maisons** = a block (of houses)

patience *noun, feminine*
• (*a virtue*)
  la patience = patience
• (*a game of cards*)
  faire une patience = to play patience, to
  play solitaire

patient/patiente
1 *adjective*
  = patient
2 *noun, masculine/feminine*
  un patient/une patiente = a patient

patienter *verb* 1
  = to wait

patin *noun, masculine*
  un patin = a skate
des patins de frein = brake blocks
des patins à glace = ice-skates
des patins à roulettes = roller-skates

patinage *noun, masculine*
  le patinage = skating

patinoire *noun, feminine*
  une patinoire = an ice rink

pâtisserie *noun, feminine*
• (*a place*)
  une pâtisserie = a cake shop
• (*a sweet*)
  une pâtisserie = a pastry, a cake

pâtissier/pâtissière *noun,*
masculine/feminine
  un pâtissier/une pâtissière = a
  confectioner

patron/patronne
1 *noun, masculine/feminine*
  le patron/la patronne = the boss
  = the manager
2 patron *noun, masculine*
  un patron = a pattern

patronne ▶ patron 1

patte *noun, feminine*
  une patte = a leg
  = a paw
  = a foot
  à quatre pattes = on all fours

---

paupière *noun, feminine*
  une paupière = an eyelid

pause *noun, feminine*
  une pause = a break
  faire une pause = to take a break

pauvre *adjective*
  = poor

pauvreté *noun, feminine*
  la pauvreté = poverty

pavé/pavée
1 *adjective*
  = cobbled
2 pavé *noun, masculine*
  un pavé = a cobblestone

payant/payante *adjective*
  (*describing a person*) = paying
  (*describing a show*) = not free

payer *verb* 21
1 (**!** + *avoir*)
  = to pay
2 se payer* (**!** + *être*)
  se payer* un repas = to treat oneself to a
  meal

pays *noun, masculine* (**!** *never changes*)
  un pays = a country

paysage *noun, masculine*
  un paysage = a landscape

Pays-Bas *noun, masculine plural*
  les Pays-Bas = the Netherlands, Holland

Pays de Galles *noun, masculine*
  le Pays de Galles = Wales

PCV *noun, masculine*
  appeler en PCV = to make a reverse-
  charge call, to call collect

péage *noun, masculine*
  le péage = the toll
  = the tollbooth

peau *noun, feminine*
(*plural*) **peaux**
  la peau = skin

pêche *noun, feminine*
• **une pêche** = a peach
• **la pêche** = fishing

péché *noun, masculine*
  un péché = a sin

pêcher
1 *verb* 1
• = to catch
• = to go fishing
2 *noun, masculine*
  un pêcher = a peach tree

pêcheur *noun, masculine*
  un pêcheur = a fisherman

pédale *noun, feminine*
  une pédale = a pedal

---

pédaler verb [1]
= to pedal

pédestre adjective
une randonnée pédestre = a ramble, a walk

peigne noun, masculine
un peigne = a comb

peignoir noun, masculine
un peignoir = a dressing gown, a robe

peindre verb [55]
= to paint

peine
1 noun, feminine
• avoir de la peine à finir un travail = to have difficulty finishing a job
• ce n'est pas la peine d'essayer = it's not worth trying
  ça vaut la peine d'y aller = it's worth going
• (sorrow)
  la peine = grief
  faire de la peine à ses amis = to upset one's friends
  avoir de la peine = to be sad
• (punishment)
  une peine de prison = a prison sentence
  la peine de mort = capital punishment
2 à peine = hardly

peint/peinte ▶ **peindre** [55]

peintre noun, masculine
un peintre = a painter

peinture noun, feminine
• la peinture (substance) = paint
  (the activity) = painting
• une peinture = a painting

pêle-mêle adverb
= higgledy-piggledy, pell-mell

peler verb [17]
= to peel

pèlerinage noun, masculine
un pèlerinage = a pilgrimage

pelle noun, feminine
une pelle = a shovel

pellicule
1 noun, feminine
une pellicule = a film
2 pellicules noun, feminine plural
des pellicules = dandruff

pelouse noun, feminine
la pelouse = the lawn

peluche noun, feminine
une peluche = a soft toy
un animal en peluche = a soft toy, a stuffed animal

pencher verb [1]
1 (! + avoir)
= to tilt
pencher la tête = to bend one's head

2 se pencher (! + être)
se pencher = to lean
= to bend down

pendant
1 preposition
• = for
  pendant des heures = for hours
  pendant tout le voyage = for the whole journey, throughout the journey
• = during
  pendant la nuit = during the night
  pendant ce temps = meanwhile
2 pendant que = while

penderie noun, feminine
une penderie = a wardrobe, a closet

pendre verb [6]
• = to hang
• = to dangle

pendu/pendue
1 ▶ **pendre** [6]
2 pendu noun, masculine
jouer au pendu = to play hangman

pendule noun, feminine
une pendule = a clock

pénétrer verb [14]
pénétrer dans un bâtiment = to enter a building, to get into a building

pénible adjective
= hard, difficult

péniblement adverb
= with difficulty

péniche noun, feminine
une péniche = a barge

pensée noun, feminine
• (an idea)
  une pensée = a thought
• (a flower)
  une pensée = a pansy

penser verb [1]
• = to think
  qu'en pensez-vous? = what do you think (about it)?
• penser à = to think of
  = to remember
  je pense à toi = I'm thinking of you
  j'y ai pensé = I thought about it

pension noun, feminine
• (money)
  une pension = a pension
• (a school)
  une pension = a boarding school
• (a hotel)
  une pension = a boarding house
  la pension complète = full board
  une pension de famille = a family hotel

pensionnaire noun, masculine|feminine
un pensionnaire/une pensionnaire (in a school) = a boarder
(in a hotel) = a resident

P

pensionnat *noun, masculine*
  un pensionnat = a boarding school

pente *noun, feminine*
  une pente = a slope
  en pente = sloping

Pentecôte *noun, feminine*
  la Pentecôte = Whitsun, Pentecost

pépé✗ *noun, masculine*
  un pépé✗ = a grandad

pépin *noun, masculine*
• un pépin = a pip, a seed
• un pépin✗ = a slight problem

perche *noun, feminine*
  une perche = a pole
  la saut à la perche = pole vaulting

perdant/perdante
1 *adjective*
  = losing
2 *noun, masculine/feminine*
  un perdant/une perdante = a loser

perdre *verb* ⑥
1 (**!** + *avoir*)
  = to lose
  perdre son temps = to waste one's time
2 se perdre (**!** + *être*)
  se perdre = to get lost

perdu/perdue
1 ▶ perdre ⑥
2 *adjective*
• = lost
  = stray
• = wasted
  c'est du temps perdu = it's a waste of time
• = remote, isolated

père *noun, masculine*
  un père = a father
le père Noël = Father Christmas, Santa
  Claus

perfectionner *verb* ①
1 (**!** + *avoir*)
  = to perfect
  = to improve
  = to refine
2 se perfectionner (**!** + *être*)
  se perfectionner = to improve

périmé/périmée *adjective*
  = out-of-date

périphérique *noun, masculine*
  le périphérique = the ring road, the
  beltway

permanence
1 *noun, feminine*
  une permanence = a permanently
  manned office
  (*in school*) = a (supervised) study room, a
  study hall

---

2 en permanence = permanently

permettre *verb* ⑥⓪
1 (**!** + *avoir*)
  = to allow
  permettre à un enfant de sortir = to allow a
  child to go out
2 se permettre (**!** + *être*)
• (*to act without asking*)
  se permettre de se servir = to take the
  liberty of helping oneself
• (*to have money*)
  pouvoir se permettre d'aller au restaurant
  = to be able to afford to eat out

permis/permise
1 ▶ permettre ⑥⓪
2 *adjective*
  = permitted, allowed
3 permis *noun, masculine* (**!** *never*
  changes)
  un permis = a permit
  = a licence, a license
un permis de conduire = a driving
  licence, a driver's license

perroquet *noun, masculine*
  un perroquet = a parrot

perruche *noun, feminine*
  une perruche = a budgerigar, a budgie

perruque *noun, feminine*
  une perruque = a wig

persienne *noun, feminine*
  une persienne = a shutter

persil *noun, masculine*
  le persil = parsley

personnage *noun, masculine*
  un personnage = a character

personne
1 *pronoun*
  = nobody
  = anybody
2 *noun, feminine*
  une personne = a person
  quelques personnes = a few people

personnel/personnelle
1 *adjective*
  = personal
2 personnel *noun, masculine*
  le personnel = the staff

perte *noun, feminine*
  une perte = a loss
  une perte de temps = a waste of time

peser *verb* ⑯
  = to weigh

pétanque *noun, feminine*
  la pétanque = pétanque, *French bowls*

pétard *noun, masculine*
  un pétard = a banger, a firecracker

pétillant/pétillante *adjective*
  = sparkling

✗ in informal situations

petit/petite
1 *adjective*
  (*in size or importance*) = small, little
  (*in duration, length*) = short
2 *noun, masculine/feminine*
  un petit/une petite = a child
  (*in school*) = a junior
3 **petit** *noun, masculine*
  un petit = a little one
  les petits = the young
4 **petit à petit** = little by little, gradually
les petits chevaux ≈ ludo, Parcheesi

petite-fille *noun, feminine*
(*plural*) **petites-filles**
  une petite-fille = a granddaughter

petit-fils *noun, masculine*
(*plural*) **petits-fils**
  un petit-fils = a grandson

petits-enfants *noun, masculine plural*
  des petits-enfants = grandchildren

pétrole *noun, masculine*
  le pétrole = oil, petroleum

peu
1 *noun, masculine*
  un peu = a little
  un tout petit peu = just a little
2 *adverb*
• = not much
  il mange peu = he doesn't eat very much
• = not very
  peu intelligent = not very intelligent
  peu après = soon afterwards
3 **peu de** *determiner*
  = few, not many
  = little, not much
  peu de livres = few books
  peu de nourriture = little food
  c'est peu de chose = it's not much
4 **peu à peu** = gradually
5 **à peu près** = more or less
  = approximately

peuple *noun, masculine*
  un peuple = a people

peur *noun, feminine*
  la peur = fear
  avoir peur = to be afraid
  faire peur à quelqu'un = to frighten
    someone

peut-être *adverb*
  = perhaps, maybe

peux ▶ pouvoir 2 49

phare *noun, masculine*
  un phare (*on a car*) = a headlight
  (*on the coast*) = a lighthouse

pharmacie *noun, feminine*
  une pharmacie = a chemist's (shop), a
    drugstore

pharmacien/pharmacienne *noun,
masculine/feminine*
  un pharmacien/une pharmacienne = a
    chemist, a pharmacist

philatélie *noun, feminine*
  la philatélie = stamp collecting

phoque *noun, masculine*
  un phoque = a seal

photo *noun, feminine*
• (*a picture*)
  une photo = a photograph
• (*the activity*)
  la photo = photography

photocopie *noun, feminine*
  une photocopie = a photocopy

photocopieuse *noun, feminine*
  une photocopieuse = a photocopier

photographe *noun, masculine/feminine*
  un photographe/une photographe = a
    photographer

photographie *noun, feminine*
• (*a picture*)
  une photographie = a photograph
• (*the activity*)
  la photographie = photography

phrase *noun, feminine*
  une phrase = a sentence

physicien/physicienne *noun,
masculine/feminine*
  un physicien/une physicienne = a
    physicist

physique
1 *adjective*
  = physical
2 *noun, feminine*
  la physique = physics
3 *noun, masculine*
  le physique = physical appearance

P

picorer *verb* 1
  = to peck

pièce *noun, feminine*
• (*in a house, an apartment*)
  une pièce = a room
  un trois-pièces cuisine = a three-roomed
    apartment with kitchen
• (*money*)
  une pièce (de monnaie) = a coin
• (*at the theatre*)
  une pièce (de théâtre) = a play
• (*a component*)
  une pièce = a part
  une pièce de rechange = a spare part
• (*an item*)
  une pièce = a piece
  ils coûtent dix francs pièce = they cost ten
    francs each
  un (maillot) deux-pièces = a two-piece
    swimsuit
• (*in a file*)
  une pièce = a document

une pièce détachée = a spare part
une pièce d'identité = identification

pied *noun, masculine*
* (*part of the body*)
un pied = a foot
à pied = on foot
il va à l'école à pied = he walks to school
pieds nus = barefoot
un coup de pied = a kick
* (*the lower end*)
le pied = the foot, the bottom
au pied de l'escalier = at the bottom of the
stairs
* (*an upright part*)
un pied (*on a table*) = a leg
(*on a lamp*) = a base
(*on a glass*) = a stem
* (*a measurement*)
un pied = a foot

piège *noun, masculine*
un piège = a trap

pierre *noun, feminine*
une pierre = a stone

piéton/piétonne *noun,*
masculine|feminine
un piéton/une piétonne = a pedestrian

pieuvre *noun, feminine*
une pieuvre = an octopus

pigeon *noun, masculine*
un pigeon = a pigeon
pigeon vole = Simon says

pile
1 *noun, feminine*
* (*in a flashlight, a toy*)
une pile = a battery
à piles = battery-operated
* (*on a coin*)
pile = tails
jouer à pile ou face = to play heads or tails
* (*things on top of one another*)
une pile = a pile, a stack
2 *adverb**✶**
à trois heures pile✶ = at three o'clock on
the dot
s'arrêter pile✶ = to stop dead
tu tombes pile✶ = you've come at just the
right moment

pilier *noun, masculine*
un pilier = a pillar

pilote *noun, masculine*
un pilote = a pilot
pilote automobile = racing driver
pilote de rallye = rally driver

pilule *noun, feminine*
une pilule = a pill

pin *noun, masculine*
un pin = a pine (tree)

pinceau *noun, masculine*
(*plural*) **pinceaux**
un pinceau = a (paint)brush

pincée *noun, feminine*
une pincée = a pinch

pincer *verb* [12]
= to pinch

pinède *noun, feminine*
une pinède = a pine forest

pingouin *noun, masculine*
un pingouin = a penguin

ping-pong *noun, masculine*
(*plural*) **ping-pongs**
le ping-pong = table tennis, ping-pong

pin's *noun, masculine* (**!** *never changes*)
un pin's = a (lapel) badge, a pin

pioche *noun, feminine*
une pioche = a pickaxe

pipe *noun, feminine*
une pipe = a pipe

pipi✶ *noun, masculine*
faire pipi✶ = to have a pee, to take a pee

pique *noun, masculine*
pique = spades

pique-nique *noun, masculine*
(*plural*) **pique-niques**
un pique-nique = a picnic

piquer *verb* [1]
1 (**!** + *avoir*)
* (*if it's a bee, a nettle, smoke*) = to sting
(*if it's a snake, a mosquito*) = to bite
(*if it's a thorn*) = to prick
* (*to take*)✶ = to pinch, to steal
= to borrow
2 se piquer (**!** + *être*)
se piquer = to prick oneself

piqûre *noun, feminine*
une piqûre (*with a syringe*) = an injection
(*from an insect*) = a sting
= a bite

pire
1 *adjective*
= worse
= worst
2 *noun, masculine*
le pire = the worst (about it)

piscine *noun, feminine*
une piscine = a swimming pool
une piscine couverte = an indoor
swimming pool

pistache *noun, feminine*
une pistache = a pistachio nut

piste *noun, feminine*
* (*a clearly marked path*)
une piste (*in a forest*) = a trail, a track
(*when skiing*) = a piste, a run

✶ in informal situations

(in racing events)
= a (race)track
= a racecourse
* *(in a circus)*
la piste = the ring
* *(in a police investigation)*
une piste = a lead
une piste d'atterrissage = a runway
une piste cyclable = a cycle lane
une piste de danse = a dance floor

pistolet *noun, masculine*
un pistolet = a gun

pitre *noun, masculine*
un pitre = a clown, a buffoon

pittoresque *adjective*
= picturesque

placard *noun, masculine*
un placard = a cupboard

place *noun, feminine*
* *(in a town)*
une place = a square
* *(for a passenger, a spectator)*
une place = a seat
une place assise = a seat
une place debout = a standing ticket
* *(a position)*
une place = a place
remettre un livre à sa place = to put a
book back in its place
obtenir la première place = to take first
place
à la place de = instead of
* *(a vacant spot)*
une place *(at a table)* = a place
(for a car) = a parking space
* *(enough empty space)*
de la place = room, space

plafond *noun, masculine*
le plafond = the ceiling

plage *noun, feminine*
la plage = the beach

plaie *noun, feminine*
une plaie = a wound

plaindre *verb* 54
1 (**!** + *avoir*)
= to feel sorry for
2 se plaindre (**!** + *être*)
se plaindre = to complain

plaint/plainte¹ ▶ plaindre 54

plainte² *noun, feminine*
* *(expressing dissatisfaction)*
une plainte = a complaint
* *(a sound of pain)*
une plainte = a moan, a groan

plaire *verb* 59
* s'il te plaît, s'il vous plaît = please
* Marc plaît aux filles = girls find Marc
attractive
le film leur a plu = they liked the film

plaisanterie *noun, feminine*
une plaisanterie = a joke

plaisir *noun, masculine*
le plaisir = pleasure
ma visite leur a fait plaisir = they were
pleased to see me

plaît ▶ plaire 59

plan *noun, masculine*
* *(of an area)*
un plan = a map
* *(for an essay)*
un plan = an outline
* *(for a line of action)*
un plan = a plan
* *(in films, photography)*
au premier plan = in the foreground
un gros plan = a close-up

planche *noun, feminine*
une planche = a plank
= a board
une planche à repasser = an ironing
board
une planche à roulettes = a skateboard
une planche à voile = a windsurfing
board

plancher *noun, masculine*
le plancher = the floor

planète *noun, feminine*
une planète = a planet

planeur *noun, masculine*
* *(the equipment)*
un planeur = a glider
* *(the sport)*
le planeur = gliding

P

planifier *verb* 2
= to plan

plante *noun, feminine*
une plante = a plant
une plante grasse = a succulent
une plante verte = a houseplant

planter *verb* 1
* = to plant
* planter une tente = to pitch a tent

plaque *noun, feminine*
une plaque *(of metal, glass)* = a plate
une plaque d'immatriculation = a
number plate, a license plate

plastique *noun, masculine*
le plastique = plastic

plat/plate
1 *adjective*
= flat
2 plat *noun, masculine*
un plat = a dish
= a course
le plat du jour = today's special

3 à plat
- (*the way something lies*)
  à plat = flat
  poser une carte à plat = to lay a map down flat
  à plat ventre = flat on one's stomach
- (*describing a tyre*)
  à plat = flat
- (*describing a person*)
  à plat✱ = run down

plateau *noun, masculine*
(*plural*) **plateaux**
  un plateau (*for serving*) = a tray
  un plateau de fromages = a cheeseboard

platine *noun, feminine*
  une platine = a turntable
  une platine CD = a CD player

plâtre *noun, masculine*
  le plâtre = plaster

plein/pleine
1 *adjective*
- = full
- **en pleine forêt** = (right) in the middle of the forest
  en plein jour = in broad daylight
  en plein air = in the open air
  en pleine forme = in great shape, really fit
2 plein *noun, masculine*
  faire le plein (d'essence) = to fill up (with petrol)

pleurer *verb* 1
  = to cry, to weep

pleut ▶ **pleuvoir** 33

pleuvoir *verb* 33
  = to rain
  il pleut = it's raining

plier *verb* 2
  = to fold
  = to bend

plombier *noun, masculine*
  un plombier = a plumber

plongée *noun, feminine*
  la plongée = diving
  la plongée sous-marine = deep-sea diving

plongeoir *noun, masculine*
  un plongeoir = a diving-board

plongeon *noun, masculine*
  un plongeon = a dive

plonger *verb* 13
- = to dive
- = to plunge

plongeur/plongeuse *noun,*
masculine/feminine
  un plongeur/une plongeuse = a diver

✱ in informal situations

plu
- ▶ **plaire** 59
- ▶ **pleuvoir** 33

pluie *noun, feminine*
  la pluie = rain

plume *noun, feminine*
- (*on a bird*)
  une plume = a feather
- (*on a pen*)
  une plume = a nib

plupart *noun, feminine*
  la plupart de = most of

pluriel *noun, masculine*
  le pluriel = the plural

plus
1 *conjunction*
  = plus
2 *adverb*
- = more
  c'est plus intéressant = it's more interesting
  arriver plus tôt que d'habitude = to arrive earlier than usual
  de plus en plus prudent = more and more careful
  deux fois plus cher = twice as expensive
- **plus de** = more
  = more than, over
  plus de la moitié = more than half
  elle a plus de seize ans = she's over sixteen
  il est plus de minuit = it's past midnight
- **plus... plus** = the more... the more
  plus... moins = the more... the less
  plus... mieux = the more... the better
  plus on lit, plus on apprend = the more you read, the more you learn
- **le plus/la plus** = the most
  = the more
  les plus belles fleurs du jardin = the most beautiful flowers in the garden
  le plus cher des deux = the more expensive of the two
- **en plus** = on top (of that)
  il fait froid et en plus il pleut = it's cold and on top of that it's raining
  en plus de mon travail = on top of my work
3 ne... plus = no more, not any more
  = no longer
  il n'y a plus de pain = there's no more bread, there's no bread left
  elle ne travaille plus = she doesn't work any more, she no longer works
  je n'ai plus que dix francs = I've only got ten francs left
  il ne reste plus rien = you've nothing left
  plus jamais = never again
  il n'y va pas, et moi non plus = he's not going and neither am I

plusieurs *adjective*
  = several

plutôt *adverb*
= rather
= instead

pluvieux/pluvieuse *adjective*
= rainy

pneu *noun, masculine*
un pneu = a tyre, a tire

pneumatique *adjective*
= inflatable

poche *noun, feminine*
une poche = a pocket

poêle
1 *noun, feminine*
une poêle (à frire) = a frying pan
2 *noun, masculine*
un poêle = a stove

poésie *noun, feminine*
• la poésie = poetry
• une poésie = a poem

poids *noun, masculine* (**!** *never changes*)
le poids = the weight
prendre du poids = to put on weight
un poids lourd = a heavy goods vehicle

poignée *noun, feminine*
• (*on a door*)
une poignée = a handle
• (*an amount*)
une poignée = a handful
une poignée de main = a handshake

poignet *noun, masculine*
un poignet = a wrist
= a cuff

poil *noun, masculine*
un poil (*on the body, on an animal*) = a hair
(*on a brush*) = a bristle

poing *noun, masculine*
le poing = the fist
un coup de poing = a punch

point
1 *noun, masculine*
• (*a punctuation mark*)
un point = a full stop, a period
deux points = a colon
• (*when scoring*)
un point = a point
• (*in sewing, in knitting*)
un point = a stitch
• (*a small round mark*)
un point = a dot, a speck
• (*a particular place or position*)
un point de rencontre = a meeting point
2 à point
un bifteck (cuit) à point = a medium rare
steak
un point de départ = a starting point
un point d'exclamation = an
exclamation mark
un point d'interrogation = a question
mark

un point de repère = a landmark
des points de suspension = suspension
points

pointe *noun, feminine*
la pointe = the point, the tip
sur la pointe des pieds = on tiptoe

pointer: **se pointer*** *verb* ⓵ (**!** + *être*)
se pointer* = to show up

pointu/pointue *adjective*
= pointed
= with a sharp point

pointure *noun, feminine*
une pointure = a shoe size

point-virgule *noun, masculine*
(*plural*) **points-virgules**
un point-virgule = a semicolon

poire *noun, feminine*
une poire = a pear

poireau *noun, masculine*
(*plural*) **poireaux**
un poireau = a leek

pois *noun, masculine* (**!** *never changes*)
• (*on material*)
un pois = a dot
à pois = polka dot, dotted
• (*in a pod*)
un pois = a pea
des petits pois = garden peas, petits pois

poisson *noun, masculine*
un poisson = a fish
un poisson d'avril = an April fool's joke
un poisson rouge = a goldfish

poissonnerie *noun, feminine*
une poissonnerie = a fishmonger's, a fish
shop

poissonnier/poissonnière *noun,*
masculine/feminine
un poissonnier/une poissonnière = a
fishmonger, a fish dealer

Poissons *noun, masculine plural*
Poissons = Pisces

poitrine *noun, feminine*
la poitrine = the chest
= the bust

poivre *noun, masculine*
le poivre = pepper

poivron *noun, masculine*
un poivron = a sweet pepper, a capsicum

poli/polie *adjective*
• (*well-mannered*) = polite
• (*shiny*) = polished

police *noun, feminine*
la police = the police
police secours ≈ emergency services

policier *noun, masculine*
un policier = a policeman

P

polluer *verb* $\boxed{1}$
= to pollute

Pologne *noun, feminine*
la Pologne = Poland

polonais/polonaise
1 *adjective*
= Polish
2 polonais *noun, masculine*
le polonais = Polish

pommade *noun, feminine*
une pommade = an ointment

pomme *noun, feminine*
une pomme = an apple
une pomme de pin = a pine cone
une pomme de terre = a potato

pommier *noun, masculine*
un pommier = an apple tree

pompe *noun, feminine*
une pompe = a pump

pompier *noun, masculine*
un pompier = a fireman, a firefighter
les pompiers = the fire brigade, the fire
department

pompiste *noun, masculine|feminine*
un pompiste/une pompiste = a petrol
pump attendant, a gas station
attendant

pont *noun, masculine*
• (*over a river*)
un pont = a bridge
• (*on a ship*)
un pont = a deck
• (*extra time off*)
faire le pont *to have the day(s) off between
a public holiday and a weekend*

populaire *adjective*
• (*describing an area*) = working-class
• (*meaning well-liked*) = popular

porc *noun, masculine*
• (*the animal*)
un porc = a pig
• (*the meat*)
le porc = pork

porc-épic *noun, masculine*
(*plural*) **porc-épics**
un porc-épic = a porcupine

porcherie *noun, feminine*
une porcherie = a pigsty

port *noun, masculine*
un port = a harbo(u)r, a port
un port de pêche = a fishing harbo(u)r
un port de plaisance = a marina

portail *noun, masculine*
un portail = a gate

porte *noun, feminine*
une porte = a door
= a gate
mettre à la porte = to throw out
une porte d'embarquement = a
departure gate
la porte d'entrée = the front door

porte-clés, **porte-clefs** *noun,
masculine* (**!** *never changes*)
un porte-clés = a key ring

porte-fenêtre *noun, feminine*
(*plural*) **portes-fenêtres**
une porte-fenêtre = a French window

portefeuille *noun, masculine*
un portefeuille = a wallet

portemanteau *noun, masculine*
(*plural*) **portemanteaux**
un portemanteau = a coat rack
= a coat stand

porte-monnaie *noun, masculine*
(**!** *never changes*)
un porte-monnaie = a purse, a coin purse

porter *verb* $\boxed{1}$
1 (**!** + *avoir*)
• = to carry
• = to wear
• porter bonheur = to bring good luck
porter malheur = to bring bad luck
2 se porter (**!** + *être*)
se porter bien = to be well

porteur *noun, masculine*
un porteur = a porter

portier *noun, masculine*
un portier = a doorman

portière *noun, feminine*
une portière = a door

portillon *noun, masculine*
un portillon = a gate, a barrier

portrait *noun, masculine*
• (*a likeness*)
un portrait = a portrait
• (*in words*)
un portrait = a description

portrait-robot *noun, masculine*
(*plural*) **portraits-robots**
un portrait-robot = a photofit , an
identikit

portugais/portugaise
1 *adjective*
= Portuguese
2 portugais *noun, masculine*
le portugais = Portuguese

Portugal *noun, masculine*
le Portugal = Portugal

✗ in informal situations

poser verb 1
1 (**!** + *avoir*)
• = to put down
  poser un sac sur une table = to put a bag
    down on a table
• = to ask
  poser une question = to ask a question
2 se poser (**!** + *être*)
  se poser (*if it's a bird*) = to settle, to alight
    (*if it's a plane*) = to land, to touch down

posséder verb 14
= to own
= to possess

possible
1 *adjective*
= possible
  le plus de temps possible = as much time
    as possible
  le plus tôt possible = as soon as possible
2 *noun, masculine*
  faire tout son possible = to do one's
    utmost

poste
1 *noun, feminine*
  la poste = the post office
2 *noun, masculine*
• (*employment*)
  un poste = a job, a position
• (*a receiver*)
  un poste de télévision = a television set
• (*a place*)
  le poste (de police) = the police station
• (*for telephoning*)
  un poste = an extension

poster verb 1
= to post, to mail

pot *noun, masculine*
• **un pot** = a pot
  = a jar
• **un pot*** = a drink

potable *adjective*
  l'eau potable = drinking water

potage *noun, masculine*
  le potage = soup

potager *noun, masculine*
  un (jardin) potager = a vegetable garden

poteau *noun, masculine*
(*plural*) **poteaux**
  un poteau = a post
  un poteau indicateur = a signpost

potier/potière *noun, masculine/feminine*
  un potier/une potière = a potter

poubelle *noun, feminine*
  une poubelle = a dustbin, a trash can

pouce *noun, masculine*
• **un pouce** = a thumb
• **un pouce** = an inch

poudre *noun, feminine*
  la poudre = powder

poule *noun, feminine*
  une poule = a hen

poulet *noun, masculine*
  un poulet = a chicken

poulpe *noun, masculine*
  un poulpe = an octopus

pouls *noun, masculine* (**!** *never changes*)
  le pouls = the pulse

poumon *noun, masculine*
  un poumon = a lung

poupée *noun, feminine*
  une poupée = a doll

pour
1 *preposition*
• = for
  c'est pour toi = it's for you
  un produit pour nettoyer les vitres = a
    product for cleaning windows
• = to, in order to, so as to
  j'ai écrit pour les remercier = I've written
    to thank them
  pour ne pas manquer le train = so as not to
    miss the train
• = per
  dix pour cent = ten per cent
2 *noun, masculine*
  le pour et le contre = the pros and the cons

pourboire *noun, masculine*
  un pourboire = a tip

pourpre *adjective*
= crimson

pourquoi *adverb, conjunction*
= why

pourrai ▶ **pouvoir 2** 49

pourri/pourrie *adjective*
= rotten

pourtant *adverb*
= yet

pousser verb 1
1 (**!** + *avoir*)
• = to push
• = to move
• = to let out
  pousser un cri = to let out a cry
• (*if it's a plant, hair*) = to grow
  faire pousser des fleurs = to grow flowers
2 se pousser (**!** + *être*)
  se pousser = to move over

poussette *noun, feminine*
  une poussette = a pushchair, a stroller

poussière *noun, feminine*
  la poussière = dust

poussin *noun, masculine*
  un poussin = a chick

pouvoir
1 *noun, masculine*
  le pouvoir = power

2 *verb* 49
- = to be able to
 il ne pourra pas venir = he won't be able to come
 elle n'a pas pu partir = she wasn't able to leave, she couldn't leave
 je ne peux pas payer ce prix = I can't pay that sort of price
 pourriez-vous me dire où se trouve la gare? = could you tell me where the station is?
 je n'en peux plus! (*after an effort*) = I've had it!
 (*after a meal*) = I'm full!
- = to be allowed to
 puis-je téléphoner? = may I use the phone?
 tu ne peux pas te garer là = you can't park there
- (*expressing a possibility*)
 attention, tu pourrais glisser = careful, you might slip
 vous auriez pu m'avertir! = you might have warned me!
 il pouvait avoir dix ans = he would have been about ten
 il pouvait être dix heures = it was probably about ten o'clock
3 il se peut (**!** + *être*)
 il se peut que j'y aille = I might go
 il se pourrait bien que l'avion ait du retard = the plane might well be delayed
 ça se peut = it's possible

prairie *noun, feminine*
 une prairie = a meadow

pratique *adjective*
 = practical
 = handy, convenient

pratiquer *verb* 1
 pratiquer le tennis = to play tennis
 pratiquer le yoga = to do yoga

pré *noun, masculine*
 un pré = a meadow

précieux/précieuse *adjective*
 = precious

précipiter: **se précipiter** *verb* 1
(**!** + *être*)
 se précipiter = to rush
 se précipiter sur le journal = to pounce on the newspaper

précis/précise *adjective*
 = precise
 = accurate
 à trois heures précises = at exactly three o'clock, at three o'clock sharp

préféré/préférée
1 ▶ préférer 14
2 *adjective*
 = favo(u)rite

préférence *noun, feminine*
 une préférence = a preference
 de préférence = preferably

préférer *verb* 14
 = to prefer

premier/première¹
1 *adjective*
 = first
2 premier *noun, masculine*
 habiter au premier (*in Britain*) = to live on the first floor
 (*in the US*) = to live on the second floor
 le premier de l'an = New Year's Day

première² *noun, feminine*
- (*in school*)
 la première *the class for secondary school students aged 16 to 17*
- (*when travelling*)
 voyager en première = to travel first class

prendre *verb* 52
1 (**!** + *avoir*)
- = to take
- = to have
 allons prendre un verre = let's go and have a drink
 qu'est-ce que tu prends? = what'll you have?
- = to go
 prenez à gauche = go left, turn left
- = to catch
 prendre froid = to catch a chill
 prendre feu = to catch fire
- **qu'est-ce qui te prend✱?** = what's up with you?
2 se prendre (**!** + *être*)
- **pour qui se prend-il?** = who does he think he is?
- **elle s'y prend mal** = she's going about it the wrong way

prénom *noun, masculine*
 un prénom = a first name

préparer *verb* 1
1 (**!** + *avoir*)
- **préparer un repas** = to prepare a meal
- **préparer un examen** = to prepare for an examination
- **préparer ses affaires** = to get one's things ready
2 se préparer (**!** + *être*)
 se préparer = to get ready

près
1 *adverb*
 = close, near(by)
 tout près du magasin = near the shop
 près de trois mètres = nearly three metres
2 de près = closely
3 à peu près = about
 = practically

présenter *verb* 1
1 (**!** + *avoir*)
- = to present
- = to show

• = to introduce
présenter son passeport = to show one's
  passport
il m'a présenté à ses amis = he introduced
  me to his friends
2 se présenter(**!** + *être*)
• (*to give one's name*)
  se présenter = to introduce oneself
• (*to show up*)
  se présenter = to present oneself
• (*if it's an opportunity*)
  se présenter = to arise

président/présidente *noun*,
masculine/feminine
  un président/une présidente = a president
  = a chairman/a chairwoman, a
  chairperson

presque *adverb*
  = nearly, almost

pressé/pressée *adjective*
  être pressé = to be in a hurry

pressing *noun, masculine*
  un pressing = a dry-cleaner's

pression *noun, feminine*
  la pression = pressure

prêt/prête
1 *adjective*
  = ready
2 prêt *noun, masculine*
  un prêt = a loan

prêt-à-porter *noun, masculine*
  le prêt-à-porter = ready-to-wear (clothes)

prêter *verb* 1
  = to lend

prêtre *noun, masculine*
  un prêtre = a priest

preuve *noun, feminine*
• **une preuve** = a piece of evidence
  des preuves = evidence
• **la preuve** = the proof
  c'est la preuve qu'il est innocent = it's
  proof that he's innocent
• **faire preuve de** = to show

prévenir *verb* 36
• = to warn
• = to prevent

prévenu/prévenue ▶ **prévenir** 36

prévision *noun, feminine*
  une prévision = a forecast
  les prévisions météorologiques = the
  weather forecast

prévoir *verb* 35
• = to predict
  = to anticipate, to expect
• = to plan
  comme prévu = as planned

prévu/prévue ▶ **prévoir** 35

prier *verb* 2
  = to request, to ask
  je vous en prie = don't mention it

primaire *adjective*
  = primary

primeurs *noun, feminine plural*
  les primeurs = early produce

principal/principale *adjective*
(*plural*) **principaux/principales**
  = main

principauté *noun, feminine*
  une principauté = a principality

printemps *noun, masculine* (**!** *never
changes*)
  le printemps = spring

priorité *noun, feminine*
  la priorité = priority
  (*on the road*) = the right of way

pris/prise¹ ▶ **prendre** 52

prise² *noun, feminine*
• (*electrical*)
  une prise = a plug
    = a socket
• (*when fishing*)
  une prise = a catch

prisonnier/prisonnière *adjective*
  être prisonnier = to be a prisoner

privé/privée *adjective*
  = private

prix *noun, masculine* (**!** *never changes*)
• (*the cost*)
  le prix = the price
  à tout prix = at all costs
• (*a reward*)
  un prix = a prize

problème *noun, masculine*
  un problème = a problem
    = an issue

procès *noun, masculine* (**!** *never changes*)
  un procès = a trial

prochain/prochaine *adjective*
  = next
  à l'année prochaine! = see you next year!

proche *adjective*
  = nearby
  le garage le plus proche = the nearest
  garage

producteur/productrice *noun,*
masculine/feminine
  un producteur/une productrice = a
  producer

produire *verb* 62
1 (**!** + *avoir*)
• = to produce
• = to cause

P

2 se produire (! + *être*)
  se produire = to happen

produit/produite
1 ▶ produire 62
2 produit *noun, masculine*
  un produit = a product
un produit de beauté = a beauty product
un produit chimique = a chemical

prof✶ *noun, masculine/feminine*
  un prof✶/une prof✶ = a teacher, a lecturer

professeur *noun, masculine*
  un professeur = a teacher, a lecturer

profiter *verb* 1
  profiter de = to take advantage of
  = to make the most of

profond/profonde *adjective*
  = deep
  peu profond = shallow

profondeur *noun, feminine*
  la profondeur = the depth
  avoir dix mètres de profondeur = to be ten
  metres deep

programmateur *noun, masculine*
  un programmateur = a timer

programme *noun, masculine*
  un programme = a program(me)
  (*for an examination*) = a syllabus
  (*for a computer*) = a program

programmer *verb* 1
  = to program

progrès *noun, masculine* (! *never
changes*)
  le progrès = progress

projecteur *noun, masculine*
• (*a light*)
  un projecteur = a floodlight
  = a searchlight
• (*for slides*)
  un projecteur = a projector

projet *noun, masculine*
  un projet = a plan
  des projets de vacances = holiday plans,
  vacation plans

projeter *verb* 20
  = to plan

promenade *noun, feminine*
  une promenade (*on foot*) = a walk
  (*by car*) = a drive
  (*on a bike*) = a ride

promener *verb* 16
1 (! + *avoir*)
  promener le chien = to take the dog for a
  walk
2 se promener (! + *être*)
  se promener (*on foot*) = to go for a walk

(*by car*) = to go for a drive
(*on a bike*) = to go for a ride

promesse *noun, feminine*
  une promesse = a promise

promettre *verb* 60
  = to promise

promis/promise ▶ promettre 60

promotion *noun, feminine*
• (*in a shop*)
  une promotion = a special offer
• (*in one's career*)
  une promotion = promotion

pronom *noun, masculine*
  un pronom = a pronoun

prononcer *verb* 12
• = to pronounce
• = to deliver

propos *noun, masculine plural*
  des propos = words
à propos = by the way
  à propos, je n'y vais pas = by the way, I'm
  not going
à propos de = about

proposer *verb* 1
• = to suggest
• = to offer
  elle m'a proposé sa voiture = she offered
  me her car

proposition *noun, feminine*
  une proposition = a suggestion
  = a proposal

propre *adjective*
• = clean
  une serviette propre = a clean towel
• = own
  avec mon propre argent = with my own
  money

propriétaire *noun, masculine/feminine*
  le propriétaire/la propriétaire = the owner
  (*with tenants*) = the landlord/the landlady

propriété *noun, feminine*
  la propriété = property
  'propriété privée' = 'private property'

prospère *adjective*
  = prosperous

protéger *verb* 15
  = to protect

protester *verb* 1
  = to protest

prouver *verb* 1
  = to prove

provenance *noun, feminine*
  la provenance = the origin
  le train en provenance de Paris = the train
  from Paris

✶ in informal situations

provençal/provençale
(plural) **provençaux/provençales**
1 adjective
= of Provence
= from Provence
2 provençal noun, masculine
le provençal = Provençal

proviseur noun, masculine
le proviseur = the headteacher, the
   principal

provision
1 noun, feminine
une provision de = a stock of, a supply of
faire une provision de papier = to stock up
   on paper
2 provisions noun, feminine plural
faire des provisions = to go shopping for
   food

provisoire adjective
= provisional, temporary

provoquer verb ①
• = to cause
• = to provoke

proximité: **à proximité** adverb
= near(by)

prudence noun, feminine
la prudence = caution

prudent/prudente adjective
= careful, cautious

prune noun, feminine
une prune = a plum

pruneau noun, masculine
(plural) **pruneaux**
un pruneau = a prune

PTT noun, feminine plural
les PTT formerly the French postal and
   telecommunications service

pu ▶ pouvoir 2 ⑭⑨

pub✱ noun, feminine ▶ **publicité**

public/publique
1 adjective
= public
(describing a school, education) = state
(in the US) = public
2 public noun, masculine
le public (all the people) = the public
(at a meeting, a show) = the audience

publicitaire
1 adjective
= advertising
2 noun, masculine/feminine
un publicitaire/une publicitaire = an
   advertising executive

publicité noun, feminine
• la publicité = advertising
• une publicité = an advertisement, a
   commercial

publier verb ②
= to publish

puer verb ①
= to stink
ça pue le poisson! = it stinks of fish!

puis adverb
= then
= next

puisque (**puisqu'** before vowel or mute
h) conjunction
= as
= since

puissant/puissante adjective
= powerful

puisse ▶ pouvoir 2 ⑭⑨

puits noun, masculine (**!** never changes)
un puits = a well

pull noun, masculine
un pull = a jumper, a sweater

punaise noun, feminine
• (for pinning)
une punaise = a drawing pin, a
   thumbtack
• (an insect)
une punaise = a bug

punir verb ③
= to punish

punition noun, feminine
une punition = a punishment

pur/pure adjective
= pure
(describing wine or spirits) = neat

purée noun, feminine
• la purée (de pommes de terre) = mashed
   potatoes
• la purée = puree

PV✱ noun, masculine
un PV✱ = a fine
= a parking ticket

pyjama noun, masculine
un pyjama = pyjamas, pajamas

Q

qu' ▶ que

quai noun, masculine
un quai (in a station) = a platform
(in a port) = a quay
(along a river) = a bank
le navire est à quai = the ship has docked

qualité *noun, feminine*
• une qualité = a quality
• nom, prénom et qualité = surname, first name and occupation
  en sa qualité de représentant = in his/her capacity as a representative

quand
1 *conjunction*
  = when
  quand il sera vieux = when he's old
  tu sortiras quand tu auras fini = you'll go out when you've finished
2 *adverb*
  = when
  quand est-ce que vous partez? = when are you leaving?
  depuis quand est-il malade? = how long has he been ill?
3 quand même = still, even so

quant à *preposition*
  = as for

quantité *noun, feminine*
  une quantité = a quantity, an amount
  des quantités de = lots of

quarante *number*
  = forty

quart *noun, masculine*
  un quart = a quarter
  un quart d'heure = a quarter of an hour
  une heure moins le quart = a quarter to one
  une heure et quart = a quarter past one

quartier *noun, masculine*
• (*part of a town*)
  un quartier = an area, a district
  les gens du quartier = the locals
• (*a segment*)
  un quartier = a quarter
  le premier quartier de la lune = the moon's first quarter
un quartier général = headquarters

quatorze *number*
  = fourteen

quatorzième *number*
  = fourteenth

quatre *number*
  = quatre

quatre-vingt(s) *number*
  = eighty

quatre-vingt-dix *number*
  = ninety

quatrième
1 *number*
  = fourth
2 *noun, feminine*
  la quatrième *the class for secondary school students aged 13 to 14*

que (**qu'** *before vowel or mute h*)
  ! *The construction* ne + verb + que *is treated under* ne.

1 *conjunction*
• = that
  elle a dit qu'elle le ferait = she said that she would do it
  je veux que tu m'accompagnes = I want you to come with me
• = than, as
  plus gros que moi = fatter than me
  aussi fort que mon père = as strong as my father
  c'est le même que le mien = it's the same as mine
• = whether
  que tu le veuilles ou non = whether you like it or not
2 *pronoun*
• = what
  que dire? = what can you say?
  je ne sais pas ce qu'il a dit = I don't know what he said
  qu'est-ce que c'est? = what's that?
• = that
  = who
  la voiture que tu as achetée = the car (that) you've bought
  l'ami que j'ai invité = the friend whom I invited
3 *adverb*
  que c'est joli! = it's so pretty!

québécois/québécoise *adjective*
  = of Quebec
  = from Quebec

quel/quelle
1 *determiner*
  = what
  = which
  quelle est la capitale du Togo? = what's the capital of Togo?
2 *adjective*
• = what
  = which
  quelle heure est-il? = what time is it?
  quels disques as-tu achetés? = which records did you buy?
• quelle coïncidence! = what a coincidence!
• quel que soit le temps = whatever the weather
  quelles que soient leurs habitudes = whatever their habits

quelque *determiner*
• (*in the singular*) = some
  depuis quelque temps = for some time
• (*in the plural*) = some, a few
  = any
  quelques élèves = some pupils, a few pupils

quelquefois *adverb*
  = sometimes

quelques-uns/quelques-unes
pronoun
= some, a few

quelqu'un *pronoun*
= someone, somebody
= anyone, anybody

quenelle *noun, feminine*
une quenelle *a dumpling made of flour and egg, flavo(u)red with meat or fish*

querelle *noun, feminine*
une querelle = a quarrel

question *noun, feminine*
• (*a sentence asking something*)
une question = a question
poser une question à un élève = to ask a pupil a question
• (*something to be examined*)
une question = a matter
= an issue
c'est une question de vie ou de mort = it's a matter of life and death
pas question! = no way!

questionnaire *noun, masculine*
un questionnaire = a questionnaire

questionner *verb* ⓵
= to question

quête *noun, feminine*
une quête = a collection
faire la quête = to pass the hat around
= to collect for charity
= to take the collection

queue *noun, feminine*
• (*on an animal*)
une queue = a tail
• (*people or cars waiting*)
une queue = a queue, a line
faire la queue = to stand in a queue, to stand in line

queue-de-cheval *noun, feminine*
(*plural*) **queues-de-cheval**
une queue-de-cheval = a ponytail

qui *pronoun*
• = who
= whom
qui est-ce? = who is it?
l'homme à qui tu as parlé = the man to whom you spoke
à qui sont ces chaussures? = whose shoes are these?
• = who
= that
= which
qui que vous soyez = whoever you are
je n'ai jamais frappé qui que ce soit = I've never hit anybody

quille *noun, feminine*
une quille = a skittle

quincaillerie *noun, feminine*
une quincaillerie = a hardware shop, a hardware store

quinzaine *noun, feminine*
• **une quinzaine** = about fifteen
• **une quinzaine (de jours)** = a fortnight, two weeks

quinze *number*
= fifteen
quinze jours = fifteen days
= a fortnight, two weeks

quinzième *number*
= fifteenth

quittance *noun, feminine*
une quittance = a receipt
= a bill

quitter *verb* ⓵
1 (**!** + *avoir*)
• = to leave
• **ne quittez pas** = hold the line please, hold on please
2 se quitter (**!** + *être*)
se quitter = to part

quoi *pronoun*
= what
quoi de neuf? = what's new?
je ne sais pas quoi faire = I don't know what to do
à quoi penses-tu? = what are you thinking about?
à quoi bon? = what's the point?
si je peux faire quoi que ce soit = if there's anything I can do
il n'y a pas de quoi = my pleasure, don't mention it
il n'y a pas de quoi s'inquiéter = there's nothing to worry about

quotidien/quotidienne
1 *adjective*
= daily, everyday
2 quotidien *noun, masculine*
un quotidien = a daily (paper)

rabais *noun, masculine* (**!** *never changes*)
un rabais = a reduction

raccompagner *verb* ⓵
raccompagner quelqu'un = to take someone home

raccourci *noun, masculine*
un raccourci = a short cut

raccourcir *verb* ⓷
= to shorten

raccrocher *verb* ⓵
(*when telephoning*) = to hang up

racine noun, feminine
une racine = a root

raconter verb 1
= to tell

radiateur noun, masculine
un radiateur = a radiator

radin/radine✘ adjective
= mean

radio noun, feminine
• (for broadcasts)
la radio = (the) radio
à la radio = on the radio
• (a medical examination)
une radio = an X-ray

radis noun, masculine (! never changes)
un radis = a radish

radoucir: se radoucir verb 3 (! + être)
se radoucir = to turn milder

rafale noun, feminine
une rafale de vent = a gust of wind

raffiné/raffinée adjective
= refined

raffinerie noun, feminine
une raffinerie = a refinery

rafraîchir verb 3
1 (! + avoir)
= to cool (down)
2 se rafraîchir (! + être)
• (if it's the weather)
se rafraîchir = to get cooler
• (if it's a person)
se rafraîchir = to freshen up, to wash up
= to have a drink

rafraîchissement noun, masculine
un rafraîchissement = a cold drink

ragoût noun, masculine
un ragoût = a stew

raide adjective
(describing a slope) = steep
(describing hair) = straight
(describing a collar, a person) = stiff

raie noun, feminine
• (in hair)
une raie = a parting, a part
• (a narrow band of colour)
une raie = a stripe

rail noun, masculine
un rail = a rail
les rails = the track(s)

raisin noun, masculine
le raisin = grapes
un grain de raisin = a grape
les raisins de Corinthe = currants
les raisins secs = raisins

raison noun, feminine
• une raison = a reason
• avoir raison = to be right

raisonnable adjective
= reasonable, moderate
= sensible

ralenti noun, masculine
le ralenti = slow motion
le moteur tourne au ralenti = the engine is
(just) ticking over

ralentir verb 3
= to slow down

ralentisseur noun, masculine
un ralentisseur = a speed ramp

râler✘ verb 1
= to moan

ramasser verb 1
= to pick (up)
= to collect

rame noun, feminine
• une rame = an oar
• une rame de métro = a (metro) train

ramer verb 1
= to row

rampe noun, feminine
une rampe (on a staircase) = a banister
une rampe d'accès
(to a motorway) = a sliproad, an entrance
ramp
(to a building) = a ramp

ramper verb 1
= to crawl

rance adjective
= rancid

rançon noun, feminine
une rançon = a ransom

randonnée noun, feminine
• (a walk)
une randonnée = a ramble, a hike
• (an activity)
la randonnée = hiking
la randonnée à cheval = pony-trekking
la randonnée pédestre = rambling, hiking

rang noun, masculine
• (a line)
un rang = a row
se mettre en rangs = to get into line
• (a position)
un rang = a rank

rangée noun, feminine
une rangée = a row

ranger verb 13
• = to put away
• = to tidy
= to sort out, to put in order

râper verb 1
= to grate

✘ in informal situations

rapide
1 *adjective*
= fast, quick
= prompt
2 *noun, masculine*
• (*a train*)
un rapide = an express
• (*in a river*)
un rapide = rapids

rapidement *adverb*
= quickly, fast

rappel *noun, masculine*
un rappel = a reminder

rappeler *verb* [19]
1 (**!** + *avoir*)
• = to call back
• = to remind
2 se rappeler (**!** + *être*)
se rappeler = to remember

rapport
1 *noun, masculine*
• (*an account*)
un rapport = a report
• (*a link*)
un rapport = a connection
2 par rapport à = compared with

rapporter *verb* [1]
1 (**!** + *avoir*)
= to take back, to bring back
2 se rapporter à (**!** + *être*)
se rapporter à = to relate to

rapprocher *verb* [1]
= to move closer
= to bring closer

raquette *noun, feminine*
une raquette (*in tennis*) = a racket
(*in table tennis*) = a bat, a paddle

rare *adjective*
= rare
= scarce

ras/rase *adjective*
• **des cheveux ras** = close-cropped hair,
short hair
• **une cuillère à café rase** = a level
teaspoonful
plein à ras bord = full to the brim
• **en rase campagne** = in (the) open country

raser: **se raser** *verb* [1] (**!** + *être*)
se raser = to shave

rasoir
1 *noun, masculine*
un rasoir = a razor
2 *adjective* **✶** (**!** *never changes*)
= boring

rassembler *verb* [1]
1 (**!** + *avoir*)
= to gather
= to bring together

2 se rassembler (**!** + *être*)
se rassembler = to gather
= to get together

rassurer *verb* [1]
= to reassure

rat *noun, masculine*
un rat = a rat

râteau *noun, masculine*
(*plural*) **râteaux**
un râteau = a rake

rater *verb* [1]
• = to miss
• = to fail

rattraper *verb* [1]
• = to catch up with
rattraper un concurrent = to catch up with
a competitor
• = to make up for
rattraper le temps perdu = to make up for
lost time
• = to recapture, to catch

ravin *noun, masculine*
un ravin = a ravine

ravissant/ravissante *adjective*
= beautiful, delightful

ravitailler *verb* [1]
ravitailler une ville = to provide a town
with fresh supplies
ravitailler un avion = to refuel a plane

rayé/rayée *adjective*
= striped

rayer *verb* [21]
• = to cross out
• = to scratch

rayon *noun, masculine*
• (*of light*)
un rayon = a ray, a beam
• (*for books, goods*)
un rayon = a shelf
• (*of a circle*)
le rayon = the radius

rayure *noun, feminine*
• (*on material*)
une rayure = a stripe
• (*on glass, on metal*)
une rayure = a scratch

réaction *noun, feminine*
une réaction = a reaction

réagir *verb* [3]
= to react

réaliser *verb* [1]
1 (**!** + *avoir*)
• (*to make something happen*)
réaliser son ambition = to achieve one's
ambition
• (*to understand*) = to realize

R

2 se réaliser (**!** + *être*)
se réaliser = to come true
= to be fulfilled

réaliste *adjective*
= realistic

réalité *noun, feminine*
la réalité = reality

réanimation *noun, feminine*
la réanimation = resuscitation

rebord *noun, masculine*
le rebord de la fenêtre = the windowsill

récemment *adverb*
= recently

récent/récente *adjective*
= recent

récepteur *noun, masculine*
un récepteur = a (telephone) receiver

recette *noun, feminine*
• (*a set of instructions*)
une recette = a recipe
• (*money*)
la recette = the takings

recevoir *verb* [5]
• = to receive, to get
• = to receive, to welcome
• être reçu à un examen = to pass an exam

rechange *noun, masculine*
une pièce de rechange = a spare part

recharge *noun, feminine*
une recharge = a refill

réchaud *noun, masculine*
un réchaud = a (portable) stove

réchauffer *verb* [1]
• (*if it's food*) = to reheat, to heat up
• (*if it's a person, a part of the body*) = to
warm up

recherche *noun, feminine*
• (*into a subject*)
la recherche = research
• (*looking for something*)
une recherche = a search

récipient *noun, masculine*
un récipient = a container

récit *noun, masculine*
un récit = a story

réciter *verb* [1]
= to recite

réclamation *noun, feminine*
une réclamation = a complaint

réclame *noun, feminine*
• la réclame = publicity
• une réclame = an advertisement
• 'en réclame' = 'on offer', 'on sale'

réclamer *verb* [1]
• = to ask for
• = to complain

récolter *verb* [1]
= to harvest, to reap

recommandé/recommandée
adjective
une lettre recommandée = a registered
letter

recommander *verb* [1]
• = to recommend
• = to advise

recommencer *verb* [12]
= to start again, to start over

récompense *noun, feminine*
une récompense = a reward

récompenser *verb* [1]
= to reward

reconnaissance *noun, feminine*
la reconnaissance = gratitude

reconnaissant/reconnaissante
adjective
= grateful

reconnaître *verb* [63]
• = to recognize
• = to admit
= to acknowledge

recopier *verb* [2]
= to copy out
= to write out

record *noun, masculine*
le record du monde = the world record

recouvrir *verb* [32]
= to cover

récréation *noun, feminine*
la récréation (*in school*) = break, recess

reçu/reçue
1 ▶ recevoir [5]
2 reçu *noun, masculine*
un reçu = a receipt

recueillir *verb* [27]
= to collect

reculer *verb* [1]
• = to move back
= to reverse
• = to postpone

reculons: à reculons *adverb*
à reculons = backwards

récupérer *verb* [14]
• (*after an illness*) = to recover
• (*having lost or lent something*) = to get
back
= to collect
• (*in order to reuse*) = to salvage

recyclage *noun, masculine*
le recyclage (*of waste*) = recycling
(*of staff*) = retraining

rédaction *noun, feminine*
une rédaction = an essay, a theme

redescendre *verb* 6
1 (! + *être*)
= to go down again, to come down again
2 (! + *avoir*)
= to take down again, to bring down again

rediffusion *noun, feminine*
une rediffusion = a repeat (broadcast)

redoubler *verb* 1
redoubler (une classe) = to repeat a year

redresser *verb* 1
• = to put up again
• = to straighten (up)

réduction *noun, feminine*
une réduction = a reduction, a discount

réduire *verb* 62
= to reduce

réduit/réduite
1 ▶ réduire 62
2 réduit *noun, masculine*
un réduit = a cubbyhole

réel/réelle *adjective*
= real

réexpédier *verb* 2
• = to forward, to redirect
• = to send back

refaire *verb* 10
= to do again
= to redo
= to make again

réfectoire *noun, masculine*
un réfectoire = a refectory, a dining hall

refermer *verb* 1
= to close

réfléchir *verb* 3
• = to reflect
réfléchir la lumière = to reflect light
• réfléchir = to think

reflet *noun, masculine*
• (*an image*)
un reflet = a reflection
• (*a flash of light*)
un reflet = a glint
= a shimmer
cheveux châtain à reflets roux = brown hair with auburn highlights

refléter *verb* 14
= to reflect

réflexion *noun, feminine*
• la réflexion = reflection
• une réflexion = a remark

refrain *noun, masculine*
• le refrain = the chorus
• c'est toujours le même refrain = it's the same old refrain

refroidir *verb* 3
• = to cool down
• = to get cold

refus *noun, masculine* (! *never changes*)
un refus = a refusal

refuser *verb* 1
= to refuse
= to turn down

regagner *verb* 1
• = to get back to, to return to
• = to regain

régaler: se régaler *verb* 1 (! + *être*)
je me suis régalé = I really enjoyed that

regard *noun, masculine*
un regard = a look

regarder *verb* 1
• = to look at
• = to watch
• = to concern
ça ne te regarde pas = it's none of your business

régime *noun, masculine*
• (*what one eats*)
un régime = a diet
• (*in politics*)
un régime = a regime

région *noun, feminine*
une région = a region, an area

règle
1 *noun, feminine*
• (*for measuring*)
une règle = a ruler
• (*to be obeyed*)
une règle = a rule
2 règles *noun, feminine plural*
avoir ses règles = to have a period

règlement *noun, masculine*
le règlement = the regulations, the rules

régler *verb* 14
• = to pay
• = to settle
• = to adjust

réglisse *noun, feminine*
la réglisse = liquorice, licorice

règne *noun, masculine*
un règne = a reign

regretter *verb* 1
• = to be sorry
• = to regret
• = to miss

régulier/régulière *adjective*
• = regular
un vol régulier = a scheduled flight
• = steady
= even

rein
1 *noun, masculine*
un rein = a kidney

R

2 reins noun, masculine plural
  les reins = the small of the back
  avoir mal aux reins = to have (a) backache

reine noun, feminine
  une reine = a queen

rejoindre verb 56
• = to join
• = to meet up with
• = to catch up with

relais noun, masculine (**!** never changes)
• (a place)
  un relais = an inn
  un relais routier = a roadside café, a truck
    stop
• (in sport)
  un relais = a relay

relever verb 16
1 (**!** + avoir)
• (after something has fallen) = to pick up
  = to put back up
• (to become aware of) = to notice
2 se relever (**!** + être)
  se relever (after a fall) = to get up

relier verb 2
• = to connect
• = to bind

religieuse¹ noun, feminine
• ▶ religieux 2
• (a cake)
  une religieuse = a round éclair

religieux/religieuse²
1 adjective
  = religious
2 noun, masculine|feminine
  un religieux/une religieuse = a monk/a
    nun

relire verb 41
  = to read again
  = to read over

reliure noun, feminine
  une reliure = a binding

remarier: se remarier verb 2 (**!** + être)
  se remarier = to remarry

remarquer verb 1
  = to notice
  faire remarquer = to point out

rembourser verb 1
  = to reimburse, to pay back

remède noun, masculine
  un remède = a medicine
    = a cure

remerciement noun, masculine
  des remerciements = thanks

remercier verb 2
  = to thank

remettre verb 60
1 (**!** + avoir)
• = to put back
  remettre une lettre dans un tiroir = to put a
    letter back in a drawer
  remettre son manteau = to put one's coat
    back on
• = to hand over, to give
  je leur ai remis les clés = I handed the
    keys over to them
2 se remettre (**!** + être)
• **se remettre** = to recover
  se remettre d'une maladie = to recover
    from an illness, to get over an illness
• **se remettre à** [travailler | marcher | pleurer …]
  = to start [working | walking | crying …] again

remonter verb 1
1 (**!** + être)
• = to go back up(stairs), to come back
    up(stairs)
• **remonter au dix-septième siècle** = to go
    back to the seventeenth century
2 (**!** + avoir)
• **remonter les escaliers** = to go back up the
    stairs
• **remonter ses bagages** = to take one's
    luggage back up(stairs)

remorque noun, feminine
  une remorque = a trailer

remplacer verb 12
  = to replace

remplir verb 3
  = to fill

remuer verb 1
• = to move
  = to wriggle
• = to stir

renard noun, masculine
  un renard = a fox

rencontre noun, feminine
• **une rencontre** = an encounter
  = a meeting
  faire la rencontre d'un garçon = to meet a
    boy
• (in sport)
  une rencontre (sportive) = a match, a
    game

rencontrer verb 1
  = to meet
  = to come across

rendez-vous noun, masculine (**!** never
changes)
  un rendez-vous = an appointment
    = a date

rendre verb 6
1 (**!** + avoir)
• = to give back, to return
• **rendre visite à un ami** = to visit a friend

2 se rendre (**!** + *être*)
• se rendre = to surrender
• se rendre à Paris = to go to Paris
• se rendre compte = to realize
  = to notice
• se rendre malade = to make oneself ill

renne *noun, masculine*
  un renne = a reindeer

renoncer *verb* 12
  renoncer à = to give up

renouveler *verb* 19
• = to renew
• = to replace

rénover *verb* 1
  = to renovate

renseignement
1 *noun, masculine*
  un renseignement = (a piece of)
  information
  des renseignements = information
2 renseignements *noun, masculine plural*
  les renseignements (*on the telephone*)
  = directory enquiries, information
  (*an office*) = enquiries, information

renseigner *verb* 1
1 (**!** + *avoir*)
  = to give information
  être bien renseigné = to be well-informed
2 se renseigner (**!** + *être*)
  se renseigner = to find out
  = to enquire, to make enquiries

rentrée *noun, feminine*
  la rentrée (scolaire *or* des classes) = the
  start of the school year

rentrer *verb* 1
1 (**!** + *être*)
• = to go in, to come in
  rentrer dans une pièce = to go/come back
  into a room
• = to go home, to come home
• = to fit
  rentrer dans une boîte = to fit into a box
• rentrer dans un mur = to crash into a wall
2 (**!** + *avoir*)
  = to take in, to bring in

renverser *verb* 1
• = to spill
• = to knock over

renvoyer *verb* 24
• = to return
  = to throw back
  = to send back
• = to expel
  = to dismiss

réparation *noun, feminine*
  une réparation = a repair

réparer *verb* 1
  = to mend, to repair

repas *noun, masculine* (**!** *never changes*)
  un repas = a meal

repassage *noun, masculine*
  le repassage = ironing

repasser *verb* 1
1 (**!** + *avoir*)
• repasser une jupe = to iron a skirt
• repasser un examen = to resit an exam
2 (**!** + *être*)
• = to go past again
• = to call again

répéter *verb* 14
• = to repeat
• = to rehearse

répétition *noun, feminine*
• (*in a text*)
  une répétition = a repetition
• (*for actors*)
  une répétition = a rehearsal

répondre *verb* 6
  = to answer, to reply

réponse *noun, feminine*
  une réponse = an answer, a reply

reportage *noun, masculine*
  un reportage = a report, an article

repos *noun, masculine* (**!** *never changes*)
  le repos = rest
  = relaxation
  mon jour de repos = my day off

reposer: se reposer *verb* 1 (**!** + *être*)
  se reposer = to rest

reprendre *verb* 52
• reprendre du pain = to have some more
  bread
• = to take back
• reprendre le travail = to go back to work
  reprendre ses études = to take up one's
  studies again
  reprendre la conversation = to continue
  the conversation
• = to start again
  l'école a repris = school has started again

représentant/représentante *noun,*
masculine/feminine
  un représentant/une représentante = a
  representative

représenter *verb* 1
  = to represent

réprimander *verb* 1
  = to tell off

repris/reprise ▶ **reprendre** 52

république *noun, feminine*
  une république = a republic

requin *noun, masculine*
  un requin = a shark

R

RER *noun, masculine*
le RER *a rapid-transit rail system in the Paris area*

réseau *noun, masculine*
(*plural*) **réseaux**
un réseau = a network

réservation *noun, feminine*
une réservation = a reservation, a booking

réserver *verb* ①
• = to reserve, to book
• = to put aside, to set aside

résidence *noun, feminine*
une résidence = a residence
= a place of residence
une résidence secondaire = a second home

résolu/résolue
1 ▶ résoudre ⑥⑤
2 *adjective*
= resolute, determined

résoudre *verb* ⑥⑤
= to solve, to resolve

respecter *verb* ①
= to respect
= to treat with respect

respiration *noun, feminine*
la respiration = breathing

respirer *verb* ①
= to breathe

responsable
1 *adjective*
= responsible
2 *noun, masculine/feminine*
• **un responsable/une responsable** = a person in charge
• **le responsable de l'accident** = the person responsible for the accident

ressembler *verb* ①
1 (**!** + *avoir*)
ressembler à = to look like, to resemble
= to be like
2 se ressembler (**!** + *être*)
se ressembler = to look alike

ressort *noun, masculine*
un ressort = a spring

reste *noun, masculine*
• (*the remaining part*)
le reste = the rest
• (*the remains of a meal*)
les restes = the leftovers

rester *verb* ① (**!** + *être*)
• = to stay
= to remain

• **il me reste dix francs** = I've got ten francs left
il ne reste que quelques personnes = there are only a few people left

restituer *verb* ①
= to return, to hand back

résultat *noun, masculine*
le résultat = the result

résumé *noun, masculine*
un résumé = a summary

rétablir *verb* ③
1 (**!** + *avoir*)
= to restore
2 se rétablir (**!** + *être*)
se rétablir = to recover

retard *noun, masculine*
un retard = a delay
avoir du retard = to be late
être en retard = to be late

retarder *verb* ①
• = to be slow
• = to postpone, to put off
• = to delay, to hold up

retenir *verb* ㊱
1 (**!** + *avoir*)
• = to reserve
retenir des places = to reserve seats
• = to hold (back)
retenir son souffle = to hold one's breath
• = to remember
2 se retenir (**!** + *être*)
• **se retenir à une branche** = to hold on to a branch
• **se retenir de pleurer** = to stop oneself from crying

retenu/retenue¹ ▶ retenir ㊱

retenue² *noun, feminine*
une retenue (*in school*) = a detention

retirer *verb* ①
= to withdraw, to take out

retour *noun, masculine*
• **le retour** = the return
• **le retour** = the return journey
au retour = on the way back

retourner *verb* ①
1 (**!** + *avoir*)
• = to turn over
= to turn inside out
= to turn upside down
• = to send back
2 (**!** + *être*)
= to go back, to return
3 se retourner (**!** + *être*)
se retourner = to turn around, to turn over

retraite *noun, feminine*
la retraite = retirement

✗ in informal situations

retraité/retraitée *noun,*
masculine/feminine
  un retraité/une retraitée = a retired person

rétrécir *verb* ③
  = to shrink

retrouver *verb* ①
1 (**!** + *avoir*)
• (*after losing something*) = to find
• (*after arranging to get together*) = to meet
• (*after losing touch*) = to see again
2 se retrouver (**!** + *être*)
• (*by arrangement*)
  se retrouver = to meet
• (*to end up*)
  se retrouver = to find oneself
  se retouver dans une situation difficile = to
   find oneself in a difficult situation

rétroviseur *noun, masculine*
  un rétroviseur = a rearview mirror

réunion *noun, feminine*
  une réunion = a meeting

réunir *verb* ③
1 (**!** + *avoir*)
• = to gather together
• = to collect
2 se réunir (**!** + *être*)
  se réunir = to meet
  = to get together

réussir *verb* ③
• = to succeed
  = to be successful
• réussir à ouvrir la porte = to manage to
  open the door
  réussir à un examen = to pass an exam

réussite *noun, feminine*
• (*an achievement*)
  une réussite = success
• (*a game*)
  une réussite = patience, solitaire

rêve *noun, masculine*
  un rêve = a dream

réveil *noun, masculine*
  un réveil = an alarm clock

réveiller *verb* ①
1 (**!** + *avoir*)
  = to wake (up)
2 se réveiller (**!** + *être*)
  se réveiller = to wake up

réveillon *noun, masculine*
  le réveillon de Noël = Christmas Eve
   celebrations
  le réveillon du Nouvel An = New Year's Eve
   celebrations

révéler *verb* ⑭
  = to reveal
  = to show

revenir *verb* ㊱ (**!** + *être*)
  = to come back

revenu/revenue
1 ▶ revenir ㊱
2 revenu *noun, masculine*
  mon revenu = my income

rêver *verb* ①
  = to dream

réverbère *noun, masculine*
  un réverbère = a streetlamp

rêveur/rêveuse *adjective*
  = dreamy

réviser *verb* ①
• = to revise
• réviser un moteur = to overhaul an engine

revoir
1 *verb* ㊼
• = to see again
• = to go over
  revoir un exercice = to go over an exercise
2 au revoir = goodbye

revu/revue¹ ▶ revoir 1 ㊼

revue² *noun, feminine*
• une revue = a magazine
• une revue = a show

rez-de-chaussée *noun, masculine*
(**!** *never changes*)
  au rez-de-chaussée (*in Britain*) = on the
   ground floor
  (*in the US*) = on the first floor

Rhin *noun, masculine*
  le Rhin = the Rhine

rhum *noun, masculine*
  le rhum = rum

rhume *noun, masculine*
  un rhume = a cold
  le rhume des foins = hay fever

riant ▶ rire 1 ㊸

riche *adjective*
  = rich, wealthy

ride *noun, feminine*
  une ride = a wrinkle

rideau *noun, masculine*
(*plural*) **rideaux**
  un rideau = a curtain
  des rideaux = curtains, drapes

ridicule *adjective*
  = ridiculous

rien *pronoun*
  = nothing
  je ne veux rien = I don't want anything
  ça ne fait rien = it doesn't matter
  de rien = don't mention it

rigoler* *verb* ①
• = to laugh
• = to have fun
• = to joke

R

rigolo/rigolote* *adjective*
= funny

rimer *verb* 1
= to rhyme

rinçage *noun, masculine*
le rinçage = rinsing

rincer *verb* 12
= to rinse

rire
1 *verb* 43
• = to laugh
• = to have fun
il a dit ça pour rire = he said that as a joke
2 *noun, masculine*
un rire = a laugh, laughter

risque *noun, masculine*
un risque = a risk

risquer *verb* 1
• = to risk
vos bagages ne risquent rien = your
luggage is quite safe
• = to venture
• tu risques de tomber = you might fall
il risque de faire froid = it might be cold
ça ne risque pas de se produire = there's
no chance of that happening

rivage *noun, masculine*
le rivage = the shore

rive *noun, feminine*
la rive (*of a river*) = the bank
(*of a lake*) = the shore

rivière *noun, feminine*
une rivière = a river

riz *noun, masculine* (**!** *never changes*)
le riz = rice

robe *noun, feminine*
une robe = a dress
une robe de chambre = a dressing gown,
a robe

robinet *noun, masculine*
un robinet = a tap, a faucet

robuste *adjective*
(*describing a person*) = robust, sturdy

rocher *noun, masculine*
un rocher = a rock

rognon *noun, masculine*
un rognon = a kidney

roi *noun, masculine*
un roi = a king

rôle *noun, masculine*
un rôle = a role
= a part

romain/romaine *adjective*
= Roman

roman *noun, masculine*
un roman = a novel
un roman policier = a detective novel, a
thriller

romarin *noun, masculine*
le romarin = rosemary

ronce *noun, feminine*
une ronce = a bramble

rond/ronde
1 *adjective*
• = round
• = chubby
2 **rond** *noun, masculine*
un rond = a circle
en rond = in a circle

rondelle *noun, feminine*
une rondelle = a slice

rond-point *noun, masculine*
(*plural*) **ronds-points**
un rond-point = a roundabout, a traffic
circle

ronfler *verb* 1
= to snore

ronger *verb* 13
1 (**!** + *avoir*)
= to gnaw
= to eat into
2 **se ronger** (**!** + *être*)
se ronger les ongles = to bite one's nails

ronronner *verb* 1
= to purr

rosbif *noun, masculine*
un rosbif = a joint of beef, a roast of beef
= roast beef

rose
1 *adjective*
= pink
2 *noun, feminine*
une rose = a rose

roseau *noun, masculine*
(*plural*) **roseaux**
un roseau = a reed

rosée *noun, feminine*
la rosée = dew

roseraie *noun, feminine*
une roseraie = a rose garden

rosier *noun, masculine*
un rosier = a rose bush

rossignol *noun, masculine*
un rossignol = a nightingale

rôti *noun, masculine*
un rôti = a joint
= a roast

---

* in informal situations

roue *noun, feminine*
une roue = a wheel
une roue de secours = a spare wheel, a spare tire

rouge
1 *adjective*
= red
2 *noun, masculine*
le rouge = red
le rouge à lèvres = lipstick

rouge-gorge *noun, masculine*
(*plural*) **rouges-gorges**
un rouge-gorge = a robin

rougeole *noun, feminine*
la rougeole = measles

rouille *noun, feminine*
la rouille = rust

rouleau *noun, masculine*
(*plural*) **rouleaux**
un rouleau = a roll

rouler *verb* [1]
• (*if it's a ball, a coin*) = to roll
• (*if it's a car*) = to go
(*if it's a driver*) = to drive
• rouler✶ = to trick

roumain/roumaine
1 *adjective*
= Romanian
2 roumain *noun, masculine*
le roumain = Romanian

Roumanie *noun, feminine*
la Roumanie = Romania

rouspéter✶ *verb* [14]
= to grumble, to complain

rousse *adjective, feminine* ▶ **roux**

route *noun, feminine*
• une route = a road, a highway
• la route = the way
en (cours de) route = on the way
se mettre en route = to set off
en route! = let's go!
il y a deux heures de route = it's a two-hour drive
une route départementale = a secondary road
une route nationale = a trunk road, a national highway

routier/routière
1 *adjective*
= road
2 routier *noun, masculine*
un routier = a lorry driver, a truck driver

roux/rousse
1 *adjective*
= red
= red-haired
2 *noun, masculine/feminine*
un roux/une rousse = a redhead

Royaume-Uni *noun, masculine*
le Royaume-Uni = the United Kingdom

ruban *noun, masculine*
un ruban = a ribbon

ruche *noun, feminine*
une ruche = a beehive

rude *adjective*
(*describing a task*) = hard, tough
(*describing a climate, a voice*) = harsh

rue *noun, feminine*
une rue = a street

ruée *noun, feminine*
une ruée = a rush
= a stampede

ruelle *noun, feminine*
une ruelle = an alley

ruine *noun, feminine*
• (*financial*)
la ruine = ruin
• (*remains*)
des ruines = ruins

ruisseau *noun, masculine*
(*plural*) **ruisseaux**
un ruisseau = a stream, a brook

rumeur *noun, feminine*
une rumeur (*gossip*) = a rumo(u)r
(*a noise*) = a rumble

ruse *noun, feminine*
• une ruse = a trick
• la ruse = cunning

rusé/rusée *adjective*
= cunning, crafty

russe
1 *adjective*
= Russian
2 *noun, masculine*
le russe = Russian

Russie *noun, feminine*
la Russie = Russia

rustine *noun, feminine*
une rustine = a patch

rythme *noun, masculine*
le rythme = (the) rhythm
= the rate, the pace

R

Ss

s'
1 *pronoun* ▶ **se**
2 *conjunction* ▶ **si 2**

sa ▶ **son²**

sable *noun, masculine*
le sable = sand

sac *noun, masculine*
un sac = a bag
un sac de couchage = a sleeping bag
un sac à dos = a rucksack, a backpack
un sac à main = a handbag, a purse
un sac à provisions = a shopping bag, a carry-all

saccade *noun, feminine*
une saccade = a jerk

saccager *verb* 13
= to wreck, to devastate
= to vandalize

sache ▶ **savoir** 47

sachet *noun, masculine*
un sachet = a packet
= a sachet
= a bag

sacoche *noun, feminine*
une sacoche = a bag
(*on a bicycle*) = a pannier, a saddlebag

sacré/sacrée *adjective*
= sacred, holy

sage *adjective*
• = good, well-behaved
• = wise

Sagittaire *noun, masculine*
le Sagittaire = Sagittarius

saignant/saignante *adjective*
(*describing steak*) = rare

saigner *verb* 1
= to bleed

sain/saine *adjective*
= healthy

sais ▶ **savoir** 47

saisir *verb* 3
• (*to catch hold of*) = to grab, to seize
saisir une balle au vol = to catch a ball
• (*to affect deeply*) = to grip
être saisi de panique = to be panic-stricken
• (*to get the meaning*) = to understand

✗ in informal situations

saison *noun, feminine*
une saison = a season
en cette saison = at this time of year
en toute saison = all year round

saisonnier/saisonnière *adjective*
= seasonal

salade *noun, feminine*
une salade = a (head of) lettuce
= a salad

salaire *noun, masculine*
un salaire = a salary, wages

sale *adjective*
= dirty

salé/salée *adjective*
= salty, salted
= savoury

saler *verb* 1
= to salt

saleté *noun, feminine*
• la saleté = dirtiness
= dirt, filth
• ramasser les saletés = to pick up the rubbish, to pick up the trash

salir *verb* 3
1 (**!** + *avoir*)
= to dirty, to soil
2 **se salir** (**!** + *être*)
se salir = to get dirty

salle *noun, feminine*
une salle = a room
= a hall
une salle de bains = a bathroom
une salle de classe = a classroom
la salle d'embarquement = the departure lounge
une salle à manger = a dining room
une salle de séjour = a living room

salon *noun, masculine*
un salon = a lounge, a sitting room, a parlor

salopette *noun, feminine*
une salopette = dungarees

saluer *verb* 1
• = to greet
• = to salute

salut✗ *exclamation*
salut✗! = hi!
= goodbye!

salutations *noun, feminine plural*
des salutations = greetings
'sincères salutations' = 'yours sincerely'
= 'yours faithfully'

samedi *noun, masculine*
samedi = Saturday

sang *noun, masculine*
le sang = blood

sang-froid noun, masculine (**!** never changes)
le sang-froid = calm, composure

sanglier noun, masculine
un sanglier = a wild boar

sangloter verb 1
= to sob

sans preposition
= without
sans doute = probably

santé noun, feminine
la santé = health
à votre santé! = cheers!

santon noun, masculine
un santon a Christmas crib figure

saoul/saoule adjective
= drunk

sapin noun, masculine
un sapin = a fir tree
un sapin de Noël = a Christmas tree

satisfaire verb 10
= to satisfy

satisfaisant/satisfaisante adjective
• = satisfactory
• = satisfying

satisfait/satisfaite adjective
= satisfied

sauce noun, feminine
une sauce = a sauce
= gravy

saucisse noun, feminine
une saucisse = a sausage

saucisson noun, masculine
le saucisson ≈ salami

sauf¹ preposition
= except
sauf si = unless

sauf²/sauve adjective
= safe
sain et sauf/saine et sauve = safe and sound

saumon noun, masculine
un saumon = a salmon

saurai ▶ savoir 47

saut noun, masculine
un saut = a jump
le saut en hauteur = the high jump

saute-mouton noun, masculine
jouer à saute-mouton = to play leapfrog

sauter verb 1
= to jump
= to skip
sauter à la corde = to skip, to jump rope

sauterelle noun, feminine
une sauterelle = a grasshopper

sauvage adjective
= wild

sauve ▶ sauf 2

sauvegarder verb 1
= to save

sauver verb 1
1 (**!** + avoir)
= to save
= to rescue
2 se sauver (**!** + être)
se sauver = to escape
= to run away

sauvetage noun, masculine
un sauvetage = a rescue

sauveteur noun, masculine
un sauveteur = a rescuer

savant/savante
1 adjective
• = learned
• **les animaux savants** = performing animals
2 noun, masculine/feminine
un savant/une savante = a scholar
= a scientist

saveur noun, feminine
la saveur = the flavo(u)r

savoir verb 47
• = to know
je n'en sais rien = I've no idea
• = to know how to

savon noun, masculine
le savon = soap

savonnette noun, feminine
une savonnette = a small bar of soap

savoureux/savoureuse adjective
= tasty

scène noun, feminine
• (in a theatre)
la scène = the stage
• (something seen)
une scène = a scene

schéma noun, masculine
un schéma = a diagram

scie noun, feminine
une scie = a saw

science noun, feminine
la science = science
les sciences (as a school subject)
= science

scier verb 2
= to saw

scintiller verb 1
= to twinkle, to sparkle, to glisten

scolaire adjective
= school

S

Scorpion noun, masculine
le Scorpion = Scorpion

scotch noun, masculine
(plural) **scotches**
• le scotch = Sellotape , Scotch tape
• le scotch = Scotch (whisky)

scout/scoute noun, masculine/feminine
un scout/une scoute = a boy scout/a girl
scout

se (**s'** before vowel or mute h) pronoun
• = oneself
= himself/herself
= itself
= themselves
se faire mal = to hurt oneself
elles se sont fait mal = they hurt
themselves
• = each other
ils s'aimaient = they loved each other

séance noun, feminine
une séance = a session
(in a cinema) = a showing

seau noun, masculine
(plural) **seaux**
un seau = a bucket

sec/sèche adjective
• (without moisture) = dry
des fruits secs = dried fruit
• (abrupt) = sharp

sèche ▶ sec

sèche-cheveux noun, masculine
(! never changes)
un sèche-cheveux = a hairdryer

sèche-linge noun, masculine (! never
changes)
un sèche-linge = a tumble dryer

sécher verb 14
= to dry (up)

sécheresse noun, feminine
la sécheresse = drought

séchoir noun, masculine
• un séchoir = a hairdryer
• un séchoir = a clothes horse, a drying rack
= a rotary clothes dryer

second/seconde¹ number
= second

secondaire
1 adjective
= secondary
2 noun, masculine
le secondaire = secondary-school
education, high-school education (for
students aged 11 to 18)

seconde² noun, feminine
• (a unit of time)
une seconde = a second
• (in school)
la seconde the class for secondary school
students aged 15 to 16
• (when travelling)
voyager en seconde = to travel second
class
un billet de seconde = a second-class
ticket

secouer verb 1
= to shake

secourir verb 26
= to rescue
= to help

secours
1 noun, masculine (! never changes)
un secours = help
au secours! = help!
une sortie de secours = an emergency exit
2 noun, masculine plural
des secours = rescuers
= (relief) supplies

secousse noun, feminine
une secousse = a jolt

secret/secrète
1 adjective
= secret
2 secret noun, masculine
un secret = a secret

secrétaire noun, masculine/feminine
un secrétaire/une secrétaire = a secretary

secrétariat noun, masculine
le secrétariat = the secretary's office

secrète ▶ secret 1

sectionner verb 1
= to cut

sécuriser verb 1
= to reassure
= to give a feeling of security

sécurité noun, feminine
la sécurité = security
= safety
se sentir en sécurité = to feel safe
la sécurité sociale the French national
health and pensions organization

séduisant/séduisante adjective
= attractive

seigneur noun, masculine
un seigneur = a lord

sein noun, masculine
un sein = a breast

seize number
= sixteen

seizième number
= sixteenth

✶ in informal situations

séjour noun, masculine
• (a room)
  un séjour = a living room, a parlor
• (time spent somewhere)
  un séjour = a stay
  faire un séjour à l'étranger = to spend
    some time abroad
un séjour linguistique = a language-
  study holiday, a language-study vacation

sel noun, masculine
  le sel = salt

sélectionner verb 1
  = to select

selle noun, feminine
  une selle = a saddle

selon preposition
• = according to
  selon moi = in my opinion
• = depending on
  selon le temps = depending on the
    weather

semaine noun, feminine
  une semaine = a week

semblable adjective
  = similar

semblant noun, masculine
  faire semblant [de dormir | d'être malade |
    d'avoir mal …] = to pretend [to be asleep | to
    be ill | to be in pain …]

sembler verb 1
  = to seem
  il me semble que = it seems to me that
  il me semble qu'il pleut = I think it's
    raining

semelle noun, feminine
  une semelle = a sole

semer verb 1
• = to sow
• = to scatter

semoule noun, feminine
  la semoule = semolina

sens noun, masculine (**!** never changes)
• **un sens** = a meaning
• **le sens** = sense
  le bon sens = common sense
  ça n'a pas de sens = it doesn't make sense
• **le sens** = the way
  = the direction
  plie-le dans l'autre sens = fold it the other
    way
  dans le sens de la flèche = in the
    direction of the arrow
  dans le sens des aiguilles d'une montre
    = clockwise
  une rue à sens unique = a one-way street
  'sens obligatoire' = 'one way'

sensationnel/sensationnelle
adjective
• (causing a stir) = sensational
• (very good)**✱** = fantastic

sensé/sensée adjective
  = sensible

sensible adjective
  = sensitive

senti ▶ sentir 30

sentier noun, masculine
  un sentier = a path
un sentier de grande randonnée = a
  long-distance footpath

sentiment noun, masculine
  un sentiment = a feeling

sentir verb 30
1 (**!** + avoir)
• = to feel
• = to sense
• = to smell
• = to smell of
  ça sent le brûlé = there's a smell of
    burning
2 se sentir (**!** + être)
  se sentir = to feel

séparer verb 1, **se séparer** (**!** + être)
  = to separate
  = to part
  = to divide

sept number
  = seven

septante number
  = seventy

septembre noun, masculine
  septembre = September

septième number
  = seventh

serai ▶ être 7

série noun, feminine
• (a succession)
  une série = a series
• (a collection)
  une série = a set

sérieux/sérieuse adjective
• = serious
• = reliable

seringue noun, feminine
  une seringue = a syringe

serpent noun, masculine
  un serpent = a snake

serre noun, feminine
  une serre = a greenhouse

serré/serrée adjective
• (not big enough) = tight
• (too close together)
  être serrés = to be packed together

S

serrer verb 1
1 (**!** + *avoir*)
- = to grip
  = to squeeze
  serrer la main d'un ami = to shake hands
  with a friend
- = to tighten
  serrer une ceinture = to tighten a belt
- = to be too tight
  ma jupe me serre à la taille = my skirt is
  too tight around the waist
- (*on the road*)
  'serrez à droite' = 'keep to the right'
2 se serrer (**!** + *être*)
  se serrer = to squeeze up
  je me suis serré contre elle = I huddled up
  against her

serrure noun, feminine
  une serrure = a lock
  le trou de la serrure = the keyhole

serrurier noun, masculine
  un serrurier = a locksmith

serveur/serveuse noun,
masculine/feminine
  un serveur/une serveuse = a waiter/a
  waitress

servi/servie ▶ **servir** 30

serviable adjective
  = obliging

service noun, masculine
- **le service** = service
  service compris = service included
- **un service** = a favo(u)r
  rendre service à un ami = to be helpful to
  a friend, to do a friend a favo(u)r

serviette noun, feminine
- (*household linen*)
  une serviette de toilette = a towel
  une serviette de table = a napkin
- (*a kind of bag*)
  une serviette = a briefcase

serviette-éponge noun, feminine
(*plural*) **serviettes-éponges**
  une serviette-éponge = a terry(-cloth) towel

servir verb 30
1 (**!** + *avoir*)
- = to serve
  qu'est-ce que je vous sers (à boire)?
  = what would you like to drink?
- = to be of use
  = to come in handy
  garde-le, ça peut servir = keep it, it might
  come in handy
- **servir à quelque chose** = to be used for
  something
  servir à quelqu'un = to be used by
  someone
  à quoi sert cet outil? = what's this tool
  used for?
  ça va me servir pour faire un coussin = I'm
  going to use it to make a cushion
  ça ne sert à rien de se mettre en colère
  = there's no point in losing one's temper
  j'ai écrit, mais ça n'a servi à rien = I wrote,
  but it didn't do any good

- **servir de** = to serve as
  = to be used as
  mon sac m'a servi d'oreiller = I used my
  bag as a pillow
2 se servir (**!** + *être*)
- **se servir** = to help oneself
- **se servir de** = to use
  il s'est servi d'un dictionnaire = he used a
  dictionary

ses ▶ **son²**

seuil noun, masculine
  le seuil = the threshold

seul/seule adjective
- = alone, by oneself, on one's own
  vivre seul = to live alone
- = lonely
  se sentir seul = to feel lonely
- = single
  pas un seul arbre = not a single tree
  une seule fois = once only

seulement adverb
  = only

sévère adjective
  = strict, harsh
  = severe

shampooing noun, masculine
  un shampooing = a shampoo

short noun, masculine
  un short = shorts

si
1 adverb
- = yes
  'tu n'y vas pas?'—'si!' = 'aren't you going?'
  —'yes I am!'
- = so
  elle est si jolie! = she's so pretty!
2 conjunction (**s'** before il or ils)
- (*introducing a supposition*) = if
  si j'étais riche = if I were rich
  si j'avais su = if only I had known, if I'd
  only known
  et s'il ne peut pas le réparer? = and what
  if he can't repair it?
  s'il vous plaît = please
- (*introducing a suggestion*)
  et si on allait en ville? = how about going
  into town?

sida noun, masculine
  le sida = Aids

siècle noun, masculine
  un siècle = a century
  au vingtième siècle = in the twentieth
  century

siège noun, masculine
- (*a piece of furniture*)
  un siège = a seat
- (*a place*)
  le siège (social) = the headquarters, the
  head office

sien/sienne *pronoun*
le sien/la sienne = his/hers
les siens/les siennes = his/hers

sieste *noun, feminine*
une sieste = a siesta, a snooze, a nap

siffler *verb* 1
* = to whistle
* = to blow one's whistle
* = to boo

sifflet *noun, masculine*
un sifflet = a whistle
un coup de sifflet = a whistle blast, a
whistle blow

sigle *noun, masculine*
un sigle = an acronym

signalement *noun, masculine*
un signalement = a description

signaler *verb* 1
* (*by informing*) = to report
rien à signaler = nothing to report
* (*by drawing attention*) = to point out
je vous signale qu'il est huit heures = may
I point out that it's eight o'clock
* (*by means of a notice, a sign*) = to indicate
= to signpost

signalisation *noun, feminine*
la signalisation = signs
la signalisation routière = road signs and
markings

signe *noun, masculine*
un signe = a sign

signer *verb* 1
= to sign

signifier *verb* 2
= to mean

silencieux/silencieuse *adjective*
= silent
= quiet

silhouette *noun, feminine*
* (*a shape*)
une silhouette = a silhouette
= an outline
* (*a person*)
une silhouette = a figure

sillon *noun, masculine*
un sillon = a furrow

simple *adjective*
* = simple
* = ordinary
c'est une simple formalité = it's just a
formality
* = single
un aller simple = a single (ticket)

singe *noun, masculine*
un singe = a monkey

sinistre
1 *adjective*
= sinister

2 *noun, masculine*
un sinistre = a (natural) disaster
= a fire

sinistré/sinistrée *adjective*
= stricken
une région sinistrée = a disaster area

sinon *conjunction*
= otherwise

sirène *noun, feminine*
une sirène = a siren

sirop *noun, masculine*
un sirop = a syrup
un sirop (de fruits) = a (fruit) cordial
un sirop (pour la toux) = a cough mixture

site *noun, masculine*
un site = a site
un site classé = a conservation area
un site pittoresque = a beauty spot, a
scenic area
un site touristique = a place of interest

situation *noun, feminine*
* (*a site*)
la situation d'une ville = the location of a
town
* (*the circumstances*)
la situation est grave = the situation is
serious
* (*a position*)
une bonne situation = a good job

situé/située *adjective*
= situated, located
la ville est bien située = the town is in a
good location

situer: se situer *verb* 1 (**!** + *être*)
* (*if it's a building, a town*)
se situer = to be situated
* (*if it's an event*)
se situer = to take place

six *number*
= six

sixième
1 *number*
= sixth
2 *noun, feminine*
la sixième *the class for secondary school
students aged 11 to 12*

ski *noun, masculine*
* (*the equipment*)
un ski = a ski
* (*the sport*)
le ski = skiing
le ski de fond = cross-country skiing
le ski nautique = water-skiing

skier *verb* 2
= to ski

slip *noun, masculine*
un slip (*for men*) = pants, shorts
(*for women*) = knickers, panties

S

slovaque
1 *adjective*
= Slovak
2 *noun, masculine*
le slovaque = Slovak

smoking *noun, masculine*
un smoking = a dinner jacket, a tuxedo

SNCF *noun, feminine*
la SNCF *the French national railway company*

snob *adjective*
= snobbish

société *noun, feminine*
• la société = society
• une société = a company

soda *noun, masculine*
le soda = soda water

sœur *noun, feminine*
une sœur = a sister

soi *pronoun*
= oneself
= itself

soi-disant
1 *adjective* (**!** *never changes*)
= so-called
2 *adverb*
= supposedly

soie *noun, feminine*
la soie = silk

soif *noun, feminine*
la soif = thirst
avoir soif = to be thirsty

soigné/soignée *adjective*
= meticulous, neat

soigner *verb* ⬚1
1 (**!** + *avoir*)
• = to treat
• = to look after
= to take care of
• = to take care over
2 se soigner (**!** + *être*)
se soigner = to look after oneself

soigneusement *adverb*
= carefully

soi-même *pronoun*
= oneself

soin
1 *noun, masculine*
le soin = care
avec soin = carefully
2 soins *noun, masculine plural*
les soins = treatment
= care
donner les premiers soins aux blessés
= to give first aid to the injured

soir *noun, masculine*
un soir = an evening
à ce soir = see you tonight

soirée *noun, feminine*
• la soirée = the evening
• une soirée = a party

soit
1 ▶ **être** ⬚7
2 *conjunction*
soit lundi soit mardi = either Monday or Tuesday

soixante *number*
= sixty

soixante-dix *number*
= seventy

soja *noun, masculine*
le soja = soya

sol *noun, masculine*
le sol = the floor
= the ground
= the soil

solaire *adjective*
= sun
= suntan
= solar

soldat *noun, masculine*
un soldat = a soldier

solde
1 *noun, masculine*
articles en solde = reduced items, sales bargains, sale items
acheter une veste en solde = to buy a jacket in a sale, to buy a jacket on sale
2 soldes *noun, masculine plural*
les soldes (*the event*) = the sales
(*the goods*) = sales goods, sale items

soleil *noun, masculine*
le soleil = the sun
au soleil = in the sun
il fait (du) soleil = it's sunny
un coup de soleil = sunburn
attraper un coup de soleil = to get sunburned

solennel/solennelle *adjective*
= solemn

solide *adjective*
= solid, strong
= sturdy

sombre *adjective*
= dark
il fait sombre = it's dark

sombrer *verb* ⬚1
= to sink

somme
1 *noun, feminine*
une somme = a sum
2 *noun, masculine*
un somme = a nap, a snooze

✘ in informal situations

sommeil *noun, masculine*
  le sommeil = sleep
  avoir sommeil = to be sleepy

sommes ▶ être 7

sommet *noun, masculine*
  le sommet = the summit, the peak, the top

sommier *noun, masculine*
  un sommier = a (bed) base

somnifère *noun, masculine*
  un somnifère = a sleeping pill

son¹ *noun, masculine*
  un son = a sound

son²/sa *determiner*
(*plural*) **ses**
  = his/her
  = its
  son mari = her husband
  sa femme = his wife
  ses livres = his/her books
  ses pattes = its paws

sondage *noun, masculine*
  un sondage = a survey
  = a(n opinion) poll

sonner *verb* 1
  = to ring
  (*if it's a clock*) = to strike

sonnerie *noun, feminine*
• (*a noise*)
  la sonnerie = the ringing
• (*a mechanism*)
  la sonnerie (*on an alarm clock*) = the alarm
  (*on a door*) = the bell

sonnette *noun, feminine*
  une sonnette = a bell

sonore *adjective*
• (*loud*) = resounding
• effets sonores = sound effects

sont ▶ être 7

sorcier *noun, masculine/feminine*
  un sorcier/une sorcière = a wizard/a witch

sordide *adjective*
  = squalid
  = sordid

sort *noun, masculine*
• le sort = fate
  tirer au sort = to draw lots
• son sort = one's lot
  être satisfait de son sort = to be satisfied
  with one's lot
• un sort = a curse, a spell
  jeter un sort à un ennemi = to put a curse
  on an enemy

sorte *noun, feminine*
  une sorte = a sort, a kind

sortie *noun, feminine*
• (*a way out*)
  une sortie = an exit
• (*the action of leaving a place*)
  il a été attaqué à sa sortie du bureau = he
  was mugged as he left the office
  se retrouver à la sortie de l'école = to meet
  after school
• (*a trip*)
  une sortie = an outing

sortir *verb* 30
1 (**!** + *être*)
• = to go out, to come out
• sortir de = to leave, to come out of
2 (**!** + *avoir*)
  = to take out
  = to get out
  sortir une lettre de sa poche = to take a
  letter out of one's pocket
  sors ton frère du lit! = get your brother out
  of bed!

sou *noun, masculine*
• un sou ≈ a penny, a cent
• avoir des sous✖ = to have money

souci *noun, masculine*
  un souci = a worry
  se faire du souci = to worry

soucoupe *noun, feminine*
  une soucoupe = a saucer

soudain/soudaine
1 *adjective*
  = sudden
2 soudain *adverb*
  = suddenly

souffler *verb* 1
• = to blow
• = to prompt
  on t'a soufflé la réponse = you were
  prompted, you were told the answer
• = to breathe out
• = to get one's breath back

souffrant/souffrante *adjective*
  = unwell

souffrir *verb* 4
  = to suffer
  = to be in pain

souhait *noun, masculine*
  un souhait = a wish

souhaiter *verb* 1
  = to wish
  souhaite-moi bonne chance = wish me
  luck
  souhaiter la bienvenue à un visiteur = to
  welcome a visitor
  je souhaite qu'il ne fasse pas froid
  = I hope that it won't be cold

soûl/soûle *adjective*
  = drunk

S

soulager verb 13
= to relieve
le comprimé m'a soulagé = the pill made me feel better

soulever verb 16
= to lift
= to raise

soulier noun, masculine
un soulier = a shoe

souligner verb 1
• = to underline
• = to emphasize, to stress

soupçon noun, masculine
un soupçon = a suspicion

soupçonner verb 1
= to suspect

soupe noun, feminine
la soupe = soup

souper
1 noun, masculine
le souper = supper
2 verb 1
= to have supper

soupir noun, masculine
un soupir = a sigh

soupirer verb 1
= to sigh

souple adjective
• = supple
• = flexible

source noun, feminine
• (water)
une source = a spring
• (the origin or cause of something)
une source = a source

sourcil noun, masculine
un sourcil = an eyebrow

sourd/sourde adjective
• (unable to hear) = deaf
• (describing a noise, a pain) = dull

souriant/souriante adjective
= smiling

sourire
1 verb 43
= to smile
2 noun, masculine
un sourire = a smile

souris noun, feminine (! never changes)
une souris = a mouse

sous
1 preposition
= under, underneath
sous terre = underground
sous la pluie = in the rain
2 ▶ sou

sous-marin/sous-marine
(plural) **sous-marins/sous-marines**
1 adjective
= submarine, underwater
= deep-sea
2 sous-marin noun, masculine
un sous-marin = a submarine

sous-sol noun, masculine
(plural) **sous-sols**
le sous-sol = the basement

sous-titre noun, masculine
(plural) **sous-titres**
un sous-titre = a subtitle

sous-vêtement noun, masculine
(plural) **sous-vêtements**
des sous-vêtements = underwear

soutenir verb 36
= to support

soutenu/soutenue ▶ soutenir 36

souterrain/souterraine
1 adjective
= underground
2 souterrain noun, masculine
un souterrain = a subway, a pedestrian underpass

soutien-gorge noun, masculine
(plural) **soutiens-gorge**
un soutien-gorge = a bra

souvenir
1 noun, masculine
• (something remembered)
un souvenir = a memory
• (an object)
un souvenir = a souvenir
2 se souvenir verb 36 (! + être)
se souvenir de = to remember

souvent adverb
= often
le plus souvent = more often than not

soyons ▶ être 7

spacieux/spacieuse adjective
= spacious

sparadrap noun, masculine
le sparadrap = (sticking) plaster, surgical tape

spatial/spatiale adjective
(plural) **spatiaux/spatiales**
= space

spécial/spéciale adjective
(plural) **spéciaux/spéciales**
• (not ordinary) = special
• (strange) = odd

spécialement adverb
= specially
= especially

spectacle noun, masculine
• (in a theatre, a circus)
un spectacle = a show

✗ in informal situations

• (*something seen*)
un spectacle = a sight

spectateur/spectatrice *noun,*
masculine/feminine
un spectateur/une spectatrice = a member
of the audience
= a spectator

spéléologie *noun, feminine*
la spéléologie = potholing, spelunking
= speleology

sponsoriser *verb* 1
= to sponsor

sport *noun, masculine*
le sport = sport

sportif/sportive
1 *adjective*
• (*describing an event, a magazine*) = sports
• (*describing a person*)
être sportif = to be the sporty type, to be
athletic
2 *noun, masculine/feminine*
un sportif/une sportive = a sportsman/a
sportswoman

square *noun, masculine*
un square = a small public garden

squelette *noun, masculine*
le squelette = the skeleton

squelettique *adjective*
= scrawny, thin as a rake

stade *noun, masculine*
un stade = a stadium

stage *noun, masculine*
un stage = a course
= (a period of) work experience

station *noun, feminine*
• (*in a town*)
une station de métro = a tube station, a
subway station
une station de taxis = a taxi rank, a taxi
stand
• (*a town or a village*)
une station balnéaire = a seaside resort
une station de ski = a ski resort
une station thermale = a spa

stationnement *noun, masculine*
le stationnement = parking

station-service *noun, feminine*
(*plural*) **stations-service**
une station-service = a service station, a
gas station

steak *noun, masculine*
un steak = a steak
un steak haché = a beefburger

sténodactylo
1 *noun, masculine/feminine*
un sténodactylo/une sténodactylo = a
shorthand typist, a stenographer

2 *noun, feminine*
la sténodactylo = shorthand typing,
stenographing

stop *noun, masculine*
• un stop = a stop sign
• le stop✗ = hitch-hiking
faire du stop✗ = to hitch-hike

store *noun, masculine*
un store = a blind
= an awning

studio *noun, masculine*
• (*accommodation*)
un studio = a studio flat, a studio
apartment
• (*a place of work*)
un studio = a studio

stupéfait/stupéfaite *adjective*
= astounded

stylo *noun, masculine*
un stylo = a (fountain) pen
un stylo (à) bille = a ball-point pen, a bic
un stylo feutre = a felt-tip pen

su/sue ▶ savoir 47

subir *verb* 3
subir une opération = to undergo an
operation
subir des dégâts = to suffer damage

subitement *adverb*
= suddenly

succès *noun, masculine* (**!** *never
changes*)
le succès = success

sucer *verb* 12
= to suck

sucette *noun, feminine*
une sucette = a lollipop, a lolly

sucre *noun, masculine*
le sucre = sugar
un sucre = a lump of sugar
le sucre d'orge = barley sugar

sucré/sucrée *adjective*
= sweet
= sweetened

sucrer *verb* 1
= to put sugar in
= to sweeten

sucreries *noun, feminine plural*
les sucreries = sweets, candies

sud
1 *noun, masculine*
le sud = the south
2 *adjective* (**!** *never changes*)
= south
= southern

Suède *noun, feminine*
la Suède = Sweden

S

suédois/suédoise
1 *adjective*
= Swedish
2 **suédois** *noun, masculine*
le Suédois = Swedish

sueur *noun, feminine*
la sueur = sweat

suffire *verb* 39
• = to be enough
ça me suffit = that's enough for me
• **il suffit de demander** = all you have to do is ask
il suffit d'une étincelle = one spark is enough

suffisamment *adverb*
= enough

suffisant/suffisante *adjective*
= sufficient

suis
• ▶ **être** 7
• ▶ **suivre** 37

suisse *adjective*
= Swiss

Suisse *noun, feminine*
la Suisse = Switzerland

suite
1 *noun, feminine*
• **la suite** = the rest
(*if it's another film or novel*) = the sequel
'suite page 45' = 'continued on page 45'
• **une suite de** = a succession of, a series of
2 **de suite** = in a row
à la suite de = following
trois jours de suite = three days in a row
3 **tout de suite** = straight away, right away
4 **par la suite** = subsequently

suivant/suivante
1 *adjective*
= next
= following
2 *noun, masculine|feminine*
le suivant/la suivante = the next (one)
au suivant! = next!
3 **suivant** = according to

suivi/suivie ▶ **suivre** 37

suivre *verb* 37
= to follow
'à suivre' = 'to be continued'
faire suivre le courrier = to forward the mail

sujet *noun, masculine*
un sujet = a subject

super
1 *adjective*✱ (**!** *never changes*)
= great

2 *noun, masculine*
le super ≈ 4-star (petrol), super

superficie *noun, feminine*
la superficie = the area

supérieur/supérieure *adjective*
• = upper, top
• = higher
• = superior

supermarché *noun, masculine*
un supermarché = a supermarket

supplémentaire *adjective*
= additional, extra

supportable *adjective*
= bearable

supporter *verb* 1
• = to support, to bear the weight of
• = to put up with, to bear

supprimer *verb* 1
= to remove
= to cancel
= to withdraw
= to do away with
= to cut

sur *preposition*
• = on
sur la table = on the table
• = over
un pont sur la rivière = a bridge over the river
• = about
un livre sur la guerre = a book about war
• = out of
9 sur 20 = 9 out of 20
• = by
faire 10 mètres sur 15 = to measure 10 metres by 15

sûr/sûre
1 *adjective*
• = sure, certain
c'est sûr = it's certain
j'en suis sûr = I'm sure of it, I'm certain of it
j'en étais sûr! = I knew it!
être sûr de soi = to be self-confident
• = safe
= reliable
un endroit sûr = a safe place
un homme sûr = a reliable man
2 **bien sûr** = of course

sûreté *noun, feminine*
la sûreté = safety
= security

surf *noun, masculine*
le surf = surfing

surface *noun, feminine*
la surface = the surface (area)

surgelé/surgelée *adjective*
= (deep-)frozen
les produits surgelés = frozen food

surligneur *noun, masculine*
un surligneur = a highlighter

surnaturel/surnaturelle *adjective*
= supernatural

surnom *noun, masculine*
un surnom = a nickname

surprenant/surprenante *adjective*
= surprising
= amazing

surprise *noun, feminine*
une surprise = a surprise

sursauter *verb* 1
= to jump, to start

surtout *adverb*
= above all
= especially

surveillant/surveillante *noun,*
masculine/feminine
un surveillant/une surveillante (*in a school*) = a supervisor
(*in a store*) = a store detective
(*in a prison*) = a warder, a guard

surveiller *verb* 1
• = to watch, to keep an eye on
• = to supervise

survenir *verb* 36
= to occur, to happen

survêtement *noun, masculine*
un survêtement = a tracksuit

survivant/survivante *noun,*
masculine/feminine
un survivant/une survivante = a survivor

survoler *verb* 1
= to fly over

sus : **en sus** *adverb*
en sus = in addition, on top

svelte *adjective*
= slender

SVP (*abbreviation of* **s'il vous plaît**)
SVP = please

sympa✽ *adjective* (**!** *never changes*)
= nice

sympathie *noun, feminine*
avoir de la sympathie pour quelqu'un = to like someone

sympathique *adjective*
= nice, pleasant

syndicat *noun, masculine*
un syndicat = a trade union
un syndicat d'initiative = a tourist information office

synthétique *adjective*
= man-made

T t

t' ▶ **te**

ta ▶ **ton²**

tabac *noun, masculine*
• (*a substance*)
le tabac = tobacco
• (*a shop*)
un tabac = a tobacconist's, a smoke shop

tabagisme *noun, masculine*
le tabagisme = tobacco addiction

table *noun, feminine*
une table = a table
mettre la table = to set the table
se mettre à table = to sit down at the table
à table! = dinner is served!
une table des matières = a table of contents
une table de nuit = a bedside table, a night stand

tableau *noun, masculine*
(*plural*) **tableaux**
• (*ornamental*)
un tableau = a painting
= a picture
• (*a surface*)
un tableau = a board
un tableau d'affichage = a noticeboard, a bulletin board
le tableau de bord = the dashboard
le tableau (noir) = the blackboard

tablier *noun, masculine*
un tablier = an apron

tabouret *noun, masculine*
un tabouret = a stool

tache *noun, feminine*
une tache = a stain

tâche *noun, feminine*
une tâche = a task, a job
les tâches ménagères = household chores

tacher *verb* 1
= to stain

tâcher *verb* 1
tâcher de = to try to

taille *noun, feminine*
• (*the middle of the body*)
la taille = the waist, the waistline
• (*overall dimensions*)
la taille = the size
quelle taille faites-vous? = what size do you take?
taille unique = one size
• (*tallness*)
la taille = the height

T

taille-crayon noun, masculine
(plural) **taille-crayons**
  un taille-crayon = a pencil sharpener

tailler verb [1]
  = to cut
  = to prune
  = to carve
  = to sharpen

tailleur noun, masculine
• (a garment)
  un tailleur = a (woman's) suit
• (a person)
  un tailleur = a tailor

taire: **se taire** verb [59] (**!** + être)
  se taire = to stop talking
  = to be silent, to fall silent
  taisez-vous! = be quiet!

talent noun, masculine
  le talent = talent
  un acteur de talent = a talented actor

talkie-walkie noun, masculine
(plural) **talkies-walkies**
  un talkie-walkie = a walkie-talkie

talon noun, masculine
  un talon = a heel

talus noun, masculine (**!** never changes)
  un talus = an embankment

tambour noun, masculine
  un tambour = a drum

Tamise noun, feminine
  la Tamise = the Thames

tampon noun, masculine
  un tampon (for documents) = a stamp

tamponner verb [1]
  1 (**!** + avoir)
• (to put a mark on) = to stamp
• (to wipe) = to mop, to dab
  2 se tamponner (**!** + être)
  se tamponner = to collide

tandis que (**tandis qu'** before vowel or
mute h) conjunction
  = while, whilst

tant adverb
• = so much
  il t'aime tant! = he loves you so much!
  tant mieux! = so much the better!
  tant mieux pour vous! = good for you!
  tant pis! = too bad!
• tant de = so much, so many
• tant que = as much as, as many as
  = as long as
  mange tant que tu veux = eat as much as
    you like
  il restera tant qu'il voudra = he'll stay as
    long as he likes

tante noun, feminine
  une tante = an aunt

tapage noun, masculine
  du tapage = a din, a racket

taper verb [1]
• taper sur un clou = to hit a nail
  il m'a tapé sur l'épaule = he tapped me on
    the shoulder
• taper des mains = to clap one's hands
  taper du pied = to tap one's foot
  taper à la porte = to knock at the door
• taper (à la machine) = to type

tapis noun, masculine (**!** never changes)
  un tapis = a rug
  = a carpet
  un tapis roulant = a moving walkway

tapisser verb [1]
• = to wallpaper
• = to line

tapisserie noun, feminine
• (woven or embroidered cloth)
  une tapisserie = a tapestry
• (paper)
  la tapisserie = the wallpaper

taquiner verb [1]
  = to tease

tard adverb
  = late
  plus tard = later
  au plus tard = at the latest
  pas plus tard qu'hier = only yesterday

tarder verb [1]
• tarder à arriver = to be a long time coming
  tes parents ne vont pas tarder = your
    parents won't be long
• tarder à répondre à une lettre = to take a
  long time replying to a letter
  = to put off replying to a letter
• il me tarde de les revoir = I'm longing to
  see them again, I can't wait to see them
  again

tarif noun, masculine
  le tarif = the price
  = the price list

tarte noun, feminine
  une tarte = a tart, a flan

tartelette noun, feminine
  une tartelette = a (small) tart

tartine noun, feminine
  une tartine = a slice of bread and butter

tas noun, masculine (**!** never changes)
• un tas = a pile, a heap
  en tas = in a pile, in a heap
• un (or des) tas✱ d'amis = loads of friends

tasse noun, feminine
  une tasse = a cup

tâter verb [1]
  = to feel

✱ in informal situations

tâtonner verb 1
= to grope about

tâtons: **à tâtons** adverb
avancer à tâtons = to grope one's way
along

taudis noun, masculine (**!** never changes)
un taudis = a slum

taupe noun, feminine
une taupe = a mole

taureau noun, masculine
(plural) **taureaux**
un taureau = a bull

Taureau noun, masculine
le Taureau = Taurus

taux noun, masculine (**!** never changes)
le taux = the rate
= the level
le taux de change = the exchange rate

tchèque
1 adjective
= Czech
2 noun, masculine
le tchèque = Czech

tchin(-tchin)* exclamation
tchin(-tchin)*! = cheers!

TD noun, masculine plural ▶ travail

te (**t'** before vowel or mute h) pronoun
• = you
je te vois = I can see you
elle te l'a donné = she gave it to you
• = yourself
tu t'es fait mal? = did you hurt yourself?

technicien/technicienne noun,
masculine/feminine
un technicien/une technicienne = a
technician

teindre verb 55
= to dye
= to stain

teint/teinte¹
1 ▶ **teindre** 55
2 teint noun, masculine
un teint = a complexion

teinte² noun, feminine
une teinte = a shade
= a colo(u)r

teinture noun, feminine
une teinture = a dye

teinturerie noun, feminine
une teinturerie = a dry cleaner's

teinturier/teinturière noun,
masculine/feminine
un teinturier/une teinturière = a dry cleaner

tel/telle adjective
= such
de telle sorte qu'il l'a cassé = in such a
way that he broke it
les pays tels que la France = countries
like France

télé* noun, feminine
la télé* = TV

télécommandé/télécommandée
adjective
= remote control

télécopieur noun, masculine
un télécopieur = a fax (machine)

téléfilm noun, masculine
un téléfilm = a TV film, a TV movie

téléphérique noun, masculine
un téléphérique = a cable car

téléphone noun, masculine
un téléphone = a (tele)phone

téléphoner verb 1
= to (tele)phone

télésiège noun, masculine
un télésiège = a chair lift

téléski noun, masculine
un téléski = a ski tow

téléspectateur/téléspectatrice
noun, masculine/feminine
un téléspectateur/une téléspectatrice = a
viewer

téléviseur noun, masculine
un téléviseur = a television (set)

télévision noun, feminine
la télévision = television, TV

tellement adverb
• = so (much)
il est tellement riche! = he's so rich!
c'est tellement mieux maintenant! = it's so
much better now!
• tellement de = so much, so many
elle a tellement de temps libre = she has so
much free time
il y avait tellement de monde que je suis
parti = there were so many people that I
left

témoignage noun, masculine
un témoignage = a personal account
(in court) = evidence

témoin noun, masculine
un témoin = a witness
être témoin d'un incident = to witness an
incident

tempérament noun, masculine
un tempérament = a disposition, a
temperament

température noun, feminine
la température = the temperature

T

tempête noun, feminine
une tempête = a storm
= a gale

temporaire adjective
= temporary

temps noun, masculine (! never changes)
* (outside conditions)
le temps = the weather
quel temps fait-il? = what's the weather like?
il fait beau temps = the weather is fine
il a fait mauvais temps = the weather has been bad
quel temps de chien! = what awful weather!, it's terrible weather!
* (as measured in hours)
le temps = time
je n'ai pas le temps de me reposer = I haven't got time to rest
il est grand temps de partir = it's high time we left
ils ont fini à temps = they finished in time
de temps en temps = from time to time
pendant ce temps = meanwhile
* (in grammar)
un temps = a tense

tenace adjective
= stubborn, persistent

tenir verb 36
1 (! + avoir)
* = to hold
* tiens!, tenez! (when giving something)
= here!
(expressing surprise) = hey!
2 tenir à (! + avoir)
tenir à sa famille = to be fond of one's family
3 se tenir (! + être)
* se tenir = to hold on
se tenir à la rampe = to hold on to the banister
* se tenir = to stand
se tenir droit (if standing) = to stand up straight
se tenir tranquille = to keep still
* se tenir = to behave
tenez-vous bien! = behave yourselves!
* ils se tenaient par la main = they were holding hands
4 si cela ne tenait qu'à moi = if I had my way

tennis noun, masculine (! never changes)
* (the sport)
le tennis = tennis
* (footwear)
un tennis = a tennis shoe

tentation noun, feminine
la tentation = temptation

tentative noun, feminine
une tentative = an attempt

tente noun, feminine
une tente = a tent

tenter verb 1
* = to attempt
= to try
tenter sa chance = to try one's luck
* = to tempt
ça ne me tente guère = it doesn't appeal to me very much

tenu/tenue¹ ▶ tenir 36

tenue² noun, feminine
une tenue = an outfit, clothes
en tenue de soirée = in evening dress

terminale noun, feminine
la terminale the class for secondary school students aged 17 to 18

terminer verb 1
1 (! + avoir)
= to finish, to end
2 se terminer (! + être)
se terminer = end
se terminer par une bagarre = to end in a fight

terminus noun, masculine (! never changes)
le terminus (for a train) = the end of the line
(for a bus) = the terminus

terne adjective
= dull

terrain noun, masculine
* (a site)
un terrain = a piece of land
(used for sport) = a pitch, a ground
* (the surface underfoot)
le terrain = the ground
un terrain d'atterrissage = a landing strip
un terrain à bâtir = a building plot
un terrain de camping = a campsite
un terrain de jeux = a playground
un terrain de sports = a sports ground, a sports field
un terrain vague = a piece of wasteland

terrasse noun, feminine
une terrasse = a terrace
= a flat roof
s'asseoir à la terrasse d'un café = to sit at a table outside a café

terre noun, feminine
* (the surface underfoot)
la terre = the ground
sous terre = underground
par terre = on the ground, on the floor
* (the substance)
la terre = the earth, the soil
(as opposed to the sea) = land
aller à terre = to go ashore
* (a type of clay)
un pot en terre = an earthenware pot

✗ in informal situations

- (*an area in private ownership*)
  une terre = a piece of land
  des terres = land

Terre *noun, feminine*
  la Terre = Earth

terrestre *adjective*
  (*describing plants or animals*) = land
  (*relating to the Earth*) = of the Earth

terrible *adjective*
- = terrible
- (*excellent*)✱ = terrific
  le livre n'est pas terrible✱ = it's not a great
  book

tes ▶ ton²

testament *noun, masculine*
  un testament = a will

tester *verb* ⬚1⬚
  = to test

tête *noun, feminine*
- (*part of the body*)
  la tête = the head
  se laver la tête = to wash one's hair
- (*the front part of the head*)
  la tête = the face
  tu fais une drôle de tête = you look funny
  faire la tête = to sulk
  n'en faire qu'à sa tête = to get one's way
- (*as opposed to the end*)
  la tête = the front
  = the head
  être en tête = to be at the front
  une tête en l'air = a scatterbrain

têtu/têtue *adjective*
  = stubborn, obstinate

TGV *noun, masculine*
  un TGV = a high speed train

thé *noun, masculine*
- **le thé** = tea
- **un thé** = a cup of tea

théâtre *noun, masculine*
  un théâtre = a theatre, a theater
  faire du théâtre = to be an actor/an actress,
  to act

théière *noun, feminine*
  une théière = a teapot

thème *noun, masculine*
- (*of a speech*)
  le thème = the theme
- (*a translation*)
  un thème = a prose

thermal/thermale *adjective*
(*plural*) **thermaux/thermales**
  une source thermale = a thermal spring
  une station thermale = a spa

thermos *noun, masculine* (❗ *never changes*)
  un thermos = a (vacuum) flask

thon *noun, masculine*
  le thon = tuna

thym *noun, masculine*
  le thym = thyme

tibia *noun, masculine*
  le tibia = the shin

ticket *noun, masculine*
  un ticket = a ticket

tiède *adjective*
  = warm
  = lukewarm, tepid

tien/tienne: *pronoun*
  le tien/la tienne = yours
  les tiens/les tiennes = yours

tiens ▶ tenir ⬚36⬚

tiers *noun, masculine* (❗ *never changes*)
  un tiers = one third

tiers-monde *noun, masculine*
  le tiers-monde = the Third World

tige *noun, feminine*
  une tige = a stem

tigre *noun, masculine*
  un tigre = a tiger

tilleul *noun, masculine*
- (*a tree*)
  un tilleul = a lime tree
- (*a drink*)
  le tilleul = lime tea

timbre *noun, masculine*
  un timbre = a (postage) stamp

timbrer *verb* ⬚1⬚
  = to put a stamp on

timide *adjective*
  = shy

timidité *noun, feminine*
  la timidité = shyness

tir *noun, masculine*
- **le tir** (*in an attack*) = firing
  (*as a sport*) = shooting
- **le tir à l'arc** = archery

tirage *noun, masculine*
- (*in a lottery*)
  le tirage (au sort) = the draw
- (*for a newspaper*)
  le tirage = the circulation
  un quotidien à grand tirage = a mass
  circulation daily

tire-bouchon *noun, masculine*
(*plural*) **tire-bouchons**
  un tire-bouchon = a corkscrew

tirelire *noun, feminine*
  une tirelire = a piggy bank

tirer *verb* ⬚1⬚
- = to pull
- = to draw

T

- = to fire
  = to shoot
- **tirer au sort** = to draw lots

tiroir *noun, masculine*
  un tiroir = a drawer

tiroir-caisse *noun, masculine*
(plural) **tiroirs-caisses**
  un tiroir-caisse = a cash register

tisane *noun, feminine*
  la tisane = herbal tea

tisser *verb* 1
  = to weave

tissu *noun, masculine*
  le tissu = material, fabric

titre *noun, masculine*
  un titre = a title

toc *exclamation*
  toc toc! = knock! knock!

toi *pronoun*
  = you
  plus jeune que toi = younger than you
  toi, tu as de la chance = you're lucky, you
    are
  ce livre est à toi = this book belongs to
    you, this book is yours
  à toi (de jouer)! = it's your turn (to play)!
  allons chez toi = let's go to your house
  lève-toi! = get up!

toile *noun, feminine*
- *(material)*
  la toile = cloth
  = canvas
- *(in art)*
  une toile = a canvas
une toile d'araignée = a cobweb, a
  spider's web
une toile cirée = an oilcloth

toilette
1 *noun, feminine*
  faire sa toilette = to have a wash
2 toilettes *noun, feminine plural*
  les toilettes *(in a house)* = the toilet, the
    bathroom
  (in a public place) = the toilets

toi-même *pronoun*
  = yourself

toise *noun, feminine*
  une toise = a height gauge

toit *noun, masculine*
  un toit = a roof
un toit ouvrant = a sunroof

tôle *noun, feminine*
  la tôle = sheet metal
la tôle ondulée = corrugated iron

tomate *noun, feminine*
  une tomate = a tomato

＊ in informal situations

tombe *noun, feminine*
  une tombe = a grave

tomber *verb* 1 (**!** + *être*)
- = to fall
  = to fall over
  c'est tombé de ma poche = it fell out of
    my pocket
  il est tombé de l'arbre = he fell off the tree
  tomber en panne = to break down
- **laisser tomber** = to drop
- *(to see or meet by chance)*
  tomber sur = to come across
  = to run into
- *(to happen)*
  ça tombe bien, moi aussi je suis libre
    = that's good, I'm free too

ton[1] *noun, masculine*
- *(a way of speaking)*
  un ton = a tone
  d'un ton sec = drily
- *(a colour)*
  un ton = a shade

ton[2]/**ta** *determiner*
(plural) **tes**
  = your

tonalité *noun, feminine*
  la tonalité = the dialling tone, the dial
    tone

tondeuse *noun, feminine*
  une tondeuse (à gazon) = a lawnmower

tondre *verb* 6
  tondre le gazon = to mow the grass
  tondre un mouton = to shear a sheep
  tondre quelqu'un = to shave someone's
    head

tondu/tondue ▶ tondre 6

tonneau *noun, masculine*
(plural) **tonneaux**
  un tonneau = a barrel

tonnerre
1 *noun, masculine*
  le tonnerre = thunder
  un coup de tonnerre = a clap of thunder
2 du tonnerre＊ = fabulous

torchon *noun, masculine*
  un torchon = a tea towel, a dish towel

tordre *verb* 6
1 (**!** + *avoir*)
  = to twist
  = to wring
  = to bend
2 se tordre (**!** + *être*)
  se tordre la cheville = to twist one's ankle

tordu/tordue *adjective*
1 ▶ tordre 6
2 *adjective*
  = crooked
  = twisted

tornade *noun, feminine*
une tornade = a tornado

torrent *noun, masculine*
un torrent = a torrent
pleuvoir à torrents = to rain very heavily

torse *noun, masculine*
le torse = the chest

tort *noun, masculine*
avoir tort = to be wrong

tortue *noun, feminine*
une tortue = a tortoise, a turtle

tôt *adverb*
= early
tôt le matin = early in the morning
le plus tôt possible = as soon as possible

toucher *verb* [1]
• = to touch
• = to get
toucher un salaire = to get a wage
• = to cash

touffe *noun, feminine*
une touffe (*of hair, grass*) = a tuft

toujours *adverb*
• (*all the time*) = always
il est toujours en retard = he's always late
• (*showing that something is continuing*)
= still
tu habites toujours Paris? = are you still
living in Paris?
il n'est toujours pas levé = he's still not up
elle est toujours aussi jolie = she's as pretty
as ever

tour
1 *noun, feminine*
• (*a building*)
une tour = a tower
= a tower block, a high rise
• (*in chess*)
une tour = a rook, a castle
2 *noun, masculine*
• (*a turning movement*)
un tour = a turn
faire un tour de manège = to have a go on
a fairground ride
faire le tour du lac (*on foot*) = to walk
round the lake
faire le tour du monde en bateau = to sail
round the world
• (*in a game, a rota*)
un tour = a turn
à tour de rôle = in turn
• (*an outing*)
(aller) faire un tour = to go for a stroll
aller faire un tour à Rome = to go to Rome
• (*a piece of mischief*)
un tour = a trick
jouer un tour à un ami = to play a trick on
a friend
• (*a size*)
un tour = a measurement
mon tour de taille = my waist
measurement

tourbillon *noun, masculine*
un tourbillon = a whirlpool
un tourbillon (de vent) = a whirlwind
un tourbillon de poussière = a whirl of
dust

tourisme *noun, masculine*
le tourisme = tourism

touristique *adjective*
− tourist
un endroit touristique = a popular tourist
spot

tournée *noun, feminine*
• une tournée (*for a postman*) = a round
(*for a singer, a theatre company*) = a tour
• (*in a café*)
une tournée = a round (of drinks)

tourner *verb* [1]
1 (**!** + *avoir*)
• = to turn
• tourner un film = to shoot a film
2 se tourner (**!** + *être*)
se tourner = to turn around

tournoi *noun, masculine*
un tournoi = a tournament

tous ▶ tout 1, 2

Toussaint *noun, feminine*
la Toussaint = All Saints' Day

tousser *verb* [1]
= to cough

tout/toute
(*plural*) **tous/toutes**
1 *adjective*
• = all
= every
il a plu toute la journée = it rained all day
(long)
c'est tout ce que tu veux? = is that all you
want?
tout le reste = everything else
tout le monde = everyone
tous les jours = every day
tous les deux ans = every other year
ils sont venus tous les deux = they both
came
• tout un/tout une = a whole
manger tout un pain = to eat a whole loaf
• − any
à toute heure = at any time
de toute façon = in any case
2 *pronoun*
= everything
= anything
= all
il a tout oublié = he's forgotten everything
tout peut arriver = anything can happen
100 francs en tout = 100 francs in all
tous ensemble = all together

T

3 *adverb*
- = quite
  = very
  c'est tout naturel = it's quite natural
  c'est tout près d'ici = it's very near
  être tout seul = to be all by oneself
  continuer tout droit = to carry straight on
  tout neuf/toute neuve = brand-new
  des rideaux tout faits = ready-made curtains
- **tout en** [marchant | travaillant | écoutant la radio …] = while [walking | working | listening to the radio …]
- (*in some phrases*)
  tout à coup = suddenly
  tout à fait = quite
  tout à l'heure = in a moment
  à tout à l'heure! = see you later!
  tout de même = all the same, even so
  tout de suite = at once

4 tout *noun, masculine*
- **le tout** = the lot
- **pas du tout** = not at all

toux *noun, feminine* (**!** *never changes*)
  une toux = a cough

TP *noun, masculine plural* ▶ **travail**

tracasser *verb* [1]
  = to bother

trace *noun, feminine*
- **une trace** = a trail, a track
- **une trace** = a mark, a trace
  des traces de pas = footprints
  des traces de doigts = fingermarks

tracer *verb* [12]
  = to draw
  = to write

traduire *verb* [62]
  = to translate

trafic *noun, masculine*
  le trafic = traffic

trafiquant/trafiquante *noun, masculine/feminine*
  un trafiquant/une trafiquante = a trafficker, a dealer

train
1 *noun, masculine*
- **un train** = a train
2 en train de = in the process of
  être en train de [travailler | dormir | se doucher …] = to be [working | sleeping | having a shower …]

traîneau *noun, masculine*
(*plural*) **traîneaux**
  un traîneau = a sledge

traîner *verb* [1]
- = to drag (along)

- **traîner dans les rues** = to hang around (on) the streets
- (*to be scattered*) = to be lying around
  laisser traîner ses affaires = to leave one's things lying around

trait
1 *noun, masculine*
  un trait = a line
2 traits *noun, masculine plural*
  des traits (*of a face*) = features

traitement *noun, masculine*
  un traitement = a treatment

traiter *verb* [1]
  = to treat

trajet *noun, masculine*
  un trajet = a journey

tranche *noun, feminine*
  une tranche (*of cheese, bread*) = a slice

tranquille *adjective*
  = quiet
  = calm, peaceful

tranquillité *noun, feminine*
  la tranquillité = peace and quiet

transmettre *verb* [60]
- = to broadcast
- = to pass on, to convey
- = to transmit

transpirer *verb* [1]
  = to sweat, to perspire

transport *noun, masculine*
- **le transport** = transport, transportation
- **les transports en commun** = public transport

transporter *verb* [1]
  = to carry

travail
(*plural*) **travaux**
1 *noun, masculine*
- **le travail** = work
- **un travail** = a job
2 travaux *noun, masculine plural*
  des travaux = work
  = roadwork(s)
  les travaux ménagers = housework
  les travaux dirigés, TD = practicals
  les travaux manuels = handicrafts
  les travaux pratiques, TP = practical work
  les travaux publics = civil engineering

travailler *verb* [1]
  = to work
  = to practise

travailleur/travailleuse
1 *adjective*
  = hardworking
2 *noun, masculine/feminine*
  un travailleur/une travailleuse = a worker

✗ in informal situations

travaux ▶ travail

travers noun, masculine
1 à travers = through
= across
2 de travers
ta cravate est de travers = your tie is
crooked
boutonné de travers = buttoned up
wrongly
j'ai avalé de travers = it went down the
wrong way
3 en travers de
= across

traversée noun, feminine
une traversée = a crossing

traverser verb [1]
• = to cross
• = to go through

traversin noun, masculine
un traversin = a bolster

trèfle noun, masculine
• (a plant)
le trèfle = clover
• (at cards)
trèfle = clubs

treille noun, feminine
une treille = a climbing vine

treize number
= thirteen

treizième number
= thirteenth

tremblement noun, masculine
un tremblement = a tremor
un tremblement de terre = an
earthquake

trembler verb [1]
= to shake
= to tremble, to quiver

trempé/trempée adjective
= soaked, sodden, soaking wet
trempé jusqu'aux os = soaked to the skin

tremper verb [1]
• = to soak
• = to dip

trente number
= thirty

très adverb
= very
avoir très faim = to be very hungry
très volontiers = gladly

trésor noun, masculine
un trésor = a treasure

tresse noun, feminine
une tresse = a plait, a braid

tribu noun, feminine
une tribu = a tribe

tribune noun, feminine
la tribune (in a stadium) = the grandstand

tricher verb [1]
= to cheat

tricolore adjective
le drapeau tricolore = the French flag

tricot noun, masculine
• (a craft)
le tricot = knitting
• (a knitted garment)
un tricot = a jumper, a sweater

tricoter verb [1]
= to knit

trier verb [2]
• = to sort (out)
• = to select

trimestre noun, masculine
un trimestre = a term

triste adjective
= sad

tristesse noun, feminine
la tristesse = sadness

trois number
= three

troisième
1 number
= third
2 noun, feminine
la troisième the class for secondary school
students aged 14 to 15

trombone noun, masculine
• (an instrument)
un trombone = a trombone
• (for fastening papers)
un trombone = a paper clip

trompe noun, feminine
une trompe d'éléphant = an elephant
trunk

tromper verb [1]
1 (! + avoir)
= to deceive
2 se tromper (! + être)
• se tromper = to make a mistake
se tromper de bus = to take the wrong bus
se tromper de date = to get the date wrong
• se tromper = to be mistaken

trompette noun, feminine
une trompette = a trumpet

tronc noun, masculine
un tronc = a trunk

trop
1 adverb = too
= too much
c'est trop petit = it's too small
tu parles trop = you talk too much
2 trop de = too much, too many

T

trottoir noun, masculine
  un trottoir = a pavement, a sidewalk
  le bord du trottoir = the kerb, the curb

trou noun, masculine
• un trou = a hole
  (in a hedge) = a gap
• (a small town)✶
  un trou✶ (perdu) = a dump

troupeau noun, masculine
(plural) **troupeaux**
  un troupeau = a herd
  = a flock

trousse noun, feminine
  une trousse = a (small) case
  = a kit
une trousse d'écolier = a pencil case
une trousse de secours = a first-aid kit
une trousse de toilette = a toilet bag

trouver verb [1]
1 (! + avoir)
• = to find
• = to think
  je trouve qu'il a raison = I think he's right
  comment trouves-tu mon copain? = what
    do you think of my friend?
2 se trouver (! + être)
• se trouver = to be
  se trouver à Nice = to be in Nice
• se trouver = to find
  se trouver une excuse = to find an excuse
• je me trouve bien ici = I like it here
  se trouver mal = to pass out, to faint

truc noun, masculine
• (when referring vaguely to something)
  un truc = a thing
• (a clever way)✶
  un truc✶ = a trick
  = a knack

truffe noun, feminine
  une truffe = a truffle

truite noun, feminine
  une truite = a trout

TTC (abbreviation of **toutes taxes comprises**)
  TTC = inclusive of tax

tu pronoun
  = you

tube noun, masculine
• un tube = a tube, a pipe
• (a song)✶
  un tube✶ = a hit

tuer verb [1]
  = to kill

tue-tête: **à tue-tête** adverb
  chanter à tue-tête = to sing at the top of
    one's voice

✶ in informal situations

tuile noun, feminine
  une tuile = a tile

Tunisie noun, feminine
  la Tunisie = Tunisia

tunisien/tunisienne adjective
  = Tunisian

tunnel noun, masculine
  un tunnel = a tunnel
  le tunnel sous la Manche = the Channel
    Tunnel

turc/turque
1 adjective
  = Turkish
2 turc noun, masculine
  le turc = Turkish

Turquie noun, feminine
  la Turquie = Turkey

tutoyer verb [23]
  tutoyer quelqu'un = to address someone
    using the 'tu' form

tuyau noun, masculine
(plural) **tuyaux**
  un tuyau = a pipe
un tuyau d'arrosage = a hosepipe
le tuyau d'échappement = the exhaust

TVA noun, feminine
  la TVA = VAT

type noun, masculine
• (a sort)
  un type = a type, a kind
• (a man)✶
  un type✶ = a bloke, a guy

typique adjective
  = typical

Uu

ULM noun, masculine (! never changes)
• (the equipment)
  un ULM = a microlight
• (the sport)
  l'ULM = microlighting

un/une
1 number
  = one
  trente et un jours = thirty-one days
  une fois = once
  un jour sur deux = every other day
2 determiner
(plural) **des**
  = a(n)
  un chat = a cat
  des enfants = children

3 *pronoun*
(*plural*) **uns/unes**
  (l')un/(l')une = one
  les uns/les unes = some
  l'un d'entre vous = one of you
  pourquoi les uns et pas les autres? = why
    some and not others?

uni/unie *adjective*
• (*not at odds*) = united
  = close-knit
• (*not patterned*) = plain

unique *adjective*
• = only
  être fils/fille unique = to be an only child
• = unique
  une occasion unique = a unique
    opportunity

uniquement *adverb*
  = only

unir *verb* ③
  = to unite

unité *noun, feminine*
• **une unité** = a unit
• **l'unité** = unity

univers *noun, masculine* (**!** *never changes*)
  l'univers = the universe

universitaire *adjective*
  = university

université *noun, feminine*
  l'université = university, college

uns/unes ▶ **un 3**

urbain/urbaine *adjective*
  = urban
  la vie urbaine = city life

urbanisme *noun, masculine*
  l'urbanisme = town planning, city
    planning

urgence *noun, feminine*
• **l'urgence** = the urgency
  téléphonez d'urgence = phone
    immediately
  des mesures d'urgence = emergency
    measures
  on l'a transporté d'urgence à l'hôpital = he
    was rushed to the hospital
• (*in a hospital*)
  une urgence = an emergency
  le service des urgences = the casualty
    department, the accident and
    emergency department

urticaire *noun, feminine*
  l'urticaire = nettle rash

usage *noun, masculine*
  l'usage = the use
  'à usage externe' = 'for external use only'

usager *noun, masculine*
  un usager (*of a service*) = a user
  les usagers de la route = road-users

usé/usée *adjective*
  = worn

user *verb* ①
1 (**!** + *avoir*)
  = to wear out
  = to wear down
2 s'user (**!** + *être*)
  s'user = to wear out

usine *noun, feminine*
  une usine = a factory

ustensile *noun, masculine*
  un ustensile = a utensil

utile *adjective*
  = useful

utiliser *verb* ①
  = to use

Vv

va ▶ **aller 1** ⑨

vacances *noun, feminine plural*
  des vacances = holidays, a vacation
  être en vacances = to be on holiday, to be
    on vacation

vacancier/vacancière *noun, masculine/feminine*
  un vacancier/une vacancière = a
    holidaymaker, a vacationer

vache *noun, feminine*
  une vache = a cow

vagabonder *verb* ①
  = to wander

vague
1 *adjective*
  = vague
2 *noun, masculine*
  il regardait dans le vague = he was staring
    into space
3 *noun, feminine*
• **une vague** = a wave
• **une vague de froid** = a cold spell

vaincre *verb* ⑤⑦
  = to defeat
  = to overcome

vaincu/vaincue
1 ▶ **vaincre** ⑤⑦
2 *noun, masculine/feminine*
  les vaincus = the losers

V

vainqueur *noun, masculine*
 un vainqueur = a winner
 = a victor

vais ▶ **aller 1** 9

vaisselle *noun, feminine*
 la vaisselle = crockery, dishes
 faire la vaisselle = to do the dishes

valable *adjective*
 = valid

valet *noun, masculine*
• (*a person*)
 un valet = a manservant
• (*at cards*)
 un valet = a jack

valeur *noun, feminine*
 la valeur (*in terms of money*) = value
 (*in terms of merit*) = worth
 les objets de valeur = valuables
 sans valeur = worthless

valise *noun, feminine*
 une valise = a suitcase
 faire ses valises = to pack

vallée *noun, feminine*
 une vallée = a valley

valoir *verb* 45
• = to be worth
 = to cost
 ça en vaut la peine = it's worth it
• il vaut mieux partir tôt = it's better to leave
 early
 il vaut mieux que tu y ailles = you'd better
 go

valu ▶ **valoir** 45

vanille *noun, feminine*
 la vanille = vanilla

vapeur
1 *noun, feminine*
 la vapeur = steam
 un bateau à vapeur = a steamboat
 faire cuire des légumes à la vapeur = to
 steam vegetables
2 vapeurs *noun, feminine plural*
 des vapeurs = fumes

vaporisateur *noun, masculine*
 un vaporisateur = a spray

vaporiser *verb* 1
 = to spray
 = to vaporize

varappe *noun, feminine*
 la varappe = rock-climbing

variable *adjective*
• = variable
• = changeable, unpredictable

variante *noun, feminine*
 une variante = a variation

varié/variée *adjective*
 = varied
 = various
 'sandwichs variés' = 'a selection of
 sandwiches'

variété
1 *noun, feminine*
• la variété = variety
• une variété = a variety
2 variétés *noun, feminine plural*
 un spectacle de variétés = a variety show

vas ▶ **aller 1** 9

vase
1 *noun, masculine*
 un vase = a vase
2 *noun, feminine*
 la vase = mud

vaste *adjective*
 = vast, huge
 = large

vaudrait ▶ **valoir** 45

vaut ▶ **valoir** 45

vautour *noun, masculine*
 un vautour = a vulture

veau *noun, masculine*
(*plural*) **veaux**
• (*the animal*)
 un veau = a calf
• (*the meat*)
 le veau = veal

vécu/vécue
1 ▶ **vivre** 38
2 *adjective*
 = real-life

vedette *noun, feminine*
• (*a person*)
 une vedette = a star
• (*a boat*)
 une vedette = a motor launch

véhicule *noun, masculine*
 un véhicule = a vehicle

veille *noun, feminine*
 la veille = the day before
 la veille au soir = the night before

veiller *verb* 1
• (*to remain awake*) = to stay up
• (*to be alert*) = to be watchful

veilleur *noun, masculine*
 un veilleur de nuit = a night watchman

veilleuse *noun, feminine*
 une veilleuse = a night light
 = a pilot light

veine *noun, feminine*
• une veine = a vein
• la veine✶ = luck
 avoir de la veine✶ = to be lucky

---

vélo *noun, masculine*
  un vélo = a bike
  un vélo tout terrain = a mountain bike
  faire du vélo = to cycle

vélomoteur *noun, masculine*
  un vélomoteur = a moped

velours *noun, masculine* (❗ *never changes*)
  le velours = velvet
  = corduroy

venais ▶ **venir** 36

vendanges *noun, feminine plural*
  les vendanges = the grape harvest

vendeur/vendeuse *noun, masculine/feminine*
  un vendeur/une vendeuse = a seller, a vendor
  = a shop assistant
  = a salesman/a saleswoman

vendre *verb* 6
1 (❗ + *avoir*)
  = to sell
  'à vendre' = 'for sale'
2 se vendre (❗ + *être*)
  se vendre = to be sold
  ça se vend bien = it sells well

vendredi *noun, masculine*
  vendredi = Friday
  le vendredi = on Fridays

vendu/vendue ▶ **vendre** 6

vénéneux/vénéneuse *adjective*
  = poisonous

vengeance *noun, feminine*
  la vengeance = revenge

venger *verb* 13
1 (❗ + *avoir*)
  = to avenge
2 se venger (❗ + *être*)
  se venger = to get one's revenge

venir *verb* 36 (❗ + *être*)
• = to come
  viens déjeuner = come for lunch
  faire venir un plombier = to call a plumber
  ça ne m'est jamais venu à l'idée = it never crossed my mind
• venir de faire = to have just done

vent *noun, masculine*
  le vent = the wind
  il y a du vent, il fait du vent = it's windy

vente *noun, feminine*
  une vente = a sale
  des médicaments en vente libre = drugs available over the counter
la vente par correspondance = mail-order selling
une vente aux enchères = an auction

ventre *noun, masculine*
  le ventre (*a person's*) = the stomach
  (*an animal's*) = the (under)belly

venu/venue ▶ **venir** 36

ver *noun, masculine*
  un ver = a worm
  = a maggot
un ver de terre = an earthworm

verbe *noun, masculine*
  un verbe = a verb

verdure *noun, feminine*
  la verdure = greenery

verger *noun, masculine*
  un verger = an orchard

verglacé/verglacée *adjective*
  = icy

verglas *noun, masculine* (❗ *never changes*)
  le verglas = black ice

vérifier *verb* 2
  = to check

véritable *adjective*
  = real, true, genuine

vérité *noun, feminine*
  la vérité = the truth

vernis *noun, masculine* (❗ *never changes*)
  le vernis = varnish
  = glaze
  du vernis à ongles = nail polish

verrai ▶ **voir** 46

verre *noun, masculine*
• (*a substance*)
  le verre = glass
• (*a container*)
  un verre = a glass
  un verre à vin = a wine glass
  un verre de vin = a glass of wine
  aller prendre un verre = to go for a drink
• (*on spectacles*)
  un verre = a lens
des verres de contact = contact lenses

vers
1 *noun, masculine* (❗ *never changes*)
  un vers = a line (of verse)
  des vers = poetry
2 *preposition*
• = toward(s)
  rouler vers Paris = to go toward(s) Paris
  vers le soir = toward(s) evening
• = about
  vers six heures = at about six o'clock

Verseau *noun, masculine*
  le Verseau = Aquarius

verser *verb* 1
• = to pour
• = to pay

V

version *noun, feminine*
- (*an exercise*)
  une version = a translation (*into one's own language*)
- (*an account, an adaptation*)
  une version = a version
  un film en version originale = a film in the original language

vert/verte *adjective*
= green

vertèbre *noun, feminine*
une vertèbre = a vertebra
se déplacer une vertèbre = to slip a disc

vertical/verticale *adjective*
(*plural*) **verticaux/verticales**
= vertical
= upright

verticalement *adverb*
- = vertically
- (*in a crossword*) = down

vertige *noun, masculine*
le vertige = dizziness
= vertigo
avoir le vertige = to feel dizzy

veste *noun, feminine*
une veste = a jacket

vestiaire *noun, masculine*
un vestiaire (*in a gym*) = a changing room
(*in a theatre, a museum*) = a cloakroom

vestibule *noun, masculine*
un vestibule = a hall
= a foyer, a lobby

veston *noun, masculine*
un veston = a (man's) jacket

vêtement *noun, masculine*
un vêtement = a garment
des vêtements = clothes, clothing
'**vêtements pour hommes**' = 'menswear'

vétérinaire *noun, masculine/feminine*
un vétérinaire/une vétérinaire = a veterinary surgeon, a veterinarian

vêtu/vêtue *adjective*
= dressed
elle était vêtue d'une robe noire = she was wearing a black dress

veuf/veuve
1 *adjective*
= widowed
2 *noun, masculine/feminine*
un veuf/une veuve = a widower/a widow

veuille ▶ **vouloir** 48

veulent ▶ **vouloir** 48

veuve ▶ **veuf**

veux ▶ **vouloir** 48

vexer *verb* 1
1 (**!** + *avoir*)
= to offend, to upset

2 se vexer (**!** + *être*)
se vexer = to take offence, to get upset

viande *noun, feminine*
la viande = meat
de la viande de bœuf = beef

victime *noun, feminine*
une victime = a victim
= a casualty

victoire *noun, feminine*
une victoire = a victory

vide
1 *adjective*
= empty, vacant
= blank
2 *noun, masculine*
- (*a space*)
  un vide = a gap
- (*absence of air*)
  le vide = a vacuum
  emballé sous vide = vacuum-packed
- **sauter dans le vide** = to jump

vidéothèque *noun, feminine*
une vidéothèque = a video library
= a video collection

vider *verb* 1
1 (**!** + *avoir*)
= to empty
2 se vider (**!** + *être*)
se vider = to empty

vie *noun, feminine*
la vie = life
être en vie = to be alive
la vie active = working life
la vie est chère = the cost of living is high

vieil ▶ **vieux 1**

vieillard/vieillarde *noun,*
masculine/feminine
un vieillard/une vieillarde = an old man/an old woman
les vieillards = old people

vieille ▶ **vieux**

vieillir *verb* 3
= to get old(er)
= to age

viendrai ▶ **venir** 36

viens ▶ **venir** 36

vierge *adjective*
= virgin
= blank
= new

Vierge *noun, feminine*
- **la Vierge** = Virgo
- **la (Sainte) Vierge** = the (Blessed) Virgin

vietnamien/vietnamienne
1 *adjective*
= Vietnamese

2 vietnamien *noun, masculine*
le vietnamien = Vietnamese

vieux/vieille
(plural) **vieux/vieilles**
1 *adjective*
= old

> ! vieil *is used instead of* vieux *before masculine nouns that begin with a vowel or a mute h. The plural of* vieil *is* vieux.

un vieil homme = an old man
de vieilles photos = old photographs
2 *noun, masculine|feminine*
un vieux/une vieille = an old man/an old woman
les vieux = old people

vif/vive¹ *adjective*
- *(describing a person)* = lively
- *(describing a pace, a movement)* = brisk
rouler à vive allure = to drive at high speed
- *(describing a light, a colour)* = bright
- *(describing the cold, the wind)* = biting
- *(describing a pain)* = sharp

vigne *noun, feminine*
la vigne = vine
une vigne = a vineyard
la vigne vierge = Virginia creeper

vigneron/vigneronne *noun, masculine|feminine*
un vigneron/une vigneronne = a winegrower

vignette *noun, feminine*
une vignette = a label
(on a car) = a tax disc

vignoble *noun, masculine*
un vignoble = a vineyard

vilain/vilaine *adjective*
- = naughty, nasty
- = ugly

villa *noun, feminine*
une villa = a detached house
= a villa

village *noun, masculine*
un village = a village

ville *noun, feminine*
une ville = a town, a city
aller en ville = to go into town

vin *noun, masculine*
le vin = wine

vinaigre *noun, masculine*
le vinaigre = vinegar

vinaigrette *noun, feminine*
la vinaigrette = vinaigrette, oil and vinegar dressing

vingt *number*
= twenty

vingtaine *noun, feminine*
une vingtaine = about twenty
= twenty

vingt et un/vingt et une *number*
= twenty-one

vingt et unième *number*
= twenty-first

vingtième *number*
= twentieth

violent/violente *adjective*
= violent

violet/violette¹ *adjective*
= purple

violette² *noun, feminine*
une violette = a violet

violon *noun, masculine*
un violon = a violin

violoncelle *noun, masculine*
un violoncelle = a cello

vipère *noun, feminine*
une vipère = an adder, a viper

virage *noun, masculine*
un virage = a bend

virgule *noun, feminine*
une virgule = a comma
= a decimal point

vis
1 ▶ **vivre** 38
2 *noun, feminine* (! *never changes*)
une vis = a screw

visage *noun, masculine*
le visage = the face

viser *verb* 1
- = to aim at
- = to be aimed at

visite *noun, feminine*
une visite = a visit
= a call
rendre visite à un ami = to pay a visit to a friend
avoir de la visite = to have visitors
une visite médicale = a medical examination

visiter *verb* 1
visiter une ville = to visit a town
visiter un appartement = to view a flat, to look at an apartment

visser *verb* 1
= to screw on

vite *adverb*
= quickly, fast
vite! = quick!
j'ai parlé trop vite = I spoke too hastily

vitesse *noun, feminine*
- la vitesse = speed
en vitesse = quickly
à toute vitesse = at top speed
- une vitesse = a gear

V

168

vitre *noun, feminine*
  une vitre = a windowpane
  = a pane of glass
  les vitres d'une voiture = the windows of a
  car

vitrine *noun, feminine*
• (*in a shop*)
  une vitrine = a (shop) window
  faire les vitrines = to go window shopping
• (*in a museum*)
  une vitrine = a display cabinet, a curio
  cabinet

vivant/vivante *adjective*
• = alive, living
  être vivant = to be alive
  les êtres vivants = living creatures
• = lively

vive²
1 *adjective, feminine* ▶ **vif**
2 *verb* ▶ **vivre** ⃞38

vivre *verb* ⃞38
  = to live
  se laisser vivre = to take things easy

vocabulaire *noun, masculine*
  le vocabulaire = vocabulary

vœu *noun, masculine*
(*plural*) **vœux**
  un vœu = a wish
  meilleurs vœux = best wishes
  les vœux du Nouvel An = New Year's
  greetings

voici *preposition*
  = here is, this is
  = here are, these are
  me voici = here I am
  voici un mois = a month ago

voie *noun, feminine*
• (*for traffic*)
  une voie = a road
  = a street
  la voie publique = the public highway
  une voie sans issue = a dead end
• (*part of a road*)
  une voie = a lane
• (*for a train*)
  une voie = a track
• en voie de = in the process of
  un pays en voie de développement = a
  developing country
  une espèce en voie de disparition = an
  endangered species
  la voie ferrée = the railway track, the
  railroad track

voilà *preposition*
  = here is, this is
  = here are, these are
  te voilà enfin! = here you are at last!
  voilà tout = that's all
  voilà un mois = a month ago

voile
1 *noun, feminine*
• une voile = a sail
• la voile = sailing
2 *noun, masculine*
  un voile = a veil

voir *verb* ⃞46
1 (**!** + *avoir*)
• = to see
  on verra = we'll see
  un film à voir = a film worth seeing
  faire voir quelque chose à quelqu'un = to
  show someone something
• = to be able to see
  je ne vois rien, je n'y vois rien = I can't see
  a thing
• (*to be connected*)
  ça n'a rien à voir = that's got nothing to do
  with it
• (*when encouraging someone*)
  voyons, soyez sages! = come on, be good!
2 se voir (**!** + *être*)
• (*to be visible*)
  se voir = to show
  ça se voit de loin = it can be seen from a
  distance
• (*to meet*)
  se voir = to see each other

voisin/voisine
1 *adjective*
  = neighbo(u)ring
  = nearby
2 *noun, masculine/feminine*
  un voisin/une voisine = a neighbo(u)r

voiture *noun, feminine*
  une voiture = a car, an automobile
  = a carriage, a car
  en voiture! = all aboard!

voix *noun, feminine* (**!** *never changes*)
• (*the way one speaks*)
  une voix = a voice
  à voix basse = in a low voice
  à haute voix = out loud
• (*in an election*)
  une voix = a vote

vol *noun, masculine*
• (*through the air*)
  un vol = a flight
  à vol d'oiseau = as the crow flies
• (*an offence*)
  un vol = a theft, a robbery
  un vol à main armée = an armed robbery
  le vol à voile = gliding

volaille *noun, feminine*
  la volaille = poultry

volant/volante
1 *adjective*
  = flying
2 volant *noun, masculine*
• (*in a car*)
  un volant = a steering wheel
  donner un coup de volant = to turn the
  wheel sharply

- (*in badminton*)
  un volant = a shuttlecock
- (*on a skirt*)
  un volant = a flounce

volcan *noun, masculine*
un volcan = a volcano

voler *verb* 1
- = to steal
  il s'est fait voler sa voiture = he had his car stolen
- **voler un passant** = to rob a passer-by
- = to fly

volet *noun, masculine*
un volet (*on a window*) = a shutter

voleur/voleuse *noun, masculine/feminine*
un voleur/une voleuse = a thief

volontaire
1 *adjective*
= deliberate
2 *noun, masculine/feminine*
un volontaire/une volontaire = a volunteer

volonté *noun, feminine*
la volonté = will
= will-power

volontiers *adverb*
= gladly, willingly
= with pleasure

vomir *verb* 3
- = to vomit, to bring up
- = to be sick, to throw up

vont ▶ **aller** 1 9

vos ▶ **votre**

voter *verb* 1
= to vote

votre *determiner*
(*plural*) **vos**
= your

vôtre *pronoun*
le vôtre/la vôtre/les vôtres = yours
à la vôtre! = cheers!

voudrais ▶ **vouloir** 48

vouloir *verb* 48
- (*expressing determination*) = to want
  je veux partir = I want to leave
  il ne voulait pas que tu viennes = he didn't want you to come
- (*expressing a wish, a polite request*)
  que veux-tu boire?, que voulez-vous boire? = what would you like to drink?
  je voudrais des poires = I'd like pears
  comme tu veux = as you wish
  veuillez vous asseoir = please sit down
- **vouloir dire** = to mean
  qu'est-ce que ça veut dire? = what does it mean?

voulu/voulue
1 ▶ **vouloir** 48

2 *adjective*
- = required
- = deliberate, planned

vous *pronoun*
- = you
  vous avez gagné = you've won
  à cause de vous = because of you
  la voiture est à vous = the car is yours
- = yourself
  = yourselves
  soignez-vous = look after yourself
  = look after yourselves
  allez vous laver les mains = go and wash your hands
- = each other
  vous vous aimez? = do you love each other?

vous-même *pronoun*
(*plural*) **vous-mêmes**
= yourself
= yourselves

vouvoyer *verb* 23
vouvoyer quelqu'un = to address someone using the "vous" form

voyage *noun, masculine*
un voyage = a trip, a journey
aimer les voyages = to love travel(l)ing
un voyage de noces = a honeymoon
un voyage organisé = a package tour

voyager *verb* 13
= to travel

voyageur/voyageuse *noun, masculine/feminine*
un voyageur/une voyageuse = a passenger
= a travel(l)er

voyant/voyante
1 *adjective*
= loud
2 *noun, masculine/feminine*
un voyant/une voyante = a clairvoyant
3 voyant *noun, masculine*
un voyant lumineux = a warning light

voyelle *noun, feminine*
une voyelle = a vowel

voyons ▶ **voir** 46

voyou *noun, masculine*
un voyou = a lout
= a rascal

vrai/vraie
1 *adjective*
= true
= real, genuine
2 vrai *noun, masculine*
le vrai = the truth
à vrai dire = to tell the truth
pour de vrai = for real

vraiment *adverb*
= really

V

vrombir verb ③
= to roar

VTT noun, masculine
un VTT = a mountain bike

vu/vue[1]
1 ▶ **voir** 46
2 adjective
• **être bien vu** = to be well thought of
  ce serait plutôt mal vu = it wouldn't go
  down well
• **bien vu!** = good point!
• **c'est tout vu** = my mind is made up
3 vu = in view of

vue[2] noun, feminine
• **la vue** = sight
  avoir une bonne vue = to have good
  eyesight
  je la connais de vue = I know her to see
  perdre un ami de vue = to lose touch with
  a friend
  à vue d'œil = visibly
• **une vue** = a view
  avoir vue sur le lac = to look out onto the
  lake

wagon noun, masculine
un wagon = a wagon, a car
= a carriage, a car

wagon-lit noun, masculine
(plural) **wagons-lits**
un wagon-lit = a sleeper, a sleeping car

wagon-restaurant noun, masculine
(plural) **wagons-restaurants**
un wagon-restaurant = a restaurant car, a
dining car

WC noun, masculine plural
les WC = the toilet, the bathroom

Yy

y pronoun
• = it
  j'y pense souvent = I often think about it
  il s'y attendait = he was expecting it
  tu n'y peux rien = you can't do anything
  about it
  elle n'y arrivera jamais = she'll never
  manage it
  je n'y comprends rien = I don't understand
  a thing

• = there
  j'y mange parfois = I sometimes eat there
  j'y vais = I'm going
• **il y a** = there is
  = there are
  il n'y en a plus = there's none left
  = there aren't any left

yaourt noun, masculine
un yaourt = a yogurt

yeux ▶ **œil**

yoga noun, masculine
le yoga = yoga

Zz

zapper✶ verb ①
= to flick through the TV channels

zèbre noun, masculine
un zèbre = a zebra

zéro
1 number
= zero
2 noun, masculine
zéro (in school) = nought, zero
(in a match) = nil, nothing
il est zéro heure quinze = it's a quarter
past midnight
trois (buts) à zéro = three nil, three
nothing
avoir le moral à zéro✶ = to feel very down
repartir à zéro = to start all over again

zeste noun, masculine
un zeste de citron = the zest of a lemon

zigzag noun, masculine
un zigzag = a zigzag
une route en zigzag = a winding
road

zodiaque noun, masculine
le zodiaque = the zodiac

zone noun, feminine
une zone = a zone, an area
une zone industrielle = an industrial
estate, an industrial park

zoo noun, masculine
un zoo = a zoo

zoologique adjective
= zoological

zut✶ exclamation
= blast!
= oh dear!

✶ in informal situations

Dictionary know-how

This section contains a number of short exercises which will help you to use your dictionary more effectively. You will find answers to all of the exercises at the end of the section p. 182.

1 Identifying French nouns and adjectives

Here is an extract from a French advertisement for a gas oven. See if you can find fourteen different nouns and underline them, and six different adjectives and circle them (or make two lists). If you are not sure of some words, look them up in the French–English half of the dictionary and see if the term 'noun' or 'adjective' is used to describe them.

GAZ DE FRANCE, LE CHOIX DE LA QUALITÉ

Pourquoi les Français préfèrent-ils le gaz naturel?

Si vous venez dîner chez moi, vous verrez un magnifique objet, écran plat, coins carrés, dont la beauté luisante saute aux yeux.

Un poste de télévision? Non, non, ce n'est pas mon téléviseur, c'est mon nouveau four au gaz naturel.

The publishers would like to thank Gaz de France for permission to reproduce copyright material.

2 Checking the gender of French nouns

Here are some English nouns which appear in the English–French half of the dictionary. Find out what their French equivalents are and make two separate lists, masculine nouns and feminine nouns.

bag	hippopotamus	magic	saddle
cake shop	island	oyster	thunderstorm
doorbell	jumper	peach	waitress
felt-tip pen	library	raincoat	worm

3 Identifying French and English pronouns

Each of the following phrases appears in the French–English half of this dictionary
in entries where a pronoun is the headword. In each one, underline the pronoun(s)
and give the English equivalent(s).

ça ne fait rien

c'est un cadeau

ce sont des détails sans importance

il l'a invitée

elle ne me parle pas

donne-la-moi

je lui ai prêté ma robe

elles se sont fait mal

il vous l'a prêté

donne-nous l'adresse

4 Recognizing French verbs

Underline the verb in each sentence.

Pierre descend la rue sur son vélo.

Sophie ne connaît pas le nom du magasin.

Les sapeurs pompiers arriveront dans cinq minutes.

Chaque année nous passons nos vacances d'été en France.

Ma sœur a un bassin avec des poissons dans son jardin.

5 Identifying French adverbs

Here is a list of twelve French words. Eight of them are adverbs and four are not.
Underline the ones which are not, or make a list, and say what they are. If you are
not sure of some of them, look them up in the French–English half of the
dictionary.

absolument	enseignement	seulement
certainement	facilement	stationnement
directement	heureusement	vêtement
énormément	médicament	vraiment

6 Identifying subjects and objects

We have left out the subjects and objects from this French newspaper report. Choose suitable words from the list below in order to complete it. When you have finished, list the subjects and objects separately.

L'OURS FÉLIX ATTAQUE

.... a dévoré ....
depuis son arrivée dans les Pyrénées. Hier, ... ,
transplanté des forêts de Slovénie, a entièrement dévoré
.... qui se trouvait près de Portet-d'Aspet en
Haute-Garonne. .... a aussitôt
compensé .... de la perte de sa bête.
.... est de 600F pour l'attaque, qui ne sont versés
qu'une seule fois, puis de 800F par mouton. Pourtant, ...
devraient se rassurer: .... sont toujours plus
prédateurs que les vieux. Avec le temps, ... perdra
.... pour la chasse.

---

l'animal	Le département	Félix
le berger	les jeunes ours	sa passion
les bergers	neuf moutons	Le 'tarif'
une brebis	L'ours Félix	

The publishers would like to thank *Libération* for permission to use copyright material.

---

7 Word search

Here is a grid in which are hidden eleven French words: 3 masculine nouns, 3 feminine nouns, 2 adjectives, 2 verbs and 1 pronoun. They may appear horizontally or vertically, and in either direction. When you have found them, circle them. If you are not sure of any of them, look them up in the French–English section of the dictionary.

B	G	R	A	N	D	K	Y	S	T
H	O	E	P	M	Q	C	E	L	A
S	T	N	D	N	O	R	U	I	V
Z	F	N	X	A	K	E	R	B	C
D	F	O	G	H	J	S	K	L	P
M	R	D	E	N	T	U	A	P	Q
M	O	N	D	E	P	C	O	A	D
P	G	A	W	C	U	X	V	R	N
C	U	B	A	G	U	E	T	T	E
R	H	A	N	F	Q	E	M	T	K

abandonner
baguette
cela
dent
excuser
fils
grand
monde
nez
part
rond

8 Accents are important!

Here is part of a letter typed by somebody who does not know how to find the accents on a word processor. Use your dictionary as necessary to help you put them in:

> Ma chere Louise,
>
> Merci pour ta lettre que j'ai recue hier. Ce matin, comme
> d'habitude, je suis allee faire mes courses au marche ou j'ai
> rencontre Madame Bonnard, que tu connais tres bien, je crois. Elle
> m'a dit que sa fille ainee, Sandrine, a fini ses etudes et qu'elle part
> en Grece faire un stage de six mois dans un hotel. Ça devrait etre
> amusant, non? Qu'est-ce que tu comptes faire toi-meme cet ete? Est-
> ce que tu restes en France ou esperes-tu toujours visiter la Norvege?
> Moi, je vais passer deux semaines dans la maison de campagne de
> mon frere a Gaillac...

9 Using page headings

In order to help you find what you are looking for quickly, every page of the main section of the dictionary has a word at the top which identifies the first entry on that page. In this exercise the left-hand column contains a list of entries and the right-hand column a selection of page headings. Choose the page where you would expect to find the entry you are looking for.

Entry	Page headings
encourager	énerver | enseigne en | énervé
historique	hâte | histoire historique | hôtesse
liquide	librairie | loge logé | luge
mener	mélanger | mesure mesurer | million
renseigner	reine | rendre renne | requin
sérieux	séjour | serré serrer | siège
vieil	version | vietnamien vieux | vitesse

10 **Masculine or feminine?**

Some French nouns can be both masculine and feminine, and change their meaning accordingly. Use your dictionary to find the following nouns and list them with their different meanings in two columns, masculine and feminine, e.g.

un livre = ...   *une* livre = ...

livre
manche
mode
moule
poêle
tour
vase
voile

11 **Which preposition, à or de?**

Many verbs in French take a preposition, either *à* or *de*, before an infinitive e.g. *il m'a demandé de venir demain; elle a réussi à ouvrir la porte.* In the following extract, all of the prepositions have been left out. Use your dictionary to check what they should be.

> Jean-Pierre a longtemps refusé . . . accepter la proposition de son ami, Michel, mais finalement il a décidé . . . dire oui. Michel avait envie . . . faire une randonnée de plusieurs semaines à vélo à travers l'Europe et avait tout fait pour convaincre son ami . . . venir avec lui. A vrai dire, Jean-Pierre préférait passer son temps . . . se faire bronzer sur la plage, mais il essayait toujours . . . faire plaisir à son copain et c'est pour cette raison que Michel est parvenu . . . le persuader. Bien entendu, c'est Michel qui s'est chargé . . . faire tous les préparatifs du voyage, alors que Jean-Pierre a commencé . . . tracer l'itinéraire sur la carte.

12 Find the verb

Some words in English can be both nouns and verbs e.g. race. In this exercise, you have to find the following English words in the English–French half of the dictionary and then give the French for the verb only.

aim	iron	question
block	joke	sail
camp	kiss	train
dance	milk	welcome
finish	paint	yell

13 Choosing the right word

Very often you cannot use a word exactly as it is given in the dictionary. In the case of adjectives with an irregular feminine form, for example, you have to make sure that you select the form which is appropriate to the noun you are using. Use your dictionary to find the correct form of the adjective to match the nouns in the following sentences.

Elle a de .... yeux et de .... dents. (*beautiful*)

Notre .... maison était très .... (*former*) (*old*)

C'est une très .... idée. (*good*)

La .... chose à faire est de trouver l'entrée ....
(*first*) (*secret*)

Elles sont si .... (*happy*)

La neige est .... (*white*)

Il a une .... voiture. (*new*)

Mon père est ...., mais ma mère est ....
(*Italian*) (*Norwegian*)

14 **Which part of speech?**

Use your dictionary to help you arrange these words in separate lists according to their parts of speech (masculine noun, feminine noun, adjective etc). Some words may belong to more than one category and will therefore appear in more than one list.

chasse	inscrire	pâle
dessous	juste	que
en	mouche	relire
facilement	notre	toi-même
gendre	ouest	vers

15 **Translating phrasal verbs**

Use your dictionary to find the correct translation for the following English sentences containing phrasal verbs.

The button's **come off**.

The dustmen have **taken** the rubbish **away**.

She is **bringing up** her children on her own.

They've **given up** smoking.

I'm going to **take** my shoes **off**.

16 **Find the plural**

Use your dictionary as necessary to find the plural of the following nouns (be careful, some of them are exceptions to the general guidelines):

un bijou, des ....

un cas, des ....

un cheval, deux ....

un cheveu, mes ....

une croix, deux ....

un manteau, deux ....

un pneu, quatre ....

du travail, des ....

un trou, deux ....

un vieux, des ....

17 **Faux amis**

Some French words look the same as, or similar to English words, but in fact have a different meaning. These are known as *faux amis* or false friends. Use your dictionary to find the meanings of the following French words:

actuellement	éventuellement
un bonnet	gentil
un car	le matériel
une cave	le pétrole
une course	un pin
décevoir	sale
délivrer	sensible
un engin	

18 **False friends**

Now use your dictionary to find a French meaning for each of these English 'lookalikes'.

actually	eventually
a bonnet	gentle
a car	material
a cave	petrol
a course	a pin
to deceive	a sale
to deliver	sensible
an engine	

19 **Male or female?**

Some French masculine nouns also have a feminine form. This is particularly true of words denoting an occupation–*un commerçant, une commerçante*. Some simply add -e to the masculine form but many do not. Use your dictionary to find the feminine form of the following nouns:

un astronaute	un piéton
un conseiller	un religieux
un enquêteur	un scout
un jongleur	un skieur
un musicien	un téléspectateur

20 **Which meaning?**

Some words have more than one meaning and it's important to check that you have chosen the right one. In this dictionary different meanings of a word are marked by a bullet point (•). We have given you one meaning of the French words below. Use your dictionary to find another one.

une baie	• a bay	• ....
blanc	• white	• ....
un centimètre	• a centimetre	• ....
enlever	• to remove	• ....
un gorille	• a gorilla	• ....
le jour	• the day	• ....
mauvais	• bad	• ....
noir	• black	• ....
un pépin	• a pip	• ....
une radio	• a radio	• ....
un tailleur	• a tailor	• ....
voler	• to steal	• ....

21 **Mots croisés**

Across

1 avoid (*verb*) (6)
4 washing (*noun*) (7)
6 stadium (*noun*) (5)
7 him (*pronoun*) (2)
8 studies (*plural noun*) (6)

Down

1 church (*noun*) (6)
2 moment (*noun*) (7)
3 thorn (*noun*) (5)
5 they (*pronoun*) (5)
7 the (*determiner*) (2)

22 **Odd one out**

Hidden in this list of nouns is a verb. See if you can find it, then use your dictionary to check whether you are right.

abattoir	givre
bagarre	injure
colorier	lecture
enfer	ordre
foudre	sentier

23 Filling in the gaps

Here is a dialogue between a market stall holder and someone shopping for fruit and vegetables. Use your dictionary to help you fill in the names of the things she buys.

CLIENTE:	Bonjour, monsieur.
MARCHAND:	Bonjour, madame. Que voulez-vous aujourd'hui?
CLIENTE:	Eh bien, nous avons des invités ce soir et j'ai besoin de plusieurs choses. Pour commencer je voudrais un kilo de belles (*tomatoes*), s'il vous plaît, et deux bottes de (*radishes*). C'est tellement bon, les (*radishes*) au beurre.
MARCHAND:	Très bien, et avec ça?
CLIENTE:	J'ai besoin d'une (*lettuce*), une grosse.
MARCHAND:	Voilà. Il y a autre chose?
CLIENTE:	Oui, oui. Je voudrais, deux kilos de (*potatoes*), une livre d'(*onions*), une livre de (*carrots*), un (*cauliflower*) et un (*cucumber*).
MARCHAND:	Et avec ça?
CLIENTE:	Les (*peaches*) sont bonnes aujourd'hui?
MARCHAND:	Oui, elles sont très bonnes.
CLIENTE:	Donnez-m'en un kilo et puis avec ça une livre de (*plums*) et une barquette de (*raspberries*).
MARCHAND:	Bien, madame. Ce sera tout?
CLIENTE:	Oui, merci, c'est tout pour aujourd'hui.

24 French reflexive verbs

Use your dictionary to find the French equivalents of the following English sentences:

(a) I'm going to get changed.

(b) We argue about money.

(c) He easily gets bored.

(d) She always parks near the office.

(e) Sometimes I get impatient.

(f) What's happening?

(g) I always wake up at 7 o'clock.

(h) The war's coming to an end.

(i) Stamps are sold in the cafés.

(j) She's great fun.

Answers

1

Nouns: gaz, France, choix, qualité, Français, objet, écran, coins, beauté, yeux, poste, télévision, téléviseur, four.

Adjectives: naturel, magnifique, plat, carrés, luisante, nouveau.

2

Masculine nouns: sac, feutre, hippopotame, pull, imperméable, orage, ver.

Feminine nouns: pâtisserie, sonnette, île, bibliothèque, magie, huître, pêche, selle, serveuse.

3

ça ne fait rien (*it doesn't matter*)

c'est un cadeau (*it's a present*)

ce sont des détails sans importance (*these are unimportant details*)

il **l'**a invitée (*he invited her*)

elle ne **me** parle pas (*she won't speak to me*)

donne-**la-moi** (*give it to me*)

je **lui** ai prêté ma robe (*I lent her my dress*)

elles **se** sont fait mal (*they hurt themselves*)

il **vous l'**a prêté (*he lent it to you*)

donne-**nous** l'adresse (*give us the address*)

4

Pierre **descend** la rue sur son vélo.

Sophie ne **connaît** pas le nom du magasin.

Les sapeurs pompiers **arriveront** dans cinq minutes.

Chaque année nous **passons** nos vacances d'été en France.

Ma sœur **a** un bassin avec des poissons dans son jardin.

5

enseignement, médicament, stationnement, vêtement (*all masculine nouns*).

6

L'ours Félix a dévoré **neuf moutons** depuis son arrivée dans les Pyrénées. Hier, **l'animal** (or **Félix**), transplanté des forêts de Slovénie, a entièrement dévoré une brebis qui se trouvait près de Portet-d'Aspet en Haute-Garonne. **Le département** a aussitôt compensé **le berger** de la perte de sa bête. **Le 'tarif'** est de 600F pour l'attaque, qui ne sont versés qu'une seule fois, puis de 800F par mouton. Pourtant, **les bergers** devraient se rassurer: **les jeunes ours** sont toujours plus prédateurs que les vieux. Avec le temps, **Félix** (or **l'animal**) perdra **sa passion** pour la chasse.

Subjects: l'ours Félix, l'animal, le département, le 'tarif', les bergers, les jeunes ours, Félix.

Objects: neuf moutons, une brebis, le berger, sa passion.

7

B	G	R	A	N	D	K	Y	S	T
H	O	E	P	M	Q	C	E	L	A
S	T	N	D	N	O	R	U	I	V
Z	E	N	X	A	K	E	B	F	C
D	F	O	G	H	J	S	K	L	P
M	R	D	E	N	T	U	A	P	Q
M	O	N	D	E	P	C	O	A	D
P	G	A	W	C	U	X	V	R	N
C	U	B	A	G	U	E	T	T	E
R	H	A	N	F	Q	E	M	T	K

8

Ma chère Louise,

Merci pour ta lettre que j'ai reçue hier. Ce matin, comme d'habitude, je suis all**é**e faire mes courses au march**é** o**ù** j'ai rencontr**é** Madame Bonnard, que tu connais tr**è**s bien, je crois. Elle m'a dit que sa fille aîn**é**e, Sandrine, a fini ses **é**tudes et qu'elle part en Gr**è**ce faire un stage de six mois dans un h**ô**tel. Ça devrait **ê**tre amusant, non? Qu'est-ce que tu comptes faire toi-m**ê**me cet **é**t**é**? Est-ce que tu restes en France ou esp**è**res-tu toujours visiter la Norv**è**ge? Moi, je vais passer deux semaines dans la maison de campagne de mon fr**è**re **à** Gaillac . . .

9

encourager	**en** | **énerver**
horreur	**historique** | **hôtesse**
liquide	**librairie** | **loge**
mener	**mélanger** | **mesure**
renseigner	**renne** | **requin**
sérieux	**séjour** | **serré**
vieil	**version** | **vietnamien**

10

un livre = *a book*
une livre = *a pound*

un manche = *a handle*
une manche = *a sleeve*

un mode (de vie) = *a (life)style*
une mode = *a fashion*

un moule = *a mould*
une moule = *a mussel*

un poêle = *a stove*
une poêle = *a frying pan*

un tour = *a trick, a turn*
une tour = *a tower*

un vase = *a vase*
la vase = *mud*

un voile = *a veil*
une voile = *a sail*

11

Jean-Pierre a longtemps refusé **d'**accepter la proposition de son ami, Michel, mais finalement il a décidé **de** dire oui. Michel avait envie **de** faire une randonnée de plusieurs semaines à vélo à travers l'Europe et avait tout fait pour convaincre son ami **de** venir avec lui. A vrai dire, Jean-Pierre préférait passer son temps **à** se bronzer sur la plage, mais il essayait toujours **de** faire plaisir à son copain et c'est pour cette raison que Michel est parvenu **à** le persuader. Bien entendu, c'est Michel qui s'est chargé **de** faire tous les préparatifs du voyage, alors que Jean-Pierre a commencé **à** tracer l'itinéraire sur la carte.

12

to aim *viser*; to block *bloquer*; to camp *camper*; to dance *danser*; to finish *finir*; to iron *repasser*; to joke *plaisanter*; to kiss *embrasser*; to milk *traire*; to paint *peindre*; to question *interroger*; to sail *voyager en bateau*; to train *former, entraîner*; to welcome *accueillir*; to yell *crier*.

13

Elle a de **beaux** yeux et de **belles** dents.

Notre **ancienne** maison était très **vieille**.

C'est une très **bonne** idée.

La **première** chose à faire est de trouver l'entrée **secrète**.

Elles sont si **heureuses**.

La neige est **blanche**.

Il a une **nouvelle** voiture.

Mon père est **italien**, mais ma mère est **norvégienne**.

14

Masculine noun: dessous, gendre, ouest, vers.

Feminine noun: chasse, mouche.

Pronoun: en, que, toi-même.

Adjective: juste, ouest, pâle.

Preposition: en, vers.

Verb: inscrire, relire.

Adverb: dessous, facilement, juste, que.

Determiner: notre.

Conjunction: que.

15

Le bouton s'est détaché.
Les éboueurs ont enlevé les déchets.
Elle élève ses enfants toute seule.
Ils ont cessé de fumer.
Je vais enlever mes chaussures.

16

bijoux, cas, chevaux, cheveux, croix, manteaux, pneus, travaux, trous, vieux

17

actuellement currently, at the moment
un bonnet a cap, a hat
un car a coach, bus
une cave a cellar
une course a race, an errand
décevoir to disappoint
délivrer to free, to issue
un engin a device, a vehicle
éventuellement possibly, if necessary
gentil kind, nice
le matériel the equipment
le pétrole oil, petroleum
un pin a pine
sale dirty
sensible sensitive

18

actually *en fait, vraiment, exactement*
a bonnet *un capot*
a cap *une casquette, un capuchon, une capsule*
a car *une voiture*
a cave *une grotte*
a course *un cours, un plat*
to deceive *tromper*
to deliver *livrer*
an engine *un moteur, une locomotive*
eventually *finalement*
gentle *doux*
material *la documentation* (a material *une matière, une substance, un tissu, une étoffe*)
petrol *l'essence*
a pin *une épingle*
a sale *une solde*
sensible *raisonnable, judicieux, pratique*

19

une astronaute
une conseillère
une enquêtrice
une jongleuse
une musicienne
une piétonne
une religieuse
une scoute
une skieuse
une téléspectatrice

20

une baie	• a bay	• a berry
blanc	• white	• blank
un centimètre	• a centimetre	• a tape measure
enlever	• to remove	• to kidnap
un gorille	• a gorilla	• a bodyguard
le jour	• the day	• daylight
mauvais	• bad	• wrong
noir	• black	• dark
un pépin	• a pip	• a slight problem
une radio	• a radio	• an X-ray
un tailleur	• a tailor	• a (woman's) suit
voler	• to steal	• to fly

21

22
The verb is *colorier*.

23
tomates, radis, salade (*or* laitue), pommes de terre, oignons, carottes, chou-fleur, concombre, pêches, prunes, framboises

24
(a) Je vais **me changer**.
(b) Nous **nous disputons** pour des questions d'argent.
(c) Il **s'ennuie** facilement.
(d) Elle **se gare** toujours près du bureau.
(e) Parfois je **m'impatiente**.
(f) Qu'est-ce qui **se passe**?
(g) Je **me réveille** toujours à sept heures.
(h) La guerre **se termine**.
(i) Les timbres **se vendent** dans les cafés.
(j) On **s'amuse** bien avec elle.

a, an *determiner*
  a, an = un/une
  a dog = un chien
  an exhibition = une exposition
  my mother's a doctor = ma mère est médecin

able *adjective*
• (*having the possibility*)
  to be able to [walk | travel | sleep ...]
  = pouvoir [marcher | voyager | dormir ...]
• (*having the skill or knowledge*)
  to be able to [drive | read | type ...] = savoir
  [conduire | lire | taper à la machine ...]

aboard *adverb*
  to go aboard = monter à bord

about

> ! *Often* about *occurs in combinations with verbs, for example:* bring about, run about *etc. To find the correct translations for this type of verb, look up the separate dictionary entries at* bring, run *etc.*

1 *preposition*
  it's a book about France = c'est un livre sur la France
  I need some information about the town = j'ai besoin de renseignements sur la ville
2 *adverb*
  = environ
  I have about 200 francs left = il me reste environ 200 francs
  Oxford is about 40 km from here = Oxford est à environ 40 km d'ici
  we arrived at about midnight = nous sommes arrivés vers minuit
3 to be about to = être sur le point de
  to be about to [leave | cry | fall asleep ...]
  = être sur le point de [partir | pleurer | s'endormir ...]

above
1 *preposition*
  = au-dessus de
  their apartment is above the shop = leur appartement se trouve au-dessus de la boutique
  there is a shelf above it = il y a une étagère au-dessus
2 above all = surtout

abroad *adverb*
  = à l'étranger
  to go abroad = aller à l'étranger

absent *adjective*
  = absent/absente

accent *noun*
  an accent = un accent

accept *verb*
  = accepter

accident *noun*
• (*causing injury or damage*)
  an accident = un accident
  a car accident = un accident de voiture
• I heard about it by accident = je l'ai appris par hasard

accommodation *noun*
  to look for accommodation = chercher un logement

accompany *verb*
  = accompagner

account *noun*
• (*in a bank or post office*)
  an account = un compte
  there's money in my account = il y a de l'argent sur mon compte
• to take travelling expenses into account = tenir compte des frais de voyage

accountant *noun* ▶ 315|
  an accountant = un comptable/une comptable

accuse *verb*
  to accuse someone of cheating = accuser quelqu'un de tricher

across *preposition*
• to go across the street = traverser la rue
  to run across the street = traverser la rue en courant
  to swim across the Channel = traverser la Manche à la nage
  a journey across the desert = un voyage à travers le désert
• (*on the other side of*) = de l'autre côté de
  he lives across the street = il habite de l'autre côté de la rue

act *verb*
• (*to do something*) = agir
• (*to play a role*) = jouer

activity *noun*
  an activity = une activité
  sports activities = les activités sportives

actor *noun* ▶ 315|
  an actor = un acteur

actress *noun* ▶ 315|
  an actress = une actrice

actually *adverb*

> ! *Note that* actually *is not translated by* actuellement.

  actually, she's a very good athlete = en fait, c'est une très bonne athlète
  what actually happened? = qu'est-ce qui s'est passé exactement?

adapt *verb*
= s'adapter (**!** + *être*)

add *verb*
• (*to put in*) = ajouter
• (*in arithmetic*) = additionner

address *noun*
an address = une adresse

admire *verb*
= admirer

admit *verb*
• (*to recognize as being true*) = reconnaître
• (*to own up*) = avouer
did she admit that she'd stolen the money? = est-ce qu'elle a avoué avoir volé l'argent?
• to be admitted to (the) hospital = être hospitalisé/hospitalisée

adolescent *noun*
an adolescent = un adolescent/une adolescente

adopt *verb*
= adopter

adult *noun*
an adult = un adulte/une adulte

advantage *noun*
• (*a positive point*)
an advantage = un avantage
• to take advantage of a situation = profiter d'une situation

adventure *noun*
an adventure = une aventure

advertisement *noun*
• (*on TV, in the cinema*)
an advertisement = une publicité
• (*in a newspaper*)
an advertisement = une (petite) annonce
to answer job advertisements = répondre aux offres d'emploi

advertising *noun*
advertising = la publicité

advice *noun*
a piece of advice = un conseil
advice = des conseils

advise *verb*
to advise someone to rest = conseiller à quelqu'un de se reposer
I've been advised not to go there = on m'a déconseillé d'y aller

aerial *noun*
an aerial = une antenne

aerobics *noun* ▶ 248 |
aerobics = l'aérobic (*masculine*)

affect *verb*
the farmers have been affected by the drought = les fermiers ont été touchés par la sécheresse
the war is bound to affect tourism = la guerre va sûrement avoir des conséquences pour le tourisme

afford *verb*
to be able to afford a car = avoir les moyens d'acheter une voiture

afraid *adjective*
to be afraid = avoir peur
to be afraid of spiders = avoir peur des araignées
to be afraid to go out = avoir peur de sortir

Africa *noun* ▶ 218 |
Africa = l'Afrique (*feminine*)

African ▶ 275 |
1 *adjective*
= africain/africaine
2 *noun*
the Africans = les Africains (*masculine*)

after
1 *preposition*
= après
we'll leave after breakfast = nous partirons après le petit déjeuner
the day after tomorrow = après-demain
2 *conjunction*
after we had eaten, we went for a walk = après avoir mangé, nous sommes allés nous promener
they went in after the film had started = ils sont entrés après le début du film
3 after all = après tout

afternoon *noun* ▶ 211 |, ▶ 356 |
an afternoon = un après-midi, une après-midi

afterwards, afterward (*US English*) *adverb*
• (*after*) = après
• (*later*) = plus tard

again *adverb*
= encore
are you going camping again this year? = est-ce que vous allez encore camper cette année?
! *Note that there will very often be a specific French verb to translate the idea of doing something again—to start again = recommencer, to do the work again = refaire le travail, to see someone again = revoir quelqu'un.*

against *preposition*
= contre

age *noun* ▶ 187 |
age = l'âge (*masculine*)
he's my age, he's the same age as me = il a mon âge

aged *adjective*
= âgé de/âgée de
a boy aged 13 = un garçon âgé de 13 ans

ago *adverb*
two weeks ago = il y a deux semaines
long ago = il y a longtemps

Age

Note that, where English says **to be X years old**, French says **avoir X ans** (*to have X years*).

How old?

*how old **are you**?*	= quel âge **as-tu**?
*what age **is she**?*	= quel âge **a-t-elle**?

The word **ans** (*years*) is never dropped:

he is forty-one (years old)	= Il a quarante et un **ans**
the house is a hundred years old	= la maison a cent **ans**
a man of fifty	= un homme de cinquante **ans**

Note the use of **de** after **âgé**:

a woman aged thirty	= une femme âgée **de** trente ans

Comparing ages

*I'm older **than** you*	= je suis plus âgé **que** toi
*she's younger **than** him*	= elle est plus jeune **que** lui
*Anne's two years **younger***	= Anne a deux ans **de moins**
*Tom's five years **older than** Jo*	= Tom a cinq ans **de plus que** Jo

Approximate ages

*he is **about** fifty*	= il a **environ** cinquante ans
*she's **just over** sixty*	= elle **vient d'**avoir soixante ans
*games for **the under** twelves*	= jeux pour **les moins de** douze ans
*only for **the over** eighteens*	= seulement pour **les plus de** dix-huit ans

---

agree *verb*
- *(to have the same opinion)* = être d'accord
  I don't agree with you = je ne suis pas d'accord avec toi
- *(to be ready)*
  to agree to come a week later = accepter de venir une semaine plus tard
- *(to reach a decision)* = se mettre d'accord
  (**!** + *être*)

agriculture *noun*
  agriculture = l'agriculture (*feminine*)

ahead *adverb*
  to go on ahead = partir en avant

Aids *noun* ▶ **266**
  Aids = le sida

aim
1 *noun*
  an aim = un but
2 *verb*
- *(to be directed at)*
  to be aimed at young people = viser les jeunes
- *(when using a weapon)*
  to aim a rifle at someone = braquer un fusil sur quelqu'un

air *noun*
  air = l'air (*masculine*)
  to throw a ball up into the air = lancer un ballon en l'air
  to let the air out of a tyre = dégonfler un pneu

air force *noun*
  the air force = l'armée de l'air
  ! *Note that* **armée** *is feminine.*

air hostess *noun* ▶ **315** (*British English*)
  an air hostess = une hôtesse de l'air

airmail *noun*
  to send a letter by airmail = envoyer une lettre par avion

airport *noun*
  an airport = un aéroport

alarm clock *noun*
  an alarm clock = un réveil

alcohol *noun*
  alcohol = l'alcool (*masculine*)

alive *adjective*
  = vivant/vivante

all
1 *determiner*
  = tout/toute (+ *singular*)
  = tous/toutes (+ *plural*)
  I spent all week working = j'ai passé toute la semaine à travailler
  all the men have left = tous les hommes sont partis
2 *pronoun*
  = tout
  that's all = c'est tout
  after all we've done = après tout ce que nous avons fait

3 *adverb*
  to be all alone = être tout seul/toute seule
  all along the street = tout le long de la rue

allow *verb*
  to allow someone to [**work** | **play** | **leave** …]
    = permettre à quelqu'un de [travailler |
    jouer | partir…]
  they don't allow me to smoke at home
    = on ne me permet pas de fumer à la
    maison
  smoking is not allowed = il est interdit de
    fumer

all right *adjective*
• (*when giving your opinion*) = pas mal✷
  the film was all right = le film n'était pas
    mal✷
• (*when talking about health*)
  are you all right? = ça va?
• (*when asking someone's opinion*)
  is it all right if I come later? = est-ce que ça
    va si je viens plus tard?
  come at about nine, all right? = viens vers
    neuf heures, d'accord?
• (*when agreeing*) = d'accord

almond *noun*
  an almond = une amande

almost *adverb*
  = presque
  we're almost there = nous sommes
    presque arrivés
  I almost forgot = j'ai failli oublier

alone
1 *adjective*
  = seul/seule
  to be all alone = être tout seul/toute seule
  leave me alone! = laisse-moi tranquille!
2 *adverb*
  [**to work** | **to live** | **to travel** …] **alone**
    = [travailler | vivre | voyager …] seul/seule

along *preposition*
  = le long de
  there are seats all along the canal = il y a
    des bancs tout le long du canal

aloud *adverb*
  to read aloud = lire à haute voix

already *adverb*
  = déjà
  it's ten o'clock already = il est déjà dix
    heures
  have you finished already? = tu as déjà
    fini?

also *adverb*
  = aussi

although *conjunction*
  = bien que
  although she's strict, she's fair = bien
    qu'elle soit sévère, elle est juste

✷ in informal situations

! *Note that the subjunctive is used after*
bien que.

always *adverb*
  = toujours
  I always go to France in (the) summer = je
    vais toujours en France en été

amazed *adjective*
  = stupéfait/stupéfaite

amazing *adjective*
  = extraordinaire

ambition *noun*
  an ambition = une ambition

ambitious *adjective*
  = ambitieux/ambitieuse

ambulance *noun*
  an ambulance = une ambulance

America *noun* ▶ 218 |
  America = l'Amérique (*feminine*)

American ▶ 275 |
1 *adjective*
  = américain/américaine
2 *noun*
  the Americans = les Américains
    (*masculine*)

among, amongst *preposition*
• (*in the middle of*) = parmi
  the ruins are hidden among the trees = les
    ruines sont cachées parmi les arbres
• (*in a particular group*) = chez
  unemployment among young people = le
    chômage chez les jeunes

amount *noun*
  an amount = une quantité

amusement arcade *noun*
  an amusement arcade = une salle de jeux
    électroniques

amusement park *noun*
  an amusement park = un parc
    d'attractions

an ▶ **a**

ancestor *noun*
  an ancestor = un ancêtre/une ancêtre

and *conjunction*
• **and** = et
  a red and white sweater = un pull rouge
    et blanc
  she stood up and went out = elle s'est
    levée et elle est sortie
  to go faster and faster = aller de plus en
    plus vite
• (*in numbers,* **and** *is not translated*)
  three hundred and sixty-five = trois cent
    soixante-cinq

anger *noun*
  anger = la colère

angry *adjective*
to be angry = être en colère
to be angry with someone = être en colère contre quelqu'un

animal *noun*
an animal = un animal
farm animals = les animaux de la ferme

ankle *noun* ► **201**
the ankle = la cheville

announcement *noun*
an announcement = une annonce

annoy *verb*
= agacer

annoyed *adjective*
to be annoyed with someone = être fâché/fâchée contre quelqu'un

another
1 *determiner*
• **another** = un autre/une autre, encore un/une
another cup of coffee? = encore un café?
I'll buy another ticket for Alison = je vais acheter un autre billet pour Alison
• (*different*) = un autre/une autre
there's another way of doing it = il y a une autre façon de le faire
she's got another boyfriend now = elle a un nouveau copain maintenant
2 *pronoun*
there are some pears left—would you like another? = il reste des poires—est-ce que tu en veux encore une?

! *Note that it is necessary to use* en, *which might be translated as* 'of it' *or* 'of them', *with pronouns like* another. *See also* any, a few, a lot *etc for this use of* en.

answer
1 *noun*
an answer = une réponse
did you get an answer? = est-ce que tu as eu une réponse?
there's no answer (*at the door*) = il n'y a personne
(*on the phone*) = ça ne répond pas
2 *verb*
= répondre
to answer a question = répondre à une question
to answer the phone = répondre au téléphone
answer back = répondre

answering machine *noun*
an answering machine = un répondeur (téléphonique)

ant *noun*
an ant = une fourmi

antique *noun*
an antique = un objet ancien

antique shop *noun*
an antique shop = un magasin d'antiquités

anxious *adjective*
= inquiet/inquiète, anxieux/anxieuse
then I started to get anxious = j'ai commencé à m'inquiéter à ce moment-là

any
1 *determiner*
• (*in questions*) = du/de la (! de l' + *vowel or mute h*)
= des (+ *plural*)
is there any tea? = est-ce qu'il y a du thé?
is there any tart left? = est-ce qu'il reste de la tarte?
have you got any money? = est-ce que vous avez de l'argent?
• (*with the negative*) = de (! d' + *vowel or mute h*)
we don't have any bread = nous n'avons pas de pain
I didn't have any friends = je n'avais pas d'amis
• (*whatever*)
take any cup you like = prenez n'importe quelle tasse
2 *pronoun*
= en
do you have any? = est-ce que vous en avez?
he doesn't have any = il n'en a pas

! *Note that it is necessary to use* en, *which might be translated as* 'of it' *or* 'of them', *with pronouns like* any. *See also* another, a few, a lot *etc for this use of* en.

anyone *pronoun* (*also* **anybody**)
• (*in questions*) = quelqu'un
do you know anyone who could help us? = est-ce que tu connais quelqu'un qui pourrait nous aider?
• (*with the negative*) = personne
there isn't anyone in the house = il n'y a personne dans la maison
• (*everyone*)
anyone could do it = n'importe qui pourrait le faire

anything *pronoun*
• (*in questions*) = quelque chose
can I do anything to help? = est-ce que je peux faire quelque chose pour vous aider?
• (*with the negative*) = rien
she didn't say anything = elle n'a rien dit
there isn't anything to do here = il n'y a rien à faire ici
• (*everything*) = tout
I like anything to do with sports = j'aime tout ce qui a rapport au sport

anyway *adverb*
= de toute façon
I didn't want to go there anyway = de toute façon je ne voulais pas y aller

anywhere *adverb*
- (*in questions*) = quelque part
  can you see a phone booth anywhere?
  = est-ce que tu vois une cabine
  téléphonique quelque part?
- (*with the negative*) = nulle part
  you can't go anywhere = on ne peut aller
  nulle part
- (*any place*)
  we can meet anywhere you like = nous
  pouvons nous retrouver où tu veux

apart
1 *adjective*
  they don't like being apart = ils n'aiment
  pas être séparés
2 apart from = à part

apartment *noun*
  an apartment = un appartement

apartment block *noun*
  an apartment block = un immeuble

apologize *verb*
  = s'excuser (**!** + *être*)

apology *noun*
  an apology = des excuses (*feminine plural*)

appear *verb*
- (*to seem*)
  to appear happy = avoir l'air
  heureux/heureuse
- (*to come into view*) = apparaître (**!** + *être*)

appetite *noun*
  the appetite = l'appétit (*masculine*)
  to have a good appetite = avoir bon
  appétit

apple *noun*
  an apple = une pomme

apple juice *noun*
  apple juice = le jus de pomme

appliance *noun*
  an appliance = un appareil

application *noun*
  an application = une candidature

apply *verb*
  to apply for a job = poser sa candidature
  pour un emploi
  to apply for a passport = faire une
  demande de passeport

appointment *noun*
  an appointment = un rendez-vous
  to make an appointment = prendre
  rendez-vous

appreciate *verb*
  ! *Note that* **apprécier** *usually means to*
  like.

  I'd appreciate it if you could let me know
  = je vous serais reconnaissant de
  m'informer

approach *verb*
  = s'approcher de (**!** + *être*)

approve *verb*
  to approve of someone = apprécier
  quelqu'un

apricot *noun*
  an apricot = un abricot

April *noun* ▶ **222** |
  April = avril (*masculine*)

Aquarius *noun*
  Aquarius = Verseau (*masculine*)

architect *noun* ▶ **315** |
  an architect = un architecte/une
  architecte

area *noun*
  an area (*of a country*) = une région
  (*of a city*) = un quartier
  in the poorer areas of Paris = dans les
  quartiers plus défavorisés de Paris

area code *noun* (*US English*)
  an area code = un indicatif

argue *verb*
- (*to quarrel*) = se disputer (**!** + *être*)
  to argue about money = se disputer pour
  des questions d'argent
- (*to discuss a subject*) = discuter
  to argue about politics = discuter de
  politique

argument *noun*
  an argument = une dispute
  to have an argument with someone = se
  disputer avec quelqu'un

Aries *noun*
  Aries = Bélier (*masculine*)

arm *noun* ▶ **201** |
  the arm = le bras
  she's hurt her arm = elle s'est fait mal au
  bras

armchair *noun*
  an armchair = un fauteuil

armed *adjective*
  = armé/armée

arms *noun*
  arms = les armes (*feminine*)

army *noun*
  an army = une armée
  to join the army = s'engager (**!** + *être*)

around

  ! *Often* **around** *occurs in combinations*
  with verbs, for example: **run around**, **turn**
  around *etc. To find the correct*
  translations for this type of verb, look up
  the separate dictionary entries at **run**, **turn**
  etc.

1 *preposition*
= autour de
there are trees all around the garden = il y
a des arbres tout autour du jardin
**the people around me were speaking
French** = les gens autour de moi
parlaient français
to go around the world = faire le tour du
monde
2 *adverb*
= environ
it costs around £200 = ça coûte environ
200 livres sterling
we'll be there at around four o'clock
= nous serons là vers quatre heures

arrange *verb*
to arrange a break in Italy = organiser des
vacances en Italie
to arrange to have lunch together
= s'arranger pour déjeuner ensemble

arrest *verb*
= arrêter

arrive *verb*
= arriver (! + *être*)
we arrived at the station at noon = nous
sommes arrivés à la gare à midi

arrow *noun*
an arrow = une flèche

art *noun*
• **art** = l'art (*masculine*)
• (*as a school subject*)
art = le dessin

art gallery *noun*
an art gallery = un musée d'art

artificial *adjective*
= artificiel/artificielle

artist *noun* ▶ 315 |
an artist = un artiste/une artiste

arts and crafts *noun*
arts and crafts = les travaux manuels
! Note that **travaux** *is masculine plural.*

as
1 *conjunction*
• **as** = comme
as you know, we're leaving = comme vous
le savez, nous partons
• (*at the time when*)
**the phone rang as I was getting out of the
bath** = le téléphone a sonné au moment
où je sortais du bain
I used to live there as a child = j'habitais
là quand j'étais enfant
• (*British English*) (*because, since*) = comme
as you were out, I left a message
= comme tu étais sorti j'ai laissé un
message
• (*when used with* the same)
my coat is the same as yours = j'ai le
même manteau que toi

2 *preposition*
she's got a job as a teacher = elle a trouvé
un poste d'enseignante
he was dressed as a sailor = il était
habillé en marin
3 *adverb*
as [intelligent | rich | strong …] as = aussi
[intelligent | riche | fort …] que
go there as fast as you can = vas-y aussi
vite que possible
I have as much work as you = j'ai autant
de travail que toi
he plays the piano as well as his sister
= il joue du piano aussi bien que sa sœur
4 as usual = comme d'habitude

ashamed *adjective*
to be ashamed = avoir honte

ashes *noun*
ashes = les cendres (*feminine*)

ashtray *noun*
an ashtray = un cendrier

Asia *noun* ▶ 218 |
Asia = l'Asie (*feminine*)

Asian *adjective* ▶ 275 |
(*from China, Japan*) = asiatique

ask *verb*
• **to ask** = demander
he asked me my name = il m'a demandé
mon nom
**to ask someone to [phone | take a message |
do the shopping …]** = demander à
quelqu'un de [téléphoner | prendre un
message | faire les courses …]
I'll ask them if they want to come = je vais
leur demander s'ils veulent venir
to ask for money = demander de l'argent
to ask to speak to someone = demander à
parler à quelqu'un
to ask a question = poser une question
• (*to invite*) = inviter
to ask some friends to dinner = inviter des
amis à dîner
he asked her out = il l'a invitée à sortir
avec lui
• (*to look for information*) = se renseigner
(! + *être*)
did you ask about the tickets? = est-ce que
tu t'es renseigné pour les billets?

asleep *adjective*
to be asleep = dormir
to fall asleep = s'endormir (! + *être*)

assemble *verb*
= se rassembler (! + *être*)

assignment *noun*
a school assignment = un devoir

assistant *noun*
an assistant = un assistant/une assistante

at *preposition*

> **!** *There are many verbs which involve the use of at, like* look at, laugh at, point at *etc. For translations, look up the entries at* look, laugh, point *etc.*

- (*when talking about a position or place*) = à
  we met at a concert = nous nous sommes rencontrés à un concert
  she's at an exhibition = elle est allée à une exposition
  he's not at his desk = il n'est pas à son bureau
  at the = au/à la (**!** à l' + *vowel or mute h*) = aux (+ *plural*)
  they're at the clinic = ils sont à la clinique
  I saw her at the races = je l'ai vue aux courses
  to be [at home | at school | at work …] = être [à la maison | à l'école | au travail …]
- (*at the house, shop, practice of*) = chez
  we'll be at Nathalie's = nous serons chez Nathalie
  he's got an appointment at the dentist's = il a rendez-vous chez le dentiste
- (*when talking about time*) = à
  the film starts at nine o'clock = le film commence à neuf heures
  I was here at dawn = j'étais ici à l'aube
- (*when talking about age*) = à
  she was able to read at four years of age = elle savait lire à l'âge de quatre ans

athlete *noun* ▶ 315 |
an athlete = un athlète/une athlète

athletics *noun* ▶ 248 |
athletics (*in Britain*) = l'athlétisme (*masculine singular*)
(*in the US*) = les sports (*masculine*)

Atlantic *noun*
the Atlantic = l'Atlantique (*masculine*)

atmosphere *noun*
- (*the air*)
  the atmosphere = l'atmosphère (*feminine*)
- (*a mood, a feeling*)
  an atmosphere = une ambiance

attach *verb*
= attacher
to be attached to the wall = être fixé/fixée au mur

attack *verb*
to attack a town = attaquer une ville
to attack someone in the street = agresser quelqu'un dans la rue

attempt
1 *verb*
to attempt to break the record = tenter de battre le record
2 *noun*
an attempt = une tentative

attend *verb*
to attend the village school = fréquenter l'école du village
to attend evening classes = suivre des cours du soir

attention *noun*
attention = l'attention (*feminine*)
to get someone's attention = attirer l'attention de quelqu'un
to pay attention to the teacher = écouter le professeur

attic *noun*
an attic = un grenier

attitude *noun*
an attitude = une attitude
he has a strange attitude toward(s) people = il a une attitude bizarre envers les gens

attract *verb*
= attirer

attractive *adjective*
to be attractive = être séduisant/séduisante

auburn *adjective* ▶ 213 |
= auburn (**!** *never changes*)

audience *noun*
an audience = un public

August *noun* ▶ 222 |
August = août (*masculine*)

aunt *noun*
an aunt = une tante

au pair *noun*
an au pair = une jeune fille au pair

Australia *noun* ▶ 218 |
Australia = l'Australie (*feminine*)

Australian ▶ 275 |
1 *adjective*
= australien/australienne
2 *noun*
the Australians = les Australiens (*masculine*)

Austria *noun* ▶ 218 |
Austria = l'Autriche (*feminine*)

Austrian ▶ 275 |
1 *adjective*
= autrichien/autrichienne
2 *noun*
the Austrians = les Autrichiens (*masculine*)

author *noun* ▶ 315 |
an author = un écrivain

automatic *adjective*
= automatique

autumn *noun*
autumn = l'automne (*masculine*)
in (the) autumn = en automne

available *adjective*
- (*on sale*)
  tickets for the concert are still available = il reste encore des billets pour le concert

- (*free*) = disponible
  are you available? = est-ce que vous êtes disponible?

average *adjective*
  = moyen/moyenne
  the average teenager = l'adolescent moyen

avoid *verb*
- (*to prevent*) = éviter
  to avoid spending money = éviter de dépenser de l'argent
- (*to stay away from*) = éviter

awake *adjective*
  to be awake (*having slept*) = être réveillé/réveillée
  to stay awake = rester éveillé/éveillée
  to keep someone awake = empêcher quelqu'un de dormir

award *noun*
  an award = un prix
  she got the award for best actress = elle a reçu le prix de la meilleure actrice

aware *adjective*
  to be aware of the [problem | danger | risk ...]
  = être conscient/consciente du [problème | danger | risque ...]

away *adverb*
- (*absent*)
  to be away = être absent/absente
  she's away on business = elle est en voyage d'affaires
- (*when talking about distances*)
  to be far away = être loin
  London is 40 km away = Londres est à 40 km d'ici

awful *adjective*
- (*no good*) = épouvantable
  I thought the film was awful = j'ai trouvé le film épouvantable
- (*causing shock*) = terrible
- **I feel awful** = je ne me sens pas bien du tout

awkward *adjective*
  (*describing a situation, a problem*)
  = délicat/délicate
  I feel awkward about telling him = ça me gêne de le lui dire

axe, **ax** (*US English*) *noun*
  an axe = une hache

Bb

baby *noun*
  a baby = un bébé

babysit *verb*
  = faire du babysitting

back

> **!** *Often* **back** *occurs in combinations with verbs, for example:* come back, get back, give back *etc. To find the correct translations for this type of verb, look up the separate dictionary entries at* come, get, give *etc.*

1 *noun*
- (*part of the body*) ▶ **201**
  the back = le dos
  I've hurt my back = je me suis fait mal au dos
- (*the rear*)
  at the back of the supermarket = derrière le supermarché
  to sit in the back of the car = s'asseoir à l'arrière de la voiture
2 *adverb*
- **to be back** = être de retour
  I'll be back in five minutes = je serai de retour dans cinq minutes
- (*before in time*)
  back in January = en janvier

back door *noun*
  the back door = la porte de derrière

background *noun*
- (*of a person*)
  a background = un milieu
- (*of a picture*)
  the background = l'arrière-plan (*masculine*)
  in the background = à l'arrière-plan

backpack *noun*
  a backpack = un sac à dos

back seat *noun*
  the back seat = le siège arrière

back to front *adverb*
  = sens devant derrière
  to put a sweater on back to front = mettre un pull sens devant derrière

backwards, **backward** (*US English*) *adverb*
  = en arrière

bacon *noun*
  bacon = le bacon

bad *adjective*
* bad = mauvais/mauvaise (**!** *before the noun*)
  a bad film = un mauvais film
  a bad idea = une mauvaise idée
  I have some bad news = j'ai une mauvaise nouvelle
  to be bad [at maths | at tennis | at chess …] = être mauvais/mauvaise [en maths | au tennis | aux échecs …]
  it's a bad time to go on holiday = ce n'est pas le bon moment pour partir en vacances
  'was the film good?'—'not bad' = 'est-ce que le film était bien?'—'pas mal**✱**'
  smoking is bad for you = fumer est mauvais pour ta santé
* (*serious*) = grave
  a bad accident = un accident grave
* (*when talking about food*) = mauvais/mauvaise (**!** *before the noun*)
* (*not kind, not honest*) = méchant/méchante
  to feel bad = culpabiliser
* (*severe*)
  to have a bad cold = avoir un gros rhume

badger *noun*
  a badger = un blaireau

badly *adverb*
* (*not well*) = mal
  she slept badly = elle a mal dormi
* (*seriously*) = gravement
  he was badly injured = il a été gravement blessé

badminton *noun* ▶ 248 |
  badminton = le badminton

bad-tempered *adjective*
  to be bad-tempered = avoir mauvais caractère

bag *noun*
  a bag = un sac

baggage *noun*
  baggage = les bagages (*masculine plural*)

bake *verb*
* (*to prepare bread or cakes*) (*bread*) = faire du pain
  (*cakes*) = faire des gâteaux
* (*to be cooked in the oven*) = cuire (au four)

baker *noun* ▶ 315 |
  a baker = un boulanger/une boulangère

bakery *noun* ▶ 315 |
  a bakery = une boulangerie

balance *noun*
  balance = l'équilibre (*masculine*)
  to lose one's balance = perdre l'équilibre

balcony *noun*
  a balcony = un balcon

bald *adjective*
  = chauve

ball *noun*
  a ball (*in football, rugby or basketball*) = un ballon
  (*in tennis, golf or cricket*) = une balle
  (*in billiards*) = une bille
  to play ball = jouer au ballon

ballet *noun*
  ballet = le ballet

balloon *noun*
  a balloon = un ballon en baudruche

ban *verb*
  = interdire

banana *noun*
  a banana = une banane

band *noun*
  a band = un groupe
  a rock band = un groupe de rock

bandage *noun*
  a bandage = un bandage

bang
1 *noun*
* (*a loud noise*)
  a bang = une détonation
* (*US English*) (*a fringe*)
  bangs = une frange
2 *verb*
* (*to close with a bang*) = claquer
* (*to hurt*)
  to bang one's head on the wall = se cogner la tête contre le mur
* (*to hit*)
  to bang one's fist on the table = taper du poing sur la table

bank *noun*
  a bank = une banque

bank account *noun*
  a bank account = un compte bancaire

bank holiday *noun* (*British English*)
  a bank holiday = un jour férié

bank manager *noun* ▶ 315 |
  a bank manager = un directeur de banque

bar *noun*
* (*a place*)
  a bar = un bar
  to go to a bar = aller dans un bar
* (*a piece of metal*)
  a bar = une barre
* (*on a cage or window*)
  a bar = un barreau
* (*other uses*)
  a bar of soap = une savonnette
  a bar of chocolate = une tablette de chocolat

barbecue *noun*
  a barbecue = un barbecue

✱ in informal situations

barely *adverb*
= à peine
he was barely able to walk = il pouvait à peine marcher

bargain *noun*
a bargain = une affaire

bark *verb*
= aboyer

barn *noun*
a barn = une grange

barrel *noun*
a barrel = un tonneau

base *verb*
to be based in London = être basé/basée à Londres
to be based on a true story = être basé/basée sur une histoire vécue

baseball *noun* ▶ 248
baseball = le base-ball

basement *noun*
a basement = un sous-sol

basically *adverb*
= au fond

basin *noun*
a basin = une cuvette

basket *noun*
a basket = un panier

basketball *noun* ▶ 248
basketball = le basket

bat *noun*
• (*in cricket or baseball*)
a bat = une batte
• (*an animal*)
a bat = une chauve-souris

bath *noun*
• **to have a bath** = prendre un bain
he's in the bath = il est dans son bain
• (*a bathtub*)
a bath = une baignoire

bathroom *noun*
• **a bathroom** = une salle de bains
• (*US English*) (*the toilet*)
to go to the bathroom = aller aux toilettes

battery *noun*
a battery (*for a torch*) = une pile
(*for a car*) = une batterie

battle *noun*
a battle = une bataille

bay *noun*
a bay = une baie

be *verb*
▶ 196 See the boxed note on **be** for more information and examples.

• **to be** = être
to be intelligent = être intelligent/intelligente
he is tall = il est grand
we are rich = nous sommes riches
be polite! = sois poli!
it's a girl = c'est une fille
it's Monday = c'est lundi
it's past midnight = il est minuit passé
it's late = il est tard
the house has been sold = la maison a été vendue
he'll be famous = il sera célèbre
• (*when talking about jobs*) ▶ 315
she is a lawyer = elle est avocat
he is a good doctor = c'est un bon médecin
• (*when describing a physical or mental state*)
to be [cold | hungry | afraid ...] = avoir [froid | faim | peur ...]
my feet are cold = j'ai froid aux pieds
I am 18 = j'ai 18 ans
• (*when describing the weather*)
the weather is [fine | awful | cold ...] = il fait [beau | mauvais | froid ...]
it's not too hot = il ne fait pas trop chaud
it's raining = il pleut
• (*when talking about travelling*)
I've never been to Spain = je ne suis jamais allé en Espagne
have you ever been to Africa? = est-ce que tu es déjà allé en Afrique?
• (*when talking about health*)
how are you? = comment allez-vous?, comment vas-tu?
I'm very well = je vais très bien
how is your mother? = comment va ta mère?
• (*in continuous tenses*)
I'm coming = j'arrive
it was snowing = il neigeait
he is reading = il lit, il est en train de lire
• (*in questions and short answers*)
it's a lovely house, isn't it? = c'est une belle maison, n'est-ce-pas?
'he's not here'—'yes he is' = 'il n'est pas là'—'si'

beach *noun*
a beach = une plage

beak *noun*
a beak = un bec

beam *noun*
a beam = une poutre

bean *noun*
a bean = un haricot

bear
1 *noun*
a bear = un ours
2 *verb*
= supporter

beard *noun*
a beard = une barbe

B

be

As an ordinary verb

When **be** is used as a simple verb in *subject + verb* sentences, it is generally translated by **être**:

I **am** tired	= je **suis** fatigué
Paul **is** a doctor	= Paul **est** médecin

As an auxiliary verb in progressive tenses

In English, **be** can be used in combination with another verb to form a progressive tense which allows us to express *an idea of duration, of something happening over a period of time*.

The present

French uses the present tense to translate both forms of the English present tense, the simple and the progressive:

I work in London	= je travaille à Londres
I am working in London	= je travaille à Londres

To emphasize the idea of duration, **être en train de** + *infinitive* can be useful:

I'm working	= je suis **en train de** travailler
he's reading the paper	= il est **en train de** lire le journal

The future

By using the progressive form of the present tense, you can also refer to the future:

we're going to Paris next week	= nous allons à Paris la semaine prochaine

The past

To express the difference between *she watched TV* and *she was watching TV*, French uses the perfect and the imperfect tenses:

she **watched** TV	= elle a **regardé** la télévision
she **was watching** TV	= elle **regardait** la télévision

Again, to emphasize the idea of an activity happening over a period of time, the phrase **être en train de** + *infinitive* is useful:

she **was watching** TV when I phoned her	= elle **était en train de regarder** la télévision quand je lui ai téléphoné

As part of the passive

In French, as in English, the passive is formed in exactly the same way using **être**:

the rabbit **was killed by** a fox	= le lapin **a été tué** par un renard
the window **has been fixed**	= la fenêtre **a été réparée**

However, in spoken French, the impersonal pronoun **on** is often used to translate the passive if there is a person clearly involved:

the window has been fixed	= **on** a réparé la fenêtre

In short questions

With questions like *aren't you?*, *wasn't she?*, the general French phrase **n'est-ce pas?** can be useful in specific cases:

you're a doctor, **aren't you?**	= vous êtes médecin, **n'est-ce pas?**

With negative questions, **par hasard** can be useful:

he's not there, **is he?**	= il n'est pas là **par hasard?**

In short answers

There is no French equivalent for the verb in short answers such as *no, he's not, yes, we were* etc.

'is he around?' — 'no, he's not'	= 'est-ce qu'il est là?' — 'non'
'are you coming?'— 'yes, I am'	= 'est-ce que tu viens?' — 'oui'

If answering 'yes' to contradict a negative statement, the most useful translation is **si**:

'you're **not** coming, are you?' — '**yes, I am**'	= 'tu **ne** viens pas?' — '**si**'

beat *verb*
- (*to hit hard*) = battre
- (*in cooking*) = battre
- (*to win against*) = battre
  Scotland beat England two nil = l'Écosse a
  battu l'Angleterre deux à zéro
beat up = battre

beautiful *adjective*
= beau/belle (**!** *before the noun*)
  ! *Note that* bol *is used instead of* beau
  *before masculine nouns beginning with a
  vowel (*endroit*) or a mute h (*hôtel*). The
  plural of* beau *and* bel *is* beaux.

  a beautiful garden = un beau jardin
  a beautiful girl = une belle fille
  a beautiful place = un bel endroit
  they are beautiful cities = ce sont de belles
  villes

beauty *noun*
  beauty = la beauté

because
1 *conjunction*
= parce que
  he did it because it was necessary = il l'a
  fait parce que c'était nécessaire
2 because of = à cause de
  we didn't go out because of the rain
  = nous ne sommes pas sortis à cause de
  la pluie

become *verb*
= devenir
  to become an adult = devenir adulte

bed *noun*
  a bed = un lit
  to go to bed = se coucher (**!** + *être*)

bedroom *noun*
  a bedroom = une chambre

bee *noun*
  a bee = une abeille

beef *noun*
  beef = le bœuf
  roast beef = le rosbif

beer *noun*
- (*the product*)
  beer = la bière
- (*a glass of beer*)
  a beer = une bière

beet, beetroot (*British English*) *noun*
  a beet(root) = une betterave

before
1 *preposition*
= avant
  before the holidays = avant les vacances
  the day before yesterday = avant-hier
  the day before the exam = la veille de
  l'examen

2 *adjective*
= précédent/précédente, d'avant
  the week before = la semaine précédente,
  la semaine d'avant
  the day before = la veille
3 *adverb*
= avant
  two months before = deux mois avant
  have you been to Paris before? = est-ce
  que tu es déjà allé à Paris?
4 *conjunction*
  I'd like to see him before I go = j'aimerais
  le voir avant de partir
  I'd like to see him before he goes
  = j'aimerais le voir avant son départ

beg *verb*
= mendier

beggar *noun*
  a beggar = un mendiant/une mendiante

begin *verb*
= commencer
  to begin [working | laughing | raining …]
  = commencer à [travailler | rire | pleuvoir …]

beginner *noun*
  a beginner = un débutant/une débutante

beginning *noun*
  the beginning = le début
  in the beginning = au début
  at the beginning of May = début mai

behave *verb*
= se conduire (**!** + *être*)
  he behaved badly = il s'est mal conduit
  to be well behaved = être sage
  behave yourself! = tiens-toi bien!

behaviour (*British English*), **behavior**
(*US English*) *noun*
  behaviour = la conduite

behind *preposition*
= derrière
  I looked behind me = j'ai regardé derrière
  moi

Belgian ▶ 275 |
1 *adjective*
= belge
2 *noun*
  the Belgians = les Belges (*masculine*)

Belgium *noun* ▶ 218 |
  Belgium = la Belgique

believe *verb*
= croire

bell *noun*
- (*in a church*)
  a bell = une cloche
- (*on a door or bicycle*)
  a bell = une sonnette

belong *verb*
• (*to be the property of*)
  to belong to someone = appartenir à
    quelqu'un
  that book belongs to me = ce livre
    m'appartient
• (*to be a member of*)
  to belong to a club = faire partie d'un club

belongings *noun*
  belongings = les affaires (*feminine*)

below *preposition*
  = au-dessous de
  the kitchen is below my bedroom = la
    cuisine se trouve au-dessous de ma
    chambre
  there's a cupboard below it = il y a un
    placard au-dessous

belt *noun*
  a belt = une ceinture

bench *noun*
  a bench = un banc

bend
1 *verb*
• (*to lean, to move*) = se pencher (**!** + *être*)
  to bend one's head = pencher la tête
  to bend one's knees = plier les genoux
• (*to make crooked*) = tordre
2 *noun*
  a bend = un tournant, un virage
bend down = se pencher (**!** + *être*)

beneath *preposition*
  = sous

beside *preposition*
  = à côté de
  he is sitting beside me = il est assis à côté
    de moi
  to live beside the sea = habiter au bord de
    la mer

best
1 *noun*
  the best = le meilleur/la meilleure
  to be the best at French = être le
    meilleur/la meilleure en français
  who is the best at drawing? = qui dessine
    le mieux?
  to do one's best = faire de son mieux
2 *adjective*
  = meilleur/meilleure
  the best hotel in town = le meilleur hôtel
    de la ville
  she speaks the best French = c'est elle
    qui parle le mieux français
  my best friend = mon meilleur ami/ma
    meilleure amie
  the best book I've ever read = le meilleur
    livre que j'aie jamais lu

  ! *Note that the subjunctive is used after
  the superlative* le meilleur... que.

  **the best thing to do would be to phone
    him** = le mieux serait de lui téléphoner

3 *adverb*
  = le mieux
  the best dressed man = l'homme le
    mieux habillé
  I like tennis best = le tennis est mon sport
    préféré

bet *verb*
  = parier

better
1 *adjective*
  = meilleur/meilleure
  her new film is better than the others
    = son nouveau film est meilleur que les
    précédents
  he is better at sports than me = il est
    meilleur en sport que moi
  the weather is going to get better = le
    temps va s'améliorer
  he was ill but now he's better = il était
    malade mais maintenant il va mieux
2 *adverb*
  = mieux
  he speaks French better than I do = il
    parle mieux le français que moi
  we'd better go = nous ferions mieux de
    partir
  it's better to [phone | write | check ...] = il
    vaut mieux [téléphoner | écrire | vérifier ...]

between
1 *preposition*
  = entre
  there is a wall between the two gardens
    = il y a un mur entre les deux jardins
  between now and next year = d'ici l'année
    prochaine
2 in between = au milieu

beyond *preposition*
  = au-delà de
  beyond the village = au-delà du village

bicycle *noun*
  a bicycle = un vélo

big *adjective*
• (*large*) = grand/grande (**!** *before the noun*)
  a big garden = un grand jardin
  a big party = une grande fête
  they have big houses = ils ont de grandes
    maisons
  a big car = une grosse voiture
• (*heavy, thick*) = gros/grosse (**!** *before the
  noun*)
  a big parcel = un gros paquet
  a big book = un gros livre
• (*important, serious*) = gros/grosse (**!** *before
  the noun*)
  a big salary = un gros salaire
  to make a big mistake = faire une grave
    erreur

bike *noun*
  a bike = un vélo

bill *noun*
• (*for gas, electricity, telephone*)
  a bill = une facture

B

- (*in a restaurant*)
  a bill = une addition
  could we have the bill please?
  = l'addition, s'il vous plaît
- (*in a hotel*)
  a bill = une note
- (*US English*) (*money*)
  a bill = un billet de banque

billiards *noun* ▶ 248 |
  billiards = le billard

bin *noun* (*British English*)
  a bin = une poubelle

biology *noun*
  biology = la biologie

bird *noun*
  a bird = un oiseau

biro *noun* (*British English*)
  a biro = un stylo-bille

birth *noun*
  a birth = une naissance
  a place of birth = un lieu de naissance

birthday *noun*
  a birthday = un anniversaire
  Happy birthday! = Bon anniversaire!

biscuit *noun* (*British English*)
  a biscuit = un gâteau sec, un biscuit

bit
1 *noun*
  (*of cheese, bread, wood*) = un morceau
  (*of string, paper*) = un bout
2 **a bit** (*British English*)
  a bit [early | nasty | odd …] = un peu [tôt |
    méchant | bizarre …]

bite *verb*
  = mordre
  to bite one's nails = se ronger les ongles

bitter *adjective*
  = amer/amère

black *adjective* ▶ 213 |
  = noir/noire

blackberry *noun*
  a blackberry = une mûre

blackboard *noun*
  a blackboard = un tableau noir

blackcurrants *noun*
  blackcurrants = le cassis (*singular*)

blade *noun*
- (*of a knife, a sword*)
  a blade = une lame
- **a blade of grass** = un brin d'herbe

blame
1 *verb*
  to blame someone = en vouloir à
    quelqu'un
2 *noun*
  to take the blame = prendre la
    responsabilité

blank *adjective*
  (*describing a page*) = blanc/blanche
  (*describing a cassette*) = vierge

blanket *noun*
  a blanket = une couverture

blaze *verb*
  = être en flammes

bleed *verb*
  = saigner
  my nose is bleeding = je saigne du nez

blind
1 *adjective*
  = aveugle
2 *verb*
- (*destroy someone's sight*) = aveugler
- (*to dazzle*) = éblouir
3 *noun*
  a blind = un store

blink *verb*
  = cligner des yeux

blister *noun*
  a blister = une ampoule

block
1 *noun*
- (*a building*)
  a block of apartments = un immeuble
- (*a group of houses*)
  a block of houses = une pâté de maisons
- (*a large piece*)
  a block = un bloc
  a block of ice = un bloc de glace
2 *verb*
  = bloquer
  to block a road = bloquer une route

blond, blonde *adjective* ▶ 213 |
  = blond/blonde
  he has blond hair = il a les cheveux blonds
  my sister's blonde = ma sœur est blonde

blood *noun*
  blood = le sang

blouse *noun*
  a blouse = un chemisier

blow
1 *verb*
- (*if it's the wind*) = souffler
  the wind blew the door shut = un coup de
    vent a fermé la porte
- (*if it's a person*) = souffler
  to blow a whistle = donner un coup de
    sifflet
  to blow one's nose = se moucher
    (**!** + *être*)
  to blow bubbles = faire des bulles
- (*if it's a light bulb*) = sauter
2 *noun*
  a blow = un coup
blow away
  to be blown away = être
    emporté/emportée par le vent

blow down
  to be blown down = être abattu/abattue
    (par le vent)
blow out = souffler
  to blow out a candle = souffler une bougie
blow up
• (to destroy) = faire sauter
  to blow up a car = faire sauter une voiture
• (to be destroyed) = sauter
• (to put air into) = gonfler

blue adjective ▶ 213
  = bleu/bleue

blush verb
  = rougir

board
1 noun
• (a piece of wood)
  a board = une planche
• (for games)
  a board (in chess) = un échiquier
  (in draughts, checkers) = un damier
• (a blackboard)
  a board = un tableau noir
2 verb
  to board a ship = monter à bord d'un
    navire
3 on board = à bord

boarding school noun
  a boarding school = une pension

boast verb
  = se vanter (! + être)

boat noun
  a boat = un bateau

body noun
  the body = le corps
  a dead body = un cadavre

boil verb
• (if it's a person)
  to boil water = faire bouillir de l'eau
  to boil an egg = faire cuire un œuf
• (if it's water, milk) = bouillir

boiled egg noun
  a boiled egg = un œuf à la coque

boiler noun
  a boiler = une chaudière

boiling adjective
  = bouillant/bouillante

bomb
1 noun
  a bomb = une bombe
2 verb
  = bombarder

bone noun ▶ 201
  a bone (in the body, in meat) = un os
  (in fish) = une arête

✗ in informal situations

bonnet noun (British English)
  the bonnet (in a car) = le capot

book
1 noun
  a book = un livre
2 verb
  = réserver
  to book a room = réserver une chambre
  the flight is fully booked = le vol est
    complet

booking noun
  a booking = une réservation

bookshop, bookstore noun ▶ 315
  a bookshop, a bookstore = une librairie

boot noun
• (worn on the feet)
  a boot = une botte
• (British English) (of a car)
  the boot = le coffre

border noun
  a border = une frontière
  to cross the border = passer la frontière

bore verb
  = ennuyer

bored adjective
  to be bored, to get bored = s'ennuyer
    (! + être)

boring adjective
  = ennuyeux/ennuyeuse

born adjective
  to be born = naître (! + être)
  he was born in February = il est né au
    mois de février
  she was born in Italy = elle est née en
    Italie

borrow verb
  = emprunter
  to borrow some money from someone
    = emprunter de l'argent à quelqu'un

boss noun
  the boss = le patron/la patronne

both
1 determiner
  both girls are blonde = les deux filles sont
    blondes
  both my sons = mes deux fils
  both Anne and Brian came = Anne et
    Brian sont venus tous les deux
2 pronoun
  = tous les deux/toutes les deux
  you are both wrong, both of you are
    wrong = vous avez tort tous les
    deux/toutes les deux

bother verb
• (to take the trouble)
  don't bother calling back = ce n'est pas la
    peine de rappeler
• (to worry, to upset) = tracasser

The human body

Note the use of **le**, **la**, **l'** or **les** in French where English uses a possessive adjective:

*he raised **his** hand*   = il a levé **la** main
*she closed **her** eyes*   = elle a fermé **les** yeux
***my** eye hurts*   = j'ai mal à **l'**œil

For expressions such as *he hurt his foot* or *she brushed her teeth*, where the action involves more than the simple movement of a body part, use a reflexive verb in French:

she has broken her leg   = **elle s'est cassé** la jambe
he was washing his hands   = **il se lavait** les mains

Note also the following:

she broke his nose   = **elle lui a cassé** le nez (literally *she broke to him the nose*)

Describing people

Here are some ways of describing people in French:

his hair is long   = il a les cheveux longs
he has long hair   = il a les cheveux longs
a boy with long hair   = un garçon aux cheveux longs
her eyes are blue   = elle a les yeux bleus
she has blue eyes   = elle a les yeux bleus
the girl with blue eyes   = la fille aux yeux bleus
his nose is red   = il a le nez rouge
he has a red nose   = il a le nez rouge
a man with a red nose   = un homme au nez rouge

▶ For other expressions with terms relating to parts of the body, **▶ 266 |**.

---

* (*in polite apologies*) = déranger
  I'm sorry to bother you = je suis désolé de
  vous déranger

bottle *noun*
  a bottle = une bouteille

bottle-opener *noun*
  a bottle-opener = un décapsuleur

bottom
1 *noun*
* (*the lowest part*)
  the bottom of the hill = le pied de la
  colline
  at the bottom of [the page | the stairs | the
  street ...] = en bas [de la page | de l'escalier |
  de la rue ...]
  at the bottom [of the lake | of the sea | of the
  garden ...] = au fond [du lac | de la mer | du
  jardin ...]
* (*at the lowest level*)
  to be bottom of the class = être
  dernier/dernière de la classe
* (*part of the body*) **▶ 201 |**
  the bottom = le derrière*
2 *adjective*
  the bottom [shelf | drawer | cupboard ...]
  = [l'étagère | le tiroir | le placard ...] du bas

bound: **to be bound to** *verb*
  it's bound to create problems = ça va
  sûrement créer des problèmes
  she's bound to complain = elle va
  sûrement se plaindre
  it was bound to happen = cela devait
  arriver

bow¹ *noun*
* (*a knot*)
  a bow = un nœud
* (*a weapon*)
  a bow = un arc

bow² *verb*
  = saluer
  to bow one's head = baisser la tête

bowl *noun*
  a bowl = un bol
  (*shallow*) = une assiette

bowling *noun* **▶ 248 |**
  bowling = le bowling

box *noun*
  a box = une boîte
  (*when moving*) = un carton

boxing *noun* **▶ 248 |**
  boxing = la boxe

boy *noun*
  a boy = un garçon

boyfriend *noun*
  a boyfriend = un copain

bra *noun*
  a bra = un soutien-gorge

bracelet *noun*
  a bracelet = un bracelet

braid *noun* (*US English*)
  a braid = une natte, une tresse

brain *noun* ▶ 201 |
the brain = le cerveau

brake *noun*
a brake = un frein

branch *noun*
a branch = une branche

brand-new *adjective*
= tout neuf/toute neuve

brandy *noun*
brandy = le cognac

brave *adjective*
= courageux/courageuse

Brazil *noun* ▶ 218 |
Brazil = le Brésil

bread *noun*
bread = le pain

break
1 *verb*
• (*to be damaged*) = se casser (**!** + *être*)
  the chair broke = la chaise s'est cassée
• (*to crack, to smash or damage*) = casser
  to break an egg = casser un œuf
• (*to injure*)
  to break one's leg = se casser la jambe
  she broke her arm = elle s'est cassé le bras
• (*not to keep*)
  to break a promise = manquer à une
    promesse
  to break the rules = enfreindre le
    règlement
2 *noun*
• a break (*a short rest*) = une pause
  (*at school*) = une récréation
  to take a break = faire une pause
• (*a holiday*)
  a break = des vacances (*feminine plural*)
break down
• (*if it's a TV, a car*) = tomber en panne
  (**!** + *être*)
• (*to get upset*) = s'effondrer (**!** + *être*)
break into = cambrioler
  to be broken into = être
    cambriolé/cambriolée
break out
  (*if it's a fire*) = se déclarer (**!** + *être*)
  (*if it's violence*) = éclater
break up
• (*if it's a crowd*) = se disperser (**!** + *être*)
• (*if it's a couple*) = se séparer (**!** + *être*)
  to break up with someone = rompre avec
    quelqu'un
• (*to put an end to*) = mettre fin à
  the police broke up the demonstration
    = la police a mis fin à la manifestation

breakfast *noun*
breakfast = le petit déjeuner
to have breakfast = prendre le petit
  déjeuner

breast *noun* ▶ 201 |
a breast = un sein

breath *noun*
breath = le souffle
to be out of breath = être hors d'haleine
to hold one's breath = retenir sa
  respiration

breathe *verb*
= respirer
breathe in = inspirer
breathe out = expirer, souffler

breeze *noun*
a breeze = une brise

brick *noun*
a brick = une brique

bride *noun*
a bride = une mariée

bridegroom *noun*
a bridegroom = un marié

bridge *noun*
a bridge = un pont

brief *adjective*
= bref/brève (**!** *before the noun*)

bright *adjective*
• (*describing colours, light*) = vif/vive
  a bright yellow dress = une robe jaune vif
• (*having plenty of light, sun*) = clair/claire
  this room is not very bright = cette pièce
    n'est pas très claire
  a bright spell = une belle éclaircie
  to get brighter = s'éclaircir (**!** + *être*)
• (*intelligent*) = intelligent/intelligente

brilliant *adjective*
• (*very intelligent*) = brillant/brillante
• (*British English*) (*used for emphasis*)
  = génial/géniale✷

bring *verb*
• to bring = apporter
  to bring someone a present = apporter un
    cadeau à quelqu'un
  it will bring us good luck = ça va nous
    porter chance
• (*to be accompanied by*) = amener
  he brought his sister to the party = il a
    amené sa sœur à la soirée
bring about
  to bring about a change = provoquer un
    changement
bring back = rapporter
  he brought me back some perfume = il
    m'a rapporté du parfum
bring up = élever
  to bring up a child = élever un enfant

Britain *noun* ▶ 218 |
Britain = la Grande-Bretagne

British ▶ 275 |
1 *adjective*
= britannique

✷ *in informal situations*

2 *noun*
the **British** = les Britanniques (*masculine plural*)

broad *adjective*
= large

broadcast *verb*
= diffuser
to be **broadcast live** = être diffusé/diffusée en direct

brochure *noun*
a **brochure** = une brochure

broke *adjective*
= fauché/fauchée✶

broken *adjective*
= cassé/cassée

bronze *noun*
bronze = le bronze

brother *noun*
a **brother** = un frère

brother-in-law *noun*
a **brother-in-law** = un beau-frère

brown *adjective* ▶ 213
* (*in colour*) = marron (**!** *never changes*)
to have **brown eyes** = avoir les yeux marron
* (*describing hair*) = châtain (**!** *never changes*)
* to go **brown** = bronzer

bruise *noun* ▶ 266
a **bruise** = un bleu

brush
1 *noun*
* (*for hair, teeth, clothes or shoes*)
a **brush** = une brosse
* (*for sweeping up*)
a **brush** = un balai
* (*for painting*)
a **brush** = un pinceau
2 *verb*
to **brush one's hair** = se brosser les cheveux
to **brush one's teeth** = se brosser les dents

Brussels *noun* ▶ 218
Brussels = Bruxelles

bubble *noun*
a **bubble** = une bulle

bucket *noun*
a **bucket** = un seau

budgerigar, budgie *noun*
a **budgerigar** = une perruche

build *verb*
= construire
to **build a house** = construire une maison

building *noun*
a **building** = un bâtiment

Bulgaria *noun* ▶ 218
Bulgaria = la Bulgarie

bull *noun*
a **bull** = un taureau

bullet *noun*
a **bullet** = une balle

bulletin *noun*
a **bulletin** = un bulletin
a **news bulletin** = un bulletin d'informations

bully *verb*
= tyranniser

bump *verb*
to **bump one's head** = se cogner la tête
bump into
* (*to hit*) = rentrer dans (**!** + *être*)
* (*to meet*) = tomber sur (**!** + *être*)

bunch *noun*
a **bunch of flowers** = un bouquet de fleurs
a **bunch of grapes** = une grappe de raisins
a **bunch of keys** = un trousseau de clés

burger *noun*
a **burger** = un hamburger

burglar *noun*
a **burglar** = un cambrioleur/une cambrioleuse

burglar alarm *noun*
a **burglar alarm** = une sirène d'alarme

burglary *noun*
a **burglary** = un cambriolage

burn
1 *verb*
* (*to destroy, to get rid of*) = brûler
to **burn rubbish** = brûler des ordures
* (*to injure*)
to **burn oneself** = se brûler (**!** + *être*)
to **burn one's finger** = se brûler le doigt
* (*to be on fire*) = brûler
* (*when cooking*) = laisser brûler
* (*in the sun*)
to **burn easily** = attraper facilement des coups de soleil
2 *noun*
a **burn** = une brûlure
burn down = brûler

burst *verb*
* (*if it's a balloon*) = éclater
* (*if it's a pipe*) = éclater
* (*if it's a river*)
to **burst its banks** = déborder
burst into
to **burst into tears** = fondre en larmes
burst out
to **burst out laughing** = éclater de rire

bury *verb*
= enterrer

bus *noun*
a **bus** = un bus

B

bus conductor *noun* ▶ 315 |
   a bus conductor = un receveur/une
   receveuse d'autobus

bus driver *noun* ▶ 315 |
   a bus driver = un conducteur/une
   conductrice d'autobus

bush *noun*
   a bush = un buisson

business *noun*
* (*commercial activities*)
   business = les affaires (*feminine plural*)
   to go to London on business = aller à
   Londres pour affaires
* (*a company*)
   a business = une entreprise
* (*when protecting one's privacy*)
   that's my business = ça me regarde
   it's none of your business = ça ne te
   regarde pas

businessman *noun* ▶ 315 |
   a businessman = un homme d'affaires

businesswoman *noun* ▶ 315 |
   a businesswoman = une femme d'affaires

bus station *noun*
   a bus station = une gare routière

bus stop *noun*
   a bus stop = un arrêt d'autobus

busy *adjective*
   = occupé/occupée
   to be busy packing = être occupé à faire
   ses valises
   to have a busy day = avoir une journée
   chargée
   to lead a busy life = mener une vie
   active

but *conjunction*
   = mais
   he understands French but he doesn't
   speak it = il comprend le français mais
   il ne le parle pas

butcher *noun* ▶ 315 |
   a butcher = un boucher

butter *noun*
   butter = le beurre

butterfly *noun*
   a butterfly = un papillon

button *noun*
   a button = un bouton

buy *verb*
   = acheter
   to buy a present for someone = acheter
   un cadeau à quelqu'un
   she bought herself a new coat = elle s'est
   acheté un nouveau manteau

buzz *verb*
   = bourdonner

by *preposition*

* by = par
   by accident = accidentellement
   by chance = par hasard
   by mistake = par erreur
   one by one = un par un/une par une
   he was bitten by a dog = il a été mordu
   par un chien
* (*on one's own*)
   by oneself = tout seul/toute seule
* (*using*)
   to travel by bus = voyager en bus
   we went there by bicycle = nous y
   sommes allés à bicyclette
   to pay by cheque = payer par chèque
   to book by phone = réserver par
   téléphone
   to come in by the back door = entrer par
   la porte de derrière
* (*as a result of*)
   he succeeded by working hard = il a
   réussi en travaillant beaucoup
* (*beside*)
   by the sea = au bord de la mer
   by the side of the road = au bord de la
   route
* (*indicating the author or painter*) = de
   a book by Charles Dickens = un livre de
   Charles Dickens
   a painting by Chagall = un tableau de
   Chagall
* (*when talking about time*)
   by next Thursday = d'ici jeudi prochain
   he should be here by now = il devrait
   déjà être là
* (*when talking about figures, rates*)
   to increase by 20% = augmenter de 20%
   to be paid by the hour = être payé/payée à
   l'heure
   8 metres by 4 metres = 8 mètres sur 4

Cc

cab *noun*
   a cab = un taxi

cabbage *noun*
   cabbage = le chou

cable car *noun*
   a cable car = un téléphérique

café *noun*
   a café = un café

cake *noun*
   a cake = un gâteau

cake shop *noun* ▶ 315 |
   a cake shop = une pâtisserie

calculator *noun*
   a calculator = une calculatrice, une
   calculette

calendar *noun*
  a calendar = un calendrier

calf *noun*
  (*the animal*)
  a calf = un veau
  (*part of the leg*) **▶ 201**
  the calf = le mollet

call *verb*
  (*to name*) = appeler
  he's called Michael = il s'appelle Michael
  it's called 'un robinet' in French = en
    français ça s'appelle 'un robinet'
  (*to describe as*)
  to call someone a coward = traiter
    quelqu'un de lâche
  (*to call out (to)*) = appeler
  the teacher is calling us = le professeur
    nous appelle
  to call the register (*British English*) = faire
    l'appel
  (*to phone*) = appeler
  who's calling? = qui est à l'appareil?
  (*to get to come*) = appeler
  to call the doctor = faire venir le médecin
  (*to wake*) = réveiller
  (*to pay a visit*) = passer (**!** + *être*)
  they called yesterday = ils sont passés
    hier
call back
  (*to come back*) = repasser (**!** + *être*)
  (*to phone back*) = rappeler
call off = annuler
call out
  to call out the numbers for the lottery
    = annoncer les numéros gagnants du
    loto
call up = appeler

calm
1 *adjective*
  = calme
2 *verb*
  = calmer
calm down = se calmer (**!** + *être*)

camcorder *noun*
  a camcorder = un caméscope

camel *noun*
  a camel = un chameau

camera *noun*
  a camera (*for taking photos*) = un appareil
    photo
  (*in a studio, for videos*) = une caméra

camp
1 *noun*
  a summer camp = un camp de vacances
2 *verb*
  = camper
  to go camping = faire du camping

camping *noun*
  camping = le camping

campsite *noun*
  a campsite = un camping

can¹ *verb*
  (*to have the possibility*)
  can you come? = est-ce que tu peux
    venir?
  where can I buy stamps? = où est-ce que
    je peux acheter des timbres?
  he can't sleep when it's hot = il ne peut
    pas dormir quand il fait chaud
  (*when talking about seeing, hearing,
  understanding, you don't usually translate*
  can)
  I can hear you better now = je t'entends
    mieux maintenant
  can they see us? = est-ce qu'ils nous
    voient?
  he can't understand Japanese = il ne
    comprend pas le japonais
  (*to be allowed to*)
  can I smoke? = est-ce que je peux fumer?
  we can't turn right here = nous ne
    pouvons pas tourner à droite ici
  (*to know how to*)
  she can swim = elle sait nager
  he can't drive yet = il ne sait pas encore
    conduire
  can you speak French? = est-ce que tu
    parles français?
  (*when asking, offering or suggesting*)
  can we borrow your car? = est-ce que
    nous pouvons emprunter ta voiture?
  can I help you? = est-ce que je peux vous
    aider?
  you can phone back later if you like
    = vous pouvez rappeler plus tard si vous
    voulez

can² *noun*
  a can = une boîte

Canada *noun* **▶ 218**
  Canada = le Canada

Canadian ▶ 275
1 *adjective*
  = canadien/canadienne
2 *noun*
  the Canadians = les Canadiens
    (*masculine*)

canal *noun*
  a canal = un canal

cancel *verb*
  = annuler

cancer *noun* **▶ 266**
  cancer = le cancer

candle *noun*
  a candle (*in a room, on a cake*) = une
    bougie
  (*in a church*) = un cierge

candy *noun* (*US English*)
  candy = la confiserie
  (*a sweet*)
  a candy = un bonbon

canoe *noun*
  a canoe = un canoë, un canoë-kayak

canoeing *noun* ▶ 248 |
  canoeing = le canoë-kayak

can-opener *noun*
  a can-opener = un ouvre-boîtes

canteen *noun*
  a canteen = une cantine

cap *noun*
  a cap = une casquette
  a baseball cap = une casquette de baseball

capable *adjective*
  to be capable of looking after oneself
  = être capable de se débrouiller tout seul
  (*having ability, skill*)
  = compétent/compétente

capital
1 *noun*
  the capital = la capitale
  Paris is the capital of France = Paris est la
  capitale de la France
2 *adjective*
  = majuscule
  capital P = P majuscule

captain *noun*
  a captain = un capitaine

car *noun*
  a car = une voiture

caravan *noun* (*British English*)
  a caravan = une caravane

card *noun*
  (*for sending to someone*)
  a card = une carte
  (*for playing games*)
  a card = une carte (à jouer)
  to play cards = jouer aux cartes

cardphone *noun*
  a cardphone = un téléphone à carte

care
1 *noun*
  (*to take care*) = faire attention
  to take care crossing the street = faire
  attention en traversant la rue
  to take care of someone = s'occuper de
  quelqu'un
2 *verb*
  I don't care = ça m'est égal
  to care about the environment
  = s'intéresser à l'environnement

career *noun*
  a career = une carrière

careful *adjective*
  to be careful = faire attention
  to be careful crossing the street = faire
  attention en traversant la rue
  to be careful not to make mistakes = faire
  attention de ne pas faire d'erreurs

careless *adjective*
  to be careless = être négligent/négligente

car ferry *noun*
  a car ferry = un ferry, un transbordeur

carnival *noun*
  (*British English*) (*a festival*)
  a carnival = un carnaval
  (*US English*) (*a fair*)
  a carnival = une fête foraine

car park *noun* (*British English*)
  a car park = un parking, un parc de
  stationnement

carpet *noun*
  carpet = la moquette

car phone *noun*
  a car phone = un téléphone de voiture

carrot *noun*
  a carrot = une carotte

carry *verb*
  (*to hold*) = porter
  I can't carry the shopping = je ne peux pas
  porter les courses
  (*to move*)
  to carry the baggage upstairs = monter
  les bagages
  to carry the boxes downstairs = descendre
  les cartons
  carry on = continuer

cartoon *noun*
  a cartoon (*a comic strip*) = une bande
  dessinée, une BD
  (*a film*) = un dessin animé

case¹: in case *conjunction*
  = au cas où
  keep the bike in case you need it = garde
  le vélo au cas où tu en aurais besoin
  ! *Note that the conditional is used after* au
  cas où.

case² *noun*
  a case = une valise

cash
1 *noun*
  cash = l'argent liquide
  ! *Note that* argent *is masculine.*
  I don't have any cash = je n'ai pas
  d'argent liquide
  to pay in cash = payer en espèces
2 *verb*
  = encaisser

cash dispenser *noun*
  a cash dispenser = un distributeur
  automatique de billets

cassette *noun*
  a cassette = une cassette

cassette player *noun*
  a cassette player = un lecteur de cassettes

castle *noun*
  a castle = un château

cat *noun*
  a cat = un chat/une chatte

catch *verb*
  (*to capture*) = attraper
  to catch a fish = attraper un poisson
  (*to take hold of*) = attraper
  (*to pinch, to stick*)
  he caught his finger in the door = il s'est
    pris le doigt dans la porte
  my shirt got caught in the thorns = ma
    chemise s'est prise dans les ronces
  (*to get*)
  he was running to catch his train = il
    courait pour attraper son train
  (*to take by surprise*)
  to catch someone stealing = surprendre
    quelqu'un en train de voler
  to get caught = se faire prendre (**!** + *être*)
  (*to become ill with*)
  to catch flu = attraper la grippe
  to catch a cold = s'enrhumer (**!** + *être*),
    attraper un rhume
  to catch fire = prendre feu
catch up
  to catch up with someone = rattraper
    quelqu'un

caterpillar *noun*
  a caterpillar = une chenille

cathedral *noun*
  a cathedral = une cathédrale

cauliflower *noun*
  cauliflower = le chou-fleur

cause *verb*
  the storm will cause damage = l'orage va
    causer des dégâts
  it has caused us a lot of problems = ça
    nous a causé beaucoup de problèmes
  it's going to cause delays = ça va
    provoquer des retards

cautious *adjective*
  = prudent/prudente

cave *noun*
  a cave = une grotte

CD *noun*
  a CD = un disque compact, un CD

CD player *noun*
  a CD player = une platine laser

ceiling *noun*
  the ceiling = le plafond

celebrate *verb*
  = faire la fête
  to celebrate someone's birthday = fêter
    l'anniversaire de quelqu'un

celery *noun*
  celery = le céleri

cell *noun*
  a cell = une cellule

cellar *noun*
  a cellar = une cave

cello *noun* ▶ 290 |
  a cello = un violoncelle

cement *noun*
  cement = le ciment

cemetery *noun*
  a cemetery = un cimetière

centimetre (*British English*),
centimeter (*US English*) *noun* ▶ 285 |
  a centimetre = un centimètre

central heating *noun*
  central heating = le chauffage central

centre (*British English*), **center** (*US
English*) *noun*
  (*a place for activities, meetings*)
  a centre = un centre
  a leisure centre = un centre de loisirs
  (*the middle*)
  the centre = le centre
  near the centre of London = près du
    centre de Londres

century *noun* ▶ 356 |
  a century = un siècle

certain *adjective*
  = certain/certaine

certainly *adverb*
  = certainement

chain *noun*
  a chain = une chaîne

chair *noun*
  a chair = une chaise

chalk *noun*
  chalk = la craie

champagne *noun*
  champagne = le champagne

champion *noun*
  a champion = un champion/une
    championne
  a tennis champion = un champion/une
    championne de tennis

chance *noun*
  (*when talking about a possibility*)
  there is a chance that she'll have a job in
    Paris = il est possible qu'elle ait un
    travail à Paris

  ! *Note that the subjunctive is used after il
  est possible que.*

  (*an opportunity*)
  a chance = une occasion
  to have a chance to meet people = avoir
    l'occasion de rencontrer des gens
  by chance = par hasard

change
1 *noun*
  a change = un changement
  a change of temperature = un
    changement de température

(*a different experience*)
it makes a change from homework = ça change des devoirs
let's go to the beach for a change = allons à la plage pour changer
(*cash*)
change = la monnaie
have you got change for 50 francs? = pouvez-vous me faire la monnaie de 50 francs?
2 *verb*
(*to become different, to make different*) = changer
the town has changed a lot = la ville a beaucoup changé
I've changed my mind = j'ai changé d'avis
(*to replace*) = changer
to change a wheel = changer une roue
(*to exchange in a shop*) = échanger
change a shirt for a smaller size = échanger une chemise pour une taille plus petite
(*to switch*) = changer de
to change places with someone = changer de place avec quelqu'un
she keeps changing channels = elle n'arrête pas de changer de chaîne
(*when talking about one's clothes*) = se changer (**!** + *être*)
to get changed = se changer (**!** + *être*)
(*when using transport*) = changer
to change dollars into French francs = changer des dollars en francs français

changing room *noun*
a changing room = un vestiaire

channel *noun*
a TV channel = une chaîne de télévision

Channel *noun*
the (English) Channel = la Manche

chapter *noun*
a chapter = un chapitre

charge
1 *verb*
to charge someone for the damage = faire payer les dégâts à quelqu'un
they'll charge you for the electricity = ils te feront payer l'électricité
2 *noun*
(*a price, a fee*)
a charge = des frais (*masculine plural*)
there's no charge = c'est gratuit
3 in charge = responsable
to be in charge of the money = être responsable de l'argent

charming *adjective*
= charmant/charmante

chase *verb*
(*on foot*) = courir après
(*in a car*) = poursuivre

chase away = chasser

chat
1 *verb*
= bavarder, discuter
2 *noun*
a chat = une conversation
chat up (*British English*) = draguer✱

cheap *adjective*
(*not expensive*) = bon marché (**!** *never changes*)
it's cheap = c'est bon marché, ça ne coûte pas cher
it's cheaper to take the bus = ça coûte moins cher de prendre le bus
(*of poor quality*) = de mauvaise qualité

cheat *verb*
= tricher

check
1 *verb*
(*to make sure*) = vérifier
you should check whether it's true = tu devrais vérifier si c'est vrai
(*to inspect*) = contrôler
they didn't even check our passports = ils n'ont même pas contrôlé nos passeports
2 *noun*
(*US English*) (*a bill*)
a check = une addition
(*US English*) (*a cheque*)
a check = un chèque
check in = se présenter à l'enregistrement
check out = partir (**!** + *être*)

checkbook *noun* (*US English*)
a checkbook = un carnet de chèques, un chéquier

checkers *noun* ▶ 248 | (*US English*)
checkers = les dames (*feminine*)

check-in *noun*
the check-in = l'enregistrement (*masculine*)

checkout *noun*
a checkout = une caisse

cheek *noun* ▶ 201 |
the cheek = la joue

cheeky *adjective*
= effronté/effrontée, insolent/insolente

cheerful *adjective*
= gai/gaie

cheese *noun*
cheese = le fromage

chef *noun* ▶ 315 |
a chef = un chef cuisinier

chemist *noun* ▶ 315 |
(*in a shop*)
a chemist = un pharmacien/une pharmacienne
(*in a laboratory*)
a chemist = un chimiste/une chimiste

✱ in informal situations

chemistry noun
chemistry = la chimie

cheque noun (British English)
a cheque = un chèque
to write a cheque for £50 = faire un chèque de 50 livres

cheque book noun (British English)
a cheque book = un carnet de chèques, un chéquier

cherry noun
a cherry = une cerise

chess noun ▶ 248 |
chess = les échecs (masculine plural)

chest noun ▶ 201 |
the chest = la poitrine

chestnut
1 noun
a chestnut = un marron, une châtaigne
2 adjective
= châtain (! never changes)
to have chestnut hair = avoir les cheveux châtain

chew verb
(if it's a person) = mâcher
(if it's an animal) = ronger

chewing gum noun
chewing gum = le chewing gum

chicken noun
(the bird)
a chicken = une poule
(the meat)
chicken = le poulet

child noun
a child = un enfant/une enfant

chilly adjective
it's chilly = il fait froid

chimney noun
a chimney = une cheminée

chin noun ▶ 201 |, ▶ 237 |
the chin = le menton

China noun ▶ 218 |
China = la Chine

Chinese ▶ 275 |
1 adjective
= chinois/chinoise
2 noun
(the people)
the Chinese = les Chinois (masculine plural)
(the language)
Chinese = le chinois

chips noun
(British English) (French fries)
chips = les frites (feminine)
(US English) (crisps)
(potato) chips = les chips (feminine)

chocolate noun
chocolate = le chocolat
a box of chocolates = une boîte de chocolats

choice noun
a choice = un choix
we had no choice = nous n'avions pas le choix

choir noun
a choir = une chorale

choke verb
= s'étouffer (! + être)

choose verb
= choisir

chore noun
a chore = une tâche
to do the chores = faire le ménage

Christian adjective
= chrétien/chrétienne

Christian name noun
a Christian name = un nom de baptême

Christmas noun
Christmas (Day) = (le jour de) Noël
Merry Christmas!, Happy Christmas! = Joyeux Noël!

Christmas carol noun
a Christmas carol = un chant de Noël

Christmas cracker noun (British English)
a Christmas cracker = un diablotin

Christmas Eve noun
Christmas Eve = la veille de Noël

Christmas tree noun
a Christmas tree = un sapin de Noël

church noun
a church (Catholic or Anglican) = une église
(Protestant) = un temple

cider noun
cider = le cidre

cigar noun
a cigar = un cigare

cigarette noun
a cigarette = une cigarette

cigarette lighter noun
a cigarette lighter = un briquet

cinema noun (British English)
a cinema = un cinéma

circle noun
a circle = un cercle
we were sitting in a circle = nous étions assis en cercle

circus noun
a circus = un cirque

citizen noun
  (of a country)
  a citizen = un citoyen/une citoyenne
  (of a city or town)
  a citizen = un habitant/une habitante

city noun
  a city = une (grande) ville

city centre (British English), **city center** (US English) noun
  the city centre = le centre-ville

civilized adjective
  = civilisé/civilisée

civil servant noun ▶ 315 |
  a civil servant = un fonctionnaire/une fonctionnaire

clap verb
  = applaudir

clarinet noun ▶ 290 |
  a clarinet = une clarinette

class noun
  (a group of students)
  a class = une classe
  (a lesson)
  a class = un cours
  a history class = un cours d'histoire
  (a social group)
  a (social) class = une classe (sociale)

classical music noun
  classical music = la musique classique

classmate noun
  a classmate = un camarade/une camarade de classe

classroom noun
  a classroom = une salle de classe

clean
1 adjective
  (not dirty) = propre
  my hands are clean = j'ai les mains propres
  to keep the house clean = tenir la maison propre
  (not polluted) = pur/pure
2 verb
  = nettoyer
  to have a jacket cleaned = faire nettoyer une veste

clear
1 adjective
  (easy to understand, making sense) = clair/claire
  is that clear? = est-ce que c'est clair?
  (obvious)
  it is clear that no-one is happy = il est clair que personne n'est content
  (easy to see or hear, distinct)
  a clear voice = une voix claire
  your writing must be clear = votre écriture doit être lisible
  (with no rain or cloud) = clair/claire
  on a clear day = par temps clair

2 verb
  (to empty, to remove from)
  to clear the table = débarrasser la table
  to clear the building = évacuer le bâtiment
  to clear the snow off the road = dégager la neige de la route
  (if it's fog, mist) = se dissiper (**!** + être)

clever adjective
  (intelligent) = intelligent/intelligente
  to be clever at mathematics = être doué/douée pour les mathématiques
  (smart) = astucieux/astucieuse

cliff noun
  a cliff = une falaise

climate noun
  a climate = un climat

climb verb
  to climb (up) a tree = grimper à un arbre
  to climb a mountain = faire l'ascension d'une montagne
  to climb over a wall = passer par-dessus un mur
  (to rise higher) = monter (**!** + être)

climbing noun ▶ 248 |
  climbing = l'escalade (feminine)

clinic noun
  a clinic = un centre médical

cloakroom noun
  a cloakroom = un vestiaire

clock noun
  a clock (on a building, in a classroom) = une horloge
  (smaller, as an ornament) = une pendule
  (in sporting events) = un chronomètre

close¹
1 adjective
  (near) = proche
  the station is quite close = la gare est assez proche
  is the house close to the school? = est-ce que la maison est près de l'école?
  (as a friend or relation) = proche
2 adverb
  to live close (by) = habiter tout près
  to come closer = s'approcher (**!** + être)

close² verb
  = fermer
  close your eyes = ferme les yeux
  the shop closes at noon = le magasin ferme à midi
  the door closed suddenly = tout d'un coup, la porte s'est fermée
close down = fermer définitivement

closed adjective
  = fermé/fermée

cloth noun
  (material)
  cloth = le tissu

The clock

What time is it?

what time is it?	= quelle heure est-il?
could you tell me the time?	= pouvez-vous me donner l'heure?
it's exactly four o'clock	= il est exactement quatre heures

It is ...	Il est ...	say
4 o'clock	4 heures	
	4 h	quatre heures
*4 o'clock in the morning	4 am*	4 h 00	quatre heures du matin
*4 o'clock in the afternoon	4 pm*	16 h 00	quatre heures de l'après-midi
		seize heures*
*4.10	ten past four*	4 h 10	quatre heures dix
4.15	4 h 15	quatre heures quinze
a quarter past four	4 h 15	quatre heures et quart
4.20	4 h 20	quatre heures vingt
4.25	4 h 25	quatre heures vingt-cinq
4.30	4 h 30	quatre heures trente
half past four	4 h 30	quatre heures et demie†
4.35	4 h 35	quatre heures trente-cinq
twenty-five to five	4 h 35	cinq heures moins vingt-cinq
4.40	4 h 40	quatre heures quarante
twenty to five	4 h 40	cinq heures moins vingt
*4.45	a quarter to five*	4 h 45	cinq heures moins le quart
4.50	4 h 50	quatre heures cinquante
ten to five	4 h 50	cinq heures moins dix
4.55	4 h 55	quatre heures cinquante-cinq
five to five	4 h 55	cinq heures moins cinq
5 o'clock	5 h 00	cinq heures
16.15	16 h 15	seize heures quinze
8 o'clock in the evening	8 h du soir	huit heures du soir
8 pm	20 h 00	vingt heures
12.00	12 h 00	douze heures
*noon	12 noon*	12 h 00	midi
*midnight	12 midnight*	24 h 00	minuit

* In timetables etc, the twenty-four hour clock is used, so that **4 pm** is **seize heures**. In ordinary usage, one says **quatre heures (de l'après-midi)**.

† Note that **demi** agrees with the noun it follows:

une heure et demie
un jour et demi
minuit et demi
midi et demi

Note also that, when it comes before the noun, **demi** is hyphenated and does not change:

une **demi**-journée
les **demi**-heures.

When?

French never drops the word **heures**: *at five* is **à cinq heures** and so on:

French always uses **à**, whether or not English includes the word *at*. The only exception is when there is another preposition present, as in **vers cinq heures** (*about five o'clock*), **avant cinq heures** (*before five o'clock*) etc:

what time did it happen?	= **à quelle** heure cela s'est-il passé?
what time will he come at?	= **à quelle** heure va-t-il venir?
it happened at two o'clock	= c'est arrivé **à** deux heures
he'll come at four	= il viendra **à** quatre heures
at about five	= **vers** cinq heures / **à** cinq heures **environ**
it must be ready by ten	= il faut que ce soit prêt **avant** dix heures
closed from 1 to 2 pm	= fermé **de** treize **à** quatorze heures
every hour on the hour	= toutes les heures **à** l'heure juste

a cloth (*for dusting*) = un chiffon
(*for the floor*) = une serpillière
(*for dishes*) = un torchon

clothes *noun*
  clothes = les vêtements (*masculine*)
  to put on one's clothes = s'habiller
    (**!** + *être*)
  to take off one's clothes = se déshabiller
    (**!** + *être*)
  to have no clothes on = être tout nu/toute
    nue

cloud *noun*
  a cloud = un nuage

clown *noun*
  a clown = un clown

club *noun*
  a club = un club
  a tennis club = un club de tennis
  to be in a club = faire partie d'un club
  (*a nightclub*)
  a club = une boîte de nuit

clue *noun*
  (*in an investigation*)
  a clue = un indice
  (*in a crossword*)
  a clue = une définition

clumsy *adjective*
  = maladroit/maladroite

coach
  1 *noun* (*British English*)
  (*a bus*)
  a coach = un car
  (*of a train*)
  a coach = un wagon
  2 *verb*
  = entraîner

coach station *noun*
  a coach station = une gare routière

coal *noun*
  coal = le charbon

coast *noun*
  the coast = la côte

coat *noun*
  a coat = un manteau
  (*of an animal*)
  the coat (*of a dog*) = le poil
  (*of a cat*) = la fourrure

coat hanger *noun*
  a coat hanger = un cintre

cobweb *noun*
  a cobweb = une toile d'araignée

cock *noun*
  a cock = un coq

cocoa *noun*
  (*the drink*)
  cocoa = le chocolat
  (*the product*)
  cocoa = le cacao

coconut *noun*
  a coconut = une noix de coco

cod *noun*
  cod = le cabillaud

coffee *noun*
  (*the product*)
  coffee = le café
  (*a cup of coffee*)
  a coffee = un café

coffee machine *noun*
  a coffee machine (*an appliance*) = une
    cafetière électrique
  (*a machine*) = une machine à café

coin *noun*
  a coin = une pièce
  a ten-franc coin = une pièce de dix francs

coincidence *noun*
  a coincidence = une coïncidence

cold
  1 *adjective*
  = froid/froide
  to be cold, to feel cold = avoir froid
  I'm very cold = j'ai très froid
  it's cold in the classroom = il fait froid
    dans la salle de classe
  you'll get cold = tu vas prendre froid
  to go cold = refroidir
  a cold meal = un repas froid
  2 *noun*
  (*the lack of heat*)
  the cold = le froid
  (*a common illness*)
  a cold = un rhume

collapse *verb*
  (*if it's a building, a chair*) = s'effondrer
    (**!** + *être*)
  (*if it's a wall*) = s'écrouler (**!** + *être*)

collar *noun*
  (*on a shirt or jacket*)
  a collar = un col
  (*for a pet*)
  a collar = un collier

colleague *noun*
  a colleague = un collègue/une collègue

collect *verb*
  (*to gather*) = ramasser
  to collect the exercise books = ramasser
    les cahiers
  (*to make a collection of*) = collectionner
  he collects stamps = il collectionne les
    timbres
  (*to take away*)
  to collect the post = faire la levée du
    courrier
  to collect the rubbish = ramasser les
    ordures

✱ in informal situations

Colours

Most colour adjectives agree with the noun they are describing:

a blue coat	= un manteau bleu
a blue dress	= une robe bleue

There are exceptions, labelled (**!** *never changes*) in the dictionary. Even with a plural noun, this type of adjective remains the same:

brown shoes	= des chaussures marron
orange curtains	= des rideaux orange

This rule also applies to shades of colour:

a dark blue dress	= une robe bleu foncé
pale blue curtains	= des rideaux bleu pâle

Describing the colour of something

what colour is your car?	= ta voiture est de quelle couleur?
	(*more formally*) de quelle couleur est ta voiture?
it's green	= elle est verte
to paint something green	= peindre quelque chose en vert

Describing people

Note the use of **les**:

to have brown eyes	= avoir **les** yeux marron

Note the use of **à**:

the girl with the blond hair	= la fille **aux** cheveux blonds

---

collection *noun*
(*a set*)
  a collection = une collection
  she has a great collection of posters
    = elle a une super✱ collection d'affiches
(*money collected*)
  a collection = une collecte

college *noun*
  a college = un établissement
    d'enseignement supérieur
  to go to college, to be at college = faire
    des études supérieures

colour (*British English*), **color** (*US English*)
1 *noun*
  a colour = une couleur
  what colour is the car? = de quelle
    couleur est la voiture?
2 *verb*
  to colour the drawings (in) = colorier les
    dessins

colourful (*British English*), **colorful** (*US English*) *adjective*
  a colourful shirt = une chemise aux
    couleurs vives

colour television (*British English*),
color television (*US English*) *noun*
  a colour television = une télévision (en)
    couleur

comb
1 *noun*
  a comb = un peigne
2 *verb*
  to comb one's hair = se peigner (**!** + *être*)

come *verb*
  to come = venir (**!** + *être*)
  she's coming today = elle vient
    aujourd'hui
  come to Paris with us = viens avec nous à
    Paris
  we came by bike = nous sommes venus à
    bicyclette
  come and see! = venez voir!
  I'm coming! = j'arrive!
  is the bus coming? = est-ce que le bus
    arrive?
  **be careful when you come down the
    stairs** = faites attention en descendant
    l'escalier
  he won't come into the house = il ne veut
    pas entrer dans la maison
  to come through the city centre = passer
    par le centre-ville
  (*to call around*) = passer (**!** + *être*)
  (*to reach*)
  **turn left when you come to the traffic
    lights** = tournez à gauche quand vous
    arriverez aux feux
  (*to attend*) = venir (**!** + *être*)
  will you be able to come to the meeting?
    = est-ce que tu pourras venir à la
    réunion?

* (*to be a native or a product of*)
 she comes from Italy = elle est italienne
 the strawberries all come from Spain
  = toutes les fraises viennent d'Espagne
* (*in a contest*)
 to come first = arriver premier/première
come around ▶ come round
come back = revenir (**!** + *être*)
 to come back home = rentrer (**!** + *être*)
come in
* (*to enter*) = entrer (**!** + *être*)
* (*if it's a plane, a train*) = arriver (**!** + *être*)
* **the tide's coming in** = la marée monte
come off
 (*if it's a cover, a lid*) = s'enlever (**!** + *être*)
 (*if it's a button, a label*) = se détacher
  (**!** + *être*)
come on
* (*to start to work*) (*if it's heating*) = se mettre
 en marche
 (*if it's a light*) = s'allumer (**!** + *être*)
* (*when encouraging someone*)
 come on, hurry up! = allez, dépêchez-
 vous!
 come on, you can do better than that!
  = allez, tu peux faire mieux!
come on to (*US English*)
 to come on to someone = draguer
 quelqu'un✸
come out
* (*to leave a place*) = sortir (**!** + *être*)
 I saw him as I was coming out of the shop
  = je l'ai vu en sortant du magasin
* (*to become available*)
 (*if it's a film*) = sortir (**!** + *être*)
 (*if it's a book*) = paraître (**!** + *être*)
* (*to wash out*) = s'en aller (**!** + *être*)
* (*if it's a photo*)
 the photo didn't come out = la photo est
 ratée
* (*if it's smoke, fire*)
 there are flames coming out of the
  windows = il y a des flammes qui
 sortent par les fenêtres
come round
* (*to visit*) = venir (**!** + *être*)
* (*after a faint*) = reprendre connaissance
come to
 the meal came to 75 francs = le repas a
 coûté 75 francs
 how much does it come to? = ça fait
 combien?
come up
* (*to be discussed*)
 to come up in conversation = être
 abordé/abordée dans la conversation
* (*if it's the sun*) = se lever (**!** + *être*)

comfortable *adjective*
* (*if it's a chair, a bed*) = confortable
 are you comfortable? = êtes-vous bien
 installés?
* (*relaxed*) = à l'aise
* (*having enough money*) = aisé/aisée

comforter *noun* (*US English*)
 a comforter = une couette

comic strip *noun*
 a comic strip = une bande dessinée, une
 BD

commercial
1 *adjective*
 = commercial/commerciale
2 *noun*
 a commercial = une publicité

commit *verb*
 to commit a crime = commettre un crime

common *adjective*
 = courant/courante

communicate *verb*
 = communiquer

community *noun*
 a community = une communauté

company *noun*
* (*a business*)
 a company = une société
* (*a group of actors*)
 a theatre company = une troupe de
 théâtre
* (*other people*)
 company = la compagnie
 to keep someone company = tenir
 compagnie à quelqu'un
 to keep bad company = avoir de
 mauvaises fréquentations

company secretary *noun* ▶ 315 |
 a company secretary = un secrétaire
 général

compare *verb*
 = comparer
 to compare France with Italy = comparer
 la France à l'Italie
 she compares herself to her older sister
  = elle se compare à sa sœur aînée

compass *noun*
 a compass = une boussole

competition *noun*
* **competition** = la concurrence
 there's a lot of competition between the
  schools = il y a beaucoup de
 concurrence entre les écoles
* (*a contest*)
 a competition = un concours
 a drawing competition = un concours de
 dessin

competitive *adjective*
 to be competitive = avoir l'esprit de la
 compétition

complain *verb*
 = se plaindre (**!** + *être*)
 to complain about the food = se plaindre
 de la nourriture

complete
1 *adjective*
  it was a complete disaster = c'était un
    désastre total
  this is a complete waste of time = c'est
    vraiment du temps perdu
2 *verb*
  = terminer
  to complete a training course = terminer
    un stage de formation

completely *adverb*
  = complètement

complicate *verb*
  = compliquer

complicated *adjective*
  = compliqué/compliquée

compliment
1 *noun*
  a compliment = un compliment
2 *verb*
  to compliment someone = faire des
    compliments à quelqu'un

comprehensive *noun (British English)*
  a comprehensive = une école (publique)
    secondaire

compulsory *adjective*
  = obligatoire

computer *noun*
  a computer = un ordinateur

computer game *noun*
  a computer game (*the game*) = un jeu
    électronique
  (*the software*) = un logiciel de jeu

computer programmer *noun* ▶ 315|
  a computer programmer = un
    programmeur/une programmeuse

computer scientist *noun* ▶ 315|
  a computer scientist = un
    informaticien/une informaticienne

computer studies *noun*
  computer studies = l'informatique
    (*feminine*)

concentrate *verb*
  = se concentrer (❗ + *être*)

concert *noun*
  a concert = un concert
  in concert at Wembley = en concert à
    Wembley

concert hall *noun*
  a concert hall = une salle de concert

concrete *noun*
  concrete = le béton

condemn *verb*
  to condemn someone to death
    = condamner quelqu'un à mort

condition
1 *noun*
  a condition = un état
  in a terrible condition = dans un état
    lamentable
  the car is in good condition = la voiture
    est en bon état
2 on condition that = à condition que
  you can go on condition that her parents
    drive you home = tu peux y aller à
    condition que ses parents te ramènent
    ❗ *Note that the subjunctive is used after* à
    condition que.

condom *noun*
  a condom = un préservatif

conductor *noun* ▶ 315|
  a conductor = un chef d'orchestre

cone *noun*
  a cone = un cornet

conference *noun*
  a conference = une conférence

confidence *noun*
  confidence = l'assurance (*feminine*)
  (*trust*)
  to have confidence in someone = avoir
    confiance en quelqu'un

confident *adjective*
  = sûr de soi
  she's a confident girl = c'est une fille sûre
    d'elle

confidential *adjective*
  = confidentiel/confidentielle

confiscate *verb*
  = confisquer

conflict *noun*
  a conflict = un conflit

confused *adjective*
  to get confused = s'embrouiller (❗ + *être*)

congratulate *verb*
  = féliciter

congratulations *noun (also
exclamation)*
  congratulations! = félicitations!

connection *noun*
  a connection = un rapport
  it has no connection with the strike = cela
    n'a aucun rapport avec la grève

conscientious *adjective*
  = consciencieux/consciencieuse

conscious *adjective*
  (*aware*) = conscient/consciente
  (*after an operation*) = réveillé/réveillée

construct *verb*
  = construire

consult *verb*
  = consulter

contact
1 *noun*
  to be in contact with someone = être en
    contact avec quelqu'un
  to lose contact = perdre contact
2 *verb*
  = contacter

contact lens *noun*
  a contact lens = une lentille de contact

contain *verb*
  = contenir

content *adjective*
  = content/contente

contest *noun*
  a contest = un concours
  the Eurovision song contest = le concours
    Eurovision de la chanson

continent *noun*
  (*a large mass of land*)
  a continent = un continent
  (*British English*) (*Europe*)
  the Continent = l'Europe continentale

continental quilt *noun* (*British English*)
  a continental quilt = une couette

continue *verb*
  = continuer
  to continue to talk, to continue talking
    = continuer à parler
  to continue down the street = continuer à
    descendre la rue

continuous *adjective*
  = incessant/incessante
  the continuous noise of the traffic = le
    bruit incessant de la circulation

contraception *noun*
  contraception = la contraception

contract *noun*
  a contract = un contrat
  to have a two-year contract = avoir un
    contrat de deux ans

contradict *verb*
  = contredire

contradiction *noun*
  a contradiction = une contradiction

contrast *noun*
  a contrast = un contraste

contribute *verb*
  (*to give money*) = donner (de l'argent)
  to contribute to a discussion = participer à
  une discussion

control
1 *noun*
  to take control of a situation = prendre
    une situation en main
  to lose control of a car = perdre le
    contrôle d'une voiture

2 *verb*
  to control a region = contrôler une région
  to control traffic = diriger la circulation

convenient *adjective*
  (*useful, practical*) = pratique
  it's more convenient to take the bus = il
    est plus pratique de prendre le bus
  (*suitable*) = pratique
  it's a convenient place to meet = c'est un
    endroit pratique pour se retrouver
  it's not convenient for me = ça ne me
    convient pas

conversation *noun*
  a conversation = une conversation
  to make conversation = faire la
    conversation

convince *verb*
  = convaincre

cook
1 *verb*
  (*to prepare food*) = faire la cuisine,
  cuisiner
  to cook a meal = préparer un repas
  to cook vegetables = faire cuire des
    légumes
  (*to be cooked in the oven*) = cuire
2 *noun* ▶ **315**
  a cook = un cuisinier/une cuisinière

cooker *noun* (*British English*)
  a cooker = une cuisinière

cookie *noun* (*US English*)
  a cookie = un gâteau sec, un biscuit

cooking *noun*
  cooking = la cuisine
  to do the cooking = faire la cuisine

cool *adjective*
  (*fresh, not hot*) = frais/fraîche
  a cool drink = une boisson fraîche
  it's much cooler today = il fait beaucoup
    plus frais aujourd'hui
  (*calm*) = calme
  (*fashionable*) = branché/branchée✶
  (*relaxed*) = décontracté/décontractée
cool down
  (*to get colder*) = refroidir
  (*to calm down*) = se calmer (**!** + *être*)

cooperate *verb*
  = coopérer

cope *verb*
  (*to manage*) = se débrouiller (**!** + *être*)
  to cope with pain = supporter la douleur

copper *noun*
  copper = le cuivre

copy
1 *noun*
  a copy = une copie
2 *verb*
  = copier
  to copy in an exam = copier à un examen

✶ in informal situations

copy down, copy out = recopier

cork noun
  a cork = un bouchon
  cork = le liège

corkscrew noun
  a corkscrew = un tire-bouchon

corner noun
  (of a street, a building)
  the corner = l'angle (masculine)
  = le coin
  the shop on the corner = le magasin qui
    fait l'angle
  to go around the corner = tourner au coin
    de la rue
  (in football, hockey)
  a corner = un corner

correct
1 adjective
  = bon/bonne (! before the noun),
    correct/correcte
  the correct answer = la bonne réponse, la
    réponse correcte
  that is correct = c'est exact
2 verb
  = corriger

correction noun
  a correction = une correction

corridor noun
  a corridor = un couloir

cost verb
  = coûter
  how much does it cost? = ça coûte
    combien?
  it costs a lot of money = ça coûte très cher

costume noun
  a costume = un costume

cosy adjective (British English)
  a cosy room = une pièce confortable

cot noun (British English)
  a cot = un lit de bébé

cottage noun
  a cottage = une petite maison

cotton noun
  (the material)
  cotton = le coton
  (the thread)
  cotton = le fil de coton

cotton wool noun (British English)
  cotton wool = le coton hydrophile

couch noun
  a couch = un canapé

cough verb
  = tousser

could verb
  (had the possibility)
  I couldn't move = je ne pouvais pas
    bouger
  he couldn't sleep for weeks = il n'a pas pu
    dormir pendant des semaines

  (knew how to)
  she could read at the age of three = elle
    savait lire à l'âge de trois ans
  he couldn't type = il ne savait pas taper à
    la machine
  I couldn't speak any German = je ne
    parlais pas allemand
  (when talking about seeing, hearing,
  understanding, you don't translate could)
  I couldn't see a thing = je n'y voyais rien
  he could hear them = il les entendait
  they couldn't understand me = ils ne me
    comprenaient pas
  (when implying that something did not
  happen)
  she could have become a doctor = elle
    aurait pu devenir médecin
  you could have apologized! = tu aurais
    pu t'excuser!
  (when indicating a possibility)
  they could be wrong = ils se trompent
    peut-être
  a bike could be useful = un vélo pourrait
    être utile
  (when asking, offering or suggesting)
  could I speak to Annie? = est-ce que je
    pourrais parler à Annie?
  could you take a message? = est-ce que
    vous pourriez prendre un message?
  we could ask Gary = nous pourrions
    demander à Gary

count verb
  = compter
count on
  to count on someone = compter sur
    quelqu'un

counter noun
  a counter (in a shop) = un comptoir
  (in a bank, a post office) = un guichet
  (in a bar) = un bar, un comptoir

country noun
  (a state)
  a country = un pays
  (the countryside)
  the country = la campagne
  to live in the country = vivre à la
    campagne

countryside noun
  the countryside = la campagne

couple noun
  a couple of days (two days) = deux jours
  (a few days) = deux ou trois jours
  (two people)
  a couple = un couple

courage noun
  courage = le courage

courageous adjective
  = courageux/courageuse

course
1 noun
  (a series of lessons or lectures)
  a course = un cours

Countries, cities, and continents

Countries and continents

Most countries and all continents are used with the definite article in French:

*I like France	Canada*	= j'aime **la** France / **le** Canada
to visit the United States	= visiter **les** États-Unis

All the continent names are feminine in French. Generally, the names of countries ending in **e** are feminine and the rest are mostly masculine. Some names of countries are plural, eg **les États-Unis**.

In, to, and from somewhere

With continent names and feminine singular names of countries, for **in** and **to** use **en**, and for **from** use **de** (or **d'** before a vowel or mute 'h'):

*to go **to** Europe / **to** France*	= aller **en** Europe / **en** France
*to come **from** France / **from** Germany*	= venir **d'**Europe / **d'**Allemagne

With masculine names of countries beginning with a consonant, use **au** for **in** and **to**, and **du** for **from** and with masculine names of countries beginning with a vowel use **en** for **in** and **to**, and **d'** for **from**

*to live **in** Canada / **in** Iraq*	= vivre **au** Canada / **en** Irak
*to come **from** Japan / **from** Iraq*	= venir **du** Japon / **d'**Irak

With plurals, use **aux** for **in** and **to**, and **des** for **from**

*to live **in the** United States*	= vivre **aux** États-Unis
*to come **from the** United States*	= venir **des** États-Unis

Towns and cities

For **in** and **to** with the name of a town, use **à** in French; if the French name includes the definite article, **à** will become **au**, **à la**, **à l'** or **aux**.

*to live **in** Toulouse / **in le** Havre /*	= vivre **à** Toulouse / **au** Havre /
***in la** Rochelle / **in les** Arcs*	**à la** Rochelle / **aux** Arcs

Similarly, **from** is **de**, becoming **du**, **de la**, **de l'** or **des** when it combines with the definite article in town names:

*to come **from** Toulouse / **from le** Havre /*	= venir **de** Toulouse / **du** Havre /
***from la** Rochelle / **from les** Arc*	**de la** Rochelle / **des** Arcs

---

a language course = un cours de langue
(*part of a meal*)
a course = un plat
what's the main course? = qu'est-ce qu'il y a comme plat principal?
2 of course = bien sûr
of course not! = bien sûr que non!

court *noun*
(*of law*)
a court = une cour, un tribunal
to go to court = aller devant les tribunaux
(*for playing sports*)
a tennis court = un court de tennis
a basketball court = un terrain de basket

court case *noun*
a court case = un procès

cousin *noun*
a cousin = un cousin/une cousine

cover
1 *verb*
to cover = couvrir
to be covered in spots = être couvert/couverte de boutons
(*to decorate*)
to cover a cake with chocolate = recouvrir un gâteau de chocolat
2 *noun*
(*a lid*)
a cover = un couvercle
(*for a cushion, a quilt*)
a cover = une housse
(*a blanket*)
a cover = une couverture
(*on a book, a magazine, an exercise book*)
the cover = la couverture

cow *noun*
a cow = une vache

coward *noun*
a coward = un lâche/une lâche

cowboy noun
  a cowboy = un cowboy

cozy adjective (US English)
  a cozy room = une pièce confortable

crab noun
  a crab = un crabe

crack verb
  (to damage) = fêler
  (to get damaged) = se fêler (**!** + être)
  (to get broken) = se casser (**!** + être)

cradle noun
  a cradle = un berceau

cramp noun
  a cramp = une crampe

crash
1 noun
  a crash = un accident
  a car crash = un accident de voiture
2 verb
  to crash into a tree = rentrer dans un
    arbre
  the plane crashed = l'avion s'est écrasé

crayon noun
  a crayon = une craie grasse

crazy adjective
  = fou/folle

cream noun
  cream = la crème

create verb
  = créer
  to create employment = créer des emplois

credit noun
  credit = le crédit
  they don't give credit = ils ne font pas
    crédit

credit card noun
  a credit card = une carte de crédit

cricket noun ▶ 248 |
  cricket = le cricket

crime noun
  (a criminal act)
  a crime (serious) = un crime
  (minor) = un délit
  (in general)
  crime = la criminalité

criminal
1 noun
  a criminal = un criminel/une criminelle
2 adjective
  = criminel/criminelle

crisis noun
  a crisis = une crise

crisps noun (British English)
  crisps = les chips (feminine)

critical adjective
  = critique

criticize verb
  = critiquer

crocodile noun
  a crocodile = un crocodile

crooked adjective
  a crooked line = une ligne brisée
  the picture is crooked = le tableau est de
    travers

cross
1 verb
  (to go across)
  to cross the road = traverser la rue
  to cross the Channel = traverser la
    Manche
  to cross the border = passer la frontière
  to cross into Italy = passer en Italie
  (other uses)
  to cross one's legs = croiser les jambes
  our letters crossed = nos lettres se sont
    croisées
2 noun
  a cross = une croix
3 adjective
  = fâché/fâchée
  to get cross = se fâcher (**!** + être)
cross out = rayer

crossroads noun
  a crossroads = un carrefour

crossword puzzle noun
  a crossword puzzle = des mots croisés
  | **!** Note that mots is masculine plural.

crow noun
  a crow = un corbeau

crowd noun
  (a large number of people)
  a crowd = une foule
  crowds of people = une foule de gens
  (watching a game)
  the crowd = les spectateurs (masculine
    plural)

crown noun
  a crown = une couronne

cruel adjective
  = cruel/cruelle

cruelty noun
  cruelty = la cruauté

cruise noun
  a cruise = une croisière

crush verb
  = écraser

crutch noun
  a crutch = une béquille

cry
1 verb
  = pleurer
2 noun
  a cry = un cri

cub *noun*
a cub = un petit

cuckoo *noun*
a cuckoo = un coucou

cucumber *noun*
a cucumber = un concombre

cuddle *noun*
a cuddle = un câlin
to give someone a cuddle = faire un câlin
à quelqu'un

culprit *noun*
a culprit = un coupable/une coupable

cultural *adjective*
= culturel/culturelle

culture *noun*
culture = la culture

cunning *adjective*
(*describing a person*) = rusé/rusée
(*describing a plan*) = habile

cup *noun*
a cup = une tasse
a cup of coffee = une tasse de café
(*in sport*)
a cup = une coupe

cupboard *noun*
a cupboard = un placard

curb *noun* (*US English*)
the curb = le bord du trottoir

cure
1 *verb*
= guérir
2 *noun*
a cure = un traitement

curious *adjective*
= curieux/curieuse

curly *adjective*
= frisé/frisée
to have curly hair = avoir les cheveux
frisés

currency *noun*
a currency = une monnaie
foreign currency = les devises étrangères
! *Note that* devises *is feminine plural.*

curry *noun*
a curry = un curry

curtain *noun*
a curtain = un rideau
to draw the curtains = tirer les rideaux

cushion *noun*
a cushion = un coussin

custard *noun* (*British English*)
custard ≈ la crème anglaise

custom *noun*
a custom = une coutume

customer *noun*
a customer = un client/une cliente

customs *noun*
customs = la douane
to go through customs = passer à la
douane

customs officer *noun* ▶ 315 |
a customs officer = un douanier/une
douanière

cut
1 *verb*
= couper
to cut an apple in half = couper une
pomme en deux
to cut [one's fingers | one's knee | one's foot ...]
= se couper [les doigts | le genou | le pied ...]
she cut herself = elle s'est coupée
to have one's hair cut = se faire couper les
cheveux
I got my hair cut = je me suis fait couper
les cheveux
2 *noun*
a cut = une coupure
cut down = abattre
cut out
to cut a photo out of a magazine
= découper une photo dans un
magazine
cut up = couper

cute *adjective*
= mignon/mignonne

CV *noun*
a CV = un CV, un curriculum vitae

cycle *verb*
to cycle to school = aller à l'école à vélo
to go cycling = faire du vélo

cycle lane, cycle path *noun*
a cycle lane = une piste cyclable

cycling *noun* ▶ 248 |
cycling = le cyclisme

cyclist *noun*
a cyclist = un cycliste/une cycliste

cynical *adjective*
= cynique

Czech Republic *noun* ▶ 218 |
the Czech Republic = la République
tchèque

Dd

dad, **Dad** noun
  a dad = un papa

daffodil noun
  a daffodil = une jonquille

daisy noun
  a daisy = une pâquerette

damage
1 verb
  to damage = abîmer
  the building was damaged by the fire = le
    bâtiment a été endommagé par
    l'incendie
  (to harm) = nuire à
  it can damage your health = cela nuit à la
    santé
2 noun
  damage = les dégâts (masculine plural)
  to cause damage = faire des dégâts

damp adjective
  = humide

dance
1 verb
  = danser
2 noun
  a dance = une danse

dancer noun ▶ 315|
  a dancer = un danseur/une danseuse

dancing noun
  dancing = la danse

danger noun
  danger = le danger
  to be in danger = être en danger

dangerous adjective
  = dangereux/dangereuse

Danish ▶ 275|
1 adjective
  = danois/danoise
2 noun
  Danish = le danois

dare verb
  (to have the courage) = oser
  (when testing someone)
  to dare someone to play a trick = défier
    quelqu'un de jouer un tour
  (when expressing anger)
  don't dare speak to me like that! = je
    t'interdis de me parler sur ce ton!

dark
1 adjective
  (lacking light) = sombre
  it's getting dark = il commence à faire
    nuit

  (describing a colour, clothes) ▶ 213|
  = sombre
  he always wears dark clothes = il porte
    toujours des vêtements sombres
  a dark blue dress = une robe bleu foncé
  (describing a person) = brun/brune
2 noun
  the dark = le noir, l'obscurité (feminine)

darts noun ▶ 248|
  darts = les fléchettes (feminine)

date noun ▶ 222|
  (in a calendar)
  a date = une date
  what date is today? = quelle est la date
    aujourd'hui?
  (with a friend)
  a date = un rendez-vous
  to go out on a date with someone = sortir
    avec quelqu'un

daughter noun
  a daughter = une fille

daughter-in-law noun
  a daughter-in-law = une belle-fille

dawn noun
  dawn = l'aube (feminine)
  at dawn = à l'aube

day noun ▶ 356|
  ! Note that day is usually translated by
  jour in French. However it is sometimes
  translated by journée, when there is an
  emphasis on the idea of duration.

  a day = un jour
  what day is it today? = quel jour sommes-
    nous aujourd'hui?
  during the day = pendant la journée
  we had a very nice day = nous avons
    passé une journée très agréable
  the next day, the day after = le lendemain
  the day before = la veille

daylight noun
  daylight = le jour, la lumière du jour

dazzle verb
  = éblouir

dead adjective
  = mort/morte
  he is dead = il est mort

deaf adjective
  = sourd/sourde

deal
1 noun
  a deal (in business) = une affaire
  (with a friend) = un marché
  a great deal [of money | of time | of energy …]
  = beaucoup [d'argent | de temps | d'énergie …]
2 verb
  to deal the cards = distribuer les cartes
deal with = s'occuper de (! + être)
  to deal with a problem = s'occuper d'un
    problème

Dates, days, and months

The days of the week

Note that French uses lower-case letters for the names of days.
Write the names of days in full; do not abbreviate as in English (*Tues*, *Sat* and so on).

Monday	= lundi
Tuesday	= mardi
Wednesday	= mercredi
Thursday	= jeudi
Friday	= vendredi
Saturday	= samedi
Sunday	= dimanche

lundi in the notes below stands for any day; they all work the same way. Note the use of **le** for regular occurrences, and no article for single ones. (*Remember: do not translate* **on**.)

on Monday	= lundi
on Mondays	= le lundi
Monday afternoon	= lundi après-midi
*last	next Monday*	= lundi dernier / prochain
last Monday night	= la nuit de lundi dernier
	(*if evening*) lundi dernier dans la soirée
early on Monday	= lundi matin de bonne heure
late on Monday	= lundi soir tard
a month from Monday	= dans un mois lundi
from Monday on	= à partir de lundi

The months of the year

As with the days of the week, do not use capitals to spell the names of the months in French, and do not abbreviate as in English (*Jan*, *Feb* and so on).

January	= janvier	*July*	= juillet
February	= février	*August*	= août
March	= mars	*September*	= septembre
April	= avril	*October*	= octobre
May	= mai	*November*	= novembre
June	= juin	*December*	= décembre

May in the notes below stands for any month; they all work the same way.

in May	= en mai / au mois de mai
next May	= en mai prochain
last May	= l'année dernière en mai
*in early	late May*	= début / fin mai

Dates

French has only one generally accepted way of writing dates: **le 10 mai** (say **le dix mai**).
If the days of the week is included, put it after the **le**:

Monday, May 1st 1901	= le lundi 1er mai 1901
what's the date?	= quel jour sommes-nous?
it's the tenth of May	= nous sommes le 10 mai / on est le 10 mai
in 1968	= en 1968
in the year 2000	= en l'an 2000
in the seventeenth century	= au dix-septième siècle

	Write	Say
May 1	le 1er mai	le premier mai
May 2	le 2 mai	le deux mai
from 4th to 16th May	du 4 au 16 mai	du quatre au seize mai
May 6 1968	le 6 mai 1968	le six mai mille neuf cent soixante-huit
in the 1980s	dans les années 80	dans les années quatre-vingt
the 16th century	le XVIe siècle	le seizième siècle

dear
1 *adjective*
(*in letters*) = cher/chère
Dear Anne = Chère Anne
Dear Anne and Paul = Chers Anne et Paul
Dear Sir/Madam = Monsieur, Madame
(*expensive*) = cher/chère
2 *exclamation* ▶ **237**
oh dear! = oh mon Dieu!

death *noun*
death = la mort

death penalty *noun*
the death penalty = la peine de mort

debate *noun*
a debate = un débat

debt *noun*
a debt = une dette
to be in debt = avoir des dettes

decade *noun*
a decade = une décennie

decaffeinated *adjective*
= décaféiné/décaféinée

deceive *verb*
= tromper

December *noun* ▶ **222**
December = décembre (*masculine*)

decide *verb*
= décider
**he decided [to accept | to stay | to get
married …]** = il a décidé [d'accepter | de
rester | de se marier …]

decision *noun*
a decision = une décision
to make a decision = prendre une
décision

deck *noun*
a deck = un pont
on deck = sur le pont

deckchair *noun*
a deckchair = une chaise longue

decorate *verb*
(*with ornaments*) = décorer
(*with wallpaper*) = tapisser
(*to paint*) = peindre

decoration *noun*
a decoration = une décoration

deep *adjective* ▶ **285**
= profond/profonde
how deep is the lake? = quelle est la
profondeur du lac?
the hole is three metres deep = le trou fait
trois mètres de profondeur

deer *noun*
a deer (*male*) = un cerf
(*female*) = une biche

defeat
1 *verb*
to defeat an enemy = vaincre un ennemi
the team was defeated = l'équipe a été
battue
2 *noun*
a defeat = une défaite

defence (British English), defense (US
English) *noun*
defence = la défense

D

defend *verb*
= défendre

definite *adjective*
(*describing a decision*) = ferme
(*describing a plan*) = précis/précise
nothing is definite = rien n'est sûr
(*obvious, visible*) = net/nette
a definite improvement = une nette
amélioration

definitely *adverb*
= sans aucun doute
they're definitely lying = ils mentent sans
aucun doute
I'm definitely coming = c'est décidé, je
viens
'definitely!' = 'absolument!'

defy *verb*
= défier

degree *noun*
(*from a university*)
a degree = un diplôme universitaire
(*in measurements*)
a degree = un degré

delay
1 *verb*
= retarder
2 *noun*
a delay = un retard

deliberate *adjective*
= délibéré/délibérée

deliberately *adverb*
= exprès
he did it deliberately = il l'a fait exprès

delicious *adjective*
= délicieux/délicieuse

delighted *adjective*
= ravi/ravie
to be delighted with a present = être
ravi/ravie d'un cadeau

deliver *verb*
= livrer
to deliver goods = livrer des marchandises
to deliver mail = distribuer le courrier

demand *verb*
= exiger

demolish *verb*
= démolir

demonstration noun
  a demonstration = une manifestation

denim jacket adjective
  a denim jacket = un blouson en jean

Denmark noun ▶ 218 |
  Denmark = le Danemark

dentist noun ▶ 315 |
  a dentist = un dentiste/une dentiste

deny verb
  = nier

department noun
  a department (in a firm) = un service
  (in a large store) = un rayon
  (in a school) = une section
  (in a university) = un département

department store noun
  a department store = un grand magasin

depend verb
  = dépendre
  to depend on someone = dépendre de
    quelqu'un
  it depends on you = cela dépend de toi
  it depends = ça dépend

depressed adjective
  = déprimé/déprimée

depressing adjective
  = déprimant/déprimante

deprive verb
  = priver

depth noun ▶ 285 |
  depth = la profondeur

describe verb
  = décrire

description noun
  a description = une description

desert noun
  a desert = un désert

deserve verb
  = mériter
  he deserves to be punished = il mérite
    d'être puni

design
1 verb
  (to plan) = concevoir
  the house was designed for a hot climate
    = la maison a été conçue pour un climat
    chaud
  (in fashion)
  to design clothes = créer des vêtements
2 noun
  (a subject of study)
  (fashion) design = le stylisme
  (a pattern)
  a design = un motif

desk noun
  a desk = un bureau

desperate adjective
  = désespéré/désespérée

dessert noun
  a dessert = un dessert

destroy verb
  = détruire

detail noun
  a detail = un détail
  to go into details = entrer dans les détails

detective noun ▶ 315 |
  a detective = un inspecteur de police
  a private detective = un détective

detective story noun
  a detective story = un roman policier

determined adjective
  = déterminé/déterminée
  to be determined to go = être
    décidé/décidée à y aller

develop verb
  = développer

development noun
  a development = un développement

diagram noun
  a diagram = un schéma

dial verb
  to dial a number = composer un numéro

dialling code noun (British English)
  a dialling code = un indicatif

dialling tone (British English), **dial tone** (US English) noun
  a dialling tone = une tonalité

diamond noun
  a diamond = un diamant

diary noun
  (for personal thoughts)
  a diary = un journal
  (for appointments)
  a diary = un agenda

dice noun
  a dice = un dé

dictionary noun
  a dictionary = un dictionnaire

die verb
  to die = mourir (! + être)
  he died in the war = il est mort à la guerre
  to be dying of cancer = être
    atteint/atteinte d'un cancer incurable
  (used for emphasis)
  I'm dying to go on holiday = je meurs
    d'envie de partir en vacances

diet noun
  a diet = un régime
  to go on a diet = se mettre au régime

difference noun
  a difference = une différence
  I can't tell the difference = je ne vois pas la différence
  it won't make any difference = ça ne changera rien
  what difference does it make? = qu'est-ce que ça change?

different adjective
  = différent/différente

difficult adjective
  = difficile
  Spanish is not difficult to learn = l'espagnol n'est pas difficile à apprendre
  to be difficult to get along with = être difficile à vivre

difficulty noun
  a difficulty = une difficulté, un problème
  to have difficulty concentrating = avoir du mal à se concentrer

dig verb
  = creuser
dig up
  (when gardening) = bêcher
  (to find what was buried) = déterrer

dim adjective
  (describing a light) = faible
  (describing a room) = sombre

diner noun (US English)
  a diner = un café-restaurant

dinghy noun
  a dinghy = un dériveur

dining room noun
  a dining room = une salle à manger

dinner noun
  a dinner = un dîner
  dinner's ready! = à table!

dip verb
  = tremper

direct
1 adjective
  = direct/directe
2 verb
  (when talking about directions)
  could you direct me to the station? = pourriez-vous m'indiquer le chemin pour aller à la gare?
  (in cinema or theatre)
  to direct a film = réaliser un film
  to direct a play = mettre en scène une pièce

direction noun
  a direction = une direction, un sens
  is this the right direction? = est-ce que c'est la bonne direction?
  they were going in the other direction = ils allaient dans l'autre sens

directions noun
  directions = les indications (feminine)
  to give someone directions = donner des indications à quelqu'un
  to ask someone for directions = demander le chemin à quelqu'un

director noun ▶ 315 |
  (of a film or play)
  a director = un metteur en scène
  (of a company)
  a director = un directeur/une directrice

D

dirt noun
  dirt = la saleté

dirty
1 adjective
  = sale
  to get dirty = se salir (! + être)
2 verb
  = salir

disabled adjective
  = handicapé/handicapée

disadvantage noun
  a disadvantage = un désavantage

disagree verb
  = ne pas être d'accord
  I disagree with you = je ne suis pas d'accord avec toi

disappear verb
  = disparaître

disappoint verb
  = décevoir

disappointed adjective
  = déçu/déçue

disappointing adjective
  = décevant/décevante

disappointment noun
  disappointment = la déception

disapprove verb
  to disapprove of someone = ne pas apprécier quelqu'un

disaster noun
  a disaster = une catastrophe, un désastre

discipline noun
  discipline = la discipline

disco noun
  a disco = une discothèque

disconnect verb
  (to pull out a plug) = débrancher
  (to cut off) = couper

discourage verb
  = décourager

discover verb
  = découvrir

discovery noun
  a discovery = une découverte

discreet *adjective*
= discret/discrète

discrimination *noun*
discrimination = la discrimination

discuss *verb*
= discuter de
to discuss politics = discuter de politique

discussion *noun*
a discussion = une discussion

disease *noun* ▶ **266**
a disease = une maladie

disguise
1 *noun*
a disguise = un déguisement
to wear a disguise = être déguisé/déguisée
2 *verb*
to disguise oneself as a woman = se
déguiser en femme

disgusting *adjective*
= dégoûtant/dégoûtante

dish *noun*
(*food*)
a dish = un plat
the dishes = la vaisselle (*singular*)
to wash the dishes = faire la vaisselle

dishonest *adjective*
= malhonnête

dishwasher *noun*
a dishwasher = un lave-vaisselle

dislike *verb*
= ne pas aimer
I dislike him = je ne l'aime pas

dismiss *verb*
= renvoyer

disobedient *adjective*
= désobéissant/désobéissante

disobey *verb*
to disobey someone = désobéir à
quelqu'un

display *noun*
a display = un étalage
a window display = une vitrine

dispute *noun*
a dispute (*between individuals*) = une
dispute
(*between groups*) = un conflit

disqualify *verb*
= disqualifier

disrupt *verb*
= perturber

dissatisfied *adjective*
= mécontent/mécontente

distance *noun*
a distance = une distance
in the distance = au loin
to keep one's distance = garder ses
distances

distinct *adjective*
(*easy to see, to hear*) = distinct/distincte
(*definite*) = net/nette (**!** *before the noun*)

distinguish *verb*
= distinguer
to distinguish between truth and lies
= faire la distinction entre la vérité et les
mensonges

distract *verb*
= distraire
to distract someone from working
= empêcher quelqu'un de travailler

distressed *adjective*
= bouleversé/bouleversée

distribute *verb*
= distribuer

disturb *verb*
= déranger

disturbing *adjective*
= troublant/troublante

dive *verb* ▶ **248**
= plonger
to go diving = faire de la plongée

divide *verb*
(*in arithmetic*) = diviser
(*to share*) = partager

diving board *noun*
a diving board = un plongeoir

divorce
1 *noun*
a divorce = un divorce
2 *verb*
= divorcer

DIY *noun* (*British English*)
DIY = le bricolage

dizzy *adjective*
to feel dizzy = avoir la tête qui tourne

do *verb* ▶ **237**
▶ **227** *See the boxed note on* do *for more
information and examples.*
to do = faire
to do the cooking = faire la cuisine
to do one's homework = faire ses devoirs
what has he done with the newspaper?
= qu'est-ce qu'il a fait du journal?
what has she done to her hair? = qu'est-ce
qu'elle a fait à ses cheveux?
do as you're told = fais ce qu'on te dit
(*in questions, negatives*)
do you like cats? = est-ce que tu aimes les
chats?
I don't like cats = je n'aime pas les chats
I didn't do anything = je n'ai rien fait
don't shout! = ne crie pas!

do

As an ordinary verb

Usually, the French equivalent of the verb **to do** is **faire**:

*she is **doing** her homework*	= elle **fait** ses devoirs
*what **has** he **done** with the newspaper?*	= qu'est-ce qu'il **a fait** du journal?

D

As an auxiliary verb

In questions

In French there is no auxiliary verb in questions equivalent to **do** in English.

When the subject is a pronoun, use either of these structures: *verb* + *hyphen* + *subject* or, less formally, **est-ce que** + *subject* + *verb*:

***do** you like Mozart?*	= aimes-tu Mozart?
	= **est-ce que** tu aimes Mozart?

When the subject is a noun, there are again two possibilities:

***did** your sister ring?*	= **est-ce que** ta sœur a téléphoné?
	= ta sœur a-t-elle téléphoné?

In negatives

Equally, auxiliaries are not used in negatives in French:

*I **don't** like Mozart*	= je n'aime pas Mozart.

In emphatic uses

There is no verbal equivalent for the use of **do** in such expressions as *I do like your dress*. In emphatic uses, French may use an adverb like *beaucoup, vraiment*:

*I **do** like your dress*	= j'aime **beaucoup** ta robe
*I **do** think you should go*	= je pense **vraiment** que tu devrais y aller

When referring back to another verb

In this case the verb **to do** is not translated at all:

*I live in Oxford and so **does** Lily*	= j'habite à Oxford et Lily aussi
*she gets paid more than I **do***	= elle est payée plus que moi
*'I don't like carrots' — 'neither **do** I'*	= 'je n'aime pas les carottes' — 'moi non plus'

In polite requests

In polite requests the phrase *je vous en prie* or *je t'en prie* is useful:

***do** sit down*	= asseyez-vous, **je vous en prie**

In imperatives

In French there is no use of an auxiliary verb in imperatives:

***don't** shut the door*	= ne ferme pas la porte
***do** be quiet*	= tais-toi!

In short questions

With questions like **doesn't he?** or **didn't he?**, there is a general French phrase question **n'est-ce pas?** which will work in many cases:

*you like fish, **don't you?***	= tu aimes les poisson, **n'est-ce pas?**

With positive tag questions, **par hasard** can often be used as a translation:

Lola didn't phone, did she?	= Lola n'a pas téléphoné **par hasard?**

In short answers

There is no direct French equivalent for the verb such as *no, he doesn't, yes, we did* etc.

'does he play tennis?' — 'no, he doesn't'	= 'est-ce qu'il joue au tennis?' — 'non'
'do you like strawberries?' — 'yes I do'	= 'aimez-vous les fraises?' — 'oui'

If answering 'yes' to contradict a negative statement, the most useful translation is **si**:

*'Marion didn't say that' — '**yes she did**'*	= 'Marion n'a pas dit ça' — '**si**'

▶ For more examples, see the entry **do**.

(in short answers and tag questions)
'do you like strawberries?'—'yes, I do'
= 'est-ce que tu aimes les fraises?'—'oui'
'I never said I liked him'—'yes, you did'
= 'je n'ai jamais dit que je l'aimais'—'si, tu l'as dit'
'I love chocolate'—'so do I!' = 'j'adore le chocolat'—'moi aussi!'
'who wrote it?'—'I did' = 'qui l'a écrit?'—'moi'
he lives in London, doesn't he? = il habite à Londres, n'est-ce-pas?
Martine didn't phone, did she? = Martine n'a pas téléphoné, par hasard?
'may I sit down?'—'yes, please do' = 'puis-je m'asseoir?'—'je t'en prie'
(to be enough) = suffire
ten pounds will do = dix livres suffiront
that box will do = cette boîte fera l'affaire
(to perform)
he did well = il s'est bien débrouillé
he did badly = il s'est mal débrouillé
do up *(British English)*
to do up one's buttons = se boutonner *(! + être)*
to do up a house = refaire une maison
do with
it's got something to do with computers = ça a quelque chose à voir avec l'informatique
it has nothing to do with him = ça n'a rien à voir avec lui
do without = se passer de *(! + être)*
I can do without a television = je peux me passer de télévision

dock *noun*
a dock = un dock

doctor *noun* ▶ **315**
a doctor = un médecin

document *noun*
a document = un document

documentary *noun*
a documentary = un documentaire

dog *noun*
a dog = un chien

doll *noun*
a doll = une poupée

dollar *noun*
a dollar = un dollar

dolphin *noun*
a dolphin = un dauphin

dominoes *noun* ▶ **248**
dominoes = les dominos *(masculine)*

donkey *noun*
a donkey = un âne

door *noun*
a door = une porte

doorbell *noun*
a doorbell = une sonnette

dormitory *noun*
a dormitory = un dortoir

dose *noun*
a dose = une dose

double
1 *adjective*
(of an amount) = double
a double helping of strawberries = une double portion de fraises
(when spelling or giving a number)
Annie is spelled with a double 'n' = Annie s'écrit avec deux 'n'
three double five *(British English)* = trois cent cinquante cinq
2 *verb*
= doubler

double bass *noun* ▶ **290**
a double bass = une contrebasse

double bed *noun*
a double bed = un grand lit

double-decker *noun*
a double-decker = un autobus à impériale

double room *noun*
a double room = une chambre pour deux personnes

doubt
1 *noun*
a doubt = un doute
there's no doubt that he is innocent = son innocence ne fait aucun doute
I've no doubt that it's true = je suis certain que c'est vrai
2 *verb*
= douter
I doubt if she'll come = je doute qu'elle vienne

! *Note that the subjunctive is used after* douter que.

dough *noun*
dough = la pâte

doughnut, donut *(US English)* *noun*
a doughnut = un beignet

down

! *Often* down *occurs in combinations with verbs, for example:* calm down, let down, slow down *etc. To find the correct translations for this type of verb, look up the separate dictionary entries at* calm, let, slow *etc.*

1 *preposition*
to go down the street = descendre la rue
he walked down the corridor = il a descendu le couloir
he ran down the hill = il a descendu la colline en courant
the kitchen is down those stairs = la cuisine est en bas de cet escalier

D

2 *adverb*
she's down in the cellar = elle est dans la cave
down in Brighton = à Brighton
to go down to the country = aller à la campagne
to go down = descendre (**!** + *être*)
to fall down = tomber (**!** + *être*)
down there = là-bas

downstairs *adverb*
= en bas
to go downstairs = descendre (l'escalier)
to bring the boxes downstairs
= descendre les cartons

dozen *noun* ▶ 317 |
a dozen = une douzaine
a dozen eggs = une douzaine d'œufs

draft *noun* (*US English*)
a draft = un courant d'air

drag *verb*
= traîner

drain *verb*
(*when cooking*) = égoutter
(*if it's water*)
to drain (away) = s'écouler (**!** + *être*)

drama *noun*
(*a play, an event*)
a drama = un drame
(*theatre*)
drama = le théâtre

dramatic *adjective*
= spectaculaire

drapes *noun* (*US English*)
drapes = les rideaux (*masculine*)

draught *noun* (*British English*)
a draught = un courant d'air

draughts *noun* ▶ 248 | (*British English*)
draughts = les dames (*feminine*)

draw
1 *verb*
(*with a pen or pencil*) = dessiner
to draw a rabbit = dessiner un lapin
to draw a picture = faire un dessin
to draw a line = tracer une ligne
she drew his portrait = elle a fait son portrait
(*to pull*) = tirer
to draw the curtains = tirer les rideaux
(*to take out*) = sortir
to draw a knife = sortir un couteau
(*in a lottery*)
to draw a ticket = tirer un ticket au sort
(*to attract*) = attirer
the circus drew a large crowd = le cirque a attiré beaucoup de monde
(*British English*) (*in sport*) = faire match nul
Christmas is drawing near = Noël approche

2 *noun*
(*in sport*)
a draw = un match nul
(*in a lottery*)
a draw = un tirage au sort

draw aside
to draw someone aside = prendre quelqu'un à part

draw back
to draw back the curtains = ouvrir les rideaux

draw up
to draw up a list = dresser une liste

drawer *noun*
a drawer = un tiroir

drawing *noun*
drawing = le dessin

dread *verb*
= appréhender

dreadful *adjective*
= épouvantable

dream
1 *noun* ▶ 237 |
a dream = un rêve
to have a dream = faire un rêve
2 *verb*
= rêver
to dream of going to Japan = rêver d'aller au Japon

dress
1 *noun*
a dress = une robe
2 *verb*
(*to put one's own clothes on*) = s'habiller (**!** + *être*)
(*to put clothes on someone*) = habiller
dress up
(*in good clothes*) = s'habiller (**!** + *être*)
(*in a disguise*) = se déguiser (**!** + *être*)
she dressed up as a clown = elle s'est déguisée en clown

dressing gown *noun*
a dressing gown = une robe de chambre

drill
1 *noun*
a drill = une perceuse
2 *verb*
to drill a hole = percer un trou
to drill through the wall = percer un trou dans le mur

drink
1 *verb*
= boire
2 *noun*
a drink = une boisson
a drink of water = un verre d'eau

drive
1 *verb*
(*in a car*) = conduire
to learn to drive = apprendre à conduire
he drives to work = il va au travail en
voiture
to drive someone home = ramener
quelqu'un en voiture
(*to make*)
to drive someone mad = rendre quelqu'un
fou/folle
2 *noun*
a drive = un tour (en voiture)
to go for a drive = aller faire un tour (en
voiture)
drive away
(*in a car*) = démarrer
(*to chase away*) = chasser
drive back = rentrer (en voiture) (**!** + *être*)

driver *noun*
a driver = un conducteur/une conductrice

driver's license (*US English*), driving licence (*British English*) *noun*
a driver's license = un permis de conduire

drizzle *verb*
= bruiner

drop
1 *verb*
(*to come down*) = baisser
the temperature has dropped = la
température a baissé
(*to let fall*) = laisser tomber
she dropped her suitcase = elle a laissé
tomber sa valise
(*to fall*) = tomber (**!** + *être*)
2 *noun*
(*a fall*)
a drop = une baisse
a drop in temperature = une baisse de
température
(*of liquid*)
a drop = une goutte
drop in = passer (**!** + *être*)
he dropped in to see me = il est passé me
voir
drop off = déposer
could you drop me off at the station?
= est-ce que tu pourrais me déposer à la
gare?
drop out
to drop out of school = abandonner ses
études
to drop out of a race = se retirer d'une
course

drought *noun*
a drought = une sécheresse

drown *verb*
= se noyer (**!** + *être*)

drug
1 *noun*
(*for illegal use*)
a drug = une drogue
to be on drugs = se droguer (**!** + *être*)
(*for medical use*)
a drug = un médicament
2 *verb*
to drug someone = droguer quelqu'un

drug addict *noun*
a drug addict = un toxicomane/une
toxicomane

drum *noun* ▶ 290 |
a drum = un tambour
to play drums = jouer de la batterie

drunk *adjective*
= ivre

dry
1 *adjective*
= sec/sèche
a dry day = une journée sans pluie
2 *verb*
to dry clothes = faire sécher des
vêtements
to dry oneself = se sécher (**!** + *être*)
he dried his hands = il s'est séché les
mains
to dry the dishes = essuyer la vaisselle

duck
1 *noun*
a duck = un canard
2 *verb*
= baisser la tête

due
1 **due to** = à cause de
**the game was cancelled due to bad
weather** = le match a été annulé à cause
du mauvais temps
2 *adjective*
(*expected*)
the train is due (in) at two o'clock = le
train doit arriver à deux heures
(*owed*) = dû/due
the amount due = la somme due

dull *adjective*
(*describing a person or book*) = terne
(*describing a colour*) = terne
(*describing the weather or a landscape*)
= morne

dumb *adjective*
(*unable to speak*) = muet/muette
(*stupid*) = bête

dump
1 *verb*
= jeter
2 *noun*
a dump = une décharge

during *preposition*
= pendant
during the summer = pendant l'été

dust
1 *noun*
dust = la poussière

2 *verb*
= épousseter

dustbin *noun* (*British English*)
a dustbin = une poubelle

dustman *noun* (*British English*)
a dustman = un éboueur

dustpan *noun*
a dustpan = une pelle (à poussière)

Dutch ▶ 275 |
1 *adjective*
= hollandais/hollandaise
2 *noun*
the Dutch = les Hollandais (*masculine plural*)

duty *noun*
(*a task, part of one's job*)
a duty = une fonction
to take up one's duties = prendre ses fonctions
(*of a soldier, a nurse*)
to be on duty = être de service
(*what one must do*)
duty = le devoir
it's my duty to go = il est de mon devoir d'y aller
(*a tax*)
customs duties = les droits de douane

| **!** *Note that* droits *is masculine.*

dye *verb*
= teindre
to dye one's hair = se teindre les cheveux

Ee

each
1 *determiner*
= chaque
each time I see him = chaque fois que je le vois
2 *pronoun*
= chacun/chacune
each of the boys = chacun des garçons
each of them has a car, they each have a car = ils ont chacun/elles ont chacune une voiture

each other *pronoun*

| **!** *Note that* each other *is very often translated by using a reflexive pronoun like* se, s', nous *or* vous.

they know each other already = ils se connaissent déjà
we write to each other every year = nous nous écrivons tous les ans

eager *adjective*
= enthousiaste

eagle *noun*
an eagle = un aigle

ear *noun* **▶ 201 |**
an ear = une oreille

early *adverb*
early = tôt
to got up early = se lever tôt
early in the afternoon = en début d'après-midi
(*ahead of time*) = en avance
to arrive early = arriver en avance

earn *verb*
to earn lots of money = gagner beaucoup d'argent

earring *noun*
an earring = une boucle d'oreille

earth *noun*
(*the planet*)
the earth = la terre
(*soil*)
earth = la terre

easily *adverb*
= facilement

east
1 *noun*
the east = l'est (*masculine*)
in the east of France = dans l'est de la France
2 *adverb*
to go east = aller vers l'est
to live east of Paris = vivre à l'est de Paris
3 *adjective*
= est (**!** *never changes*)
to work in east London = travailler dans l'est de Londres

Easter *noun*
Easter = Pâques (*feminine plural*)
Happy Easter! = Joyeuses Pâques!

Easter egg *noun*
an Easter egg = un œuf de Pâques

easy *adjective*
= facile
it's easy to fix = c'est facile à réparer
it's not easy to find work there = il n'est pas facile d'y trouver du travail

eat *verb*
= manger
eat out = manger au restaurant

EC *noun*
the EC = la Communauté Européenne

echo *noun*
an echo = un écho

economic *adjective*
= économique

economics noun
  economics = les sciences économiques
  ! *Note that* **sciences** *is feminine plural.*

economy noun
  the economy = l'économie (*feminine*)

edge noun
  (*of a road, table, an object*)
  the edge = le bord
  the edge of the lake = le bord du lac
  at the edge of the town = aux abords de la
    ville
  (*of a forest, a wood or field*)
  the edge = la lisière
  (*of a blade or knife*)
  the edge = le tranchant

educate verb
  = instruire
  he was educated in Paris = il a fait ses
    études à Paris

education noun
  education = l'instruction (*feminine*)
  to get a good education = recevoir une
    bonne instruction

effect noun
  an effect = un effet

effective adjective
  = efficace

efficient adjective
  = efficace

effort noun
  an effort = un effort
  to make an effort = faire un effort

egg noun
  an egg = un œuf

eggcup noun
  an eggcup = un coquetier

eight number ▶ 187 |, ▶ 211 |
  eight = huit
  eight apples = huit pommes
  I've got eight (of them) = j'en ai huit

eighteen number ▶ 187 |, ▶ 211 |
  eighteen = dix-huit

eighteenth number
  (*in a series*) = dix-huitième
  (*in dates*) ▶ 222 |
  the eighteenth of August = le dix-huit
    août

eighth number
  (*in a series*) = huitième
  (*in dates*) ▶ 222 |
  the eighth of August = le huit août

eighty number ▶ 187 |
  eighty = quatre-vingts

either
  1 *conjunction*
    they're coming on either Tuesday or
      Wednesday = ils viendront soit mardi,
      soit mercredi
    he didn't contact either Helen or Paul = il
      n'a contacté ni Helen ni Paul
  2 *pronoun*
    take either (of them) = prends l'un ou
      l'autre/l'une ou l'autre
    I don't know either (of them) = je ne
      connais ni l'un ni l'autre/l'une ni l'autre
  3 *determiner*
    take either road = prenez l'une ou l'autre
      route
    I don't want to live in either country = je ne
      veux habiter dans aucun des deux pays
  4 *adverb*
    = non plus
    she can't do it either = elle ne peut pas le
      faire non plus

elbow noun ▶ 201 |
  the elbow = le coude

elder adjective
  = aîné/aînée

elderly adjective
  = âgé/âgée

eldest adjective
  = aîné/aînée
  the eldest daughter = l'aînée

elect verb
  = élire

election noun
  an election = une élection
  to win an election = remporter les
    élections

electric adjective
  = électrique

electrician noun ▶ 315 |
  an electrician = un électricien/une
    électricienne

electricity noun
  electricity = l'électricité (*feminine*)

elegant adjective
  = élégant/élégante

elephant noun
  an elephant = un éléphant

elevator noun (*US English*)
  an elevator = un ascenseur

eleven number ▶ 187 |, ▶ 211 |
  eleven = onze
  eleven apples = onze pommes
  I've got eleven (of them) = j'en ai onze

eleventh number
  (*in a series*) = onzième
  (*in dates*) ▶ 222 |
  the eleventh of May = le onze mai

else
1 *adverb*
= d'autre
someone else = quelqu'un d'autre
nothing else = rien d'autre
what else did he say? = qu'est-ce qu'il a
  dit d'autre?
something else = autre chose
everything else = tout le reste
2 or else = sinon
be quiet or else I'll get angry – taisez-vous
  sinon je vais me fâcher

elsewhere *adverb*
= ailleurs

embarrassed *adjective*
= gêné/gênée

embarrassing *adjective*
= gênant/gênante

embassy *noun*
an embassy = une ambassade

emergency *noun*
an emergency = une urgence
in an emergency = en cas d'urgence

emergency exit *noun*
an emergency exit = une sortie de secours

emigrate *verb*
= émigrer

emotion *noun*
an emotion = une émotion

emotional *adjective*
(*describing a scene or moment*)
= émouvant/émouvante
(*describing a person*) = émotif/émotive

emperor *noun*
an emperor = un empereur

employ *verb*
= employer

employed *adjective*
to be employed = avoir un emploi

employee *noun*
an employee = un employé/une employée

employer *noun*
an employer = un employeur

employment *noun*
employment = le travail, l'emploi
(*masculine*)

empty
1 *adjective*
= vide
2 *verb*
= vider

encourage *verb*
= encourager

end
1 *noun*
(*the final part*)
the end = la fin

at the end of the film = à la fin du film
at the end of May = fin mai
in the end = finalement
(*the furthest part*)
the end = le bout
at the end of the street = au bout de la rue
2 *verb*
(*to come to an end*) = se terminer
(**!** + *être*)
(*to put an end to*) = mettre fin à
to end the war – mettre fin à la guerre
(*to finish*) = terminer
to end a concert = terminer un concert
end up
to end up in London = se retrouver à
  Londres
to end up going abroad = finir par aller à
  l'étranger

ending *noun*
the ending = la fin

enemy *noun*
an enemy = un ennemi/une ennemie

energetic *adjective*
= énergique

energy *noun*
energy = l'énergie (*feminine*)

engaged *adjective*
to get engaged = se fiancer (**!** + *être*)
to be engaged = être fiancé/fiancée
(*British English*) (*describing a phone, toilet*)
= occupé/occupée

engine *noun*
(*of a car*)
an engine = un moteur
(*for a train*)
an engine = une locomotive

engineer *noun* ▶ 315 |
an engineer = un ingénieur

England *noun* ▶ 218 |
England = l'Angleterre (*feminine*)

English ▶ 275 |
1 *adjective*
= anglais/anglaise
2 *noun*
(*the people*)
the English = les Anglais (*masculine
plural*)
(*the language*)
English – l'anglais (*masculine*)

enjoy *verb*
(*to like*) = aimer
he enjoys fishing = il aime la pêche
did you enjoy your holiday? = est-ce que
  tu as passé de bonnes vacances?
(*to have a good time*) ▶ 237 |
to enjoy oneself = s'amuser (**!** + *être*)

enjoyable *adjective*
= agréable

E

enormous *adjective*
= énorme

enough
1 *determiner*
= assez de
I don't have enough [money | time |
friends …] = je n'ai pas assez [d'argent | de
temps | d'amis …]
there's enough room for everyone = il y a
assez de place pour tout le monde
2 *adverb*
= assez
is it big enough? = est-ce que c'est assez
grand?
you're not old enough = tu n'es pas assez
grand
3 *pronoun*
= assez
we have enough to eat = nous avons assez
à manger
I've had enough = j'en ai assez
that's enough = ça suffit

enquire *verb*
= se renseigner (**!** + *être*)
I'll enquire about the price = je vais me
renseigner sur le prix

enter *verb*
(*to go into*) = entrer dans (**!** + *être*)
(*to take part in*) = participer à
to enter a competition = participer à un
concours

entertain *verb*
= divertir

entertaining *adjective*
= divertissant/divertissante

entertainment *noun*
entertainment = le divertissement, les
distractions (*feminine plural*)

enthusiasm *noun*
enthusiasm = l'enthousiasme (*masculine*)

enthusiastic *adjective*
= enthousiaste

entrance *noun*
an entrance = une entrée
the entrance to the castle = l'entrée du
château

envelope *noun*
an envelope = une enveloppe

environment *noun*
the environment = l'environnement
(*masculine*)

envy
1 *noun*
envy = l'envie (*feminine*)
2 *verb*
= envier

episode *noun*
an episode = un épisode

equal
1 *adjective*
= égal/égale
to fight for equal rights = lutter pour
l'égalité des droits
2 *verb*
= égaler
six and four equals ten = six et quatre
égalent dix

equality *noun*
equality = l'égalité (*feminine*)

equator *noun*
the equator = l'équateur (*masculine*)

equipment *noun*
equipment (*in an office, a laboratory, a
factory*) = le matériel
(*for an activity*) = l'équipement (*masculine*)

eraser *noun*
an eraser = une gomme

escalator *noun*
an escalator = un escalier mécanique

escape *verb*
(*to get away*) = s'échapper (**!** + *être*)
he escaped from prison = il s'est échappé
de prison
(*to avoid*) = échapper à
to escape death = échapper à la mort

especially *adverb*
= surtout

essay *noun*
an essay (*by a pupil*) = une rédaction
(*by a student*) = une dissertation

essential *adjective*
= essentiel/essentielle

ethnic *adjective*
= ethnique

eurocheque *noun*
a eurocheque = un Eurochèque

Europe *noun* ▶ 218 |
Europe = l'Europe (*feminine*)

European *adjective* ▶ 275 |
= européen/européenne

European Union *noun*
the European Union = l'Union
européenne
| **!** *Note that* **Union** *is feminine.*

evacuate *verb*
= évacuer

even[1]
1 *adverb*
(*when expressing surprise*) = même
he didn't even try = il n'a même pas essayé
she even works on weekends = elle
travaille même le week-end
(*in comparisons*) = encore
it's even colder today = il fait encore plus
froid aujourd'hui

2 even though = bien que
he's bored even though he's with other
  people = bien qu'il soit avec d'autres
  personnes, il s'ennuie

> **!** Note that the subjunctive is used after
> bien que.

even² adjective
(flat, smooth) = régulier/régulière
(when talking about numbers)
an even number = un nombre pair

evening noun ▶ 211 |, ▶ 356 |

> **!** Note that evening is usually translated
> by soir in French. However it is sometimes
> translated by soirée, when there is an
> emphasis on the idea of duration.

an evening = un soir
at eight o'clock in the evening = à huit
  heures du soir
to spend the evening at home = passer la
  soirée à la maison

event noun
an event = un événement

eventually adverb

> **!** Note that eventually is never translated
> by éventuellement.

= finalement

ever adverb
(at any time)
nothing ever happens here = il ne se
  passe jamais rien ici
no-one will ever know = personne ne le
  saura jamais
have you ever been to Greece? = est-ce
  que tu es déjà allé en Grèce?
I hardly ever go there = je n'y vais presque
  jamais
(always)
he's as lazy as ever = il est toujours aussi
  paresseux

every determiner ▶ 356 |
= tous les/toutes les
every time I meet her = toutes les fois que
  je la rencontre
every day = tous les jours
every second day, every other day = tous
  les deux jours
two out of every three people = deux
  personnes sur trois

everyone pronoun (also **everybody**)
= tout le monde
everyone else = tous les autres

everything pronoun
= tout

everywhere adverb
= partout
everywhere else = partout ailleurs

evidence noun
a piece of evidence = une preuve
to give evidence = témoigner

evil noun
evil = le mal

exact adjective
= exact/exacte

exactly adverb
= exactement

exaggerate verb
= exagérer

exam noun
an exam = un examen
to pass an exam = réussir à un examen
to take an exam = passer un examen

examine verb
= examiner

example noun
an example = un exemple
for example = par exemple

excellent adjective
= excellent/excellente

except preposition
= sauf

exchange verb
= échanger
to exchange a hat for a scarf = échanger
  un chapeau contre une écharpe

exchange rate noun
the exchange rate = le taux de change

excited adjective
= excité/excitée

exciting adjective
= passionnant/passionnante

exclude verb
= exclure

excuse
1 noun
an excuse = une excuse
to make excuses = trouver des excuses
2 verb
= excuser
excuse me! = excusez-moi!

exercise noun
(to keep fit)
an exercise = un exercice
to take exercise, to do exercise = faire de
  l'exercice
(a piece of work)
an exercise = un exercice

exercise book noun
an exercise book = un cahier

exhausted adjective
= épuisé/épuisée

exhibition noun
an exhibition = une exposition

exit noun
an exit = une sortie

E

expect *verb*
　(*to be prepared for*) = s'attendre à (**!** + *être*)
　to expect bad news = s'attendre à de
　　mauvaises nouvelles
　they expect to win = ils s'attendent à
　　gagner
　(*to wait for*) = attendre
　(*to want*) = vouloir
　they expect us to do the work = ils
　　veulent que nous fassions le travail
　| **!** *Note that the subjunctive is used after*
　| *vouloir que.*

expenses *noun*
　expenses = les frais (*masculine*)

expensive *adjective*
　= cher/chère

experience *noun*
　an experience = une expérience

experienced *adjective*
　= expérimenté/expérimentée

experiment
1 *noun*
　an experiment = une expérience
2 *verb*
　= expérimenter

expert *noun*
　an expert = un spécialiste/une spécialiste
　a computer expert = un spécialiste/une
　　spécialiste en informatique

explain *verb*
　= expliquer
　to explain a rule to someone = expliquer
　　une règle à quelqu'un

explanation *noun*
　an explanation = une explication

explode *verb*
　= exploser

exploit *verb*
　= exploiter

explosion *noun*
　an explosion = une explosion

export *verb*
　= exporter

express
1 *verb*
　to express oneself = s'exprimer (**!** + *être*)
2 *adverb*
　to send a letter express = envoyer une
　　lettre en exprès

expression *noun*
　an expression = une expression

express train *noun*
　an express train = un rapide

extinct *adjective*
　(*describing an animal*) = disparu/disparue
　(*describing a volcano*) = éteint/éteinte

extra
1 *adjective*
　= supplémentaire
　an extra bed = un lit supplémentaire
　to pay an extra ten pounds = payer dix
　　livres de plus
2 *adverb*
　to pay extra = payer un supplément

extraordinary *adjective*
　= extraordinaire

extreme *adjective*
　= extrême

extremely *adverb*
　= extrêmement

eye *noun* ▶ **201** |
　an eye = un œil
　to have green eyes = avoir les yeux verts

eyebrow *noun* ▶ **201** |
　an eyebrow = un sourcil

eyelash *noun* ▶ **201** |
　an eyelash = un cil

eyelid *noun* ▶ **201** |
　an eyelid = une paupière

eye shadow *noun*
　eye shadow = le fard à paupières

eyesight *noun*
　eyesight = la vue
　to have good eyesight = avoir une bonne
　　vue

Ff

face
1 *noun*
　the face = le visage, la figure
　to make a face = faire une grimace
2 *verb*
　(*to be opposite*) = être face à
　she was facing me = elle était face à moi
　(*to have to deal with*) = confronter
　I can't face seeing them again = je n'ai pas
　　le courage de les revoir
　(*to look toward(s)*)
　my room faces the sea = ma chambre
　　donne sur la mer
face up to = faire face à

fact
1 *noun*
　a fact = un fait
2 in fact = en fait

factory *noun*
　a factory = une usine

Useful everyday expressions in spoken French

When things are going well

well done!	= bravo!	*congratulations!*	= félicitations!
	= chapeau✱!	*good luck!*	= bonne chance!
	(*I take my hat*	*way to go! (US English)*	= bravo!
	off to him / you etc)	*wow!*	= super✱!, génial✱!

When things are not so good

hard luck!	= pas de chance!	*good luck! (you'll need it)*	= bon courage!
too bad !	= tant pis!	*ouch!*	= aïe!, ouïlle!
cheer up!, chin up!	= courage!	*shit!*	= merde♦!
oh dear!	= oh là là✱!	*yuck!, ugh!*	= beurk✱!
	= ça alors!	*phew! (that was close)*	= ouf!
damn!	= oh, mince✱!	*get well soon!*	= bon rétablissement!,
blast!	= zut✱!		remets-toi vite!

Coming

welcome!	= bienvenue!
nice to meet you, pleased to meet you	= enchanté/enchantée de faire votre connaissance
hello!	= bonjour! (*face to face*)
	= allô, bonjour! (*on the phone*)
hi!	= salut✱!
hi again!	= rebonjour✱!

Going

goodbye!	= au revoir!
bye!	= salut✱! tchao✱!
cheers! (British English)	= salut✱!
see you soon / later / next week!	= à biontôt! / plus tard! / la semaine prochaine!
see you around!	= à un de ces jours!
(have a) safe journey!	= bon voyage!
all the best!	= bonne continuation!

Wishing someone well

have a nice day!	= bonne journée!
have a good weekend!	= bon week-end!
have a great holiday or *vacation!*	= bonnes vacances!
have a good time!, enjoy yourself!	= amuse-toi bien!, amusez-vous bien!
have a good trip!	= bon voyage!

Special greetings

Happy birthday!	= Bon anniversaire!	*Happy New Year!*	= Bonne année!
Happy Christmas!	= Joyeux Noël!	*April fool!*	= poisson d'avril!

In reply to: 'Would you like ...?'

yes, please	= volontiers
	= oui, je veux bien!
	= pourquoi pas?

In reply to: 'Thank you'

you're very welcome	= je t'en prie, je vous en prie
don't mention it	= (il n'y a) pas de quoi
no problem, not at all	= de rien

Eating and drinking

enjoy your meal!	= bon appétit!
cheers!	= santé!, à la tienne!, à la vôtre!, tchin! tchin!

Sleeping

good night!	= bonne nuit!	*sweet dreams!*	= fais de beaux rêves!
sleep well!	= dors bien!		

✱ in informal situations   ♦ may be considered offensive

fade *verb*
  (*if it's a material*) = se décolorer (**!** + *être*)
  (*if it's a colour*) = passer (**!** + *être*)

fail *verb*
  = échouer
  to fail an exam = échouer à un examen

failure *noun*
  a failure (*an event, an attempt*) = un échec
  (*a person*) = un raté/une ratée

faint *verb*
  = s'évanouir (**!** + *être*)

fair
1 *adjective*
  (*just*) = juste
  it's not fair = ce n'est pas juste
  (*in colour*)
  to have fair hair = avoir les cheveux
    blonds
  to have fair skin = avoir le teint clair
2 *noun*
  (*British English*) (*a funfair*)
  a fair = une fête foraine
  (*a display of goods*)
  a (trade) fair = une foire

fairly *adverb*
  = assez

faith *noun*
  to have faith in someone = avoir
    confiance en quelqu'un

faithful *adjective*
  = fidèle

fall
1 *verb*
  (*if it's a person*) = tomber (**!** + *être*)
  she fell to the ground = elle est tombée
    par terre
  (*to come down, to be reduced*) = baisser
  (*other uses*)
  to fall asleep = s'endormir (**!** + *être*)
  to fall ill = tomber malade (**!** + *être*)
  to fall in love with someone = tomber
    amoureux/amoureuse de quelqu'un
2 *noun*
  (*in prices, temperature*)
  a fall = une baisse
  a fall in prices = une baisse des prix
  (*US English*) (*autumn*)
  fall = l'automne (*masculine*)
fall down
  (*if it's a person*) = tomber (**!** + *être*)
  (*if it's a building*) = s'effondrer (**!** + *être*)
fall off = tomber (**!** + *être*)
  to fall off a chair = tomber d'une chaise
fall out
  (*from somewhere*) = tomber (**!** + *être*)
  the letter fell out of his pocket = la lettre
    est tombée de sa poche
  (*to quarrel*) = se brouiller (**!** + *être*)

fall over = tomber (par terre) (**!** + *être*)
fall through = tomber à l'eau

false *adjective*
  = faux/fausse

false teeth *noun*
  false teeth = un dentier (*singular*)

familiar *adjective*
  = familier/familière

family *noun*
  a family = une famille

famous *adjective*
  = célèbre

fan *noun*
  (*of a pop star, an actor, a sport*)
  a fan = un fan/une fan
  (*for cooling*)
  a fan (*electric*) = un ventilateur
  (*hand-held*) = un éventail

fancy dress party *noun* (*British
English*)
  a fancy dress party = une soirée costumée

fantastic *adjective*
  = formidable, super**✶**

far
1 *adverb*
  ▶ **285** |
  far (away) = loin
  how far is it to London? = Londres est à
    combien de kilomètres?
  how far is Oxford from London? = Oxford
    est à quelle distance de Londres?
  we went as far as the coast = nous
    sommes allés jusqu'à la côte
  (*in time*)
  as far back as 1950 = déjà en 1950
  (*very much*) = beaucoup
  you're eating far too much bread = tu
    manges beaucoup trop de pain
  we know far fewer people here = on
    connaît beaucoup moins de monde ici
2 *adjective*
  = autre (**!** *before the noun*)
  at the far side of the room = de l'autre côté
    de la pièce
3 so far = jusqu'ici

fare *noun*
  the fare (*on a bus or the underground*) = le
    prix du ticket
  (*on a train or plane*) = le prix du billet

farm *noun*
  a farm = une ferme

farmer *noun* ▶ **315** |
  a farmer = un fermier

fascinating *adjective*
  = fascinant/fascinante

fashion *noun*
  fashion = la mode
  to be in fashion = être à la mode
  to go out of fashion = se démoder
    (**!** + *être*)

✶ *in informal situations*

fashionable adjective
= à la mode

fast
1 adjective
(describing movement) = rapide
to be fast = avancer
my watch is ten minutes fast = ma montre avance de dix minutes
2 adverb
= vite, rapidement

fasten verb
to fasten a seatbelt = attacher une ceinture de sécurité

fast-forward verb
to fast-forward a cassette = faire avancer rapidement une cassette

fat adjective
= gros/grosse (! before the noun)
to get fat = grossir

fatal adjective
= mortel/mortelle

father noun
a father = un père

Father Christmas noun (British English)
Father Christmas = le père Noël

father-in-law noun
a father-in-law = un beau père

faucet noun (US English)
a faucet = un robinet

fault noun
to be someone's fault = être (de) la faute de quelqu'un
it's not my fault = ce n'est pas (de) ma faute
whose fault was it? = à qui la faute?

favour (British English), **favor** (US English)
1 noun
a favour = un service
to do someone a favour = rendre (un) service à quelqu'un
to ask someone a favour = demander un service à quelqu'un
2 in favour of
to be in favour of a change in the law = être pour un changement de la loi

favourite (British English), **favorite** (US English) adjective
= préféré/préférée
it's my favourite film = c'est mon film préféré

fax noun
a fax = un fax

fear noun
fear = la peur

feather noun
a feather = une plume

February noun ▶ 222 |
February = février (masculine)

fed up adjective
to be fed up = en avoir marre✶

fee noun
a fee (to attend an event, a show) = un droit d'entrée
(to join a club, a union) = une cotisation

feeble adjective
= faible

feed verb
= nourrir
I must feed the children = je dois donner à manger aux enfants

feel verb
(referring to an emotion, an impression)
to feel happy = être heureux/heureuse
he's feeling uncomfortable = il se sent mal à l'aise
to feel afraid = avoir peur
I feel as if I'm being followed = j'ai l'impression qu'on me suit
it feels like winter = on se croirait en hiver
it feels good to be back home = ça fait du bien d'être chez soi
(referring to a physical feeling)
to feel [hot | cold | sleepy ...] = avoir [chaud | froid | sommeil ...]
to feel ill = se sentir malade
to feel a draught = sentir un courant d'air
I don't feel a thing = je ne sens rien
(describing how something seems)
the box felt very heavy = la boîte était lourde
the room feels very cold = la pièce est très froide
(to touch) = tâter, toucher
to feel like [going out | eating | dancing ...] = avoir envie de [sortir | manger | danser ...]
I don't feel like it = je n'en ai pas envie

feeling noun
(emotional)
a feeling = un sentiment
to hurt someone's feelings = blesser quelqu'un
(physical)
a feeling = une sensation
I have a feeling he's right = j'ai l'impression qu'il a raison

felt-tip pen noun
a felt-tip pen = un crayon feutre

female adjective
(in biology) = femelle
(relating to women) = féminin/féminine

feminine adjective
= féminin/féminine

fence noun
a fence = une clôture

fencing noun ▶ 248 |
fencing = l'escrime (feminine)

F

festival noun
a festival = une fête

fetch verb
= aller chercher
go and fetch some water = va chercher de l'eau

fever noun
to have a fever = avoir de la fièvre

few ▶ 317 |
1 a few
a few [people | houses | books ...] = quelques [personnes | maisons | livres ...]
a few of the houses were burned down = quelques-unes des maisons ont été brûlées
a few of them speak Greek = quelques-uns d'entre eux parlent grec
I would like a few more = j'en voudrais quelques-uns/quelques-unes de plus
! Note that it is necessary to use en, which may be translated as 'of them', with phrases like a few. See also another, a lot, none etc for this use of en.

2 determiner
(not many) = peu de
few [visitors | letters | meals ...] = peu de [visiteurs | lettres | repas ...]
(several)
the first few weeks = les premières semaines
3 pronoun
= peu
few of us succeeded = peu d'entre nous ont réussi
there are so few of them (of people) = ils sont si peu nombreux
(of things) = il y en a tellement peu

fewer ▶ 317 |
1 determiner
= moins de
fewer shops = moins de magasins
2 pronoun
= moins
fewer than ten people = moins de dix personnes

fewest
1 determiner
the fewest = le moins de
they have the fewest advantages = ce sont eux qui ont le moins d'avantages
2 pronoun
the fewest = le moins

field noun
a field = un champ

fifteen number ▶ 187 |, ▶ 211 |
fifteen = quinze

fifteenth number
(in a series) = quinzième
(in dates) ▶ 222 |
the fifteenth of May = le quinze mai

fifth number
(in a series) = cinquième
(in dates) ▶ 222 |
the fifth of June = le cinq juin

fifty number ▶ 187 |, ▶ 211 |
fifty = cinquante

fight
1 verb
to fight (against) prejudice = lutter contre les préjugés
to fight for justice = lutter pour la justice
(in war) = se battre (! + être)
to fight the enemy = combattre l'ennemi
(physically) = se battre (! + être)
(to quarrel) = se disputer (! + être)
2 noun
(a campaign)
a fight = une lutte
(physical)
a fight = une bagarre
fight back = se défendre (! + être)

figure noun
(a number)
a figure = un chiffre
to have a good figure = être bien fait/bien faite

file noun
a file (for documents) = un dossier
(in a computer) = un fichier
in single file = en file indienne

fill verb
(to make full) = remplir
(to become full) = se remplir (! + être)
fill in = remplir

film
1 noun
(in cinema or on TV)
a film = un film
(for a camera)
a film = une pellicule
2 verb
= filmer

filthy adjective
= sale

final
1 adjective
= dernier/dernière (! before the noun)
2 noun
a final = une finale

finally adverb
= finalement

find verb
= trouver
find out
to find out the truth = découvrir la vérité
if he ever finds out he'll be furious = si jamais il l'apprend il sera furieux

fine
1 adjective
(very good, excellent) = beau/belle (! before the noun)
the weather is fine = il fait beau

(in good health)
I feel fine = je me sens très bien
(expressing agreement)
(that's) fine = d'accord
2 *noun*
a fine = une amende

finger *noun* ▶ **201 |**
  a finger = un doigt

finish
1 *verb*
(to end) = finir
to finish writing a letter = finir d'écrire
  une lettre
(to come to an end) = finir
2 *noun*
the finish *(in a race)* = l'arrivée *(feminine)*

Finland *noun* ▶ **218 |**
  Finland = la Finlande

fire
1 *noun*
fire = le feu
a fire *(for heat)* = un feu
(causing damage) = un incendie
to catch fire = prendre feu
to be on fire = être en feu
2 *verb*
(to shoot) = tirer
(to dismiss) = renvoyer

fire alarm *noun*
  a fire alarm = une sonnerie d'alarme
  incendie

fire brigade *(British English)*, **fire department** *(US English) noun*
  the fire brigade = les pompiers *(masculine plural)*

fire engine *noun*
  a fire engine = une voiture de pompiers

fireman *noun* ▶ **315 |**
  a fireman = un pompier

fire station *noun*
  a fire station = une caserne de pompiers

fireworks display *noun*
  a fireworks display = un feu d'artifice

firm
1 *noun*
a firm = une entreprise
2 *adjective*
= ferme

first
1 *adjective*
= premier/première *(**!** before the noun)*
the first time = la première fois
the first three weeks = les trois premières
  semaines
2 *adverb*
(to begin with) = d'abord
first of all = tout d'abord
(for the first time) = pour la première fois

to arrive first = arriver le premier/la
  première
3 *noun*
(in a series or group)
the first = le premier/la première
he was the first to congratulate us = il a
  été le premier à nous féliciter
(in dates) ▶ **222 |**
the first of June = le premier juin
4 at first = au début

first aid *noun*
  first aid = les premiers soins
  ! Note that **soins** is masculine plural.

first class *adverb*
  to travel first class = voyager en première
  classe

first floor *noun*
  the first floor *(in Britain)* = le premier étage
  (in the US) = le rez-de-chaussée

first name *noun*
  a first name = un prénom

fish
1 *noun*
a fish = un poisson
2 *verb*
to go fishing = aller à la pêche

fisherman *noun* ▶ **315 |**
  a fisherman = un pêcheur

fishing *noun* ▶ **248 |**
  fishing = la pêche

fishing rod *noun*
  a fishing rod = une canne à pêche

fist *noun* ▶ **201 |**
  the fist = le poing

fit
1 *verb*
the shoes don't fit me = les chaussures ne
  me vont pas
the photo won't fit into the envelope = la
  photo ne rentre pas dans l'enveloppe
will the table fit here? = est-ce qu'il y a de
  la place pour la table ici?
2 *adjective*
(suitable, capable)
the house isn't fit to live in = la maison
  n'est pas habitable
to be fit to drive = être en état de conduire
he's not fit to be a minister = il n'est pas
  capable d'être ministre
(healthy)
to be fit = être en forme
fit in
(in a room or car)
can you all fit in? = est-ce qu'il y a de la
  place pour vous tous?
(in a group or team) = s'intégrer *(**!** + être)*

fitness *noun*
  (physical) fitness = la forme (physique)

five *number* ▶ **187** |, ▶ **211** |
  five = cinq
  five apples = cinq pommes
  I've got five (of them) = j'en ai cinq

fix *verb*
  (*to decide on, to set*) = fixer
  (*to repair*) = réparer
  to get a watch fixed = faire réparer une
    montre
  (*to prepare*) = préparer

flag *noun*
  a flag = un drapeau

flame *noun*
  a flame = une flamme
  to go up in flames = s'enflammer
    (**!** + *être*)

flash
1 *noun*
  a flash (*for a camera*) = un flash
2 *verb*
  to flash (on and off) = clignoter

flashlight *noun*
  a flashlight = une lampe de poche

flask *noun*
  a flask = un thermos

flat
1 *noun* (*British English*)
  a flat = un appartement
2 *adjective*
  = plat/plate
  to have a flat tyre = avoir un pneu à plat

flavour (*British English*), **flavor** (*US English*) *noun*
  a flavour (*of food*) = une saveur, un goût
  (*of ice cream, yogurt*) = un parfum

flea *noun*
  a flea = une puce

flight *noun*
  a flight = un vol

flight attendant *noun* ▶ **315** |
  a flight attendant = un steward/une
    hôtesse de l'air

float *verb*
  = flotter
  to float up into the air = s'envoler (**!** + *être*)

flock *noun*
  (*of sheep, goats, geese*)
  a flock = un troupeau
  (*of birds*)
  a flock = une volée

flood *noun*
  a flood = une inondation

floor *noun*
  (*a surface*)
  a floor = un plancher
  to sit on the floor = s'asseoir par terre
  (*a storey*)
  a floor = un étage

florist *noun* ▶ **315** |
  a florist = un fleuriste/une fleuriste

flour *noun*
  flour = la farine

flow *verb*
  (*if it's a liquid*) = couler
  (*if it's traffic*) = circuler

flower
1 *noun*
  a flower = une fleur
2 *verb*
  = fleurir

flu *noun* ▶ **266** |
  flu = la grippe

fluently *adverb*
  = couramment

flush *verb*
  to flush the toilet = tirer la chasse d'eau

flute *noun* ▶ **290** |
  a flute = une flûte

fly
1 *noun*
  a fly = une mouche
2 *verb*
  (*if it's a bird, a kite, a plane, an insect*)
  = voler
  (*if it's a passenger*) = prendre l'avion
  to fly from London to Paris = aller de
    Londres à Paris en avion
  to fly a plane = piloter un avion
  (*if it's a flag*) = flotter
fly away = s'envoler (**!** + *être*)

fog *noun*
  fog = le brouillard

fold *verb*
  to fold a shirt = plier une chemise
  to fold one's arms = croiser les bras

folder *noun*
  a folder (*for work*) = une chemise
  (*in computing*) = un dossier

follow *verb*
  (*to go or come after*) = suivre
  (*to use, to look at*) = suivre
  I followed the signposts = j'ai suivi les
    panneaux indicateurs

following *adjective*
  = suivant/suivante

fond *adjective*
  I'm very fond of you = je t'aime beaucoup

food *noun*
  food = la nourriture

fool *verb*
  = tromper, duper

foot *noun*
  (*part of the leg*) ▶ **201** |
  the foot = le pied
  on foot = à pied

(of a rabbit, a cat, a dog, a cow)
the foot = la patte
(in measurements) ▶ **285 |**
a foot = un pied
| **!** Note that a **foot** = 30.48 cm.

football *noun* ▶ **248 |**
  football *(soccer)* = le football
  (American football) = le football américain
  (a ball)
  a football = un football

footballer *(British English)*, **football player** *(US English) noun* ▶ **315 |**
  a footballer = un joueur/une joueuse de football

footprint *noun*
  a footprint = une trace de pas

footstep *noun*
  a footstep = un pas

for *preposition*
▶ **244 |** *See the boxed note on* **for** *for more information and examples.*
  for = pour
  the letter is for you = la lettre est pour toi
  to work for a company = travailler pour une entreprise
  he cooked dinner for us = il nous a préparé à manger
  (when talking about time)
  we've been living here for two years = on habite ici depuis deux ans, ça fait deux ans qu'on habite ici
  he's going to Paris for a year = il va à Paris pour un an
  she read for two hours = elle a lu pendant deux heures
  I've been waiting for three hours = ça fait trois heures que j'attends
  he won't arrive for another two weeks = il ne va pas arriver avant deux semaines
  (when talking about distance)
  we drove for 80 kilometres = nous avons roulé pendant 80 kilomètres
  (when talking about money)
  he bought it for £50 = il l'a acheté pour 50 livres
  a cheque for £20 = un chèque de 20 livres
  (in favour (of)) = pour
  say hello to her for me = donne-lui le bonjour de ma part
  (other uses)
  T for Tom = T comme Tom
  the Minister for Education = le ministre de l'éducation
  what is the French for 'badger'? = comment dit-on 'badger' en français?
  we went [for a swim | for a run | for a walk ...] = nous sommes allés [nager | courir | nous promener ...]

forbid *verb*
  = interdire
  to forbid someone to go out = interdire à quelqu'un de sortir
  smoking is forbidden = il est interdit de fumer

force
1 *verb*
  = forcer
  to force someone to leave = forcer quelqu'un à partir
2 *noun*
  force = la force
  by force = de force

forecast *noun*
  the forecast = les prévisions *(feminine plural)*
  the forecast is for rain = la météo prévoit de la pluie

forehead *noun* ▶ **201 |**
  the forehead = le front

foreign *adjective*
  = étranger/étrangère

foreigner *noun*
  a foreigner = un étranger/une étrangère

forest *noun*
  a forest = une forêt

forever, **for ever** *adverb*
  = pour toujours

forget *verb*
  = oublier
  to forget about someone = oublier quelqu'un
  to forget [to do the shopping | to eat | to call ...] = oublier [de faire les courses | de manger | de téléphoner ...]

forgive *verb*
  to forgive someone = pardonner à quelqu'un

fork *noun*
  a fork = une fourchette

form
1 *noun* ▶ **245 |**
  (a shape)
  a form = une forme
  (a document)
  a form = un formulaire
  (referring to mood or fitness)
  to be in good form = être en bonne forme
  (British English) (a class)
  a form = une classe
  to be in the sixth form = être en terminale
2 *verb*
  (to create, to make) = former
  to form a circle = former un cercle
  (to start, to set up) = créer

formal *adjective*
  (describing language) = soutenu/soutenue
  to wear formal clothes *(for the evening)* = être en tenue de soirée
  (official) = officiel/officielle

former *adjective*
  = ancien/ancienne (**!** *before the noun*)

fortnight *noun* ▶ **356 |** *(British English)*
  a fortnight = quinze jours *(masculine plural)*

F

for

Some general uses

for is generally translated by **pour**:

for my sister	= **pour** ma sœur
for me	= **pour** moi

When **for** followed by a verb is used to explain the purpose of something, it is translated by **pour** + *infinitive*:

a product *for* losing weight	= un produit **pour** maigrir

When talking about time

for in time expressions may be translated by **depuis**, **pendant** or **pour**. The following examples are designed to show you which translation to choose. Note that tense is very important in distinguishing between them.

- When **for** is used to express the time period of something that started in the past and is still going on, French uses either *present tense* + **depuis** or **ça fait✻** ... **que** + *present tense*:

I have been waiting for three hours	= j'attends **depuis** trois heures
(and I am still waiting)	= **ça fait✻** trois heures **que** j'attends
we've been together for two years	= nous sommes ensemble **depuis** deux ans
(and we're still together)	= **ça fait✻** deux ans **que** nous sommes ensemble

When **for** is used after a verb in the past perfect tense placing an event even further back in time, French uses either *imperfect* + **depuis** or **ça faisait✻** ... **que** + *imperfect*:

I had been waiting for two hours	= j'attendais **depuis** deux heures
(and was still waiting)	= **ça faisait✻** deux heures **que** j'attendais

- When **for** is used in negative sentences with the present perfect tense to express the time that has elapsed since something has happened, French uses the same tense as English, either *perfect* + **depuis** or **ça fait✻** ... **que** + *perfect*:

I haven't seen him for ten years	= je ne l'ai pas vu **depuis** dix ans
(and I still haven't seen him)	= **ça fait✻** dix ans que je ne l'ai pas vu

When **for** is used in negative sentences after a verb in the past perfect tense, again placing events further back in time, French uses either *past perfect* + **depuis** or **ça faisait✻** ... **que** + *past perfect*:

I hadn't seen him for ten years	= je ne l'avais pas vu **depuis** dix ans
	= **ça faisait✻** dix ans que je ne l'avais pas vu

- When **for** is used to express the time period of something that happened in the past and is no longer going on, French uses *present perfect* + **pendant**:

last Sunday I read for two hours	= dimanche dernier j'ai lu **pendant** deux heures

- When **for** is used to express a time period in the future, French uses *present* or *future* + **pour**:

I'm going to Montreal for six weeks	= je vais à Montréal **pour** six semaines
I will go to Montreal for six weeks	= j'irai à Montréal **pour** six semaines

- When the verb **to be** is used in the future with **for** to emphasize the period of time, French uses *future* + **pendant**:

I will be in Brussels for six weeks	= je serai à Bruxelles **pendant** six semaines

✻ in informal situations

---

fortunately *adverb*
= heureusement

fortune *noun*
a fortune = une fortune
to make a fortune = faire fortune
to tell someone's fortune = dire la bonne aventure à quelqu'un

forty *number* ▶ **187** |, ▶ **211** |
forty = quarante

forward
1 *adverb*
= en avant
to step forward = faire un pas en avant

Forms of address (Miss, Mr, Mrs)

When speaking to someone

Where English puts the surname after the title, French normally uses the title alone:

Good morning, **Miss Jones**	= bonjour, **Mademoiselle**
Good evening, **Mr Halpin**	= bonsoir, **Monsieur**
Good morning, **Mrs Davies**	= bonjour, **Madame**

When speaking about someone

In this case, French and English behave the same:

Miss Jones | Mr Halpin | Mrs Davies = Mademoiselle Jones / Monsieur Halpin /
is here   Madame Davies est là

When writing to someone

When starting a letter, translations will differ according to the degree of formality involved:

	formal	less formal
Dear Miss Jones	= Mademoiselle	= Chère Mademoiselle
Dear Mr Halpin	= Monsieur	= Cher Monsieur
Dear Mrs Davies	= Madame	= Chère Madame

▶ There is no French equivalent of **Ms** but one can use **Madame** in similar circumstances.

---

2 *verb*
  to forward a letter to someone = faire
  suivre une lettre à quelqu'un

found *verb*
  – fonder

fountain *noun*
  a fountain = une fontaine

four *number* ▶ **187** |, ▶ **211** |
  four = quatre
  four apples = quatre pommes
  I've got four (of them) = j'en ai quatre

fourteen *number* ▶ **187** |, ▶ **211** |
  fourteen = quatorze

fourteenth *number*
  (*in a series*) = quatorzième
  (*in dates*) ▶ **222** |
  the fourteenth of July = le quatorze juillet

fourth *number*
  (*in a series*) = quatrième
  (*in dates*) ▶ **222** |
  the fourth of July = le quatre juillet

fox *noun*
  a fox = un renard

fragile *adjective*
  = fragile

frame *noun*
  a frame = un cadre

France *noun* ▶ **218** |
  France = la France

frank *adjective*
  = franc/franche

freckle *noun*
  a freckle = une tache de rousseur

free
1 *adjective*
  (*costing nothing*) = gratuit/gratuite
  (*independent, able to come and go*) = libre
  he is free to do what he likes = il est libre
  de faire ce qu'il veut
  (*not occupied, available*) = libre
  are you free on Monday? = est-ce que tu
  es libre lundi?
2 *verb*
  = libérer
3 *adverb*
  = gratuitement

freedom *noun*
  freedom = la liberté

freeway *noun* (*US English*)
  a freeway = une autoroute

freeze *verb*
  (*in cold weather*) = geler
  the river froze = la rivière a gelé
  the ground was frozen = le sol était gelé
  (*in a freezer*) = congeler
  to freeze to death = mourir de froid

freezer *noun*
  a freezer = un congélateur

freezing *adjective*
  it's freezing = il fait un temps glacial
  this room is freezing = cette pièce est
    glaciale
  to be freezing (*if it's a person*) = être
    gelé/gelée

French ▶ 275 |
1 *adjective*
  = français/française
2 *noun*
  (*the people*)
  the French = les Français (*masculine
    plural*)
  (*the language*)
  French = le français

French fries *noun*
  French fries = les frites (*feminine*)

fresh *adjective*
  = frais/fraîche

Friday *noun* ▶ 222 |
  Friday = vendredi (*masculine*)

fridge *noun*
  a fridge = un frigo✗

fried *adjective*
  = frit/frite

fried egg *noun*
  a fried egg = un œuf sur le plat

friend *noun*
  a friend = un ami/une amie
  to make friends = se faire des amis
  to make friends with someone = devenir
    ami/amie avec quelqu'un

friendly *adjective*
  = gentil/gentille

fright *noun*
  to get a fright = avoir peur
  to give someone a fright = faire peur à
    quelqu'un

frightened *adjective*
  to be frightened = avoir peur

fringe *noun* (*British English*)
  a fringe = une frange

frog *noun*
  a frog = une grenouille

from *preposition*

  > ! There are many verbs which involve the
  > use of from, like borrow from, escape from
  > etc. For translations, look up the entries at
  > borrow, escape etc.

from = de (**!** d' + *vowel or mute h*)
  the boy from London = le garçon (qui
    vient) de Londres
  where is she from? = d'où vient-elle?
  to come back from the office = rentrer du
    bureau
  to return from a holiday = rentrer de
    vacances
  there's a message from Paul = il y a un
    message de Paul
  the train from Oxford is late = le train en
    provenance d'Oxford est en retard
  we live ten minutes from the city centre
    = nous habitons à dix minutes du
    centre-ville
  (*when talking about time*) = de, à partir de
  the shop is open from eight to six = le
    magasin est ouvert de huit heures à
    dix-huit heures
  from Monday to Saturday = du lundi au
    samedi
  from April on = à partir du mois d'avril
  from then on = à partir de ce moment-là
  fifty years from now = d'ici cinquante ans
  (*British English*) (*in arithmetic*)
  5 from 8 leaves 3 = 5 ôté de 8, il reste 3

front
1 *noun*
  (*of a building*)
  the front of a house = la façade d'une
    maison
  the front of a shop = la devanture d'un
    magasin
  my room is at the front of the house = ma
    chambre est sur le devant de la maison
  (*of a car, a train or queue*)
  at the front of the bus = à l'avant du bus
  at the front of the queue = au début de la
    queue
2 **in front of** = devant

front door *noun*
  the front door = la porte d'entrée

front page *noun*
  the front page = la première page

front seat *noun*
  the front seat = le siège avant

frost *noun*
  frost = le givre, la gelée

frozen *adjective*
  = congelé/congelée

fruit *noun*
  a piece of fruit = un fruit
  he likes fruit = il aime les fruits

frustrated *adjective*
  = frustré/frustrée

fry *verb*
  to fry potatoes = faire frire des pommes de
    terre

frying pan *noun* (*British English*)
  a frying pan = une poêle

✗ in informal situations

full *adjective*
(*not empty*) = plein/pleine
the streets were full of people = les rues
  étaient pleines de monde
(*describing a flight, a hotel*)
= complet/complète
(*maximum*)
to travel at full speed = rouler à toute
  vitesse
to get full marks = obtenir la note
  maximale
(*complete*)
to pay the full fare = payer plein tarif
his full name = ses nom et prénom

full-time *adverb*
= à plein temps
to work full-time = travailler à plein temps

fumes *noun*
fumes = les fumées (*feminine*)

fun *noun*
it's fun = c'est amusant
skiing is fun = c'est amusant de faire du
  ski
to have fun = s'amuser (**!** + *être*)
she's fun = on s'amuse bien avec elle

function *verb*
= fonctionner

funeral *noun*
a funeral = un enterrement

funfair *noun* (*British English*)
a funfair = une fête foraine

funny *adjective*
(*amusing*) = drôle, amusant/amusante
(*odd*) = drôle, bizarre

fur *noun*
fur (*an animal's coat*) = les poils (*masculine
  plural*)
(*on a garment*) = la fourrure

furious *adjective*
= furieux/furieuse

furniture *noun*
a piece of furniture = un meuble
furniture = les meubles

further *adverb*
= plus loin
he lives further away from the school = il
  habite plus loin de l'école
how much further is it? = c'est encore
  loin?

fuss *noun*
a fuss = des histoires (*feminine plural*)

future
1 *noun*
the future = l'avenir (*masculine*)
in the future = dans l'avenir
in future, let us know = à l'avenir, préviens-
  nous
2 *adjective*
= futur/future

Gg

gallery *noun*
a gallery = un musée

game *noun*
a game = un jeu
a game of football = un match de football
a game of tennis = une partie de tennis

games *noun* (*British English*)
games = le sport

game show *noun*
a game show = un jeu télévisé

gang *noun*
a gang (*a group of friends, young people*)
= une bande
(*of criminals*) = un gang

gap *noun*
a gap (*in a fence or hedge*) = un trou
(*between buildings, cars*) = un espace
(*a period of time*)
a gap = un intervalle

garage *noun*
a garage = un garage

garbage *noun* (*US English*)
garbage = les ordures (*feminine plural*)

garden
1 *noun*
a garden = un jardin
2 *verb*
= faire du jardinage

gardener *noun* ▶ 315 |
a gardener = un jardinier/une jardinière

gardening *noun*
gardening = le jardinage

garlic *noun*
garlic = l'ail (*masculine*)

gas *noun*
(*for cooking, heating*)
gas = le gaz
(*US English*) (*gasoline*)
gas = l'essence (*feminine*)

gas station *noun* (*US English*)
a gas station = une station-service

gate *noun*
a gate (*to a garden, a town, a prison*) = une
  porte
(*to a field*) = une barrière

gather *verb*
(*to come together*) = se rassembler
(**!** + *être*)

G

Games and sports

With or without the definite article?

French normally uses **le**, **la**, **l'** or **les** with names of games and sports:

football	= le football
chess	= les échecs (*masculine plural*)
to play football	= jouer au football
to play tennis	= jouer au tennis
to play chess	= jouer aux échecs
to go climbing	= faire de l'escalade
to beat somebody at tennis	= battre quelqu'un au tennis
to win at chess	= gagner aux échecs
to lose at marbles	= perdre aux billes

Players and events

a tennis player	= un joueur de tennis

but

I'm not a tennis player	= je ne joue pas au tennis
he's a good tennis player	= il joue bien au tennis
a game of tennis	= une partie de tennis
a tennis champion	= un champion de tennis
the French tennis champion	= le champion de France de tennis
a tennis championship	= un championnat de tennis
the rules of tennis	= les règles du tennis

• (*to collect*)
to gather wood = ramasser du bois
to gather fruit = cueillir des fruits

gay *adjective*
= homosexuel/homosexuelle

gear *noun*
• (*in a car or bus, on a bike*)
a gear = une vitesse
• (*equipment*)
gear = le matériel
fishing gear = le matériel de pêche
• (*clothes*)
my football gear = ma tenue de football
your swimming gear = tes affaires pour la piscine

Gemini *noun*
Gemini = Gémeaux (*masculine*)

general
1 *noun*
a general = un général
2 *adjective*
= général/générale
3 in general = en général

generation *noun*
a generation = une génération

generous *adjective*
= généreux/généreuse

Geneva *noun* ▶ 218 |
Geneva = Genève

genius *noun*
a genius = un génie

gentle *adjective*
= doux/douce

gentleman *noun*
a gentleman = un monsieur

geography *noun*
geography = la géographie

germ *noun*
a germ = un microbe

German ▶ 275 |
1 *adjective*
= allemand/allemande
2 *noun*
• (*the people*)
the Germans = les Allemands (*masculine*)
• (*the language*)
German = l'allemand (*masculine*)

Germany *noun* ▶ 218 |
Germany = l'Allemagne (*feminine*)

get *verb*
▶ *See the boxed note on* **get** *for more information and examples.*
get away
• (*to escape*) = s'échapper (**!** + *être*)
• **he won't get away with it** = il ne va pas s'en tirer comme ça
get back
• (*to return*) = revenir (**!** + *être*)
• (*to have back*) = récupérer
I got my bike back = j'ai récupéré mon vélo
he'll get his money back = il va être remboursé

get

A multi-purpose verb

The word **get** is extremely common in English and does not have a multi-purpose French equivalent.

However, it is helpful to try to find a synonym (a word which has the same sense) and from there, a suitable translation:

he's gone to get (or *fetch*) *help* — il est parti **chercher** de l'aide
I'll call when we get (or *arrive*) *there* = j'appellerai quand **nous arriverons**

Main senses

When changing from one state (of mind) to another

French very often has a specific verb for the various combinations of **to get** + *adjective*:

to get old | angry | worried = vieillir / se fâcher / s'inquiéter

devenir + *adjective* is also useful:

to get jealous = **devenir** jaloux / jalouse

When asking, telling or persuading

The translations **dire (à quelqu'un)** and **demander (à quelqu'un)** are helpful:

get him to call me = **dis-lui** de m'appeler
I'll get her to help me = je **lui demanderai** de m'aider

When getting things done by someone else

The construction **faire** + *infinitive verb* is useful here:

to get the car cleaned = **faire nettoyer** la voiture
to get a TV repaired = **faire réparer** une télévision
to get one's hair cut = **se faire couper** les cheveux

When to get means to obtain

to get (or *buy*)*someone a present* = **acheter** un cadeau à quelqu'un
I got (or *found*) *a job in Paris* = j'**ai trouvé** un travail à Paris

When to get means to receive

The best translation is **recevoir**:

we got a letter from Mark = nous **avons reçu** une lettre de Mark

but

to get good grades = **avoir** de bonnes notes

When cooking

A translation which will work well is **préparer**:

to get dinner = **préparer** le déjeuner

With illnesses:

In this context **attraper** is useful:

to get measles = **attraper** la rougeole
to get a cold = s'enrhumer (+ *être*)

When using transport

The most reliable translation is **prendre**:

we can get the bus = on peut **prendre** le bus
to get a taxi to the station = **prendre** un taxi pour aller à la gare

▶ To find translations for other expressions using **get**—**to get sick**, **to get a surprise**, **to get better**, etc. —look up the entries at **sick**, **surprise**, **better**, etc.

▶ You will also find translations for *phrasal verbs* using **get** (**get down**, **get away**, **get on**, **get up**) listed separately in the dictionary.

get down
  (*to come or go down*) = descendre
  (**!** + *être*)
  can he get down from the tree? = est-ce
    qu'il peut descendre de l'arbre?
  (*to take down*) = descendre (**!** + *avoir*)
  I got the box down from the shelf = j'ai
    descendu la boîte de l'étagère
  (*to depress*) = déprimer
  it gets him down = ça le déprime
get in = entrer (**!** + *être*)
get off
  (*to leave a bus or train*) = descendre
  (**!** + *être*)
  I'm getting off at the next stop = je
    descends au prochain arrêt
  he fell as he was getting off the train = il
    est tombé en descendant du train
  (*to remove*) = enlever
  to get a stain off = enlever une tache
get on
  (*to climb on board a bus or train*) = monter
  (**!** + *être*)
  to get on the bus = monter dans le bus
  to get on well = bien s'entendre (**!** + *être*)
  I get on well with her = je m'entends bien
    avec elle
  (*in polite enquiries*)
  how did you get on? = comment est-ce
    que ça s'est passé?
  how is she getting on at school? = et ses
    études, ça marche**✱**?
get out
  (*to leave*) = sortir (**!** + *être*)
  she got out of the building = elle est sortie
    du bâtiment
  (*to take out*) = sortir (**!** + *avoir*)
  to get the furniture out of the house
    = sortir les meubles de la maison
get over
  to get over a shock = se remettre d'un
    choc
get through to
  to get through to someone = avoir
    quelqu'un au téléphone
get together = se réunir (**!** + *être*)
get up = se lever (**!** + *être*)

ghost *noun*
  a ghost = un fantôme

gift *noun*
  (*a present*)
  a gift = un cadeau
  (*an ability*)
  a gift = un don
  to have a gift for languages = avoir le don
    des langues

ginger *adjective* ▶ **213 |**
  = roux/rousse
  to have ginger hair (*British English*) = avoir
    les cheveux roux

girl *noun*
  a girl = une fille

girlfriend *noun*
  a girlfriend (*in a couple*) = une (petite)
    amie
  (*a female friend*) = une amie

give *verb*
  ! *For translations of expressions like* to
  give someone a lift, to give someone an
  injection, to give someone a fright *etc,*
  look up the entries lift, injection, fright.

  to give = donner
  to give someone a book = donner un livre
    à quelqu'un
  I gave him the photos = je lui ai donné les
    photos
  give me the newspapers = donne-moi les
    journaux
  give them to me = donne-les-moi
  to give someone a drink = donner à boire
    à quelqu'un
  to give one's seat to someone = laisser sa
    place à quelqu'un
  (*to offer*) = offrir
  he gave us one of his pictures = il nous a
    offert un de ses tableaux
  to give someone a present = faire un
    cadeau à quelqu'un
  to give someone a message = transmettre
    un message à quelqu'un
give away
  (*to make a present of*) = donner
  to give away a secret = révéler un secret
give back = rendre
give in = céder
give off
  to give off fumes = dégager des vapeurs
give out
  to give out the exercise books
    = distribuer les cahiers
give up
  (*to stop*)
  to give up smoking = cesser de fumer
  to give up the idea of working abroad
    = renoncer à l'idée de travailler à
    l'étranger
  to give oneself up to the police = se livrer à
    la police

glad *adjective*
  = content/contente

glass *noun*
  a glass = un verre

glasses *noun*
  glasses = les lunettes (*feminine*)

glove *noun*
  a glove = un gant

glow *verb*
  = luire

glue
1 *noun*
  glue = la colle

2 *verb*
= coller

go *verb*
▶ **253** See the boxed note on go for more information and examples.

go across = traverser
go after = poursuivre
go ahead
- (*if it's an event*) = avoir lieu
  the concert's going ahead after all = le concert aura finalement lieu
- (*if it's a person*)
  go ahead, there's no-one there = vas-y, il n'y a personne
go around ▶ **go round**
go around with ▶ **go round with**
go away = partir (**!** + *être*)
  go away! = allez-vous-en!, va-t'en!
go back = retourner (**!** + *être*)
  Gary went back to Paris = Gary est retourné à Paris
  to go back to school = reprendre les cours
  to go back to work = reprendre le travail
  to go back to sleep = se rendormir (**!** + *être*)
go by = passer (**!** + *être*)
go down
- (*if it's quality, a price, a salary*) = baisser
- (*if it's a person*) = descendre
  she went down into the basement = elle est descendue au sous-sol
  we went down the hill = nous avons descendu la pente
- (*if it's the sun*) = se coucher (**!** + *être*)
- (*if it's a computer*) = tomber en panne (**!** + *être*)
go in
- (*to enter*) = entrer (**!** + *être*)
- (*to return inside*) = rentrer (**!** + *être*)
go off
- (*to explode*) = exploser
- (*to ring*) (*if it's an alarm clock*) = sonner (*if it's an alarm*) = se déclencher (**!** + *être*)
- (*to leave*) = partir (**!** + *être*)
- the milk will go off = le lait va tourner
- (*to be switched off*) = s'éteindre (**!** + *être*)
go on
- (*to continue*) = continuer
  to go on talking = continuer à parler
- (*to happen*)
  what's going on? = qu'est-ce qui se passe?
- (*to keep talking*)
  he goes on (and on) about his work = il n'arrête pas de parler de son travail
- (*to be switched on*) (*if it's a light*) = s'allumer (**!** + *être*)
  (*if it's heating, a machine*) = se mettre en marche (**!** + *être*)
go out
- (*to leave the house*) = sortir (**!** + *être*)
  are you going out this evening? = est-ce que tu sors ce soir?
- (*as a boyfriend, a girlfriend*)
  to go out with someone = sortir avec quelqu'un

- (*to be switched off, to stop burning*) = s'éteindre (**!** + *être*)
- the tide's going out = la marée descend
go over
- (*to check*)
  to go over some grammar = vérifier quelques points de grammaire
- (*to revise*) = revoir
go round
- (*British English*) (*to call on*) = passer (**!** + *être*)
  to go round to see someone = passer voir quelqu'un
- (*to walk around, to visit*) = visiter
  to go round the museums = visiter les musées
  to go round the shops = faire les magasins
- (*to be enough*)
  is there enough bread to go round? = est-ce qu'il y a assez de pain pour tout le monde?
go round with
- (*British English*) (*to spend time with*) = fréquenter
go through
- (*to have, to live through*)
  to go through a difficult time = traverser une période difficile
  I don't want to go through that again = je ne voudrais pas revivre ça
- (*to search*) = fouiller
- (*to check*) = examiner
go together = aller ensemble
  the skirt and blouse go well together = la jupe et la chemise vont bien ensemble
go up
- (*if it's a person*) = monter
  he went up to bed = il est monté se coucher
  he went up the stairs = il a monté l'escalier
  to go up to the top of the hill = monter jusqu'en haut de la colline
  to go up to the top floor = monter jusqu'au dernier étage
- (*if it's a price, a salary*) = augmenter
go with = aller avec (**!** + *être*)
  the trousers don't really go with your jacket = le pantalon ne va pas très bien avec la veste

goal *noun*
  a goal = un but

goalkeeper *noun*
  a goalkeeper = un gardien de but

goat *noun*
  a goat = une chèvre

god *noun*
  a god = un dieu
  God = Dieu

goddaughter *noun*
  a goddaughter = une filleule

godfather *noun*
  a godfather = un parrain

G

godmother noun
a godmother = une marraine

godson noun
a godson = un filleul

going: **to be going to**
= aller
I'm going to [leave | go to Ireland | learn to drive …] = je vais [partir | aller en Irlande | apprendre à conduire …]
we were going to phone you = on allait te téléphoner

gold
1 noun
gold = l'or (*masculine*)
2 adjective
= en or
a gold ring = une bague en or

goldfish noun
a goldfish = un poisson rouge

golf noun ▶ **248**
golf = le golf

golf course noun
a golf course = un terrain de golf

good
1 adjective
• good = bon/bonne (**!** before the noun)
a good book = un bon livre
a good party = une bonne soirée
we've got some good news = nous avons de bonnes nouvelles
to have good eyesight = avoir une bonne vue
to be good [at chemistry | at drawing | at chess …] = être bon/bonne [en chimie | en dessin | aux échecs …]
it's a good time to visit Paris = c'est le bon moment pour visiter Paris
exercise is good for you = ça fait du bien de faire de l'exercice
to look good (*healthy*) = avoir bonne mine
I don't feel too good = je ne me sens pas très bien
I had a good time = je me suis bien amusé
• (*talking about food*) = bon/bonne (**!** before the noun)
• (*obedient*) = sage
• (*kind*) = gentil/gentille
it's very good of you to let me know = c'est très gentil de votre part de me prévenir
2 noun
it's no good shouting = ça ne sert à rien de crier
to be no good at Latin = être nul/nulle✘ en latin
the change will do you good = le changement te fera du bien
3 exclamation
• (*when pleased*)
good = c'est bien

• (*when relieved*)
'he's much better'—'good' = 'il va beaucoup mieux'—'tant mieux'
• (*when praising*)
good! = très bien!
4 for good = pour toujours

good afternoon noun (also exclamation)
good afternoon (*when meeting*) = bonjour
(*when leaving*) = au revoir

goodbye noun (also exclamation)
goodbye = au revoir

good evening noun (also exclamation)
good evening = bonsoir

good-looking adjective
= beau/belle (**!** before the noun)

good morning noun (also exclamation)
good morning (*when meeting*) = bonjour
(*when leaving*) = au revoir

goodnight noun (also exclamation)
goodnight = bonne nuit

goods noun
goods = la marchandise (*singular*)

goose noun
a goose = une oie

gooseberry noun
a gooseberry = une groseille à maquereau

gorilla noun
a gorilla = un gorille

gossip verb
• (*to chat*) = bavarder
• (*to talk in a harmful way*) = faire des commérages

got: **to have got** verb
▶ See the boxed note on **got** for more information and examples.
• (*to have*) = avoir
I've got work to do = j'ai du travail
have you got a cold? = est-ce que tu as un rhume?
• (*to be obliged to*)
to have got to = devoir
I've got to [go | work | get dressed …] = je dois [partir | travailler | m'habiller …], il faut que [je parte | je travaille | je m'habille …]
! Note that the subjunctive is used after **il faut que**.

government noun
a government = un gouvernement

GP noun ▶ **315** (British English)
a GP = un médecin, un généraliste

grab verb
to grab someone by the arm = saisir quelqu'un par le bras
he tried to grab my handbag = il a essayé d'arracher mon sac à main

✘ in informal situations

go

▶ You will find translations for phrasal verbs like **go away**, **go back**, **go round**, etc listed separately in the dictionary.

▶ For translations of expressions like **I'm going to leave** / **go to London** / **learn to drive**, see the entry **going**.

Getting from A to B

Generally **go** is translated by **aller** (**!** + *être*):

we went to the cinema	= nous sommes allés au cinéma
to go to town | to school | to the market	= aller en ville | à l'école | au marché
to go to Brussels | to Germany | to Japan	= aller à Bruxelles | en Allemagne | au Japon
to go to the dentist's | the doctor's | the chemist's	= aller chez le dentiste | le médecin | le pharmacien
to go for a swim | for a coffee | for a walk	= aller nager | prendre un café | se promener

Translating verbs of movement in French

Moving in, out, back, away etc is usually translated using a single verb in French which takes **être**:

to go into a room	= entrer dans une pièce
to go away on vacation	= partir en vacances
to go back to work in France	= retourner travailler en France
to go home	= rentrer
to go outside	= sortir
to go upstairs	= monter

See also the phrasal verbs listed separately for further translations.

go meaning *to become*

There is often a single French verb to translate the structure **to go** + *adjective*:

to go pale	= pâlir
to go red	= rougir

but

the light went red	= le feu est passé au rouge

devenir + *adjective* is a useful alternative:

to go crazy	= devenir fou | folle
to go blind	= devenir aveugle

In polite inquiries

how's it going?	= comment ça va?
everything's going very well	= tout va très bien
how did the exam go?	= comment s'est passé l'examen?

Talking about time, money, food ...

the time goes so quickly	= le temps passe si vite
200 francs won't go far here	= on n'ira pas loin avec 200 francs ici
the money's | bread's | petrol's gone	= il n'y a plus d'argent | de pain | d'essence

Describing how (and if) something works

is the car going?	= est-ce que la voiture marche?
it's still not going	= ça ne marche toujours pas
to get the heating going	= mettre le chauffage en marche

grade *noun*
• (*a mark*)
  a grade = une note
• (*US English*) (*a class*)
  a grade = une classe
  he's in the eighth grade = il est en
    quatrième

grade school *noun* (*US English*)
  grade school = l'école primaire
  | **!** *Note that* école *is feminine.*

gradually *adverb*
= peu à peu

gram(me) *noun* ▶ 285 |
  a gram = un gramme

grammar *noun*
  grammar = la grammaire

grandchild *noun*
  a grandchild = un petit-fils/une petite-
    fille
  the grandchildren = les petits-enfants

granddaughter *noun*
  a granddaughter = une petite-fille

grandfather *noun*
  a grandfather = un grand-père

grandmother *noun*
  a grandmother = une grand-mère

grandparents *noun*
  grandparents = les grands-parents
    (*masculine*)

grandson *noun*
  a grandson = un petit-fils

grapefruit *noun*
  a grapefruit = un pamplemousse

grapes *noun*
  grapes = le raisin (*singular*)
  a bunch of grapes = une grappe de raisin

grass *noun*
  grass = l'herbe (*feminine*)
  (*in gardens*) = la pelouse
  to cut the grass = tondre la pelouse

grasshopper *noun*
  a grasshopper = une sauterelle

grateful *adjective*
= reconnaissant/reconnaissante
  I would be grateful if you could let me
    know = je vous serais reconnaissant de
    me prévenir

grave *noun*
  a grave = une tombe

gray (*US English*) ▶ **grey**

grease *noun*
  grease = la graisse

greasy *adjective*
= gras/grasse

great *adjective*
• (*stressing size, amount, importance*)
  = grand/grande (**!** *before the noun*)
  a great improvement = une grande
    amélioration
  to have great difficulty reading = avoir
    beaucoup de mal à lire
  the guide book was a great help = le
    guide a été très utile
• (*showing enthusiasm*)
  that's great! = c'est formidable!, c'est
    génial✶!
  I had a great time = je me suis bien amusé

Great Britain *noun* ▶ 218 |
  Great Britain = la Grande-Bretagne

great grandfather *noun*
  a great grandfather = un arrière-grand-
    père

great grandmother *noun*
  a great grandmother = une arrière-grand-
    mère

Greece *noun* ▶ 218 |
  Greece = la Grèce

greedy *adjective*
= gourmand/gourmande

Greek ▶ 275 |
1 *adjective*
= grec/grecque
2 *noun*
• (*the people*)
  the Greeks = les Grecs (*masculine*)
• (*the language*)
  Greek = le grec

green *adjective* ▶ 213 |
= vert/verte

greenhouse *noun*
  a greenhouse = une serre

grey (*British English*), **gray** (*US English*)
adjective ▶ 213 |
= gris/grise
  to have grey hair = avoir les cheveux gris

grill *verb*
= faire griller

grin *verb*
= sourire

grocer *noun* ▶ 315 |
  a grocer = un épicier/une épicière

grocery *noun* ▶ 315 |
  a grocery = une épicerie

ground *noun*
• the ground = le sol
  the ground is hard in winter = le sol est
    dur en hiver
  to throw papers on the ground = jeter des
    papiers par terre
  to get up off the ground = se lever
    (**!** + *être*)

✶ in informal situations

(land used for sports)
a sports ground = un terrain de sport

ground floor *noun* *(British English)*
the ground floor = le rez-de-chaussée

group *noun*
(a number of people)
a group = un groupe
(a band)
a (rock) group = un groupe (de rock)

grow *verb*
(to get big, strong) *(if it's a person, an animal)* = grandir
(if it's a plant) = pousser
(as a gardener, a farmer) = cultiver
to grow vegetables = cultiver des légumes
(to get long) = pousser
she's decided to let her hair grow = elle a décidé de se laisser pousser les cheveux
(to let grow)
to grow a beard = se laisser pousser la barbe
(to become) = devenir (**!** + *être*)
she's grown more cynical = elle est devenue plus cynique
to grow old = vieillir
(to increase in size)
the population will grow = la population va augmenter
grow up = grandir
when I grow up, I want to be a doctor = je veux être médecin quand je serai grand

grumble *verb*
= ronchonner

guard *noun*
(in a prison, at a bank)
a guard = un gardien/une gardienne
(in the army)
a guard = un garde
to be on guard = être de garde

guard dog *noun*
a guard dog = un chien de garde

guess *verb*
= deviner

guest *noun*
(a person invited to stay)
a guest = un invité/une invitée
(at a hotel)
a guest = un client/une cliente

guesthouse *noun*
a guesthouse = une pension de famille

guide
1 *noun*
(a person)
a (tour) guide = un guide
(British English) *(a Girl Guide)*
a guide = une guide
2 *verb*
= guider

guide book *noun*
a guide book = un guide

guided tour *noun*
a guided tour = une visite guidée

guilty *adjective*
= coupable
to feel guilty = culpabiliser

guinea pig *noun*
a guinea pig = un cochon d'Inde

guitar *noun* ▶ **290**|
a guitar = une guitare

gum *noun*
the gum = la gencive

gun *noun*
a gun *(a weapon)* = une arme à feu
(a rifle) = un fusil
(a revolver) = un revolver

gym *noun*
a gym = une salle de gym✶

gymnasium *noun*
a gymnasium = un gymnase

gymnastics *noun* ▶ **248**|
gymnastics = la gymnastique

gypsy *noun*
a gypsy = un gitan/une gitane

habit *noun*
a habit = une habitude

hail *noun*
hail = la grêle

hair *noun*
hair *(on the head)* = les cheveux *(masculine plural)*
(on the body) = les poils *(masculine plural)*

hairbrush *noun*
a hairbrush = une brosse à cheveux

hairdresser *noun* ▶ **315**|
a hairdresser = un coiffeur/une coiffeuse

hairdryer *noun*
a hairdryer = un sèche-cheveux

hairstyle *noun*
a hairstyle = une coiffure

half ▶ **317**|
1 *noun*
a half = une moitié
to cut a melon in half = couper un melon en deux
(in a game)
the first half = la première mi-temps

2 *adjective*
a half-litre of milk, half a litre of milk = un demi-litre de lait
3 *pronoun*
(*when talking about quantities, numbers*)
to spend half of one's pocket money = dépenser la moitié de son argent de poche
half the pupils speak French = la moitié des élèves parlent français
(*when talking about time, age*) ▶ **211**|, ▶ **187**|
an hour and a half = une heure et demie
he's three and a half = il a trois ans et demi
it's half (past) three (*British English*) = il est trois heures et demie
4 *adverb*
Sam's half French half Irish = Sam est moitié français moitié irlandais

half hour *noun* ▶ **356**|
a half hour = une demi-heure

half term *noun* (*British English*)
half term = les vacances de la mi-trimestre
| ! *Note that* vacances *is feminine plural.*

hall *noun*
(*in a house, an apartment*)
a hall = une entrée
(*for public events*)
a hall = une grande salle

ham *noun*
ham = le jambon

hamburger *noun*
a hamburger = un hamburger

hammer *noun*
a hammer = un marteau

hamster *noun*
a hamster = un hamster

hand *noun*
(*the part of the body*) ▶ **201**|
the hand = la main
he had a pencil in his hand = il avait un crayon à la main
to hold someone's hand = tenir quelqu'un par la main
(*help*)
a hand = un coup de main
(*on a clock or watch*)
a hand = une aiguille
(*when judging a situation or subject*)
on the one hand…, on the other… = d'un côté…, d'un autre côté…

handbag *noun*
a handbag = un sac à main

handball *noun* ▶ **248**|
handball = le handball

handicapped *adjective*
= handicapé/handicapée

handkerchief *noun*
a handkerchief = un mouchoir

handle *noun*
a handle = une poignée

handsome *adjective*
= beau/belle (! *before the noun*)
a handsome man = un bel homme

handwriting *noun*
handwriting = l'écriture (*feminine*)

handy *adjective*
(*practical*) = pratique
(*helpful*) = utile

hang *verb*
(*on a hook, a coat hanger, a line*)
to hang a picture (up) on the wall = accrocher un tableau au mur
to hang clothes (up) in a wardrobe = suspendre des vêtements dans une armoire
to hang clothes on a line = étendre du linge
(*to be attached*)
the portrait hangs over the piano = le portrait est accroché au-dessus du piano
to be hanging from the ceiling = être suspendu/suspendue au plafond
(*to kill*) = pendre
hang around
(*to wait*) = attendre
(*to waste time, to do nothing*) = traîner
hang on to = s'agripper à (! + *être*)
she was hanging on to the rope = elle s'agrippait à la corde
hang up
(*on a hook, a coat hanger, a line*)
to hang up one's coat = accrocher son manteau
to hang clothes up to dry = mettre des vêtements à sécher
your coat's hanging up in the hall = ton manteau est suspendu dans l'entrée
(*when phoning*) = raccrocher

hang-gliding *noun* ▶ **248**|
hang-gliding = le deltaplane

happen *verb*
(*to occur*) = se passer (! + *être*), arriver (! + *être*)
what happened? = qu'est-ce qui s'est passé?, qu'est-ce qui est arrivé?
the accident happened last week = l'accident est arrivé la semaine dernière
to happen again = se reproduire (! + *être*)
(*to affect someone*)
what happened to you? = qu'est-ce qui t'est arrivé?
something odd happened to me = il m'est arrivé quelque chose de bizarre

happy *adjective*
(*content*) = heureux/heureuse
to make someone happy = rendre
  quelqu'un heureux
they were happy to hear from you = ils
  ont été heureux d'avoir de tes nouvelles
he's happy with the language course = le
  cours de langue lui plaît
(*in greetings*)
Happy birthday! = Bon anniversaire!
Happy New Year! = Bonne année!

hard
1 *adjective*
(*firm, stiff*) = dur/dure
the ground is hard = le sol est dur
(*difficult*) = difficile
a hard question = une question difficile
it's not hard to change a light bulb = ce
  n'est pas difficile de changer une
  ampoule
it's hard to understand = c'est difficile à
  comprendre
I find it hard to concentrate = j'ai du mal à
  me concentrer
(*harsh, tough*)
a hard winter = un hiver rude
to be having a hard time = traverser une
  période difficile
(*severe*) = dur/dure, sévère
2 *adverb*
to work hard = travailler dur
they hit him hard = ils l'ont frappé fort
to try hard to concentrate = faire
  beaucoup d'efforts pour se concentrer

hardly *adverb*
= à peine
I hardly know them = je les connais à
  peine

hardware *noun*
hardware (*for computers*) = le matériel
  (informatique)

hard-working *adjective*
= travailleur/travailleuse

hare *noun*
a hare = un lièvre

harm *verb*
to harm someone = faire du mal à
  quelqu'un
to harm the environment = nuire à
  l'environnement

harmful *adjective*
= nocif/nocive

harmless *adjective*
= inoffensif/inoffensive

harp *noun* ▶ 290 |
a harp = une harpe

harvest *noun*
the harvest (*of wheat*) = la moisson
(*of fruit*) = la récolte
(*of grapes*) = la vendange

hat *noun*
a hat = un chapeau

hate *verb*
(*to feel a strong dislike for*)
to hate someone = détester quelqu'un
(*to feel hatred for*) = haïr

hatred *noun*
hatred = la haine

have
1 *verb*
▶ 258 | *See the boxed note on* **have** *for more
information and examples.*
(*to eat, to drink*)
to have a sandwich = manger un
  sandwich
to have a glass of wine = boire un verre de
  vin
to have dinner = dîner
(*to get*)
I had a letter from Bob yesterday = j'ai
  reçu une lettre de Bob hier
I'll let you have the money soon = je te
  donnerai l'argent bientôt
(*to hold or organize*)
to have a party = faire une fête
to have a competition = organiser un
  concours
(*to spend*) ▶ 237 |
we had a nice day at the beach = nous
  avons passé une journée agréable à la
  plage
I'll have a good time in Paris = je
  m'amuserai bien à Paris
(*to suffer*)
to have [flu | a headache | a toothache ...]
  = avoir [la grippe | mal à la tête | mal aux
  dents ...]
(*to get something done*)
to have the house painted = faire peindre
  la maison
she had her hair cut = elle s'est fait couper
  les cheveux
to have a baby = avoir un enfant
2 *auxiliary verb*

! *For a detailed note on the use of* **have** *as
an auxiliary verb, see the boxed note on*
have. *All verbs which don't take* **avoir** *as
an auxiliary verb are marked (***! + être***) in
this dictionary.*

you've seen her, haven't you? = tu l'as
  vue, n'est-ce pas?
he hasn't called, has he? = il n'a pas
  téléphoné, par hasard?
'I've no money'—'yes you have!' = 'je n'ai
  pas d'argent'—'mais si tu en as!'
3 to have to = devoir
I have to [study | pay | go home ...] = je dois
  [étudier | payer | rentrer ...]
you don't have to go back to France = tu
  n'es pas obligé de retourner en France

hay *noun*
hay = le foin

H

have

As an ordinary verb

● When **have** or **have got** is used as a verb meaning *possess*, it can generally be translated by **avoir**:

    I have (got) a car   = j'**ai** une voiture
    she has (got) a good memory = elle **a** une bonne mémoire
    they have (got) problems   = ils **ont** des problèmes

For examples and particular usages see the entry **have**; see also the entry **got**.

● **have** is also used with certain noun objects where the whole expression is equivalent to a verb: *to have dinner* = to dine; *to have a walk* = to walk; *to have a swim* = to swim. In such cases, the phrase is very often translated by the equivalent verb in French (*dîner, se promener, se baigner*).

As an auxiliary verb

● When used as an auxiliary in present perfect and past perfect tenses, **have** is normally translated by **avoir**:

    I have seen = j'**ai** vu
    I had seen = j'**avais** vu

● However, some verbs in French, especially verbs of movement and change of state (*aller, venir, descendre, mourir*), always take **être** in these tenses:

    he has left   = il **est** parti
    she's fallen = elle **est** tombée

In this case, remember the past participle agrees with the subject of the verb:

    she has gone   = elle **est** allée
    they had come back   = ils **étaient** revenus
    we had stayed at home = nous **étions** restés chez nous

If you are in doubt as to whether a verb conjugates with **être** or **avoir**, consult the French entry, where verbs taking **être** will be indicated like this: (**!** + *être*).

● Reflexive verbs (*se lever, se coucher*) always conjugate with **être**:

    she has fainted   = elle s'**est** évanouie
    have you had a rest? = est-ce que tu **t'es** reposé?
    he had fallen asleep = il s'**était** endormi
    I had changed my clothes = je m'**étais** changé

In this case, the past participle agrees with the reflexive pronoun only when the pronoun is a direct object. Otherwise there is no agreement:

    she has hurt herself = elle s'**est** fait mal
    I've washed my hair = je **me suis** lavé les cheveux
    he's broken his leg = il s'**est** cassé la jambe

to have (got) to

● **to have (got) to** meaning *must* is translated by either **devoir** or the impersonal construction **il faut que** + *subjunctive*:

    I have to leave now   = je **dois** partir maintenant
                             = **il faut que** je parte maintenant
    you've got to understand = tu **dois** comprendre
                             = **il faut que** tu comprennes

● In negative sentences, **not to have to** is usually translated by **ne pas être obligé / obligée de**:

    you don't have to go   = tu **n'es pas obligé d'**y aller
    we don't have to accept = nous **ne sommes pas obligés d'**accepter

▶ For **have** used with illnesses, see usage note **Illnesses, aches, and pains ▶ 266 ⟩**.

hazel adjective ▶ 213 |
= noisette (! never changes)

hazelnut noun
a hazelnut = une noisette

he pronoun
he = il
he's coming next week = il vient la
semaine prochaine
there he is = le voilà!
HE didn't write the letter = ce n'est pas lui
qui a écrit la lettre
I work in London but he doesn't = je
travaille à Londres mais lui non
he's a strange man = c'est un homme
bizarre

head
1 noun
(the part of the body) ▶ 201 |
the head = la tête
(the mind)
he's got it into his head that he's ugly = il
s'est mis dans la tête qu'il était laid
a head of cabbage = un chou
a head of lettuce = une laitue
(the person in charge)
the head = le responsable/la responsable,
le directeur/la directrice
a head of State = un chef d'État
2 verb
(to be in charge of)
to head a team = être à la tête d'une
équipe
(in soccer)
to head the ball = faire une tête
head for = se diriger vers (! + être)

headache noun ▶ 266 |
to have a headache = avoir mal à la tête
my headache's gone = mon mal de tête
est passé

headlamp, **headlight** noun
a headlamp = un phare

headline noun
a headline = un gros titre
to hit the headlines = faire la une des
journaux
the news headlines = les grands titres de
l'actualité

headquarters noun
the headquarters (of a company, a
business) = le siège social
(of an army) = le quartier général

headteacher noun ▶ 315 |
a headteacher = un directeur/une
directrice

health noun
health = la santé

healthy adjective
(in good health) = en bonne santé
(good for the health) = sain/saine

hear verb
to hear = entendre
he can't hear anything = il n'entend rien
I heard someone coming in = j'ai entendu
quelqu'un entrer
you can hear him practising the piano
= on l'entend qui travaille le piano
(to learn, to discover)
to hear the news = apprendre la nouvelle
I've heard about that school = j'ai
entendu parler de cette école
we've heard a lot about you = nous avons
beaucoup entendu parler de vous
(to listen to) = écouter
hear from = avoir des nouvelles de
have you heard from Cathy? = est-ce que
tu as eu des nouvelles de Cathy?
hear of = entendre parler de
I've never heard of the place = je n'ai
jamais entendu parler de cet endroit

heart noun
(part of the body) ▶ 201 |
the heart = le cœur
(the centre)
right in the heart of London = en plein
cœur de Londres
by heart = par cœur

heart attack noun ▶ 266 |
a heart attack = une crise cardiaque

heat
1 verb
= chauffer
2 noun
the heat = la chaleur
I can't stand the heat = je ne supporte pas
la chaleur
(on a cooker)
to cook at a low heat = faire cuire à feu
doux
(in a sporting contest)
a heat = une épreuve éliminatoire
heat up
(to cook) = faire chauffer
(to warm up again) = réchauffer

heater noun
a heater = un appareil de chauffage

heating noun
heating = le chauffage

heatwave noun
a heatwave = une vague de chaleur

heaven noun
heaven = le paradis

heavy adjective
(in weight) ▶ 285 | = lourd/lourde
(in quantity, intensity)
the traffic is very heavy = il y a beaucoup
de circulation
to be a heavy smoker = beaucoup fumer
to have a heavy cold = avoir un gros
rhume
(describing food) = lourd/lourde

H

it's very heavy today = il fait très lourd aujourd'hui

hedge noun
a hedge = une haie

hedgehog noun
a hedgehog = un hérisson

heel noun ▶ 201 |
the heel = le talon

height noun ▶ 285 |
height (of a person) = la taille
(of a building, a tree) = la hauteur
to be afraid of heights = avoir le vertige

helicopter noun
a helicopter = un hélicoptère

hell noun
hell = l'enfer

hello noun (also exclamation) ▶ 237 |
hello! (when greeting someone) = bonjour!
(on the phone) = allô!

helmet noun
a helmet = un casque

help
1 verb
to help = aider
to help someone to [walk | do the
housework | escape ...] = aider quelqu'un
à [marcher | faire le ménage | s'échapper ...]
the medicine helps to cure the illness = le
médicament aide à guérir la maladie
to help each other = s'aider, s'entraider
(! + être)
(at a meal)
to help oneself = se servir (! + être)
help yourselves! = servez-vous!
I can't help thinking about it = je ne peux
pas m'empêcher d'y penser
2 exclamation
help! = au secours!
3 noun
help (a helping hand) = l'aide (feminine)
(urgent assistance) = le secours
to ask someone for help = demander de
l'aide à quelqu'un
to shout for help = crier au secours
help out = donner un coup de main

helpful adjective
(ready to help) = serviable, aimable
(useful) = utile

helping noun
a helping = une portion

helpless adjective
(having no power)
= impuissant/impuissante
(because of weakness, ill health)
= impotent/impotente

✘ in informal situations

hen noun
a hen = une poule

her
1 pronoun

> ! Note that there is a boxed usage note at
> them. The entries me, him, her and us are
> modelled on this note where you will find
> detailed grammatical information and
> fuller explanations.

her = la (! l' + vowel or mute h)
I know her = je la connais
I don't know her = je ne la connais pas
do I know her? = est-ce que je la connais?
he's seen her = il l'a vue
he hasn't seen her = il ne l'a pas vue
has he seen her? = est-ce qu'il l'a vue?
catch her! = attrape-la!
help her! = aide-la!
don't help her! = ne l'aide pas!
don't hit her! = ne la frappe pas!
I gave the book to her = je lui ai donné le
livre
I didn't give the book to her = je ne lui ai
pas donné le livre
did I give the book to her? = est-ce que je
lui ai donné le livre?
her = lui
write to her! = écris-lui!
say it to her! = dis-le-lui!
don't show it to her! = ne le lui montre
pas!
her = elle
he did it for her = il l'a fait pour elle
it's her = c'est elle
stand in front of her = mets-toi devant elle
2 determiner
her = son/sa (+ singular)
= ses (+ plural)

> ! Note that sa becomes son before a
> vowel or mute h.

I hate her dog = je déteste son chien
what do you think of her house? = qu'est-
ce que tu penses de sa maison?
she licked her plate = elle a léché son
assiette
did you see all her CDs? = est-ce que tu as
vu tous ses disques compacts?
she broke her leg = elle s'est cassé la jambe

> ! Note that, when talking about parts of
> the body, son, sa, ses are not used. See
> the usage note on The human body
> ▶ 201 | for further examples.

herd noun
a herd = un troupeau

here adverb
(when talking about location) = ici
is it far from here? = est-ce que c'est loin
d'ici?
I'm up here = je suis là

(*when drawing attention*)
here's the post office = voici la poste
here they are = les voici
here's my telephone number = voici mon numéro de téléphone
here comes the train = voilà le train
here—take my pencil = tiens—prends mon crayon
(*in general statements*) = là
tell him I'm not here = dis-lui que je ne suis pas là
we're here to help you = nous sommes là pour vous aider

hers *pronoun*
the green pen is hers = le stylo vert est à elle
which bag is hers? = lequel de ces sacs est le sien?
my jacket is red but hers is green = ma veste est rouge mais la sienne est verte
my parents are younger than hers = mes parents sont plus jeunes que les siens

! Note that, when comparing objects, people, etc, one of the following translations—le sien, la sienne, les siens or les siennes—will be used. To know which one to use, find out whether the object, person, etc being described is masculine or feminine, singular or plural.

herself *pronoun*
(*when used as a reflexive pronoun*)
she wants to enjoy herself = elle veut s'amuser
she's cut herself with a knife = elle s'est coupée avec un couteau
(*when used for emphasis*)
she said it herself = elle l'a dit elle-même
she did it all by herself = elle l'a fait toute seule

hesitate *verb*
= hésiter

hi *exclamation*
hi! = salut*!

hiccups *noun*
to have hiccups = avoir le hoquet

hidden *adjective*
= caché/cachée

hide *verb*
(*to avoid showing*) = cacher
to hide documents from the police = cacher des documents à la police
(*to avoid being seen*) = se cacher (! + *être*)

hi-fi *noun*
a hi-fi = une chaîne hi-fi

high
1 *adjective* ▶ 285
(*having a great height*) = haut/haute
the mountains are high = les montagnes sont hautes
(*describing a level, a price, a speed*) = élevé/élevée
prices are high = les prix sont élevés
the train travels at high speed = le train roule très vite

(*describing a standard, grades*)
the standard is high = le niveau est élevé
to get high grades = avoir de très bonnes notes
(*describing a voice*) = aigu/aiguë
2 *adverb*
don't go any higher = ne montez pas plus haut

high rise block *noun*
a high rise block = une tour d'habitation

high school *noun*
a high school (*in the US*) = un établissement secondaire
(*in Britain*) = un lycée

hijack *verb*
= détourner

hike *verb*
to go hiking = faire de la randonnée

hiking *noun* ▶ 248
hiking = la randonnée

hill *noun*
a hill = une colline
(*a rise in the road*) = une pente

him *pronoun*

! Note that there is a boxed usage note at them. The entries me, him, her and us are modelled on this note where you will find detailed grammatical information and fuller explanations.

him = le (! l' + vowel or mute h)
I know him = je le connais
I don't know him = je ne le connais pas
do I know him? = est-ce que je le connais?
she's seen him = elle l'a vu
she hasn't seen him = elle ne l'a pas vu
has she seen him? = est-ce qu'elle l'a vu?
catch him! = attrape-le!
help him! = aide-le!
don't help him! = ne l'aide pas!
don't hit him! = ne le frappe pas!
I gave the book to him = je lui ai donné le livre
I didn't give the book to him = je ne lui ai pas donné le livre
did I give the book to him? = est-ce que je lui ai donné le livre?
him = lui
write to him! = écris-lui!
say it to him! = dis-le-lui!
don't show it to him! = ne le lui montre pas!
him = lui
he did it for him = il l'a fait pour lui
it's him = c'est lui
stand in front of him = mets-toi devant lui

himself *pronoun*
(*when used as a reflexive pronoun*)
he wants to enjoy himself = il veut s'amuser
he's cut himself with a knife = il s'est coupé avec un couteau

(when used for emphasis)
he said it himself = il l'a dit lui-même
he did it all by himself = il l'a fait tout seul

hip *noun* ▶ **201**
the hip = la hanche

hippopotamus, **hippo** *noun*
a hippopotamus = un hippopotame

hire *verb*
(to employ) = embaucher
(British English) *(to rent)* = louer
to hire a car = louer une voiture
(to lend for a fee) = louer
they hire (out) the skates = ils louent les patins

his
1 *determiner*
his = son/sa *(+ singular)*
= ses *(+ plural)*

! Note that **sa** becomes **son** before a vowel or mute h.

I hate his dog = je déteste son chien
what do you think of his house? = qu'est-ce que tu penses de sa maison?
he licked his plate = il a léché son assiette
did you see all his CDs? = est-ce que tu as vu tous ses disques compacts?
he broke his arm = il s'est cassé le bras

! Note that, when talking about parts of the body, **son, sa, ses** are not used. See the usage note on **The human body** ▶ **201** for further examples.

2 *pronoun*
the blue pen is his = le stylo bleu est à lui
which house is his? = laquelle de ces maisons est la sienne?
my shirt is white but his is yellow = ma chemise est blanche mais la sienne est jaune
my brother is taller than his = mon frère est plus grand que le sien

! Note that, when comparing objects, people, etc, one of the following translations—**le sien, la sienne, les siens** or **les siennes**—will be used. To know which one to use, find out whether the object, person, etc which is being described is masculine or feminine, singular or plural.

history *noun*
history = l'histoire *(feminine)*

hit
1 *verb*
(to strike) = frapper
to hit someone on the head = frapper quelqu'un à la tête
to hit one's head on a chair = se cogner la tête contre une chaise

(to crash into)
to hit a wall = heurter un mur
to hit a pedestrian = renverser un piéton
2 *noun*
a hit *(a song)* = un tube✶
(a film, a play) = un succès
hit back = riposter
to hit someone back = rendre un coup à quelqu'un

hitchhike *verb*
= faire de l'auto-stop, faire du stop✶

hitchhiker *noun*
a hitchhiker = un auto-stoppeur/une auto-stoppeuse

hoarse *adjective*
to be hoarse = être enroué/enrouée

hobby *noun*
a hobby = un passe-temps

hockey *noun* ▶ **248**
hockey = le hockey

hold
1 *verb*
to hold = tenir
he held some coins in his hand = il avait quelques pièces dans la main
(to arrange)
to hold a competition = organiser un concours
the party will be held in the school = la fête aura lieu dans l'école
(to keep or hide) = détenir
to hold someone hostage = garder quelqu'un en otage
(to keep back) = garder
to hold a seat for someone = garder une place pour quelqu'un
(other uses)
to hold the world record = détenir le record mondial
to hold someone responsible = tenir quelqu'un pour responsable
to hold, to hold the line = patienter
2 *noun*
to get hold of the ball = attraper le ballon
to get hold of someone *(to find)* = trouver quelqu'un
(by phone) = joindre quelqu'un
hold on
(to wait) = attendre
hold on tight! = tiens-toi bien!
hold on to = s'agripper à (! + *être*)
hold up
(to raise) = lever
to hold up one's hand ≈ lever le doigt
(to delay)
to hold someone up = retarder quelqu'un
to hold up the traffic = ralentir la circulation
(to rob) = attaquer

hole *noun*
a hole = un trou

✶ in informal situations

holiday *noun*
(*British English*) (*a vacation*)
a holiday = des vacances (*feminine plural*)
to go on holiday = partir en vacances
(*a national or religious festival*)
a (public) holiday = un jour férié
(*British English*) (*time taken off work*)
a day's holiday = un jour de congé
to take two weeks' holiday = prendre
quinze jours de congé

Holland *noun* ▶ 218 |
Holland = la Hollande

holly *noun*
holly = le houx

home
1 *noun*
a home (*a place to live*) = un logement
(*a house*) = une maison
to leave home = quitter la maison
to work from home = travailler à domicile
(*for elderly, ill or disabled people*)
a home for handicapped children = un
établissement pour enfants handicapés
an old people's home = une maison de
retraite
2 *adverb*
! *Note that* chez soi *changes to* chez moi,
chez lui, chez eux, *etc depending on the
person whose home is being talked
about.*

to go home (*to one's house*) = retourner à
la maison, rentrer (chez soi)
(*to one's home country*) = rentrer (dans son
pays)
on my way home = en rentrant chez moi
to be home (*from school, work*) = être
rentré/rentrée
I can take you home = je peux te
raccompagner chez toi
3 at home
(*in one's house*) = à la maison, chez soi
she's working at home = elle travaille à la
maison, elle travaille chez elle
he lives at home = il habite chez ses
parents
to feel at home = se sentir à l'aise
make yourselves at home = faites comme
chez vous
(*when talking about a sports team*) = à
domicile

homeless *adjective*
to be homeless = être sans abri, être sans
logement

homesick *adjective*
to be homesick (*when abroad*) = avoir le
mal du pays

homework *noun*
homework = les devoirs (*masculine plural*)

homosexual *noun*
a homosexual = un homosexuel/une
homosexuelle

honest *adjective*
honest = honnête
(*frank, sincere*) = franc/franche
to be honest, I'd rather stay here = à vrai
dire, je préfère rester ici

honestly *adverb*
= franchement, honnêtement

honey *noun*
honey = le miel

honeymoon *noun*
a honeymoon = un voyage de noces

hood *noun*
(*to cover the head*)
a hood = un capuchon
(*US English*) (*of a car*)
the hood = le capot

hoof *noun*
a hoof = un sabot

hook *noun*
(*for hanging clothes, pictures*)
a hook = un crochet
(*for fishing*)
a hook = un hameçon

hooligan *noun*
a hooligan = un voyou, un vandale
a football hooligan = un hooligan

hoover *verb* (*British English*)
to hoover the house = passer l'aspirateur
dans la maison

hop *verb*
= sauter à cloche-pied

hope
1 *verb*
= espérer
I hope you don't mind = j'espère que cela
ne vous dérange pas
I hope she remembers to come = j'espère
qu'elle pensera à venir
! *Note that, when talking about the future,*
espérer que *is followed by the future
tense.*

we hope to meet lots of people = nous
espérons rencontrer beaucoup de
monde
I hope so = j'espère que oui
2 *noun*
hope = l'espoir (*masculine*)
to give up hope = abandonner tout espoir

hopeless *adjective*
(*without hope of success*)
= désespéré/désespérée
(*without any ability*) = nul/nulle
to be hopeless at cooking = être
incapable de faire la cuisine

horn *noun*
(*on a car, a bus*)
a horn = un klaxon
to blow a horn = klaxonner

H

(of an animal)
a horn = une corne
(an instrument) **▶ 290 |**
a horn = un cor

horoscope noun
the horoscope = l'horoscope (masculine)

horrible adjective
= affreux/affreuse

horror film noun
a horror film = un film d'épouvante

horse noun
a horse = un cheval
he likes horses = il aime les chevaux

horseracing noun **▶ 248 |**
horseracing = les courses (feminine plural)

horseriding noun **▶ 248 |**
horseriding = l'équitation (feminine)

hospital noun
a hospital = un hôpital
he's still in (the) hospital = il est toujours
à l'hôpital
to be taken to (the) hospital = être
hospitalisé/hospitalisée

host noun
a host = un hôte

hostage noun
a hostage = un otage

hostel noun
a hostel = un foyer

hostess noun
a hostess = une hôtesse

hot adjective
(very warm) = chaud/chaude
to be hot, to feel hot = avoir chaud
I'm very hot = j'ai très chaud
it's too hot in the office = il fait trop chaud
au bureau
a hot meal = un repas chaud
(strong, with a lot of spices)
a hot mustard = une moutarde forte
a very hot dish = un plat très épicé

hot air balloon noun
a hot air balloon = une montgolfière

hot dog noun
a hot dog = un hot dog

hotel noun
a hotel = un hôtel

hour noun **▶ 211 |, ▶ 356 |**
an hour = une heure
I earn two pounds an hour = je gagne
deux livres (de) l'heure

house noun
a house = une maison
to go to someone's house = aller chez
quelqu'un
the bike is at my house = le vélo est chez
moi

housewife noun **▶ 315 |**
a housewife = une femme au foyer

housework noun
to do the housework = faire le ménage

housing estate (British English),
housing development (US English)
noun
a housing estate = une cité (ouvrière)

hovercraft noun
a hovercraft = un aéroglisseur

how adverb
(in what way) = comment
how did you find us? = comment est-ce
que tu nous as trouvés?
I know how [to swim | to ride a horse | to cook
a curry …] = je sais [nager | monter à cheval |
préparer un curry …]
(in polite questions)
how are you? = comment allez-vous?,
comment vas-tu?
how is your sister? = comment va ta sœur?
how was your holiday? = est-ce que tes
vacances se sont bien passées?
(in questions requiring specific information)
how long will it take? = combien de temps
faudra-t-il?
how tall are you? = combien mesures-tu?
how old is he? = quel âge a-t-il?
(when making a suggestion)
how would you like to eat out? = est-ce
que ça te dirait d'aller au restaurant?
how about going to the cinema tonight?
= et si on allait au cinéma ce soir?

however adverb
(nevertheless) = toutefois, cependant
however hard I try, I can't understand
grammar = j'ai beau essayer, je ne
comprends pas la grammaire

how many ▶ 317 |
1 pronoun
= combien
how many do you want? = combien en
voulez-vous?
how many of you are there? = combien
êtes-vous?
2 determiner
= combien de
how many children are going on the trip?
= combien d'enfants vont participer à
l'excursion?

how much ▶ 317 |
1 pronoun
= combien
how much does it come to? = ça fait
combien?
how much is the jacket? = combien coûte
la veste?
2 determiner
= combien de
how much money do you have left?
= combien d'argent est-ce qu'il te reste?

huge adjective
= énorme

human being noun
a human being = un être humain

humour (British English), **humor** (US English) noun
humour = l'humour (masculine)
to have a sense of humour = avoir le sens de l'humour

hundred number ▶ 187 |
one hundred, a hundred = cent
three hundred = trois cents
five hundred and fifty francs = cinq cent cinquante francs
about a hundred people = une centaine de personnes

Hungary noun ▶ 218 |
Hungary = la Hongrie

hungry adjective
to be hungry = avoir faim
I'm very hungry = j'ai très faim

hunt verb ▶ 248 |
= chasser
to go hunting = aller à la chasse

hurdles noun ▶ 248 |
the hurdles = la course de haies

hurrah, hurray noun (also exclamation)
hurrah! = hourra!

hurry
1 verb
= se dépêcher (**!** + être)
hurry home! = dépêche-toi de rentrer!
to hurry someone = bousculer quelqu'un
2 noun
to be in a hurry = être pressé/pressée
there's no hurry = ça ne presse pas
hurry up = se dépêcher (**!** + être)

hurt verb
(to injure)
to hurt oneself = se faire mal (**!** + être)
to hurt one's leg = se faire mal à la jambe
(to be painful)
my throat hurts = j'ai mal à la gorge
that hurts = ça fait mal
(to upset) = blesser
to hurt someone's feelings = blesser quelqu'un

husband noun
a husband = un mari

I i

I pronoun
I = je (**!** j' + vowel or mute h)
I've got to go = je dois m'en aller
here I am = me voilà
I didn't do it = ce n'est pas moi qui l'ai fait
I'M the one who does all the work = c'est moi qui fais tout le travail
she drives but I don't = elle conduit mais moi non

ice noun
(frozen water)
ice = la glace
(on roads)
ice = le verglas
(in a drink)
ice = des glaçons (masculine plural)

ice cream noun
ice cream = la glace
an ice cream = une glace

ice hockey noun ▶ 248 |
ice hockey = le hockey sur glace

ice rink noun
an ice rink = une patinoire

ice-skate noun
an ice-skate = un patin à glace

ice-skating noun ▶ 248 |
ice-skating = le patin à glace

icing noun
icing = le glaçage

idea noun
an idea = une idée
what a good idea! = quelle bonne idée!
I've no idea how much it costs = je ne sais pas du tout combien ça coûte

identity card noun
an identity card = une carte d'identité

idiot noun
an idiot = un idiot/une idiote

if conjunction
= si
if you like = si tu veux
if it rains, we won't go = s'il pleut, nous n'irons pas
if I were rich, I would travel = si j'étais riche, je voyagerais
I wonder if they'll come = je me demande s'ils vont venir
if I were you, I'd refuse = à ta place, je refuserais

Illnesses, aches, and pains

Where does it hurt?

where does it hurt?	= où est-ce que ça vous fait mal?
his leg hurts	= il a mal à la jambe

(Do not confuse, **faire mal à quelqu'un** with **faire du mal à quelqu'un**, which means *to harm somebody*.)

Note that with **avoir mal à** French uses the definite article (**le, la, les,** or **l'**) with the part of the body, where English has a possessive, hence:

*he **has a pain in his** leg*	= il **a mal à la** jambe
*his head **was hurting***	= il **avait mal à la** tête

Accidents

*she broke **her** leg*	= elle s'est cassé **la** jambe
*I twisted **my** ankle*	= je me suis foulé **la** cheville

Being ill

French mostly uses the definite article with the name of an illness:

*to have flu	measles*	= avoir **la** grippe / **la** rougeole

but

to have cancer	= avoir **un** cancer

Falling ill

French has no general equivalent of **to get**. However, where English can use **catch**, French can use **attraper**:

*to **catch** measles*	= **attraper** la rougeole
*to **catch** a cold*	= **attraper** un rhume

Treatment

to be treated for rabies	= **se faire soigner contre** la rage
to take tablets for indigestion	= **prendre des comprimés contre** l'indigestion
to be operated on for cancer	= **être opéré d'**un cancer

---

ignore *verb*
  to ignore a person = faire semblant de ne
  pas voir quelqu'un
  to ignore a problem = ne prêter aucune
  attention à un problème

ill *adjective*
  = malade

illegal *adjective*
  = illégal/illégale

illness *noun*
  an illness = une maladie

imagination *noun*
  imagination = l'imagination (*feminine*)
  to have imagination = avoir de
  l'imagination

imagine *verb*
  = imaginer

imitate *verb*
  = imiter

immediately *adverb*
  = immédiatement

impatient *adjective*
  = impatient/impatiente
  to get impatient = s'impatienter (**!** + *être*)

import *verb*
  = importer

important *adjective*
  = important/importante
  it is important to eat well = il est
  important de bien manger

impossible *adjective*
  = impossible
  it's impossible to argue with him = c'est
  impossible de discuter avec lui

impress *verb*
  = impressionner

impression *noun*
  an impression = une impression
  to make a good impression = faire bonne
  impression

improve *verb*
(*to make better*) = améliorer
to improve living conditions = améliorer
les conditions de vie
to improve one's French = se
perfectionner en français
(*to get better*) = s'améliorer (**!** + *être*)

improvement *noun*
an improvement = une amélioration

in

> **!** *Often* in *occurs in combinations with verbs, for example:* drop in, fit in, move in *etc. To find the correct translations for this type of verb, look up the separate dictionary entries at* drop, fit, move *etc.*

1 *preposition*
(*inside*) = dans
in the house = dans la maison
I read it in the newspaper = je l'ai lu dans
le journal
there's a letter in the envelope = il y a une
lettre dans l'enveloppe
there's a letter in it = il y a une lettre
dedans
the woman in the photograph = la femme
sur la photo
(*at*) = à
I learned German in school = j'ai fait de
l'allemand à l'école
in the countryside = à la campagne
(*when talking about countries or cities*)
to live [in Ireland | in Japan | in Paris ...]
= vivre [en Irlande | au Japon | à Paris ...]
(*dressed in*) = en
in a skirt = en jupe
to be dressed in black = être
habillé/habillée en noir
(*showing the way in which something is
done*) = en
written in French = écrit en français
we paid in cash = nous avons payé en
espèces
they were sitting in a circle = ils étaient
assis en cercle
in ink = à l'encre
(*during*)
in October = en octobre
in the night = pendant la nuit
in the morning = le matin
(*within*)
I'll be ready in ten minutes = je serai prêt
en dix minutes
she'll be back in half an hour = elle sera de
retour dans une demi-heure
(*other uses*)
to stay in the rain = rester sous la pluie
she's in her twenties = elle a entre vingt
et trente ans
one in ten = un sur dix
to cut an apple in two = couper une
pomme en deux

2 *adverb*
(*at home, available*) = là
tell her I'm not in = dis-lui que je ne suis
pas là
(*arrived*)
the train is in = le train est en gare
the tide is in = c'est la marée haute

inch *noun* ▶ **285** |
an inch = un pouce
> **!** *Note that an inch = 2.54 cm.*

include *verb*
= comprendre
service is included in the bill = le service
est compris dans la note

including *preposition*
= y compris
**they were all invited, including the
children** = ils étaient tous invités, y
compris les enfants

income *noun*
an income = un revenu

income tax *noun*
income tax = l'impôt sur le revenu
> **!** *Note that* impôt *is masculine.*

inconvenient *adjective*
it's an inconvenient place to meet = c'est
un endroit peu pratique pour se
retrouver
an inconvenient time = un moment
inopportun
I hope that's not inconvenient for you
= j'espère que cela ne vous dérange pas

increase
1 *verb*
= augmenter
to increase in value = augmenter de
valeur
to increase by 10% = augmenter de 10%
2 *noun*
an increase = une augmentation

incredible *adjective*
= incroyable

independent *adjective*
= indépendant/indépendante

India *noun* ▶ **218** |
= l'Inde (*feminine*)

Indian ▶ **275** |
1 *adjective*
= indien/indienne
2 *noun*
(*from India*)
the Indians = les Indiens (*masculine*)
(*from North America*)
the Indians = les Indiens d'Amérique

indicate *verb*
= indiquer

indifferent *adjective*
= indifférent/indifférente

indigestion noun ▶ 266 |
  to have indigestion = avoir mal à
  l'estomac

individual
1 adjective
  = individuel/individuelle
2 noun
  an individual = un individu

indoor adjective
  = couvert/couverte
  an indoor swimming pool = une piscine
  couverte

indoors adverb
  = à l'intérieur

industrial adjective
  = industriel/industrielle

industry noun
  industry = l'industrie (feminine)

inevitable adjective
  = inévitable

infant school noun (British English)
  an infant school = une école maternelle

infection noun
  an infection = une infection

influence
1 noun
  an influence = une influence
  to have influence = avoir de l'influence
2 verb
  (to persuade) = influencer
  (to make a strong impression on)
  to influence someone = avoir une
  influence sur quelqu'un
  to be too influenced by someone = se
  laisser trop influencer par quelqu'un

inform verb
  to inform the police of an accident
  = signaler un accident à la police
  to keep someone informed = tenir
  quelqu'un au courant

informal adjective
  (describing a person, a person's manner)
  = simple
  (describing a word, a language)
  = familier/familière
  (describing a discussion or an interview)
  = informel/informelle

information noun
  a piece of information = un
  renseignement
  information = des renseignements

information desk noun
  the information desk = l'accueil
  (masculine)

information technology noun
  information technology = l'informatique
  (feminine)

ingredient noun
  an ingredient = un ingrédient

inhabitant noun
  an inhabitant = un habitant/une habitante

injection noun
  an injection = une piqûre
  to give someone an injection = faire une
  piqûre à quelqu'un

injured adjective
  = blessé/blessée

injury noun
  an injury = une blessure

ink noun
  ink = l'encre (feminine)

innocent adjective
  = innocent/innocente

inquiry noun
  an inquiry = une enquête

insect noun
  an insect = un insecte

inside
1 preposition
  = à l'intérieur de
  inside the house = à l'intérieur de la
  maison
2 adverb
  = à l'intérieur
  he's inside = il est à l'intérieur
  I looked inside = j'ai regardé à l'intérieur
  let's bring the chairs inside = rentrons les
  chaises
3 noun
  the inside = l'intérieur (masculine)
  the inside of the palace = l'intérieur du
  palais
4 adjective
  = intérieur/intérieure
5 inside out = à l'envers
  to put one's shirt on inside out = mettre sa
  chemise à l'envers

inspect verb
  (if it's an official) = inspecter
  (if it's a conductor) = contrôler

inspector noun
  (of a school)
  an inspector = un inspecteur/une
  inspectrice
  (on a bus, a train)
  an inspector = un contrôleur/une
  contrôleuse
  (in the police)
  a police inspector = un inspecteur de
  police

instantly adverb
  = immédiatement

instead

1 instead of
(rather than) = au lieu de
he hired a van instead of a car = il a loué une camionnette au lieu d'une voiture
instead of working he watched TV = au lieu de travailler il a regardé la télévision
(in place of) = à la place de
use oil instead of butter = utilisez de l'huile à la place du beurre
his wife came instead of him = sa femme est venue à sa place
2 *adverb*
I don't feel like going to the cinema—let's stay at home instead = je n'ai pas envie d'aller au cinéma–restons plutôt à la maison

instruction *noun*
an instruction = une instruction
to give someone instructions to check the baggage = donner l'ordre à quelqu'un de vérifier les bagages
the instructions for use = le mode d'emploi

instrument *noun* ▶ 290 |
an instrument = un instrument
to play an instrument = jouer d'un instrument

insult *verb*
= insulter

insurance *noun*
insurance = l'assurance *(feminine)*

insure *verb*
= assurer
to insure a car against theft = assurer une voiture contre le vol

intelligent *adjective*
= intelligent/intelligente

intend *verb*
he intends [to leave | to learn Spanish | to travel abroad ...] = il a l'intention [de partir | d'apprendre l'espagnol | d'aller à l'étranger ...]

intense *adjective*
= intense

intensive care *noun*
to be in intensive care = être en soins intensifs

interest
1 *noun*
(enthusiasm)
interest = l'intérêt *(masculine)*
to have an interest in music = s'intéresser à la musique
(financial)
interest = l'intérêt *(masculine)*
2 *verb*
= intéresser

interested *adjective*
= intéressé/intéressée
to be interested [in politics | in sport | in painting ...] = s'intéresser [à la politique | au sport | à la peinture ...]
are you interested? = ça t'intéresse?

interesting *adjective*
= intéressant/intéressante

interfere *verb*
(to get involved in)
to interfere in someone's business = se mêler des affaires de quelqu'un
(to have a bad effect on)
it's going to interfere with his work = ça va l'empêcher de travailler

intermission *noun*
an intermission = un entracte

international *adjective*
= international/internationale

interpreter *noun* ▶ 315 |
an interpreter = un interprète/une interprète

interrupt *verb*
= interrompre

interval *noun*
(in time or at a location)
an interval = un intervalle
at regular intervals = à intervalles réguliers
(British English) *(during a play, a show)*
an interval = un entracte

interview
1 *noun*
an interview *(for a job)* = un entretien
(with a journalist) = une interview
2 *verb*
to interview someone *(if it's an employer)* = faire passer un entretien à quelqu'un
(if it's a journalist) = interviewer quelqu'un
(if it's the police) = interroger quelqu'un

intimidate *verb*
= intimider

into *preposition*
(when talking about a location) = dans
to go into the garden = aller dans le jardin
to get into a car = monter dans une voiture
to get into bed = se mettre au lit
(indicating a change) = en
to translate a letter into French = traduire une lettre en français
to turn someone into a frog = transformer quelqu'un en grenouille

introduce *verb*
(to bring in) = introduire
to introduce a law = introduire une loi
(when people meet) = présenter
he introduced me to Peter = il m'a présenté à Peter

it

- When **it** is used as a subject pronoun to stand for a specific object (or animal), **il** or **elle** is used in French depending on whether the object referred to is masculine or feminine:

  'where is the book / chair?' — *'it's* = 'où est le livre / la chaise?' — 'il / elle est
  in the kitchen'   dans la cuisine'

- When **it** is used as an object pronoun, it is translated by **le** or **la** (**l'** before a vowel or mute h) depending on whether the object referred to is masculine or feminine:

  it's my book / my chair and I want it = c'est mon livre / ma chaise et je le / la veux

  Note that the object pronoun normally comes before the verb in French and that in tenses like the perfect and past perfect, the past participle agrees with it:

  I liked his shirt, did you notice it? = sa chemise m'a plu, est-ce que tu l'as remarquée?
                         sa chemise m'a plu, l'as-tu remarquée?

  In imperatives the pronoun comes after the verb:

  it's my book, give it to me = c'est mon livre, donne-**le**-moi*

  * Note the hyphens.

  However, in negative commands, the pronoun comes before the verb:

  it's my book, don't give it to him! = c'est mon livre, ne **le** lui donne pas!

- When **it** is used after a preposition in English, the two words (*preposition* + **it**) are often translated by one word in French. If the preposition would normally be translated by **de** in French (**of**, **about**, **from** etc), the preposition + **it** = **en**:

  we talked a lot about it = on **en** a beaucoup parlé
  have you heard of it? = est-ce que tu **en** as entendu parler?

  If the preposition would normally be translated by **à** in French (**to**, **in**, **at** etc), the preposition + **it** = **y**:

  they went to it = ils **y** sont allés

  For translations of **it** following prepositions not normally translated by **de** or **à** (*above, under, over, etc*) consult the entry for the preposition.

- When **it** is used in expressions like *it's raining, it will snow* etc, the translation will always be **il**: **il** pleut, **il** va neiger. See the entry for the verb in question.

  ▶ For translations of *it's Friday, it's five o'clock* etc, consult the usage notes on **Dates, days, and months** and **The clock**.

(*on radio or television*) = présenter
to introduce a programme = présenter
    une émission

invade *verb*
= envahir

invent *verb*
= inventer

invention *noun*
an invention = une invention

investigate *verb*
to investigate a crime = enquêter sur un
    crime

investigation *noun*
an investigation = une enquête

invisible *adjective*
= invisible

invitation *noun*
an invitation = une invitation

invite *verb*
= inviter
to invite someone to a party = inviter
    quelqu'un à une fête

involved *adjective*
to be involved in an accident = avoir un
    accident
to get involved in someone's problems
    = se mêler des problèmes de quelqu'un

Ireland *noun* ▶ **218**
Ireland = l'Irlande (*feminine*)

Irish ▶ **275**
1 *adjective*
= irlandais/irlandaise
2 *noun*
(*the people*)
the Irish = les Irlandais (*masculine
    plural*)
(*the language*)
Irish = l'irlandais (*masculine*)

iron
1 *noun*
iron = le fer
an iron = un fer à repasser
2 *verb*
= repasser

island *noun*
an island = une île

it *pronoun*
▶ **270** *See the boxed note on* it *for more information and examples.*
where is it? (*if it's an object*) = où est-il/elle?
(*if it's a place*) = où est-ce?
who is it? = qui est-ce?
it's me = c'est moi
it's a nice house = c'est une jolie maison
it is [difficult | easy | complicated ...] = c'est [difficile | facile | compliqué ...]
it doesn't matter = ça ne fait rien
it's easy to make a mistake = il est facile de se tromper
it's [cold | warm | mild ...] = il fait [froid | chaud | doux ...]
I've heard about it = j'en ai entendu parler
did you go to it? = est-ce que tu y es allé?

Italian ▶ **275**
1 *adjective*
= italien/italienne
2 *noun*
(*the people*)
the Italians = les Italiens (*masculine*)
(*the language*)
Italian = l'italien (*masculine*)

Italy *noun* ▶ **218**
Italy = l'Italie (*feminine*)

itchy *adjective*
my leg is itchy = j'ai la jambe qui me démange

its *determiner*
its = son/sa (+ *singular*)
= ses (+ *plural*)
! *Note that* sa *becomes* son *before a vowel or mute h.*

its nose = son nez
its tail = sa queue
its ear = son oreille
its eyes = ses yeux

itself *pronoun*
(*when used as a reflexive pronoun*)
the cat's going to hurt itself = le chat va se faire mal
(*when used for emphasis*)
the car itself was not damaged = la voiture elle-même n'a pas été endommagée
the heating comes on by itself = le chauffage se met en marche tout seul

jacket *noun*
a jacket = une veste
(*gathered at the waist*) = un blouson

jail *noun*
a jail = une prison

jam *noun* (*British English*)
jam = la confiture

Jamaica *noun* ▶ **218**
Jamaica = la Jamaïque

January *noun* ▶ **222**
January = janvier (*masculine*)

Japan *noun* ▶ **218**
Japan = le Japon

Japanese ▶ **275**
1 *adjective*
= japonais/japonaise
2 *noun*
(*the people*)
the Japanese = les Japonais (*masculine plural*)
(*the language*)
japanese = le japonais

jaw *noun* ▶ **201**
the jaw = la mâchoire

jazz *noun*
jazz = le jazz

jealous *adjective*
= jaloux/jalouse
he is jealous of her = il est jaloux d'elle

jeans *noun*
jeans = un jean (*singular*)

jeer *verb*
to jeer someone = se moquer de quelqu'un

jelly *noun*
(*US English*) (*jam*)
jelly = la confiture
(*British English*) (*a dessert*)
jelly = la gelée de fruits

Jesus *noun*
Jesus = Jésus

jet *noun*
a jet = un jet, un avion à réaction

jewellery (*British English*), **jewelry** (*US English*) *noun*
a piece of jewellery = un bijou
jewellery = les bijoux (*plural*)

Jewish *adjective*
= juif/juive

jigsaw puzzle *noun*
 a jigsaw puzzle = un puzzle

job *noun*
 (*work*)
 a job = un emploi
 to look for a job = chercher un emploi
 (*a task*)
 a job = un travail, une tâche

jogging *noun* ▶ 248
 jogging = le jogging

join *verb*
 (*meet up with*) = rejoindre
 I'll join you in half an hour = je vous
  rejoins dans une demi-heure
 (*become a member of*)
 to join a club = s'inscrire dans un club
 to join a company = entrer dans une
  entreprise
join in
 to join in a game = participer à un jeu

joke
1 *noun*
 a joke = une plaisanterie, une blague✗
2 *verb*
 = plaisanter

journalist *noun* ▶ 315
 a journalist = un journaliste/une
  journaliste

journey *noun*
 a journey = un voyage
 to go on a journey = partir en voyage

joy *noun*
 joy = la joie

judge
1 *noun* ▶ 315
 a judge = un juge
2 *verb*
 = juger

judo *noun* ▶ 248
 judo = le judo

jug *noun*
 a jug = un pichet

juice *noun*
 juice = le jus
 fruit juice = le jus de fruits

July *noun* ▶ 222
 July = juillet (*masculine*)

jump *verb*
 = sauter
 the children were jumping on the bed
  = les enfants sautaient sur le lit
 to jump across the stream = franchir le
  ruisseau d'un bond
 to jump rope = sauter à la corde
 to jump out of the window = sauter par la
  fenêtre

 to jump the queue (*British English*) = passer
  devant tout le monde

jumper *noun* (*British English*)
 a jumper = un pull

June *noun* ▶ 222
 June = juin (*masculine*)

junior high school *noun* (*US English*)
 a junior high school ≈ un collège

junior school *noun* (*British English*)
 a junior school = une école primaire

jury *noun*
 the jury = le jury

just¹ *adverb*
 (*very recently*)
 I have just [arrived | seen her | received the
  letter …] = je viens [d'arriver | de la voir | de
  recevoir la lettre …]
 I had just turned on the TV = je venais
  d'allumer la télévision
 (*at this or that very moment*) = juste
 I was just about to phone you = j'étais
  juste sur le point de t'appeler, j'allais
  t'appeler
 you've just missed him = il vient juste de
  partir
 I arrived just as he was leaving = je suis
  arrivé juste au moment où il partait
 (*only*) = juste
 just two days ago = il y a juste deux jours
 he's just a child = ce n'est qu'un enfant
 (*barely*) = tout juste
 I got there just in time = je suis arrivé juste
  à temps
 she's just 18 = elle a tout juste 18 ans
 (*when comparing*)
 she is just as intelligent as he is = elle est
  tout aussi intelligente que lui
 (*immediately*) = juste
 just before the weekend = juste avant le
  week-end

just² *adjective*
 = juste

justice *noun*
 justice = la justice

Kk

kangaroo *noun*
 a kangaroo = un kangourou

karate *noun* ▶ 248
 karate = le karaté

✗ in informal situations

keen *adjective*
a keen student = un étudiant/une
étudiante enthousiaste
to be keen on swimming = aimer la
natation

keep *verb*
= garder
to keep someone in (the) hospital
= garder quelqu'un à l'hôpital
we keep the wine in the cellar = nous
gardons le vin dans la cave
this sweater will keep you warm = ce pull
te tiendra chaud
to keep someone waiting = faire attendre
quelqu'un
(*to delay*) = retenir
what kept you? – qu'est-ce qui t'a retenu?
I won't keep you long = je n'en ai pas pour
longtemps
(*to put*) = ranger
where do you keep the cups? = où est-ce
que tu ranges les tasses?
(*not to break, not to reveal*)
to keep a promise = tenir une promesse
to keep a secret = garder un secret
(*to continue*)
to keep [walking | talking | running ...]
= continuer à [marcher | parler | courir ...]
to keep going = continuer
to keep calm = rester calme
(*if it's food*) = se conserver (**!** + *être*)
keep away = ne pas s'approcher (**!** + *être*)
keep away from the fire! = ne t'approche
pas du feu!
keep back = retenir
he kept the children back after school = il
a retenu les enfants après l'école
keep on
to keep on [talking | walking | singing ...]
= continuer à [parler | marcher | chanter ...]
keep out
to keep out of the sun = ne pas se mettre
au soleil
to keep the rain out = empêcher la pluie
d'entrer
keep up = suivre
to keep up with the other pupils = suivre
en classe

kerb *noun* (*British English*)
the kerb = le bord du trottoir

kettle *noun*
a kettle = une bouilloire

key *noun*
a key = une clé

keyhole *noun*
a keyhole = un trou de serrure

kick *verb*
to kick someone = donner un coup de
pied à quelqu'un
he kicked the ball = il a donné un coup de
pied dans le ballon
kick off = donner le coup d'envoi

kick out
to kick someone out = mettre quelqu'un à
la porte

kid *noun*
(*a child*)
a kid = un enfant/une enfant, un
gamin/une gamine*****
(*a young goat*)
a kid = un chevreau

kidnap *noun*
= enlever

kill *verb*
= tuer
to kill oneself = se suicider (**!** + *être*)

kilo *noun* ▶ **285** |
a kilo = un kilo

kilogram(me) *noun* ▶ **285** |
a kilogram = un kilogramme

kilometre (*British English*), **kilometer**
(*US English*) *noun* ▶ **285** |
a kilometre = un kilomètre

kind
1 *noun*
it's a kind of [fish | novel | hotel ...] = c'est
une sorte [de poisson | de roman | d'hôtel ...]
what kind of film is it? = c'est quel genre
de film?
what kind of car is it? = qu'est-ce que c'est
comme voiture?
2 *adjective*
= gentil/gentille

king *noun*
a king = un roi

kingdom *noun*
a kingdom = un royaume

kiss
1 *verb*
to kiss someone = embrasser quelqu'un
to kiss (each other) = s'embrasser
(**!** + *être*)
2 *noun*
a kiss = un baiser

kitchen *noun*
a kitchen = une cuisine

kite *noun*
a kite = un cerf-volant

kitten *noun*
a kitten = un chaton

knee *noun* ▶ **201** |
the knee = le genou

kneel down *verb*
= se mettre à genoux (**!** + *être*)

knife *noun*
a knife = un couteau

knit *verb*
= tricoter

K

knock
1 *verb*
to knock on the door = frapper à la porte
2 *noun*
a knock = un coup
to get a knock on the head = recevoir un coup sur la tête
knock down
(*in an accident*) = renverser
(*to demolish*) = démolir
knock out
(*to make unconscious*) = assommer
(*in a contest*) = éliminer
knock over = renverser

knot *noun*
a knot = un nœud

know *verb*
(*when talking about facts, information*) = savoir
he thinks he knows everything = il croit tout savoir
I know why he phoned = je sais pourquoi il a téléphoné
she knows how to swim = elle sait nager
I don't know the French word for it = je ne sais pas comment ça se dit en français
let me know = tenez-moi au courant
does he know about the party? = est-ce qu'il est au courant pour la soirée?
to know all about art = s'y connaître en art
(*when talking about people, places*) = connaître
do you know Paris? = est-ce que tu connais Paris?
to get to know someone = faire la connaissance de quelqu'un

knowledge *noun*
knowledge = les connaissances (*feminine plural*)

L1

laboratory *noun*
a laboratory = un laboratoire

lace *noun*
(*the material*)
lace = la dentelle
(*for shoes*)
a lace = un lacet
to tie one's laces = lacer ses chaussures

lack
1 *noun*
a lack [of food | of money | of interest …] = un manque [de nourriture | d'argent | d'intérêt …]

2 *verb*
= manquer de
he lacks confidence = il manque d'assurance

ladder *noun*
a ladder = une échelle

lady *noun*
a lady = une dame

lake *noun*
a lake = un lac

lamb *noun*
a lamb = un agneau

lamp *noun*
a lamp = une lampe

lampshade *noun*
a lampshade = un abat-jour

land
1 *noun*
(*for farming, as opposed to the sea*)
land = la terre
(*property*)
a piece of land = un terrain
to own land = posséder des terres
(*the countryside*)
the land = la campagne
2 *verb*
(*to fall*) = tomber (**!** + *être*)
(*if it's a plane*) = atterrir
(*if it's a passenger*) = débarquer

landscape *noun*
a landscape = un paysage

language *noun*
a language = une langue
foreign languages = les langues étrangères
bad language = le langage grossier

language laboratory *noun*
a language laboratory = un laboratoire de langues

large *adjective*
(*big*) = grand/grande (**!** *before the noun*)
a large garden = un grand jardin
a large house = une grande maison
(*when talking about numbers*) = gros/grosse (**!** *before the noun*)
a large sum of money = une grosse somme
a large population = une forte population
(*bulky*) = gros/grosse (**!** *before the noun*)
a large parcel = un gros paquet

last
1 *adjective*
= dernier/dernière
last week = la semaine dernière
that's the last time I saw her = c'est la dernière fois que je l'ai vue
2 *adverb*
(*most recently*)
when I was last here = la dernière fois que je suis venu ici

Languages and nationalities

Languages

The names of languages in French are always written with a small letter, not a capital as in English. French almost always uses the definite article **le** or **l'** with languages:

to learn French   = apprendre **le** français

except after **en**:

*to translate a word **into** French* = traduire un mot **en** français

and it may be omitted with **parler**:

to speak French   = parler français / parler le français

but

*to speak **in** French*   = parler **en** français

When **French** means **in French** or **of the French**, it is translated by **français**:

*the **French** language*   = la langue **française**

If you want to make it clear you mean **in French** and not **from France**, use **en français**:

*a **French** book*   = un livre **en français**

When **French** means **relating to French** or **about French**, it is translated by **de français**:

*a **French** class*   = une classe **de français**

Nationalities

Adjectives indicating nationality **never** have capitals in French:

*a **French** student*   = un étudiant **français** / une étudiante **française**

Nouns have capitals in French when they mean *a person of a specific nationality*:

*a **Frenchman** | a **Frenchwoman*** = un **Français** / une **Française**
French** people or the **French = les **Français** (*masculine plural*)

English sometimes has a special word for a person *of a specific nationality*; in French, the same word is almost always either an adjective (no capitals) or a noun (with capitals):

Spanish   = espagnol
*a **Spaniard***   = un **Espagnol** / une **Espagnole**
*the **Spaniards***   = les **Espagnols** (*masculine plural*)

You can use either the adjective or the noun to refer to nationality:

*he | she is **French***   = il est **français** / elle est **française**
                                     = c'est un **Français** / c'est une **Française**

L

(*at the end*) = en dernier
I'll do the dishes last (of all) = je ferai la
  vaisselle en dernier
(*in final position*)
he came last in the race = il est arrivé
  dernier dans la course
3 *pronoun*
  the last = le dernier/la dernière
  they were the last to arrive = ils ont été les
    derniers à arriver
  the night before last = avant-hier soir
4 *verb*
  = durer
  the film lasts two hours = le film dure
    deux heures

late
1 *adverb*
  (*far into the day or night*) = tard
  late in the afternoon = tard dans l'après-
    midi
  it's getting late = il se fait tard

(*not on time*) = en retard
to arrive half an hour late = arriver avec
  une demi-heure de retard
2 *adjective*
  = en retard
  to be late for work = arriver en retard au
    travail
  the train was two hours late = le train a eu
    deux heures de retard
  to make someone late = retarder
    quelqu'un

later *adverb*
  = plus tard
  I'll call back later = je rappellerai plus tard
  see you later! = à plus tard!

latest
1 *adjective*
  = dernier/dernière (**!** *before the noun*)
  the latest news = les dernières nouvelles
2 **at the latest** = au plus tard

Latin noun
Latin = le latin

laugh
1 verb
= rire
to laugh at a joke = rire d'une plaisanterie
to make someone laugh = faire rire
quelqu'un
to laugh at someone = se moquer de
quelqu'un
2 noun
a laugh = un rire

laundry noun
the laundry = le linge (sale)
to do the laundry = faire la lessive

law noun
(a set of rules in a country)
the law = la loi
to obey the law = respecter la loi
it's against the law = c'est interdit par la
loi
(a rule)
a law = une loi
(as a subject)
law = le droit

lawn noun
a lawn = une pelouse

lawnmower noun
a lawnmower = une tondeuse à gazon

lawyer noun ▶ 315 |
a lawyer = un avocat/une avocate

lay verb
(to put) = poser, mettre
lay some newspapers on the floor = mets
des journaux par terre
to lay the table = mettre le couvert
(of a chicken)
to lay an egg = pondre un œuf
lay down = poser, mettre
he laid the tray down on the table = il a
posé le plateau sur la table
lay off = licencier

lazy adjective
= paresseux/paresseuse

lead¹ verb
(to guide) = mener, conduire
this road will lead you to the village
= cette route vous mènera au village
(in a match) = mener
(in a race) = être en tête
to lead a busy life = mener une vie active
(to have as a result)
to lead to an accident = entraîner un
accident

lead² noun
lead = le plomb

leader noun
a leader (of a political party) = un leader,
un dirigeant
(of a state) = un chef d'État

leaf noun
a leaf = une feuille

leak verb
(if it's a container) = fuir
the pipe leaks = il y a une fuite dans le
tuyau
(if it's a boat, shoes) = prendre l'eau

lean
1 verb
(to support oneself)
to lean against the wall = s'appuyer contre
le mur
(to put)
to lean a bicycle against the wall
= appuyer un vélo contre le mur
to lean out of the window = se pencher par
la fenêtre
2 adjective
= maigre
lean back = se pencher en arrière
(! + être)
lean forward = se pencher en avant
(! + être)
lean on = s'appuyer sur (! + être)

learn verb
= apprendre
to learn how to drive = apprendre à
conduire

leash noun
a leash = une laisse

least
1 determiner
the least
= le moins de
they have the least money = ce sont eux
qui ont le moins d'argent
2 pronoun
it was the least I could do! = c'était la
moindre des choses!
3 adverb
the least = le moins/la moins (+ singular)
= les moins (+ plural)
the least expensive shop = le magasin le
moins cher
the least difficult question = la question la
moins difficile
4 at least
(at the minimum) = au moins
he's at least thirty = il a au moins trente
ans
(when expressing some doubt) = du moins
he's gone out—at least, I think so = il est
sorti—du moins, il me semble

leather noun
leather = le cuir

leave verb
(to go away from) = quitter
to leave school = quitter l'école
she left her husband = elle a quitté son
mari

(*to go away*) = partir (**!** + *être*)
he left the next day = il est parti le
 lendemain
(*to go out of*) = sortir de (**!** + *être*)
she left the room = elle est sortie de la
 pièce
(*to allow to remain*) = laisser
leave your coat here = laisse ton manteau
 ici
she left the window open = elle a laissé la
 fenêtre ouverte
(*to put, to give*) = laisser
he didn't leave a message = il n'a pas
 laissé de message
she left him some money = elle lui a laissé
 de l'argent
(*to put off*) = laisser
leave it until tomorrow = laisse ça pour
 demain
(*to remain*)
there's nothing left = il ne reste rien
we've got ten minutes left = il nous reste
 dix minutes
(*other uses*)
I left them to clean the windows = je les ai
 laissés nettoyer les fenêtres
leave behind = laisser
 he left his belongings behind = il a laissé
  ses affaires
leave out
 (*not to show or talk about*) (*by accident*)
  = oublier
 (*deliberately*) = omettre
 (*to exclude*) = exclure
 to feel left out = se sentir exclu/exclue
leave over
 there was not much left over = il ne restait
  plus grand-chose
 there is some food left over = il reste un
  peu de nourriture

lecture *noun*
 a lecture (*to students*) = un cours
  magistral
 (*to the public*) = une conférence

left
1 *noun*
 the left = la gauche
 the first street on the left = la première rue
  à gauche
2 *adjective*
 = gauche
 his left hand = sa main gauche
3 *adverb*
 = à gauche
 to turn left = tourner à gauche

leg *noun*
 (*of a person*) ▶ **201** |
 the leg = la jambe
 (*of animals*)
 the leg = la patte
 (*of meat*)
 a leg of lamb = un gigot d'agneau

legal *adjective*
 = légal/légale

leisure *noun*
 leisure = les loisirs (*masculine plural*)

leisure centre (*British English*),
leisure center (*US English*) *noun*
 a leisure centre = un centre de loisirs

lemon *noun*
 a lemon = un citron

lemonade *noun*
 lemonade = la limonade

lend *verb*
 = prêter
 to lend someone money = prêter de
  l'argent à quelqu'un

length *noun* ▶ **285** |
 (*in measurements*)
 length = la longueur
 length (*of a book, a film, a list*) = la
  longueur
 (*of an event*) = la durée

leopard *noun*
 a leopard = un léopard

less ▶ **317** |
1 *determiner*
 = moins de
 less [money | food | time …] = moins
  [d'argent | de nourriture | de temps …]
 I have less work than he does = j'ai moins
  de travail que lui
2 *pronoun*
 = moins
 to cost less = coûter moins cher
 he reads less than she does = il lit moins
  qu'elle
 they have less than you = ils en ont
  moins que toi

 ! *Note that it is necessary to use* **en**,
 *which might be translated as 'of it', with
 pronouns like* **less**. *See also* **another, a
 few, a lot** *etc for this use of* **en**.

3 *adverb*
 = moins
 we travel less in winter = nous voyageons
  moins l'hiver
4 *preposition*
 (*minus*) = moins
5 less and less = de moins en moins
 less and less often = de moins en moins
  souvent
6 less than = moins de
 in less than half an hour = en moins d'une
  demi-heure

lesson *noun*
 a lesson = un cours
 a riding lesson = une leçon d'équitation

let¹ *verb*
 (*when making suggestions*)
 let's go home = rentrons
 let's go! = allons-y!

L

(*to allow*) = laisser
to let someone in = laisser entrer
  quelqu'un
he let me help him = il m'a laissé l'aider
she lets him do what he likes = elle le
  laisse faire ce qu'il veut
he's letting his hair grow = il se laisse
  pousser les cheveux
let down = décevoir
let go
  (*to stop holding*) = lâcher prise
  he let go of me = il m'a lâché
  (*to release*) = relâcher
  he let the prisoners go = il a relâché les
    prisonniers
let in
  (*to a room or house*) = faire entrer
  he let me in = il m'a fait entrer
  to let in the rain = laisser entrer la pluie
let out
  (*to allow to go out*) = laisser sortir
  let me out! = laisse-moi sortir!
  to let out a scream = laisser échapper un
    cri
let through
  to let someone through = laisser passer
    quelqu'un

let² *verb* (*British English*)
  = louer

letter *noun*
  a letter = une lettre

letter box *noun* (*British English*)
  a letter box = une boîte aux lettres

lettuce *noun*
  a lettuce = une laitue

level
1 *noun*
  a level = un niveau
2 *adjective*
  = plat/plate

library *noun*
  a library = une bibliothèque

licence (*British English*), **license** (*US English*) *noun*
  a licence = un permis

license plate *noun* (*US English*)
  a license plate = une plaque
    minéralogique

lick *verb*
  = lécher

lid *noun*
  a lid = un couvercle

lie
1 *verb*
  (*on the ground, on a bed*) = s'allonger
  (**!** + *être*)
  he lay down on the sofa = il s'est allongé
    sur le canapé
  he was lying on the sofa = il était allongé
    sur le canapé

(*to be situated*) = se trouver (**!** + *être*)
(*not to tell the truth*) = mentir
2 *noun*
  a lie = un mensonge
  to tell a lie = mentir
lie around = traîner
  he always leaves his keys lying around
    = il laisse toujours traîner ses clés
lie down = s'allonger (**!** + *être*)

life *noun*
  life = la vie
  a way of life = un mode de vie

lifestyle *noun*
  a lifestyle = un style de vie

lift
1 *verb*
  to lift one's arm = lever le bras
  to lift a lid = soulever un couvercle
2 *noun*
  (*British English*) (*an elevator*)
  a lift = un ascenseur
  (*in a car*)
  to give someone a lift to the station
    = conduire quelqu'un à la gare
lift up = soulever

light
1 *noun*
  (*from the sun, moon*)
  light = la lumière
  (*in a room, on a machine*)
  a light = une lumière
  to switch on a light = allumer
  (*for traffic*)
  the lights are green = le feu est au vert
  (*in a street*)
  a light = un réverbère
  have you got a light? = est-ce que vous
    avez du feu?
2 *adjective*
  (*not dark*) ▶ **213** = clair/claire
  it's still light outside = il fait encore jour
    dehors
  a light blue dress = une robe bleu clair
  (*not heavy*) = léger/légère
3 *verb*
  = allumer
  he lit a cigarette = il a allumé une
    cigarette
  to light a fire = faire un feu

light bulb *noun*
  a light bulb = une ampoule

lighthouse *noun*
  a lighthouse = un phare

lightning *noun*
  a flash of lightning = un éclair

like¹ *preposition*
  = comme
  people like you and me = des gens comme
    toi et moi
  what's it like? = c'est comment?

like² *verb*
(*when expressing an interest*) = aimer
I like [swimming | reading | dancing ...]
= j'aime (bien) [nager | lire | danser ...]
I like it! = ça me plaît!
how do you like America? = est-ce que
l'Amérique te plaît?
(*when expressing a wish*) = vouloir, aimer
I'd like coffee please = je voudrais un café
s'il vous plaît
I'd like to live here – j'aimerais vivre ici

limit *noun*
a limit = une limite

line
1 *noun*
a line = une ligne
a straight line = une ligne droite
(*US English*) (*a queue*)
a line = une queue
to stand in line = faire la queue
(*a row*)
a line = une rangée
the line is bad = la ligne est mauvaise
2 *verb*
to be lined with trees = être bordé/bordée
d'arbres

link *verb*
(*by train*) = relier
to link Paris to Brussels = relier Paris à
Bruxelles
(*to make a connection between*) = lier
the two murders are linked = les deux
meurtres sont liés

lion *noun*
a lion = un lion

lip *noun*
a lip = une lèvre

lipstick *noun*
lipstick = le rouge à lèvres

list *noun*
a list – une liste

listen *verb*
= écouter
to listen to someone = écouter quelqu'un

litre (*British English*), **liter** (*US English*)
noun
a litre = un litre

little¹
1 *determiner*
= peu de
little [food | wine | money ...] = peu [de
nourriture | de vin | d'argent ...]
there is very little time = il y a très peu de
temps
2 *pronoun*
a little = un peu
I only ate a little = je n'en ai mangé qu'un
peu

! *Note that it is necessary to use* en,
which might be translated as 'of it', *with
pronouns like* a little. *See also* a lot, more,
none, *etc for this use of* en.

3 *adverb*
= peu
4 a little (bit) = un peu
5 little by little = peu à peu

little² *adjective*
= petit/petite (**!** *before the noun*)

live¹ *verb*
(*to have one's home*) = vivre, habiter
he lives in London = il habite à Londres, il
vit à Londres
(*to be alive*) = vivre
that's not enough to live on = ça ne suffit
pas pour vivre

live² *adjective*
(*alive*) = vivant/vivante
(*of a match, a show*) = en direct

lively *adjective*
= vivant/vivante

living room *noun*
a living room = une salle de séjour

load *noun*
(*on a truck, being carried*)
a load = un chargement
loads of money = beaucoup d'argent

loaf *noun*
a loaf (of bread) = un pain

loan *noun*
a loan (*money lent*) = un prêt
(*money borrowed*) = un emprunt

lobster *noun*
a lobster = un homard

local *adjective*
a local newspaper = un journal local
the local people = les gens du coin

lock
1 *verb*
= fermer à clé
she locked the door = elle a fermé la porte
à clé
2 *noun*
a lock = une serrure
a bicycle lock = un antivol
lock in
to lock someone in = enfermer quelqu'un
to lock oneself in = s'enfermer (**!** + *être*)

locker *noun*
a locker = un casier

logical *adjective*
= logique

London *noun* ▶ 218 |
= Londres

lonely *adjective*
= seul/seule

long

1 *adjective* ▶ **285**
= long/longue
a long letter = une longue lettre
to have long hair = avoir les cheveux longs
the film is two hours long = le film dure
deux heures
I haven't seen him for a long time = ça fait
longtemps que je ne l'ai pas vu
2 *adverb*
= longtemps
long ago = il y a longtemps
you can stay as long as you like = tu peux
rester aussi longtemps que tu veux
I won't be long = je n'en ai pas pour
longtemps
3 as long as = à condition que
as long as the weather is nice = à
condition qu'il fasse beau

! *Note that the subjunctive is used after* à
condition que.

look

1 *verb*
= regarder
to look at a picture = regarder un tableau
to look out of the window = regarder par
la fenêtre
(to appear)
to look tired = avoir l'air fatigué/fatiguée
to look well = avoir bonne mine
he looks young = il fait jeune
she looks like her mother = elle ressemble
à sa mère
what does he look like? = il est comment?
2 *noun*
a look = un regard
look after = s'occuper de (**!** + *être*)
to look after a child = s'occuper d'un
enfant
look down
(to lower one's eyes) = baisser les yeux
to look down on someone = regarder
quelqu'un de haut
look for = chercher
he is looking for a job = il cherche un
emploi
look forward to
I am looking forward to meeting her
= j'attends avec impatience le plaisir de
faire sa connaissance
look onto = donner sur
my bedroom looks onto the garden = ma
chambre donne sur le jardin
look out = faire attention
look through
to look through a book = feuilleter un
livre
look up
to look up a word in a dictionary
= chercher un mot dans un dictionnaire
(to raise one's eyes) = lever les yeux

loose *adjective*
(describing clothes) = ample
(describing a screw) = desserré/desserrée

lorry *noun* (*British English*)
a lorry = un camion

lose *verb*
= perdre

lost *adjective*
= perdu/perdue
to get lost = se perdre (**!** + *être*)

lot *pronoun* ▶ **317**
a lot = beaucoup
he eats a lot = il mange beaucoup
a lot [of money | of time | of books ...]
= beaucoup [d'argent | de temps | de livres ...]
there's not a lot left = il n'en reste pas
beaucoup

! *Note that it is necessary to use* en,
which may be translated as 'of it' *or* 'of
them', *with pronouns like* a lot. *See also*
another, a few, any *etc for this use of* en.

lottery *noun*
a lottery = une loterie

loud *adjective*
= fort/forte
to talk in a loud voice = parler fort

loudspeaker *noun*
a loudspeaker = un haut-parleur

lounge *noun*
a lounge = un salon

love

1 *verb*
(when talking about people) = aimer
to love each other = s'aimer (**!** + *être*)
(when talking about things, activities)
= adorer
2 *noun*
love = l'amour (*masculine*)
to be in love = être amoureux/amoureuse
to make love = faire l'amour

lovely *adjective*
(beautiful) = beau/belle (**!** *before the noun*)
a lovely apartment = un bel appartement
you've got lovely eyes = tu as de beaux
yeux
(very nice, kind) = charmant/charmante

low

1 *adjective*
= bas/basse
to speak in a low voice = parler à voix
basse
2 *adverb*
= bas
to turn the lights down low = baisser les
lumières

lower *verb*
= baisser

loyal *adjective*
= loyal/loyale

✱ in informal situations

luck *noun* ▶ **237**
luck = la chance
good luck! = bonne chance!
to bring someone (good) luck = porter
bonheur à quelqu'un

lucky *adjective*
to be lucky = avoir de la chance

lunch *noun*
lunch = le déjeuner

lung *noun*
the lung = le poumon

Luxembourg *noun* ▶ **218**
Luxembourg = le Luxembourg

luxury
1 *noun*
luxury = le luxe
2 *adjective*
a luxury hotel = un hôtel de luxe

Mm

machine *noun*
a machine = une machine

mad *adjective*
(*crazy*) = fou/folle
to go mad = devenir fou/folle
(*very angry*) = furieux/furieuse
to be mad about someone = être fou/folle✱
de quelqu'un

magazine *noun*
a magazine = un magazine

magic *adjective*
= magique

maiden name *noun*
a maiden name = un nom de jeune fille

mail
1 *noun*
(*the postal system*)
the mail = la poste
(*letters*)
mail = le courrier
2 *verb* (*US English*)
to mail a letter to someone = envoyer une
lettre à quelqu'un

mailbox *noun* (*US English*)
a mailbox = une boîte aux lettres

mailman *noun* ▶ **315** (*US English*)
a mailman = un facteur

main *adjective*
= principal/principale

main course *noun*
a main course = un plat principal

major
1 *adjective*
= majeur/majeure
a major event = un événement majeur
2 *noun*
a major = un commandant

majority *noun*
a majority = une majorité

make *verb*

> **!** Note that the word **make** can often be
> translated by **faire**. This entry covers the
> most frequent uses of **make** but to find
> translations for other expressions like *to
> make a mess, to make a mistake, to make
> sure etc, look up the entries at* **mess,
> mistake, sure** *etc.*

to make = faire
to make [the bed | a film | some coffee ...]
= faire [le lit | un film | du café ...]
to make room = faire de la place
to make a phone call = passer un coup de
fil
to make friends = se faire des amis
(**!** + *être*)
to make breakfast = préparer le petit
déjeuner
to be made of [gold | metal | wood ...] = être
en [or | métal | bois ...]
to be made in France = être
fabriqué/fabriquée en France
(*to cause a particular reaction*)
to make someone [happy | ill | jealous ...]
= rendre quelqu'un [heureux | malade |
jaloux ...]
to make someone [annoyed | tired |
sleepy ...] = [agacer | fatiguer | endormir ...]
quelqu'un
to make someone [cry | laugh | eat ...]
= faire [pleurer | rire | manger ...] quelqu'un
to make someone wait = faire attendre
quelqu'un
(*to earn*)
to make a lot of money = gagner
beaucoup d'argent
to make a living = gagner sa vie
to make a profit = faire un bénéfice
make do = faire avec
make out = faire
to make out a list = faire une liste
to make a cheque out to someone = faire
un chèque à quelqu'un
make up
(*to be friends again*) = se réconcilier
(**!** + *être*)
to make up an excuse = inventer un
prétexte
to make up a parcel = faire un paquet

make-up *noun*
make-up = le maquillage
to wear make-up = se maquiller (**!** + *être*)

male *adjective*
(*in biology*) = mâle
(*relating to men*) = masculin/masculine

M

man noun
a man = un homme
a single man = un célibataire
man = l'homme

manage verb
(to run) = gérer
to manage to finish one's homework
= réussir à finir ses devoirs

manager noun ▶ 315 |
a manager (of a company, a bank, a
project) = un directeur/une directrice
(of a shop) = un gérant/une gérante
(of a football team) = un manager

manner noun
a manner = une attitude

manners noun
manners = les manières (feminine)
it's bad manners not to say hello = c'est
impoli de ne pas dire bonjour

manufacture verb
= fabriquer

many ▶ 317 |
1 determiner
(a lot of) = beaucoup de
were there many tourists? = est-ce qu'il y
avait beaucoup de touristes?
there weren't many people there = il n'y
avait pas beaucoup de monde
(when used with how, too, so, as)
how many cases have you got?
= combien de valises avez-vous?
you eat too many chips = tu manges trop
de frites
there are so many things to do here = il y
a tant de choses à faire ici
I got as many presents as you did = j'ai
reçu autant de cadeaux que toi
2 pronoun
are there many left? = est-ce qu'il en reste
beaucoup?
I've got too many = j'en ai trop
take as many as you like = prends-en
autant que tu veux

! Note that it is necessary to use en,
which might be translated as 'of them',
with pronouns like many. See also
another, a few, a lot etc for this use of en.

many (of them) speak English = beaucoup
(d'entre eux) parlent anglais

map noun
a map (of a country or region) = une carte
(of a town or a transport system) = un plan

marble noun
marble = le marbre

marbles noun ▶ 248 |
marbles = les billes (feminine)

march verb
(in the army) = marcher au pas
(in a demonstration) = manifester

March noun ▶ 222 |
March = mars (masculine)

margarine noun
margarine = la margarine

mark
1 noun
a mark (on a surface) = une tache
(on a person's body) = une marque
to leave marks on the table = laisser des
taches sur la table
(British English) (a grade)
a mark = une note
to get good marks = avoir de bonnes
notes
2 verb
(to stain) = tacher
to mark the homework = corriger les
devoirs
(to indicate) = indiquer

marker noun
a marker (a pen) = un marqueur
(a felt-tip pen) = un feutre

market noun
(the place)
a market = un marché
a flea market = un marché aux puces
(the system)
the market = le marché
the job market = le marché du travail

marmalade noun
marmalade = la confiture d'oranges

marriage noun
marriage = le mariage

married adjective
= marié/mariée
to be married to someone = être
marié/mariée à quelqu'un

marry verb
to marry someone = se marier avec
quelqu'un (! + être)

marsh noun
a marsh = un marécage

masculine adjective
= masculin/masculine

mashed potatoes noun
mashed potatoes = la purée de pommes
de terre

mask noun
a mask = un masque

mat noun
a mat = un (petit) tapis

---

* in informal situations

match
1 *noun*
(*British English*) (*a game*)
a match = un match
a football match = un match de football
(*a matchstick*)
a match = une allumette
2 *verb*
the shoes match the belt = les chaussures
sont assorties à la ceinture

mate *noun* (*British English*)
a mate = un copain/une copine

material *noun*
a material = un tissu, une étoffe

math (*US English*), maths (*British English*) *noun*
math(s) = les maths (*feminine plural*)

mathematics *noun*
mathematics = les mathématiques
(*feminine plural*)

matter
1 *noun*
what's the matter? = qu'est-ce qu'il y a?
what's the matter with her? = qu'est-ce
qu'elle a?
2 *verb*
does it really matter? = est-ce que c'est
vraiment important?
it doesn't matter = ça ne fait rien, ça n'a
pas d'importance

maximum
1 *adjective*
the maximum price = le prix maximum
a maximum temperature of 80 degrees
= une température maximale de 80
degrés
2 *noun*
the maximum = le maximum

may *verb*
(*when talking about a possibility*)
they may be able to come = ils pourront
peut-être venir
she may not have seen him = elle ne l'a
peut-être pas vu
it may rain = il risque de pleuvoir
(*when asking for or giving permission*)
may I come in? = est-ce que je peux
entrer?, puis-je entrer?
you may sit down = vous pouvez vous
asseoir

May *noun* ▶ 222 |
May = mai (*masculine*)

maybe *adverb*
= peut-être

mayor *noun* ▶ 315 |
a mayor = un maire

me *pronoun*
! Note that there is a boxed usage note at
them. The entries me, him, her *and* us *are*
modelled on this note where you will find
detailed grammatical information and
fuller explanations.

me = me (! m' + *vowel or mute h*)
they know me = ils me connaissent
they don't know me = ils ne me
connaissent pas
do they know me? = est-ce qu'ils me
connaissent?
he's seen me = il m'a vu
he hasn't seen me = il ne m'a pas vu
has he seen me? = est-ce qu'il m'a vu?
help me! = aide-moi!
hold me! = tiens-moi!
don't bother me! = ne m'embête pas!
don't hit me! = ne me frappe pas!
she gave the book to me = elle m'a donné
le livre
she didn't give the book to me = elle ne
m'a pas donné le livre
did she give the book to me? = est-ce
qu'elle m'a donné le livre?
write to me! = écris-moi!
say it to me! = dis-le-moi!
don't show it to me! = ne me le montre
pas!
me = moi
he did it for me = il l'a fait pour moi
it's me = c'est moi
stand in front of me = mets-toi devant moi

meal *noun*
a meal = un repas

mean
1 *verb*
to mean = vouloir dire
what does that mean? = qu'est-ce que ça
veut dire?
what does the word 'bête' mean? = que
veut dire le mot 'bête'?
(*to have as a result*)
it means giving up my job = ça veut dire
que je dois abandonner mon travail
(*to intend*)
I meant to order a pizza = je voulais
commander une pizza
she didn't mean to upset you = elle ne
voulait pas te faire de la peine
he meant it as a joke = il voulait
plaisanter
(*to intend to say*) = vouloir dire
what do you mean? = qu'est-ce que tu
veux dire?
her work means a lot to her = son travail
compte beaucoup pour elle
money doesn't mean much to him
= l'argent n'a pas beaucoup
d'importance pour lui
2 *adjective*
(*British English*) (*not generous*) = avare,
radin/radine*

M

to be mean to someone = être méchant/méchante avec quelqu'un

meaning *noun*
a meaning = un sens

means *noun*
a means = un moyen
a means of transport = un moyen de transport
a means of earning money = un moyen de gagner de l'argent

meant : **to be meant to** *verb*
to be meant to = être censé/censée
I'm meant to be at my parents' house = je suis censé être chez mes parents

meanwhile *adverb*
= pendant ce temps

measles *noun* ▶ 266 |
measles = la rougeole

measure *verb*
= mesurer

meat *noun*
meat = la viande

mechanic *noun* ▶ 315 |
a mechanic = un mécanicien/une mécanicienne

medal *noun*
a medal = une médaille
the gold medal = la médaille d'or

media *noun*
the media = les médias (*masculine*)

medical *adjective*
= médical/médicale
to have medical treatment = suivre un traitement médical

medicine *noun*
a medicine = un médicament

Mediterranean *noun*
the Mediterranean = la (mer) Méditerranée

medium *adjective*
= moyen/moyenne

meet *verb*
(*by accident or appointment*) = rencontrer
she met him at the butcher's = elle l'a rencontré à la boucherie
can we meet (up) next week? = est-ce qu'on peut se voir la semaine prochaine?
to meet again = se revoir (**!** + *être*)
(*to be introduced to*) ▶ 237 | = faire la connaissance de
she met him at a wedding = elle a fait sa connaissance à un mariage
have you met Tom? = est-ce que vous connaissez Tom?

(*to fetch*)
I can meet you at the station = je peux aller te chercher à la gare
can you meet me at the station? = peux-tu venir me chercher à la gare?
(*to have a meeting*) = se réunir (**!** + *être*)

meeting *noun*
a meeting = une réunion

melon *noun*
a melon = un melon

melt *verb*
the snow is starting to melt = la neige commence à fondre
the salt will melt the ice = le sel fera fondre le verglas

member *noun* ▶ 315 |
a member = un membre
a member of staff (*in a school*) = un enseignant/une enseignante
(*in a bank, a firm*) = un membre du personnel

memory *noun*
memory = la mémoire
to have a good memory = avoir bonne mémoire
he's got a bad memory = il n'a pas de mémoire
(*of a person, a place or time*)
a memory = un souvenir

mend *verb*
(*to fix*) = réparer
(*by sewing*) = raccommoder

mental *adjective*
= mental/mentale

menu *noun*
a menu = un menu

mess *noun*
a mess = le désordre
your room is in a mess = ta chambre est en désordre
to make a mess in the kitchen = mettre du désordre dans la cuisine

message *noun*
a message = un message

metal *noun*
a metal = un métal

method *noun*
a method = une méthode

metre (*British English*), **meter** (*US English*) *noun* ▶ 285 |
a metre = un mètre

Mexico *noun* ▶ 218 |
Mexico = le Mexique

microphone *noun*
a microphone = un microphone

microwave *noun*
a microwave = un four à micro-ondes

Length and weight measurements

Length measurements

Note that French has a *comma* where English has a *decimal point*:

1 inch	= 2,54 cm	*1 yard*	= 91,44 cm
1 foot	= 30,48 cm	*1 mile*	= 1,61 km (kilomètres)

Length

how long is the rope?	= quelle est la longueur de la corde?
it's ten metres long	= elle fait dix mètres
the rope is three metres too short	= la corde est trop courte de trois mètres

Height

People	*how tall is he?*	= combien mesure-t-il?
	he's six feet tall	= il mesure un mètre quatre-vingts
	*Tom is taller	smaller than Jane*	= Tom est plus grand / plus petit que Jane
Things	*how high is the tower?*	= quelle est la hauteur de la tour?
	it's 100 metres high	= elle fait cent mètres de† haut / de† hauteur
	*A is higher	lower than B*	= A est plus haut / moins haut que B

Distance

how far is it from Paris to Nice?	= quelle distance y a-t-il entre Paris et Nice?
it's about 800 kilometres	= il y a environ 800 kilomètres

M

Width / breadth

how wide is the river?	= quelle est la largeur de la rivière?
it's seven metres wide	= elle fait sept mètres de† large / de† largeur

Depth

how deep is the lake	= quelle est la profondeur du lac?
it's four metres deep	= il fait quatre mètres de† profondeur

Note the French construction with **de**, coming after the noun it describes:

a street two kilometres long	= une rue **de** deux kilomètres de† long
a 100-metre-high tower	= une tour **de** cent mètres de† haut
a ten-kilometre walk	= une promenade **de** dix kilomètres
a river 50 metres wide	= une rivière **de** 50 mètres de† largeur

Weight measurements

Again, note that French has a *comma* where English has a *decimal point*:

1 ounce	= 28,35 g (grammes)	*1 stone*	= 6,35 kg (kilos)
1 pound *	= 453,60 g	*1 ton*	= 1 014,60 kg

* a pound (£1) is translated by **une livre** in French, but the French **livre** = 500 grammes (half a kilo).

People	*how much does he weigh?*	= combien pèse-t-il?
	*he weighs 10st	140 lbs*	= il pèse 63 kg 500 (soixante-trois kilos cinq cents)
Things	*what does the parcel weigh?*	= combien pèse le colis?
	how heavy is it?	– quel est son poids?
	it weighs 10 kilos	= il pèse 10 kilos
	A weighs more than B	= A pèse plus lourd que B
	sold by the kilo	= vendu au kilo

† The use of **de** is obligatory in these constructions.

midday noun ▶ 211 |, ▶ 356 |
  midday = midi (*masculine*)
  at midday = à midi

middle noun
  the middle = le milieu
  in the middle of the road = au milieu de la route
  to be in the middle of cooking a meal = être en train de préparer un repas

middle-aged adjective
  = d'âge mûr (❗ *never changes*)

midnight noun ▶ 211 |, ▶ 356 |
  midnight = minuit (*masculine*)
  at midnight = à minuit

might verb
  (*when talking about a possibility*)
  she might be right = elle a peut-être raison
  they might have got lost = ils se sont peut-être perdus
  'will you come?'—'I might' = 'est-ce tu viendras?'—'peut-être'
  we might miss the plane = nous risquons de rater l'avion
  he said he might not come = il a dit qu'il ne viendrait peut-être pas
  (*when implying something didn't happen*)
  you might have been killed! = tu aurais pu te faire tuer!
  she might have warned us = elle aurait pu nous prévenir
  (*when making suggestions*)
  you might try leaving a message = vous pourriez laisser un message
  it might be better to wait = ce serait peut-être mieux d'attendre

mild adjective
  = doux/douce
  the weather's mild, it's mild = il fait doux

mile noun ▶ 285 |
  a mile = un mile
  ❗ *Note that a* **mile** = *1609 m.*

military adjective
  = militaire

milk
1 noun
  milk = le lait
2 verb
  = traire

milkman noun ▶ 315 |
  a milkman = un laitier

million number
  one million, a million = un million
  three million dollars = trois millions de dollars
  a million inhabitants = un million d'habitants

mind
1 noun
  the mind = l'esprit (*masculine*)
  to have a logical mind = avoir l'esprit logique
  I have a lot on my mind = j'ai beaucoup de soucis
  to make up one's mind to change jobs = se décider à changer de travail
  to change one's mind = changer d'avis
2 verb
  (*when expressing an opinion*)
  'where shall we go?'—'I don't mind' = 'où irons-nous?'—'ça m'est égal'
  she doesn't mind the heat = la chaleur ne la dérange pas
  I wouldn't mind some cake = je prendrais volontiers du gâteau
  (*in polite questions or requests*)
  do you mind if I smoke? = est-ce que cela vous dérange si je fume?
  would you mind coming? = est-ce que ça vous ennuierait de venir?
  (*to be careful*)
  mind the steps! = fais attention aux marches!
  mind you don't break the plates = fais attention de ne pas casser les assiettes
  (*to take care of*) = s'occuper de (❗ + *être*)
  never mind, she'll get the next train = ne t'en fais pas, elle prendra le train suivant

mine¹ pronoun
  the green pen is mine = le stylo vert est à moi
  guess which house is mine = devine laquelle de ces maisons est la mienne
  her coat is brown but mine is dark green = son manteau est marron mais le mien est vert foncé
  his sister's the same age as mine = sa sœur a le même âge que la mienne
  ❗ *Note that, when comparing objects, people, etc, one of the following translations—le mien, la mienne, les miens or les miennes—will be used. To know which one to use, find out whether the object, person, etc which is being described is masculine or feminine, singular or plural.*

mine² noun
  a mine = une mine

miner noun ▶ 315 |
  a miner = un mineur

mineral water noun
  a mineral water = une eau minérale

minimum
1 adjective
  the minimum price = le prix minimum
  a minimum temperature of 15 degrees = une température minimale de 15 degrés
2 noun
  the minimum = le minimum

minister *noun* ▶ 315 |
* (*in government*)
  a minister = un ministre
  the minister for Education = le ministre de
    l'Éducation
* (*in religion*)
  a minister = un ministre du culte

minor *adjective*
  = mineur/mineure
  a minor injury = une blessure légère

minority *noun*
  a minority = une minorité

minus *preposition*
  = moins
  it's minus four outside = il fait moins
    quatre dehors

minute *noun* ▶ 211 |, ▶ 356 |
  a minute = une minute
  they'll be here any minute now = ils vont
    arriver d'une minute à l'autre

mirror *noun*
  a mirror (*on a wall*) = un miroir, une glace
  (*on a car*) = un rétroviseur

miserable *adjective*
  = malheureux/malheureuse
  to feel miserable = avoir le cafard

miss *verb*
* (*to fail to hit*)
  to miss the target = manquer la cible
  the stone just missed his head = la pierre
    lui a frôlé la tête
* (*to fail to see*) = rater
  you can't miss it = tu ne peux pas le rater
* (*to fail to take*)
  to miss an opportunity = laisser passer
    une occasion
* (*to feel sad not to see*)
  I miss you = tu me manques
  we'll miss Oxford = Oxford va nous
    manquer
* (*other uses*)
  don't miss this film = ne rate pas ce film
  she missed her plane = elle a raté son
    avion
  to miss school (*due to illness*) = manquer
    l'école
  (*by skipping classes*) = sauter les cours

Miss *noun*
  ▶ See the boxed note on **Forms of address.**
  Miss = mademoiselle (*feminine*)

missing *adjective*
  to be missing = manquer
  there's a book missing = il manque un
    livre

mist *noun*
  mist = la brume

mistake *noun*
  a mistake = une erreur
  a spelling mistake = une faute
    d'orthographe
  to make a mistake = se tromper (**!** + *être*)

mistletoe *noun*
  mistletoe = le gui

mix *verb*
* (*to put together*) = mélanger
* (*to go together*) = se mélanger (**!** + *être*)
* **to mix with the other students** = fréquenter
  les autres étudiants
  mix up = confondre
    to get the two languages mixed up
      = confondre les deux langues
    I'm always mixing him up with his brother
      = je le confonds toujours avec son frère

mixture *noun*
  a mixture = un mélange

model *noun*
* (*of a train, a car, a building*)
  a model = un modèle réduit, une
    maquette
* ▶ 315 |
  a (fashion) model = un mannequin

modern *adjective*
  = moderne

Mohammed *noun*
  Mohammed = Mahomet

mole *noun*
  a mole = une taupe

mom, Mom *noun* (*US English*)
  a mom = une maman

moment *noun*
  a moment = un instant
  there's no-one there at the moment = il
    n'y a personne en ce moment

Monday *noun* ▶ 222 |
  Monday = lundi (*masculine*)

money *noun*
  money = l'argent (*masculine*)

monkey *noun*
  a monkey = un singe

month *noun* ▶ 356 |
  a month = un mois
  he'll be back in two months' time = il sera
    de retour dans deux mois

Montreal *noun* ▶ 218 |
  Montreal = Montréal

monument *noun*
  a monument = un monument

mood *noun*
  to be in a good mood = être de bonne
    humeur
  I'm in a very bad mood = je suis de très
    mauvaise humeur

M

moon *noun*
the moon = la lune

moped *noun*
a moped = un vélomoteur

moral *adjective*
= moral/morale

more ▶ 317 |
1 *determiner*
= plus de
more [friends | books | CDs ...] = plus [d'amis | de livres | de disques compacts ...]
more [money | food | time ...] = plus [d'argent | de nourriture | de temps ...]
I have more work than him = j'ai plus de travail que lui
there's no more bread = il n'y a plus de pain
there's more tea = il y a encore du thé
would you like more coffee? = voulez-vous encore du café?
he bought two more tickets = il a acheté deux billets de plus
2 *pronoun*
= plus
to cost more = coûter plus cher
I did more than you = j'en ai fait plus que toi
I can't tell you any more = je ne peux pas t'en dire plus
we need more (of them) = il nous en faut plus
we need more (of it) = il nous en faut davantage

! Note that it is necessary to use en, which might be translated as 'of it' or 'of them', with pronouns like more. See also another, a few, a lot etc for this use of en.

3 *adverb*
(when comparing) = plus
it's more complicated than that = c'est plus compliqué que ça
(when talking about time)
he doesn't live there any more = il n'habite plus là
4 more and more = de plus en plus
more and more expensive = de plus en plus cher
5 more or less = plus ou moins
6 more than = plus de
there were more than 20 people there = il y avait plus de 20 personnes

morning *noun* ▶ 211 |, ▶ 356 |

! Note that morning is usually translated by matin in French. However it is sometimes translated by matinée, when there is an emphasis on the idea of duration.

a morning = un matin
at three o'clock in the morning = à trois heures du matin
to spend the morning reading the paper = passer la matinée à lire le journal

mosquito *noun*
a mosquito = un moustique

most
1 *determiner*
(the majority of) = la plupart de
most schools will be closed = la plupart des écoles seront fermées
(in superlatives)
the most = le plus de
who has the most money? = qui a le plus d'argent?
2 *pronoun*
= la plupart de
most of the time they phone each other = la plupart du temps ils se téléphonent
most (of them) speak Greek = la plupart (d'entre eux) parlent grec
3 *adverb*
the most
= le plus/la plus (+ singular)
= les plus (+ plural)
the most expensive shop in London = le magasin le plus cher de Londres
the most beautiful town in France = la plus belle ville de France
4 at (the) most = au maximum, au plus
5 most of all = par-dessus tout

mostly *adverb*
= pour la plupart

mother *noun*
a mother = une mère

mother-in-law *noun*
a mother-in-law = une belle-mère

motor *noun*
a motor = un moteur

motorbike *noun*
a motorbike = une moto

motorcyclist *noun*
a motorcyclist = un motocycliste/une motocycliste

motorist *noun*
a motorist = un automobiliste/une automobiliste

motor racing *noun* ▶ 248 |
motor racing = la course automobile

motorway *noun* (British English)
a motorway = une autoroute

mountain *noun*
a mountain = une montagne
to go camping in the mountains = faire du camping en montagne

mountain bike *noun*
a mountain bike = un vélo tout terrain, un VTT

mountain climbing *noun* ▶ 248 |
mountain climbing = l'alpinisme (masculine)

mouse *noun*
a mouse = une souris

moustache, mustache (*US English*)
noun
  a moustache = une moustache

mouth *noun* ▶ **201** |
• (*of a person*)
  the mouth = la bouche
  to have a big mouth = avoir une grande
    gueule✗
• (*of an animal*)
  the mouth = la gueule
• (*of a river*)
  the mouth = l'embouchure (*feminine*)

move *verb*
• (*to make a movement*) = bouger
  don't move! = ne bouge pas!
  the train's starting to move = le train
    démarre
• (*to put elsewhere*) = déplacer
  to move the car = déplacer la voiture
  to move a chair (out of the way)
    = déplacer une chaise
• (*to make a movement with*) = bouger
  I couldn't move my leg = je n'arrivais pas à
    bouger la jambe
  don't move the camera = ne bouge pas
    l'appareil photo
• (*to act*) = agir
• (*to move (house)*) = déménager
  to move to Paris = déménager à Paris
move away
• (*to live elsewhere*) = déménager
• (*to make a movement away*) = s'éloigner
  (❗ + *être*)
  to move away from the window
    = s'éloigner de la fenêtre
move back = reculer
move forward = s'avancer (❗ + *être*)
move in = emménager
  to move in with friends = s'installer avec
    des amis
move out = déménager
move over = se pousser (❗ + *être*)
  move over please = pousse-toi s'il te plaît

movement *noun*
  a movement = un mouvement

movie *noun* (*US English*)
  a movie = un film

movies *noun* (*US English*)
  the movies = le cinéma

movie theater *noun* (*US English*)
  a movie theater = un cinéma

moving *adjective*
  = émouvant/émouvante

mow *verb*
  to mow the lawn = tondre le gazon

MP *noun* ▶ **315** | (*British English*)
  an MP = un député

Mr *noun*
▶ *See the boxed note on* Forms of address.
  Mr = monsieur (*masculine*)

Mrs *noun*
▶ *See the boxed note on* Forms of address.
  Mrs = madame (*feminine*)

much ▶ **317** |
1 *adverb*
• (*a lot*) = beaucoup
  her work is much more tiring = son travail
    est beaucoup plus fatigant
  he doesn't read much = il ne lit pas
    beaucoup
• (*often*) = beaucoup
  they don't go out much = ils ne sortent
    pas beaucoup
• (*when used with* very, too *or* so)
  he misses her very much = elle lui
    manque beaucoup
  you talk too much = tu parles trop
  she loves him so much = elle l'aime
    tellement
2 *pronoun*
  (*in questions*) = beaucoup
  (*in negative statements*) = grand-chose
  is there much to be done? = est-ce qu'il y a
    beaucoup à faire?
  he didn't eat much = il n'a pas mangé
    grand-chose
3 *determiner*
• (*a lot of*) = beaucoup de
  I haven't got much time = je n'ai pas
    beaucoup de temps
  do you have much work? = est-ce que
    vous avez beaucoup de travail?
• (*when used with* how, very, too, so *or* as)
  how much money have you got?
    = combien d'argent as-tu?
  she doesn't eat very much meat = elle ne
    mange pas beaucoup de viande
  I spent too much money = j'ai dépensé
    trop d'argent
  don't use so much salt = ne mets pas tant
    de sel
  she has as much work as me = elle a
    autant de travail que moi

mud *noun*
  mud = la boue

mug
1 *noun*
  a mug = une grande tasse
2 *verb*
  to be mugged = se faire agresser (❗ + *être*)

multiply *verb*
  = multiplier

mum, Mum *noun* (*British English*)
  a mum = une maman

mumps *noun* ▶ **266** |
  mumps = les oreillons (*masculine plural*)

murder
1 *noun*
  a murder = un meurtre

M

Musical instruments

Playing an instrument

Note the use of **de** with **jouer**:

to play the piano	= **jouer du** piano
to play the flute	= **jouer de la** flûte

but

to learn the piano	= **apprendre le** piano
to learn the guitar	= **apprendre la** guitare

Players

English **-ist** is very often French **-iste**. The gender will reflect the sex of the player:

a pianist	= **un** pian**iste** / **une** pian**iste**
a violonist	= **un** violon**iste** / **une** violon**iste**

But note the French when these words are used with **good** and **bad** like this:

he's a good pianist	= **il joue bien du** piano
he's a bad pianist	= **il joue mal du** piano

Use with another noun

de is usually correct:

to take piano lessons	= prendre des leçons **de** piano
a guitar solo	= un solo **de** guitare
a piano teacher	= un professeur **de** piano

---

2 *verb*
= assassiner

murderer *noun*
a murderer = un meurtrier

muscle *noun*
a muscle = un muscle

museum *noun*
a museum = un musée

mushroom *noun*
a mushroom = un champignon

music *noun*
music = la musique

musical *noun*
a musical = une comédie musicale

musical instrument *noun*
a musical instrument = un instrument de musique

musician *noun* ▶ 315 |
a musician = un musicien/une musicienne

Muslim *adjective*
= musulman/musulmane

mussel *noun*
a mussel = une moule

must *verb*

! *The verbs* **devoir** *and* **falloir** *are used to translate* **must***. Note that the subjunctive is used after* **il faut que***.*

(when stressing the importance of something)
you must go to the doctor = il faut que tu ailles chez le médecin
we mustn't tell anyone = il ne faut en parler à personne
(when talking about a rule)
she must take the exam in June = elle doit passer l'examen au mois de juin
visitors must go to (the) reception = les visiteurs doivent se présenter au bureau d'accueil
(when assuming that something is true)
it must be nice to live there = ça doit être agréable de vivre là-bas
you must be David's sister = tu dois être la sœur de David
they must have been bored = ils ont dû s'ennuyer

mustard *noun*
mustard = la moutarde

mutton *noun*
mutton = le mouton

Using the subjunctive

There are a number of examples in this dictionary which use the subjunctive. They are highlighted in the text with a note. The type of examples generating the subjunctive fall into three main categories. They are examples which contain:

- certain verbs, mainly:
  falloir
  vouloir

- certain conjunctions:
  bien que ...
  jusqu'à ce que ...
  à condition que ...
  pour que ...
  à moins que ...

- certain phrases, often expressing a personal opinion:
  il est bizarre que ...
  c'est dommage que ...
  je suis content que ...
  je doute que ...

Verbs

- *falloir* is by far the most common verb requiring the subjunctive in this dictionary. The impersonal form **il faut que** is most often used to translate **must**.

I **must** go	= il **faut que** je m'en aille
you **must** come	= il **faut que** tu viennes

- *vouloir*, meaning **to want**, requires the subjunctive in specific cases. Compare:

I want **to come**	= je veux **venir**
I want you **to come**	= je veux que **tu viennes**

The second example uses the subjunctive because there are two 'subjects' involved, I and you. In the first example, there is only one subject, which means that no subjunctive is required.

Conjunctions

The most common conjunctions requiring the subjunctive in French in this dictionary are:

- **bien que** (= *although, even though, though*)

  although she's quite old, she has lots of energy
  = **bien qu**'elle soit assez âgée, elle a beaucoup d'énergie

- **jusqu'à ce que** (= *until*)

  let's watch television **until** they arrive
  = regardons la télévision **jusqu'à ce qu**'ils arrivent

- **à condition que** (= *provided, on condition that, as long as*)

  you can go out with them **provided** they bring you home
  = tu peux sortir avec eux **à condition qu**'ils te ramènent

- **pour que** (= *so that*)

  be quiet **so that** I can sleep
  = tais-toi **pour que** je puisse dormir!

- **à moins que** (= *unless*)

  I am not going **unless** you come with me
  – je n'y vais pas **à moins que** tu viennes avec moi

Phrases

When stating an opinion, the subjunctive is always used with the following phrases:

it's strange that she's never there	= il est bizarre qu'elle ne soit jamais là
it's a pity we can't go there	= c'est dommage qu'on ne puisse pas y aller
I'm glad he has lots of friends	= je suis content qu'il ait beaucoup d'amis
I doubt if he'll come	= je doute qu'il vienne

Superlatives

it's the best book (that) I have ever read	= c'est le meilleur livre que j'aie jamais lu
it's the most expensive watch (that) he's seen	= c'est la montre la plus chère qu'il ait vue

In French, the subjunctive is always used in clauses with **que** following a superlative adjective like *le meilleur | la meilleure, le plus mauvais | la plus mauvaise* etc.

▶ For more information on the subjunctive forms of French verbs, see the **verb tables ▶ 381**.

▶ For information on grammar terms used in this note, see the **glossary page x**.

M

my *determiner*
my = mon/ma (+ *singular*)
= mes (+ *plural*)

! *Note that* ma *becomes* mon *before a
vowel or mute h.*

they hate my dog = ils détestent mon
chien
what do you think of my house? = qu'est-
ce que tu penses de ma maison?
he's my age = il a mon âge
I sold all my CDs = j'ai vendu tous mes
disques compacts
I broke my leg = je me suis cassé la
jambe

! *Note that, when talking about parts of
the body,* mon, ma *and* mes *are not used.
See the usage note on* The human
body ▶ 201 | *for further examples.*

myself *pronoun*
(*when used as a reflexive pronoun*)
I want to enjoy myself = je veux m'amuser
I didn't hurt myself = je ne me suis pas fait
mal
(*when used for emphasis*)
I told them myself = je le leur ai dit moi-
même
I did it all by myself = je l'ai fait tout seul

mystery *noun*
a mystery = un mystère

Nn

nail *noun* ▶ 201 |
(*for use in attaching, repairing*)
a nail = un clou
(*on the fingers or toes*)
a nail = un ongle

nail polish *noun*
nail polish = le vernis à ongles

naked *adjective*
= nu/nue

name *noun*
(*of a person*)
a name = un nom
what's your name? = comment t'appelles-
tu?, comment vous appelez-vous?
my name is Louis = je m'appelle Louis
(*of a book, a play or film*)
a name = un titre

narrow *adjective*
= étroit/étroite

nasty *adjective*
(*mean, unkind*) = méchant/méchante
(*unpleasant*) = désagréable

national *adjective*
= national/nationale

native *adjective*
a native language = une langue
maternelle
a native French speaker = une personne
de langue maternelle française

natural *adjective*
= naturel/naturelle
it's natural to be disappointed = c'est
normal d'être déçu

naturally *adverb*
= naturellement

nature *noun*
nature = la nature

naughty *adjective*
= vilain/vilaine

navy *noun*
the navy = la marine

navy blue *adjective* ▶ 213 |
= bleu marine (! *never changes*)

near
1 *preposition*
= près de
he was sitting near us = il était assis près
de nous
2 *adverb*
they live quite near = ils habitent tout
près

3 *adjective*
= proche
the school is quite near = l'école est assez
   proche
the nearest shops are several miles away
   = les magasins les plus proches sont à
   plusieurs kilomètres d'ici

nearby *adverb*
= à proximité

nearly *adverb*
= presque
we're nearly there = nous sommes
   presque arrivés
I nearly [forgot | gave up | fell asleep …] = j'ai
   failli [oublier | abandonner | m'endormir …]

neat *adjective*
(*in one's habits*) = ordonné/ordonnée
(*in how one looks*) = net/nette
(*describing work, handwriting*)
   = soigné/soignée

necessary *adjective*
= nécessaire

neck *noun* ▶ 201 |
the neck = le cou

necklace *noun*
a necklace = un collier

need *verb*
• (*(to) have to*)
  you don't need to ask permission = tu
    n'es pas obligé de demander la
    permission
  they'll need to come early = il va falloir
    qu'ils viennent de bonne heure
  ! *Note that the subjunctive is used after*
  falloir que.

• (*to want*) = avoir besoin de
  they need [money | help | friends …] = ils ont
    besoin [d'argent | d'aide | d'amis …]
  we need to see the doctor = nous avons
    besoin de voir le médecin
  everything you need = tout ce qu'il vous
    faut

needle *noun*
a needle = une aiguille

negative
1 *adjective*
• (*pessimistic*) = négatif/négative
• (*harmful*) = néfaste
2 *noun*
a negative = un négatif

neighbour (*British English*), **neighbor**
(*US English*) *noun*
a neighbour = un voisin/une voisine

neither
1 *conjunction*
• (*in* neither… nor *sentences*) = ni… ni

she speaks neither French nor English
   = elle ne parle ni français ni anglais
I have neither the time nor the energy to
   argue = je n'ai ni le temps ni la force de
   discuter
• (*nor*)
  'I can't sleep'—'neither can I' = 'je
    n'arrive pas à dormir'—'moi non plus'
2 *determiner*
= aucun des deux/aucune des deux
neither girl answered = aucune des deux
   filles n'a répondu
3 *pronoun*
= ni l'un/l'une ni l'autre
neither of them is coming = ni l'un ni
   l'autre ne vient

  ! *Note that, in sentences with a verb, the
  negative* ne *or* n' (*before a vowel or mute
  h*) *is used together with* ni… ni,
  aucun/aucune des deux *and* ni l'un/l'une
  ni l'autre *to translate* neither. *Remember
  that* ne *comes before the verb or the
  auxiliary verb.*

nephew *noun*
a nephew = un neveu

nerves *noun*
nerves = les nerfs (*masculine*)
to get on someone's nerves = énerver
   quelqu'un

nervous *adjective*
• (*frightened*)
  to be nervous = avoir peur
• (*anxious*) = angoissé/angoissée
  to feel nervous = être angoissé/angoissée

nest *noun*
a nest = un nid

net *noun*
• (*for fishing*)
  a net = un filet
• (*in sport*)
  the net (*in football*) = les filets (*masculine
   plural*)
  (*in tennis*) = le filet

Netherlands *noun* ▶ 218 |
the Netherlands = les Pays-Bas (*masculine
   plural*)

network *noun*
a network = un réseau

neutral *adjective*
= neutre

never *adverb*
  ! *Note that, in sentences with a verb, the
  negative* ne *or* n' (*before a vowel or mute
  h*) *is used together with* jamais *to
  translate* never. *Remember that* ne *comes
  before the verb or the auxiliary verb.*

N

* (*not ever*) = jamais
  they never come to see us = ils ne
  viennent jamais nous voir
  she has never been to the opera = elle
  n'est jamais allée à l'opéra
  I'll never go back there again = je n'y
  retournerai plus jamais
* (*when used for emphasis*)
  she never even apologized = elle ne s'est
  même pas excusée

nevertheless *adverb*
= pourtant, néanmoins

new *adjective*
= nouveau/nouvelle (**!** *before the noun*)

> **!** *Note that* **nouvel** *is used instead of*
> **nouveau** *before masculine nouns*
> *beginning with a vowel (* **endroit, ordina-**
> **teur** *) or a mute h (* **hôtel** *). The plural of*
> **nouveau** *and* **nouvel** *is* **nouveaux.**

a new bike = un nouveau vélo
a new car = une nouvelle voiture
a new computer = un nouvel ordinateur
new dresses = de nouvelles robes

newborn baby *noun*
a newborn baby = un nouveau-né

news *noun*
* **a piece of news** = une nouvelle
  have you heard the news? = est-ce que tu
  connais la nouvelle?
  that's good news = c'est une bonne
  nouvelle
  have you any news of John? = est-ce que
  tu as des nouvelles de John?
* (*on radio, TV*)
  the news = le journal (*singular*)= , les
  informations (*feminine*)

newsagent's *noun* ▶ 315 | (*British
English*)
a newsagent's = un magasin de journaux

newspaper *noun*
a newspaper = un journal

New Year *noun*
the New Year = le nouvel an
Happy New Year! = Bonne année!

New Year's Day, **New Year's** (*US
English*) *noun*
New Year's (Day) = le jour de l'an

New Year's Eve *noun*
New Year's Eve = la Saint-Sylvestre

New Zealand *noun* ▶ 218 |
New Zealand = la Nouvelle-Zélande

next
1 *adjective*
* (*when talking about what is still to come*)
  = prochain/prochaine

I'll take the next train to London = je
prendrai le prochain train pour Londres
he'll be here next week = il sera là la
semaine prochaine
* (*when talking about what followed*)
  = suivant/suivante
  I took the next train = j'ai pris le train
  suivant
  they arrived the next day = ils sont arrivés
  le lendemain
* (*in a queue*)
  'who's next?' = 'à qui le tour?'
  'I'm next' = 'c'est mon tour'
2 *adverb*
* (*in the past*) = ensuite
  what happened next? = qu'est-ce qui s'est
  passé ensuite?
* (*now*) = maintenant
  what'll we do next? = qu'est-ce qu'on fait
  maintenant?
* (*in the future*)
  **when you next go to Paris, give Gary a
  call** = la prochaine fois que tu iras à
  Paris, passe un coup de fil à Gary
3 next to = à côté de

next door *adverb*
= à côté

nice *adjective*
* (*enjoyable*) = agréable
  it's nice to be able to relax = c'est agréable
  de pouvoir se détendre
* (*kind, friendly*) = sympathique, sympa✕
  to be nice to someone = être
  gentil/gentille avec quelqu'un
* (*attractive*) = beau/belle (**!** *before the noun*)

nickname *noun*
a nickname = un surnom

niece *noun*
a niece = une nièce

night *noun* ▶ 356 |
* (*as opposed to day*)
  a night = une nuit
  I didn't sleep last night = je n'ai pas dormi
  cette nuit
  he stayed out all night = il n'est pas rentré
  de la nuit
* (*evening*)
  a night = un soir
  last night = hier soir
  a night at the cinema = une soirée au
  cinéma

> **!** *See the note at* **evening** *for information
> on* **soir** *and* **soirée.**

nightclub *noun*
a nightclub = une boîte de nuit

nightdress *noun*
a nightdress = une chemise de nuit

nightmare *noun*
  a nightmare = un cauchemar
  to have a nightmare = faire un cauchemar

nil *noun*
  nil = zéro

nine *number* ▶ **187** |, ▶ **211** |
  nine = neuf
  nine books = neuf livres
  I have nine (of them) – j'en ai neuf

nineteen *number* ▶ **187** |, ▶ **211** |
  nineteen = dix-neuf

nineteenth *number*
* (*in a series*) = dix-neuvième
* (*in dates*) ▶ **222** |
  the nineteenth of July = le dix-neuf juillet

ninety *number* ▶ **187** |
  ninety = quatre-vingt-dix

ninth *number*
* (*in a series*) = neuvième
* (*in dates*) ▶ **222** |
  the ninth of December = le neuf décembre

no
1 *adverb*
* no = non
  no thanks = non merci
* he no longer works here = il ne travaille
  plus ici
2 *determiner*
* (*not any*)
  we have no money = nous n'avons pas
    d'argent
  there are no trains = il n'y a pas de trains
* (*when refusing permission*)
  no smoking = défense de fumer
  no talking! = silence!
* (*when used for emphasis*)
  this is no time to argue = ce n'est pas le
    moment de discuter
  it's no problem = ce n'est pas du tout un
    problème

nobody ▶ **no-one**

noise *noun*
  noise = le bruit
  to make noise = faire du bruit

noisy *adjective*
  = bruyant/bruyante

none *pronoun*

> ! *Note that, when there is a verb in the
> sentence, the negative ne or n' (before a
> vowel or mute h) is used together with
> aucun/aucune to translate none.
> Remember that ne comes before the verb
> or the auxiliary verb.*

  none = aucun/aucune
  none of the girls went to the class
    = aucune des filles n'est allée au cours
  none of [us | you | them …] can speak
    German = aucun [de nous | de vous | d'entre
    eux …] ne parle allemand
  there's none left = il n'y en a plus
  I've got none, I have none = je n'en ai pas

> ! *Note that it is necessary to use en which
> might be translated as 'of it' or 'of them',
> with pronouns like none. See also another,
> a few, a lot etc for this use of en.*

nonsense *noun*
  that's nonsense! = c'est absurde!

noon *noun* ▶ **211** |, ▶ **356** |
  noon = midi (*masculine*)
  at noon = à midi

no-one *pronoun* (*also* **nobody**)

> ! *Note that, when there is a verb in the
> sentence, the negative ne or n' (before a
> vowel or mute h) is used together with
> personne to translate no-one. Remember
> that ne comes before the verb or the
> auxiliary verb.*

  no-one = personne
  no-one tells me anything = personne ne
    me dit rien
  no-one saw him = personne ne l'a vu
  there's no-one else in the office = il n'y a
    personne d'autre au bureau

nor *conjunction*

> ! *For translations of nor when used in
> combination with neither, look at the entry
> for neither in this dictionary.*

  'I don't like him'—'nor do I' = 'je ne l'aime
    pas'—'moi non plus'

normal *adjective*
  = normal/normale

normally *adverb*
  = normalement

north
1 *noun*
  the north = le nord
  in the north of France = dans le nord de la
    France
2 *adverb*
  to go north = aller vers le nord
  to live north of Paris = vivre au nord de
    Paris
3 *adjective*
  = nord (! *never changes*)
  to work in north London = travailler dans
    le nord de Londres

North America *noun* ▶ **218** |
  North America = l'Amérique du Nord
  ! *Note that Amérique is feminine.*

northeast *noun*
  the northeast = le nord-est

Northern Ireland *noun* ▶ **218** |
  Northern Ireland = l'Irlande du Nord
  ! *Note that Irlande is feminine.*

northwest *noun*
  the northwest = le nord-ouest

Norway *noun* ▶ **218** |
  Norway = la Norvège

N

not

Used without a verb

When **not** is used without a verb before an adjective, a noun, an adverb, a verb or a pronoun it is translated by **pas**:

not at all	= **pas** du tout
not bad	= **pas** mal
it's a cat *not* a dog	= c'est un chat **pas** un chien
you should walk, *not* run	= il faut marcher, **pas** courir
she should apologise, *not* me	= c'est elle qui devrait s'excuser, **pas** moi

Used with a verb

When **not** is used with the verbs *be*, *do*, *have*, *will* and *would*, the translation is **ne ... pas** (**n'** before a vowel or mute h): **ne** comes before the verb or the auxiliary, and **pas** comes after the verb or auxiliary:

it's *not* a cat	= ce n'est **pas** un chat
he doesn't like oranges	= il n'aime **pas** les oranges
I haven't seen him	= je ne l'ai **pas** vu
she hasn't arrived yet	= elle n'est **pas** encore arrivée
she won't come by car	= elle ne viendra **pas** en voiture
it wouldn't matter	= ce ne serait **pas** grave

When used with a verb in the infinitive, **ne** and **pas** are placed together before the verb:

he decided *not* to go	= il a décidé de **ne pas** y aller
you were wrong *not* to tell her	= tu as eu tort de **ne pas** le lui dire

Used in short questions

When **not** is used in short questions, the whole question can usually be translated by the French **n'est-ce pas**:

she bought it, *didn't she*?	= elle l'a acheté, **n'est-ce pas**?
you were there too, *weren't you*?	= tu y étais aussi, **n'est-ce pas**?
they're living in Germany, *aren't they*?	= ils habitent en Allemagne, **n'est-ce pas**?
he's got a lot of money, *hasn't he*?	= il a beaucoup d'argent, **n'est-ce pas**?
you'll come too, *won't you*?	= vous viendrez vous aussi, **n'est-ce pas**?
he likes fish, *doesn't he*?	= il aime le poisson, **n'est-ce pas**?

▶ For more examples, see the entry **not**.

Norwegian ▶ 275 |
1 *adjective*
= norvégien/norvégienne
2 *noun*
the Norwegians = les Norvégiens

nose *noun* ▶ 201 |
the nose = le nez

not
▶ *See the boxed note on* not *for more information and examples*
1 *adverb*
= ne... pas (**!** n' + *vowel or mute h...* pas)

! *Remember that* ne *or* n' *(before a vowel or mute h) comes before the verb or auxiliary verb and* pas *after.*

she's not at home = elle n'est pas chez elle
hasn't he phoned you? = il ne t'a pas téléphoné?
I hope not = j'espère que non

we're going to go out whether it rains or not = qu'il pleuve ou non, nous allons sortir
not everyone likes football = le football ne plaît pas à tout le monde
2 not at all
• (*in no way*) = pas du tout
  he's not at all worried = il n'est pas du tout inquiet
• 'thanks a lot'—'not at all' = 'merci beaucoup'—'de rien'

note
1 *noun*
• (*to remind oneself*)
  a note = une note
• (*a message*)
  a note = un mot
  I left you a note = je t'ai laissé un mot
• (*British English*) (*money*)
  a note = un billet
  a 50-franc note = un billet de 50 francs

- (*in music*)
  a note = une note
2 *verb*
  to note (down) = noter

notebook *noun*
  a notebook = un carnet

nothing *pronoun*
  nothing = rien

  ! *Note that, when there is a verb in the
  sentence, the negative ne or n' (before a
  vowel or mute h) is used together with
  rien to translate nothing. Remember that
  ne or n' comes before the verb or the
  auxiliary verb.*

  nothing has changed = rien n'a changé
  there's nothing left = il ne reste rien
  she said nothing = elle n'a rien dit
  I knew nothing about it = je n'en savais
    rien
  there's nothing we can do about it = nous
    n'y pouvons rien
  I had nothing to do with it! = je n'y étais
    pour rien!
  it's nothing to do with us = ça ne nous
    regarde pas

notice
1 *verb*
  = remarquer
2 *noun*
- (*a written sign*)
  a notice = une pancarte
- (*warning people*)
  notice = le préavis
  a month's notice = un mois de préavis
  to be cancelled at short notice = être
    annulé/annulée à la dernière minute
- **don't take any notice, take no notice** = ne
  fais pas attention

novel *noun*
  a novel = un roman

November *noun* ▶ **222** |
  November = novembre (*masculine*)

now
1 *adverb*
  = maintenant
  we have to do it now = il faut le faire
    maintenant
  I'm phoning her now = je suis en train de
    lui téléphoner
  do it right now = fais-le tout de suite
  now is the time to contact them = c'est le
    moment de les contacter
  I should have told you before now
    = j'aurais dû te le dire avant
  it hasn't been a problem until now = ça n'a
    pas posé de problème jusqu'à présent
  between now and next Monday = d'ici
    lundi prochain
  from now on = à partir de maintenant
2 now and again, now and then = de
  temps en temps

nowhere *adverb*
  = nulle part
  I go nowhere without my dog = je ne vais
    nulle part sans mon chien
  there's nowhere to sit = il n'y a pas
    d'endroit pour s'asseoir

nuclear *adjective*
  = nucléaire

nuisance *noun*
  to be a nuisance = être pénible
  it's a nuisance having to pay in cash
    = c'est agaçant de devoir payer en
    espèces

numb *adjective*
- **to go numb** = s'engourdir (! + *être*)
  my hands are numb = j'ai les mains
    engourdies
- (*before an operation*) = insensible

number
1 *noun*
- **a number** (*a figure*) = un chiffre
  (*of a house, a bus, a telephone, a passport*)
    = un numéro
  to dial the wrong number = faire un faux
    numéro
- (*when talking about quantities*) ▶ **317** |
  a number of [demonstrations | people |
    times ...] = un certain nombre de
    [manifestations | personnes | fois ...]
  a small number of tourists = quelques
    touristes
2 *verb*
  = numéroter

numberplate *noun* (*British English*)
  a numberplate = une plaque
    minéralogique

nun *noun* ▶ **315** |
  a nun = une religieuse

nurse *noun* ▶ **315** |
  a nurse = un infirmier/une infirmière

nursery *noun*
  a nursery = une crèche

nursery school *noun*
  a nursery school = une école maternelle

nut *noun*
  a nut (*a walnut*) = une noix

nylon *noun*
  nylon = le nylon

N

Oo

oak *noun*
  an oak = un chêne

oar *noun*
  an oar = une rame

obedient *adjective*
  = obéissant/obéissante

obey *verb*
  = obéir
  to obey someone = obéir à quelqu'un
  to obey the law = se conformer à la loi

object
1 *noun*
  an object = un objet
2 *verb*
  = soulever des objections

oblige *verb*
  to be obliged to leave = être obligé/obligée
  de partir
  to oblige someone = rendre service à
  quelqu'un

obtain *verb*
  = obtenir

obvious *adjective*
  = évident/évidente

obviously *adverb*
  = manifestement

occasion *noun*
  an occasion = une occasion
  on special occasions = dans les grandes
  occasions

occasionally *adverb*
  = de temps à autre

occupy *verb*
  (*to take over*) = occuper
  (*to keep busy*)
  to keep oneself occupied = s'occuper
  (**!** + *être*)
  to keep the children occupied = occuper
  les enfants

occur *verb*
  = se produire (**!** + *être*)

ocean *noun*
  the ocean = l'océan (*masculine*)

o'clock *adverb* ▶ **211**
  it's five o'clock = il est cinq heures
  at one o'clock = à une heure

October *noun* ▶ **222**
  October = octobre (*masculine*)

octopus *noun*
  an octopus = une pieuvre

odd *adjective*
  (*strange*) = bizarre
  (*not matching*) = dépareillé/dépareillée
  (*when talking about numbers*)
  an odd number = un nombre impair

odour (*British English*), **odor** (*US English*)
noun
  an odour = une odeur

of *preposition*
  of = de (**!** d' + *vowel or mute h*)
  the sound of an engine = le bruit d'un
  moteur
  it's in the centre of Paris = c'est au centre
  de Paris
  a photo of the dog = une photo du chien
  half of the salad = la moitié de la salade
  at the top of the stairs = en haut de
  l'escalier
  the names of the pupils = le nom des
  élèves
  (*when talking about quantities*) ▶ **317**
  of = de (**!** d' + *vowel or mute h*)
  a kilo of potatoes = un kilo de pommes
  de terre
  a bottle of mineral water = une bouteille
  d'eau minérale
  two cans of beer = deux cannettes de
  bière
  the flowers are lovely so we bought some
  of them = les fleurs sont belles alors
  nous en avons acheté
  have you heard of it? = est-ce que tu en as
  entendu parler?
  there are six of them in the family = ils
  sont six dans la famille
  there were too many of them = ils étaient
  trop nombreux

  ! *Note that* en *is used to translate* 'of it' *or*
  'of them' *when talking about things, but*
  not usually when referring to people.

off

  ! *Often* off *occurs in combinations with*
  verbs, for example: get off, go off, take off
  etc. To find the correct translations for this
  type of verb, look up the separate
  dictionary entries at get, go, take *etc.*

1 *adverb*
  (*leaving*)
  I'm off (*British English*) = je m'en vais
  they're off to Italy tomorrow = ils partent
  pour l'Italie demain
  (*away*)
  the coast is a long way off = la côte est
  loin d'ici
  we could see them from a long way off
  = on les voyait de loin
  (*free*)
  to take a day off = prendre un jour de
  congé
  today's her day off = elle ne travaille pas
  aujourd'hui

(*not working, switched off*)
the lights are all off = toutes les lumières
sont éteintes
2 *adjective*
the milk is off = le lait a tourné

offence (*British English*), **offense** (*US English*) *noun*
(*a crime*)
an offence = un délit
to take offence = s'offenser (**!** + *être*)

offend *verb*
= vexer

offer *verb*
to offer someone a job = offrir un emploi
à quelqu'un
to offer to water the plants = se proposer
pour arroser les plantes

office *noun*
an office = un bureau

office block *noun* (*British English*)
an office block = un immeuble de
bureaux

officer *noun*
an officer (*in the army or navy*) = un
officier
(*in the police*) = un policier

office worker *noun* ▶ 315 |
an office worker = un employé/une
employée de bureau

official *adjective*
= officiel/officielle

often *adverb*
= souvent

oil *noun*
(*for heating, energy*)
oil = le pétrole
(*for a car*)
oil = l'huile (*feminine*)
(*for cooking, for health*)
oil = l'huile (*feminine*)

okay, OK
1 *adjective*
(*when asking or giving opinions*)
is it okay if I come later? = est-ce que je
peux venir plus tard?
it's okay to invite them = on peut les
inviter
(*when talking about health*)
to feel okay = aller bien
are you okay? = ça va?
2 *adverb*
okay = d'accord

old *adjective*
(*not new, not young*) = vieux/vieille
(**!** *before the noun*)

! *Note that* **vieil** *is used instead of* **vieux**
*before masculine nouns beginning with a
vowel* (**ordinateur**) *or a mute h* (**hôtel**). *The
plural of* **vieux** *and* **vieil** *is* **vieux**.

an old oak = un vieux chêne
an old woman = une vieille femme
an old man = un vieil homme
old houses = de vieilles maisons
old people = les personnes âgées
(*when talking about a person's age*) ▶ 187 |
how old are you? = quel âge as tu?
a three-year old girl = une fillette de trois
ans
I'm as old as he is = j'ai le même âge que
lui
she's eight years older than her brother
= elle a huit ans de plus que son frère
to be the oldest = être l'aîné/l'aînée
to be old enough to go out at night = être
en âge de sortir le soir
(*previous*) = ancien/ancienne (**!** *before the
noun*)
that's my old address = c'est mon
ancienne adresse
in the old days = autrefois

old-fashioned *adjective*
(*describing attitudes, ideas*)
= démodé/démodée
(*describing people*) = vieux jeu (**!** *never
changes*)

olive
1 *noun*
an olive = une olive
2 *adjective* ▶ 213 |
= vert olive (**!** *never changes*)

olive oil *noun*
olive oil = l'huile d'olive
! *Note that* **huile** *is feminine.*

Olympics *noun*
the Olympics = les jeux Olympiques
! *Note that* **jeux** *is masculine plural.*

omelette *noun*
an omelette = une omelette

on
! *Often* **on** *occurs in combinations with
verbs, for example:* **count on, get on, keep
on** *etc. To find the correct translations for
this type of verb, look up the separate
dictionary entries for* **count, get, keep** *etc.*

1 *preposition*
on = sur
it's on the table = c'est sur la table
it's on top of the wardrobe = c'est sur
l'armoire
you've got a spot on your nose = tu as un
bouton sur le nez
there's a stain on it = il y a une tache
dessus
to fall on the floor = tomber par terre
I like the picture on the wall = j'aime le
tableau qui est au mur
to live on Park Avenue = habiter Park
Avenue

(*when talking about transport*)
to travel on the bus = voyager en bus
I'm on my bike today = je suis à vélo
aujourd'hui
(*about*) = sur
it's a book on Africa = c'est un livre sur
l'Afrique
a programme on primary schools = une
émission sur les écoles primaires
(*when talking about time*)
she was born on the sixth of December
= elle est née le six décembre
I'll be there on Saturday = j'y serai samedi
we went there on my birthday = nous y
sommes allés le jour de mon
anniversaire
(*when talking about the media*)
on television = à la télévision
I saw it on the news = je l'ai vu aux
informations
is the film out on video? = est-ce que le
film est sorti en vidéo?
(*using*)
to be on drugs = se droguer (**!** + *être*)
2 *adverb*
(*when talking about what one wears*)
to have a sweater on = porter un pull
to have make-up on = être
maquillé/maquillée
(*working, switched on*)
why are all the lights on? = pourquoi est-
ce que toutes les lumières sont
allumées?
the radio was on all evening = la radio a
marché toute la soirée
(*showing*)
what's on? (*on TV*) = qu'est-ce qu'il y a à la
télévision?
(*in the cinema*) = qu'est-ce qu'on joue (au
cinéma)?
(*when talking about time*)
from Tuesday on, I'll be here = à partir de
mardi, je serai là
a little later on = un peu plus tard

once
1 *adverb*
(*one time*) = une fois
once a day = une fois par jour
(*in the old days*) = autrefois
2 *conjunction*
= une fois que
it'll be easier once we've found a house
= ce sera plus facile une fois que nous
aurons trouvé une maison
3 at once = tout de suite

one
1 *number* ▶ **187 |**, ▶ **211 |**
one = un/une
one child = un enfant/une enfant
one of my colleagues = un/une de mes
collègues
one hundred = cent

2 *determiner*
(*the only*)
she's the one person who can help him
= c'est la seule personne capable de
l'aider
it's the one thing that annoys me = c'est la
seule chose qui m'agace
(*the same*)
to take three exams in the one day
= passer trois examens dans la même
journée
3 *pronoun*
(*when referring to something generally*)
I need an umbrella—have you got one?
= j'ai besoin d'un parapluie—est-ce que
tu en as un?

> **!** *Note that it is necessary to use* en,
> *which might be translated as* 'of them',
> *with pronouns like* one. *See also* any, a
> few, many *etc for this use of* en.

(*when referring to a specific person or
thing*)
**I like the new house but she prefers the
old one** = j'aime la nouvelle maison
mais elle préfère l'ancienne
he's the one who told me to be quiet
= c'est lui qui m'a dit de me taire
which one? = lequel/laquelle?
this one = celui-ci/celle-ci
(*when used to mean* 'you' *or* 'people')
one never knows = on ne sait jamais
4 one by one = un par un/une par une

one another *pronoun*

> **!** *Note that* one another *is very often
> translated by using a reflexive pronoun
> like* se, s', nous *or* vous.

to love one another = s'aimer (**!** + *être*)
**we don't like being apart from one
another** = nous n'aimons pas être
séparés (l'un de l'autre)

oneself *pronoun*
= se (**!** *s'* + vowel or mute h)
to enjoy oneself = s'amuser (**!** + *être*)
to hurt oneself = se blesser (**!** + *être*)

onion *noun*
an onion = un oignon

only
1 *adverb*

> **!** *Note that in sentences with a verb, the
> negative* ne *is often used together with*
> que *to translate* only. *Remember that* ne
> *comes before the verb or the auxiliary
> verb.*

only = ne... que
it's only a game = ce n'est qu'un jeu
you only have to ask = vous n'avez qu'à
demander
they've only met once = ils ne se sont
rencontrés qu'une fois
he only hit his elbow = il s'est juste cogné
le coude

2 *adjective*
= seul/seule (**!** *before the noun*)
she was the only one who didn't speak French = elle était la seule à ne pas parler français
the only problem is that I can't drive = le seul problème c'est que je ne conduis pas
an only daughter = une fille unique
3 only just
I've only just [arrived | heard the news | moved house …] = je viens juste [d'arriver | d'apprendre la nouvelle | de déménager …]
she had only just bought a car = elle venait d'acheter une voiture

onto *preposition*
= sur

open
1 *verb*
to open = ouvrir
to open a letter = ouvrir une lettre
what time do you open? = à quelle heure est-ce que vous ouvrez?
the shop opens at eight = le magasin ouvre à huit heures
the door opens very easily = la porte s'ouvre facilement
(*to start*) (*when talking about a film*) = sortir (**!** + *être*)
(*when talking about a play*) = commencer
2 *adjective*
(*not closed*) = ouvert/ouverte
leave the door open = laisse la porte ouverte
the pool isn't open = la piscine n'est pas ouverte
(*frank*) = franc/franche
3 *noun*
out in the open = dehors, en plein air

opener *noun*
an opener (*for bottles*) = un décapsuleur
(*for cans*) = un ouvre-boîtes

open-minded *adjective*
to be open-minded = avoir l'esprit ouvert

opera *noun*
an opera = un opéra

operate *verb*
(*to make something work*) = faire marcher
(*to carry out an operation*) = opérer
to operate on someone = opérer quelqu'un
to operate on someone's leg = opérer quelqu'un à la jambe

operation *noun*
an operation = une opération
to have an operation = se faire opérer
(**!** + *être*)

operator *noun* ▶ 315 |
an operator = un standardiste/une standardiste

opinion *noun*
an opinion (*a point of view*) = un avis
(*when judging a person, a situation*) = une opinion
in my opinion, they're lying = à mon avis, ils mentent

opponent *noun*
an opponent = un adversaire/une adversaire

opportunity *noun*
an opportunity = une occasion
to take the opportunity to visit Paris = profiter de l'occasion pour visiter Paris

oppose *verb*
to oppose a plan = s'opposer à un projet
to be opposed to nuclear weapons = être contre les armes nucléaires

opposite
1 *preposition*
= en face de
she was sitting opposite me = elle était assise en face de moi
2 *adjective*
the opposite sex = le sexe opposé
he was walking in the opposite direction = il allait dans l'autre sens
3 *adverb*
= en face
4 *noun*
the opposite = le contraire
it's the exact opposite = c'est tout le contraire

optician *noun* ▶ 315 |
an optician = un opticien/une opticienne

optimist *noun*
an optimist = un optimiste/une optimiste

optimistic *adjective*
= optimiste

or *conjunction*
or = ou
once or twice a week = une ou deux fois par semaine
we'll stay either here or at Martine's = nous resterons soit ici soit chez Martine
do you have any brothers or sisters? = est-ce que tu as des frères et sœurs?
(*in negative sentences*)
I can't come today or tomorrow = je ne peux venir ni aujourd'hui ni demain
don't tell Mum or Dad = ne le dis ni à maman ni à papa
(*otherwise*) = sinon
be careful or you'll break the cups = fais attention sinon tu vas casser les tasses

oral *adjective*
= oral/orale

orange
1 *noun*
an orange = une orange

2 *adjective* ▶ **213** |
= orange (**!** *never changes*)

orange juice *noun*
 orange juice = le jus d'orange

orchard *noun*
 an orchard = un verger

orchestra *noun*
 an orchestra = un orchestre

order
1 *verb*
 (*to tell*)
 to order someone to leave = ordonner à
  quelqu'un de partir
 (*to ask for*) = commander
 to order goods from a magazine
  = commander des articles dans un
  magazine
2 *noun*
 (*an instruction*)
 an order = un ordre
 to give orders = donner des ordres
 the right order = le bon ordre
 the list is in alphabetical order = la liste
  est dans l'ordre alphabétique
3 in order to = pour
 I phoned them in order to change the date
  = je leur ai téléphoné pour changer la
  date

ordinary *adjective*
 (*not unusual*) = ordinaire
 an ordinary family = une famille ordinaire
 (*average*) = moyen/moyenne

organ *noun*
 (*the musical instrument*) ▶ **290** |
 an organ = un orgue
 (*a part of the body*)
 an organ = un organe

organization *noun*
 an organization = une organisation

organize *verb*
 = organiser
 to get organized = s'organiser (**!** + *être*)

original *adjective*
 (*first*) = original/originale
 (*true, real*) = originel/originelle
 (*new, fresh*) = original/originale

ornament *noun*
 an ornament = un bibelot

orphan *noun*
 an orphan = un orphelin/une orpheline

ostrich *noun*
 an ostrich = une autruche

other
1 *adjective*
 = autre (+ *singular*)
 = autres (+ *plural*)
 not that dress, the other one = pas cette
  robe-là, l'autre
 they sold the other car = ils ont vendu
  l'autre voiture
 to annoy the other pupils = embêter les
  autres élèves

**some people like driving, other people
  hate it** = certains aiment conduire,
  d'autres détestent ça
 every other Saturday = un samedi sur
  deux
2 *pronoun*
 he makes the others laugh = il fait rire les
  autres
 **some students learn French easily,
  others have problems** = certains élèves
  apprennent le français facilement,
  d'autres ont des problèmes
 they came in one after the other = ils sont
  entrés l'un après l'autre

otherwise *conjunction*
 = sinon
 **it's not dangerous, otherwise I wouldn't
  go** = ce n'est pas dangereux, sinon je
  n'irais pas

otter *noun*
 an otter = une loutre

ought *verb*
 (*when talking about what should be done*)
 you ought not to say things like that = tu
  ne devrais pas dire des choses pareilles
 (*when making a polite suggestion*)
 you ought to be in bed = tu devrais être au
  lit
 (*when saying something may happen*)
 they ought to arrive tomorrow = ils
  devraient arriver demain
 (*when saying something didn't happen*)
 someone ought to have gone with them
  = quelqu'un aurait dû les accompagner

our *determiner*
 our = notre (+ *singular*)
 = nos (+ *plural*)
 he ran over our dog = il a écrasé notre
  chien
 what do you think of our house? = qu'est-
  ce que tu penses de notre maison?
 all our CDs have been stolen = on a volé
  tous nos disques compacts

ours *pronoun*
 the grey car is ours = la voiture grise est à
  nous
 which case is ours? = laquelle de ces
  valises est la nôtre?
 their garden is bigger than ours = leur
  jardin est plus grand que le nôtre
 their children are younger than ours
  = leurs enfants sont plus jeunes que les
  nôtres

 ! *Note that, when comparing objects,
 people, etc, one of the following
 translations—le nôtre, la nôtre or les
 nôtres—will be used. To know which one
 to use, find out whether the object,
 person etc which is being described is
 masculine singular, feminine singular or
 just plural.*

ourselves pronoun
(when used as a reflexive pronoun)
we want to enjoy ourselves = nous
  voulons nous amuser, on veut s'amuser
we didn't hurt ourselves = nous ne nous
  sommes pas fait mal, on ne s'est pas fait
  mal

! Note that on is more usual in spoken
French.

(when used for emphasis)
we organized everything ourselves
  = nous avons tout organisé nous-mêmes
we like to be by ourselves = nous aimons
  être seuls

out

! Often out occurs in combinations with
verbs, for example: blow out, come out,
find out, give out etc. To find the correct
translations for this type of verb, look up
the separate dictionary entries at blow,
come, find, give etc.

1 adverb
(outside) = dehors
they're out there = ils sont dehors
to stay out in the rain = rester dehors sous
  la pluie
she's out in the garden = elle est dans le
  jardin
I'm looking for the way out = je cherche la
  sortie
(absent)
to be out = être sorti/sortie
someone called while you were out
  = quelqu'un a téléphoné pendant que tu
  étais sorti
(not lighting, not on)
to be out = être éteint/éteinte
all the lights were out = toutes les
  lumières étaient éteintes
2 out of
to walk out of the building = sortir du
  bâtiment
to get out of the city = sortir de la ville
to take a pencil out of the drawer
  = prendre un crayon dans le tiroir

outdoor adjective
= en plein air
an outdoor swimming pool = une piscine
  en plein air

outdoors adverb
= dehors

outer space noun
outer space = l'espace (masculine)

outside
1 preposition
(in front of) = devant
to wait outside the school = attendre
  devant l'école
(beyond)
outside the city = en dehors de la ville

2 adverb
= dehors
let's go outside = allons dehors
let's bring the chairs outside = sortons les
  chaises
3 noun
the outside = l'extérieur (masculine)
the outside of the building = l'extérieur du
  bâtiment
4 adjective
= extérieur/extérieure

oven noun
an oven = un four

over

! Often over occurs in combinations with
verbs, for example: get over, move over
etc. To find the correct translations for this
type of verb, look up the separate
dictionary entries at get, move etc.

1 preposition
over = par-dessus
to climb over a wall = passer par-dessus un
  mur
we climbed over it = nous sommes passés
  par-dessus
(across)
it's somewhere over there = c'est quelque
  part par là
come over here = viens par ici
(above) = au-dessus de
the picture over the piano = le tableau au-
  dessus du piano
young people over 18 = les jeunes de plus
  de 18 ans
(during)
we saw them over the weekend = nous les
  avons vus pendant le week-end
(everywhere)
I've looked all over the house for my keys
  = j'ai cherché mes clés partout dans la
  maison
2 adverb
(finished)
the term is over = le trimestre est terminé
is the film over? = est-ce que le film est
  fini?
(to one's home)
to ask someone over = inviter quelqu'un
to start over again = recommencer à zéro

overdose noun
an overdose = une surdose

overtake verb
= dépasser

overweight adjective
= trop gros/trop grosse

owe verb
= devoir
to owe money to someone = devoir de
  l'argent à quelqu'un

owl noun
an owl = un hibou, une chouette

own

1 *adjective*
= propre (**!** *before the noun*)
you should clean your own room = tu devrais ranger ta propre chambre
he'd like his own car = il voudrait une voiture à lui, il voudrait sa propre voiture

2 *pronoun*

> **!** *Note that, when comparing objects, people etc, the translations given for the pronouns* mine, yours, his, hers, ours *or* theirs *work for* my own, your own *etc.*

I didn't use his pencil—I've got my own = je n'ai pas utilisé son crayon—j'ai le mien
they have a house of their own = ils ont une maison à eux, ils ont leur propre maison

3 *verb*
= avoir
he owns a shop in town = il a un magasin en ville
who owns that dog? = à qui est ce chien?
4 on one's own = tout seul/toute seule
own up = avouer

owner *noun*
an owner = un propriétaire/une propriétaire

ox *noun*
an ox = un bœuf

oxygen *noun*
oxygen = l'oxygène (*masculine*)

oyster *noun*
an oyster = une huître

Pacific *noun*
the Pacific = le Pacifique

pack

1 *verb*
= faire ses bagages
I've got to pack my suitcase = je dois faire ma valise

2 *noun*
a pack = un paquet
a pack of cigarettes = un paquet de cigarettes
a pack of cards = un jeu de cartes
pack up = faire ses bagages
to pack up one's belongings = emballer ses affaires

package *noun*
a package = un paquet, un colis

packed *adjective*
(*describing a room*) = plein/pleine à craquer
(*describing a train, a bus*) = bondé/bondée

packet *noun*
a packet = un paquet

page *noun*
a page = une page
on page six = (à la) page six

pain *noun*
pain = la douleur
I've got a pain in my back = j'ai mal au dos
to be in pain = souffrir

painful *adjective*
= douloureux/douloureuse

paint

1 *noun*
paint = la peinture

2 *verb*
= peindre

paintbrush *noun*
a paintbrush = un pinceau

painter *noun* ▶ 315 |
a painter = un peintre

painting *noun*
(*a picture*)
a painting = un tableau
(*the activity*)
painting = la peinture

pair *noun*
a pair = une paire
a pair of shoes = une paire de chaussures

pajamas *noun* (*US English*)
pajamas = un pyjama (*singular*)

Pakistan *noun* ▶ 218 |
Pakistan = le Pakistan

palace *noun*
a palace = un palais

pale *adjective*
= pâle
to go pale, to turn pale = pâlir

pancake *noun*
a pancake = une crêpe

panic *verb*
= s'affoler (**!** + *être*)

pants *noun*
(*British English*) (*underwear*)
pants = un slip (*singular*)
(*US English*) (*trousers*)
pants = un pantalon (*singular*)

pantyhose *noun* (*US English*)
pantyhose = un collant

paper *noun*
(*for writing or drawing on*)
paper = le papier
a piece of paper = un bout de papier

(*a newspaper*)
a paper = un journal

parachuting *noun* ▶ **248**
parachuting = le parachutisme

parade *noun*
a parade = un défilé

paragliding *noun* ▶ **248**
paragliding = le parapente

paralysed (*British English*), **paralyzed**
(*US English*) *adjective*
= paralysé/paralysée

parcel *noun*
a parcel = un paquet, un colis

parents *noun*
parents = les parents (*masculine*)

Paris *noun* ▶ **218**
Paris = Paris

park
1 *noun*
a park = un jardin public, un parc
2 *verb*
to park a car = garer une voiture
to park near the office = se garer près du bureau

parking lot *noun* (*US English*)
a parking lot = un parking, un parc de stationnement

parking meter *noun*
a parking meter = un parcmètre

parliament *noun*
a parliament = un parlement

parrot *noun*
a parrot = un perroquet

part
a part = une partie
part of the [book | film | time ...] = une partie du [livre | film | temps ...]
It's part of the job = ça fait partie du travail
in this part of the country = dans cette région
(*a piece for a machine, a car*)
a part = une pièce
(*a section*)
a part (*in a programme*) = une partie
(*in a series*) = un épisode
(*a role*)
a part = un rôle
to play the part of Tommy = jouer le rôle de Tommy

participate *verb*
= participer

particular
1 *adjective*
= particulier/particulière
2 in particular = en particulier

partner *noun*
(*in a relationship*)
a partner = un compagnon/une compagne
(*in dancing, sport*)
a partner = un partenaire/une partenaire

part-time *adverb*
= à temps partiel
to work part-time = travailler à temps partiel

party *noun*
(*a social event*)
a party = une fête
(*held in the evening*) = une soirée
a birthday party = une fête d'anniversaire, un anniversaire
a children's party = un goûter d'enfants
a political party = un parti politique

pass *verb*
(*to go past*) = passer (**!** + *être*)
to let someone pass = laisser passer quelqu'un
to pass the school = passer devant l'école
to pass a car = dépasser une voiture
to pass someone in the street = croiser quelqu'un dans la rue
(*to give*) = passer
pass me the salt, please = passe-moi le sel, s'il te plaît
to pass the ball to someone = passer le ballon à quelqu'un
(*to spend*) = passer
to pass the time [reading | painting | listening to the radio ...] = passer le temps [en lisant | en faisant de la peinture | en écoutant la radio ...]
(*to succeed in an exam*) = réussir
to pass an exam = réussir un examen
pass around
to pass around the biscuits = faire passer les biscuits
pass on = transmettre
to pass on a message to someone = transmettre un message à quelqu'un

passage *noun*
a passage (*indoors*) = un couloir
(*outdoors*) = un passage

passenger *noun*
a passenger = un passager/une passagère

passport *noun*
a passport = un passeport

past
1 *noun*
the past = le passé
in the past = dans le passé
2 *adjective*
= dernier/dernière (**!** *before the noun*)
the past few days have been difficult = ces derniers jours ont été difficiles
3 *preposition*
(*when talking about time*) ▶ **211**
it's twenty past four = il est quatre heures vingt
it's past midnight = il est minuit passé

P

(by)
to go past someone = passer devant
quelqu'un
she ran past me = elle est passée devant
moi en courant
(beyond) = après
it's just past the traffic lights = c'est juste
après les feux
4 adverb
to go past, to walk past = passer (**!** + être)

pasta noun
pasta = les pâtes (feminine)

pastry noun
(for baking)
pastry = la pâte
to make pastry = faire de la pâte
(a cake)
a pastry = une pâtisserie, un gâteau

patch noun
(on a garment)
a patch = une pièce
(on a tyre)
a patch = une rustine

path noun
a path = un chemin
(narrower) = un sentier
(in a garden) = une allée

patience noun
patience = la patience
to lose patience with someone = perdre
patience avec quelqu'un

patient
1 noun
a patient = un patient/une patiente
2 adjective
= patient/patiente

patrol car noun
a patrol car = une voiture de police

pattern noun
(a design)
a pattern = un dessin, un motif
(when making garments)
a pattern (for knitting) = un modèle
(for sewing) = un patron

pavement noun (British English)
a pavement = un trottoir

paw noun
a paw = une patte

pay
1 verb
to pay = payer
to pay the bills = payer les factures
to pay for the shopping = payer les
courses
he paid for my meal = il a payé mon repas
(when talking about wages)
the work doesn't pay very well = le travail
est mal payé
I'm paid eight pounds an hour = je suis
payé huit livres de l'heure

(to give)
to pay attention to the teacher = écouter
le professeur
to pay someone a visit = rendre visite à
quelqu'un
to pay someone a compliment = faire des
compliments à quelqu'un
2 noun
pay = le salaire
the pay is very good = c'est très bien payé
pay back = rembourser

PE noun
PE = l'éducation physique
! Note that éducation is feminine.

pea noun
a pea = un petit pois

peace noun
peace = la paix

peach noun
a peach = une pêche

peacock noun
a peacock = un paon

peanut noun
a peanut = une cacahuète

pear noun
a pear = une poire

pearl noun
a pearl = une perle

pebble noun
a pebble (on a beach) = un galet

pedestrian noun
a pedestrian = un piéton

pedestrian crossing noun
a pedestrian crossing = un passage pour
piétons

peel verb
= éplucher

pen noun
a pen = un stylo

penalty noun
a penalty (in soccer) = un tir de
réparation, un penalty
(in rugby) = une pénalité

pencil noun
a pencil = un crayon

pencil case noun
a pencil case = une trousse à crayons

pencil sharpener noun
a pencil sharpener = un taille-crayon

penfriend (British English), **penpal**
noun
a penfriend = un correspondant/une
correspondante

penguin noun
a penguin = un pingouin

penknife noun
  a penknife = un canif

pensioner noun
  a pensioner = un retraité/une retraitée

people noun
  people (in general) = les gens (masculine plural)
  (if counting) = les personnes (feminine plural)
  we met very nice people = nous avons fait la connaissance de gens très sympathiques
  most people don't know what's going on = la plupart des gens ne savent pas ce qui se passe
  there were three people at the meeting = il y avait trois personnes à la réunion
  there are too many people here = il y a trop de monde ici
  to help other people = aider les autres

pepper noun
  (the spice)
  pepper = le poivre
  (the vegetable)
  a pepper = un poivron

per preposition
  per person = par personne

per cent, **percent** (US English) noun
  per cent = pour cent, %

perfect adjective
  = parfait/parfaite
  to speak perfect French = parler un français parfait
  it's the perfect place for a picnic = c'est l'endroit idéal pour un pique-nique

perform verb
  (to do)
  to perform a task = exécuter une tâche
  (to act, to play) = jouer

perfume noun
  perfume = le parfum
  to wear perfume = mettre du parfum

perhaps adverb
  = peut-être

period noun
  (in time)
  a period = une période
  a trial period = une période d'essai
  (in history)
  a period = une époque
  (for women)
  a period = des règles (feminine plural)
  to have one's period = avoir ses règles
  (a school lesson)
  a period = un cours

permanent adjective
  = permanent/permanente

permission noun
  permission = la permission
  to get permission to leave the country = obtenir la permission de quitter le pays

person noun
  a person = une personne
  an old person = une personne âgée
  to be a kind person – être gentil/gentille
  he's not a very patient person = il n'est pas très patient

personal adjective
  = personnel/personnelle

personality noun
  a personality = une personnalité

perspire verb
  = transpirer

persuade verb
  = persuader
  to persuade someone to buy a car = persuader quelqu'un d'acheter une voiture

pessimist noun
  a pessimist = un pessimiste/une pessimiste

pessimistic adjective
  = pessimiste

pet noun
  a pet = un animal de compagnie
  do you have any pets? = est-ce que tu as des animaux?

petrol noun (British English)
  petrol = l'essence (feminine)
  to run out of petrol = tomber en panne d'essence

petrol station noun (British English)
  a petrol station = une station d'essence

pet shop noun ▶ 315 |
  a pet shop = une animalerie

phone
1 noun
  a phone = un téléphone
  the phone's ringing = le téléphone sonne
  to answer the phone = répondre au téléphone
  he's on the phone = il est au téléphone
2 verb
  = téléphoner
  to phone someone = téléphoner à quelqu'un, passer un coup de fil à quelqu'un

phone book noun
  a phone book = un annuaire téléphonique

phone booth noun
  a phone booth = une cabine téléphonique

P

phone call *noun*
 a phone call = un coup de fil, un appel téléphonique
 to receive a phone call = recevoir un appel téléphonique, recevoir un coup de fil
 to make a phone call = téléphoner, passer un coup de fil

phone card *noun*
 a phone card = une télécarte

phone number *noun*
 a phone number = un numéro de téléphone

photo *noun*
 a photo = une photo

photocopier *noun*
 a photocopier = une photocopieuse

photocopy *noun*
 a photocopy = une photocopie

photograph *noun*
 a photograph = une photo
 to take a photograph of someone = prendre quelqu'un en photo

photographer *noun* ▶ 315 |
 a photographer = un photographe/une photographe

physical *adjective*
 = physique

physics *noun*
 physics = la physique

piano *noun* ▶ 290 |
 a piano = un piano

pick *verb*
 (*to choose*) = choisir
 to pick a number = choisir un chiffre
 (*to collect*) = cueillir
 to pick blackberries = cueillir des mûres
 (*to take*)
 to pick a book off the shelf = prendre un livre sur l'étagère
pick on = s'en prendre à (**!** + *être*)
 he's always picking on me = il s'en prend toujours à moi
pick out = choisir
pick up
 (*to lift*) = ramasser
 to pick the clothes up off the floor = ramasser les vêtements par terre
 to pick a baby up = prendre un bébé dans ses bras
 to pick up the phone = décrocher le téléphone
 (*to collect*)
 to pick up passengers = prendre des passagers
 he's coming to pick me up = il vient me chercher

 (*to buy*) = prendre
 I stopped to pick up some milk = je me suis arrêté pour prendre du lait
 (*to learn*)
 to pick up a little German = apprendre un peu d'allemand

picnic *noun*
 a picnic = un pique-nique
 to go on a picnic = aller faire un pique-nique

picture *noun*
 a picture (*painted*) = une peinture, un tableau
 (*drawn*) = un dessin
 to paint someone's picture = faire le portrait de quelqu'un
 (*a photograph*)
 a picture = une photo
 the pictures = le cinéma (*singular*)

piece *noun*
 (*a bit*)
 a piece = un morceau
 a piece of cheese = un morceau de fromage
 a piece of string = un bout de ficelle
 (*a part of a machine*)
 a piece = une pièce
 (*a broken part*)
 a piece = un morceau
 to fall to pieces = tomber en morceaux
 (*a coin*)
 a 50-pence piece = une pièce de 50 pence
 (*other uses*)
 a piece of furniture = un meuble
 a piece of information = un renseignement
 a piece of advice = un conseil

pierce *verb*
 = percer

pig *noun*
 a pig = un porc, un cochon

pigeon *noun*
 a pigeon = un pigeon

pile *noun*
 a pile = une pile
 (*untidy*) = un tas
 a pile of old shoes = un tas de vieilles chaussures
 (*lots*)
 piles of [toys | records | books …] = des tas✷ de [jouets | disques | livres …]

pill *noun*
 (*a tablet*)
 a pill = un comprimé
 (*a method of contraception*)
 the pill = la pilule

pillow *noun*
 a pillow = un oreiller

pilot *noun* ▶ 315 |
 a pilot = un pilote

pin
1 *noun*
 a pin = une épingle
2 *verb*
 = accrocher

pinball *noun* ▶ 248 |
 pinball = le flipper

pinch *verb*
 to pinch = pincer
 **he pinched my arm, he pinched me on the
  arm** = il m'a pincé le bras
 (to hurt by being too tight) = serrer
 my shoes are pinching = mes chaussures
  me serrent

pineapple *noun*
 a pineapple = un ananas

pine tree *noun*
 a pine tree = un pin

pink *adjective* ▶ 213 |
 = rose

pint *noun*
 (the quantity)
 a pint ≈ un demi-litre

 ! *Note that a pint = 0.57 l in Britain and
 0.47 l in the US.*

 a pint of milk ≈ un demi-litre de lait
 (British English) (a drink)
 to go for a pint = aller boire une bière

pipe *noun*
 (for gas, water)
 a pipe = un tuyau
 (for smoking)
 a pipe = une pipe

pirate *noun*
 a pirate = un pirate

Pisces *noun*
 Pisces = Poissons *(masculine plural)*

pitch *noun (British English)*
 a pitch = un terrain
 a football pitch = un terrain de football

pity
1 *noun*
 pity = la pitié
 (when expressing regret)
 what a pity! = quel dommage!
 it's a pity you can't come = c'est dommage
  que tu ne puisses pas venir

 ! *Note that the subjunctive is used after*
 c'est dommage que.

2 *verb*
 = plaindre

pizza *noun*
 a pizza = une pizza

place *noun*
 a place = un endroit
 it's the best place to buy salmon = c'est le
  meilleur endroit pour acheter du
  saumon
 Oxford is a nice place = Oxford est une
  belle ville
 they come from all over the place = ils
  viennent de partout
 this place is dirty = c'est sale ici
 (a home)
 at Alison's place = chez Alison
 I'd like a place of my own = j'aimerais
  avoir un chez-moi
 *(in a queue, on a bus, in a car park, at
 table)*
 a place = une place
 is this place free? = est-ce que cette place
  est libre?
 to take someone's place = prendre la
  place de quelqu'un
 to find a place to park = trouver une place
  pour se garer
 (on a team, a course, in a firm)
 a place = une place
 to get a place on a course = obtenir une
  place dans un cours
 (in a contest)
 a place = une place
 to win first place = gagner la première
  place

plain
1 *adjective*
 (simple) = simple
 a plain dress = une robe simple
 (not good-looking) = quelconque
2 *noun*
 a plain = une plaine

plait *noun (British English)*
 a plait = une natte, une tresse

plan
1 *noun*
 (what one intends to do)
 a plan = un plan
 we need a plan = il nous faut un plan
 (what one has arranged to do)
 a plan = un projet
 do you have any plans for the future?
  = est-ce que tu as des projets pour
  l'avenir?
 I don't have any plans for tonight = je n'ai
  rien de prévu pour ce soir
2 *verb*
 (to prepare, to organize)
 to plan [a trip | a school timetable | a
  meeting ...] = organiser [un voyage | un
  emploi du temps | une réunion ...]
 (to intend) = avoir l'intention de
 I'm planning to visit Scotland = j'ai
  l'intention de visiter l'Écosse

plane *noun*
 a plane = un avion

P

planet *noun*
  a planet = une planète

plant
1 *noun*
  a plant = une plante
2 *verb*
  = planter

plaster *noun* (*British English*)
  a plaster = un pansement adhésif

plastic
1 *noun*
  plastic = le plastique
2 *adjective*
  = en plastique

plate *noun*
  a plate = une assiette

platform *noun*
  a platform = un quai
  on platform 4 = au quai numéro 4

play
1 *verb*
  (*to have fun*) = jouer
  to play with friends = jouer avec des amis
  to play a trick on someone = jouer un
    tour à quelqu'un
  to play cards = jouer aux cartes
  (*when talking about sports*) ▶ **248** | = jouer
  to play [**football** | **cricket** | **tennis** …] = jouer
    [au football | au cricket | au tennis …]
  France is playing (against) Ireland = la
    France joue contre l'Irlande
  (*when talking about music*) ▶ **290** | = jouer
  to play [**the piano** | **the flute** | **drums** …] = jouer
    [du piano | de la flûte | de la batterie …]
  (*to put on*) = mettre
  to play [**a video** | **a CD** | **a record** …] = mettre
    [une cassette vidéo | un disque compact | un
    disque …]
  (*when talking about theatre, cinema*)
  to play the role of Richard II = jouer le rôle
    de Richard II
  the film will be playing at the Phoenix = le
    film va passer au Phoenix
2 *noun*
  a play = une pièce
play around = faire l'imbécile
play back
  to play back a tape = repasser une cassette

player *noun* ▶ **248** |
  a player = un joueur/une joueuse
  a tennis player = un joueur/une joueuse
    de tennis

playground *noun*
  a playground = une aire de jeu
  the school playground = la cour de
    récréation

please *adverb*
  (*formal, to several people*) = s'il vous plaît
  (*informal*) = s'il te plaît
  please come in = entrez, je vous en prie
  'more cake?'—'yes please' = 'encore du
    gâteau?'—'oui, je veux bien'

pleased *adjective*
  = content/contente
  I was very pleased with myself = j'étais
    très content de moi
  pleased to meet you = enchanté

plenty *pronoun*
  to have plenty [**of time** | **of money** | **of
    friends** …] = avoir beaucoup [de temps |
    d'argent | d'amis …]

plot *noun*
  (*a plan*)
  a plot = un complot
  (*the story in a film, a novel, a play*)
  a plot = une intrigue

plug *noun*
  (*on an appliance*)
  a plug = une prise
  to pull out the plug = débrancher la prise
  (*in a sink or bath*)
  a plug = une bonde
plug in = brancher

plum *noun*
  a plum = une prune

plumber *noun* ▶ **315** |
  a plumber = un plombier

plus *preposition*
  = plus
  three plus three are six = trois plus trois
    font six

pocket *noun*
  a pocket = une poche

pocketbook *noun* (*US English*)
  a pocketbook = un sac à main

pocket money *noun*
  pocket money = l'argent de poche
  ! Note that *argent* is masculine.

poem *noun*
  a poem = un poème

point
1 *noun*
  (*a statement in a discussion*)
  a point = une remarque
  to make a point = faire une remarque
  (*the most important idea*)
  the point = le point essentiel
  that's not the point = là n'est pas la
    question
  (*use*)
  there's no point in shouting = ça ne sert à
    rien de crier
  (*when talking about time*)
  to be on the point of [**moving** | **leaving** |
    selling the house …] = être sur le point de
    [déménager | partir | vendre la maison …]
  (*the sharp end*)
  the point = la pointe
  the point of a pencil = la pointe d'un
    crayon
  (*in a contest, a game*)
  a point = un point

2 *verb*
(*to indicate*)
to point (one's finger) at someone
= montrer quelqu'un du doigt
to point at a house = indiquer une maison
to point the way to the station = indiquer
 la direction de la gare
(*to aim*)
to point a gun at someone = braquer un
 pistolet sur quelqu'un
point out = montrer
can you point them out to me? = est-ce
 que tu peux me les montrer?

poison
1 *noun*
 poison = le poison
2 *verb*
 = empoisonner

Poland *noun* ▶ **218**
 Poland = la Pologne

pole *noun*
 a pole = une perche

police *noun*
 the police = la police

policeman *noun* ▶ **315**
 a policeman = un policier

police station *noun*
 a police station = un poste de police

policewoman *noun* ▶ **315**
 a policewoman = une femme policier

polish *verb*
 to polish shoes = cirer des chaussures
 to polish the car = lustrer la voiture

polite *adjective*
 = poli/polie

political *adjective*
 = politique

politician *noun* ▶ **315**
 a politician = un homme/une femme
  politique

politics *noun*
 politics = la politique

pollute *verb*
 = polluer

pollution *noun*
 pollution = la pollution

pond *noun*
 a pond (*large*) = un étang
 (*smaller*) = une mare
 (*in a garden*) = un bassin

pony *noun*
 a pony = un poney

ponytail *noun*
 a ponytail = une queue de cheval

pool *noun*
 (*a swimming pool*)
 a pool = une piscine

(*on the ground, the floor*)
a pool of water = une flaque d'eau
(*the game*) ▶ **248**
pool = le billard américain

poor *adjective*
(*not wealthy*) = pauvre
(*not satisfactory*) = mauvais/mauvaise
(! *before the noun*)
to be poor at languages = être faible en
 langues
(*expressing sympathy*) = pauvre (! *before*
 the noun)
the poor boy is exhausted = le pauvre
 garçon est épuisé

popular *adjective*
> ! Note that **popular** *is not usually*
> *translated by* **populaire**.

a popular hobby = un passe-temps
 répandu
she's very popular = elle a beaucoup
 d'amis
to be popular with the girls = avoir du
 succès auprès des filles

population *noun*
 a population = une population

pork *noun*
 pork = le porc

port *noun*
 a port = un port

portrait *noun*
 a portrait = un portrait

Portugal *noun* ▶ **218**
 Portugal = le Portugal

Portuguese ▶ **275**
1 *adjective*
 = portugais/portugaise
2 *noun*
 (*the people*)
 the Portuguese = les Portugais (*masculine*
  plural)
 (*the language*)
 Portuguese = le portugais

positive *adjective*
 = positif/positive

possibility *noun*
 a possibility = une possibilité

possible *adjective*
 = possible
 they came as quickly as possible = ils
  sont venus le plus vite possible
 I did as much as possible = j'ai fait tout ce
  que j'ai pu

post (*British English*)
1 *noun*
 the post (*the system*) = la poste
 (*the letters*) = le courrier
 has the post come yet? = est-ce que le
  courrier est arrivé?

P

2 *verb*
  to post a letter = poster une lettre

postbox *noun* (*British English*)
  a postbox = une boîte aux lettres

postcard *noun*
  a postcard = une carte postale

postcode *noun* (*British English*)
  a postcode = un code postal

poster *noun*
  a poster (*giving information*) = une affiche
  (*used as a picture*) = un poster

postman *noun* ▶ **315** (*British English*)
  a postman = un facteur

post office *noun*
  a post office = un bureau de poste

postpone *verb*
  to postpone a concert = reporter un
    concert
  let's postpone the party until next week
    = reportons la fête à la semaine
    prochaine

pot *noun*
  (*a container*)
  a pot = un pot
  to make a pot of tea = faire du thé
  (*a saucepan*)
  a pot = une casserole

potato *noun*
  a potato = une pomme de terre

pottery *noun*
  pottery = la poterie

pound *noun*
  (*the currency*)
  a pound = une livre
  (*the measurement*)
  a pound ≈ une livre
  | **!** *Note that a pound = 453.6 g.*

  two pounds of apples ≈ un kilo de
    pommes

pour *verb*
  (*from a container*) = verser
  to pour milk into a bowl = verser du lait
    dans un bol
  (*to serve*) = servir
  to pour someone a vodka = servir une
    vodka à quelqu'un
  (*to flow*) = couler (à flots)
  the water was pouring into the kitchen
    = l'eau coulait dans la cuisine
  (*to escape*)
  there is smoke pouring out of the window
    = il y a de la fumée qui sort par la
    fenêtre
  (*to rain*)
  it's pouring (with rain) = il pleut à verse

✗ in informal situations

(*to enter or leave in large numbers*)
  to pour into the city = affluer dans la ville
  to pour out of the stadium = sortir en
    grand nombre du stade

powder *noun*
  a powder = une poudre

power *noun*
  (*control*)
  power = le pouvoir
  to be in power = être au pouvoir
  (*influence*)
  to have great power = avoir une grande
    influence
  (*electricity*)
  power = le courant

practical *adjective*
  = pratique

practise (*British English*), **practice** (*US
English*) *verb*
  (*at the piano, guitar*) = s'exercer (**!** + *être*)
  (*at a sport*) = s'entraîner (**!** + *être*)
  (*for a play, a concert*) = répéter
  to practise [the violin | one's French | a
    song ...] = travailler [le violon | son français |
    une chanson ...]

praise *verb*
  to praise someone (*when talking to
    someone else*) = faire l'éloge de
    quelqu'un
  (*when talking directly to someone*)
    = féliciter quelqu'un

prawn *noun* (*British English*)
  a prawn = une crevette rose

prayer *noun*
  a prayer = une prière

precaution *noun*
  a precaution = une précaution

precious *adjective*
  = précieux/précieuse

precise *adjective*
  = précis/précise

prefer *verb*
  = préférer, aimer mieux
  to prefer chocolate to vanilla = mieux
    aimer le chocolat que la vanille
  I'd prefer to phone = j'aimerais mieux
    téléphoner

pregnant *adjective*
  = enceinte

prejudice *noun*
  a prejudice = un préjugé

prepare *verb*
  (*to get something or someone ready*)
  = préparer
  to prepare pupils for an exam = préparer
    des élèves à un examen

(to get ready)
to prepare for [an exam | a trip | a party …]
= se préparer pour [un examen | un voyage | une fête …]

prepared *adjective*
(willing)
to be prepared to wait = être prêt/prête à attendre
(ready)
to be prepared for an exam = être prêt/prête pour un examen

prescription *noun*
a prescription = une ordonnance

present
1 *noun*
(a gift)
a present = un cadeau
to give someone a present = offrir un cadeau à quelqu'un
(now)
the present = le présent
I'm staying here for the present = je reste ici pour l'instant
2 *verb*
(to give)
to present a prize to someone = remettre un prix à quelqu'un
(on radio or TV)
to present a programme = présenter une émission

president *noun* ▶ 315|
a president = un président/une présidente

press
1 *verb*
= appuyer sur
to press the bell = appuyer sur la sonnette
to press (oneself) against the wall = se plaquer contre le mur
2 *noun*
the press = la presse

pressure *noun*
pressure = la pression
to put pressure on someone = faire pression sur quelqu'un

pretend *verb*
= faire semblant
he's pretending to be annoyed = il fait semblant d'être vexé

pretty
1 *adjective*
= joli/jolie
2 *adverb*
= assez
that's pretty good = ce n'est pas mal du tout✶

prevent *verb*
to prevent a war = éviter une guerre
to prevent someone from [working | having fun | sleeping …] = empêcher quelqu'un de [travailler | s'amuser | dormir …]

previous *adjective*
= précédent/précédente

price *noun*
a price = un prix

pride *noun*
pride = la fierté
(self-respect)
pride = l'amour-propre *(masculine)*

priest *noun* ▶ 315|
a priest = un prêtre

primary school *noun*
a primary school = une école primaire

primary school teacher *noun* ▶ 315|
a primary school teacher = un instituteur/une institutrice, un professeur des écoles

prime minister *noun* ▶ 315|
the prime minister = le premier ministre

prince *noun*
a prince = un prince

princess *noun*
a princess = une princesse

principal *noun*
a principal *(in a senior school)* = un proviseur
(in a junior school) = un directeur/une directrice

print
1 *verb*
= imprimer
to print a book = imprimer un livre
2 *noun*
(of a photo)
a print = une épreuve
(of a finger, a foot)
a print = une empreinte

priority *noun*
a priority = une priorité

prison *noun*
a prison = une prison
to put someone in prison = mettre quelqu'un en prison

prisoner *noun*
a prisoner = un prisonnier/une prisonnière
to be taken prisoner = être fait prisonnier/faite prisonnière

private
1 *adjective*
(personal) = privé/privée
my private life = ma vie privée
(not run by the state) = privé/privée
a private school = une école privée
2 in private = en privé

prize *noun*
a prize = un prix

probably *adverb*
= probablement

P

problem noun
a problem = un problème
to cause a problem = poser un problème

process noun
a process = un processus
to be in the process of writing a letter
= être en train d'écrire une lettre

produce
1 verb
• (to make) = produire
• (to create)
to produce a film = produire un film
to produce a play = mettre en scène une
pièce
2 noun
produce = les produits (masculine plural)

product noun
a product = un produit

production noun
production (of food) = la production
(of machinery, cars) = la fabrication

profession noun
a profession = une profession

professional adjective
= professionnel/professionnelle

professor noun ▶ 315|
a professor = un professeur d'université

profit noun
a profit = un bénéfice

program
1 noun
• (for a computer)
a program = un programme
• (US English) ▶ **programme**
2 verb
= programmer

programme (British English), **program**
(US English)
1 noun
• (on radio, TV)
a programme = une émission
a programme about China = une émission
sur la Chine
• (for a play, a concert)
a programme = un programme
2 verb
= programmer

progress noun
progress = le progrès
to make progress = faire des progrès

project noun
a project (at school) = un dossier

promise
1 verb
= promettre
to promise [to write | to repay a loan | to say
nothing …] = promettre [d'écrire | de
rembourser un prêt | de ne rien dire …]

2 noun
a promise = une promesse

pronounce verb
= prononcer

proof noun
proof = une preuve

properly adverb
= correctement

property noun
property = la propriété

protect verb
= protéger
to protect oneself = se protéger (! + être)

protest verb
• (to complain) = protester
• (to demonstrate) = manifester

protester noun
a protester = un manifestant/une
manifestante

proud adjective
= fier/fière
she's proud of her work = elle est fière de
son travail

prove verb
= prouver

provide verb
to provide meals = fournir des repas
to provide work for people = fournir du
travail aux gens
to provide a transport service = assurer
un service de transport

provided conjunction
I'll lend you my car provided you pay me
= je te prête ma voiture à condition que
tu me paies
! Note that the subjunctive is used after à
condition que.

psychiatrist noun ▶ 315|
a psychiatrist = un psychiatre/une
psychiatre

psychologist noun ▶ 315|
a psychologist = un psychologue/une
psychologue

pub noun (British English)
a pub = un pub

public
1 noun
the public = le public
2 adjective
a public park = un jardin public
a public library = une bibliothèque
municipale
3 in public = en public

public holiday noun
a public holiday = un jour férié

Shops, trades, and professions

Work and Jobs

what does she do?	= qu'est-ce qu'elle fait comme métier?
what do you do for a living?	= qu'est-ce que vous faites dans la vie?

- There are various ways of saying what someone works at in French. In this area, the major difference between the two languages is the *absence of article* in French, whereas in the singular English always has a.

Note the following examples:

*he's got a job as **a** mechanic*	= il travaille comme mécanicien
*to work as **a** translator*	= travailler comme traducteur / traductrice
*Paul is **a** dentist*	= Paul est dentiste
*I want to be **a** policeman*	= je voudrais devenir agent de police

- The only case where you would use the article **un** / **une** or **des** in the plural would be in combination with **c'est** or **ce sont**, so:

she is a teacher	= elle est professeur
but	= **c'est un** professeur*
she's a judge	= elle est juge
but	= **c'est un** juge*
they are all doctors	= ils sont tous médecins
but	= **ce sont** tous **des** médecins*

- When using an adjective to describe what kind of doctor / teacher / worker a person is, you must use **c'est un** / **une** ...

*she's a **good** journalist*	= c'est une **bonne** journaliste
*he's a **bad** teacher*	= c'est un **mauvais** professeur
*he's an **excellent** chef*	= c'est un chef **excellent**

* Note that some professions do not have a feminine form and the article will always be masculine as in the examples using **professeur**, **juge**, **médecin**, **ministre**, ...

Shops

In English you can say *at the baker's* or *at the baker's shop*. French also has this possibility but the translation for *at* will also differ depending on what follows:

***at** the baker's*	= **chez** le boulanger
***at** the baker's shop*	= **à** la boulangerie

chez means *at the house or premises of* and is used with the French word for the particular tradesman or professional:

*I'm going **to** the chemist's*	= je vais **chez** le pharmacien
*she's gone **to** the hairdresser's*	= elle est allée **chez** le coiffeur
*I've got an appointment **at** the dentist's*	= j'ai rendezvous **chez** le dentiste
*is he **at** the doctor's?*	= est-ce qu'il est **chez** le médecin?

However you can also use **à la** / **au** (or **à l'** + *vowel* or *mute h*) with the French word for a shop:

*I'm going **to** the chemist's*	= je vais **à la** pharmacie
*he's **at** the grocer's*	= il est **à l'**épicerie
*they've gone **to** the baker's*	= ils sont allés **à la boulangerie**

So in French you could have translations using either **à la** or **chez** in the following example:

*go **to** the butcher's*	= va **à la** boucherie
	= va **chez** le boucher

---

public transport *noun*
  public transport = les transports en commun

  ! Note that **transports** is *masculine plural*.

pudding *noun* (British English)
  a pudding = un dessert

puddle *noun*
  a puddle = une flaque

pull *verb*
  to pull = tirer
  to pull someone's hair = tirer les cheveux de quelqu'un
  to pull (on) a rope = tirer sur une corde
  (*to move*)
  to pull the piano into the hall = traîner le piano dans l'entrée
  to pull someone away from the door = éloigner quelqu'un de la porte
  (*to take out*)
  to pull a handkerchief out of one's pocket = tirer un mouchoir de sa poche
  to pull someone out of the river = sortir quelqu'un de la rivière
  to pull a face (*British English*) = faire une grimace
pull down
  (*to knock down*) = démolir
  (*to lower*) = baisser
pull out
  to pull a tooth out = arracher une dent
pull up
  (*to stop*) = s'arrêter (**!** + *être*)
  (*to remove*)
  to pull up the flowers = arracher les fleurs
  to pull up one's socks = remonter ses chaussettes

pullover *noun*
  a pullover = un pull

pump *noun*
  a pump = une pompe
  a bicycle pump = une pompe à bicyclette
pump up = gonfler

pumpkin *noun*
  a pumpkin = une citrouille

punch *verb*
  = donner des coups de poing
  she punched him in the face = elle lui a donné un coup de poing dans la figure

puncture *noun*
  a puncture = une crevaison

punish *verb*
  = punir

pupil *noun*
  a pupil = un élève/une élève

puppet *noun*
  a puppet = une marionnette

puppy *noun*
  a puppy = un chiot

pure *adjective*
  = pur/pure

purple *adjective* ▶ 213|
  = violet/violette

purpose
1 *noun*
  a purpose = un but
2 on purpose = exprès
  you did it on purpose! = tu l'as fait exprès!

purse *noun*
  (*for money*)
  a purse = un porte-monnaie
  (*US English*) (*a handbag*)
  a purse = un sac à main

push *verb*
  to push = pousser
  to push a car = pousser une voiture
  to push someone down the stairs = pousser quelqu'un dans l'escalier
  to push someone out of the way = écarter quelqu'un
  to push past someone = bousculer quelqu'un
  (*to sell*) = vendre
  to push drugs = vendre de la drogue

pushchair *noun* (*British English*)
  a pushchair = une poussette

pusher *noun*
  a pusher = un revendeur/une revendeuse de drogue

put *verb*
  = mettre
  to put the cards on the table = mettre les cartes sur la table
  don't put sugar in my coffee = ne mets pas de sucre dans mon café
  to put someone in prison = mettre quelqu'un en prison
  to put someone in a bad mood = mettre quelqu'un de mauvaise humeur
put away = ranger
put back
  (*to return to its place*) = remettre
  to put a book back on a shelf = remettre un livre sur une étagère
  (*to change the time*)
  to put the clocks back = retarder les pendules
put down
  (*on a surface*) = poser
  put your cases down here, Laurence = pose tes valises ici, Laurence
  (*when phoning*)
  to put the phone down = raccrocher
  (*British English*) (*to give an injection to*) = piquer
  our dog had to be put down = on a dû faire piquer notre chien
put forward = avancer
  to put the clocks forward = avancer les pendules
put off
  (*to delay*)
  we'll have to put the party off till next week = il va falloir reporter la fête à la semaine prochaine
  (*to switch off*) = éteindre
put on
  (*when dressing*) = mettre
  to put jeans on = mettre un jean

Quantities

Note the use of **en** (*of it* or *of them*) in the following examples. This word must be included when the thing you are talking about is not expressed. However, **en** is not needed when the commodity is specified (*there is a lot of butter* = il y a beaucoup de beurre):

How much?

how much is there?	= combien y **en** a-t-il?
there's a lot	= il y **en** a beaucoup
there's not much	= il n'y **en** a pas beaucoup
there's two kilos	= il y **en** a deux kilos
how much sugar have you?	= combien de sucre as-tu?
I've got a lot	= j'**en** ai beaucoup
I haven't got (very) much	= je n'**en** ai pas beaucoup
I've got two kilos	= j'**en** ai deux kilos

How many?

how many are there?	= combien y **en** a-t-il?*
there are a lot	= il y **en** a beaucoup*
there aren't many	= il n'y **en** a pas beaucoup*
there are twenty	= il y **en** a vingt
how many apples have you?	= combien de pommes as-tu?*
	tu as combien de pommes?
I've got a lot	= j'**en** ai beaucoup
I haven't got many	= je n'**en** ai pas beaucoup

Comparisons

I've got twenty	= j'**en** ai vingt
Tim has got more than Tom	= Tim **en** a plus que Tom
Tim has got more money than Tom	= Tim a plus d'argent que Tom
much more than	= beaucoup plus que
a little more than	= un peu plus que
Tim has got more apples than Tom	= Tim a plus de pommes que Tom
many more apples than Tom	= beaucoup plus de pommes que Tom
a few more apples than Tom	= quelques pommes de plus que Tom
a few more people than yesterday	= quelques personnes de plus qu'hier
Tom has got less than Tim	= Tom **en** a moins que Tim
Tom has got less money than Tim	= Tom a moins d'argent que Tim
much less than	= beaucoup moins que
a little less than	= un peu moins que
Tom has got fewer than Tim	= Tom **en** a moins que Tim
Tom has got fewer apples than Tim	= Tom a moins de pommes que Tim
many fewer than	= beaucoup moins que

Relative quantities

how many are there to the kilo?	= combien y **en** a-t-il au kilo?*
there are ten to the kilo	= il y **en** a dix au kilo*
how many do you get for ten francs?	= combien peut-on **en** avoir pour dix francs?
you get five for ten francs	= il y **en** a cinq pour dix francs
how much does it cost a litre?	= combien coûte le litre?
it costs £5 a litre	= ça coûte cinq livres le litre
how much do apples cost a kilo?	= combien coûte le kilo de pommes?
how many glasses do you get to the bottle?	= combien y a-t-il de verres par bouteille?
you get six glasses to the bottle	= il y a six verres par bouteille

* Note the use of a singular verb in French in these examples.

(to switch on)
to put the heating on = allumer le
    chauffage
to put the kettle on = mettre la bouilloire à
    chauffer
to put a CD on = mettre un disque
    compact
to put on weight = prendre du poids
(to organize, to produce) = monter
to put on a play = monter une pièce
put out
to put out a cigarette = éteindre une
    cigarette
(to take out) = sortir
to put the bins out = sortir les
    poubelles
put up
(to lift)
to put one's hair up = remonter ses
    cheveux
to put up one's hand *(in class)* ≈ lever le
    doigt
(to attach)
to put a sign up = mettre une pancarte
(when camping)
to put up a tent = planter une tente
(British English) *(to raise)* = augmenter
to put the rent up = augmenter le loyer
(to give someone a place to stay)
    = héberger
put up with = supporter

puzzle *noun*
    a puzzle = un casse-tête

pyjamas *noun (British English)*
    pyjamas = un pyjama *(singular)*

Qq

qualified *adjective*
    (having studied) = diplômé/diplômée
    (having experience, skills)
    = qualifié/qualifiée

quality *noun*
    quality = la qualité

quantity *noun* ▶ 317|
    a quantity = une quantité

quarrel
1 *noun*
    a quarrel = une dispute
2 *verb*
    = se disputer *(! + être)*

quarter
1 *noun*
    a quarter = un quart
    a quarter of an hour = un quart d'heure
    to cut the tomatoes in quarters = couper
        les tomates en quatre
2 *pronoun*
    *(when talking about quantities,
    numbers)* ▶ 317|
    a quarter of the population can't read
        = un quart de la population ne sait pas
        lire
    (when talking about time) ▶ 211|
    an hour and a quarter = une heure et
        quart
    it's (a) quarter past five = il est cinq
        heures et quart

quay *noun*
    a quay = un quai

queen *noun*
    a queen = une reine

question
1 *noun*
    (a request for information)
    a question = une question
    to ask someone a question = poser une
        question à quelqu'un
    (a problem, a matter)
    a question = un problème
2 *verb*
    = interroger

queue *(British English)*
1 *noun*
    a queue *(of people)* = une queue, une file
        d'attente
    (of cars, trucks) = une file
    to join the queue = se mettre à la queue
2 *verb*
    = faire la queue

quick *adjective*
    = rapide
    a quick answer = une réponse rapide
    it's quicker to go by train = c'est plus
        rapide d'y aller en train
    it's the quickest way [to get to London | to
    save money | to make friends ...] = c'est le
    moyen le plus rapide [d'aller à Londres | de
    gagner de l'argent | de se faire des amis ...]

quickly *adverb*
    = vite, rapidement

quiet
1 *adjective*
    (silent) = silencieux/silencieuse
    to keep quiet = garder le silence
    to go quiet = se taire *(! + être)*
    be quiet! = taisez-vous!
    (not talkative) = réservé/réservée
    (calm) = tranquille
    it's a quiet little village = c'est un petit
        village tranquille

2 noun
  quiet = le silence
  quiet please! = silence, s'il vous plaît!

quietly adverb
  to speak quietly = parler doucement
  to [play | sit | read ...] quietly = [jouer | s'asseoir | lire ...] en silence

quit verb
  (to resign) = démissionner
  (US English) (to give up)
  to quit [smoking | drinking | working ...] = arrêter de [fumer | boire | travailler ...]

quite adverb
  (rather) = assez
  they go back to France quite often = ils rentrent assez souvent en France
  I quite like Chinese food = j'aime assez la cuisine chinoise
  she earns quite a lot of money = elle gagne pas mal* d'argent
  (completely)
  I'm not quite ready yet = je ne suis pas encore tout à fait prêt
  you're quite right = vous avez entièrement raison
  are you quite sure? = en êtes-vous certain?
  (exactly)
  'is it true?'—'not quite' = 'est-ce que c'est vrai?'—'pas exactement'
  I don't quite know what he does = je ne sais pas exactement ce qu'il fait

quiz noun
  a quiz = un jeu de questions-réponses

Rr

---

rabbit noun
  a rabbit = un lapin

rabies noun ▶ 266 |
  rabies = la rage

race
1 noun
  (a contest)
  a race = une course
  to have a race = faire une course
  (for horse-racing)
  the races = les courses (feminine)
2 verb
  (to compete with)
  to race (against) someone = faire la course avec quelqu'un
  I'll race you to the car = on fait la course jusqu'à la voiture
  (to take part in a contest) = courir

racehorse noun
  a racehorse = un cheval de course

racetrack noun
  a racetrack (for horses) = un champ de courses
  (for cars) = un circuit

racism noun
  racism = le racisme

racket, racquet noun
  a racket = une raquette

radiator noun
  a radiator = un radiateur

radio noun
  a radio = une radio
  on the radio = à la radio

radio station noun
  a radio station = une station de radio

rage noun
  rage = la rage, la colère
  to fly into a rage = se mettre en colère

raid verb
  to raid a bank = attaquer une banque
  the police raided the building = la police a fait une descente dans le bâtiment

rail noun
  (for holding on to)
  a rail = une rampe, une main courante
  (for trains)
  rails = les rails (masculine)

railway (British English), **railroad** (US English) noun
  (a track)
  a railway = une voie ferrée
  (the rail system)
  the railway = le chemin de fer

railway line noun (British English)
  a railway line = une ligne de chemin de fer

railway station noun (British English)
  a railway station = une gare

rain
1 noun
  rain = la pluie
  to stand in the rain = rester sous la pluie
2 verb
  = pleuvoir
  it's raining = il pleut

rainbow noun
  a rainbow = un arc-en-ciel

raincoat noun
  a raincoat = un imperméable

raise verb
  (to lift) = lever
  (to increase) = augmenter
  to raise prices = augmenter les prix
  (in anger)
  to raise one's voice = hausser le ton

R

(to talk about)
to raise a subject = soulever une question
(to bring up)
to raise children = élever des enfants

range *noun*
(a selection)
a range *(of goods, prices)* = une gamme
(of activities, school subjects) = un grand choix
(of mountains)
a range = une chaîne
(US English) (for cooking)
a range = une cuisinière

rare *adjective*
(not common) = rare
(very slightly cooked) = saignant/saignante

rarely *adverb*
= rarement

rasher *noun (British English)*
a rasher (of bacon) = une tranche (de bacon)

raspberry *noun*
a raspberry = une framboise

rat *noun*
a rat = un rat

rather *adverb*
(when saying what one would prefer)
I'd rather [leave | stay here | read the paper …] = j'aimerais mieux [partir | rester ici | lire le journal …]
I'd rather you came with me = j'aimerais mieux que tu viennes avec moi

❗ *Note that the subjunctive is used after j'aimerais mieux que.*

(quite) = plutôt
I think he's rather nice = je le trouve plutôt sympathique

raw *adjective*
= cru/crue

razor *noun*
a razor = un rasoir

razor blade *noun*
a razor blade = une lame de rasoir

reach *verb*
(to arrive at) = atteindre
they reached the town at midnight = ils ont atteint la ville à minuit
(to be delivered to) = parvenir à (❗ + *être*)
the letter never reached him = la lettre ne lui est pas parvenue
(by stretching)
to reach up = lever le bras
I can't reach the shelf = je n'arrive pas à atteindre l'étagère
(to come to) = arriver à (❗ + *être*)
to reach a decision = arriver à une décision
(to contact by phone) = joindre
I can be reached at this number = on peut me joindre à ce numéro

reach out = tendre le bras

react *verb*
= réagir

read *verb*
= lire
the writing is difficult to read = l'écriture est difficile à lire
to read to someone = faire la lecture à quelqu'un
read out
to read out the names = lire les noms à haute voix
read through *(once)* = lire
(a second time) = relire

reading *noun*
reading = la lecture

ready *adjective*
(prepared) = prêt/prête
are you ready to leave? = est-ce que vous êtes prêts à partir?
to get ready = se préparer (❗ + *être*)
to get a meal ready = préparer le repas
(happy) = prêt/prête
I'm ready to help them = je suis prêt à les aider

real *adjective*
(not imagined) = réel/réelle
(not artificial) = vrai/vraie (❗ *before the noun*)
are they real diamonds? = est-ce que ce sont de vrais diamants?
it's a real shame = c'est vraiment dommage

reality *noun*
reality = la réalité

realize *verb*
= se rendre compte (❗ + *être*)
I didn't realize (that) he was your boss = je ne me suis pas rendu compte que c'était ton patron

really *adverb*
= vraiment
it's really easy to make = c'est vraiment facile à faire
what really happened? = qu'est-ce qui s'est réellement passé?
really? = c'est vrai?

rear
1 *noun*
the rear = l'arrière *(masculine)*
2 *verb*
= élever

reason *noun*
a reason = une raison
that's a good reason to learn French = c'est une bonne raison d'apprendre le français
is there any reason why you shouldn't drive? = pourquoi est-ce que vous ne devriez pas conduire?
tell me the reason why = dis-moi pourquoi

reassure verb
= rassurer

receipt noun
a receipt = un reçu
a till receipt = un ticket de caisse

receive verb
(to get) = recevoir
we received a letter from the teacher
= nous avons reçu une lettre du
professeur
(to meet) = accueillir, recevoir
to be well received = être bien reçu/reçue

recent adjective
= récent/récente

recently adverb
= récemment

reception noun
(in a hotel, a hospital, a company)
the reception = la réception
ask at (the) reception = adressez-vous à la
réception
(a formal event)
a reception = une réception

receptionist noun ▶ 315 |
a receptionist = un réceptionniste/une
réceptionniste

recipe noun
a recipe = une recette

recognize verb
= reconnaître

recommend verb
= recommander

record
1 noun
(information)
the records (historical, public) = les
archives (feminine)
(personal, medical) = le dossier (singular)
(for playing music)
a record = un disque
(in sport)
a record = un record
to break the world record = battre le
record du monde
2 verb
= enregistrer

recorder noun ▶ 290 |
a recorder = une flûte à bec

record player noun
a record player = un électrophone

recover verb
= se remettre (**!** + être)
to recover from an illness = se remettre
d'une maladie

recycle verb
= recycler

red adjective ▶ 213 |
= rouge
to go red, to turn red = rougir
to have red hair = avoir les cheveux roux

red-haired adjective
= roux/rousse

reduce verb
to reduce prices = baisser les prix
to reduce the number of employees
= réduire le nombre d'employés
to reduce speed = ralentir

reduction noun
a reduction = une réduction

redundant adjective (British English)
to be made redundant = être
licencié/licenciée pour raisons
économiques

referee noun ▶ 315 |
a referee = un arbitre

reflection noun
a reflection = un reflet

refreshing adjective
= rafraîchissant/rafraîchissante

refrigerator noun
a refrigerator = un réfrigérateur, un
frigidaire

refugee noun
a refugee = un réfugié/une réfugiée

refuse¹ verb
= refuser
to refuse [to listen | to stop | to pay …]
= refuser [d'écouter | de s'arrêter | de payer …]

refuse² noun (British English)
refuse = les ordures (feminine plural)

regards noun
give her my regards = transmettez-lui
mes amitiés

region noun
a region = une région

regional adjective
= régional/régionale

register noun
the register = le cahier d'appel
to take the register = faire l'appel

regret verb
= regretter
I regret changing my mind = je regrette
d'avoir changé d'avis
he regrets that he can't come = il regrette
de ne pas pouvoir venir
I regret that he can't come = je regrette
qu'il ne puisse pas venir
! Note that the subjunctive is used after
regretter que.

regular adjective
regular = régulier/régulière

regularly *adverb*
= régulièrement

rehearsal *noun*
a rehearsal = une répétition

rehearse *verb*
= répéter

reject *verb*
to reject someone's advice = rejeter les conseils de quelqu'un
to reject a candidate = refuser un candidat

relationship *noun*
a relationship = une relation, des relations (*plural*)
to have a good relationship = bien s'entendre (**!** + *être*)
she has a good relationship with her parents = elle s'entend bien avec ses parents

relative *noun*
a relative = un parent/une parente
my relatives = ma famille

relax *verb*
= se détendre (**!** + *être*)

relaxed *adjective*
= détendu/détendue, décontracté/décontractée

relay race *verb*
a relay race = une course de relais

release *verb*
= libérer

reliable *adjective*
a reliable person = une personne digne de confiance
a reliable car = une voiture fiable

relieved *adjective*
= soulagé/soulagée

religion *noun*
religion = la religion

religious education ,**RE** (*British English*) *noun*
religious education = l'instruction religieuse

  ! *Note that* **instruction** *is feminine.*

rely *verb*
(*to depend on*) = dépendre de
(*to count on*) = compter sur
can we rely on you? = est-ce qu'on peut compter sur toi?

remain *verb*
= rester

remark *noun*
a remark = une remarque, une réflexion

remarkable *adjective*
= remarquable

remember *verb*
= se souvenir (**!** + *être*)
do you remember her? = est-ce que tu te souviens d'elle?
I remember writing down the address = je me souviens d'avoir noté l'adresse
to remember to [write the letter | water the plants | turn off the lights ...] = penser à [écrire la lettre | arroser les plantes | éteindre les lumières ...]

remind *verb*
= rappeler
to remind someone to buy milk = rappeler à quelqu'un d'acheter du lait
she reminds me of my sister = elle me rappelle ma sœur

remote control *noun*
a remote control = une télécommande

remove *verb*
= enlever
to remove the stains from a carpet = enlever les taches d'une moquette

rent
1 *verb*
= louer
to rent an apartment = louer un appartement
2 *noun*
a rent = un loyer
rent out = louer

repair *verb*
= réparer
to have a bicycle repaired = faire réparer un vélo

repeat *verb*
(*to say again*) = répéter
to repeat a year = redoubler une classe

replace *verb*
= remplacer
they replaced the fence with a wall = ils ont remplacé la clôture par un mur

reply
1 *verb*
= répondre
to reply to a letter = répondre à une lettre
2 *noun*
a reply = une réponse

report
1 *verb*
(*to tell about*) = signaler
to report an accident = signaler un accident
(*in the news*)
to report on an event = faire un reportage sur un événement
(*to complain about*)
to report the noise = se plaindre du bruit
2 *noun*
(*in the news*)
a report = un communiqué
(*longer*) = un reportage

(*an official document*)
a report = un rapport
(*British English*) (*from school*)
a (school) report = un bulletin scolaire

report card *noun* (*US English*)
a report card = un bulletin scolaire

reporter *noun* ▶ 315 |
a reporter = un journaliste/une
journaliste, un reporter

represent *verb*
= représenter

republic *noun*
a republic = une république

request *noun*
a request = une demande

rescue *verb*
(*from danger*) = sauver

resemble *verb*
= ressembler à
to resemble each other = se ressembler
(**!** + *être*)

resent *verb*
to resent someone = en vouloir à
quelqu'un
he resents her for winning = il lui en veut
d'avoir gagné

reservation *noun*
a reservation = une réservation

reserve *verb*
= réserver

resign *verb*
= démissionner

resist *verb*
= résister

respect
1 *verb*
= respecter
2 *noun*
respect = le respect
out of respect = par respect

responsibility *noun*
responsibility = la responsabilité

responsible *adjective*
(*the cause of*) = responsable
to be responsible for the damage = être
responsable des dégâts
(*in charge*) = responsable
to be responsible for organizing a trip
= être chargé/chargée d'organiser une
sortie

rest
1 *noun*
(*what is left*)
the rest = le reste
we spent the rest of the day in the garden
= on a passé le reste de la journée dans
le jardin

(*time to recover*)
rest = le repos
to need rest = avoir besoin de repos
(*a break*)
a rest = une pause
to have a rest = se reposer (**!** + *être*)
2 *verb*
= se reposer (**!** + *être*)

restaurant *noun*
a restaurant = un restaurant

result *noun*
a result = un résultat
the exam results = les résultats des
examens
as a result of an accident = à la suite d'un
accident

résumé *noun* (*US English*)
a résumé = un CV, un curriculum vitae

retire *verb*
= prendre sa retraite

return *verb*
(*to go back*) = retourner (**!** + *être*)
(*to come back*) = revenir (**!** + *être*)
(*from abroad, to one's home*) = rentrer
(**!** + *être*)
(*to give back*) = rendre
can you return my book? = est-ce que tu
peux me rendre mon livre?
(*to send back*) = renvoyer
to return goods = renvoyer des articles
(*to start again*)
to return to work = reprendre le travail
to return to school = reprendre l'école

return ticket *noun*
a return ticket = un billet aller-retour

reveal *verb*
to reveal a secret = révéler un secret

revenge *noun*
revenge = la vengeance
to get one's revenge = se venger (**!** + *être*)

revolution *noun*
a revolution = une révolution

reward
1 *noun*
a reward = une récompense
2 *verb*
= récompenser

rewind *verb*
= rembobiner

rhinoceros, **rhino** *noun*
a rhinoceros = un rhinocéros

rhythm *noun*
rhythm = le rythme

rib *noun* ▶ 201 |
a rib = une côte

rice *noun*
rice = le riz

R

rich *adjective*
= riche
to get rich = s'enrichir (**!** + *être*)

rid :to get rid of *verb*
= se débarrasser de (**!** + *être*)

ride
1 *verb* ▶ **248 |**
to ride, to go riding = faire du cheval
to ride a horse = monter à cheval
to be riding a bike = rouler à vélo
2 *noun*
to go for a ride (*in a car, on a bike*) = aller
faire un tour
(*on a horse*) = aller faire une promenade à
cheval

ridiculous *adjective*
= ridicule

rifle *noun*
a rifle = un fusil

right
1 *adjective*
(*not left*) = droit/droite
his right hand = sa main droite
(*honest, good*) = bien
it's not right to steal = ce n'est pas bien de
voler
to do the right thing = faire ce qu'il faut
(*correct*) = bon/bonne (**!** *before the noun*)
the right answer = la bonne réponse
is this the right direction? = est-ce que
c'est la bonne direction?
what's the right time? = quelle est l'heure
exacte?
you're right = tu as raison
that's right = c'est ça
2 *noun*
(*the direction*)
the right = la droite
the first street on the right = la première
rue à droite
(*what one is entitled to*)
a right = un droit
to have a right to education = avoir droit à
l'instruction
human rights = les droits de l'homme
3 *adverb*
= à droite
to turn right = tourner à droite

ring
1 *verb*
(*British English*) (*to phone*) = appeler
to ring for a taxi = appeler un taxi
(*to make a sound*) = sonner
to ring the bell = sonner
the doorbell rang = on a sonné à la porte
2 *noun*
(*a piece of jewellery*)
a ring = une bague
a wedding ring = une alliance
(*a circle*)
a ring = un cercle
(*in a circus*)
the ring = la piste

ring up (*British English*) = téléphoner

rinse *verb*
= rincer

ripe *adjective*
= mûr/mûre

rise *verb*
(*if it's smoke, water*) = monter (**!** + *être*)
(*if it's a price*) = augmenter
(*if it's a plane*) = s'élever (**!** + *être*)
(*if it's the sun or moon*) = se lever (**!** + *être*)

risk
1 *noun*
a risk = un risque
2 *verb*
= risquer
to risk losing one's job = risquer de perdre
son travail

river *noun*
a river = une rivière
(*flowing into the sea*) = un fleuve

riverbank *noun*
a riverbank = une berge

road *noun*
a road = une route
the road to London = la route de Londres

road sign *noun*
a road sign = un panneau de signalisation

roadworks *noun*
roadworks = les travaux (*masculine*)

roar *verb*
(*if it's a lion*) = rugir
(*if it's a person*) = hurler
(*if it's an engine*) = vrombir

roast
1 *verb*
= rôtir
2 *adjective*
= rôti/rôtie
to eat roast beef = manger du rôti de bœuf
3 *noun*
a roast = un rôti

rob *verb*
to rob someone = voler quelqu'un
to rob a bank = dévaliser une banque

robbery *noun*
a robbery = un vol

robin *noun*
a robin = un rouge-gorge

robot *noun*
a robot = un robot

rock *noun*
(*the material*)
rock = la roche
(*a large stone*)
a rock = un rocher
(*music*)
rock = le rock

rock climbing *noun* ▶ 248 |
　rock climbing = la varappe

rocket *noun*
　a rocket = une fusée

role *noun*
　a role = un rôle

roll
1 *verb*
　= rouler
　the ball rolled under a car = le ballon a
　　roulé sous une voiture
　to roll the pastry into a ball = faire une
　　boule de la pâte
2 *noun*
　(*of paper, cloth, plastic*)
　a roll = un rouleau
　a roll of film = une pellicule
　(*bread*)
　a roll = un petit pain
　(*US English*) (*at school*)
　to call the roll = faire l'appel
roll about, roll around (*if it's an object*)
　= rouler
roll over = se retourner (**!** + *être*)
roll up = enrouler
　to roll up a newspaper = rouler un journal

roller coaster *noun*
　a roller coaster = des montagnes russes
　! *Note that* **montagnes** *is feminine plural.*

roller-skate *noun*
　a roller-skate = un patin à roulettes

roller-skating *noun* ▶ 248 |
　roller-skating = le patin à roulettes

Romania *noun* ▶ 218 |
　Romania = la Roumanie

romantic *adjective*
　= romantique

roof *noun*
　a roof = un toit

room *noun*
　a room = une pièce
　(*for sleeping*) = une chambre
　(*for working*) = un bureau
　(*for teaching, holding meetings*) = une salle
　(*space*)
　room = la place
　to make room = faire de la place
　is there room? = est-ce qu'il y a de la
　　place?

root *noun*
　a root = une racine

rope *noun*
　a rope = une corde

rose *noun*
　a rose = une rose

rosy *adjective*
　= rose
　to have rosy cheeks = avoir les joues roses

rotten *adjective*
　= pourri/pourrie

rough *adjective*
　(*not smooth*) = rugueux/rugueuse
　to have rough skin = avoir la peau
　　rugueuse
　(*not gentle*) = brutal/brutale
　(*tough*) = dur/dure
　to live in a rough area = habiter un
　　quartier dur
　(*not exact, precise*)
　a rough figure = un chiffre approximatif
　(*difficult*) = dur/dure, difficile
　to have a rough time = traverser une
　　période difficile
　(*caused by bad weather*)
　a rough sea = une mer agitée

round
　! *Often* **round** *occurs in combinations with
　verbs. For more information, see the note
　at* **around.**

1 *preposition*
　= autour de
　to be sitting round a table = être
　　assis/assises autour d'une table
　to sail round the world = faire le tour du
　　monde en bateau
　to go round Oxford = visiter Oxford
2 *adverb*
　to go round and round = tourner en rond
　to go round to John's = passer chez John
　to invite someone round = inviter
　　quelqu'un chez soi
3 *noun*
　a round (*in a quiz*) = une manche
　(*in showjumping*) = un parcours
　(*in boxing*) = un round
　(*in an election*) = un tour
4 *adjective*
　= rond/ronde

roundabout *noun*
　(*British English*) (*in a fair*)
　a roundabout = un manège
　(*for traffic*)
　a roundabout = un rond-point

route *noun*
　a route = un itinéraire
　a bus route = une ligne d'autobus

routine *noun*
　a routine = une routine

row[1]
1 *noun*
　a row (*of people, trees*) = un rang
　(*of houses, seats*) = une rangée
　(*of cars*) = une file
　the pupils were sitting in rows = les élèves
　　étaient assis en rangs
　(*when talking about frequency*)
　to be absent five days in a row = être
　　absent/absente cinq jours de suite

R

2 verb
(as an activity) = ramer
(as a sport) ▶ **248** | = faire de l'aviron
to row across a lake = traverser un lac à la
rame

row² noun (British English)
a row = une dispute
to have a row with someone = se disputer
avec quelqu'un

rowing noun ▶ **248** |
rowing = l'aviron (masculine)

rowing boat (British English),
rowboat (US English) noun
a rowing boat = un bateau à rames

royal adjective
= royal/royale

rub verb
to rub a stain = frotter une tache
to rub one's eyes = se frotter les yeux
rub out (British English) = s'effacer
(**!** + être)
to rub out a mistake = effacer une erreur

rubber noun
(the material)
rubber = le caoutchouc
(British English) (an eraser)
a rubber = une gomme

rubbish noun (British English)
(refuse)
rubbish (household) = les ordures
(feminine plural)
(in the street, in a dump) = les déchets
(masculine plural)
(poor quality goods)
rubbish = la camelote✱

rubbish bin noun (British English)
a rubbish bin = une poubelle

rucksack noun
a rucksack = un sac à dos

rude adjective
(not polite) = impoli/impolie
to be rude to someone = être
impoli/impolie envers quelqu'un
(vulgar) = grossier/grossière
a rude word = un gros mot

rug noun
a rug = un tapis

rugby noun ▶ **248** |
rugby = le rugby

ruin
1 verb
(to spoil) = gâcher
to ruin a meal = gâcher un repas
(to damage) = abîmer
you'll ruin your shoes = tu vas abîmer tes
chaussures

2 noun
a ruin = une ruine

rule
1 noun
a rule (of a game, a language) = une règle
(in a school, an organization) = un
règlement
it's against the rules = c'est contraire au
règlement
2 verb
(if it's a leader) = gouverner
(if it's a king, queen) = régner sur
(if it's a party) = diriger

ruler noun
a ruler = une règle

rumour (British English), **rumor** (US
English) noun
a rumour = une rumeur

run
1 verb
to run = courir
to run after someone = courir après
quelqu'un
to run across the street = traverser la rue
en courant
to run a race = faire une course
(from danger) = fuir, s'enfuir (**!** + être)
(to manage) = diriger
(to work, to operate) = marcher
the car runs on unleaded petrol = la
voiture marche à l'essence sans plomb
the system is running well = le système
marche bien
(to organize) = organiser
to run a competition = organiser un
concours
(when talking about transport) = circuler
the buses don't run after midnight = les
bus ne circulent pas après minuit
(to flow) = couler
(to fill with water)
to run a bath = faire couler un bain
(to come off) (when talking about dyes)
= déteindre
(when talking about make-up) = couler
(in an election)
to run for president = être
candidat/candidate à la présidence
(other uses)
to be running late = être en retard
to be running a temperature = avoir de la
fièvre
2 noun
a run = une course
to go for a run = aller courir
run about, run around = courir
run away = s'enfuir (**!** + être)
run off = partir en courant (**!** + être)

runner noun
a runner = un coureur/une coureuse (à
pied)

---

rush
1 *verb*
(*to hurry*) = se dépêcher (**!** + *être*)
to rush to finish one's homework = se dépêcher de finir ses devoirs
to rush into a shop = se précipiter dans un magasin
to rush out of the house = se précipiter hors de la maison
to be rushed to the hospital = être emmené/emmenée d'urgence à l'hôpital
(*to put pressure on*) = bousculer
2 *noun*
to be in a rush = être pressé/pressée
to do one's homework in a rush = faire ses devoirs à la va-vite

rush hour *noun*
the rush hour = les heures de pointe
| **!** *Note that* **heures** *is feminine plural.*

Russia *noun* ▶ 218 |
Russia = la Russie

Russian ▶ 275 |
1 *adjective*
= russe
2 *noun*
(*the people*)
the Russians = les Russes (*masculine*)
(*the language*)
Russian = le russe

rusty *adjective*
= rouillé/rouillée

Ss

sad *adjective*
= triste

saddle *noun*
a saddle = une selle

safe ▶ 237 |
1 *adjective*
(*without risk*) = sûr/sûre
a safe place = un endroit sûr
it's not safe for children = c'est dangereux pour les enfants
is it safe to go there? = est-ce qu'on peut y aller sans danger?
(*free from danger*)
to feel safe = se sentir en sécurité
your car is safe here = ici, votre voiture ne risque rien
(*out of danger*) = sain et sauf/saine et sauve
2 *noun*
a safe = un coffre-fort

safety *noun*
safety = la sécurité

Sagittarius *noun*
Sagittarius = Sagittaire (*masculine*)

sail
1 *noun*
a sail = une voile
to set sail = prendre la mer
2 *verb*
to sail around the world = faire le tour du monde en bateau
to go sailing = faire de la voile

sailing *noun* ▶ 248 |
sailing = la voile

sailing boat (*British English*), **sailboat** (*US English*) *noun*
a sailing boat = un bateau à voiles

sailor *noun* ▶ 315 |
a sailor = un marin

saint *noun*
a saint = un saint/une sainte

salad *noun*
a salad = une salade

salary *noun*
a salary = un salaire

sale *noun*
to be on sale (*British English*) = être en vente
for sale = à vendre
the sales = les soldes (*masculine*)

sales assistant *noun* ▶ 315 | (*British English*)
a sales assistant = un vendeur/une vendeuse

salmon *noun*
a salmon = un saumon

salt *noun*
salt = le sel

same
1 *adjective*
= même
she's got the same coat as me = elle a le même manteau que moi
they go to the same school = ils vont à la même école
it's the same as the car I had before = c'est la même voiture que celle que j'avais avant
it's all the same to me = ça m'est complètement égal
the houses all look the same = les maisons sont toutes pareilles
people are the same everywhere = les gens sont partout pareils
things aren't the same without them = ce n'est pas la même chose sans eux
it's the same as ever = c'est toujours la même chose

2 *pronoun*
the same = la même chose
I'll have the same = je prendrai la même chose
to do the same as the others = faire comme les autres
'Happy New Year!'—'the same to you!' = 'Bonne année!'—'à toi de même!'

sand *noun*
sand = le sable

sandal *noun*
a sandal = un nu-pied

sandwich *noun*
a sandwich = un sandwich
a ham sandwich = un sandwich au jambon

Santa (Claus) *noun*
Santa (Claus) = le Père Noël

sardine *noun*
a sardine = une sardine

satellite TV *noun*
satellite TV = la télévision par satellite

satisfactory *adjective*
= satisfaisant/satisfaisante

satisfied *adjective*
= satisfait/satisfaite

Saturday *noun* ▶ 222 |
Saturday = samedi (*masculine*)

sauce *noun*
a sauce = une sauce

saucepan *noun*
a saucepan = une casserole

saucer *noun*
a saucer = une soucoupe

sausage *noun*
a sausage = une saucisse

save *verb*
(*to rescue*) = sauver
they saved his life = ils lui ont sauvé la vie
(*to avoid spending*)
to save (up) = faire des économies
to save money = mettre de l'argent de côté
(*to avoid wasting*)
to save [time | energy | money …]
= économiser [du temps | de l'énergie | de l'argent …]
(*to keep*) = garder
to save a piece of cake for someone = garder un morceau de gâteau pour quelqu'un
to save a file = sauvegarder un fichier
(*to spare*)
to save someone a lot of work = éviter beaucoup de travail à quelqu'un
it will save us from having to drive all night = ça nous évitera de conduire toute la nuit

savings *noun*
savings = les économies (*feminine*)

saw *noun*
a saw = une scie

saxophone *noun* ▶ 290 |
a saxophone = un saxophone

say *verb*
= dire
to say goodbye = dire au revoir
she says (that) she can't go out tonight = elle dit qu'elle ne peut pas sortir ce soir
he said to wait here = il a dit d'attendre ici
they say she's very rich = on dit qu'elle est très riche
I can't say who did it = je ne peux pas dire qui a fait ça
she wouldn't say = elle n'a pas voulu le dire
I said to myself that you'd like that = je me suis dit que ça te ferait plaisir
what does the message say? = que dit le message?
it says here that smoking is not allowed = il est dit ici qu'on n'a pas le droit de fumer
I'd say she was forty = je lui donne quarante ans
let's say there are twenty people at the party = supposons qu'il y ait vingt personnes à la fête

! Note that the subjunctive is used after supposer que.

scandal *noun*
a scandal = un scandale

scare *verb*
= faire peur à
you scared me! = tu m'as fait peur!
scare away = faire fuir

scared *adjective*
to be scared = avoir peur

scarf *noun*
a scarf (*long*) = une écharpe
(*square*) = un foulard

scenery *noun*
scenery = le paysage

school
1 *noun*
a school = une école
to be at school = être à l'école
2 *adjective*
= scolaire
a school bus = un car de ramassage scolaire

schoolbag *noun*
a schoolbag = un cartable

schoolboy *noun*
a schoolboy = un élève

schoolgirl *noun*
  a schoolgirl = une élève

schoolwork *noun*
  schoolwork = le travail de classe

science *noun*
  science = la science
  to study science = étudier les sciences

scientist *noun* ▶ 315 |
  a scientist = un scientifique/une
  scientifique

scissors *noun*
  scissors = les ciseaux (*masculine*)
  a pair of scissors = une paire de ciseaux

score *verb*
  to score a goal = marquer un but

Scorpio *noun*
  Scorpio = Scorpion (*masculine*)

Scotland *noun* ▶ 218 |
  Scotland = l'Écosse

Scottish *adjective* ▶ 275 |
  = écossais/écossaise

scratch *verb*
  (*when itchy*) = se gratter (**!** + *être*)
  to scratch one's arm = se gratter le bras
  (*if it's a person or an animal*) = griffer
  (*if it's a bush, thorns*) = égratigner
  (*to mark, to damage*) = érafler

scream *verb*
  = hurler

screen *noun*
  a screen = un écran

screw *noun*
  a screw = une vis

sea *noun*
  a sea = une mer
  beside the sea, by the sea = au bord de la
  mer

seagull *noun*
  a seagull = une mouette

seal *verb*
  a seal = un phoque

search *verb*
  to search = chercher
  to search for someone = chercher
  quelqu'un
  (*to examine a place, a person*) = fouiller
  they searched me at the airport = on m'a
  fouillé à l'aéroport

seashell *noun*
  a seashell = un coquillage

seasick *adjective*
  to be seasick, to get seasick = avoir le
  mal de mer

seaside *noun*
  at the seaside = au bord de la mer
  to go to the seaside = aller à la mer

season *noun*
  a season = une saison
  strawberries are in season = c'est la
  saison des fraises

seat *noun*
  (*a chair, a bench*)
  a seat = un siège
  have a seat = asseyez-vous
  (*on transport, in a theatre*)
  a seat = une place

seatbelt *noun*
  a seatbelt = une ceinture de sécurité

second
1 *adjective*
  = deuxième, second/seconde
  it's the second time I've called her = c'est
  la deuxième fois que je l'appelle
  every second Monday = un lundi sur
  deux
2 *noun*
  (*in a series*)
  the second = le deuxième/la deuxième, le
  second/la seconde
  (*in time*)
  a second = une seconde
  (*a very short time*) = un instant
  (*in dates*) ▶ 222 |
  the second of May = le deux mai
3 *adverb*
  = deuxième
  to come second = arriver deuxième

secondary school *noun*
  a secondary school = une école
  secondaire

second-hand *adjective*
  a second-hand [car | coat | book ...] = [une
  voiture | un manteau | un livre ...] d'occasion

secret
1 *adjective*
  = secret/secrète
2 *noun*
  a secret = un secret
  to tell someone a secret = confier un
  secret à quelqu'un
3 in secret = en secret

secretary *noun* ▶ 315 |
  a secretary = un secrétaire/une secrétaire

see *verb* ▶ 237 |
  to see = voir
  what can you see? = qu'est-ce que tu vois?
  I can't see them = je ne les vois pas
  he saw the people running = il a vu les
  gens qui couraient
  do they see each other often? = est-ce
  qu'ils se voient souvent?
  see you tomorrow! = à demain!
  I'll go and see = je vais voir
  (*to accompany*)
  I'll see you home = je vais te
  raccompagner chez toi

S

seem verb
- (to appear)
  she seems [happy | annoyed | tired …] = elle
  a l'air [contente | vexée | fatiguée …]
  they seem to be looking for someone = on
  dirait qu'ils cherchent quelqu'un
- (when talking about one's impressions)
  = sembler
  it seems (that) there are a lot of problems
  = il semble qu'il y ait beaucoup de
  problèmes
  it seems strange (to me) = ça (me) paraît
  bizarre

seldom adverb
= rarement

self-confident ▶confident

selfish adjective
= égoïste

sell verb
= vendre
to sell books to the students = vendre des
livres aux étudiants
he sold me his car = il m'a vendu sa
voiture
water is sold in bottles = l'eau se vend en
bouteilles

send verb
= envoyer
to send help = envoyer des secours
to send a package to someone = envoyer
un paquet à quelqu'un
he sent her a letter = il lui a envoyé une
lettre
to send someone to post a letter
= envoyer quelqu'un mettre une lettre à
la poste
to send a pupil home from school
= renvoyer un élève chez lui/une élève
chez elle
send away = faire partir
send back = renvoyer
send for = faire venir
to send for the doctor = faire venir le
médecin
send off
to send a player off = expulser un joueur
send on
to send on baggage = expédier des
bagages à l'avance
to send on post = faire suivre du courrier

senior high school (US English),
senior school (British English) noun
a senior (high) school ≈ un lycée

sense noun
- (common) sense = le bon sens
  to have the sense to go home = avoir le
  bon sens de rentrer chez soi
- (allowing one to see, hear, smell etc)
  a sense = un sens
  the sense of taste = le goût
- (a meaning)
  a sense = un sens
  it doesn't make sense = ça n'a pas de sens
  it makes sense to check first = c'est une
  bonne idée de vérifier d'abord

sensible adjective
> ! Note that sensible in English is never
> translated by sensible in French.

(describing a person) = raisonnable
(describing a decision)
= judicieux/judicieuse
(describing clothes) = pratique

sensitive adjective
(describing a person) = sensible
(describing a situation) = délicat/délicate

sentence
1 noun
- (in grammar)
  a sentence = une phrase
- (for a crime)
  a (prison) sentence = une peine (de
  prison)
2 verb
to sentence someone to one year in
prison = condamner quelqu'un à un an
de prison

separate
1 adjective
a separate room = une pièce à part
the children have separate rooms = les
enfants ont chacun leur chambre
there are two separate problems = il y a
deux problèmes différents
2 verb
- to separate = séparer
- (if it's a couple) = se séparer (! + être)

separated adjective
= séparé/séparée

separately adverb
= séparément

September noun ▶ 222 |
September = septembre (masculine)

serial noun
a serial = un feuilleton
a TV serial = un feuilleton télévisé

series noun
a series = une série

serious adjective
- (causing worry) = grave
  a serious accident = un accident grave
- (describing a personality)
  = sérieux/sérieuse
- to be serious about football = prendre le
  football au sérieux
  to be serious about going to college
  = avoir vraiment l'intention d'aller à
  l'université

serve *verb*
(*in a shop*) = servir
are you being served? = est-ce qu'on
s'occupe de vous?
(*at table*) = faire le service
to serve the soup = servir la soupe
(*in sport*) = servir

service *noun*
(*which people need or find useful*)
a **service** = un service
(*in a shop, a restaurant*)
service = le service
(*in a church*)
a **service** = un office

service station *noun*
a **service station** = une station-service

set
1 *noun*
(*a collection*)
a **set of keys** = un jeu de clés
a **set of stamps** = une série de timbres
(*in tennis*)
a **set** = un set
2 *verb*
(*to decide on*) = fixer
to set [a date | a price | a goal ...] = fixer [une
date | un prix | un but ...]
(*for a particular time*)
to set an alarm clock = mettre un réveil
to set a video (*British English*)
= programmer un magnétoscope
(*in school*)
to set homework = donner des devoirs
to set an exam = préparer les sujets d'un
examen
(*to be responsible for*)
to set a record = établir un record
to set a good example to someone
= montrer le bon exemple à quelqu'un
(*when talking about a story, a film*)
the film is set in Paris = le film se passe à
Paris
(*when talking about the sun*) = se coucher
(**!** + *être*)
(*other uses*)
to set the table = mettre la table
to set fire to a house = mettre le feu à une
maison
to set someone free = libérer quelqu'un
set off
(*to leave*) = partir (**!** + *être*)
(*to cause to go off*)
to set off fireworks = faire partir un feu
d'artifice
to set off a bomb = faire exploser une
bombe
to set off a burglar alarm = déclencher
une sirène d'alarme
set up = monter (**!** + *avoir*)
to set up a company = monter une
entreprise

settle *verb*
(*to end*)
to settle an argument = mettre fin à une
dispute

(*to decide on*) = fixer
nothing is settled yet = rien n'est encore
fixé
(*to make one's home*) = s'installer
(**!** + *être*)
settle down
(*to get comfortable*) = s'installer (**!** + *être*)
(*to marry*) = se ranger (**!** + *être*)
settle in = s'adapter (**!** + *être*)

seven *number* **▶ 187 |** , **▶ 211 |**
seven = sept
seven exams = sept examens
I've got seven (of them) = j'en ai sept

seventeen *number* **▶ 187 |** , **▶ 211 |**
seventeen = dix-sept

seventeenth *number*
(*in a series*) = dix-septième
(*in dates*) **▶ 222 |**
the seventeenth of May = le dix-sept mai

seventh *number*
(*in a series*) = septième
(*in dates*) **▶ 222 |**
the seventh of July = le sept juillet

seventy *number* **▶ 187 |**
seventy = soixante-dix

several *determiner*
= plusieurs

severe *adjective*
(*serious*) = grave
(*harsh*) = sévère

sew *verb*
= coudre

sewing *noun*
sewing = la couture

sewing machine *noun*
a **sewing machine** = une machine à
coudre

sex *noun*
sex = le sexe
to have sex = avoir des rapports sexuels

shade *noun*
(*out of the sun*)
shade = l'ombre (*feminine*)
to sit in the shade = s'asseoir à l'ombre
(*a colour*)
a **shade** = un ton
(*for a lamp*)
a **shade** = un abat-jour

shadow *noun*
a **shadow** = une ombre

shake *verb*
to shake = secouer
the earthquake shook the building = le
tremblement de terre a ébranlé le
bâtiment
to shake a bottle = agiter une bouteille
to shake hands with someone = serrer la
main de quelqu'un

S

(*when saying no*)
to shake one's head = faire non de la tête
(*with cold, fear, shock*) = trembler
he was shaking with fear = il tremblait de peur
(*during an explosion, an earthquake*) = trembler

shall *verb*

> **!** *Note that, when referring to the future, French uses the future tense of the verb to translate* shall + *verb:* I shall leave = je partirai.

(*when talking about the future*)
I shall see you next Tuesday = je te verrai mardi prochain
(*when making suggestions*)
shall I set the table? = est-ce que je mets la table?
shall we go to the cinema? = et si nous allions au cinéma?

shame *noun*
shame = la honte
shame on you! = tu devrais avoir honte!
(*when expressing regret*)
that's a shame = c'est dommage

shampoo *noun*
shampoo = le shampooing

shape *noun*
(*a form*)
a shape = une forme
a square shape = une forme carrée
in the shape of a square = en forme de carré
(*when talking about health*)
to be in good shape = être en forme
to get in shape = se mettre en forme

share
1 *verb*
= partager
to share a house = partager une maison
2 *noun*
a share = une part
to pay one's fair share = payer sa part
share out (*British English*) (*amongst others*) = répartir
(*within a group*) = partager

shark *noun*
a shark = un requin

sharp *adjective*
(*used for cutting*) = tranchant/tranchante
(*with a point*) = pointu/pointue
(*sudden*) = brusque
a sharp bend = un virage serré
(*intelligent*) = vif/vive
(*aggressive*) = acerbe
(*in taste*) = acide

shave *verb*
= se raser (**!** + *être*)

she *pronoun*
she = elle
she'll be there too = elle sera là aussi
there she is! = la voilà!
SHE **didn't say it** = ce n'est pas elle qui l'a dit
he works in London but she doesn't = il travaille à Londres mais elle non
she's an intelligent girl = c'est une fille intelligente

sheep *noun*
a sheep = un mouton
(*female*) = une brebis

sheet *noun*
(*for a bed*)
a sheet = un drap
(*a piece*)
a sheet (*of paper*) = une feuille
(*of glass*) = une plaque

shelf *noun*
a shelf (*for books, ornaments*) = une étagère
(*in a shop*) = un rayon
a set of shelves = une étagère

shell *noun*
a shell (*of an egg, a nut, a snail*) = une coquille
(*of a crab, a tortoise*) = une carapace

shelter
1 *noun*
(*from rain, danger*)
a shelter = un abri
(*for homeless people*)
a shelter = un refuge
2 *verb*
(*to take shelter*) = se mettre à l'abri
(*to help*) = donner refuge à

shin *noun* ▶ **201** |
the shin = le tibia

shine *verb*
(*to give out light*) = briller
the light is shining in my eyes = j'ai la lumière dans les yeux
(*to point*)
to shine a torch at someone = braquer une lampe sur quelqu'un
(*to reflect light*) = reluire

ship *noun*
a ship (*large*) = un navire
(*smaller*) = un bateau
a passenger ship = un paquebot

shirt *noun*
a shirt = une chemise

shiver *verb*
(*with cold*) = grelotter
(*with fear*) = trembler

shock
1 noun
  (an upsetting experience)
  a shock = un choc
  to get a shock = avoir un choc
  to give someone a shock = faire un choc à
    quelqu'un
  (the medical state)
  to be in shock = être en état de choc
  (from electricity)
  a shock = une décharge
  to get a shock = recevoir une décharge
2 verb
  (to upset) = consterner
  (to cause a scandal) = choquer

shoe noun
  a shoe (for a person) = une chaussure
  (for a horse) = un fer

shoot verb
  (using a weapon) = tirer
  to shoot someone = tirer sur quelqu'un
  they shot him in the leg = ils lui ont tiré
    dans la jambe
  to shoot someone dead = abattre
    quelqu'un
  (to move very fast)
  to shoot past = passer en trombe
  (to make)
  to shoot a film = tourner un film

shop
1 noun
  a shop = un magasin
  (small, fashionable) = une boutique
2 verb
  to go shopping = aller faire des courses

shop assistant noun ▶ 315 | (British English)
  a shop assistant = un vendeur/une
    vendeuse

shopkeeper noun ▶ 315 |
  a shopkeeper = un commerçant/une
    commerçante

shopping noun
  shopping = les courses (feminine plural)
  to do the shopping = faire les courses

shopping cart noun (US English)
  a shopping cart = un caddie

shopping centre (British English),
shopping mall (US English) noun
  a shopping centre, a shopping mall = un
    centre commercial

shopping trolley noun (British English)
  a shopping trolley = un caddie

shop window noun
  a shop window = une vitrine

shore noun
  (the edge of the sea)
  the shore = la côte, le rivage
  (dry land)
  the shore = la terre

short
1 adjective
  (not lasting long) = court/courte (**!** before
  the noun)
  to go for a short walk = faire une petite
    promenade
  a short speech = un bref discours
  the days are getting shorter = les jours
    diminuent
  (not long) = court/courte
  a short skirt = une jupe courte
  to have short hair = avoir les cheveux
    courts
  (not tall) = petit/petite (**!** + être)
  to be short of [money | food | ideas ...] = être à
    court [d'argent | de nourriture | d'idées ...]
2 in short = bref

short cut noun
  a short cut = un raccourci

shortly adverb
  (soon) = bientôt
  (not long) = peu de temps
  shortly before we left = peu de temps
    avant notre départ

shorts noun
  shorts = un short (singular)

shot noun
  (from a gun)
  a shot = un coup (de feu)
  to fire a shot at someone = tirer sur
    quelqu'un
  (in sports) ▶ 248 |
  a shot (in football) = un tir
  (in tennis, golf, cricket) = un coup

should verb

  ! Note that, in general, **should** is
  translated by **devoir** in the conditional,
  either present (you shouldn't smoke = tu
  ne devrais pas fumer) or past (he
  shouldn't have left = il n'aurait pas dû
  partir).

  (when talking about what is right, what one
  ought to do)
  she should learn to drive = elle devrait
    apprendre à conduire
  shouldn't he be at school? = est-ce qu'il
    ne devrait pas être à l'école?
  you shouldn't have said that! = tu n'aurais
    pas dû dire ça!
  (when saying something may happen)
  we should be there by midday = nous
    devrions être là vers midi
  it shouldn't be too difficult = cela ne
    devrait pas être trop difficile
  (when implying that something, though
  likely, didn't happen)
  the letter should have arrived yesterday
    = la lettre aurait dû arriver hier
  (when asking for advice or permission)
  should I call the doctor? = est-ce que je
    devrais appeler le médecin?

S

shoulder *noun* ▶ 201 |
the shoulder = l'épaule
to wear a sweater over one's shoulders
  = porter un pull sur les épaules
to have round shoulders = avoir le dos
  rond

shout
1 *verb*
  = crier
  to shout at someone = crier après
    quelqu'un
2 *noun*
  a shout = un cri
shout out = pousser un cri

shovel *noun*
  a shovel = une pelle

show
1 *verb*
  (*to let someone see*) = montrer
  to show someone a photo = montrer une
    photo à quelqu'un
  I'll show you how it works = je vais te
    montrer comment ça marche
  (*to go with*)
  I'll show you to your room = je vais vous
    accompagner à votre chambre
  (*to point to, to indicate*) = indiquer
  to show someone where to go = indiquer
    à quelqu'un où aller
  there's a sign showing the way to the
    pool = il y a un panneau qui indique la
    direction de la piscine
  (*to be on TV, at the cinema*) = passer
    (**!** + *être*)
  the film is showing at the Phoenix = le
    film passe au Phoenix
  to be shown on TV = passer à la télévision
2 *noun*
  a show (*on a stage*) = un spectacle
  (*on TV, radio*) = une émission
  (*an exhibition*)
  a show = une exposition
show off = faire le fier/la fière
show round
  to show someone around the town = faire
    visiter la ville à quelqu'un
show up = se pointer✶ (**!** + *être*)

shower *noun*
  (*for washing*)
  a shower = une douche
  to have a shower = prendre une douche
  (*rain*)
  a shower = une averse

showjumping *noun* ▶ 248 |
  showjumping = le saut d'obstacles

shrimp *noun*
  a shrimp = une crevette grise

shrink *verb*
  = rétrécir

shut
1 *adjective*
  = fermé/fermée
  my eyes were shut = j'avais les yeux
    fermés
2 *verb*
  = fermer
  to shut the windows = fermer les fenêtres
  the door doesn't shut properly = la porte
    ne ferme pas bien
shut down = fermer
  the factory shut down in May = l'usine a
    fermé au mois de mai
shut out
  to shut someone out = laisser quelqu'un
    dehors
shut up
  (*to be quiet*) = se taire (**!** + *être*)
  shut up! = tais-toi!
  (*to lock inside*) = enfermer

shy *adjective*
  = timide

sick *adjective*
  (*ill*) = malade
  to get sick = tomber malade (**!** + *être*)
  to feel sick = avoir mal au cœur
  to be sick (*British English*) (*to vomit*)
    = vomir
  (*fed up*)
  he's sick of the neighbours = il en a
    marre✶ des voisins

sickness *noun*
  a sickness = une maladie

side *noun*
  a side = un côté
  it's an apartment block with shops on
    either side = c'est un immeuble avec des
    magasins de chaque côté
  to be driving on the wrong side of the
    road = rouler du mauvais côté de la
    route
  by the side of the river = au bord de la
    rivière
  the north side of the city = le nord de la
    ville
  he works on the other side of London = il
    travaille à l'autre bout de Londres
  (*of a person's body*)
  the side = le côté
  to be lying on one's side = être
    allongé/allongée sur le côté
  on my right side = à ma droite
  (*in a conflict, a contest*)
  a side = un camp
  (*a team*)
  a side = une équipe
side with = se mettre du côté de

sidewalk *noun* (*US English*)
  a sidewalk = un trottoir

sigh *verb*
  = soupirer

✶ in informal situations

sight *noun*
  sight = la vue
  to have good sight = avoir une bonne vue
  to catch sight of someone = apercevoir
    quelqu'un
  to be out of sight = être caché/cachée

sightseeing *noun*
  sightseeing = le tourisme

sign
1 *noun*
  (a mark)
  a sign = un signe
  the dollar sign = le symbole du dollar
  (for traffic, for advertising)
  a sign = un panneau
  (a notice)
  a sign = une pancarte
2 *verb*
  = signer
sign on *(British English)* = pointer au
chômage

signal
1 *noun*
  a signal = un signal
2 *verb*
  (to make signs) = faire des signes
  to signal to someone to come = faire
    signe à quelqu'un de venir
  (when driving) = mettre son clignotant

signature *noun*
  a signature = une signature

signpost *noun*
  a signpost = un panneau indicateur

silence *noun*
  silence = le silence

silent *adjective*
  (quiet) = silencieux/silencieuse
  (without sound or words) = muet/muette

silk *noun*
  silk = la soie

silly *adjective*
  = idiot/idiote

silver
1 *noun*
  silver = l'argent *(masculine)*
2 *adjective*
  = en argent
  a silver ring = une bague en argent

simple *adjective*
  = simple

since
1 *preposition*
  ! Note that, when **since** *is used to
  describe an event or an action that is still
  going on, rather than an event or an
  action that belongs to the past and has
  finished, the present tense +* **depuis** *is
  used. In the same way, if the
  event or action has its starting point
  further back in the past, in French the
  imperfect tense +* **depuis** *is used.*

  = depuis
  I haven't seen him since yesterday = je ne
    l'ai pas vu depuis hier
  I haven't been feeling well since Monday
    = je ne me sens pas bien depuis lundi
  she had been living in France since 1988
    = elle vivait en France depuis 1988
2 *conjunction*
  (from the time when) = depuis que
  since she left = depuis qu'elle est partie,
    depuis son départ
  I've lived here since I was ten = j'habite
    ici depuis l'âge de dix ans
  it's ten years since she died = cela fait dix
    ans qu'elle est morte
  (because) = comme
  since she was ill, she couldn't go
    = comme elle était malade, elle ne
    pouvait pas y aller
3 *adverb*
  = depuis

sincere *adjective*
  = sincère

sincerely *adverb*
  = sincèrement
  Yours sincerely *(British English)*,
  Sincerely yours *(US English)* = Veuillez
    agréer, Monsieur/Madame, l'expression
    de mes sentiments les meilleurs
  (less formal) = Meilleures salutations

sing *verb*
  = chanter

singer *noun* ▶ 315 |
  a singer = un chanteur/une chanteuse

singing *noun*
  singing = le chant

single *adjective*
  (one) = seul/seule *(**!** before the noun)*
  we visited three towns in a single day
    = nous avons visité trois villes en une
    seule journée
  (when used for emphasis)
  every single day = tous les jours sans
    exception
  I didn't see a single person = je n'ai vu
    absolument personne
  (without a partner) = célibataire

single bed *noun*
  a single bed = un lit pour une personne

single room *noun*
  a single room = une chambre à une
    personne

single ticket *noun (British English)*
  a single ticket = un aller simple

sink
1 *noun*
  a sink = un évier
2 *verb*
  = couler

S

sister *noun*
  a sister = une sœur

sister-in-law *noun*
  a sister-in-law = une belle-sœur

sit *verb*
  (*to take a seat*) = s'asseoir (**!** + *être*)
  to be sitting on the floor = être assis/assise
    par terre
  (*British English*) (*to take*)
  to sit an exam = passer un examen
sit down = s'asseoir (**!** + *être*)
  to be sitting down = être assis/assise
sit up = se redresser (**!** + *être*)
  sit up straight! = tiens-toi droit!

sitting room *noun*
  a sitting room = un salon

situated *adjective*
  = situé/située
  situated near the town centre
    = situé/située près du centre-ville

situation *noun*
  a situation = une situation

six *number* ▶ **187** |, ▶ **211** |
  six = six
  six weeks = six semaines
  I've got six (of them) = j'en ai six

sixteen *number* ▶ **187** |, ▶ **211** |
  sixteen = seize

sixteenth *number*
  (*in a series*) = seizième
  (*in dates*) ▶ **222** |
  the sixteenth of July = le seize juillet

sixth *number*
  (*in a series*) = sixième
  (*in dates*) ▶ **222** |
  the sixth of February = le six février

sixty *number* ▶ **187** |
  sixty = soixante

size *noun*
  (*when talking about a person*)
  a size = une taille
  she's about your size = elle est à peu près
    de ta taille
  (*when talking about clothes*)
  a size (*of garment*) = une taille
  (*of shoe*) = une pointure
  I'd like this in a smaller size = je voudrais
    ce modèle en plus petit
  what size do you take? (*in clothes*)
    = quelle taille faites-vous?
  (*in shoes*) = vous chaussez du combien?
  (*when talking about how big something is*)
  the size (*of a building, a region*) = la
    grandeur
  (*of an apple, a parcel*) = la grosseur

skateboard *noun* ▶ **248** |
  a skateboard = un skateboard, une
    planche à roulettes

skating *noun* ▶ **248** |
  skating = le patin

skating rink *noun*
  a skating rink (*for ice-skating*) = une
    patinoire
  (*for roller-skating*) = une piste de patin à
    roulettes

sketch *noun*
  (*a drawing*)
  a sketch = un croquis
  (*a funny scene*)
  a sketch = un sketch

ski
1 *noun*
  a ski = un ski
2 *verb*
  to go skiing = faire du ski

skiing *noun* ▶ **248** |
  skiing = le ski

skilful (*British English*), **skillful** (*US
English*) *adjective*
  = habile, adroit/adroite

skill *noun*
  (*the quality*)
  skill (*mental*) = l'habileté (*feminine*)
  (*physical*) = la dextérité
  (*a particular ability*)
  a skill (*learned*) = une compétence
  (*natural*) = une aptitude

skin *noun*
  the skin = la peau

skinny *adjective*
  = maigre

skip *verb*
  (*to give little jumps*) = sautiller
  (*with a rope*) = sauter à la corde
  to skip classes = sauter les cours

ski resort *noun*
  a ski resort = une station de ski

skirt *noun*
  a skirt = une jupe

sky *noun*
  the sky = le ciel
  a clear sky = un ciel dégagé

skydiving *noun* ▶ **248** |
  skydiving = le parachutisme (en chute
    libre)

slap *verb*
  to slap someone = donner une tape à
    quelqu'un
  (*across the face*) = gifler quelqu'un

sled, **sledge** (*British English*)
1 *noun*
  a sled (*for fun*) = une luge
  (*for transport*) = un traîneau
2 *verb*
  to go sledging (*British English*) = faire de
    la luge

sleep
1 *noun*
  sleep = le sommeil
  to go to sleep = s'endormir (**!** + *être*)
  to go back to sleep = se rendormir
    (**!** + *être*)
  to put someone to sleep = endormir
    quelqu'un
2 *verb*
  (*to be asleep*) = dormir
  to sleep with someone = coucher avec
    quelqu'un
sleep in = faire la grasse matinée

sleeping bag *noun*
  a sleeping bag = un sac de couchage

sleepy *adjective*
  to be sleepy, to feel sleepy = avoir
    sommeil, avoir envie de dormir

sleet *noun*
  sleet = la neige fondue

sleeve *noun*
  a sleeve = une manche
  to roll up one's sleeves = retrousser ses
    manches

slice
1 *noun*
  a slice (*of bread, meat*) = une tranche
  (*of lemon, cucumber*) = une rondelle
2 *verb*
  to slice bread = couper du pain en
    tranches

slide
1 *verb*
  = glisser
  the plates slid off the table = les assiettes
    ont glissé de la table
2 *noun*
  (*an image*)
  a slide = une diapositive
  (*in a playground*)
  a slide = un toboggan

slim
1 *adjective*
  = mince
2 *verb* (*British English*)
  = maigrir

slip *verb*
  (*to slide*) = glisser
  the glass slipped out of my hands = le
    verre m'a échappé des mains

slipper *noun*
  a slipper = une pantoufle

slippery *adjective*
  = glissant/glissante

slot machine *noun*
  a slot machine = une machine à sous

Slovakia *noun* ▶ 218 |
  Slovakia = la Slovaquie

slow *adjective*
  (*not fast*) = lent/lente
  to make slow progress = avancer
    lentement
  (*not bright*) = lent/lente (d'esprit)
  (*describing a watch, a clock*)
  to be slow = retarder
  the clock is 20 minutes slow = la pendule
    retarde de 20 minutes
slow down = ralentir

slowly *adverb*
  = lentement

sly *adjective*
  = rusé/rusée

small *adjective*
  = petit/petite (**!** *before the noun*)
  a small car = une petite voiture
  a small quantity = une faible quantité

small ad *noun* (*British English*)
  a small ad = une petite annonce

smart *adjective*
  (*British English*) (*elegant*)
  = élégant/élégante
  (*intelligent*) = intelligent/intelligente
  (*expensive*) = chic (**!** *never changes*)

smash *verb*
  (*to break*) = briser, fracasser
  (*to get broken*) = se briser, se fracasser
    (**!** + *être*)
smash up = démolir

smell
1 *noun*
  (*an odour*)
  a smell = une odeur
  (*the sense*)
  the sense of smell = l'odorat (*masculine*)
2 *verb*
  = sentir
  that smells nice = ça sent bon
  I can smell burning = ça sent le brûlé

smile
1 *verb*
  = sourire
  to smile at someone = sourire à quelqu'un
2 *noun*
  a smile = un sourire

smoke
1 *noun*
  smoke = la fumée
2 *verb*
  = fumer

smooth *adjective*
  (*not rough*) = lisse
  a smooth road = une route plane
  a smooth crossing = une traversée sans
    heurts

smother *verb*
  = étouffer

snack *noun*
  a snack = un casse-croûte

S

snail noun
  a snail = un escargot

snake noun
  a snake = un serpent

snapshot noun
  a snapshot = une photo

sneaker noun
  a sneaker (high) = une basket
  (low) = un tennis

sneeze verb
  = éternuer

snobbish adjective
  = snob

snooker noun ▶ 248 |
  snooker = le billard anglais

snore verb
  = ronfler

snow
1 noun
  snow = la neige
2 verb
  = neiger
  it's snowing = il neige

snowball noun
  a snowball = une boule de neige

snowman noun
  a snowman = un bonhomme de neige

so
1 adverb
  so = si, tellement
  he's so [happy | stupid | smart …] = il est si
    [content | bête | malin …]
  they speak so fast = ils parlent si vite, ils
    parlent tellement vite
  it's so much easier = c'est tellement plus
    facile
  she has so many clothes = elle a tant de
    vêtements
  I've so much work to do = j'ai tant de
    travail à faire
  (also)
  I'm fifteen and so is he = j'ai quinze ans et
    lui aussi
  if you go, so will I = si tu y vas, j'y vais
    aussi
  (other uses)
  I think so = je pense que oui
  I'm afraid so = j'ai bien peur que oui
  I told you so = je te l'avais bien dit
  who says so? = qui dit ça?
  so what? = et alors?
  and so on = et ainsi de suite
2 so (that) = pour que
  be quiet so I can work = tais-toi pour que
    je puisse travailler

! Note that the subjunctive is used after
pour que.

3 so as = pour
  we left early so as not to miss the train
    = nous sommes partis tôt pour ne pas
    rater le train

soap noun
  (for washing)
  soap = le savon
  (on TV)
  a soap = un feuilleton

soccer noun ▶ 248 |
  soccer = le football
  = sociable

social adjective
  = social/sociale

social studies noun
  social studies = l'instruction civique
  ! Note that instruction is feminine.

social worker noun ▶ 315 |
  a social worker = un travailleur social/une
    travailleuse sociale

sock noun
  a sock = une chaussette

sofa noun
  a sofa = un canapé

soft adjective
  (not hard or tough) = doux/douce
  to have soft skin = avoir la peau douce
  the ground is soft here = la terre est
    meuble ici
  a soft toffee = un caramel mou
  (not harsh or severe) = doux/douce
  (not strict) = indulgent/indulgente

software noun
  a software = un logiciel

soldier noun ▶ 315 |
  a soldier = un soldat

sole noun
  the sole (of the foot) = la plante du pied
  (of a shoe)
  a sole = une semelle

solicitor noun ▶ 315 | (British English)
  a solicitor (for documents) ≈ un notaire
  (for court work) ≈ un avocat/une avocate

solution noun
  a solution = une solution

solve verb
  = résoudre
  to solve a problem = résoudre un
    problème

some

1 *determiner*
(*an amount or a number of*) = du/de la (**!** de l' + *vowel or mute h*)
= des (+ *plural*)
I have to buy **some** bread = je dois acheter du pain
have **some** water = prenez de l'eau
we bought **some** beer = nous avons acheté de la bière
she ate **some** strawberries = elle a mangé des fraises
we visited **some** beautiful towns = nous avons visité des villes superbes
(*certain*) = certains/certaines
some people don't like travelling by plane = certaines personnes n'aiment pas voyager en avion

2 *pronoun*
(*an amount or a number of*) = en
I know where you can find **some** = je sais où tu peux en trouver
have **some** more! = reprenez-en!

! Note that it is necessary to use en, which might be translated as 'of it' or 'of them', with pronouns like some. See also any, a few, a lot etc for this use of en.

(*certain people or things*)
some are quite expensive = certains sont assez chers/certaines sont assez chères
some (of them) are French = certains d'entre eux sont français/certaines d'entre elles sont françaises

someone *pronoun* (*also* **somebody**)
= quelqu'un
someone famous = quelqu'un de célèbre

something *pronoun*
= quelque chose
I saw **something** interesting = j'ai vu quelque chose d'intéressant
there's **something** odd about him = il a quelque chose de bizarre

sometimes *adverb*
= quelquefois, parfois

somewhere *adverb*
= quelque part
they live **somewhere** in Ireland = ils habitent quelque part en Irlande
let's go **somewhere** else = allons ailleurs

son *noun*
a **son** = un fils

song *noun*
a **song** = une chanson

son-in-law *noun*
a **son-in-law** = un gendre

soon *adverb*
(*in a short time*) = bientôt
see you **soon**! = à bientôt!
(*early*)
the **sooner** the better = le plus tôt sera le mieux
as **soon** as possible = dès que possible
come as **soon** as you can = viens dès que tu pourras

! Note that, if talking about future time, the future tense is used after dès que.

sore *adjective*
to have a **sore** |throat | leg | back ...] = avoir mal [à la gorge | à la jambe | au dos ...]
it's very **sore** = ça fait très mal

sorry

1 *exclamation*
(*when apologizing*)
sorry! = pardon!, désolé/désolée!
(*when asking someone to repeat*)
sorry? = pardon?

2 *adjective*
(*when apologizing*) = désolé/désolée
I'm **sorry** I'm late = je suis désolé d'être en retard
to say **sorry** = s'excuser (**!** + *être*)
(*when expressing regret*)
I'm **sorry** you can't come = je suis désolé que tu ne puisses pas venir

! Note that the subjunctive is used after être désolé que.

(*to feel pity for*)
to feel **sorry** for someone = plaindre quelqu'un
to feel **sorry** for oneself = s'apitoyer sur son sort

sort

1 *noun*
it's a **sort** of [bird | computer | loan ...] = c'est une sorte [d'oiseau | d'ordinateur | de prêt ...]
I don't like that **sort** of thing = je n'aime pas ce genre de choses
he's not that **sort** of person = ce n'est pas son genre

2 *verb*
to **sort** files = classer des dossiers
to **sort** the books into piles = ranger les livres en piles

sort out
(*to solve*) = régler
to **sort out** a problem = régler un problème
(*to deal with*) = s'occuper de (**!** + *être*)
I'll **sort** it **out** = je m'en occuperai
(*to organize*) = classer
to **sort out** the documents = classer les documents
(*to pick out, to choose*)
to **sort out** the photos = trier les photos
to **sort out** the old clothes from the new = séparer les vieux vêtements des neufs

sound

1 *noun*
a **sound** (*a noise*) = un bruit
(*of an instrument, a bell*) = un son

I heard the sound of voices = j'ai entendu un bruit de voix
(of a radio, a television)
the sound = le son
to turn the sound up = monter le son
2 *verb*
it sounds [dangerous | odd | interesting ...] = ça a l'air [dangereux | bizarre | intéressant ...]
it sounds like a piano = on dirait un piano

soup *noun*
a soup = une soupe, un potage

sour *adjective*
= aigre
to go sour = tourner

south
1 *noun*
the south = le sud
in the south of France = dans le sud de la France
2 *adverb*
to go south = aller vers le sud
to live south of Paris = vivre au sud de Paris
3 *adjective*
= sud (**!** *never changes*)
to work in south London = travailler dans le sud de Londres

South Africa *noun* ▶ 218 |
South Africa = l'Afrique du Sud
! *Note that* **Afrique** *is feminine.*

South America *noun* ▶ 218 |
South America = l'Amérique du Sud
! *Note that* **Amérique** *is feminine.*

southeast *noun*
the southeast = le sud-est

southwest *noun*
the southwest = le sud-ouest

souvenir *noun*
a souvenir = un souvenir

space *noun*
(room)
space = la place
to take up space = prendre de la place
(an area of land)
an open space = un espace libre
(outer space)
space = l'espace (*masculine*)
(a gap)
a space = un espace

Spain *noun* ▶ 218 |
Spain = l'Espagne (*feminine*)

Spanish ▶ 275 |
1 *adjective*
= espagnol/espagnole
2 *noun*
Spanish = l'espagnol (*masculine*)

spare *adjective*
(extra) = en plus
I've got a spare ticket = j'ai un billet en plus
(available) = disponible
are there any spare seats? = est-ce qu'il y a des places disponibles?

spare part *noun*
a spare part = une pièce de rechange

spare room *noun*
a spare room = une chambre d'amis

spare time *noun*
spare time = les loisirs (*masculine plural*)

speak *verb*
= parler
to speak German = parler (l')allemand
they're not speaking (to each other) = ils ne se parlent pas
who's speaking, please? = qui est à l'appareil?
generally speaking = en règle générale
speak up = parler plus fort

special *adjective*
= spécial/spéciale

! *Note that* **spécial** *can also mean* **odd** *or* **strange** *in French:* il est assez spécial = he's rather strange.

a special offer = une offre spéciale
she's a special friend = c'est une amie très chère

speciality (*British English*), **specialty** (*US English*) *noun*
a speciality = une spécialité

specially *adverb*
= spécialement

spectator *noun*
a spectator = un spectateur/une spectatrice

speech *noun*
a speech = un discours

speed
1 *noun*
speed = la vitesse
2 *verb*
to speed away = s'éloigner à toute allure
(to drive too fast) = conduire trop vite
speed up = accélérer

speed limit *noun*
a speed limit = une limitation de vitesse

spell *verb*
(when speaking) = épeler
(when writing) = écrire
how do you spell it? = comment ça s'écrit?

spelling *noun*
spelling = l'orthographe (*feminine*)

spend *verb*
(to pay money) = dépenser

(*to pass*)
to spend (some) time [reading | painting | writing letters ...] = passer du temps [à lire | à faire de la peinture | à écrire des lettres ...]

spider *noun*
  a spider = une araignée

spill *verb*
  (*if it's a person*) = renverser
  don't spill the milk = ne renverse pas le lait
  (*if it's a liquid*) = se répandre (**!** + *être*)

spinach *noun*
  spinach = les épinards (*masculine plural*)

spit *verb*
  = cracher

spite: **in spite of** *preposition*
  = malgré
  we went out in spite of the weather = nous sommes sortis malgré le temps

spiteful *adjective*
  = méchant/méchante

spoil *verb*
  (*to take away from*) = gâcher
  to spoil the evening = gâcher la soirée
  (*to ruin, to damage*) = abîmer
  (*as a parent*) = gâter
  to spoil a child = gâter un enfant

sponge *noun*
  a sponge = une éponge

spoon *noun*
  a spoon = une cuillère

sport *noun* ▶ 248
  a sport = un sport
  to be good at sports = être bon/bonne en sport

sports centre (*British English*), **sports center** (*US English*) *noun*
  a sports centre = un centre sportif

sports club *noun*
  a sports club = un club sportif

spot
  1 *noun*
  (*on an animal*)
  a spot = une tache
  (*British English*) (*on the face or body*)
  a spot = un bouton
  (*a place*)
  a spot = un endroit
  on the spot (*there and then*) = sur le champ
  2 *verb*
  (*to see*) = apercevoir
  (*to recognize*) = repérer

sprain *verb*
  to sprain one's wrist = se fouler le poignet

spring *noun*
  spring = le printemps
  in spring = au printemps

spy *noun*
  a spy = un espion/une espionne

square
  1 *noun*
  (*the shape*)
  a square = un carré
  (*in a town*)
  a square = une place
  2 *adjective*
  = carré/carrée

squash
  1 *noun* ▶ 248
  squash = le squash
  2 *verb*
  = écraser

squeak *verb*
  (*if it's a door, a wheel*) = grincer
  (*if it's a shoe, a chair*) = craquer

squeeze *verb*
  to squeeze a lemon = presser un citron
  to squeeze someone's hand = serrer la main de quelqu'un

squirrel *noun*
  a squirrel = un écureuil

stable *noun*
  a stable = une écurie

stadium *noun*
  a stadium = un stade

staff *noun*
  the staff (*of a company*) = le personnel
  (*of a school, a college*) = le personnel enseignant

stage *noun*
  a stage = une scène

stain
  1 *noun*
  a stain = une tache
  2 *verb*
  = tacher

stairs *noun*
  the stairs = l'escalier (*masculine singular*)
  to fall down the stairs = tomber dans l'escalier

stamp *noun*
  (*for an envelope*)
  a stamp = un timbre
  a three-franc stamp = un timbre à trois francs
  (*on a document, a passport*)
  a stamp = un cachet

stamp-collecting *noun*
  stamp-collecting = la philatélie

stand *verb*
  to be standing = être debout
  to stay standing, to remain standing = rester debout (**!** + *être*)
  to be able to stand = tenir debout
  you're standing in my way = tu me bloques le passage

(*to put*)
to stand a vase on a table = mettre un
vase sur une table
(*to step*)
to stand on a nail = marcher sur un clou
(*to bear*)
I can't stand French = je déteste le
français
he can't stand playing football = il déteste
jouer au football
(*other uses*)
to stand for election (*British English*) = se
présenter aux élections
to stand trial = passer en jugement
stand back = reculer
stand for
(*to represent*) = représenter
(*to mean*) = vouloir dire
stand out
(*if it's a person*) = sortir de l'ordinaire
stand up
to stand up = se lever (**!** + *être*)
to stand someone up = poser un lapin✱ à
quelqu'un
stand up for = défendre
to stand up for oneself = se défendre
(**!** + *être*)
stand up to = tenir tête à
to stand up to someone = tenir tête à
quelqu'un

star *noun*
(*in space*)
a star = une étoile
(*a famous person*)
a star = une vedette, une star

stare *verb*
to stare at someone = dévisager
quelqu'un

start
1 *verb*
(*to begin*) = commencer
to start [working | writing | running …]
= commencer à [travailler | écrire | courir …]
you should start by phoning them = tu
devrais commencer par leur téléphoner
(*to begin one's working life*)
to start (out) as a teacher = débuter
comme professeur
(*to set up*) = lancer
to start a fashion = lancer une mode
(*to cause*) = déclencher
to start a war = déclencher une guerre
(*to begin working*) = démarrer
the car won't start = la voiture ne veut pas
démarrer
(*to put into action*)
to start a car = faire démarrer une voiture
to start a machine = mettre une machine
en marche

---

2 *noun*
a start = un début
at the start of the week = au début de la
semaine
start off = commencer
start over (*US English*) = recommencer

starter *noun* (*British English*)
a starter = un hors-d'œuvre

state *noun*
(*a country, part of a country*)
a state = un état
(*a government*)
the State = l'État
(*a condition*)
a state = un état
to be in a bad state (of repair) = être en
mauvais état
she's in no state to work = elle n'est pas
en état de travailler

statement *noun*
a statement = une déclaration
(*official*) = un communiqué

station *noun*
(*for trains*)
a station = une gare
(*on TV*)
a station = une chaîne

statue *noun*
a statue = une statue

stay
1 *verb*
(*to remain*) = rester (**!** + *être*)
we stayed there for a week = nous
sommes restés là une semaine
(*to have accommodation*) = loger
to stay with friends = loger chez des amis
2 *noun*
a stay = un séjour
stay away from = éviter
to stay away from school = ne pas aller à
l'école
stay in = rester à la maison
stay out
to stay out late = rentrer tard
stay up (*to wait*) = veiller
(*to keep late hours*) = se coucher tard

steady *adjective*
(*continuous*)
to make steady progress = faire des
progrès réguliers
(*not likely to move*) = stable

steak *noun*
a steak = un steak

steal *verb*
= voler
to steal from someone = voler quelqu'un
to steal money from someone = voler de
l'argent à quelqu'un

steam *noun*
steam = la vapeur

steel *noun*
  steel = l'acier (*masculine*)

steep *adjective*
  = raide

steering wheel *noun*
  a steering wheel = un volant

step
1 *noun*
  (*when walking*)
  a step = un pas
  to take a step = faire un pas
  (*in stairs, at a door*)
  a step = une marche
  (*a series of actions*)
  to take steps = prendre des mesures
2 *verb*
  to step in a puddle = marcher dans une
    flaque
step aside = s'écarter (**!** + *être*)

stepbrother *noun*
  a stepbrother = un demi-frère

stepfather *noun*
  a stepfather = un beau-père

stepmother *noun*
  a stepmother = une belle-mère

stepsister *noun*
  a stepsister = une demi-sœur

stereo *noun*
  a stereo = une chaîne stéréo

stewardess *noun* ▶ 315 |
  a stewardess = une hôtesse de l'air

stick
1 *verb*
  (*using glue or tape*) = coller
  (*to become attached*) = coller
  (*to get blocked*) = se coincer (**!** + *être*)
  the door is stuck = la porte est coincée
2 *noun*
  (*a piece of wood*)
  a stick = un bâton
  (*for walking*)
  a stick = une canne
stick at
  to stick at a task = persévérer dans une
    tâche
stick out = dépasser
  there's a nail sticking out = il y a un clou
    qui dépasse
  his ears stick out = il a les oreilles
    décollées

sticky tape *noun* (*British English*)
  sticky tape = le scotch , le ruban adhésif

stiff *adjective*
  (*not soft, not supple*) = raide
  to have stiff legs (*after sport, walking*)
    = avoir des courbatures dans les jambes
  (*not easy to use*)
  to be stiff (*if it's a door, a drawer*) = être
    dur/dure à ouvrir

(*if it's a handle*) = être dur/dure à tourner

still¹ *adverb*
  (*when there has been no change*)
  = toujours
  does she still play the piano? = est-ce
    qu'elle joue toujours du piano?
  I still don't understand why you left = je
    ne comprends toujours pas pourquoi tu
    es parti
  (*when referring to the future*) = encore
  she could still win = elle pourrait encore
    gagner

still²
1 *adverb*
  to sit still = se tenir tranquille
2 *adjective*
  = calme

sting *verb*
  = piquer

stir *verb*
  = remuer

stomach *noun* ▶ 201 |, ▶ 266 |
  the stomach = l'estomac (*masculine*)
  to have a pain in one's stomach = avoir
    mal au ventre

stone *noun*
  a stone = une pierre
  (*a pebble*) = un caillou

stop
1 *verb*
  (*to put an end to*) = arrêter
  to stop [smoking | laughing | working ...]
    = arrêter de [fumer | rire | travailler ...]
  stop it! = arrête!
  (*to prevent*)
  to stop someone from [leaving | winning |
    talking ...] = empêcher quelqu'un de
    [partir | gagner | parler ...]
  (*to come to a halt*) = s'arrêter (**!** + *être*)
  the bus didn't stop = le bus ne s'est pas
    arrêté
  (*when talking about machines, noise,
    weather*) = s'arrêter (**!** + *être*)
  suddenly the noise stopped = tout à
    coup, le bruit s'est arrêté
  it's stopped raining = il s'est arrêté de
    pleuvoir, la pluie s'est arrêtée
2 *noun*
  a (bus) stop = un arrêt (de bus)
  to miss one's stop = rater son arrêt

store *noun*
  a store = un magasin
  (*smaller*) = une boutique

storey (*British English*), **story** (*US
English*) *noun*
  a storey = un étage

storm *noun*
  a storm = une tempête
  (*with thunder*) = un orage

S

story noun
* **a story** = une histoire
  a true story = une histoire vécue
  a ghost story = une histoire de fantômes
* (*in a newspaper*)
  a story = un article
* (*a rumour*)
  a story = une rumeur
* (*US English*) ▶ **storey**

stove noun (*US English*)
  a stove = une cuisinière

straight
1 adjective
* **straight** = droit/droite
  a straight line = une ligne droite
* (*not curly*) = raide
  to have straight hair = avoir les cheveux
    raides
* (*in the right position*) = bien droit/droite
  the picture isn't straight = le tableau est
    de travers
* (*honest*) = honnête, droit/droite
2 adverb
* **straight** = droit
  to stand up straight = se tenir droit
  to go straight ahead = aller tout droit
* (*without delay*) = directement
  to go straight home = rentrer directement

strange adjective
* (*odd*) = bizarre
  **it's strange that she doesn't come any
    more** = il est bizarre qu'elle ne vienne
    plus

  ! Note that the subjunctive is used after il
  est bizarre que.

* (*unknown*) = inconnu/inconnue

stranger noun
  a stranger = un inconnu/une inconnue
  (*a foreigner*) = un étranger/une étrangère

straw noun
* (*for feeding animals*)
  straw = la paille
* (*for drinking*)
  a straw = une paille

strawberry noun
  a strawberry = une fraise

stream noun
  a stream = un ruisseau

street noun
  a street = une rue

streetlamp noun
  a streetlamp = un réverbère

strength noun
  strength = la force

stressful adjective
  = stressant/stressante

stretch verb
  = s'étirer (**!** + être)
  to stretch one's arms = s'étirer les bras

strict adjective
  = strict/stricte

strike noun
  a strike = une grève
  to go on strike = se mettre en grève

string noun
  string = la ficelle
  a piece of string = un bout de ficelle

striped adjective
  = rayé/rayée

stroke verb
  = caresser

stroller noun (*US English*)
  a stroller = une poussette

strong adjective
* (*having physical, mental strength*)
  = fort/forte
  she's strong = elle a de la force, elle est
    forte
* (*not easily damaged*) = solide
* (*having force, power*) = fort/forte
  a strong wind = un vent fort
  it's strong tea = c'est du thé fort
* (*obvious, noticeable*) = fort/forte (**!** before
    the noun)
  a strong German accent = un fort accent
    allemand
  a strong smell of garlic = une forte odeur
    d'ail
* (*having military power*)
  = puissant/puissante

stubborn adjective
  = entêté/entêtée

student noun ▶ **315**
  a student (*at university*) = un étudiant/une
    étudiante
  (*at school*) = un élève/une élève

study
1 verb
  to study history = étudier l'histoire, faire
    des études d'histoire
  to study to be a teacher = faire des études
    pour être professeur
  to study for an exam = réviser pour un
    examen
2 noun
  a study = un bureau

stuff
1 noun
  stuff (*things*) = les choses (*feminine plural*)
  (*belongings*) = les affaires (*feminine plural*)
2 verb
  to stuff a suitcase with clothes = bourrer
    une valise de vêtements
  to stuff oneself = s'empiffrer✶ (**!** + être)

stuffing noun
  a stuffing = une farce

✶ in informal situations

stupid *adjective*
= bête, stupide

style *noun*
(*a way of dressing, behaving*)
style = la classe
to have style = avoir de la classe
(*a design, a type*)
a style (*of car, garment*) = un modèle
(*of building*) = un type
(*a fashion*)
a style = une mode

stylish *adjective*
= élégant/élégante

subject *noun*
(*of a conversation*)
a subject = un sujet
to change the subject = parler d'autre chose
(*being studied*)
a subject (*at school, college*) = une matière
(*for an essay, a report*) = un sujet

suburb *noun*
the suburbs = la banlieue (*singular*)

subway *noun*
(*US English*) (*the underground*)
the subway = le métro
(*British English*) (*an underground passage*)
a subway = un passage souterrain

succeed *verb*
= réussir

success *noun*
success = le succès, la réussite
to be a success (*if it's a party*) = être réussi/réussie
(*if it's a film, a book*) = avoir du succès

successful *adjective*
to be successful (*in an attempt*) = réussir
(*describing a film, a book*) = avoir du succès

such
1 *determiner*
there's no such thing = ça n'existe pas
2 *adverb*
they have such a lot of money = ils ont tant d'argent
she's such a strange person = elle est si bizarre
I've never seen such a mess = je n'ai jamais vu une pagaille✻ pareille

suddenly *adverb*
= tout à coup

suffer *verb* ▶ 266 |
= souffrir

sugar *noun*
sugar = le sucre

suggestion *noun*
a suggestion = une suggestion

suicide *noun*
to commit suicide = se suicider (**!** + *être*)

suit
1 *noun*
a suit (*a man's*) = un costume
(*a woman's*) = un tailleur
2 *verb*
(*to be convenient*) = convenir
to suit someone = convenir à quelqu'un
does Friday suit you? = est-ce que vendredi te convient?
(*to look well on*)
the hat suits you = le chapeau te va bien

suitable *adjective*
a suitable present = un cadeau approprié
to be suitable for children = convenir aux enfants

suitcase *noun*
a suitcase = une valise

sum *noun*
a sum of money = une somme d'argent
a sum = un calcul
to be good at sums = être bon/bonne en calcul
sum up = récapituler

summer *noun*
summer = l'été (*masculine*)
in summer = en été

summer holiday (*British English*),
summer vacation (*US English*) *noun*
the summer holiday = les vacances d'été
(*from school*) = les grandes vacances
> **!** Note that **vacances** is feminine plural.

sun *noun*
the sun = le soleil
to sit in the sun = s'asseoir au soleil

sunbathe *verb*
= se faire bronzer (**!** + *être*)

sunburn *noun*
sunburn = un coup de soleil

sunburned *adjective*
to get sunburned = attraper un coup de soleil

Sunday *noun* ▶ 222 |
Sunday = dimanche (*masculine*)

sunglasses *noun*
sunglasses = les lunettes de soleil
> **!** Note that **lunettes** is feminine plural.

sunny *adjective*
= ensoleillé/ensoleillée
it's going to be sunny = il va faire du soleil

sunset *noun*
sunset = le coucher du soleil

sunshade *noun*
a sunshade = un parasol

sunshine *noun*
sunshine = le soleil

S

suntan *noun*
a suntan = un bronzage
to get a suntan = bronzer

suntan oil *noun*
a suntan oil = une huile solaire

supermarket *noun*
a supermarket = un supermarché

supper *noun*
a supper (*an evening meal*) = un dîner
(*after a show*) = un souper

support *verb*
(*to agree with, to help*) = soutenir
to support the strike = soutenir la grève
(*to keep*)
to support a family = subvenir aux besoins
   d'une famille
to support oneself = subvenir à ses
   propres besoins
(*to hold, to help physically*) = soutenir

supporter *noun*
a supporter (*of a team*) = un supporter
(*of a party*) = un sympathisant/une
   sympathisante

suppose *verb*
(*to imagine*) = supposer
I don't suppose you know yet? = je
   suppose que tu n'es pas encore au
   courant?
(*to be meant to*)
to be supposed to = être censé/censée
I'm supposed to pay for the shopping = je
   suis censé payer les courses

sure *adjective*
(*certain*) = sûr/sûre
I'm sure he said nine o'clock = je suis sûr
   qu'il a dit neuf heures
are you sure? = est-ce que tu en es sûr?
I'm not sure if she's coming = je ne sais
   pas trop si elle vient
to make sure that the door is closed
   = s'assurer que la porte est fermée
(*bound*)
he's sure to win = il va sûrement gagner
sure of oneself = sûr/sûre de soi

! *Note that* soi *will change to* moi, lui, elle,
eux *etc, depending on the person or
people being described.*

she's sure of herself = elle est sûre d'elle

surf *verb* ▶ 248
to go surfing = faire du surf

surface
1 *noun*
a surface = une surface
2 *verb*
= remonter à la surface

surfboard *noun*
a surfboard = une planche de surf

surgeon *noun* ▶ 315
a surgeon = un chirurgien

surgery *noun*
to have surgery = se faire opérer (**!** + *être*)
(*British English*) (*the place*)
a surgery = un cabinet médical

surname *noun*
a surname = un nom de famille

surprise
1 *noun*
(*an event, a gift*)
a surprise = une surprise
(*being amazed*)
surprise = la surprise, l'étonnement
   (*masculine*)
to take someone by surprise = prendre
   quelqu'un au dépourvu
2 *verb*
= surprendre

surprised *adjective*
= étonné/étonnée
I'm not surprised = ça ne m'étonne pas

surrender *verb*
= se rendre (**!** + *être*)

surround *verb*
= entourer
to be surrounded by trees = être
   entouré/entourée d'arbres

surroundings *noun*
the surroundings (*of a town*) = les
   environs (*masculine*)

survey *noun*
a survey = un sondage

survive *verb*
= survivre
to survive the winter = survivre à l'hiver
to survive an accident = réchapper d'un
   accident

suspect
1 *verb*
= soupçonner
she's suspected of stealing money = elle
   est soupçonnée d'avoir volé de l'argent
2 *noun*
a suspect = un suspect/une suspecte

suspicious *adjective*
= méfiant/méfiante
to be suspicious of someone = se méfier
   de quelqu'un

swan *noun*
a swan = un cygne

swap *verb*
= échanger

sweat *verb*
= transpirer

sweater *noun*
a sweater = un pull

sweatshirt *noun*
a sweatshirt = un sweatshirt

Sweden noun ▶ 218 |
  Sweden = la Suède

Swedish ▶ 275 |
1 *adjective*
  = suédois/suédoise
2 *noun*
  Swedish = le suédois

sweep *verb*
  = balayer

sweet
1 *adjective*
  sweet (*tasting of sugar*) = sucré/sucrée
  (*not bitter or dry*) = doux/douce
  to have a sweet tooth = aimer les
    sucreries
  (*describing a smell*) = bon/bonne (**!** *before
    the noun*)
  (*kind, gentle*) = gentil/gentille
  (*cute*) = mignon/mignonne
2 *noun* (*British English*)
  a sweet = un bonbon

swim
1 *verb*
  = nager
  to swim across a lake = traverser un lac à
    la nage
2 *noun*
  a swim = une baignade
  to go for a swim (*in the sea*) = aller se
    baigner (**!** + *être*)

swimming *noun* ▶ 248 |
  swimming = la natation

swimming pool *noun*
  a swimming pool = une piscine

swimsuit *noun*
  a swimsuit = un maillot de bain

swing
1 *verb*
  (*to move back and forth*) = se balancer
    (**!** + *être*)
  to swing on a gate = se balancer sur un
    portillon
  (*to move something back and forth*)
    = balancer
  to swing one's legs = balancer les jambes
2 *noun*
  a swing = une balançoire

Swiss ▶ 275 |
1 *adjective*
  = suisse
2 *noun*
  the Swiss = les Suisses (*masculine plural*)

switch
1 *noun*
  a switch (*for a light*) = un interrupteur
  (*on a radio, an appliance*) = un bouton
2 *verb*
  = changer
  to switch seats = changer de place
  to switch from English to French = passer
    de l'anglais au français

switch off = éteindre
  to switch off the light = éteindre la
    lumière
switch on = allumer
  to switch the radio on = allumer la radio

Switzerland *noun* ▶ 218 |
  Switzerland = la Suisse

sympathetic *adjective*
  (*showing pity*)
    = compatissant/compatissante
  (*showing understanding*)
    = compréhensif/compréhensive

syringe *noun*
  a syringe = une seringue

system *noun*
  a system = un système

Tt

table *noun*
  a table = une table

tablet *noun*
  a tablet = un comprimé

table tennis *noun* ▶ 248 |
  table tennis = le tennis de table, le ping-
    pong

tail *noun*
  a tail = une queue

take *verb*
  ! *See the usage note on* Talking about
    time ▶ 356 | *for more information and*
    examples.

  (*to take hold of*) = prendre
  to take someone by the hand = prendre
    quelqu'un par la main
  (*to carry with one*) = emporter, prendre
  I took my umbrella = j'ai emporté mon
    parapluie
  I'll take the letters to Jack = je vais porter
    les lettres à Jack
  (*to accompany, to bring*) = emmener
  to take the children for a walk = emmener
    les enfants faire une promenade
  to take someone home = raccompagner
    quelqu'un
  (*to remove*) = prendre
  to take a book off the shelf = prendre un
    livre sur l'étagère
  (*to steal*) = prendre, voler
  (*to cope with, to bear*) = supporter
  he can't take the pain = il ne supporte pas
    la douleur
  I can't take any more = je n'en peux plus

(when talking about what is necessary)
it takes [time | courage | patience …] = il faut
[du temps | du courage | de la patience …]
it takes two hours to get to Paris = il faut
deux heures pour aller à Paris
to take a long time to do one's homework
= mettre longtemps pour faire ses
devoirs
it won't take long = ça ne prendra pas
longtemps
(to accept) = accepter
(to react to) = prendre
he took the news badly = il a mal pris la
nouvelle
(to use when travelling) = prendre
to take a taxi = prendre un taxi
take the first turn on the right = prenez la
première rue à droite
(to do)
to take exams = passer des examens
(to have) = prendre
to take [a vacation | a shower | driving
lessons …] = prendre [des vacances | une
douche | des leçons de conduite …]
I don't take sugar = je ne prends pas de
sucre
(to wear)
to take a size 10 *(in clothes)* = s'habiller en
38
to take a size 5 *(in shoes)* = chausser du
38
take apart = démonter
take away
to take away the rubbish = enlever les
déchets
to take someone away = emmener
quelqu'un
take back = rapporter
I had to take the dress back = j'ai dû
rapporter la robe
take down
(to remove)
to take a poster down = enlever une
affiche
to take down a tent = démonter une tente
(to write down) = noter
take hold of = prendre
take off
(from an airport) = décoller
(to remove) = enlever
I took off my shoes = j'ai enlevé mes
chaussures
to take off one's clothes = se déshabiller
(✘ + *être*)
take out
(from a box, a pocket, a bag) = sortir
he took a pen out of his pocket = il a sorti
un stylo de sa poche
(from a bank account) = retirer
to take money out = retirer de l'argent
(to be nasty to)
to take it out on someone = s'en prendre à
quelqu'un

take part
to take part in a game = participer à un
jeu
take place = avoir lieu
take up
(as a hobby)
to take up windsurfing = se mettre à faire
de la planche à voile
(to use up) = prendre
to take up space = prendre de la place

talented *adjective*
= doué/douée

talk
1 *verb*
(to speak) = parler
to talk on the phone = parler au téléphone
to talk in French = parler en français
to talk to someone = parler à quelqu'un
I talked to them about the trip = je leur ai
parlé de la sortie
they were talking about you = ils parlaient
de toi
to talk to oneself = parler tout seul/toute
seule
(to chat) = bavarder
2 *noun*
(a conversation)
a talk = une conversation
(about a special subject)
a talk *(in class)* = un exposé
(to a club, a group) = une causerie
(discussions)
talks = les négociations *(feminine)*

talkative *adjective*
= bavard/bavarde

tall *adjective* ▶ 285 |
(describing a person) = grand/grande
(! *before the noun*)
(describing a building, a tree) = haut/haute
to be six feet tall ≈ mesurer un mètre
quatre-vingts
to get tall = grandir

tan *noun*
a tan = un bronzage
to get a tan = bronzer

tanned *adjective*
= bronzé/bronzée

tap
1 *noun (British English)*
a tap = un robinet
to turn the tap off = fermer le robinet
2 *verb*
to tap on the door = frapper à la porte

tape
1 *noun*
a tape *(for a tape recorder)* = une cassette
(for a video) = une cassette vidéo
(for repairs, for sticking)
tape = le scotch
2 *verb*
= enregistrer

✘ in informal situations

tape recorder noun
a tape recorder = un magnétophone

target
1 noun
a target = une cible
2 verb
= viser

tart noun (British English)
a tart = une tarte
an apple tart = une tarte aux pommes

task noun
a task = une tâche

taste
1 noun
(when eating, drinking)
a taste = un goût
(when talking about preferences)
taste = le goût
to have good taste = avoir du goût
2 verb
(when describing a flavour)
to taste good = être bon/bonne
to taste awful = avoir mauvais goût
it tastes like cabbage = ça a le goût du chou
(when eating, drinking) = goûter

Taurus noun
Taurus = Taureau (masculine)

tax noun
a tax (on income, profits) = un impôt
(on goods, property) = une taxe

taxi noun
a taxi = un taxi

taxi rank (British English), **taxi stand** (US English) noun
a taxi rank = une station de taxis

tea noun
(the product)
tea = le thé
(a cup of tea)
a tea = un thé
(British English) (a meal)
tea (in the afternoon) = le thé
(in the evening) = le dîner

teach verb
(to help someone to learn skills)
to teach someone [to read | to drive | to ride a horse ...] = apprendre à quelqu'un à [lire | conduire | monter à cheval ...]
(to work as a teacher) = enseigner
to teach French to adults = enseigner le français à des adultes

teacher noun ▶ 315 |
a teacher = un enseignant/une enseignante
(in a primary school) = un professeur des écoles, un instituteur/une institutrice
(in a secondary school) = un professeur

team noun
a team = une équipe

teapot noun
a teapot = une théière

tear¹ verb
(to cause damage to) = déchirer
to tear a page out of a book = arracher une page d'un livre
(to get damaged) = se déchirer (! + être)
tear off = détacher
tear up = déchirer

tear² noun
a tear = une larme
to burst into tears = fondre en larmes

tease verb
= taquiner

teaspoon noun
a teaspoon = une petite cuillère

technical adjective
= technique

teenager noun
a teenager = un adolescent/une adolescente

telephone noun
a telephone = un téléphone

telephone directory noun
a telephone directory = un annuaire

telescope noun
a telescope = un télescope

television noun
a television = un téléviseur
I saw the film on television = j'ai vu le film à la télévision

tell verb
(to say to) = dire à
did you tell your parents? = est-ce que tu l'as dit à tes parents?
to tell someone about a problem = parler d'un problème à quelqu'un
(for interest, fun) = raconter
to tell jokes = raconter des blagues✲
(when giving orders or instructions)
to tell someone to leave the classroom = dire à quelqu'un de quitter la salle de classe
to tell someone not to smoke = interdire à quelqu'un de fumer
(to work out, to know)
I can tell (that) she's disappointed = je vois bien qu'elle est déçue
you can tell he's lying = on voit bien qu'il ment
(when making distinctions)
to tell the twin brothers apart = distinguer les jumeaux
I can't tell which is which = je n'arrive pas à les distinguer
(to reveal) = répéter
don't tell anyone = ne le répète pas
tell off
to tell someone off = réprimander quelqu'un

T

temper *noun*
to be in a temper = être en colère
to lose one's temper = se mettre en colère

temperature *noun* ▶ **266** |
the temperature = la température
to have a temperature = avoir de la
température, avoir de la fièvre

temporary *adjective*
(*describing a job*) = temporaire
(*describing accommodation*) = provisoire

ten *number* ▶ **187** |, ▶ **211** |
ten = dix
ten houses = dix maisons
I've got ten (of them) = j'en ai dix

tennis *noun* ▶ **248** |
tennis = le tennis

tennis court *noun*
a tennis court = un court de tennis

tense *adjective*
= tendu/tendue

tent *noun*
a tent = une tente

tenth *number*
(*in a series*) = dixième
(*in dates*) ▶ **222** |
the tenth of December = le dix décembre

term *noun*
a term = un trimestre

terrible *adjective*
(*expressing shock*) = épouvantable
(*used for emphasis*) = affreux/affreuse

terrified *adjective*
= terrifié/terrifiée

terror *noun*
terror = la terreur

terrorist *noun*
a terrorist = un terroriste/une terroriste

test
1 *verb*
(*to try out*) = essayer, tester
(*in exams*) = contrôler
2 *noun*
a test = un test
(*in school, college*) (*written*) = un contrôle
(*oral*) = un contrôle oral
a driving test = un examen du permis de
conduire
to have an eye test = se faire faire un
examen de la vue

than
1 *preposition*
(*in comparisons*) = que
to be [stronger | more intelligent | faster ...]
than = être [plus fort | plus intelligent | plus
rapide ...] que
I've got more money than you = j'ai plus
d'argent que toi

(*when talking about quantities*) ▶ **317** | = de
more than half of the pupils are absent
= plus de la moitié des élèves sont
absents
it's worth less than £100 = ça vaut moins
de 100 livres
2 *conjunction*
= que
he's older than I am = il est plus âgé que
moi

thank *verb*
= remercier

thanks
1 *adverb* = merci
2 thanks to = grâce à

thank you *adverb*
= merci
thank you for coming = merci d'être venu
'more wine?'—'thank you' = 'encore un
peu de vin?'—'volontiers'

that *pronoun*
▶ **351** | *See the boxed note on* that *for more
information and examples.*
what's that? = qu'est-ce que c'est?
who's that? = qui est-ce?
is that Louis? = c'est Louis?
that's how they make butter = c'est
comme ça qu'on fait le beurre
that's not true = ce n'est pas vrai
that's the kitchen = ça, c'est la cuisine

the *determiner*
▶ **352** | *See the boxed note on* the *for
detailed information and examples.*

theatre (*British English*), **theater** (*US
English*) *noun*
a theatre = un théâtre

their *determiner*
their = leur (*+ singular*)
= leurs (*+ plural*)
I don't like their house = je n'aime pas
leur maison
they're selling their CDs = ils vendent
leurs disques compacts

theirs *pronoun*
the new house is theirs = la nouvelle
maison est à eux
which car is theirs? = laquelle est leur
voiture?
my car is red but theirs is green = ma
voiture est rouge mais la leur est verte
our parents are younger than theirs = nos
parents sont plus jeunes que les leurs

! *Note that, when comparing objects,
people etc, one of the following
translations—le leur, la leur or les
leurs—will be used. To know which one to
use, find out whether the object, person
etc. being described is masculine
singular, feminine singular or just plural.*

that

As a determiner

In French, determiners agree with the noun that follows; so **that** is translated as follows:

ce or **cet**	+	*masculine singular noun*	**ce** monsieur, **cet** homme
cette	+	*feminine singular noun*	**cette** femme
ces	+	*noun plural*	**ces** livres, **ces** histoires

Note, however, that the above translations are also used for the English **this** (plural *these*). So when it is necessary to insist on **that** as opposed to another or others of the same sort, the adverbial tag **-là** is added to the noun:

    I prefer that colour   = je préfère **cette** couleur-**là**

As a pronoun

● In French, pronouns reflect the gender and number of the noun they are standing for.

So **that** (meaning *that one*) is translated by

    celui-là   *for a masculine noun*
    celle-là   *for a feminine noun*

and **those** (meaning *those ones*) is translated by

    ceux-là   *for a masculine noun*
    celles-là   *for a feminine noun*

    all the dresses are nice but   = toutes les robes sont jolies mais
    I like that best   je préfère **celle-là**

● When used as a relative pronoun, **that** is translated by **qui** when it is the subject of the verb and by **que** when it is the object:

    the man that stole the car   = l'homme **qui** a volé la voiture
    the film that I saw   = le film **que** j'ai vu

Remember that in the present perfect and past perfect tenses, the past participle agrees with the noun that **que** is referring back to:

    the girl that I met   = la fille **que** j'ai rencontrée
    the apples that I bought   = les pommes **que** j'ai achetées

● When that is used as a relative pronoun with a preposition, it is translated by **lequel** when standing for a masculine singular noun, by **laquelle** when standing for a feminine singular noun, by **lesquels** when standing for a masculine plural noun, and by **lesquelles** when standing for a feminine plural noun:

    the chair that I was sitting on   – la chaise sur **laquelle** j'étais assis
    the children that I bought the   = les enfants pour **lesquels** j'ai acheté les livres
    books for

If the preposition would normally be translated by **à** in French (**to, at** etc), the translation of the whole (*preposition + relative pronoun*) will be:

    auquel   *for a masculine noun*
    à laquelle   *for a feminine noun*
    auxquels   *for a masculine plural noun*
    auxquelles   *for a feminine plural noun*

    the girls that I was talking to   = les filles **auxquelles** je parlais

If the preposition used would normally be translated by **de** in French (**of, from** etc), the translation of the whole (*preposition + relative pronoun*) will be **dont** in all cases.

    the people that I've talked about = les personnes **dont** j'ai parlé

As a conjunction

When used as a conjunction, **that** can almost always be translated by **que** (**qu'** before a vowel or mute h):

    she said that she would do it   = elle a dit **qu'**elle le ferait

T

the

- In French the definite article, like determiners, agrees with the noun that follows; so **the** is translated as follows:

le or **l'** +	*masculine singular noun*	**le** chien, **l'**ami
la or **l'** +	*feminine singular noun*	**la** chaise, **l'**amie
les +	*masculine plural noun*	**les** hommes, **les** avions
les +	*feminine plural noun*	**les** femmes, **les** autos

- When **the** is used after a preposition in English, the two words (*preposition* + **the**) are often translated by one word in French. If the preposition would normally be translated by **de** in French (**of**, **about**, **from** etc), the *preposition* + **the** is translated according to whether the noun is masculine or feminime, singular or plural:

	le or **l'** + *masculine singular noun*	**du** chien, **de l'**ami
de +	**la** or **l'** + *feminine singular noun*	**de la** chaise, **de l'**amie
	les + *masculine plural noun*	**des** hommes, **des** avions
	les + *feminine plural noun*	**des** femmes, **des** autos

If the preposition would usually be translated by **à** (**at**, **to** etc) the *preposition* + **the** is translated according to whether the noun is masculine or feminine, singular or plural:

	le or **l'** + *masculine singular noun*	**au** chien, **à l'**ami
à +	**la** or **l'** + *feminine singular noun*	**à la** chaise, **à l'**amie
	les + *masculine plural noun*	**aux** hommes, **aux** avions
	les + *feminine plural noun*	**aux** femmes, **aux** autos

- Other than this, there are few problems in translating **the** into French. The following cases are, however, worth remembering as not following exactly the pattern of the English:

the good, the poor, the unemployed	= **les** bons, **les** pauvres, **les** chômeurs
Charles the First, Elizabeth the Second	= Charles 1er (Premier), Elizabeth II (Deux)
she's the actress of the year	= c'est **la plus grande** actrice de l'année
the Tudors, the Batemans, the Kennedys	= **les** Tudor, **les** Bateman, **les** Kennedy
the sporting event of the year	= **le grand** événement sportif de l'année
it's the film to see	= c'est **le** film à voir

▶ This dictionary contains usage notes on such topics as **days of the week**, **illnesses**, **the human body**, and **musical instruments**, many of which use **the**; for the index to these notes see ▶ **400 |**.

---

them *pronoun*
▶ **353 |** *See the boxed note on* **them** *for detailed information and examples.*

themselves *pronoun*
(*when used as a reflexive pronoun*)
they want to enjoy themselves = ils/elles veulent s'amuser
they didn't hurt themselves = ils/elles ne se sont pas fait mal
(*when used for emphasis*)
they said it themselves = ils l'ont dit eux-mêmes/elles l'ont dit elles-mêmes
they did it all by themselves = ils l'ont fait tout seuls/elles l'ont fait toutes seules

! *Remember that, when talking about mixed groups, the masculine form* **eux-mêmes** *is used to translate* **themselves**.

then *adverb*
(*at that point in time*) = alors, à ce moment-là
I was living in Paris then = j'habitais alors Paris

× *in informal situations*

we saw each other a lot then = on se voyait beaucoup à ce moment-là
from then on = à partir de ce moment-là
(*after, next*) = puis, ensuite
I went for a drink and then had dinner = je suis allé prendre un pot**×** et puis j'ai dîné

there
1 *pronoun*
there is a problem = il y a un problème
there aren't any shops = il n'y a pas de magasins
there was no room = il n'y avait pas de place
there will be a lot of people = il y aura beaucoup de monde
2 *adverb*
(*when talking about location*) = là
who's there? = qui est là?
the train wasn't there = le train n'était pas là
go over there = va là-bas
when do we get there? = quand est-ce qu'on arrive?
they don't go there very often = ils n'y vont pas très souvent

them

● When used as a direct object pronoun, referring to people, animals or things, **them** is translated by **les**:

I know them	= je **les** connais
I don't know them	= je ne **les** connais pas
do I know them?	= est-ce que je **les** connais?

Note that the object pronoun normally comes before the verb in French and that, in tenses like the present perfect and past perfect, the past participle agrees with the direct object pronoun:

he's seen them	= il **les** a vus
	(***them** being masculine or of mixed gender*)
	= il **les** a vues
	(***them** being all feminine gender*)
he hasn't seen them	= il ne **les** a pas vus
	= il ne **les** a pas vues
has he seen them?	= est-ce qu'il **les** a vus?
	= est-ce qu'il **les** a vues?

● In imperatives, the direct object pronoun is translated by **les** and comes after the verb:

catch them!	= attrape-**les**!*
take them!	= prenez-**les**!*

But in negative commands, **les** comes before the verb:

don't take them!	= ne **les** prenez pas!
don't hit them!	= ne **les** frappe pas!

● When used as an indirect object pronoun, **them** is translated by **leur**:

I gave it to them	= je le **leur** ai donné
I didn't give it to them	= je ne le **leur** ai pas donné
did I give it to them?	= est-ce que je le **leur** ai donné?

● In imperatives, the indirect object pronoun is translated by **leur** and comes after the verb:

write to them!	= écris-**leur**!*
say it to them!	= dis-le-**leur**!*

But in negative commands, **leur** comes before the verb:

don't show it to them!	= ne le **leur** montre pas!

● After prepositions and the verb **to be**, the translation is **eux** for masculine or mixed gender and **elles** for feminine gender:

he did it for them	= il l'a fait pour **eux**
	(***them** being masculine or of mixed gender*)
	= il l'a fait pour **elles**
	(***them** being all feminine gender*)
it's them	= ce sont **eux**
	ce sont **elles**

* Note the hyphen(s).

Note that the entries for **her, him, me** and **us** are modelled in this note.

(when drawing attention)
there's [the sea | my watch | Natalie] = voilà [la mer | ma montre | Natalie …]
there they are = les voilà
there you are, there you go = et voilà

therefore *adverb*
= donc, par conséquent

these
1 *determiner*
these = ces

these books aren't mine = ces livres ne sont pas à moi
2 *pronoun*
what are these? = qu'est-ce que c'est?
these are your things = ce sont tes affaires
these are my friends = ce sont mes amis
I prefer THESE = je préfère ceux-ci/celles-ci

! See the note on **this** for further information about the use of -ci.

they *pronoun*
  they = ils/elles
  they'll be there too = ils/elles seront là
    aussi
  there they are! = les voilà!
  they're intelligent girls = ce sont des filles
    intelligentes
  that's how they make yogurt = c'est
    comme ça qu'on fait le yaourt

  ! *Note that* on *is used to translate* they
  *when talking in an impersonal or vague
  way about people.*

thick *adjective*
  = épais/épaisse

thief *noun*
  a thief = un voleur/une voleuse

thigh *noun* ▶ 201 |
  the thigh = la cuisse

thin *adjective*
  = mince
  to get thin = maigrir

thing *noun*
  a thing = une chose, un truc
  I've got things to do = j'ai des choses à
    faire
  that was a stupid thing to do = c'était
    stupide de faire ça
  the best thing would be to call him = le
    mieux serait de l'appeler
  I can't hear a thing = je n'entends rien
    (*belongings*)
  things = les affaires (*feminine*)

think *verb*
  (*when talking about opinions*) = penser,
    croire
  what do you think of it? = qu'est-ce que tu
    en penses?
  I think it's unfair = je pense que c'est
    injuste
  'will they come?'—'I don't think so' = 'est-
    ce qu'ils vont venir?'—'je ne crois pas'
  who do you think will win? = qui va
    gagner à ton avis?
  (*to concentrate on an idea*) = réfléchir
  think hard before answering = réfléchis
    bien avant de répondre
  (*to remember*)
  I can't think of his name = je ne me
    rappelle plus son nom
  (*to take into account, to have in mind*)
  to think of someone = penser à quelqu'un
  I thought of you when I saw the dress
    = j'ai pensé à toi quand j'ai vu la robe
  we didn't think of closing the window
    = nous n'avons pas pensé à fermer la
    fenêtre
  (*to have vague plans to*)
  to be thinking of changing jobs
    = envisager de changer de travail
  (*to have an idea about*)
  to think of a solution = trouver une
    solution

third
1 *adjective*
  = troisième
2 *noun*
  (*in a series*)
  the third = le troisième/la troisième
  (*in dates*) ▶ 222 |
  the third of June = le trois juin
  (*when talking about quantities*) ▶ 317 |
  a third of the population = un tiers de la
    population
3 *adverb*
  = troisième
  to come third = arriver troisième

thirsty *adjective*
  to be thirsty = avoir soif
  I'm very thirsty = j'ai très soif

thirteen *number* ▶ 187 |, ▶ 211 |
  thirteen = treize

thirteenth *number*
  (*in a series*) = treizième
  (*in dates*) ▶ 222 |
  Friday the thirteenth = vendredi treize

thirty *number* ▶ 187 |, ▶ 211 |
  thirty = trente

this
1 *determiner*
  this = ce/cette (! cet + *masculine* + *vowel
    or mute h*)
  I like this garden = j'aime bien ce jardin
  do you know this place? = est-ce que tu
    connais cet endroit?
  who is this woman? = qui est cette
    femme?
  I prefer THIS hotel to the others = je préfère
    cet hôtel-ci aux autres

  ! *Note that, since the translations for* this
  and that *are the same, the tag* -ci *must be
  added to the noun and pronoun if a clear
  distinction is to be made.*

2 *pronoun*
  what's this? = qu'est-ce que c'est?
  who's this? = qui est-ce?
  this is the kitchen = voici la cuisine
  this is my sister = voici ma sœur
  this isn't the right address = ce n'est pas la
    bonne adresse
  how much is THIS? = combien coûte celui-
    ci/celle-ci?

those
1 *determiner*
  those = ces
  those books are yours = ces livres sont à
    toi
2 *pronoun*
  what are those? = qu'est-ce que c'est?
  those are my letters = ce sont mes lettres
  those are my cousins = ce sont mes
    cousins
  I prefer THOSE = je préfère ceux-là/celles-là
  ▶ 351 | *See the boxed note on* that *for further
  information about the use of* -là.

though *conjunction*
= bien que
though it's expensive, it's still a good buy
= bien que ce soit cher, ça reste un bon
achat

! *Note that the subjunctive is used after*
bien que.

thought *noun*
a thought = une pensée

thousand *number*
one thousand, a thousand = mille
four thousand pounds = quatre mille
livres
about a thousand people = un millier de
personnes

thread *noun*
thread = le fil

threat *noun*
a threat = une menace

threaten *verb*
= menacer

three *number* ▶ **187** |, ▶ **211** |
three = trois
three sisters = trois sœurs
I've got three (of them) = j'en ai trois

throat *noun* ▶ **201** |
the throat = la gorge

through

! *Often* **through** *occurs in combinations
with verbs, for example:* go through, let
through, read through *etc. To find the
correct translations for this type of verb,
look up the separate dictionary entries at*
go, let, read *etc.*

preposition
• (*from one side to the other*) = à travers
to see through the fog = voir à travers le
brouillard
to drive through the desert = traverser le
désert (en voiture)
• (*via, by way of*)
to go through the town centre = passer par
le centre-ville
to look through a window = regarder par
une fenêtre
• (*past*)
to go through a red light = brûler un feu
rouge
to go through customs = passer la douane
• (*when talking about time*)
right through the day = toute la journée
from Friday through to Sunday = de
vendredi jusqu'à dimanche
open April through September (*US
English*) = ouvert d'avril à fin septembre

throw *verb*
= lancer
to throw stones at someone = lancer des
pierres à quelqu'un
throw me the ball = lance-moi le ballon
to throw a book on the floor = jeter un
livre par terre

throw away, throw out = jeter

thumb *noun* ▶ **201** |
the thumb = le pouce

thunder *noun*
thunder = le tonnerre

thunderstorm *noun*
a thunderstorm = un orage

Thursday *noun* ▶ **222** |
Thursday = jeudi (*masculine*)

ticket *noun*
a ticket (*for a plane, a train, a film, an
event*) = un billet
(*for a bus, the underground, a locker*) = un
ticket

tickle *verb*
= chatouiller

tide *noun*
the tide = la marée
the tide is out = c'est la marée basse
the tide is coming in = la marée monte

tidy *adjective*
(*describing a place, a desk*) = bien
rangé/rangée
(*describing a person*) = ordonné/ordonnée
tidy up = ranger

tie
1 *verb*
= attacher
to tie a dog to a tree = attacher un chien à
un arbre
to tie a parcel (up) with string = ficeler un
paquet
2 *noun*
• (*worn with a shirt*)
a tie = une cravate
• (*in sport*)
a tie = un match nul
tie up = ligoter

tiger *noun*
a tiger = un tigre

tight *adjective*
= serré/serrée

tights *noun* (*British English*)
tights = un collant (*singular*)

till¹ ▶ **until**

till² *noun*
a till = une caisse

timber *noun*
timber = le bois (de construction)

time *noun*
• **time** = le temps
I don't have time to go there = je n'ai pas
le temps d'y aller
we haven't seen them for some time = ça
fait un moment qu'on ne les a pas vus
a long time ago = il y a longtemps

T

Talking about time

▶ For time by the clock, ▶ **211** |; for days of the week, months, and dates, ▶ **222** |.

How long?

Note the various ways of translating **take** into French:

how long does it take?	= combien de temps faut-il?
it took me a week	= il m'a fallu une semaine / cela m'a pris une semaine
it'll take at least a year	= il faudra au moins un an
it'll only take a minute	= ça ne prendra qu'une minute

Use **en** for **in** when expressing the time something took or will take:

*he did it **in** an hour*	= il l'a fait **en** une heure

The commonest translation of **for** in the 'how long' sense is **pendant**:

*I worked in a factory **for** a year*	= j'ai travaillé en usine **pendant** un an

But use **pour** to translate **for** when the length of time is seen as being still to come:

*we're here **for** a month*	= nous sommes là **pour** un mois

And use **depuis** to translate **for** when the action began in the past and is still going on:

*she has been here **for** a week*	= elle est ici **depuis** une semaine
*I haven't seen her **for** years*	= je ne l'ai pas vue **depuis** des années

When?

Use **dans** for **in** when something is seen as happening in the future:

*I'll be there **in** an hour*	= j'y serai **dans** une heure
***in** three weeks' time*	= **dans** trois semaines
when did it happen?	= quand est-ce que c'est arrivé?
a month ago	= il y a un mois
a week ago yesterday	= il y a eu huit jours hier
when will you see him?	= quand est-ce que tu le verras?
***in** a few days*	= **dans** quelques jours
a month from tomorrow	= **dans** un mois demain
when you see him, tell him to call me	= quand tu le verras,* dis-lui de m'appeler

How often?

how often does it happen?	= cela arrive tous les combien?
every year	= tous les ans
five times a day	= cinq fois par jour
once every three months	= une fois tous les trois mois

How much an hour (etc)?

*how much do you get **an** hour?*	= combien gagnez-vous **de** l'heure?
*to be paid $20 **an** hour*	= être payé 20 dollars **de** l'heure
*to be paid **by** the hour*	= être payé **à** l'heure
*how much do you get **a** week?*	= combien gagnez-vous **par** semaine?
*$3,000 **a** month*	= 3 000 dollars **par** mois

* Note that, when talking about future time, the future tense of the verb is used after **quand**.

(*when talking about a specific hour or period of time*)
the time = l'heure (*feminine*)
what's the time?, what time is it? = quelle heure est-il?
what time does the film start? = à quelle heure commence le film?

to arrive on time = arriver à l'heure
in [five days' | a week's | six months' ...] time = dans [cinq jours | une semaine | six mois ...]
this time last year = il y a exactement un an
by this time next week = d'ici la semaine prochaine
it's time we left = il est temps de partir

(a moment)
a time = un moment
at times = par moments
at the right time = au bon moment
this is no time to argue = ce n'est pas le moment de se disputer
any time now = d'un moment à l'autre
for the time being = pour le moment
(a period in the past)
a time = une époque
they didn't know each other at the time = ils ne se connaissaient pas à l'époque
(an experience)
to have a good time = bien s'amuser (**!** + *être*)
to have a hard time concentrating = avoir du mal à se concentrer
(an occasion)
the first time we met = la première fois que nous nous sommes rencontrés
from time to time = de temps en temps
(when comparing)
three times more expensive = trois fois plus cher
ten times quicker = dix fois plus rapide

timetable *noun*
(for trains, buses)
a timetable = un horaire
(in school, at work)
a timetable = un emploi du temps

tin *noun*
(the metal)
tin = l'étain *(masculine)*
(British English) (a can)
a tin = une boîte (de conserve)
a tin of beans = une boîte de haricots

tin opener *noun (British English)*
a tin opener = un ouvre-boîtes

tiny *adjective*
= tout petit/toute petite

tip *noun*
(the point, the end)
the tip *(of a pen, a stick, a shoe)* = la pointe
(of the finger, nose, tongue) = le bout
on the tips of one's toes = sur la pointe des pieds
(given in a hotel, a restaurant)
a tip = un pourboire
(a piece of advice)
a tip = un conseil

tire *noun (US English)*
a tire = un pneu

tired *adjective*
(needing rest) = fatigué/fatiguée
to get tired = se fatiguer (**!** + *être*)
(needing a change)
I'm tired of being a waitress = j'en ai assez d'être serveuse

tiring *adjective*
= fatigant/fatigante

tissue *noun*
a tissue = un mouchoir en papier

to *preposition* ▶ **211**
▶ **358** *See the boxed note on* **to**. *There are many adjectives like* **mean**, **nice**, **rude** *etc and verbs like* **belong**, **write** *etc which involve the use of* **to**. *For translations, look up the adjective entries at* **mean**, **nice**, **rude** *or the verb entries at* **belong**, **write**.

toast *noun*
toast = le pain grillé
a piece of toast = une tranche de pain grillé

toaster *noun*
a toaster = un grille-pain

today *adverb* ▶ **356**
= aujourd'hui

toe *noun* ▶ **201**
the toe = l'orteil *(masculine)*

toffee *noun*
toffee = le caramel

together *adverb*
= ensemble

toilet *noun*
a toilet = des toilettes *(feminine plural)*

toilet paper *noun*
toilet paper = le papier hygiénique

tomato *noun*
a tomato = une tomate

tomorrow *adverb* ▶ **356**
= demain

tongue *noun* ▶ **201**
the tongue = la langue

tonight *adverb*
(this evening) = ce soir
(during the night) = cette nuit

too *adverb*
(also) = aussi
I'm going too = j'y vais aussi
(more than is necessary or desirable) = trop
it's too [big | dear | far ...] = c'est trop [grand | cher | loin ...]
there were too many people = il y avait trop de monde
I ate too much = j'ai trop mangé

tool *noun*
a tool = un outil

tooth *noun* ▶ **201**
a tooth = une dent
a set of false teeth = un dentier

toothache *noun* ▶ **266**
to have a toothache = avoir mal aux dents

toothbrush *noun*
a toothbrush = une brosse à dents

toothpaste *noun*
toothpaste = le dentifrice

to

▶ This dictionary contains usage notes on such topics as **The clock**, **Length and weight measurements**, **Games and sports** etc. Many of these use the preposition **to**. For the index to these notes ▶ **400**].

As a preposition

● When **to** is used as a preposition with verbs of movement (*go*, *travel* etc), it is often translated by **à** (*à Paris*, *à Londres*), but remember to use **en** with feminine countries (*en France*) and **au** with masculine countries (*au Portugal*).

Remember when using **à** in French that **à** + **le** always becomes **au**:

to the office	= **au** bureau

and **à** + **les** always becomes **aux**:

to the shops	= **aux** magasins

● When **to** is used as a preposition with verbs such as *speak*, *give*, *say* etc, it is usually translated by **à**:

give the book to Jane	= donne le livre **à** Jane
I'll speak to the headmistress	= je vais parler **à** la directrice
she said it to my father	= elle l'a dit **à** mon père
show it to the policeman	= montre-le **à** l'agent
I pointed it out to the stewardess	= je l'ai signalé **à** l'hôtesse
give the ball to the little boy	= donne le ballon **au*** petit garçon
we gave it to the children	= nous l'avons donné **aux*** enfants

* Remember that **à** + **le** = **au** and **à** + **les** = **aux**

● When **to** is used as a preposition with personal pronouns (*me*, *you*, *him*, *her*, *us*, *them*), the two words (*preposition* + *pronoun*) are translated by **me/te/lui/lui/nous/vous/leur**:

she gave it to them	= elle le **leur** a donné
I'll say it to her	= je vais le **lui** dire
will you lend it to me?	= est-ce que tu **me** le prêtes?

As part of an infinitive

● When **to** forms the infinitive of a verb taken alone, it needs no translation:

to go	= aller
to sing	= chanter

However, when **to** is used as part of an infinitive giving the meaning **in order to**, it is translated by **pour**:

he's gone into town to buy a shirt	= il est parti en ville **pour acheter** une chemise
I need it to do my homework	= j'en ai besoin **pour faire** mes devoirs

● **to** is also used as part of an infinitive after certain adjectives: **easy to read** etc. Here **to** is usually translated by **à**:

her writing is easy to read	= son écriture est facile **à** lire
his accent is difficult to understand	= son accent est dur **à** comprendre

However, when the infinitive has an object, **to** is usually translated by **de**:

it's easy to lose one's way	= il est facile **de** perdre son chemin
it's difficult to work at night	= c'est difficile **de** travailler la nuit

▶ **to** is also used as part of an infinitive after certain verbs: *she told me* **to** *wash my hands*, *I'll help him* **to** *tidy the room* etc. Here the translation, usually either **à** or **de**, depends on the verb used in French. To find the correct translation, consult the appropriate verb entry: **tell**, **help** etc.

---

top
1 *noun*
(*the highest part*)
the top of the hill = le sommet de la colline
the top of the stairs = le haut de l'escalier

at the top of [the page | the stairs | street ...] = en haut [de la page | de l'escalier | de la rue ...]
(*a cover, a lid*)
a top (*on a bottle*) = un bouchon
(*on a pan*) = un couvercle
(*on a pen*) = un capuchon

(the highest level)
to get to the top = réussir
to be at the top of the class = être premier/première de la classe
2 *adjective*
the top [shelf | drawer | button ...] = [l'étagère | le tiroir | le bouton ...] du haut

torch *noun (British English)*
a torch = une lampe de poche

torn *adjective*
= déchiré/déchirée

tortoise *noun*
a tortoise = une tortue

total
1 *noun*
a total = un total
2 *adjective*
= total/totale

touch
1 *verb*
(with one's hand) = toucher
(to interfere with) = toucher à
don't touch my things = ne touche pas à mes affaires
2 *noun*
to [be | get | stay ...] **in touch with someone** = [être | se mettre | rester ...] en contact avec quelqu'un

tough *adjective*
(not soft, not sensitive) = coriace
(rough) = dur/dure
a tough area = un quartier dur
(difficult) = difficile
(severe)
a tough law = une loi sévère

tour
1 *noun*
(by a team, a band, a theatre group)
a tour = une tournée
on tour = en tournée
(by tourists, pupils, visitors)
a tour = une visite
to go on a tour of the castle = visiter le château
2 *verb*
to go touring = faire du tourisme
to tour the United States = visiter les États-Unis

tourism *noun*
tourism = le tourisme

tourist *noun*
a tourist = un touriste/une touriste

tourist office *noun*
a tourist office *(local)* = un syndicat d'initiative

toward(s) *preposition*
(when talking about place, time) = vers

towards the east = vers l'est
towards evening = vers le soir
(when talking about attitudes) = envers
to be friendly towards someone = se montrer cordial envers quelqu'un

towel *noun*
a towel = une serviette

tower *noun*
a tower = une tour

tower block *noun (British English)*
a tower block = une tour d'habitation

town *noun*
a town = une ville
to go into town = aller en ville

town hall *noun*
a town hall = une mairie

toy *noun*
a toy = un jouet

track *noun*
(a path)
a track = un sentier, un chemin
(for sports)
a track = une piste
(the rails)
the track(s) = la voie ferrée
(left by a person, an animal, a car)
tracks = des traces *(feminine)*

tracksuit *noun*
a tracksuit = un survêtement

trade *noun*
trade = le commerce
a trade = un métier

tradition *noun*
a tradition = une tradition

traffic *noun*
traffic = la circulation

traffic jam *noun*
a traffic jam = un embouteillage, un bouchon

traffic lights *noun*
traffic lights = les feux *(masculine)*

train
1 *noun*
a train = un train
the train to Paris = le train à destination de Paris
2 *verb*
(to teach, to prepare)
to train employees = former des employés
to train athletes = entraîner des athlètes
(to learn a job)
to train as a doctor = suivre une formation de médecin
she trained as a teacher = elle a reçu une formation d'enseignante
(for a sporting event) = s'entraîner
(! + être)

T

trainer *noun* (*British English*)
a trainer (*high*) = une basket
(*low*) = un tennis

training course *noun*
a training course = un stage de formation

tramp *noun*
a tramp = un clochard/une clocharde

translate *verb*
= traduire

translator *noun* ▶ 315
a translator = un traducteur/une traductrice

transport, transportation (*US English*) *noun*
transport = le transport
a means of transport = un moyen de transport

trap *noun*
a trap = un piège
to set a trap for someone = tendre un piège à quelqu'un

trash *noun* (*US English*)
trash = les ordures (*feminine plural*)

trash can *noun* (*US English*)
a trash can = une poubelle

travel *verb*
= voyager
to travel abroad = aller à l'étranger
to travel a long way = faire beaucoup de chemin

travel agency *noun* ▶ 315
a travel agency = une agence de voyages

traveller (*British English*), **traveler** (*US English*) *noun*
a traveller = un voyageur/une voyageuse

traveller's cheque (*British English*), **traveler's check** (*US English*) *noun*
a traveller's cheque = un chèque-voyage

tray *noun*
a tray = un plateau

treat *verb*
(*to deal with, to behave with*) = traiter
to treat someone badly = mal se conduire envers quelqu'un
(*to pay for*)
to treat someone to a glass of wine = payer un verre de vin à quelqu'un

treatment *noun*
treatment = le traitement
to receive treatment = être sous traitement

tree *noun*
a tree = un arbre

tremble *verb*
= trembler

trendy *adjective*
= branché/branchée✕

trial *noun*
a trial = un procès
to go on trial = passer en jugement

triangle *noun*
a triangle = un triangle

trick
1 *noun*
(*a joke*)
a trick = un tour, une blague✕
to play a trick on someone = jouer un tour à quelqu'un
(*a means of deceiving*)
a trick = une combine
(*to entertain*)
a trick = un tour
2 *verb*
= duper, rouler✕

trip
1 *noun*
a trip (*abroad*) = un voyage
(*a day out*) = une excursion, une sortie
to be on a business trip = être en voyage d'affaires
2 *verb*
to trip (up) = trébucher
to trip someone (up) = faire trébucher quelqu'un

trouble *noun*
(*difficulties*)
trouble = les ennuis (*masculine plural*)
to be in trouble = avoir des ennuis
to get someone into trouble = créer des ennuis à quelqu'un
to make trouble = faire des histoires✕
(*an effort*)
to take the trouble to check = se donner la peine de vérifier
to go to a lot of trouble = se donner beaucoup de mal

trousers *noun*
trousers = un pantalon (*singular*)

trout *noun*
a trout = une truite

truck *noun*
a truck = un camion

truck driver *noun* ▶ 315
a truck driver = un routier

true *adjective*
= vrai/vraie
is it true that he's leaving? = est-ce que c'est vrai qu'il part?
to come true = se réaliser (✕ + être)

trumpet *noun* ▶ 290
a trumpet = une trompette

✕ in informal situations

trunk *noun*
  (*of a tree*)
  a trunk = un tronc
  (*of an elephant*)
  a trunk = une trompe
  (*US English*) (*in a car*)
  the trunk = le coffre

trust *verb*
  (*to believe*) = se fier à (**!** + *être*)
  to trust a friend = se fier à un ami
  I don't trust them = je me méfie d'eux
  (*to rely on*) = faire confiance à
  you can't trust him = on ne peut pas lui
    faire confiance

truth *noun*
  the truth = la vérité

try
 1 *verb*
  to try = essayer
  to try [**to understand** | **to come** | **to forget** ...]
    = essayer [de comprendre | de venir |
    d'oublier ...]
  try phoning him = essaie de lui téléphoner
  (*to test*) = essayer
  to try (out) a recipe = essayer une recette
  to try (on) a pair of jeans = essayer un jean
  (*to taste*) = goûter
  (*in court*) = juger
 2 *noun*
  to score a try = marquer un essai

T-shirt *noun*
  a T-shirt = un T-shirt

tube *noun*
  a tube = un tube
  (*British English*) (*the underground*)
  the tube = le métro

Tuesday *noun* ▶ **222** |
  Tuesday = mardi (*masculine*)

tuna *noun*
  tuna = le thon

tunnel *noun*
  a tunnel = un tunnel

turkey *noun*
  a turkey = une dinde

Turkey *noun* ▶ **218** |
  Turkey = la Turquie

turn
 1 *verb*
  (*to move one's body*) = se retourner
  (**!** + *être*)
  to turn one's face toward(s) the sun
    = tourner le visage vers le soleil
  (*to change direction*) = tourner
  to turn right = tourner à droite
  to turn the corner = tourner au coin de la
    rue
  (*to twist*) = tourner
  to turn the handle = tourner la poignée

  (*to change*)
  to turn the bedroom into an office
    = transformer la chambre en bureau
  to turn someone into a criminal = faire un
    criminel de quelqu'un
  (*to become*)
  to turn into a butterfly = se transformer en
    papillon
  to turn red = rougir
 2 *noun*
  (*a bend*)
  a turn = un tournant, un virage
  (*in games*)
  a turn = un tour
  whose turn is it? = c'est à qui le tour?
turn around, turn round
  (*to face the other way*) (*if it's a person*) = se
    retourner (**!** + *être*)
  (*if it's a car*) = faire demi-tour
  to turn the table around = tourner la table
    dans l'autre sens
  (*to go round and round*) = tourner
turn away = se détourner (**!** + *être*)
turn back = faire demi-tour
turn down
  (*to lower*) = baisser
  to turn down the radio = baisser la radio
  (*to reject*) = refuser
  to turn someone down = refuser
    quelqu'un
turn off
  to turn the oven off = éteindre le four
  to turn off the light = éteindre la lumière
  to turn the tap off = fermer le robinet
turn on = allumer
  to turn on the TV = allumer la télévision
  to turn the tap on = ouvrir le robinet
turn out
  to turn out all right (in the end)
    = s'arranger (**!** + *être*)
  to turn out to be easy = se révéler facile
turn over
  (*to roll over*) = se retourner (**!** + *être*)
  to turn over the page = tourner la page
turn up
  (*to show up*) = arriver
  (*to increase*)
  to turn up the heating = augmenter le
    chauffage
  to turn the music up = mettre la musique
    plus fort

turtle *noun*
  a (sea) turtle = une tortue marine
  (*US English*) (*a tortoise*)
  a turtle = une tortue

TV *noun*
  a TV = une télévision, une télé✷

twelfth *number*
  (*in a series*) = douzième
  (*in dates*) ▶ **222** |
  the twelfth of July = le douze juillet

twelve *number* ▶ **187** |, ▶ **211** |
  twelve = douze
  twelve pupils = douze élèves
  I've got twelve (of them) = j'en ai douze

T

twenty number ▶187 |, ▶211 |
twenty = vingt

twice adverb
= deux fois
twice as many people = deux fois plus de
monde
twice as much time = deux fois plus de
temps

twin
1 noun
a twin = un jumeau/une jumelle
2 adjective
a twin brother = un frère jumeau
a twin sister = une sœur jumelle

twist verb
(to bend out of shape) = tordre
(to injure) ▶266 |
to twist one's ankle = se tordre la cheville

two number ▶187 |, ▶211 |
two = deux
two brothers = deux frères
I've got two (of them) = j'en ai deux

type
1 noun
a type = un type, un genre
this type of [person | book | building ...] = ce
genre de [personne | livre | bâtiment ...]
he's not my type = ce n'est pas mon genre
2 verb
= taper (à la machine)

typewriter noun
a typewriter = une machine à écrire

typical adjective
= typique

typist noun ▶315 |
a typist = un dactylo/une dactylo

tyre noun (British English)
a tyre = un pneu

Uu

ugly adjective
= laid/laide

umbrella noun
an umbrella = un parapluie

unbelievable adjective
= incroyable

uncle noun
an uncle = un oncle

uncomfortable adjective
(awkward) = pénible
to make someone (feel) uncomfortable
= mettre quelqu'un mal à l'aise

(describing shoes, seats) = inconfortable
(describing heat, conditions) = pénible

unconscious adjective
= sans connaissance
to knock someone unconscious
= assommer quelqu'un

under preposition
under = sous
to hide under the bed = se cacher sous le
lit
I found the newspaper under it = j'ai
trouvé le journal dessous
(less than)
to earn under three pounds an hour
= gagner moins de trois livres de l'heure
children under five = les enfants de moins
de cinq ans

underground noun (British English)
the underground = le métro

underline verb
= souligner

underneath
1 adverb
= en dessous
I want to see what's underneath = je veux
voir ce qu'il y a dessous
2 preposition
= au-dessous de, sous
underneath the building = au-dessous du
bâtiment

underpants noun
underpants = un slip (singular)

understand verb
= comprendre
I can't understand what they're saying
= je ne comprends pas ce qu'ils disent
to make oneself understood = se faire
comprendre

understanding adjective
= compréhensif/compréhensive

underwater adverb
= sous l'eau

underwear noun
underwear = les sous-vêtements
(masculine plural)

undo verb
= défaire
to undo a button = défaire un bouton

undress verb
= se déshabiller (! + être)

uneasy adjective
= inquiet/inquiète

unemployed adjective
to be unemployed = être au chômage, être
sans emploi

unemployment noun
unemployment = le chômage

unfair *adjective*
= injuste

unfortunately *adverb*
= malheureusement

unfriendly *adjective*
(*describing a person*) = peu amical/peu
amicale
(*describing a place*)
= inhospitalier/inhospitalière

ungrateful *adjective*
= ingrat/ingrate

unhappy *adjective*
(*sad*) = malheureux/malheureuse
(*not satisfied*) = mécontent/mécontente

unhealthy *adjective*
(*describing a way of life, food*)
= malsain/malsaine
(*describing a person*) = maladif/maladive
(*describing conditions*) = insalubre

uniform *noun*
a uniform = un uniforme

union *noun*
a union = un syndicat

unique *adjective*
= unique

United Kingdom *noun* ▶ 218 |
the United Kingdom = le Royaume-Uni

United States (of America) *noun*
▶ 218 |
the United States (of America) = les États-
Unis (d'Amérique)
! *Note that* États *is masculine plural.*

universe *noun*
a universe = un univers

university *noun*
a university = une université

unkind *adjective*
to be unkind (*describing a person, an
action*) = ne pas être très gentil/gentille
(*describing a remark*) = être
désobligeant/désobligeante

unknown *adjective*
= inconnu/inconnue

unless *conjunction*
it won't work unless you plug it in = ça ne
marchera pas si tu ne le branches pas
she can't work unless she finds an au pair
= elle ne peut pas travailler à moins de
trouver une jeune fille au pair
she can't work unless we find an au pair
= elle ne peut pas travailler à moins
qu'on ne lui trouve une jeune fille au
pair
! *Note that the subjunctive is used after* à
moins que.

unlock *verb*
= ouvrir

unlucky *adjective*
= malchanceux/malchanceuse
you were unlucky = tu n'as pas eu de chance

unpack *verb*
to unpack a suitcase = défaire une valise
to unpack one's belongings = déballer ses
affaires

unsuitable *adjective*
= inapproprié/inappropriée

untidy *adjective*
(*in one's habits*)
= désordonné/désordonnée
(*in how one looks*) = peu soigné/peu soignée

until
1 *preposition*
= jusqu'à
I'm staying until Thursday = je reste
jusqu'à jeudi
until now = jusqu'à présent
I'm going to wait until after Christmas = je
vais attendre que Noël soit passé
she won't get an answer until next week
= elle n'aura pas de réponse avant la
semaine prochaine
2 *conjunction*
I'll wait until I get back home = j'attendrai
d'être rentré
we'll stay until they come = nous
resterons jusqu'à ce qu'ils arrivent
don't look until it's ready = ne regarde pas
avant que ce soit prêt
! *Note that the subjunctive is used after*
jusqu'à ce que *and* avant que.

unusual *adjective*
(*rare*) = peu commun/peu commune
it's unusual to see so few people = il est
rare de voir si peu de monde
(*different, out of the ordinary*)
= original/originale

up
! *Often* up *occurs in combinations with
verbs, for example:* blow up, give up, own
up, *etc. To find the correct translations for
this type of verb, look up the separate
dictionary entries at* blow, give, own *etc.*

1 *preposition*
the cat's up the tree = le chat est dans
l'arbre
to go up the street = remonter la rue
she ran up the stairs = elle a monté
l'escalier en courant
the library is up those stairs = la
bibliothèque se trouve en haut de cet
escalier
2 *adverb*
up in the sky = dans le ciel
up on (top of) the wardrobe = sur l'armoire
to go up = monter (! + *être*)
to go up to Scotland = aller en Écosse
up there = là-haut
put the picture a bit further up = mets le
tableau un peu plus haut
to climb all the way up = monter jusqu'en
haut

U

3 *adjective*
(*out of bed*)
to be up = être debout
to be up all night = veiller toute la nuit
(*higher in amount, level*)
to be up by 20% = avoir augmenté de 20%
4 up to
(*well enough*)
to be up to going out = avoir la force de
sortir
I'm not up to it = je n'en ai pas la force
(*when talking about who is responsible*)
it's up to [me | you | them …] to decide
= c'est à [moi | toi | eux …] de décider
(*until*) = jusqu'à
up to now = jusqu'à présent
up to 1996 = jusqu'en 1996

upset
1 *adjective*
to be upset (*annoyed*) = être
contrarié/contrariée
(*distressed*) = être très affecté/affectée
to get upset (*annoyed*) = se fâcher
(**!** + *être*)
(*distressed*) = se mettre dans tous ses états
(**!** + *être*)
2 *verb*
(*to make someone unhappy*) (*if it's an
event*) = bouleverser
(*if it's a person*) = faire de la peine à
(*to annoy*) = contrarier

upside down *adverb*
= à l'envers
you're holding the book upside down = tu
tiens le livre à l'envers

upstairs *adverb*
= en haut
to go upstairs = monter (l'escalier)
to bring the cases upstairs = monter les
valises

urgent *adjective*
= urgent/urgente

us *pronoun*

> **!** *us is always translated by* **nous**. *Note
> that there is a boxed usage note at* **them**.
> *The entries* **me**, **him**, **her** *and* **us** *are
> modelled on this note where you will find
> detailed grammatical information and
> fuller explanations.*

they know us = ils nous connaissent
they don't know us = ils ne nous
connaissent pas
do they know us? = est-ce qu'ils nous
connaissent?
he's seen us = il nous a vus
he hasn't seen us = il ne nous a pas vus
has he seen us? = est-ce qu'il nous a vus?
help us! = aide-nous!
catch us! = attrape-nous!
don't bother us! = ne nous embête pas!
don't hit us! = ne nous frappe pas!

she gave the book to us = elle nous a
donné le livre
she didn't give the book to us = elle ne
nous a pas donné le livre
did she give the book to us? = est-ce
qu'elle nous a donné le livre?
write to us! = écris-nous!
say it to us! = dis-le-nous!
don't show it to us! = ne nous le montre
pas!
he did it for us = il l'a fait pour nous
it's us = c'est nous
stand in front of us = mets-toi devant nous

USA *noun* ▶ **218**
the USA = les USA (*masculine plural*)

use
1 *verb*
(*to make use of*) = se servir de (**!** + *être*)
I use the car to go to work = je me sers de
la voiture pour aller au travail
he uses the room as an office = il se sert
de la pièce comme bureau
what is it used for? = ça sert à quoi?
to use the opportunity to learn French
= profiter de l'occasion pour apprendre
le français
to use a different word = employer un
autre mot
(*to operate on*)
to use petrol = marcher à l'essence
to use water = utiliser de l'eau
(*to go through*) = consommer
it uses a lot of petrol = ça consomme
beaucoup d'essence
(*to take advantage of*)
to use someone = se servir de quelqu'un
2 *noun*
to make use of a room = utiliser une pièce
to have the use of a car = avoir l'usage
d'une voiture
to lose the use of one's legs = perdre
l'usage de ses jambes
(*when talking about what is useful*)
to be of use to someone = être utile à
quelqu'un, servir à quelqu'un
to be no use = ne servir à rien
the bike is no use any more = le vélo est
hors d'usage
what's the use of complaining? = à quoi
bon se plaindre?
use up
to use up all the money = dépenser tout
l'argent
to use up the milk = finir le lait

used
1 *verb*

> **!** *Note that the imperfect tense in French
> is generally used to translate* **used to** +
> *verb:* **she used to live in Toulouse** = elle
> habitait Toulouse.

I used to read a lot = je lisais beaucoup
you used not to smoke = tu ne fumais pas
avant
there used to be a castle here = il y avait
un château ici dans le temps

2 *adjective*
  to be used to [children | animals | tourists …]
  = avoir l'habitude des [enfants | animaux | touristes …]
  he's not used to living on his own = il n'a pas l'habitude de vivre seul
  to get used to a new job = s'habituer à un nouveau travail

useful *adjective*
  = utile

useless *adjective*
  (*not working, having no use*) = inutilisable
  (*having no point or purpose*) = inutile
  it's useless complaining = il est inutile de se plaindre, ça ne sert à rien de se plaindre
  (*describing a person*) = nul/nulle
  to be useless at chemistry = être nul/nulle en chimie

usually *adverb*
  = d'habitude, normalement

Vv

---

vacant *adjective*
  = libre

vacation *noun* (*US English*)
  a vacation = des vacances (*feminine plural*)
  to take a vacation = prendre des vacances

vacuum *verb*
  to vacuum a room = passer l'aspirateur dans une pièce

vacuum cleaner *noun*
  a vacuum cleaner = un aspirateur

vague *adjective*
  = vague

vain *adjective*
  = vaniteux/vaniteuse

valid *adjective*
  (*describing a licence, a passport*) = valide
  (*describing a ticket, an offer*) = valable

valley *noun*
  a valley = une vallée

valuable *adjective*
  (*very useful*) = précieux/précieuse
  (*worth a lot of money*)
  to be valuable = avoir de la valeur

van *noun*
  a van (*small*) = une camionnette
  (*larger*) = un fourgon

vandalize *verb*
  = vandaliser

vanilla *noun*
  vanilla = la vanille

various *adjective*
  = divers/diverses
  there are various ways of saying it = on peut le dire de diverses façons

vary *verb*
  = varier
  to vary from town to town = varier d'une ville à l'autre

vase *noun*
  a vase = un vase

veal *noun*
  veal = le veau

vegetable *noun*
  a vegetable = un légume

vegetarian *noun*
  a vegetarian = un végétarien/une végétarienne

vein *noun* ▶ **201**
  a vein = une veine

velvet *noun*
  velvet = le velours

versus *preposition*
  = contre

very
1 *adverb*
  very = très
  I don't know him very well = je ne le connais pas très bien
  to eat very little = manger très peu
  you haven't said very much = tu n'as pas dit grand-chose
  we like them very much = on les aime beaucoup
  for the very first time = pour la toute première fois
  they called me the very next day = ils m'ont appelé dès le lendemain
2 *adjective*
  at the very beginning = au tout début
  to sit at the very front = s'asseoir tout devant
  to stay to the very end = rester jusqu'au bout
  you are the very person I need = tu es exactement la personne qu'il me faut

vest *noun*
  (*British English*) (*a piece of underwear*)
  a vest = un maillot de corps
  (*US English*) (*a waistcoat*)
  a vest = un gilet

vet *noun* ▶ **315**
  a vet = un vétérinaire/une vétérinaire

via *preposition*
  (*on tickets, timetables*) = via
  (*in general*) = en passant par
  we came via Paris = nous sommes venus en passant par Paris

V

vicious adjective
* (violent) = brutal/brutale
* (nasty, meant to hurt)
 = malveillant/malveillante

victory noun
 a victory = une victoire
 to win a victory = remporter une victoire

video
1 noun
* (a recorded film, programme, event)
 a video = une cassette vidéo
* ▶ video cassette, video recorder
2 verb
* (to record) = enregistrer
* (to film)
 to video a wedding = filmer un mariage
 en vidéo

video camera noun
 a video camera = une caméra vidéo

video cassette noun
 a video cassette = une cassette vidéo

video game noun
 a video game = un jeu vidéo

video recorder noun
 a video recorder = un magnétoscope

view noun
* a view = une vue
 you're blocking my view = tu me bouches
 la vue
 if you want to get a better view, come
 here = si tu veux mieux voir, viens ici
* (an opinion, an attitude)
 a view = un avis, une opinion
 a point of view = un point de vue

village noun
 a village = un village

vinegar noun
 vinegar = le vinaigre

vineyard noun
 a vineyard = un vignoble

violent adjective
 = violent/violente

violin noun ▶ 290 |
 a violin = un violon

Virgo noun
 Virgo = Vierge (feminine)

visit
1 verb
 to visit Paris (to see) = visiter Paris
 (to stay) = faire un séjour à Paris
 to visit someone (to call on) = aller voir
 quelqu'un
 (more formally) = rendre visite à quelqu'un
 (to stay with) = aller passer quelques jours
 chez quelqu'un
2 noun
 a visit (a call) = une visite

 (a stay) = un séjour
 to pay someone a visit = rendre visite à
 quelqu'un

visitor noun
* (a guest)
 a visitor = un invité/une invitée
 to have visitors = avoir de la visite
* (a tourist)
 a visitor = un visiteur/une visiteuse

vocabulary noun
 vocabulary = le vocabulaire

voice noun
 a voice = une voix
 to have a good voice = avoir une jolie
 voix
 to speak in a low voice = parler à voix
 basse
 to sing at the top of one's voice = chanter
 à tue-tête

volleyball noun ▶ 248 |
 volleyball = le volley-ball

vomit verb
 = vomir

vote verb
 = voter

Ww

wages noun
 wages = le salaire (singular)

waist noun ▶ 201 |
 the waist = la taille

waistcoat noun (British English)
 a waistcoat = un gilet

wait verb
* to wait = attendre
 to wait for someone = attendre quelqu'un
 I'm waiting to use the phone = j'attends de
 pouvoir téléphoner
 to wait for someone to leave = attendre
 que quelqu'un s'en aille
 let's have a beer while we're waiting for
 them = allons prendre une bière en
 attendant qu'ils arrivent

 ! Note that the subjunctive is used after
 attendre que.

 I can't wait to see them = j'ai hâte de les
 voir
* (in a restaurant)
 to wait on table, to wait table (US English)
 = travailler comme serveur/serveuse
wait up = veiller
 to wait up for someone = veiller jusqu'au
 retour de quelqu'un

waiter *noun* ▶ 315 |
  a waiter = un serveur

waiting room *noun*
  a waiting room = une salle d'attente

waitress *noun* ▶ 315 |
  a waitress = une serveuse

wake *verb*
  to wake someone = réveiller quelqu'un
wake up = se réveiller (**!** + *être*)

Wales *noun* ▶ 218 |
  Wales = le pays de Galles

walk
1 *verb*
  (*rather than run*) = marcher
  (*rather than drive or ride*) = aller à pied
  (*for pleasure*) = se promener (**!** + *être*)
  let's walk to the pool = allons à la piscine
    à pied
  to walk down the street = descendre la rue
  to walk the dog = promener le chien
2 *noun*
  a walk = une promenade
  to go for a walk = faire une promenade
  it's five minutes' walk from here = c'est à
    cinq minutes à pied d'ici
walk around = se promener (**!** + *être*)
  to walk around town = se promener en
    ville
  to walk around the lake = faire le tour du
    lac
walk away = s'éloigner (**!** + *être*)
walk back = revenir à pied
  to walk back home = rentrer à pied
walk by = passer (**!** + *être*)
walk in = entrer (**!** + *être*)
walk out = sortir (**!** + *être*)
  to walk out of the room = sortir de la pièce
walk round = faire le tour
  to walk round the exhibition = visiter
    l'exposition
walk up to = s'approcher de (**!** + *être*)

walkman *noun*
  a walkman = un baladeur, un walkman

wall *noun*
  a wall = un mur

wallet *noun*
  a wallet = un portefeuille

wallpaper *noun*
  wallpaper = le papier peint

walnut *noun*
  a walnut = une noix

wander *verb*
  to wander around town = se balader en
    ville
wander away, wander off = s'éloigner
(**!** + *être*)

want *verb*
  to want = vouloir
  do you want another coffee? = est-ce que
    tu veux un autre café?
  he wants [to go out | to go home | to play …]
    = il veut [sortir | rentrer | jouer …]
  she didn't want to stay = elle n'a pas voulu
    rester
  do you want me to come with you? = est-
    ce que tu veux que je vienne avec toi?
  ! *Note that the subjunctive is used after*
  vouloir que.

  (*to need*) = avoir besoin de
  do you want anything in town? = est-ce
    que tu as besoin de quelque chose en
    ville?

war *noun*
  a war = une guerre

wardrobe *noun*
  a wardrobe = une armoire

warm
1 *adjective*
  = chaud/chaude
  to be warm, to feel warm = avoir chaud
  I'm very warm = j'ai très chaud
  it's nice and warm in the classroom = il
    fait bon dans la salle de classe
  to get warm = se réchauffer (**!** + *être*)
  to keep warm = rester au chaud
  to keep a meal warm = tenir un repas au
    chaud
2 *verb*
  to warm the plates = chauffer les assiettes
  to warm one's hands = se réchauffer les
    mains
warm up
  (*to get warm*) = se réchauffer (**!** + *être*)
  (*for a sporting event*) = s'échauffer
    (**!** + *être*)
  (*to make warm*) = réchauffer

warn *verb*
  = avertir, prévenir
  to warn someone about the risks = mettre
    quelqu'un en garde contre les risques
  to warn someone to be careful
    = conseiller à quelqu'un de faire
    attention
  I warned him not to take the car = je lui ai
    déconseillé de prendre la voiture

wash *verb*
  (*to clean*) = laver
  to wash one's clothes = laver ses
    vêtements
  to wash one's face = se laver le visage
  (*to get clean*) = se laver (**!** + *être*)
wash out
  to wash out = partir au lavage
  to wash a stain out = faire partir une
    tache au lavage
wash up
  (*British English*) (*to do the dishes*) = faire la
    vaisselle

(*US English*) (*to clean oneself*) = se
rafraîchir (**!** + *être*)

washbasin (*British English*), **wash-
hand basin** *noun*
   a washbasin = un lavabo

washing *noun*
   the washing = le linge
   to do the washing = faire la lessive

washing machine *noun*
   a washing machine = une machine à laver

washing-up *noun* (*British English*)
   the washing-up = la vaisselle
   to do the washing-up = faire la vaisselle

wasp *noun*
   a wasp = une guêpe

waste
1 *verb*
   = gaspiller
   to waste energy = gaspiller de l'énergie
   to waste one's time = perdre son temps
2 *noun*
   it's a waste of money = c'est de l'argent
      gaspillé
   a waste of time = une perte de temps
   it's a waste of time going there = y aller
      est une perte de temps
   to let food go to waste = gaspiller de la
      nourriture
   waste = les déchets (*masculine plural*)

watch
1 *verb*
   (*to look at*) = regarder
   to watch television = regarder la
      télévision
   she watched me making the meal = elle
      m'a regardé préparer le repas
   (*to observe, to follow*) = surveiller
   I feel I'm being watched = j'ai l'impression
      qu'on me surveille
   (*to pay attention to*)
   watch what you're doing = fais attention à
      ce que tu fais
   watch you don't fall = fais attention de ne
      pas tomber
2 *noun*
   a watch = une montre
   watch out = faire attention

water
1 *noun*
   water = l'eau (*feminine*)
   drinking water = l'eau potable
   to let in water = prendre l'eau
2 *verb*
   = arroser

waterfall *noun*
   a waterfall = une cascade

water-skiing *noun* ▶ **248**
   water-skiing = le ski nautique

wave
1 *verb*
   (*to signal with one's hand*)
   to wave to someone = saluer quelqu'un
      de la main
   to wave goodbye = faire au revoir de la
      main
   (*to direct*)
   to wave someone on = faire signe à
      quelqu'un d'avancer
   to wave flags = agiter des drapeaux
2 *noun*
   a wave = une vague

way
1 *noun*
   (*a means, a method*)
   a way = un moyen
   it's a way of earning money = c'est un
      moyen de gagner de l'argent
   it's a good way to make friends = c'est un
      bon moyen de se faire des amis
   he does it the wrong way = il s'y prend
      mal
   that's not the way to do it = ce n'est pas
      comme ça qu'on fait
   (*how one does something*)
   a way = une façon
   I like the way she dresses = j'aime sa
      façon de s'habiller
   I prefer to do it my way = je préfère le faire
      à ma façon
   (*a route, a road*)
   a way = un chemin
   I can't remember the way to the station
      = je ne me souviens plus du chemin
      pour aller à la gare
   we can buy something to eat along the
      way = on peut acheter quelque chose à
      manger en chemin
   on the way back = sur le chemin du
      retour
   I met them on the way back from town = je
      les ai rencontrés en revenant de la ville
   on the way to Paris = en allant à Paris
   where's the way out? = où est la sortie?
   to make one's way to the stairs = se
      diriger vers l'escalier
   to lose one's way = se perdre (**!** + *être*)
   (*a direction*)
   which way are you going? = dans quelle
      direction est-ce que tu vas?
   they went that way = ils sont partis par là
   come this way = venez par ici
   (*someone's route*)
   to be in someone's way = empêcher
      quelqu'un de passer, bloquer le passage
      à quelqu'un
   to be in the way = gêner le passage
   to get out of the way = s'écarter (**!** + *être*)
   (*when talking about distances*)
   it's a long way from here = c'est loin d'ici
   to go all the way to Portugal = aller
      jusqu'au Portugal

(what one wants)
she always wants her own way = elle ne
  veut en faire qu'à sa tête
if I had my own way, I'd go alone = si cela
  ne tenait qu'à moi, j'irais tout seul
2 by the way = au fait
what's his name, by the way? = comment
  s'appelle-t-il, au fait?

we *pronoun*

> **!** *Note that* **we** *is generally translated by*
> **nous** *but that, in informal French,* **on** *is*
> *also very common:* **we're going to the**
> **cinema** = nous allons au cinéma, on va au
> cinéma.

we = nous
we saw her yesterday = nous l'avons vue
  hier, on l'a vue hier
we didn't agree = nous, nous n'étions pas
  d'accord
we all make mistakes = tout le monde
  peut se tromper

weak *adjective*
(not healthy) = faible
to have a weak heart = avoir le cœur
  fragile
(not good or able) = faible
to be weak at languages = être faible en
  langues
(easily damaged) = fragile
(having very little power) = faible
(describing tea or coffee) = léger/légère

wealthy *adjective*
= riche

wear *verb*
(to be dressed in) = porter
to be wearing jeans = porter un jean
to wear black = s'habiller en noir
(to put on) = mettre
what will you wear? = qu'est-ce que tu vas
  mettre?
I've got nothing to wear = je n'ai rien à me
  mettre
(to damage) = user
wear out
to wear out = s'user (**!** + être)
to wear one's shoes out = user ses
  chaussures
to wear someone out = épuiser quelqu'un

weather *noun*
the weather = le temps
what's the weather like? = quel temps
  fait-il?
the weather is [bad | nice | hot ...] = il fait
  [mauvais | bon | chaud ...]
in [cold | warm | wet ...] **weather** = quand [il
  fait froid | il fait bon | il pleut ...]

weather forecast *noun*
the weather forecast = les prévisions
  météorologiques, la météo

> **!** *Note that* **prévisions** *is feminine plural.*

wedding *noun*
a wedding = un mariage

Wednesday *noun* ▶ **222** |
Wednesday = mercredi *(masculine)*

week *noun* ▶ **356** |
a week = une semaine
in two weeks' time = dans quinze jours

weekend *noun* ▶ **356** |
a weekend = un week-end

weigh *verb* ▶ **285** |
= peser
what do you weigh? = combien pèses-tu?
to weigh oneself = se peser (**!** + être)

weight *noun* ▶ **285** |
weight = le poids
to lose weight = maigrir

weird *adjective*
= bizarre

welcome
1 *verb* ▶ **237** |
to welcome someone = accueillir
  quelqu'un
2 *adjective*
(when receiving people)
to be welcome = être le bienvenu/la
  bienvenue
welcome to the United States!
  = bienvenue aux États-Unis!
(when acknowledging thanks)
'thanks'—'you're welcome' = 'merci'—'de
  rien'
3 *noun*
a welcome = un accueil

well
1 *adverb* ▶ **237** |
well = bien
he dresses well = il s'habille bien
I'd like to speak French well = j'aimerais
  parler bien le français
the [exam | interview | class ...] **went well**
  = [l'examen | l'entretien | le cours ...] s'est bien
  passé
the work is well paid = le travail est bien
  payé
she is well able to defend herself = elle est
  tout à fait capable de se défendre
he's not eating well = il n'a pas d'appétit
(other uses)
we may as well go home = on ferait aussi
  bien de rentrer
you may well be right = il se pourrait bien
  que tu aies raison

> **!** *Note that the subjunctive is used after* il
> se pourrait bien que.

2 *adjective*
to feel well = se sentir bien
I hope everyone is well = j'espère que tout
  le monde va bien
I'm very well = je vais très bien
to get well = se rétablir (**!** + être)
3 as well = aussi

W

4 as well as = ainsi que

well-known *adjective*
= célèbre

Welsh ▶ 275 |
1 *adjective*
= gallois/galloise
2 *noun*
• (*the people*)
the Welsh = les Gallois (*masculine plural*)
• (*the language*)
Welsh = le gallois

west
1 *noun*
the west = l'ouest (*masculine*)
in the west of France = dans l'ouest de la
France
2 *adverb*
to go west = aller vers l'ouest
to live west of Paris = vivre à l'ouest de
Paris
3 *adjective*
= ouest (**!** *never changes*)
to work in west London = travailler dans
l'ouest de Londres

West Indies *noun* ▶ 218 |
the West Indies = les Antilles (*feminine*)

wet
1 *adjective*
• (*damp*) = mouillé/mouillée
your hair is wet = tu as les cheveux
mouillés
to get wet = se faire mouiller (**!** + *être*)
she got her feet wet = elle s'est mouillé les
pieds
• (*when talking about weather*) = humide
in wet weather = par temps humide
on a wet day = quand il pleut
2 *verb*
= mouiller

what
▶ See the boxed note on **what** for more
information and examples.
1 *pronoun*
• (*used in questions*)
what's her phone number? = quel est son
numéro de téléphone?
what's that box? = qu'est-ce que c'est que
cette boîte?
what's this button for? = à quoi sert ce
bouton?
what's the French for 'boring'?
= comment dit-on 'boring' en français?
what does he look like? = il est comment?
• (*used as a relative pronoun*)
do what you want = faites ce que vous
voulez
what we need is a timetable = ce qu'il
nous faut c'est un horaire
2 *determiner*
do you know what train to take? = est-ce
que tu sais quel train il faut prendre?
what a great idea! = quelle bonne idée!

3 *exclamation*
= quoi!, comment!
4 what if = et si
what if I don't get there on time? = et si je
n'y suis pas à l'heure?

whatever *pronoun*
• (*when anything is possible*)
take whatever you want = prends tout ce
que tu veux
whatever you think is useful = tout ce qui
vous paraît utile
• (*when it doesn't matter*)
whatever they do, it won't change
anything = quoi qu'ils fassent, ça ne
changera rien

! *Note that the subjunctive is used after* quoi
que *(*quoi qu'* before vowel or mute h).*

wheat *noun*
wheat = le blé

wheel *noun*
a wheel = une roue

wheelchair *noun*
a wheelchair = un fauteuil roulant

when
1 *adverb*
= quand
when did she leave? = quand est-ce
qu'elle est partie?
when is your birthday? = c'est quand ton
anniversaire?
I don't know when the film starts = je ne sais
pas à quelle heure le film commence

! *See the usage note on* The clock ▶ 356 |
for further information on time expressions.

2 *conjunction*
= quand
I was asleep when the phone rang = je
dormais quand le téléphone a sonné
he didn't like French when he was at
school = il n'aimait pas le français
quand il était au collège
when I'm 18 I'll have my own car = quand
j'aurai 18 ans j'aurai ma propre voiture

! *Note that, when talking about future
time, the future tense is used after* quand.

3 *pronoun*
• (*used as a relative pronoun*) = où
in the days when there was no TV = à
l'époque où il n'y avait pas de télévision
• (*used in questions*) = quand

where
1 *adverb*
= où
where are you going? = où vas-tu?
where do they work? = où est-ce qu'ils
travaillent?
do you know where [he is | Tom is | we're
going ...]? = est-ce que tu sais où [il est | est
Tom | nous allons ...]?
I wonder where he lives = je me demande
où il habite
the village where we live = le village où
nous habitons

what

As a pronoun

In questions

● When used in questions as an object pronoun, **what** is translated by **qu'est-ce que** (**qu'est-ce qu'** in front of a vowel or mute h):

what is he doing?	= qu'est-ce qu'il fait?
what did you say?	= qu'est-ce que tu as dit?
what are we going to do?	= qu'est-ce que nous allons faire?

● Alternatively, you can use **que** (**qu'** before a vowel or mute h), but note that, after **que**, the order of subject and verb is reversed and a hyphen is inserted between them if the subject is a pronoun:

what is he doing?	= que fait-il?
what did you say?	= qu'as tu dit?
what are we going to do?	= qu'allons-nous faire?

● When used in questions as a subject pronoun, what is translated by **qu'est-ce qui**:

what is happening?	= qu'est-ce qui se passe?
what happened?	= qu'est-ce qui s'est passé?
what is going to happen?	= qu'est-ce qui va se passer?

Again, if you use **que**, the order of subject and verb is reversed, the subject becomes **il** and a hyphen is inserted between them:

what is happening?	= que se passe-t-il?*
what happened?	= que s'est-il passé?
what is going to happen?	= que va-t-il se passer?

* In this case, an additional -t- is required for the liaison between the two vowels to be made.

To introduce a clause

● When used to introduce a clause as the object of the verb, **what** is translated by **ce que** (**ce qu'** before a vowel or mute h):

I don't know what he wants	= je ne sais pas ce qu'il veut
did they have what you wanted?	= est-ce qu'ils avaient ce que tu voulais?
what he said was that he didn't care	= ce qu'il a dit c'est que ça lui était égal

● When **what** is the subject of the verb, it is translated by **ce qui**:

tell me what happened	= raconte-moi ce qui s'est passé
I want to know what's happening	= je veux savoir ce qui se passe
what matters is that we won	= ce qui compte, c'est que nous avons gagné

With prepositions

What, when it is used with a preposition in English, is translated by **quoi**. In French, however, the preposition always comes before **quoi**:

what are you thinking about?	= à quoi penses-tu?
I don't know what he is talking about	= je ne sais pas de quoi il parle

As a determiner

When what is used as a determiner, it is translated by **quel, quelle, quels** or **quelles**, according to whether the noun that follows is masculine or feminine, singular or plural:

what train did you catch?	= quel train as-tu pris?
what time is it?	= quelle heure est-il?
what books do you like?	= quels livres aimes-tu?
what colours do you like?	= quelles couleurs aimes-tu?

▶ For more examples, see the entry **what**.

2 *conjunction*
   that's where she fell = c'est là qu'elle est
   tombée
   I'll leave the key where you can see it = je
   laisserai la clé là où tu peux la voir

whether *conjunction*
   = si
   I don't know whether or not to accept = je
   ne sais pas si je dois accepter

which
▶ *See the boxed note on* **which** *for more
information and examples.*
1 *pronoun*
   the house which I told you about = la
   maison dont je t'ai parlé
2 *determiner*
   which one of the nurses speaks French?
   = laquelle des infirmières parle
   français?
   ask him which bus leaves first
   = demande-lui quel bus va partir le
   premier

while *conjunction*
   = pendant que
   **I had a party while my parents were in
   Spain** = j'ai fait une fête pendant que
   mes parents étaient en Espagne
   she fell asleep while watching TV = elle
   s'est endormie en regardant la
   télévision

whisper *verb*
   = chuchoter

whistle
1 *verb*
   = siffler
2 *noun*
   a whistle = un sifflet

white *adjective* ▶ **213** |
   = blanc/blanche

who *pronoun*
• (*used in questions*) = qui
   who told you? = qui (est-ce qui) te l'a dit?
   who did you invite? = qui est-ce que tu as
   invité?
   who did he buy the book for? = pour qui
   a-t-il acheté le livre?
• (*used as a relative pronoun*)
   my friend who lives in Paris = mon ami
   qui habite Paris
   those who can't come by car = ceux/celles
   qui ne peuvent pas venir en voiture
   a friend who I see at work = un ami que je
   vois au travail

whole
1 *noun*
   the whole of [the country | London |
   August…] = tout [le pays | Londres | le mois
   d'août…]

2 *adjective*
   a whole day = toute une journée, une
   journée entière
   three whole weeks = trois semaines
   entières
   I don't want to spend my whole life here
   = je ne veux pas passer toute ma vie ici

whom *pronoun*
• (*used in questions*) = qui
   whom did you meet? = qui as-tu
   rencontré?
• (*used as a relative pronoun*)
   the person to whom I spoke on the phone
   = la personne à qui j'ai parlé au téléphone

whose
1 *pronoun*
• (*used in questions*) = à qui
   whose is the dog? = à qui est le chien?
• (*used as a relative pronoun*) = dont
   the boy whose bike was stolen = le
   garçon dont le vélo a été volé
   the woman whose house I'm buying = la
   femme dont j'achète la maison
2 *determiner*
   whose car is that? = à qui est cette voiture?
   whose pen did you borrow? = à qui as-tu
   emprunté un stylo?

why
1 *adverb*
• (*used in questions*) = pourquoi
   why did you do that? = pourquoi est-ce
   que tu as fait ça?
   why aren't they coming? = pourquoi est-
   ce qu'ils ne viennent pas?
   why not? = pourquoi pas?
• (*when making suggestions*)
   why don't we eat out tonight? = et si on
   allait au restaurant ce soir?
2 *conjunction*
   = pour ça
   that's why I can't stand him = c'est pour ça
   que je le déteste

wide *adjective* ▶ **285** |
• (*in size*) = large
   a wide garden = un jardin large
   the room is ten metres wide = la pièce a
   dix mètres de large
• (*in range*)
   a wide range of games = un très grand
   choix de jeux

width *noun* ▶ **285** |
   width = la largeur

wife *noun*
   a wife = une femme

wild *adjective*
• (*describing animals, birds*) = sauvage
• (*noisy, out of control*) = fou/folle
   to go wild = se déchaîner (**!** + *être*)

wildlife *noun*
   wildlife = la faune

which

As a pronoun

In questions

When **which** (meaning *which one* or *which ones*) is used as a pronoun in questions, it is translated by **lequel**, **laquelle**, **lesquels** or **lesquelles**, according to whether the noun it is standing for is masculine or feminine, singular or plural:

there are three peaches,	= Il y a trois pêches,
which do you want?	**laquelle** veux-tu?

When **which** is followed by a superlative adjective, then the translation is **quel**, **quelle**, **quels** or **quelles**, according to whether the noun it is standing for is masculine or feminine, singular or plural:

(of the apples) which is the biggest?	= **quelle** est la plus grosse?
(of the books) which is the most useful?	= **quel** est le plus utile?
(of the cars) which are the fastest?	= **quelles** sont les plus rapides?
(of the computers) which are the cheapest?	= **quels** sont les moins chers?

In relative clauses

When used as a pronoun, **which** is translated by **qui** when it is the subject of the verb, and by **que** when it is the object:

the book which is on the table	= le livre **qui** est sur la table
the book which Tina is reading	= le livre **que** lit Tina

Note the different word order of subject and verb; this is the case where the subject is a noun but not where the subject is a pronoun:

the book which I am reading	= le livre **que** je lis
the book which he's writing	= le livre **qu'**il écrit
the film which we're going to see	= le film **que** nous allons voir

Remember that in the present perfect and past perfect tenses, the past participle agrees with the noun **que** is referring back to:

the film which we saw	= le film **que** nous avons vu
the car which they stole	= la voiture **qu'**ils ont volée
the books which I gave you	= les livres **que** je t'ai donnés *(masculine plural)*
the dresses which she bought yesterday	= les robes **qu'**elle a achetées hier *(feminine plural)*

As a determiner

When **which** is used as a determiner in questions, it is translated by **quel**, **quelle**, **quels** or **quelles** according to whether the noun that follows is masculine or feminine, singular or plural:

which car is yours?	= **quelle** voiture est la vôtre?
which dress did she buy?	= **quelle** robe a-t-elle achetée?*
which houses are for sale?	= **quelles** maisons sont à vendre?
which computer doesn't work?	= **quel** ordinateur ne marche pas?
which books did he borrow?	= **quels** livres a-t-il empruntés?*

Note that, in the second and third examples, the object precedes the verb or auxiliary verb so that the past participle agrees with it.

* In this case, an additional **-t-** is required for the liaison between the two vowels to be made.

---

will *verb*

! *Note that, when referring to the future, French generally uses the future tense of the verb to translate will + verb:* I will sing = je chanterai. *When talking about something in the near future, the present tense of* aller + *verb is also possible:* je vais chanter.

(when talking about the future)

she won't agree = elle ne sera pas d'accord

it will be sunny tomorrow = il va faire beau demain

what will we do? = qu'est-ce que nous allons faire?

(when talking about intentions)
I'll wait for you at the airport = je t'attendrai à l'aéroport
we won't stay too long = nous ne resterons pas trop longtemps
(in invitations and requests)
will you have some coffee? = est-ce que vous voulez du café?, voulez-vous du café?
will you ask him for me? = est-ce que tu peux lui demander de ma part?
(when making assumptions)
they won't know what's happened = ils ne doivent pas savoir ce qui s'est passé
(in short questions and answers)
you'll come again, won't you? = tu reviendras, n'est-ce pas?
that will be cheaper, won't it? = ça sera moins cher, non?
'he won't be ready'—'yes he will' = 'il ne sera pas prêt'—'si'

win *verb*
= gagner

wind *noun*
a wind = un vent

window *noun*
a window *(in a house)* = une fenêtre
(in a shop) = une vitrine
(in a car, a bus) = une vitre

windsurfing *noun* ▶ **248**
windsurfing = la planche à voile

windy *adjective*
it's windy = il fait du vent

wine *noun*
wine = le vin

wing *noun*
a wing = une aile

winter *noun*
winter = l'hiver *(masculine)*
in winter = en hiver

wipe *verb*
= essuyer
to wipe one's feet = s'essuyer les pieds
to wipe one's nose = se moucher
(**!** + *être*)

wise *adjective*
(describing a person) = sage
(describing a decision, a choice) = judicieux/judicieuse

wish
1 *noun*
a wish = un souhait
to make a wish = faire un vœu
(in greetings)
best wishes = meilleurs vœux
(in a letter) = amicalement

2 *verb*
(expressing what one would like)
I wish they could come = si seulement ils pouvaient venir
she wished she hadn't lied = elle regrettait d'avoir menti
(in greetings) = souhaiter
to wish someone a happy birthday = souhaiter un bon anniversaire à quelqu'un

with *preposition*
with = avec
to go away with friends = partir avec des amis
I'm living with my parents = j'habite chez mes parents
to be pleased with the house = être content/contente de la maison
(when describing)
a girl with black hair = une fille aux cheveux noirs
the boy with the broken leg = le garçon à la jambe cassée
his clothes were covered with mud = ses vêtements étaient couverts de boue
he was walking along with his hands in his pockets = il se promenait les mains dans les poches
she's married with two children = elle est mariée et mère de deux enfants

without *preposition*
= sans
we got in without paying = on est entré sans payer

wolf *noun*
a wolf = un loup

woman *noun*
a woman = une femme
a single woman = une célibataire

wonder *verb*
(to ask oneself) = se demander (**!** + *être*)
I wonder [how | why | who ...] = je me demande [comment | pourquoi | qui ...]
I was wondering when you'd arrive = je me demandais quand tu arriverais
(in polite requests)
I wonder if you could help me? = pourriez-vous m'aider?

wonderful *adjective*
= merveilleux/merveilleuse

wood *noun*
(timber)
wood = le bois
made of wood = en bois
(a small forest)
a wood = un bois

wool *noun*
wool = la laine

word *noun*
a word = un mot
what's the French word for 'break'? = comment dit-on 'break' en français?
in other words = autrement dit

work

1 *verb*

(*to have or do a job*) = travailler
to work at home = travailler à domicile
to work as a doctor = être médecin
(*to operate properly*) = marcher
the TV isn't working = la télévision ne
  marche pas, la télévision est en panne
(*to be successful*) (*if it's an idea, a trick*)
  = marcher
(*if it's a plan*) = réussir
(*if it's a medicine, a treatment*) = agir
(*to use, to operate*) = se servir de (**!** + *être*)
do you know how to work the computer?
  = est-ce que tu sais te servir de
  l'ordinateur?

2 *noun*

work = le travail
I've got work to do = j'ai du travail
to be out of work = être au chômage
the students' work = le travail des élèves
it's hard work learning French = c'est dur
  d'apprendre le français
(*for building, for repairs*)
work(s) = les travaux (*masculine plural*)
there are road works at the moment = il y
  a des travaux en ce moment
(*by an artist, a musician*)
a work = une œuvre

work out

(*to find*) = trouver
to work out the answer = trouver la
  réponse
(*to understand*) = comprendre
(*with figures*) = calculer
(*to go well*) = marcher
(*to take exercise*) = s'entraîner (**!** + *être*)

work up

to get worked up = s'énerver (**!** + *être*)

worker *noun*

a worker (*in a factory*) = un ouvrier/une
  ouvrière
(*in an office, a bank*) = un employé/une
  employée

world *noun*

the world = le monde
all over the world = dans le monde entier
the biggest city in the world = la plus
  grande ville du monde

World Cup *noun*

the World Cup = la Coupe du Monde

worm *noun*

a worm = un ver

worried *adjective*

= inquiet/inquiète
to be worried about someone = se faire du
  souci pour quelqu'un

worry *verb*

(*to be worried*) = s'inquiéter (**!** + *être*)
there's nothing to worry about = il n'y a
  pas de quoi s'inquiéter
(*to make someone worried*) = inquiéter
it's worrying me = ça m'inquiète

worse *adjective*

= pire
this book is worse than the others = ce
  livre est pire que les autres
she's worse than me at sports = elle est
  pire que moi en sport
the weather is going to get worse = le
  temps va empirer
he's getting worse (*in health*) = il va plus
  mal

worst

1 *noun*

the worst = le pire/la pire
to be the worst at French = être le plus
  mauvais/la plus mauvaise en français

2 *adjective*

= plus mauvais/plus mauvaise
the worst hotel in town = le plus mauvais
  hôtel de la ville
the worst film I've ever seen = le plus
  mauvais film que j'aie jamais vu

! *Note that the subjunctive is used after
the superlative* le plus mauvais... que.

his worst enemy = son pire ennemi
the worst thing to do would be to tell him
  = le pire serait de le lui dire

worth *adjective*

to be worth £100 = valoir 100 livres
it's not worth the trouble = ça n'en vaut
  pas la peine

would *verb*

! *Note that French usually uses verbs in
the conditional to translate* would + *verb:*
I would buy = j'achèterais.

(*when talking about hypothetical rather
than real situations*)
if I had more money, I would buy a car = si
  j'avais plus d'argent, j'achèterais une
  voiture
**we would have missed the train if we'd
  left later** = nous aurions raté le train si
  nous étions partis plus tard
(*in reported speech*)
I thought you'd forget to come = je
  pensais que tu oublierais de venir
we were sure she would like it = nous
  étions sûrs que ça lui plairait
(*when making an assumption*)
she'd be 30 now = elle doit avoir 30 ans
  maintenant
it would have been about midday = il
  devait être à peu près midi
(*to be prepared to*)
he wouldn't listen to me = il ne voulait pas
  m'écouter
(*when talking about one's wishes*)
I'd like a beer = je voudrais une bière
we would like to stay another night = nous
  aimerions rester une nuit de plus

W

(*when asking, offering or advising*)
would you turn the TV off? = est-ce que tu veux bien éteindre la radio?
would you excuse me? = excusez-moi
would you like something to eat? = voulez-vous manger quelque chose?
you would do well to check = tu ferais mieux de vérifier

wrap *verb*
= envelopper
to wrap (up) a present = emballer un cadeau

wreck
1 *verb*
(*if it's a person*) = détruire
(*if it's a fire, a bomb*) = dévaster
2 *noun*
a wreck = une épave

wrestling *noun* ▶ 248 |
wrestling = le catch

wrist *noun* ▶ 201 |
the wrist = le poignet

write *verb*
= écrire
to write to someone, to write someone
(*US English*) = écrire à quelqu'un
to write [an essay | a cheque | a note ...]
= faire [une rédaction | un chèque | un mot ...]
write back = répondre
write down = noter
write out = écrire

writing *noun*
writing = l'écriture (*feminine*)
your writing is good = tu écris bien

writing pad *noun*
a writing pad = un bloc de papier à lettres

wrong *adjective*
(*not as it should be*)
there's something wrong = il y a quelque chose qui ne va pas
what's wrong? = qu'est-ce qu'il y a?
what's wrong with you? (*if ill, in pain*)
= qu'est-ce que tu as?
(*if behaving oddly*) = qu'est-ce qui t'arrive?
(*not proper or suitable*)
= mauvais/mauvaise (**!** before the noun)
I took the wrong key = j'ai pris la mauvaise clé
to say the wrong thing = faire une gaffe
to go the wrong way = se tromper de chemin
(*not correct*)
that's wrong = c'est faux
to dial the wrong number = faire un faux numéro, se tromper de numéro
it's the wrong answer = ce n'est pas la bonne réponse
to be wrong (*if it's a person*) = avoir tort, se tromper (**!** + *être*)

(*not honest, not good*)
it's wrong to steal = c'est mal de voler
she hasn't done anything wrong = elle n'a rien fait de mal
there's nothing wrong with trying = il n'y a pas de mal à essayer

X-ray
1 *noun*
an X-ray = une radiographie, une radio
to have an X-ray = se faire radiographier
2 *verb*
= radiographier

yacht *noun*
a yacht = un yacht

yard *noun*
(*when measuring*) ▶ 285 |
a yard ≈ un yard
! *Note that a* **yard** *= 0.9144 m.*

(*of a building*)
a yard = une cour
(*US English*) (*a garden*)
a yard = un jardin

yawn *verb*
= bâiller

year *noun*
! *Note that* **year** *is usually translated by* **an** *in French. However it is sometimes translated by* **année***, when there is an emphasis on the idea of duration.*

(*when talking about time*) ▶ 356 |
a year = un an
last year = l'an dernier, l'année dernière
two years ago = il y a deux ans
to work all year round = travailler toute l'année
he's lived there for years = il y habite depuis des années
that'll take years! = ça va prendre une éternité!
(*when talking about age*) ▶ 187 |
a year = un an
to be 15 years old, to be 15 years of age
= avoir 15 ans
a four-year old = un enfant/une enfant de quatre ans

- (*in a school system*)
  first year, year one ≈ la sixième
  to be in second year, to be in year two ≈ être en cinquième
  a first year ≈ un élève/une élève de sixième

yell
1 *verb*
= hurler
to yell at someone = crier après quelqu'un
2 *noun*
a yell = un hurlement

yellow *adjective* ▶ 213|
= jaune
to go yellow = jaunir

yes *adverb*
yes = oui
'are you coming with us?'—'yes I am'
= 'est-ce que tu viens avec nous?'—'oui'
'they don't know each other'—'yes they do' = 'ils ne se connaissent pas'—'(mais) si'
'didn't he tell you?'—'yes he did' = 'il ne te l'a pas dit?'—'si'

yesterday *adverb*
= hier

yet
1 *adverb*
= encore
not yet = pas encore
it's not ready yet = ce n'est pas encore prêt
have they arrived yet? = est-ce qu'ils sont arrivés?
has she met them yet? = est-ce qu'elle les a déjà rencontrés?
2 *conjunction*
= pourtant

yogurt *noun*
yogurt = le yaourt

you *pronoun*
▶ 378| *See the boxed note on* you *for detailed information and examples.*

young
1 *adjective*
= jeune
a young lady = une jeune femme
young people = les jeunes (*masculine*)
she is a year younger than me = elle a un an de moins que moi
a younger brother = un frère cadet
a younger sister = une sœur cadette
to look young = faire jeune
2 *noun*
the young (*of an animal*) = les petits (*masculine plural*)

your *determiner*
▶ 379| *See the boxed note on* your *for detailed information and examples. See also the usage note on* The human body ▶ 201|.

yours *pronoun*
▶ *See also the boxed notes on* you *and* your *for more information.*
the red car is yours (*informal*) = la voiture rouge est à toi
(*polite or to several people*) = la voiture rouge est à vous
my garden is bigger than yours (*informal*) = mon jardin est plus grand que le tien
(*polite or to several people*) = mon jardin est plus grand que le vôtre
her children are older than yours
(*informal*) = ses enfants sont plus âgés que les tiens
(*polite or to several people*) = ses enfants sont plus âgés que les vôtres

! *Note that, when comparing objects, people, etc, one of the following translations—le tien, la tienne, les tiens/tiennes, le/la vôtre or les vôtres—will be used. To know which one to use, find out whether the object, person, etc being described is masculine or feminine, singular or plural and whether you are using the polite or the informal form of address.*

yourself *pronoun*
- (*when used as a reflexive pronoun*)
  you'll enjoy yourself (*informal*) = tu vas t'amuser
  (*polite*) = vous allez vous amuser
  did you hurt yourself? (*informal*) = est-ce que tu t'es fait mal?
  (*polite*) = est-ce que vous vous êtes blessé?
- (*when used for emphasis*)
  you did it yourself (*informal*) = tu l'as fait toi-même
  (*polite*) = vous l'avez fait vous-même

yourselves *pronoun*
- (*when used as a reflexive pronoun*)
  you'll enjoy yourselves = vous allez vous amuser
  did you hurt yourselves? = est-ce que vous vous êtes fait mal?
- (*when used for emphasis*)
  are you going to organize it yourselves? = est-ce que vous allez l'organiser vous-mêmes?
  you want to be by yourselves = vous voulez être seuls

youth *noun*
- (*a young man*)
  a youth = un jeune
- (*young people*)
  the youth = les jeunes (*masculine plural*)

youth club *noun*
a youth club = un club de jeunes

youth hostel *noun*
a youth hostel = une auberge de jeunesse

youth worker *noun*
a youth worker = un éducateur/une éducatrice

you

Used to address people

- In English **you** is used to address everybody, whereas French has two forms: **tu** and **vous**. The usual word to use when you are speaking to anyone you do not know very well is **vous**. This is sometimes called the polite form:

where are you going?	= où allez-**vous**?
I'm thinking of you	= je pense à **vous**
would you like some coffee?	= voulez-**vous** du café?
can I help you?	= est-ce que je peux **vous** aider?
what can I do for you?	= qu'est-ce que je peux faire pour **vous**?

The more informal pronoun **tu** is used between close friends and family members, within groups of children and young people, by adults when talking to children and always when talking to animals; **tu** is the subject form, the direct and indirect object form is **te** (**t'** before a vowel or mute h) and the form for emphatic use or use after a preposition is **toi**:

where are you going?	= où vas-**tu**?
I'm thinking of you	= je pense à **toi**
would you like some coffee?	= veux-**tu** du café?
can I help you?	= est-ce que je peux **t'**aider?
there's a letter for you	= il y a une lettre pour **toi**

As a general rule, when talking to a French person use **vous**, wait to see how they address you and follow suit. It is safer to wait for the French person to suggest using **tu**.

Note that **tu** is only a singular pronoun and **vous** is its plural form.

Remember that in French the object and indirect object pronouns are always placed before the verb:

she knows you	= elle **vous** connaît
	= elle **te** connaît
I'll give you my address	= je **vous** donnerai mon adresse
	je **te** donnerai mon adresse

- In tenses like the present perfect and the past perfect, the past participle agrees with the direct object:

I saw you on Saturday	
(to one male: polite form)	= je **vous** ai vu samedi
(to one female: polite form)	= je **vous** ai vue samedi
(to one male: informal form)	= je **t'**ai vu samedi
(to one female: informal form)	= je **t'**ai vue samedi
(to two or more people, male or mixed)	= je **vous** ai vus samedi
(to two or more females)	= je **vous** ai vues samedi

Used impersonally

When **you** is used impersonally as the more informal form of **one**, it is translated by **on** for the subject form and by **vous** or **te** for the object form, depending on whether the comment is being made amongst friends or in a more formal context:

you can do as you like here	= **on** peut faire ce qu'**on** veut ici
you could easily lose your bag here	= **on** pourrait facilement perdre son sac ici
you never know	= **on** ne sait jamais
these mushrooms can make you ill	= ces champignons peuvent **vous** rendre malade
	= ces champignons peuvent **te** rendre malade

▶ For a guide to the correct verb forms with **vous**, **tu** and **on**, consult the verb in the French-English part of the dictionary and check the number in the box, which will refer you to the French verb tables at the back of the dictionary.

your

▶ For a full note on the use of the **vous** and **tu** forms in French, see the note on **you ▶ 378 |**.

● In French, determiners agree with the noun that follows:

> **your** + *masculine singular noun*
> (to one person: polite form or to two or more people)   **votre** chien, **votre** ami
> (to one person: informal form)   **ton** chien, **ton** ami
>
> **your** + *feminine singular noun*
> (to one person: polite form or to two or more people)   **votre** pomme, **votre** orange
> (to one person: informal form)   **ta** pomme, **ton*** orange

* Note that **ton** is used with a feminine noun beginning with a vowel or mute h.

> **your** + *plural noun*
> (to one person: polite form or   **vos** chiens, **vos** amis,
> to two or more people)   **vos** pommes, **vos** oranges
> (to one person: informal form)   **tes** chiens, **tes** amis,
>   **tes** pommes, **tes** oranges

When **your** is stressed, **à vous** or **à toi** is added after the noun:

> (to one person: polite form) *your* house   = **votre** maison **à vous**
> (to two or more people)   = **vos** maisons **à vous**
> (to one person: informal form) *your* house   = **ta** maison **à toi**
> (to one person: polite form) *your* parents   = **vos** parents **à vous**
> (to two or more people)   = **vos** parents **à vous**
> (to one person: informal form) *your* parents   = **tes** parents **à toi**

● When used impersonally to mean **one's**, **your** is translated by **son, sa** or **ses**, when **you** is translated by **on**:

> *you pay your bills at the end of the week*   = on paie **ses** factures à la fin de la semaine
> *you get good value for your money*   = on en a pour **son** argent

The translation after an impersonal verb in French is **son, sa, ses**:

> *you have to buy your tickets at the door*   = il faut acheter **ses** billets à l'entrée

Note, however, the following:

> *smoking is bad for your health*   = le tabac est mauvais pour **la** santé
> *your average student*   = **l'**étudiant moyen

▶ For **your** used with parts of the body, see the usage note on **The human body ▶ 201 |**.

Zz

zap *verb*
- (*to destroy*) = détruire
- (*British English*) (*to switch channels*)
  to zap from channel to channel = zapper*
- (*to remove from a computer screen*)
  = supprimer

zapper *noun* (*British English*)
   a **zapper** = une télécommande

zebra *noun*
   a **zebra** = un zèbre

---

zebra crossing *noun* (*British English*)
   a **zebra crossing** = un passage pour piétons

zero *number*
   zero = zéro

zip (*British English*), **zipper** (*US English*) *noun*
   a **zip** = une fermeture éclair
   to undo a zip = ouvrir une fermeture éclair

zip code *noun* (*US English*)
   a **zip code** = un code postal

zodiac *noun*
   the zodiac = le zodiaque

zone *noun*
   a **zone** = une zone

zoo *noun*
   a **zoo** = un zoo

---

* in informal situations

Z

French verbs

Present
je chante = *I sing, I'm singing*

Future
je chanterai = *I will sing*

Imperfect
je chantais = *I was singing*

Perfect
j'ai chanté = *I sang, I have sung*

Past participle
chanté/chantée = *sung*

Present subjunctive
bien que je chante = *although I sing*

Conditional
s'il y avait une chorale, je chanterais = *if there was a choir, I would sing*

Pluperfect
j'avais chanté = *I had sung*

1 chanter

Present		Perfect			Conditional	
je	chante	j'	ai	chanté	je	chanterais
tu	chantes	tu	as	chanté	tu	chanterais
il	chante	il	a	chanté	il	chanterait
nous	chantons	elle	a	chanté	nous	chanterions
vous	chantez				vous	chanteriez
ils	chantent	nous	avons	chanté	ils	chanteraient
		vous	avez	chanté		

Future

					Pluperfect		
je	chanterai	ils	ont	chanté	j'	avais	chanté
tu	chanteras	elles	ont	chanté	tu	avais	chanté
il	chantera				il	avait	chanté
nous	chanterons	**Past participle**			elle	avait	chanté
vous	chanterez		chanté/chantée				
ils	chanteront				nous	avions	chanté

Imperfect

Present subjunctive

					vous	aviez	chanté
je	chantais	(que) je	chante		ils	avaient	chanté
tu	chantais	(que) tu	chantes		elles	avaient	chanté
il	chantait	(qu') il	chante				
nous	chantions	(que) nous	chantions				
vous	chantiez	(que) vous	chantiez				
ils	chantaient	(qu') ils	chantent				

2 oublier

Present		Perfect			Conditional	
j'	oublie	j'	ai	oublié	j'	oublierais
tu	oublies	tu	as	oublié	tu	oublierais
il	oublie	il	a	oublié	il	oublierait
nous	oublions	elle	a	oublié	nous	oublierions
vous	oubliez				vous	oublieriez
ils	oublient	nous	avons	oublié	ils	oublieraient
		vous	avez	oublié		

Future

					Pluperfect		
j'	oublierai	ils	ont	oublié	j'	avais	oublié
tu	oublieras	elles	ont	oublié	tu	avais	oublié
Il	oubliera				il	avait	oublié
nous	oublierons	**Past participle**			elle	avait	oublié
vous	oublierez		oublié/oubliée				
ils	oublieront				nous	avions	oublié

Imperfect

Present subjunctive

					vous	aviez	oublié
j'	oubliais	(que) j'	oublie		ils	avaient	oublié
tu	oubliais	(que) tu	oublies		elles	avaient	oublié
il	oubliait	(qu') il	oublie				
nous	oubliions	(que) nous	oubliions				
vous	oubliiez	(que) vous	oubliiez				
ils	oubliaient	(qu') ils	oublient				

3 finir

Present			Perfect			Conditional		
je	finis		j'	ai	fini	je	finirais	
tu	finis		tu	as	fini	tu	finirais	
il	finit		il	a	fini	il	finirait	
nous	finissons		elle	a	fini	nous	finirions	
vous	finissez		nous	avons	fini	vous	finiriez	
ils	finissent		vous	avez	fini	ils	finiraient	
			ils	ont	fini			
Future			elles	ont	fini	**Pluperfect**		
je	finirai					j'	avais	fini
tu	finiras		**Past participle**			tu	avais	fini
il	finira		fini/finie			il	avait	fini
nous	finirons					elle	avait	fini
vous	finirez		**Present subjunctive**			nous	avons	fini
ils	finiront		(que) je	finisse		vous	aviez	fini
			(que) tu	finisses		ils	avaient	fini
Imperfect			(qu') il	finisse		elles	avaient	fini
je	finissais		(que) nous	finissions				
tu	finissais		(que) vous	finissiez				
il	finissait		(qu') ils	finissent				
nous	finissions							
vous	finissiez							
ils	finissaient							

4 offrir

Present			Perfect			Conditional		
j'	offre		j'	ai	offert	j'	offrirais	
tu	offres		tu	as	offert	tu	offrirais	
il	offre		il	a	offert	il	offrirait	
nous	offrons		elle	a	offert	nous	offririons	
vous	offrez		nous	avons	offert	vous	offririez	
ils	offrent		vous	avez	offert	ils	offriraient	
			ils	ont	offert			
Future			elles	ont	offert	**Pluperfect**		
j'	offrirai					j'	avais	offert
tu	offriras		**Past participle**			tu	avais	offert
il	offrira		offert/offerte			il	avait	offert
nous	offrirons					elle	avait	offert
vous	offrirez		**Present subjunctive**			nous	avons	offert
ils	offriront		(que) j'	offre		vous	aviez	offert
			(que) tu	offres		ils	avaient	offert
Imperfect			(qu') il	offre		elles	avaient	offert
j'	offrais		(que) nous	offrions				
tu	offrais		(que) vous	offriez				
il	offrait		(qu') ils	offrent				
nous	offrions							
vous	offriez							
ils	offraient							

5 apercevoir

Present

j'	aperçois
tu	aperçois
il	aperçoit
nous	apercevons
vous	apercevez
ils	aperçoivent

Future

j'	apercevrai
tu	apercevras
il	apercevra
nous	apercevrons
vous	apercevrez
ils	apercevront

Imperfect

j'	apercevais
tu	apercevais
il	apercevait
nous	apercevions
vous	aperceviez
ils	apercevaient

Perfect

j'	ai	aperçu
tu	as	aperçu
il	a	aperçu
elle	a	aperçu
nous	avons	aperçu
vous	avez	aperçu
ils	ont	aperçu
elles	ont	aperçu

Past participle

aperçu/aperçue

Present subjunctive

(que)	j'	aperçoive
(que)	tu	aperçoives
(qu')	il	aperçoive
(que)	nous	apercevions
(que)	vous	aperceviez
(qu')	ils	aperçoivent

Conditional

j'	apercevrais
tu	apercevrais
il	apercevrait
nous	apercevrions
vous	apercevriez
ils	apercevraient

Pluperfect

j'	avais	aperçu
tu	avais	aperçu
il	avait	aperçu
elle	avait	aperçu
nous	avions	aperçu
vous	aviez	aperçu
ils	avaient	aperçu
elles	avaient	aperçu

6 attendre

Present

j'	attends
tu	attends
il	attend
nous	attendons
vous	attendez
ils	attendent

Future

j'	attendrai
tu	attendras
il	attendra
nous	attendrons
vous	attendrez
ils	attendront

Imperfect

j'	attendais
tu	attendais
il	attendait
nous	attendions
vous	attendiez
ils	attendaient

Perfect

j'	ai	attendu
tu	as	attendu
il	a	attendu
elle	a	attendu
nous	avons	attendu
vous	avez	attendu
ils	ont	attendu
elles	ont	attendu

Past participle

attendu/attendue

Present subjunctive

(que)	j'	attende
(que)	tu	attendes
(qu')	il	attende
(que)	nous	attendions
(que)	vous	attendiez
(qu')	ils	attendent

Conditional

j'	attendrais
tu	attendrais
il	attendrait
nous	attendrions
vous	attendriez
ils	attendraient

Pluperfect

j'	avais	attendu
tu	avais	attendu
il	avait	attendu
elle	avait	attendu
nous	avions	attendu
vous	aviez	attendu
ils	avaient	attendu
elles	avaient	attendu

7 être

Present			Perfect			Conditional	
je	suis		j'	ai	été	je	serais
tu	es		tu	as	été	tu	serais
il	est		il	a	été	il	serait
nous	sommes		elle	a	été		
vous	êtes					nous	serions
ils	sont		nous	avons	été	vous	seriez
			vous	avez	été	ils	seraient

Future

		Perfect (cont.)			Pluperfect		
je	serai	ils	ont	été	j'	avais	été
tu	seras	elles	ont	été	tu	avais	été
il	sera				il	avait	été
nous	serons	**Past participle**			elle	avait	été
vous	serez		été (invariable)				
ils	seront				nous	avions	été

Imperfect

Present subjunctive

j'	étais	(que) je	sois	vous aviez été
tu	étais	(que) tu	sois	ils avaient été
il	était	(qu') il	soit	elles avaient été
nous	étions	(que) nous	soyons	
vous	étiez	(que) vous	soyez	
ils	étaient	(qu') ils	soient	

8 avoir

Present			Perfect			Conditional	
j'	ai		j'	ai	eu	j'	aurais
tu	as		tu	as	eu	tu	aurais
il	a		il	a	eu	il	aurait
nous	avons		elle	a	eu		
vous	avez					nous	aurions
ils	ont		nous	avons	eu	vous	auriez
			vous	avez	eu	ils	auraient

Future

		Perfect (cont.)			Pluperfect		
j'	aurai	ils	ont	eu	j'	avais	eu
tu	auras	elles	ont	eu	tu	avais	eu
il	aura				il	avait	eu
nous	aurons	**Past participle**			elle	avait	eu
vous	aurez		eu/eue				
ils	auront				nous	avions	eu

Imperfect

Present subjunctive

j'	avais	(que) j'	aie	vous aviez eu
tu	avais	(que) tu	aies	ils avaient eu
il	avait	(qu') il	ait	elles avaient eu
nous	avions	(que) nous	ayons	
vous	aviez	(que) vous	ayez	
ils	avaient	(qu') ils	aient	

9 aller

Present		
je	vais	
tu	vas	
il	va	
nous	allons	
vous	allez	
ils	vont	

Future	
j'	irai
tu	iras
il	ira
nous	irons
vous	irez
ils	iront

Imperfect	
j'	allais
tu	allais
il	allait
nous	allions
vous	alliez
ils	allaient

Perfect		
je	suis	allé
tu	es	allé
il	est	allé
elle	est	allée
nous	sommes	allés
vous	êtes	allés
ils	sont	allés
elles	sont	allées

Past participle

allé/allée

Present subjunctive		
(que)	j'	aille
(que)	tu	ailles
(qu')	il	aille
(que)	nous	allions
(que)	vous	alliez
(qu')	ils	aillent

Conditional	
j'	irais
tu	irais
il	irait
nous	irions
vous	iriez
ils	iraient

Pluperfect		
j'	étais	allé
tu	étais	allé
il	était	allé
elle	était	allée
nous	étions	allés
vous	étiez	allés
ils	étaient	allés
elles	étaient	allées

10 faire

Present		
je	fais	
tu	fais	
il	fait	
nous	faisons	
vous	faites	
ils	font	

Future	
je	ferai
tu	feras
il	fera
nous	ferons
vous	ferez
ils	feront

Imperfect	
je	faisais
tu	faisais
il	faisait
nous	faisions
vous	faisiez
ils	faisaient

Perfect		
j'	ai	fait
tu	as	fait
il	a	fait
elle	a	fait
nous	avons	fait
vous	avez	fait
ils	ont	fait
elles	ont	fait

Past participle

fait/faite

Present subjunctive		
(que)	je	fasse
(que)	tu	fasses
(qu')	il	fasse
(que)	nous	fassions
(que)	vous	fassiez
(qu')	ils	fassent

Conditional	
je	ferais
tu	ferais
il	ferait
nous	ferions
vous	feriez
ils	feraient

Pluperfect		
j'	avais	fait
tu	avais	fait
il	avait	fait
elle	avait	fait
nous	avions	fait
vous	aviez	fait
ils	avaient	fait
elles	avaient	fait

11 créer

Present		Perfect			Conditional	
je	crée	j'	ai	créé	je	créerais
tu	crées	tu	as	créé	tu	créerais
il	crée	il	a	créé	il	créerait
nous	créons	elle	a	créé	nous	créerions
vous	créez				vous	créeriez
ils	créent	nous	avons	créé	ils	créeraient
		vous	avez	créé		
		ils	ont	créé		

Future		Perfect (cont.)			Pluperfect		
je	créerai	elles	ont	créé	j'	avais	créé
tu	créeras				tu	avais	créé
il	créera	**Past participle**			il	avait	créé
nous	créerons		créé/créée		elle	avait	créé
vous	créerez				nous	avions	créé
ils	créeront	**Present subjunctive**			vous	aviez	créé

Imperfect		Present subjunctive			Pluperfect (cont.)		
je	créais	(que) je	crée		ils	avaient	créé
tu	créais	(que) tu	crées		elles	avaient	créé
il	créait	(qu') il	crée				
nous	créions	(que) nous	créions				
vous	créiez	(que) vous	créiez				
ils	créaient	(qu') ils	créent				

12 avancer

Present		Perfect			Conditional	
j'	avance	j'	ai	avancé	j'	avancerais
tu	avances	tu	as	avancé	tu	avancerais
il	avance	il	a	avancé	il	avancerait
nous	avançons	elle	a	avancé	nous	avancerions
vous	avancez				vous	avanceriez
ils	avancent	nous	avons	avancé	ils	avanceraient
		vous	avez	avancé		
		ils	ont	avancé		

Future		Perfect (cont.)			Pluperfect		
j'	avancerai	elles	ont	avancé	j'	avais	avancé
tu	avanceras				tu	avais	avancé
il	avancera	**Past participle**			il	avait	avancé
nous	avancerons		avancé/avancée		elle	avait	avancé
vous	avancerez				nous	avions	avancé
ils	avanceront	**Present subjunctive**			vous	aviez	avancé

Imperfect		Present subjunctive			Pluperfect (cont.)		
j'	avançais	(que) j'	avance		ils	avaient	avancé
tu	avançais	(que) tu	avances		elles	avaient	avancé
il	avançait	(qu') il	avance				
nous	avancions	(que) nous	avancions				
vous	avanciez	(que) vous	avanciez				
ils	avançaient	(qu') ils	avancent				

13 changer

Present		Perfect			Conditional	
je	change	j'	ai	changé	je	changerais
tu	changes	tu	as	changé	tu	changerais
il	change	il	a	changé	il	changerait
nous	changeons	elle	a	changé	nous	changerions
vous	changez				vous	changeriez
ils	changent	nous	avons	changé	ils	changeraient
		vous	avez	changé		
Future		ils	ont	changé		
je	changerai	elles	ont	changé	Pluperfect	
tu	changeras				j'	avais	changé
il	changera	Past participle			tu	avais	changé
nous	changerons	changé/changée			il	avait	changé
vous	changerez				elle	avait	changé
ils	changeront	Present subjunctive			nous	avions	changé
		(que) je	change		vous	aviez	changé
Imperfect		(que) tu	changes		ils	avaient	changé
je	changeais	(qu') il	change		elles	avaient	changé
tu	changeais					
il	changeait	(que) nous	changions			
nous	changions	(que) vous	changiez			
vous	changiez	(qu') ils	changent			
ils	changeaient					

14 espérer

Present		Perfect			Conditional	
j'	espère	j'	ai	espéré	j'	espérerais
tu	espères	tu	as	espéré	tu	espérerais
il	espère	il	a	espéré	il	espérerait
nous	espérons	elle	a	espéré	nous	espérerions
vous	espérez				vous	espéreriez
ils	espèrent	nous	avons	espéré	ils	espéreraient
		vous	avez	espéré		
Future		ils	ont	espéré		
j'	espérerai	elles	ont	espéré	Pluperfect	
tu	espéreras				j'	avais	espéré
il	espérera	Past participle			tu	avais	espéré
nous	espérerons	espéré/espérée			il	avait	espéré
vous	espérerez				elle	avait	espéré
ils	espéreront	Present subjunctive			nous	avions	espéré
		(que) j'	espère		vous	aviez	espéré
Imperfect		(que) tu	espères		ils	avaient	espéré
j'	espérais	(qu') il	espère		elles	avaient	espéré
tu	espérais					
il	espérait	(que) nous	espérions			
nous	espérions	(que) vous	espériez			
vous	espériez	(qu') ils	espèrent			
ils	espéraient					

15 protéger

Present			Perfect			Conditional	
je	protège		j'	ai	protégé	je	protégerais
tu	protèges		tu	as	protégé	tu	protégerais
il	protège		il	a	protégé	il	protégerait
nous	protégeons		elle	a	protégé		
vous	protégez					nous	protégerions
ils	protègent		nous	avons	protégé	vous	protégeriez
			vous	avez	protégé	ils	protégeraient
Future			ils	ont	protégé		
je	protégerai		elles	ont	protégé	Pluperfect	
tu	protégeras					j'	avais	protégé
il	protégera		Past participle			tu	avais	protégé
				protégé/protégée		il	avait	protégé
nous	protégerons					elle	avait	protégé
vous	protégerez		Present subjunctive					
ils	protégeront		(que)	je	protège	nous	avions	protégé
			(que)	tu	protèges	vous	aviez	protégé
Imperfect			(qu')	il	protège	ils	avaient	protégé
je	protégeais							
tu	protégeais		(que)	nous	protégions			
il	protégeait		(que)	vous	protégiez			
			(qu')	ils	protègent			
nous	protégions							
vous	protégiez							
ils	protégeaient							

16 mener

Present			Perfect			Conditional	
je	mène		j'	ai	mené	je	mènerais
tu	mènes		tu	as	mené	tu	mènerais
il	mène		il	a	mené	il	mènerait
nous	menons		elle	a	mené		
vous	menez					nous	mènerions
ils	mènent		nous	avons	mené	vous	mèneriez
			vous	avez	mené	ils	mèneraient
Future			ils	ont	mené		
je	mènerai		elles	ont	mené	Pluperfect	
tu	mèneras					j'	avais	mené
il	mènera		Past participle			tu	avais	mené
				mené/menée		il	avait	mené
nous	mènerons					elle	avait	mené
vous	mènerez		Present subjunctive					
ils	mèneront		(que)	je	mène	nous	avions	mené
			(que)	tu	mènes	vous	aviez	mené
Imperfect			(qu')	il	mène	ils	avaient	mené
je	menais					elles	avaient	mené
tu	menais		(que)	nous	menions			
il	menait		(que)	vous	meniez			
			(qu')	ils	mènent			
nous	menions							
vous	meniez							
ils	menaient							

17 peler

Present		Perfect			Conditional	
je	pèle	j'	ai	pelé	je	pèlerais
tu	pèles	tu	as	pelé	tu	pèlerais
il	pèle	il	a	pelé	il	pèlerait
nous	pelons	elle	a	pelé	nous	pèlerions
vous	pelez				vous	pèleriez
ils	pèlent	nous	avons	pelé	ils	pèleraient
		vous	avez	pelé		

Future		Past participle
je	pèlerai	pelé/pelée
tu	pèleras	
il	pèlera	
nous	pèlerons	
vous	pèlerez	
ils	pèleront	

Present subjunctive

(que)	je	pèle
(que)	tu	pèles
(qu')	il	pèle
(que)	nous	pelions
(que)	vous	peliez
(qu')	ils	pèlent

Perfect continued:
| ils | ont | pelé |
| elles | ont | pelé |

Imperfect

je	pelais
tu	pelais
il	pelait
nous	pelions
vous	peliez
ils	pelaient

Pluperfect

j'	avais	pelé
tu	avais	pelé
il	avait	pelé
elle	avait	pelé
nous	avions	pelé
vous	aviez	pelé
ils	avaient	pelé
elles	avaient	pelé

18 acheter

Present		Perfect			Conditional	
j'	achète	j'	ai	acheté	j'	achèterais
tu	achètes	tu	as	acheté	tu	achèterais
il	achète	il	a	acheté	il	achèterait
nous	achetons	elle	a	acheté	nous	achèterions
vous	achetez				vous	achèteriez
ils	achètent	nous	avons	acheté	ils	achèteraient
		vous	avez	acheté		
		ils	ont	acheté		
		elles	ont	acheté		

Future		Past participle
j'	achèterai	acheté/achetée
tu	achèteras	
il	achètera	
nous	achèterons	
vous	achèterez	
ils	achèteront	

Present subjunctive

(que)	j'	achète
(que)	tu	achètes
(qu')	il	achète
(que)	nous	achetions
(que)	vous	achetiez
(qu')	ils	achètent

Imperfect

j'	achetais
tu	achetais
il	achetait
nous	achetions
vous	achetiez
ils	achetaient

Pluperfect

j'	avais	acheté
tu	avais	acheté
il	avait	acheté
elle	avait	acheté
nous	avions	acheté
vous	aviez	acheté
ils	avaient	acheté
elles	avaient	acheté

19 rappeler

Present		Perfect			Conditional	
je	rappelle	j'	ai	rappelé	je	rappellerais
tu	rappelles	tu	as	rappelé	tu	rappellerais
il	rappelle	il	a	rappelé	il	rappellerait
nous	rappelons	elle	a	rappelé	nous	rappellerions
vous	rappelez				vous	rappelleriez
ils	rappellent	nous	avons	rappelé	ils	rappelleraient
		vous	avez	rappelé		
		ils	ont	rappelé		

Future

		elles	ont	rappelé	**Pluperfect**		
je	rappellerai				j'	avais	rappelé
tu	rappelleras	**Past participle**			tu	avais	rappelé
il	rappellera		rappelé/rappelée		il	avait	rappelé
nous	rappellerons				elle	avait	rappelé
vous	rappellerez	**Present subjunctive**			nous	avions	rappelé
ils	rappelleront	(que)	je	rappelle	vous	aviez	rappelé
		(que)	tu	rappelles	ils	avaient	rappelé
Imperfect		(qu')	il	rappelle	elles	avaient	rappelé
je	rappelais						
tu	rappelais	(que)	nous	rappelions			
il	rappelait	(que)	vous	rappeliez			
nous	rappelions	(qu')	ils	rappellent			
vous	rappeliez						
ils	rappelaient						

20 jeter

Present		Perfect			Conditional	
je	jette	j'	ai	jeté	je	jetterais
tu	jettes	tu	as	jeté	tu	jetterais
il	jette	il	a	jeté	il	jetterait
nous	jetons	elle	a	jeté	nous	jetterions
vous	jetez				vous	jetteriez
ils	jettent	nous	avons	jeté	ils	jetteraient
		vous	avez	jeté		
		ils	ont	jeté		

Future

		elles	ont	jeté	**Pluperfect**		
je	jetterai				j'	avais	jeté
tu	jetteras	**Past participle**			tu	avais	jeté
il	jettera		jeté/jetée		il	avait	jeté
nous	jetterons				elle	avait	jeté
vous	jetterez	**Present subjunctive**			nous	avions	jeté
ils	jetteront	(que)	je	jette	vous	aviez	jeté
		(que)	tu	jettes	ils	avaient	jeté
Imperfect		(qu')	il	jette	elles	avaient	jeté
je	jetais						
tu	jetais	(que)	nous	jetions			
il	jetait	(que)	vous	jetiez			
nous	jetions	(qu')	ils	jettent			
vous	jetiez						
ils	jetaient						

21 essayer

Present		Perfect			Conditional	
j'	essaie	j'	ai	essayé	j'	essaierais
tu	essaies	tu	as	essayé	tu	essaierais
il	essaie	il	a	essayé	il	essaierait
nous	essayons	elle	a	essayé	nous	essaierions
vous	essayez				vous	essaieriez
ils	essaient	nous	avons	essayé	ils	essaieraient
		vous	avez	essayé		
		ils	ont	essayé	

Future

		elles	ont	essayé	**Pluperfect**	
j'	essaierai				j'	avais	essayé
tu	essaieras				tu	avais	essayé
il	essaiera	**Past participle**			il	avait	essayé
nous	essaierons		essayé/essayée		elle	avait	essayé
vous	essaierez				nous	avions	essayé
ils	essaieront	**Present subjunctive**			vous	aviez	essayé

Imperfect

		(que)	j'	essaie	ils	avaient	essayé
j'	essayais	(que)	tu	essaies	elles	avaient	essayé
tu	essayais	(qu')	il	essaie			
il	essayait						
nous	essayions	(que)	nous	essayions			
vous	essayiez	(que)	vous	essayiez			
ils	essayaient	(qu')	ils	essaient			

22 appuyer

Present		Perfect			Conditional	
j'	appuie	j'	ai	appuyé	j'	appuierais
tu	appuies	tu	as	appuyé	tu	appuierais
il	appuie	il	a	appuyé	il	appuierait
nous	appuyons	elle	a	appuyé	nous	appuierions
vous	appuyez				vous	appuieriez
ils	appuient	nous	avons	appuyé	ils	appuieraient
		vous	avez	appuyé		
		ils	ont	appuyé	

Future

		elles	ont	appuyé	**Pluperfect**	
j'	appuierai				j'	avais	appuyé
tu	appuieras	**Past participle**			tu	avais	appuyé
il	appuiera		appuyé/appuyée		il	avait	appuyé
nous	appuierons				elle	avait	appuyé
vous	appuierez	**Present subjunctive**			nous	avions	appuyé
ils	appuieront	(que)	j'	appuie	vous	aviez	appuyé
		(que)	tu	appuies	ils	avaient	appuyé

Imperfect

		(qu')	il	appuie	elles	avaient	appuyé
j'	appuyais						
tu	appuyais	(que)	nous	appuyions			
il	appuyait	(que)	vous	appuyiez			
nous	appuyions	(qu')	ils	appuient			
vous	appuyiez						
ils	appuyaient						

23 nettoyer

Present		Perfect			Conditional	
je	nettoie	j'	ai	nettoyé	je	nettoierais
tu	nettoies	tu	as	nettoyé	tu	nettoierais
il	nettoie	il	a	nettoyé	il	nettoierait
nous	nettoyons	elle	a	nettoyé	nous	nettoierions
vous	nettoyez				vous	nettoieriez
ils	nettoient	nous	avons	nettoyé	ils	nettoieraient
		vous	avez	nettoyé		
		ils	ont	nettoyé		
Future		elles	ont	nettoyé		
je	nettoierai				**Pluperfect**	
tu	nettoieras	**Past participle**			j'	avais	nettoyé
il	nettoiera		nettoyé/nettoyée		tu	avais	nettoyé
nous	nettoierons				il	avait	nettoyé
vous	nettoierez	**Present subjunctive**			elle	avait	nettoyé
ils	nettoieront	(que)	je	nettoie	nous	avions	nettoyé

23 nettoyer

Present
- je nettoie
- tu nettoies
- il nettoie
- nous nettoyons
- vous nettoyez
- ils nettoient

Future
- je nettoierai
- tu nettoieras
- il nettoiera
- nous nettoierons
- vous nettoierez
- ils nettoieront

Imperfect
- je nettoyais
- tu nettoyais
- il nettoyait
- nous nettoyions
- vous nettoyiez
- ils nettoyaient

Perfect
- j' ai nettoyé
- tu as nettoyé
- il a nettoyé
- elle a nettoyé
- nous avons nettoyé
- vous avez nettoyé
- ils ont nettoyé
- elles ont nettoyé

Past participle
- nettoyé/nettoyée

Present subjunctive
- (que) je nettoie
- (que) tu nettoies
- (qu') il nettoie
- (que) nous nettoyions
- (que) vous nettoyiez
- (qu') ils nettoient

Conditional
- je nettoierais
- tu nettoierais
- il nettoierait
- nous nettoierions
- vous nettoieriez
- ils nettoieraient

Pluperfect
- j' avais nettoyé
- tu avais nettoyé
- il avait nettoyé
- elle avait nettoyé
- nous avions nettoyé
- vous aviez nettoyé
- ils avaient nettoyé
- elles avaient nettoyé

24 envoyer

Present
- j' envoie
- tu envoies
- il envoie
- nous envoyons
- vous envoyez
- ils envoient

Future
- j' enverrai
- tu enverras
- il enverra
- nous enverrons
- vous enverrez
- ils enverront

Imperfect
- j' envoyais
- tu envoyais
- il envoyait
- nous envoyions
- vous envoyiez
- ils envoyaient

Perfect
- j' ai envoyé
- tu as envoyé
- il a envoyé
- elle a envoyé
- nous avons envoyé
- vous avez envoyé
- ils ont envoyé
- elles ont envoyé

Past participle
- envoyé/envoyée

Present subjunctive
- (que) j' envoie
- (que) tu envoies
- (qu') il envoie
- (que) nous envoyions
- (que) vous envoyiez
- (qu') ils envoient

Conditional
- j' enverrais
- tu enverrais
- il enverrait
- nous enverrions
- vous enverriez
- ils enverraient

Pluperfect
- j' avais envoyé
- tu avais envoyé
- il avait envoyé
- elle avait envoyé
- nous avions envoyé
- vous aviez envoyé
- ils avaient envoyé
- elles avaient envoyé

25 mourir

Present		Perfect			Conditional	
je	meurs	je	suis	mort	je	mourrais
tu	meurs	tu	es	mort	tu	mourrais
il	meurt	il	est	mort	il	mourrait
nous	mourons	elle	est	morte		
vous	mourez				nous	mourrions
ils	meurent	nous	sommes	morts	vous	mourriez
		vous	êtes	morts	ils	mourraient

Future

je	mourrai	ils	sont	morts	**Pluperfect**		
tu	mourras	elles	sont	mortes	j'	étais	mort
il	mourra				tu	étais	mort
nous	mourrons	**Past participle**			il	était	mort
vous	mourrez		mort/morte		elle	était	morte
ils	mourront				nous	étions	morts

Imperfect

		Present subjunctive		vous	étiez	morts
je	mourais	(que) je	meure	ils	étaient	morts
tu	mourais	(que) tu	meures	elles	étaient	mortes
il	mourait	(qu') il	meure			
nous	mourions	(que) nous	mourions			
vous	mouriez	(que) vous	mouriez			
ils	mouraient	(qu') ils	meurent			

26 courir

Present		Perfect			Conditional	
je	cours	j'	ai	couru	je	courrais
tu	cours	tu	as	couru	tu	courrais
il	court	il	a	couru	il	courrait
nous	courons	elle	a	couru		
vous	courez				nous	courrions
ils	courent	nous	avons	couru	vous	courriez
		vous	avez	couru	ils	courraient

Future

je	courrai	ils	ont	couru	**Pluperfect**		
tu	courras	elles	ont	couru	j'	avais	couru
il	courra				tu	avais	couru
nous	courrons	**Past participle**			il	avait	couru
vous	courrez		couru/courue		elle	avait	couru
ils	courront				nous	avions	couru

Imperfect

		Present subjunctive		vous	aviez	couru
je	courais	(que) je	coure	ils	avaient	couru
tu	courais	(que) tu	coures	elles	avaient	couru
il	courait	(qu') il	coure			
nous	courions	(que) nous	courions			
vous	couriez	(que) vous	couriez			
ils	couraient	(qu') ils	courent			

27 cueillir

Present		Perfect			Conditional	
je	cueille	j'	ai	cueilli	je	cueillerais
tu	cueilles	tu	as	cueilli	tu	cueillerais
il	cueille	il	a	cueilli	il	cueillerait
nous	cueillons	elle	a	cueilli	nous	cueillerions
vous	cueillez				vous	cueilleriez
ils	cueillent	nous	avons	cueilli	ils	cueilleraient
		vous	avez	cueilli		

Future

		ils	ont	cueilli	**Pluperfect**	
je	cueillerai	elles	ont	cueilli	j'	avais	cueilli
tu	cueilleras				tu	avais	cueilli
il	cueillera	**Past participle**			il	avait	cueilli
nous	cueillerons		cueilli/cueillie		elle	avait	cueilli
vous	cueillerez						
ils	cueilleront	**Present subjunctive**			nous	avions	cueilli

Imperfect

		(que)	je	cueille	vous	aviez	cueilli
je	cueillais	(que)	tu	cueilles	ils	avaient	cueilli
tu	cueillais	(qu')	il	cueille	elles	avaient	cueilli
il	cueillait						
nous	cueillions	(que)	nous	cueillions			
vous	cueilliez	(que)	vous	cueilliez			
ils	cueillaient	(qu')	ils	cueillent			

28 faillir

Perfect			Past participle	Pluperfect		
j'	ai	failli	failli	j'	avais	failli
tu	as	failli		tu	avais	failli
il	a	failli		il	avait	failli
elle	a	failli		elle	avait	failli
nous	avons	failli		nous	avions	failli
vous	avez	failli		vous	aviez	failli
ils	ont	failli		ils	avaient	failli
elles	ont	failli		elles	avaient	failli

29 fuir

Present		Perfect			Conditional	
je	fuis	j'	ai	fui	je	fuirais
tu	fuis	tu	as	fui	tu	fuirais
il	fuit	il	a	fui	il	fuirait
nous	fuyons	elle	a	fui		
vous	fuyez				nous	fuirions
ils	fuient	nous	avons	fui	vous	fuiriez
		vous	avez	fui	ils	fuiraient
		ils	ont	fui		

Future		elles	ont	fui	Pluperfect	
je	fuirai				j'	avais	fui
tu	fuiras	Past participle			tu	avais	fui
il	fuira	fui/fuie			il	avait	fui
nous	fuirons				elle	avait	fui
vous	fuirez						
ils	fuiront	Present subjunctive			nous	avions	fui

Imperfect		(que) je	fuie	vous	aviez	fui
je	fuyais	(que) tu	fuies	ils	avaient	fui
tu	fuyais	(qu') il	fuie	elles	avaient	fui
il	fuyait					
nous	fuyions	(que) nous	fuyions			
vous	fuyiez	(que) vous	fuyiez			
ils	fuyaient	(qu') ils	fuient			

30 sortir

Present		Perfect			Conditional	
je	sors	je	suis	sorti	je	sortirais
tu	sors	tu	es	sorti	tu	sortirais
il	sort	il	est	sorti	il	sortirait
		elle	est	sortie		
nous	sortons				nous	sortirions
vous	sortez	nous	sommes	sortis	vous	sortiriez
ils	sortent	vous	êtes	sortis	ils	sortiraient
		ils	sont	sortis		

Future		elles	sont	sorties	Pluperfect	
je	sortirai				j'	étais	sorti
tu	sortiras	Past participle			tu	étais	sorti
il	sortira	sorti/sortie			il	était	sorti
nous	sortirons				elle	était	sortie
vous	sortirez	Present subjunctive			nous	étions	sortis
ils	sortiront	(que) je	sorte	vous	étiez	sortis

Imperfect		(que) tu	sortes	ils	étaient	sortis
je	sortais	(qu') il	sorte	elles	étaient	sorties
tu	sortais					
il	sortait	(que) nous	sortions			
		(que) vous	sortiez			
nous	sortions	(qu') ils	sortent			
vous	sortiez					
ils	sortaient					

31 bouillir

Present			Perfect			Conditional	
je	bous		j'	ai	bouilli	je	bouillirais
tu	bous		tu	as	bouilli	tu	bouillirais
il	bout		il	a	bouilli	il	bouillirait
nous	bouillons		elle	a	bouilli		
vous	bouillez					nous	bouillirions
ils	bouillent		nous	avons	bouilli	vous	bouilliriez
			vous	avez	bouilli	ils	bouilliraient
Future			ils	ont	bouilli		
je	bouillirai		elles	ont	bouilli	Pluperfect	
tu	bouilliras					j'	avais	bouilli
il	bouillira		Past participle			tu	avais	bouilli
nous	bouillirons			bouilli/bouillie		il	avait	bouilli
vous	bouillirez					elle	avait	bouilli
ils	bouilliront		Present subjunctive			nous	avions	bouilli
Imperfect			(que) je	bouille		vous	aviez	bouilli
je	bouillais		(que) tu	bouilles		ils	avaient bouilli
tu	bouillais		(qu') il	bouille		elles	avaient bouilli
il	bouillait		(que) nous	bouillions			
nous	bouillions		(que) vous	bouilliez			
vous	bouilliez		(qu') ils	bouillent			
ils	bouillaient						

32 découvrir

Present			Perfect			Conditional	
je	découvre		j'	ai	découvert	je	découvrirais
tu	découvres		tu	as	découvert	tu	découvrirais
il	découvre		il	a	découvert	il	découvrirait
nous	découvrons		elle	a	découvert	nous	découvririons
vous	découvrez		nous	avons	découvert	vous	découvririez
ils	découvrent		vous	avez	découvert	ils	découvriraient
			ils	ont	découvert		
Future			elles	ont	découvert	Pluperfect	
je	découvrirai					j'	avais	découvert
tu	découvriras		Past participle			tu	avais	découvert
il	découvrira		découvert/			il	avait	découvert
nous	découvrirons		découverte			elle	avait	découvert
vous	découvrirez					nous	avions	découvert
ils	découvriront		Present subjunctive			vous	aviez	découvert
Imperfect			(que) je	découvre		ils	avaient découvert
je	découvrais		(que) tu	découvres		elles	avaient découvert
tu	découvrais		(qu') il	découvre			
il	découvrait		(que) nous	découvrions			
nous	découvrions		(que) vous	découvriez			
vous	découvriez		(qu') ils	découvrent			
ils	découvraient						

33 pleuvoir

Present		Perfect			Conditional	
il	pleut	il	a	plu	il	pleuvrait
ils	pleuvent	ils	ont	plu	ils	pleuvraient

Future		Past participle	Pluperfect		
il	pleuvra	plu	il	avait	plu
ils	pleuvront		ils	avaient	plu

Imperfect		Present subjunctive	
il	pleuvait	(qu') il	pleuve
ils	pleuvaient	(qu') ils	pleuvent

34 asseoir

Present		Perfect			Conditional	
j'	assieds	j'	ai	assis	j'	assiérais
tu	as sieds	tu	as	assis	tu	assiérais
il	assied	il	a	assis	il	assiérait
nous	asseyons	elle	a	assis	nous	assiérions
vous	asseyez				vous	assiériez
ils	asseyent	nous	avons	assis	ils	assiéraient
		vous	avez	assis		
		ils	ont	assis		

Future					Pluperfect		
j'	assiérai	elles	ont	assis	j'	avais	assis
tu	assiéras				tu	avais	assis
il	assiéra	Past participle			il	avait	assis
nous	assiérons	assis/assise			elle	avait	assis
vous	assiérez				nous	avions	assis
ils	assiéront	Present subjunctive			vous	aviez	assis
		(que) j'	asseye		ils	avaient	assis
Imperfect		(que) tu	asseyes		elles	avaient	assis
j'	asseyais	(qu') il	asseye				
tu	asseyais						
il	asseyait	(que) nous	asseyions				
		(que) vous	asseyiez				
nous	asseyions	(qu') ils	asseyent				
vous	asseyiez						
ils	asseyaient						

35 prévoir

Present		Perfect			Conditional	
je	prévois	j'	ai	prévu	je	prévoirais
tu	prévois	tu	as	prévu	tu	prévoirais
il	prévoit	il	a	prévu	il	prévoirait
		elle	a	prévu		
nous	prévoyons				nous	prévoirions
vous	prévoyez	nous	avons	prévu	vous	prévoiriez
ils	prévoient	vous	avez	prévu	ils	prévoiraient
		ils	ont	prévu		

Future		Perfect (elles)			Pluperfect		
je	prévoirai	elles	ont	prévu	j'	avais	prévu
tu	prévoiras				tu	avais	prévu
il	prévoira	**Past participle**			il	avait	prévu
		prévu/prévue			elle	avait	prévu
nous	prévoirons						
vous	prévoirez	**Present subjunctive**			nous	avions	prévu
ils	prévoiront	(que)	je	prévoie	vous	aviez	prévu
		(que)	tu	prévoies	ils	avaient	prévu
Imperfect		(qu')	il	prévoie	elles	avaient	prévu
je	prévoyais						
tu	prévoyais	(que)	nous	prévoyions			
il	prévoyait	(que)	vous	prévoyiez			
		(qu')	ils	prévoient			
nous	prévoyions						
vous	prévoyiez						
ils	prévoyaient						

36 devenir

Present		Perfect			Conditional	
je	deviens	je	suis	devenu	je	deviendrais
tu	deviens	tu	es	devenu	tu	deviendrais
il	devient	il	est	devenu	il	deviendrait
		elle	est	devenue		
nous	devenons				nous	deviendrions
vous	devenez	nous	sommes	devenus	vous	deviendriez
ils	deviennent	vous	êtes	devenus	ils	deviendraient
		ils	sont	devenus		

Future		Perfect (elles)			Pluperfect		
je	deviendrai	elles	sont	devenues	j'	étais	devenu
tu	deviendras				tu	étais	devenu
il	deviendra	**Past participle**			il	était	devenu
		devenu/devenue			elle	était	devenue
nous	deviendrons						
vous	deviendrez	**Present subjunctive**			nous	étions	devenus
ils	deviendront	(que)	je	devienne	vous	étiez	devenus
		(que)	tu	deviennes	ils	étaient	devenus
Imperfect		(qu')	il	devienne	elles	étaient	devenues
je	devenais						
tu	devenais	(que)	nous	devenions			
il	devenait	(que)	vous	deveniez			
		(qu')	ils	deviennent			
nous	devenions						
vous	deveniez						
ils	devenaient						

37 suivre

Present		Perfect			Conditional	
je	suis	j'	ai	suivi	je	suivrais
tu	suis	tu	as	suivi	tu	suivrais
il	suit	il	a	suivi	il	suivrait
nous	suivons	elle	a	suivi	nous	suivrions
vous	suivez				vous	suivriez
ils	suivent	nous	avons	suivi	ils	suivraient
		vous	avez	suivi		
		ils	ont	suivi		
Future		elles	ont	suivi	Pluperfect	
je	suivrai				j'	avais	suivi
tu	suivras	Past participle			tu	avais	suivi
il	suivra	suivi/suivie			il	avait	suivi
nous	suivrons				elle	avait	suivi
vous	suivrez	Present subjunctive			nous	avions	suivi
ils	suivront	(que) je	suive		vous	aviez	suivi
		(que) tu	suives		ils	avaient	suivi
Imperfect		(qu') il	suive		elles	avaient	suivi
je	suivais					
tu	suivais	(que) nous	suivions			
il	suivait	(que) vous	suiviez			
nous	suivions	(qu') ils	suivent			
vous	suiviez					
ils	suivaient					

38 vivre

Present		Perfect			Conditional	
je	vis	j'	ai	vécu	je	vivrais
tu	vis	tu	as	vécu	tu	vivrais
il	vit	il	a	vécu	il	vivrait
nous	vivons	elle	a	vécu	nous	vivrions
vous	vivez				vous	vivriez
ils	vivent	nous	avons	vécu	ils	vivraient
		vous	avez	vécu		
		ils	ont	vécu		
Future		elles	ont	vécu	Pluperfect	
je	vivrai				j'	avais	vécu
tu	vivras	Past participle			tu	avais	vécu
il	vivra	vécu/vécue			il	avait	vécu
nous	vivrons				elle	avait	vécu
vous	vivrez	Present subjunctive			nous	avions	vécu
ils	vivront	(que) je	vive		vous	aviez	vécu
		(que) tu	vives		ils	avaient	vécu
Imperfect		(qu') il	vive		elles	avaient	vécu
je	vivais					
tu	vivais	(que) nous	vivions			
il	vivait	(que) vous	viviez			
nous	vivions	(qu') ils	vivent			
vous	viviez					
ils	vivaient					

39 suffire

Present	
je	suffis
tu	suffis
il	suffit
nous	suffisons
vous	suffisez
ils	suffisent

Future	
je	suffirai
tu	suffiras
il	suffira
nous	suffirons
vous	suffirez
ils	suffiront

Imperfect	
je	suffisais
tu	suffisais
il	suffisait
nous	suffisions
vous	suffisiez
ils	suffisaient

Perfect		
j'	ai	suffi
tu	as	suffi
il	a	suffi
elle	a	suffi
nous	avons	suffi
vous	avez	suffi
ils	ont	suffi
elles	ont	suffi

Past participle
suffi

Present subjunctive
(que)	je	suffise
(que)	tu	suffises
(qu')	il	suffise
(que)	nous	suffisions
(que)	vous	suffisiez
(qu')	ils	suffisent

Conditional
je	suffirais
tu	suffirais
il	suffirait
nous	suffirions
vous	suffiriez
ils	suffiraient

Pluperfect
j'	avais	suffi
tu	avais	suffi
il	avait	suffi
elle	avait	suffi
nous	avions	suffi
vous	aviez	suffi
ils	avaient	suffi
elles	avaient	suffi

40 dire

Present	
je	dis
tu	dis
il	dit
nous	disons
vous	dites*
ils	disent

Future	
je	dirai
tu	diras
il	dira
nous	dirons
vous	direz
ils	diront

Imperfect	
je	disais
tu	disais
il	disait
nous	disions
vous	disiez
ils	disaient

Perfect		
j'	ai	dit
tu	as	dit
il	a	dit
elle	a	dit
nous	avons	dit
vous	avez	dit
ils	ont	dit
elles	ont	dit

Past participle
dit/dite

Present subjunctive
(que)	je	dise
(que)	tu	dises
(qu')	il	dise
(que)	nous	disions
(que)	vous	disiez
(qu')	ils	disent

Conditional
je	dirais
tu	dirais
il	dirait
nous	dirions
vous	diriez
ils	diraient

Pluperfect
j'	avais	dit
tu	avais	dit
il	avait	dit
elle	avait	dit
nous	avions	dit
vous	aviez	dit
ils	avaient	dit
elles	avaient	dit

* vous interdisez

41 lire

Present

je	lis
tu	lis
il	lit
nous	lisons
vous	lisez
ils	lisent

Future

je	lirai
tu	liras
il	lira
nous	lirons
vous	lirez
ils	liront

Imperfect

je	lisais
tu	lisais
il	lisait
nous	lisions
vous	lisiez
ils	lisaient

Perfect

j'	ai	lu
tu	as	lu
il	a	lu
elle	a	lu
nous	avons	lu
vous	avez	lu
ils	ont	lu
elles	ont	lu

Past participle

lu/lue

Present subjunctive

(que)	je	lise
(que)	tu	lises
(qu')	il	lise
(que)	nous	lisions
(que)	vous	lisiez
(qu')	ils	lisent

Conditional

je	lirais
tu	lirais
il	lirait
nous	lirions
vous	liriez
ils	liraient

Pluperfect

j'	avais	lu
tu	avais	lu
il	avait	lu
elle	avait	lu
nous	avions	lu
vous	aviez	lu
ils	avaient	lu
elles	avaient	lu

42 écrire

Present

j'	écris
tu	écris
il	écrit
nous	écrivons
vous	écrivez
ils	écrivent

Future

j'	écrirai
tu	écriras
il	écrira
nous	écrirons
vous	écrirez
ils	écriront

Imperfect

j'	écrivais
tu	écrivais
il	écrivait
nous	écrivions
vous	écriviez
ils	écrivaient

Perfect

j'	ai	écrit
tu	as	écrit
il	a	écrit
elle	a	écrit
nous	avons	écrit
vous	avez	écrit
ils	ont	écrit
elles	ont	écrit

Past participle

écrit/écrite

Present subjunctive

(que)	j'	écrive
(que)	tu	écrives
(qu')	il	écrive
(que)	nous	écrivions
(que)	vous	écriviez
(qu')	ils	écrivent

Conditional

j'	écrirais
tu	écrirais
il	écrirait
nous	écririons
vous	écririez
ils	écriraient

Pluperfect

j'	avais	écrit
tu	avais	écrit
il	avait	écrit
elle	avait	écrit
nous	avions	écrit
vous	aviez	écrit
ils	avaient	écrit
elles	avaient	écrit

43 rire

Present		
je	ris	
tu	ris	
il	rit	
nous	rions	
vous	riez	
ils	rient	

Future	
je	rirai
tu	riras
il	rira
nous	rirons
vous	rirez
ils	riront

Imperfect	
je	riais
tu	riais
il	riait
nous	riions
vous	riiez
ils	riaient

Perfect		
j'	ai	ri
tu	as	ri
il	a	ri
elle	a	ri
nous	avons	ri
vous	avez	ri
ils	ont	ri
elles	ont	ri

Past participle

ri

Present subjunctive

(que)	je	rie
(que)	tu	ries
(qu')	il	rie
(que)	nous	riions
(que)	vous	riiez
(qu')	ils	rient

Conditional	
je	rirais
tu	rirais
il	rirait
nous	ririons
vous	ririez
ils	riraient

Pluperfect		
j'	avais	ri
tu	avais	ri
il	avait	ri
elle	avait	ri
nous	avions	ri
vous	aviez	ri
ils	avaient	ri
elles	avaient	ri

44 devoir

Present		
je	dois	
tu	dois	
il	doit	
nous	devons	
vous	devez	
ils	doivent	

Future	
je	devrai
tu	devras
il	devra
nous	devrons
vous	devrez
ils	devront

Imperfect	
je	devais
tu	devais
il	devait
nous	devions
vous	deviez
ils	devaient

Perfect		
j'	ai	dû
tu	as	dû
il	a	dû
elle	a	dû
nous	avons	dû
vous	avez	dû
ils	ont	dû
elles	ont	dû

Past participle

dû/due

Present subjunctive

(que)	je	doive
(que)	tu	doives
(qu')	il	doive
(que)	nous	devions
(que)	vous	deviez
(qu')	ils	doivent

Conditional	
je	devrais
tu	devrais
il	devrait
nous	devrions
vous	devriez
ils	devraient

Pluperfect		
j'	avais	dû
tu	avais	dû
il	avait	dû
elle	avait	dû
nous	avions	dû
vous	aviez	dû
ils	avaient	dû
elles	avaient	dû

45 valoir

Present		
je	vaux	
tu	vaux	
il	vaut	
nous	valons	
vous	valez	
ils	valent	

Future		
je	vaudrai	
tu	vaudras	
il	vaudra	
nous	vaudrons	
vous	vaudrez	
ils	vaudront	

Imperfect		
je	valais	
tu	valais	
il	valait	
nous	valions	
vous	valiez	
ils	valaient	

Perfect		
j'	ai	valu
tu	as	valu
il	a	valu
elle	a	valu
nous	avons	valu
vous	avez	valu
ils	ont	valu
elles	ont	valu

Past participle
valu/value

Present subjunctive

(que)	je	vaille
(que)	tu	vailles
(qu')	il	vaille
(que)	nous	valions
(que)	vous	valiez
(qu')	ils	vaillent

Conditional		
je	vaudrais	
tu	vaudrais	
il	vaudrait	
nous	vaudrions	
vous	vaudriez	
ils	vaudraient	

Pluperfect

j'	avais	valu
tu	avais	valu
il	avait	valu
elle	avait	valu
nous	avions	valu
vous	aviez	valu
ils	avaient	valu
elles	avaient	valu

46 voir

Present		
je	vois	
tu	vois	
il	voit	
nous	voyons	
vous	voyez	
ils	voient	

Future		
je	verrai	
tu	verras	
il	verra	
nous	verrons	
vous	verrez	
ils	verront	

Imperfect		
je	voyais	
tu	voyais	
il	voyait	
nous	voyions	
vous	voyiez	
ils	voyaient	

Perfect		
j'	ai	vu
tu	as	vu
il	a	vu
elle	a	vu
nous	avons	vu
vous	avez	vu
ils	ont	vu
elles	ont	vu

Past participle
vu/vue

Present subjunctive

(que)	je	voie
(que)	tu	voies
(qu')	il	voie
(que)	nous	voyions
(que)	vous	voyiez
(qu')	ils	voient

Conditional		
je	verrais	
tu	verrais	
il	verrait	
nous	verrions	
vous	verriez	
ils	verraient	

Pluperfect

j'	avais	vu
tu	avais	vu
il	avait	vu
elle	avait	vu
nous	avions	vu
vous	aviez	vu
ils	avaient	vu
elles	avaient	vu

47 savoir

Present	
je	sais
tu	sais
il	sait
nous	savons
vous	savez
ils	savent

Future	
je	saurai
tu	sauras
il	saura
nous	saurons
vous	saurez
ils	sauront

Imperfect	
je	savais
tu	savais
il	savait
nous	savions
vous	saviez
ils	savaient

Perfect		
j'	ai	su
tu	as	su
il	a	su
elle	a	su
nous	avons	su
vous	avez	su
ils	ont	su
elles	ont	su

Past participle
su/sue

Present subjunctive
(que) je	sache
(que) tu	saches
(qu') il	sache
(que) nous	sachions
(que) vous	sachiez
(qu') ils	sachent

Conditional	
je	saurais
tu	saurais
il	saurait
nous	saurions
vous	sauriez
ils	sauraient

Pluperfect		
j'	avais	su
tu	avais	su
il	avait	su
elle	avait	su
nous	avions	su
vous	aviez	su
ils	avaient	su
elles	avaient	su

48 vouloir

Present	
je	veux
tu	veux
il	veut
nous	voulons
vous	voulez
ils	veulent

Future	
je	voudrai
tu	voudras
il	voudra
nous	voudrons
vous	voudrez
ils	voudront

Imperfect	
je	voulais
tu	voulais
il	voulait
nous	voulions
vous	vouliez
ils	voulaient

Perfect		
j'	ai	voulu
tu	as	voulu
il	a	voulu
elle	a	voulu
nous	avons	voulu
vous	avez	voulu
ils	ont	voulu
elles	ont	voulu

Past participle
voulu/voulue

Present subjunctive
(que) je	veuille
(que) tu	veuilles
(qu') il	veuille
(que) nous	voulions
(que) vous	vouliez
(qu') ils	veuillent

Conditional	
je	voudrais
tu	voudrais
il	voudrait
nous	voudrions
vous	voudriez
ils	voudraient

Pluperfect		
j'	avais	voulu
tu	avais	voulu
il	avait	voulu
elle	avait	voulu
nous	avions	voulu
vous	aviez	voulu
ils	avaient	voulu
elles	avaient	voulu

49 pouvoir

Present		Perfect			Conditional	
je	peux	j'	ai	pu	je	pourrais
tu	peux	tu	as	pu	tu	pourrais
il	peut	il	a	pu	il	pourrait
nous	pouvons	elle	a	pu	nous	pourrions
vous	pouvez				vous	pourriez
ils	peuvent	nous	avons	pu	ils	pourraient
		vous	avez	pu		
		ils	ont	pu		

Future		Perfect (cont.)			Pluperfect		
je	pourrai	elles	ont	pu	j'	avais	pu
tu	pourras				tu	avais	pu
il	pourra	**Past participle**			il	avait	pu
nous	pourrons	pu			elle	avait	pu
vous	pourrez				nous	avions	pu
ils	pourront				vous	aviez	pu

Present subjunctive

Imperfect						
je	pouvais	(que) je	puisse	ils	avaient	pu
tu	pouvais	(que) tu	puisses	elles	avaient	pu
il	pouvait	(qu') il	puisse			
nous	pouvions	(que) nous	puissions			
vous	pouviez	(que) vous	puissiez			
ils	pouvaient	(qu') ils	puissent			

50 falloir

Present		Perfect			Conditional	
il	faut	il	a	fallu	il	faudrait

Future		Past participle	Pluperfect		
il	faudra	fallu	il	avait	fallu

Imperfect		Present subjunctive	
il	fallait	(qu') il	faille

51 boire

Present		Perfect			Conditional	
je	bois	j'	ai	bu	je	boirais
tu	bois	tu	as	bu	tu	boirais
il	boit	il	a	bu	il	boirait
nous	buvons	elle	a	bu		
vous	buvez				nous	boirions
ils	boivent	nous	avons	bu	vous	boiriez
		vous	avez	bu	ils	boiraient

Future		Past participle	Pluperfect		
je	boirai	bu/bue	j'	avais	bu
tu	boiras		tu	avais	bu
il	boira		il	avait	bu
nous	boirons	**Present subjunctive**	elle	avait	bu
vous	boirez				
ils	boiront	(que) je boive	nous	avions	bu

Imperfect		(que) tu boives	vous	aviez	bu
je	buvais	(qu') il boive	ils	avaient	bu
tu	buvais		elles	avaient	bu
il	buvait	(que) nous buvions			
nous	buvions	(que) vous buviez			
vous	buviez	(qu') ils boivent			
ils	buvaient				

Perfect:
j' ai bu
tu as bu
il a bu
elle a bu
nous avons bu
vous avez bu
ils ont bu
elles ont bu

Past participle: bu/bue

Present subjunctive:
(que) je boive
(que) tu boives
(qu') il boive
(que) nous buvions
(que) vous buviez
(qu') ils boivent

---

52 comprendre

Present		Perfect			Conditional	
je	comprends	j'	ai	compris	je	comprendrais
tu	comprends	tu	as	compris	tu	comprendrais
il	comprend	il	a	compris	il	comprendrait
nous	comprenons	elle	a	compris		
vous	comprenez	nous	avons	compris	nous	comprendrions
ils	comprennent	vous	avez	compris	vous	comprendriez
		ils	ont	compris	ils	comprendraient
		elles	ont	compris		

Future		Past participle	Pluperfect		
je	comprendrai	compris/comprise	j'	avais	compris
tu	comprendras		tu	avais	compris
il	comprendra		il	avait	compris
nous	comprendrons	**Present subjunctive**	elle	avait	compris
vous	comprendrez	(que) je comprenne	nous	avions	compris
ils	comprendront	(que) tu comprennes	vous	aviez	compris
		(qu') il comprenne	ils	avaient	compris

Imperfect			elles	avaient	compris
je	comprenais	(que) nous comprenions			
tu	comprenais	(que) vous compreniez			
il	comprenait	(qu') ils comprennent			
nous	comprenions				
vous	compreniez				
ils	comprenaient				

53 croire

Present		Perfect			Conditional	
je	crois	j'	ai	cru	je	croirais
tu	crois	tu	as	cru	tu	croirais
il	croit	il	a	cru	il	croirait
nous	croyons	elle	a	cru	nous	croirions
vous	croyez	nous	avons	cru	vous	croirioz
ils	croient	vous	avez	cru	ils	croiraient
		ils	ont	cru		
Future		elles	ont	cru		
je	croirai				**Pluperfect**	
tu	croiras	**Past participle**			j'	avais	cru
il	croira	cru/crue			tu	avais	cru
nous	croirons				il	avait	cru
vous	croirez				elle	avait	cru
ils	croiront	**Present subjunctive**			nous	avions	cru
		(que) je	croie		vous	aviez	cru
Imperfect		(que) tu	croies		ils	avaient	cru
je	croyais	(qu') il	croie		elles	avaient	cru
tu	croyais					
il	croyait	(que) nous	croyions			
nous	croyions	(que) vous	croyiez			
vous	croyiez	(qu') ils	croient			
ils	croyaient					

54 plaindre

Present		Perfect			Conditional	
je	plains	j'	ai	plaint	je	plaindrais
tu	plains	tu	as	plaint	tu	plaindrais
il	plaint	il	a	plaint	il	plaindrait
nous	plaignons	elle	a	plaint	nous	plaindrions
vous	plaignez	nous	avons	plaint	vous	plaindriez
ils	plaignent	vous	avez	plaint	ils	plaindraient
		ils	ont	plaint		
Future		elles	ont	plaint		
je	plaindrai				**Pluperfect**	
tu	plaindras	**Past participle**			j'	avais	plaint
il	plaindra	plaint/plainte			tu	avais	plaint
nous	plaindrons				il	avait	plaint
vous	plaindrez				elle	avait	plaint
ils	plaindront	**Present subjunctive**			nous	avions	plaint
		(que) je	plaigne		vous	aviez	plaint
Imperfect		(que) tu	plaignes		ils	avaient	plaint
je	plaignais	(qu') il	plaigne		elles	avaient	plaint
tu	plaignais					
il	plaignait	(que) nous	plaignions			
nous	plaignions	(que) vous	plaigniez			
vous	plaigniez	(qu') ils	plaignent			
ils	plaignaient					

55 éteindre

Present		Perfect			Conditional	
j'	éteins	j'	ai	éteint	j'	éteindrais
tu	éteins	tu	as	éteint	tu	éteindrais
il	éteint	il	a	éteint	il	éteindrait
nous	éteignons	elle	a	éteint	nous	éteindrions
vous	éteignez				vous	éteindriez
ils	éteignent	nous	avons	éteint	ils	éteindraient
		vous	avez	éteint		
Future		ils	ont	éteint		
j'	éteindrai	elles	ont	éteint	Pluperfect	
tu	éteindras				j'	avais	éteint
il	éteindra	Past participle			tu	avais	éteint
nous	éteindrons		éteint/éteinte		il	avait	éteint
vous	éteindrez				elle	avait	éteint
ils	éteindront	Present subjunctive			nous	avions	éteint
		(que)	j'	éteigne	vous	aviez	éteint
Imperfect		(que)	tu	éteignes	ils	avaient	éteint
j'	éteignais	(qu')	il	éteigne	elles	avaient	éteint
tu	éteignais					
il	éteignait	(que)	nous	éteignions		
nous	éteignions	(que)	vous	éteigniez		
vous	éteigniez	(qu')	ils	éteignent		
ils	éteignaient					

56 joindre

Present		Perfect			Conditional	
je	joins	j'	ai	joint	je	joindrais
tu	joins	tu	as	joint	tu	joindrais
il	joint	il	a	joint	il	joindrait
nous	joignons	elle	a	joint	nous	joindrions
vous	joignez				vous	joindriez
ils	joignent	nous	avons	joint	ils	joindraient
		vous	avez	joint		
Future		ils	ont	joint		
je	joindrai	elles	ont	joint	Pluperfect	
tu	joindras				j'	avais	joint
il	joindra	Past participle			tu	avais	joint
nous	joindrons		joint/jointe		il	avait	joint
vous	joindrez				elle	avait	joint
ils	joindront	Present subjunctive			nous	avions	joint
		(que)	je	joigne	vous	aviez	joint
Imperfect		(que)	tu	joignes	ils	avaient	joint
je	joignais	(qu')	il	joigne	elles	avaient	joint
tu	joignais					
il	joignait	(que)	nous	joignions		
nous	joignions	(que)	vous	joigniez		
vous	joigniez	(qu')	ils	joignent		
ils	joignaient					

57 vaincre

Present	
je	vaincs
tu	vaincs
il	vainc
nous	vainquons
vous	vainquez
ils	vainquent

Future	
je	vaincrai
tu	vaincras
il	vaincra
nous	vaincrons
vous	vaincrez
ils	vaincront

Imperfect	
je	vainquais
tu	vainquais
il	vainquait
nous	vainquions
vous	vainquiez
ils	vainquaient

Perfect		
j'	ai	vaincu
tu	as	vaincu
il	a	vaincu
elle	a	vaincu
nous	avons	vaincu
vous	avez	vaincu
ils	ont	vaincu
elles	ont	vaincu

Past participle

vaincu/vaincue

Present subjunctive		
(que)	je	vainque
(que)	tu	vainques
(qu')	il	vainque
(que)	nous	vainquions
(que)	vous	vainquiez
(qu')	ils	vainquent

Conditional	
je	vaincrais
tu	vaincrais
il	vaincrait
nous	vaincrions
vous	vaincriez
Ils	vaincraient

Pluperfect		
j'	avais	vaincu
tu	avais	vaincu
il	avait	vaincu
elle	avait	vaincu
nous	avions	vaincu
vous	aviez	vaincu
ils	avaient	vaincu
elles	avaient	vaincu

58 distraire

Present	
je	distrais
tu	distrais
il	distrait
nous	distrayons
vous	distrayez
ils	distraient

Future	
je	distrairai
tu	distrairas
il	distraira
nous	distrairons
vous	distrairez
ils	distrairont

Imperfect	
je	distrayais
tu	distrayais
il	distrayait
nous	distrayions
vous	distraylez
ils	distrayaient

Perfect		
j'	ai	distrait
tu	as	distrait
il	a	distrait
elle	a	distrait
nous	avons	distrait
vous	avez	distrait
ils	ont	distrait
elles	ont	distrait

Past participle

distrait/distraite

Present subjunctive		
(que)	je	distraie
(que)	tu	distraies
(qu')	il	distraie
(que)	nous	distrayions
(que)	vous	distrayiez
(qu')	ils	distraient

Conditional	
je	distrairais
tu	distrairais
il	distrairait
nous	distrairions
vous	distrairiez
ils	distrairaient

Pluperfect		
j'	avais	distrait
tu	avais	distrait
il	avait	distrait
elle	avait	distrait
nous	avions	distrait
vous	aviez	distrait
ils	avaient	distrait
elles	avaient	distrait

59 plaire

Present			Perfect			Conditional		
je	plais		j'	ai	plu	je	plairais	
tu	plais		tu	as	plu	tu	plairais	
il	plaît		il	a	plu	il	plairait	
nous	plaisons		elle	a	plu			
vous	plaisez					nous	plairions	
ils	plaisent		nous	avons	plu	vous	plairiez	
			vous	avez	plu	ils	plairaient	
Future			ils	ont	plu			
je	plairai		elles	ont	plu	**Pluperfect**		
tu	plairas					j'	avais	plu
il	plaira		**Past participle**			tu	avais	plu
			plu/plue			il	avait	plu
nous	plairons					elle	avait	plu
vous	plairez		**Present subjunctive**					
ils	plairont		(que) je	plaise		nous	avions	plu
			(que) tu	plaises		vous	aviez	plu
Imperfect			(qu') il	plaise		ils	avaient	plu
je	plaisais					elles	avaient	plu
tu	plaisais		(que) nous	plaisions				
il	plaisait		(que) vous	plaisiez				
			(qu') ils	plaisent				
nous	plaisions							
vous	plaisiez							
ils	plaisaient							

60 mettre

Present			Perfect			Conditional		
je	mets		j'	ai	mis	je	mettrais	
tu	mets		tu	as	mis	tu	mettrais	
il	met		il	a	mis	il	mettrait	
nous	mettons		elle	a	mis			
vous	mettez					nous	mettrions	
ils	mettent		nous	avons	mis	vous	mettriez	
			vous	avez	mis	ils	mettraient	
Future			ils	ont	mis			
je	mettrai		elles	ont	mis	**Pluperfect**		
tu	mettras					j'	avais	mis
il	mettra		**Past participle**			tu	avais	mis
			mis/mise			il	avait	mis
nous	mettrons					elle	avait	mis
vous	mettrez		**Present subjunctive**					
ils	mettront		(que) je	mette		nous	avions	mis
			(que) tu	mettes		vous	aviez	mis
Imperfect			(qu') il	mette		ils	avaient	mis
je	mettais					elles	avaient	mis
tu	mettais		(que) nous	mettions				
il	mettait		(que) vous	mettiez				
			(qu') ils	mettent				
nous	mettions							
vous	mettiez							
ils	mettaient							

61 battre

Present		Perfect			Conditional	
je	bats	j'	ai	battu	je	battrais
tu	bats	tu	as	battu	tu	battrais
il	bat	il	a	battu	il	battrait
nous	battons	elle	a	battu		
vous	battez				nous	battrions
ils	battent	nous	avons	battu	vous	battriez
		vous	avez	battu	ils	battraient
		ils	ont	battu		
Future		elles	ont	battu	**Pluperfect**	
je	battrai				j'	avais	battu
tu	battras	**Past participle**			tu	avais	battu
il	battra		battu/battue		il	avait	battu
nous	battrons				elle	avait	battu
vous	battrez	**Present subjunctive**				
ils	battront	(que)	je	batte	nous	avons	battu
		(que)	tu	battes	vous	aviez	battu
Imperfect		(qu')	il	batte	ils	avaient	battu
je	battais				elles	avaient	battu
tu	battais	(que)	nous	battions		
il	battait	(que)	vous	battiez		
nous	battions	(qu')	ils	battent		
vous	battiez					
ils	battaient					

62 traduire

Present		Perfect			Conditional	
je	traduis	j'	ai	traduit	je	traduirais
tu	traduis	tu	as	traduit	tu	traduirais
il	traduit	il	a	traduit	il	traduirait
nous	traduisons	elle	a	traduit		
vous	traduisez				nous	traduirions
ils	traduisent	nous	avons	traduit	vous	traduiriez
		vous	avez	traduit	ils	traduiraient
		ils	ont	traduit		
Future		elles	ont	traduit	**Pluperfect**	
je	traduirai				j'	avais	traduit
tu	traduiras	**Past participle**			tu	avais	traduit
il	traduira		traduit/traduite		il	avait	traduit
nous	traduirons				elle	avait	traduit
vous	traduirez	**Present subjunctive**				
ils	traduiront	(que)	je	traduise	nous	avons	traduit
		(que)	tu	traduises	vous	aviez	traduit
Imperfect		(qu')	il	traduise	ils	avaient	traduit
je	traduisais				elles	avaient	traduit
tu	traduisais	(que)	nous	traduisions		
il	traduisait	(que)	vous	traduisiez		
nous	traduisions	(qu')	ils	traduisent		
vous	traduisiez					
ils	traduisaient					

63 connaître

Present		Perfect			Conditional	
je	connais	j'	ai	connu	je	connaîtrais
tu	connais	tu	as	connu	tu	connaîtrais
il	connaît	il	a	connu	il	connaîtrait
		elle	a	connu		
nous	connaissons				nous	connaîtrions
vous	connaissez	nous	avons	connu	vous	connaîtriez
ils	connaissent	vous	avez	connu	ils	connaîtraient
		ils	ont	connu		

Future			Pluperfect		
je	connaîtrai		j'	avais	connu
tu	connaîtras	**Past participle**	tu	avais	connu
il	connaîtra	connu/connue	il	avait	connu
			elle	avait	connu
nous	connaîtrons				
vous	connaîtrez	**Present subjunctive**	nous	avions	connu
ils	connaîtront	(que) je	connaisse	vous	aviez	connu

Imperfect						
je	connaissais	(que) je	connaisse	ils	avaient	connu
tu	connaissais	(que) tu	connaisses	elles	avaient	connu
il	connaissait	(qu') il	connaisse			
nous	connaissions	(que) nous	connaissions			
vous	connaissiez	(que) vous	connaissiez			
ils	connaissaient	(qu') ils	connaissent			

64 naître

Present		Perfect			Conditional	
je	nais	je	suis	né	je	naîtrais
tu	nais	tu	es	né	tu	naîtrais
il	naît	il	est	né	il	naîtrait
		elle	est	née		
nous	naissons				nous	naîtrions
vous	naissez	nous	sommes	nés	vous	naîtriez
ils	naissent	vous	êtes	nés	ils	naîtraient
		ils	sont	nés		
		elles	sont	nées		

Future			Pluperfect		
je	naîtrai		j'	étais	né
tu	naîtras	**Past participle**	tu	étais	né
il	naîtra	né/née	il	était	né
			elle	était	née
nous	naîtrons				
vous	naîtrez	**Present subjunctive**	nous	étions	nés
ils	naîtront	(que) je	naisse	vous	étiez	nés
		(que) tu	naisses	ils	étaient	nés
		(qu') il	naisse	elles	étaient	nées

Imperfect			
je	naissais	(que) nous	naissions
tu	naissais	(que) vous	naissiez
il	naissait	(qu') ils	naissent
nous	naissions		
vous	naissiez		
ils	naissaient		

65 résoudre

Present		Perfect			Conditional	
je	résous	j'	ai	résolu	je	résoudrais
tu	résous	tu	as	résolu	tu	résoudrais
il	résout	il	a	résolu	il	résoudrait
nous	résolvons	elle	a	résolu		
vous	résolvez				nous	résoudrions
ils	résolvent	nous	avons	résolu	vous	résoudriez
		vous	avez	résolu	ils	résoudraient
Future		ils	ont	résolu		
je	résoudrai	elles	ont	résolu	**Pluperfect**	
tu	résoudras				j'	avais	résolu
il	résoudra	**Past participle**			tu	avais	résolu
nous	résoudrons		résolu/résolue		il	avait	résolu
vous	résoudrez				elle	avait	résolu
ils	résoudront	**Present subjunctive**				
		(que) je	résolve		nous	avions	résolu
Imperfect		(que) tu	résolves		vous	aviez	résolu
je	résolvais	(qu') il	résolve		ils	avaient	résolu
tu	résolvais				elles	avaient	résolu
il	résolvait	(que) nous	résolvions			
nous	résolvions	(que) vous	résolviez			
vous	résolviez	(qu') ils	résolvent			
ils	résolvaient					

66 coudre

Present		Perfect			Conditional	
je	couds	j'	ai	cousu	je	coudrais
tu	couds	tu	as	cousu	tu	coudrais
il	coud	il	a	cousu	il	coudrait
nous	cousons	elle	a	cousu		
vous	cousez				nous	coudrions
ils	cousent	nous	avons	cousu	vous	coudriez
		vous	avez	cousu	ils	coudraient
Future		ils	ont	cousu		
je	coudrai	elles	ont	cousu	**Pluperfect**	
tu	coudras				j'	avais	cousu
il	coudra	**Past participle**			tu	avais	cousu
nous	coudrons		cousu/cousue		il	avait	cousu
vous	coudrez				elle	avait	cousu
ils	coudront	**Present subjunctive**				
		(que) je	couse		nous	avions	cousu
Imperfect		(que) tu	couses		vous	aviez	cousu
je	cousais	(qu') il	couse		ils	avaient	cousu
tu	cousais				elles	avaient	cousu
il	cousait	(que) nous	cousions			
nous	cousions	(que) vous	cousiez			
vous	cousiez	(qu') ils	cousent			
ils	cousaient					

Numbers

Cardinal numbers in French

0	zéro*	80	quatre-vingts‡§
1	un†	81	quatre-vingt-un¶
2	deux	82	quatre-vingt-deux
3	trois	90	quatre-vingt-dix‡
4	quatre	91	quatre-vingt-onze
5	cinq	92	quatre-vingt-douze
6	six	99	quatre-vingt-dix-neuf
7	sept	100	cent
8	huit	101	cent un†
9	neuf	102	cent deux
10	dix	110	cent dix
11	onze	187	cent quatre-vingt-sept
12	douze	200	deux cents
13	treize	250	deux cent◊ cinquante
14	quatorze	1 000◻ mille
15	quinze	1 001	mille un†
16	seize	1 002	mille deux
17	dix-sept	1 020	mille vingt
18	dix-huit	1 200	mille** deux cents
19	dix-neuf	2 000	deux mille††
20	vingt	10 000	dix mille
21	vingt et un	100 000	cent mille
22	vingt-deux	100 200	cent deux mille
30	trente	1 000 000	un million‡‡
40	quarante	1 264 932	un million deux cent
50	cinquante		soixante-quatre mille
60	soixante		neuf cent trente-deux
70	soixante-dix‡	1 000 000 000	un milliard‡‡
71	soixante et onze	1 000 000 000 000	un billion‡‡

* In English *0* may be called *nought, zero, nil* or even *nothing*; French is always *zéro*: **a nought = un zéro**.

† **one is une** in French when it agrees with a feminine noun, so *un crayon* but *une table, des tables, vingt et une tables*, etc.

‡ (70) Also **septante** in Belgium and Switzerland. (80) Also **octante** in Switzerland and Canada, **huitante** in Switzerland. (90) Also **nonante** in Belgium and Switzerland.

§ Note that when *80* is used as a page number it has no *s*: **page eighty = page quatre-vingt**.

¶ **vingt** has no *s* when it is in the middle of a number. The only exception to this rule is when *quatre-vingts* is followed by *millions, milliards* or *billions*, e.g. **quatre-vingts millions, quatre-vingts billions** etc.

◊ **cent** does not take an *s* when it is in the middle of a number. The only exception to this rule is when it is followed by *millions, six cents billions* etc. It has a normal plural when it modifies other nouns: **200 inhabitants = deux cents habitants**.

◻ Where English would have a comma, French has simply a space. A full stop (period) can be used, e.g. **1.000**. As in English, there is no separation in dates between thousands and hundreds: **in 1995 = en 1995**.

In dates, the spelling **mil is preferred to **mille**, i.e. **en 1200 = en mil deux cents**. However, when the year is a round number of thousands, the spelling is always **mille**, so **en l'an mille, en l'an deux mille** etc.

††**mille** is invariable; it never takes an *s*.

‡‡The French words **million, milliard** and **billion** are nouns, and when written out in full they take **de** before another noun, e.g. **a million inhabitants = un million d'habitants**. However, when written in figures, **1,000,000 inhabitants = 1 000 000 habitants**, but is still spoken as **un million d'habitants**. When *million* etc. is part of a complex number, *de* is not used before the nouns, e.g. **6,000,210 people = six millions deux cent dix personnes**.

Use of *en*

Note the use of **en** in the following examples:

there are six	= il y **en** a six
I've got a hundred	= j'**en** ai cent

en must be used when the thing you are talking about is not expressed (the French says literally *there of them are six, I of them have a hundred* etc.). However, **en** is not needed when the object is specified:

there are six apples	= il y a six pommes

Approximate numbers

When you want to say **about** …, remember the French ending **-aine**:

about ten	= une diz**aine**
about ten books	= une diz**aine** de livres
about fifteen	= une quinz**aine**
about fifteen people	= une quinz**aine** de personnes

Similarly *une trentaine, une quarantaine, une cinquantaine, une soixantaine* and *une centaine* (and *une douzaine* means a *dozen*). For other numbers, use **environ** (*about*):

about thirty-five	= **environ** trente-cinq
about four	= **environ** quatre
thousand pages	mille pages

Note the use of *centaines* and *milliers* to express approximate quantities:

hundreds *of books*	= **des centaines** de livres
thousands *of books*	= **des milliers** de livres
I've got ***thousands***	= j'en ai **des milliers**

Phrases

numbers up to ten	= les nombres jusqu'à dix
to count up to ten	= compter jusqu'à dix
almost ten	= presque dix
less than ten	= moins de dix
more than ten	= plus de dix
all ten of them	= tous les dix
all ten boys	= les dix garçons

Note the French word order:

my last ten pounds	= mes dix dernières livres
the next twelve weeks	= les douze prochaines semaines
the other two	= les deux autres
the last four	= les quatre derniers

Calculations in French

$10 + 3 = 13$	dix et trois font *or* égale treize
$10 - 3 = 7$	trois ôté de dix il reste sept *or* dix moins trois égale sept
$10 \times 3 = 30$	dix fois trois égale trente
$30 : 3 = 10$	$(30 \div 3 = 10)$ trente divisé par trois égale dix

Note how the French division sign differs from the English.

5^2	cinq au carré
5^3	cinq puissance trois
5^{100}	cinq puissance cent
$\sqrt{2}$	racine carrée de deux
$\sqrt{25} = 5$	racine carrée de vingt-cinq égale cinq
$B > A$	B est plus grand que A
$A < B$	A est plus petit que B

Decimals in French

Note that French uses a comma where English has a decimal point.

	say
0,25	zéro virgule vingt-cinq
0,05	zéro virgule zéro cinq
0,75	zéro virgule soixante-quinze
3,45	trois virgule quarante-cinq
8,195	huit virgule cent quatre-vingt-quinze
9,1567	neuf virgule quinze cent soixante-sept *or* neuf virgule mille cinq cent soixante-sept
9,3456	neuf virgule trois mille quatre cent cinquante-six

Percentages in French

	say
25%	vingt-cinq pour cent
50%	cinquante pour cent
100%	cent pour cent
200%	deux cents pour cent
365%	trois cent soixante cinq pour cent
4,25%	quatre virgule vingt-cinq pour cent

Fractions in French

	say
$\frac{1}{2}$	un demi*
$\frac{1}{3}$	un tiers
$\frac{1}{4}$	un quart
$\frac{1}{5}$	un cinquième
$\frac{1}{6}$	un sixième
$\frac{1}{7}$	un septième
$\frac{1}{8}$	un huitième
$\frac{1}{9}$	un neuvième
$\frac{1}{10}$	un dixième
$\frac{1}{11}$	un onzième
$\frac{1}{12}$	un douzième (etc)
$\frac{2}{3}$	deux tiers†
$\frac{2}{5}$	deux cinquièmes
$\frac{2}{10}$	deux dixièmes (etc)
$\frac{3}{4}$	trois quarts
$\frac{3}{5}$	trois cinquièmes
$\frac{3}{10}$	trois dixièmes (etc)
$1\frac{1}{2}$	un et demi
$1\frac{1}{3}$	un (et) un tiers
$1\frac{1}{4}$	un et quart
$1\frac{1}{5}$	un (et) un cinquième
$1\frac{1}{6}$	un (et) un sixième
$1\frac{1}{7}$	un (et) un septième (etc)
$5\frac{2}{3}$	cinq (et) deux tiers
$5\frac{3}{4}$	cinq (et) trois quarts
$5\frac{4}{5}$	cinq (et) quatre cinquièmes
45/100ths of a second	= quarante-cinq centièmes de seconde

Ordinal numbers in French§

1st	1er‡	premier (*fem.* première)
2nd	2e	second *or* deuxième
3rd	3e	troisième
4th	4e	quatrième
5th	5e	cinquième
6th	6e	sixième
7th	7e	septième
8th	8e	huitième
9th	9e	neuvième
10th	10e	dixième
11th	11e	onzième
12th	12e	douzième
13th	13e	treizième
14th	14e	quatorzième
15th	15e	quinzième
16th	16e	seizième
17th	17e	dix-septième
18th	18e	dix-huitième
19th	19e	dix-neuvième
20th	20e	vingtième
21st	21e	vingt et unième
22nd	22e	vingt-deuxième
23rd	23e	vingt-troisième
24th	24e	vingt-quatrième
25th	25e	vingt-cinquième
30th	30e	trentième
31st	31e	trente et unième
40th	40e	quarantième
50th	50e	cinquantième
60th	60e	soixantième
70th	70e	soixante-dixième¶
71st	71e	soixante et onzième
72nd	72e	soixante-douzième
73rd	73e	soixante-treizième
74th	74e	soixante-quartorzième
75th	75e	soixante-quinzième
79th	79e	soixante-dix-neuvième
80th	80e	quatre-vingtième¶
81st	81e	quatre-vingt-unième
90th	90e	quatre-vingt-dixième¶
91st	91e	quatre-vingt-onzième
99th	99e	quatre-vingt-dix-neuvième
100th	100e	centième
101st	101e	cent unième
102nd	102e	cent deuxième
196th	196e	cent quatre-vingt-seizième
200th	200e	deux centième
300th	300e	trois centième
400th	400e	quatre centième
1,000th	1 000e	millième
2,000th	2 000e	deux millième
1,000,000th	1 000 000e	millionième

Like English, French makes nouns by adding the definite article:

***the** first*	= **le** premier (*or* **la** première, *or* **les** premiers *m pl or* **les** premières *f pl*)
***the** second*	= **le** second (*or* **la** seconde etc)
***the** first three*	= **les** trois premiers *or* **les** trois premières

Note the French word order in:

***the** third richest country in the world*	= **le** troisième pays **le** plus riche du monde

* Note that **half**, when not a fraction, is translated by the noun **moitié** or the adjective **demi**; see the dictionary entry.

† Note the use of **les** and **d'entre** when these fractions are used about a group of people or things: **two-thirds of them = les deux tiers d'entre eux**.

§ All the ordinal numbers in French behave like ordinary adjectives and take normal plural endings where appropriate.

‡ This is the masculine form; the feminine is **1re** and the plural **1ers** (*m*) or **1res** (*f*). All the other abbreviations of ordinal numbers are invariable.

¶ (70e) Also **septantième** in Belgium and Switzerland. (80e) Also **huitantième** in Switzerland. (90e) Also **nonantième** in Belgium and Switzerland.

Index of lexical and grammar notes

Lexical notes

Age	187
The human body	201
The clock	211
Colours	213
Countries, cities, and continents	218
Dates, days, and months	222
Everyday expressions	237
Forms of address	245
Games and sports	248
Illnesses, aches, and pains	266
Languages and nationalities	275
Length and weight measurements	285
Musical instruments	290
Numbers	398
Shops, trades, and professions	315
Quantities	317
Talking about time	356

English grammar notes

be	196
do	227
for	244
get	249
go	253
have	258
it	270
not	296
that	351
the	352
them	353
to	358
what	371
which	373
you	378
your	379
Using the subjunctive	291

French grammar notes

avoir	12
être	64

A guide to French grammar

This section expands on many of the terms found in the glossary and used in this dictionary to help you to find the information that you need. The numbers in brackets refer to the appropriate exercises in the Dictionary know-how section p. 171.

Adjective (1, 14) An adjective is used to add extra information to a noun—*a worried farmer, a black cat, a thick book*. In French: *un fermier inquiet, un chat noir, un livre épais*. Note that in English, the adjective usually comes before the noun, whereas in French it usually comes after the noun.

Sometimes, of course, the adjective is separated from its noun:

> *Your garden is beautiful.*
> *Votre jardin est beau.*

Adverb (5, 16) An adverb is used to add extra information to a verb, an adjective or another adverb—*to walk slowly, extremely satisfied, quite often*. In French: *marcher lentement, extrêmement satisfait, assez souvent*.

Agreement There are two kinds of agreement in French which you must be careful about.

The first is the agreement of nouns and adjectives. All nouns in French have a gender, and most can also be either singular or plural. Any adjective which describes a noun must 'agree' with it in both gender (masculine or feminine) and number (singular or plural). In other words, the adjective must also be masculine or feminine, singular or plural: *un garçon intelligent, une fille intelligente, deux garçons intelligents, deux filles intelligentes*.

The other kind of agreement is that between a verb and its subject. You must always ensure that the ending of the verb is the one which matches the subject. If the subject is a pronoun, this is fairly straightforward since we usually learn the various forms of a verb together with the appropriate pronoun: *je vais, tu vas, il/elle va, nous allons, vous allez, ils/elles vont*.

If the subject of the verb is a noun, or a pronoun like *moi, toi* etc, you have to be more careful to get the form of the verb right.

> *Pierre et son ami vont au cinéma.*
> *(Pierre + son ami = ils)*
>
> *La banque ouvre à neuf heures.*
> *(la banque = elle)*
>
> *Hélène et moi avons deux enfants.*
> *(Hélène + moi = nous)*
>
> *C'est toi qui as acheté ces carottes?*
> *(c'est toi qui = tu)*

Auxiliary verbs An auxiliary verb is a verb which is combined with another verb in order to form the so-called compound tenses of that verb (the main compound tenses in French are the perfect, the pluperfect and the future perfect). There are two auxiliary verbs in French, *avoir* and *être*, and each is used with a particular group of verbs.

The auxiliary verb *être* is used first of all to form the compound tenses of all reflexive verbs:

> *Vous vous êtes levé à quelle heure?*
> *(What time did you get up?)*
>
> *Je m'étais couché tard.*
> *(I had gone to bed late).*

It is also used to form the compound tenses of a small group of verbs. These verbs are:

aller	to go
arriver	to arrive
descendre	to go|come down
entrer	to enter
monter	to go|come up
mourir	to die
naître	to be born
partir	to leave, to set out
passer	to go past, to drop in on
rester	to remain, to stay
retourner	to return
sortir	to go|come out
tomber	to fall
venir	to come

> *il est allé au marché.*
> *(he went to the market.)*
>
> *je suis descendu.*
> *(I went down.)*

The auxiliary verb *avoir* is used to form the compound tenses of all other verbs:

> *j'ai fait le ménage.*
> *(I've done the housework.)*
>
> *elle a fini son travail.*
> *(she has finished her work.)*
>
> *nous avions déjà mangé.*
> *(we had already eaten.)*

Comparative The comparative, as its name indicates, is the form of the adjective or adverb which enables us to compare two or more nouns or pronouns. In English, this is usually done by putting *more, less* or *as* before the appropriate adjective or adverb:

> *Anne is more sensitive (than her sister).*
> *Louise is less tired (than Jacqueline).*
> *Léa is as intelligent (as Louise).*

In French, the equivalent comparatives are *plus, moins* and *aussi*:

> *Anne est plus sensible (que sa sœur).*
> *Louise est moins fatiguée (que Jacqueline).*
> *Léa est aussi intelligente (que Louise).*

Note that the French for both *than* and *as* is *que*.

In English, a few adjectives have an irregular comparative form (*good*/**better**, *bad*/**worse**, *little*/**less**, *much* or *many*/**more**) and some shorter English adjectives have a special comparative form ending in *-er* (for example, *bigger*, *smaller*, *happier*, *slower*). In French, there are only three adjectives with a special form: *bon*/**meilleur** (*good*/*better*); *mauvais*/**pire** (*bad*/*worse*); *petit*/**moindre** (*small*/*less*). However, note that *plus petit* is used instead of *moindre* when referring to size: *ma voiture est **plus petite** que la tienne* (*my car is smaller than yours*). The only irregular form which is always used is *meilleur*—don't forget that, like all comparative adjectives, it must agree with its noun: *une **meilleure** chanson* (*a better song*), *de **meilleurs** chanteurs* (*better singers*).

The comparative of adverbs is formed in much the same way:

> Paul walks **more** slowly (than his brother).
> Peter speaks **less** quickly (than Paul).
> Paul goes to Paris **as** often (as Peter).
>
> Paul marche **plus** lentement (que son frère).
> Peter parle **moins** vite (que Paul).
> Paul va à Paris **aussi** souvent (que Peter).

In both English and French, there are four irregular forms: *beaucoup*/**plus** (*much* or *a lot*/**more**); *bien*/**mieux** (*well*/**better**); *peu*/**moins** (*little*/**less**); *mal*/**pis** or *plus mal* (*badly*/**worse**). However, *pis* is only found in a few fixed expressions and the usual comparative of *mal* is *plus mal*: *je chante **plus mal** que lui* (*I sing worse than he does*).

Conditional A conditional sentence is one in which the statement contained in the main clause can only be fulfilled if the condition stated in the subordinate clause is also fulfilled. This condition is usually introduced by *if* in English and by *si* in French.

> If it's fine tomorrow, we'll go to the beach.
> I would be surprised if he came today.
>
> S'il fait beau demain, nous irons à la plage.
> Je serais surpris s'il venait aujourd'hui.

Conjunction (14) A conjunction can be either (i) a word like *and* or *but* which is used to join words or simple sentences together, or (ii) a word like *when*, *although*, *if*, *where*, which is used to form a complex sentence. Look at these examples:

> (i) John **and** Sarah
> Tired **but** happy
> They came down the steps **and** got into the car.
>
> Sophie **et** Pierre
> Fatigué **mais** heureux
> Ils ont descendu les marches **et** sont montés dans la voiture.

> (ii) **Although** he doesn't like the rain, he agreed to go for a walk.
> He was about to go to bed **when** he heard the noise of an aircraft.
>
> **Bien qu'**il n'aime pas la pluie, il a accepté de faire une promenade.
> Il était sur le point de se coucher, **quand** il a entendu le bruit d'un avion.

Determiner (16) A determiner is used before a noun in order to identify more precisely what is being referred to. Here are some examples of determiners in English: **a** car, **the** car, **my** car, **this** car, **these** cars, **some** cars. Examples of French determiners are: **une** voiture, **la** voiture, **ma** voiture, **cette** voiture, **ces** voitures, **certaines** voitures.

Exclamation An exclamation is a word or phrase conveying a reaction such as surprise, shock, disapproval, indignation, amusement etc. In both English and French, it is usually followed by an exclamation mark.

> Well, well!
> What!
> Ça alors!
> Quoi!

Feminine (10, 13, 19) ► Gender

Gender (2, 10, 13, 19) You will see when using the French–English half of this dictionary that some French words are marked (*noun, masculine*) or (*noun, feminine*). Unlike English nouns, every French noun has a gender—it is either masculine or feminine. For example, the French words for *office, pen, tree, roof* are masculine (**un** bureau, **un** stylo, **un** arbre, **un** toit), and the words for *car, table, house, photo* are feminine (**une** voiture, **une** table, **une** maison, **une** photo). When looking up a noun in the dictionary, it is important to note whether the French word is masculine or feminine, because this will determine the form of most adjectives and determiners which go with it—**un grand** arbre, but **une grande** maison.

Imperative The imperative is the form of the verb which we use when we want to order someone to do something. In English, there are two imperatives: for example, *leave* and *let's leave*. In French, there are three in order to allow for the *tu* and *vous* forms of the verb: for example, *pars* (*tu* form), *partons*, *partez* (*vous* form).

Indicative ► Subjunctive

Infinitive The infinitive is a form of the verb which has no indication of person or tense. In English, it is often preceded by *to*: *to walk, to run, to read, to receive*. In French, the infinitive ends in *-er*, *-ir*, *-re* or *-oir*: *marcher, courir, écrire, recevoir*. The infinitive is the form you will find at the beginning of verb entries in this and other dictionaries.

Masculine (10) ▶ Gender

Noun (1, 16, 17) A noun is used to identify a person, an animal, an object, an idea or an emotion—*farmer, cat, book, suggestion, happiness* are all nouns. It can also be the name of an individual, a company or an institution—*Emma, Peter, Robertson's, Parliament* are nouns. Equivalent French nouns are *fermier, chat, livre, suggestion, bonheur, Sophie, Pierre, Boulangerie Fauré, Conseil d'État*.

Number (16) As in English, most nouns in French may be singular or plural and change their ending accordingly (usually by adding '-s' in the plural: *a tree, two tree**s***; *un arbre, deux arbre**s***). Unlike English, however, adjectives in French may also be singular or plural and in most cases change their ending in order to agree with the noun they describe: *un grand arbre, deux grand**s** arbres*.

In the French–English half of this dictionary, when a noun has an irregular plural, the plural form is given after the noun. A noun which doesn't change in the plural has the warning (**!** *never changes*).

Object (6) The object of a sentence is the word or group of words which is immediately affected by the action indicated by the verb. So, in the sentence *The dog chewed the bone, dog* is the subject, *chewed* is the verb and **bone** is the object. Similarly, in the sentence *Le chien a rongé l'os, chien* is the subject, *a rongé* is the verb and **os** is the object.

There may be two kinds of object in a sentence, a direct object and an indirect object. In the examples above, *bone* and *os* are strictly direct objects. However, in the sentence *John gave the dog a bone, John* is the subject, *gave* is the verb, *bone* is the direct object and *dog* is the indirect object. Similarly, in the French sentence *Jean a donné un os au chien, Jean* is the subject, *a donné* is the verb, *os* is the direct object and *chien* is the indirect object. So, in general terms, the indirect object indicates the person or thing which 'benefits' from the action of the verb upon the direct object.

Phrasal verb (19) A phrasal verb is a verb combined with a preposition or an adverb and having a particular meaning. For example, *to **run away***, meaning to flee, or *to **see to*** something, meaning to ensure that something is done.

Phrasal verbs don't exist in French and you therefore need to use your dictionary carefully in order to select the correct translation. If you look up *to run away* for example, you will see that phrasal verbs are listed after all the other meanings of the word *run*, and in alphabetical order of the following adverb or preposition.

Plural ▶ Number

Preposition (11) A preposition is a word, such as *under, beside, across, in*, which is usually followed by a noun: *under the table, beside the road, in the garden; **sous** la table, **au bord de** la route, **dans** le jardin*. Most preposition + noun groups indicate movement

> he ran **towards the house**
> il a couru **vers la maison**

position

> your books are **on the table**
> vos livres sont **sur la table**

or time

> I'll be there **at 4 o'clock**
> je serai là **à six heures**.

Pronoun (3, 14) A pronoun is used instead of a noun in order to avoid repeating it unnecessarily. English pronouns are *I, me, you, he, him, she, her, it, we, us, they, them, mine, yours, his, hers, ours, theirs, this, that, these* and *those*. Equivalent French pronouns are: *je, me, tu, te, il, le, elle, la, nous, vous, ils, les, elles, leur, lui, le mien, la mienne, les miens, les miennes* etc, *ceci, cela, celui, celle, ceux, celles*. All of these are labelled as pronouns in this dictionary. However, some of the English pronouns (but *not* their French equivalents) can also be used as determiners and you must be careful not to confuse them. Compare these sentences:

> He lent me **his** book. (determiner)
> He lent me **his**. (pronoun)

> **These** ideas are important. (determiner)
> **These** are important. (pronoun)

> **Those** people have just arrived. (determiner)
> **Those** have just arrived. (pronoun)

Now look at the French equivalents:

> Il m'a prêté **son** livre. (determiner)
> Il m'a prêté **le sien**. (pronoun)

> **Ces** idées-ci sont importantes. (determiner)
> **Celles**-ci sont importantes. (pronoun)

> **Ces** gens-là viennent d'arriver. (determiner)
> **Ceux**-là viennent d'arriver. (pronoun)

Reflexive verb (24) A reflexive verb is one whose action is 'reflected back' upon the subject of the verb. In English, this is indicated by the use of reflexive pronouns such as *myself, yourself, herself, themselves, each other* etc. For example:

> When he hurts **himself**, he cries.
> We speak to **each other** every day.

In French, this reflexive action is conveyed by the use of the pronouns *me, te, se, nous* or *vous*:

> *Quand il* **se** *fait mal, il pleure.*
> *Nous* **nous** *parlons tous les jours.*

Here are the full present tense forms of the reflexive verb *se baigner* (*to go for a swim*):

je **me** *baigne*	*nous* **nous** *baignons*
tu **te** *baignes*	*vous* **vous** *baignez*
il **se** *baigne*	*ils* **se** *baignent*
elle **se** *baigne*	*elles* **se** *baignent*

Remember that many reflexive verbs in French have English equivalents which are not reflexive. Other examples are *se souvenir de* (*to remember*), *se laver* (*to wash*).

Singular ▶ Number

Subject (6) The subject of a sentence is the word or group of words which performs the action indicated by the verb. So, in the sentence *John coughed*, John is the subject of the verb *coughed*. Of course, the verb doesn't necessarily express an action as such. For example, in the sentence *John is tall*, John is the subject of the verb *is*. In the French sentence *Jean a toussé*, Jean is similarly the subject of the verb *a toussé*, and in the sentence *Jean est grand*, Jean is the subject of the verb *est*.

Subjunctive The subjunctive is a special form of some tenses of the verb, which in French is mostly used to express doubt and possibility, rather than fact or certainty. It is also used when expressing an emotional reaction to something. This form of the verb is much more widely used in French than in English, where it has almost disappeared, and you will find a fuller explanation and examples on p. 291. Note that the usual form of the various tenses of a verb is known as the indicative because it 'indicates' fact or certainty.

Superlative The superlative is the form of the adjective or adverb which is used to express the highest or lowest degree. In English, the adjective or adverb is usually preceded by *most* or *least*, **most** *important*, **least** *important*, **most** *carefully*, **least** *carefully*. Some adjectives and adverbs (usually of one syllable) have their own form: *best, worst, biggest, smallest, fastest, slowest* etc. In French, the superlative adjective (which must agree with its noun) 's usually formed by putting *le plus, la plus*, ~~·~~ *plus, le moins, la moins* or *les moins* the adjective: *le livre* **le plus** *long, le* ~~·~~ **oins** *long, la question* **la plus** ~~·~~ *la question* **la moins** ~~·~~ *avions* **les plus** *rapides, les* ~~·~~ *rapides.* The superlative ~~·~~ preceded by *le plus* or *le* ~~·~~ *te,* **le moins** *vite,* **le plus** ~~·~~ *t,* **le moins** *soigneusement.*

Some French adjectives and adverbs have their own form of the superlative, for example:

bon/bonne	**le meilleur/la meilleure**
mauvais/mauvaise	**le pire/la pire**
bien	**le mieux**
mal	**le plus mal**

Tense The tense is the particular form of the verb which tells us the approximate time when the action of the verb takes place:

Present tense
> *He* **is telephoning** *all his friends.*
> *Il téléphone à tous ses amis.*

Future tense
> *He* **will telephone** *all his friends.*
> *Il téléphonera à tous ses amis.*

The main past and future tenses used in French are:

Past tenses	(i) Imperfect
	(ii) Present perfect (or Perfect)
	(iii) Past perfect (or Pluperfect)
Future tenses	(iv) Future (simple)
	(v) Future perfect

For example:

(i) *Il* **téléphonait** *souvent à tous ses amis.*
   (*He often used to telephone all his friends.*)

(ii) *Hier, il* **a téléphoné** *à tous ses amis.*
   (*Yesterday he telephoned all his friends.*)

(iii) *Il* **avait** *déjà* **téléphoné** *à tous ses amis.*
   (*He had already telephoned all his friends.*)

(iv) *Demain, il* **téléphonera** *à tous ses amis.*
   (*Tomorrow he will telephone all his friends.*)

(v) *Avant 6 heures il* **aura téléphoné** *à tous ses amis.*
   (*By 6 o'clock he will have telephoned all his friends.*)

Verb (4, 12, 16) The verb propels the sentence along, telling us what is happening. Look at these examples:

> *Paul* **carried** *the boxes upstairs to the attic.*
> *The storm* **did** *a lot of damage.*

> *Paul* **a monté** *les cartons au grenier.*
> *La tempête* **a fait** *beaucoup de dégâts.*

Sometimes, of course, the verb doesn't describe an action, but rather a state of affairs:

> *Paul* **has** *a back problem.*
> *He* **is** *often ill.*
> *The damage* **appears** *less serious than we expected.*

> *Paul* **a** *un problème de dos.*
> *Il* **est** *souvent malade.*
> *Les dégâts* **semblent** *moins importants que prévu.*